Women Writers of Spanish America

Recent Titles in
Bibliographies and Indexes in Women's Studies

Women in China: A Selected and Annotated Bibliography
Karen T. Wei

Women Writers of Spain: An Annotated Bio-Bibliographical Guide
Carolyn L. Galerstein and Kathleen McNerney, editors

The Equal Rights Amendment: An Annotated Bibliography of the Issues, 1976-1985
Renee Feinberg, compiler

Childbearing Among Hispanics in the United States: An Annotated Bibliography
Katherine F. Darabi, compiler

Women Writers of Spanish America

An Annotated Bio-Bibliographical Guide

EDITED BY DIANE E. MARTING

BIBLIOGRAPHIES AND INDEXES IN WOMEN'S STUDIES,
NUMBER 5

GREENWOOD PRESS
NEW YORK • WESTPORT, CONNECTICUT • LONDON

Library of Congress Cataloging-in-Publication Data

Women writers of Spanish America.

(Bibliographies and indexes in women's studies,
ISSN 0742-6941 ; no. 5)
Includes index.
1. Spanish American literature—Women authors—
Bio-bibliography. 2. Women authors, Spanish American—
Bibliography. 3. Women authors, Spanish American—
Biography. I. Marting, Diane E. II. Series.
Z1609.L7W63 1987   016.89'09'9287   86-33552
[PQ7081]
ISBN 0-313-24969-5 (lib. bdg. : alk. paper)

Library of Congress Catalog Card Number: 86-33552
ISBN: 0-313-24969-5
ISSN: 0742-6941

First published in 1987

Greenwood Press, Inc.
88 Post Road West, Westport, Connecticut 06881

Printed in the United States of America

The paper used in this book complies with the
Permanent Paper Standard issued by the National
Information Standards Organization (Z39.48-1984).

10 9 8 7 6 5 4 3 2 1

CONTENTS

PREFACE

All seventy-two contributors to this volume have their initials at the end of their annotations and an all-too-brief description of their related areas of research or published works appearing at the end of this volume. While this does not recognize sufficiently the work that they donated to this project, there are still others whose equally important gifts of time, knowledge, and skills would go unrecognized without this space that I wish to devote to them.

The process of discovering a basic list of authors and titles, described briefly in the introduction, took place over periods lasting months during the years 1978 to 1980. The person who was always willing to help in the mailing of surveys, in the bibliographical work in the Rutgers University library, and in the tabulation of surveys, was my friend and English Department colleague, Joseph Boles. His generosity is all the greater because his interest in the subject is theoretical. Not being fluent in Spanish, he cannot read the works he donated over a hundred hours to recovering from the dust of libraries, yet as a feminist, he believes that Spanish-American women authors are important. Nancy Paxton, also at that time of the Rutgers University English Department and also a feminist, significantly affected the magnitude of the project. The summers when Joe and Nancy worked beside me on the <u>National Union Catalogue</u> were crucial for locating the unannotated authors listed on the following pages and for encouraging me in a monumental project that at times I feared would never be completed.

After the early collection of information, I approached sources at Rutgers University, several of which helped to cover some of the expenses of <u>Women Writers of Spanish America</u> with small grants. I would like to thank the Center for Research on Women for employing me for a summer for the purpose of working on this project and for providing funds for duplicating and mailing; the Spanish Department for the use of their Apple II; and the Comparative Literature Department, the Spanish Department, and the Office of the Graduate Dean for travel grants to conferences to speak about bibliographies of Spanish-American women writers.

During the 1985-86 academic year, I received the valuable support of both personnel and facilities at the University of California at Los Angeles. One of my students, Anahit Hakoupian, checked the library for more recent works by the annotated authors. Many contributors from UCLA reviewed quickly those recently published works Anahit found and other important writers whose works had not been annotated yet. Mary Berg has read over the final text for errors. Furthermore, Irene Chow of Word Processing for Social Sciences and Humanities has typed this difficult book over four months time, meaningfully contributing to the design of the pages and to the format with her suggestions and advice.

I would like to thank World Literature Today for permission to use in a revised form Malva Filer's review of Open to the Sun: A Bilingual Anthology of Latin-American Women Poets in the "Partially Annotated List of Anthologies." Filer's review previously appeared in the Winter 1982 issue (volume 56, number 1), p. 85 of World Literature Today.

I would also like to thank the following for their review copies of books and articles: Scarecrow Press for Lucía Fox-Lockert's Women Novelists in Spain and Spanish America; the University of California Press for Beth Miller's Women in Hispanic Literature: Icons and Fallen Idols; the Feminist Press for The Defiant Muse; the University of Massachusetts at Amherst's International Area Studies Programs for Women in Latin American Literature: A Symposium; and the University of Indiana's Chicano-Riqueño's Studies Program for Bibliography of Hispanic Women Writers by Norma Alarcón and Sylvia Kossnar.

Finally, special thanks go to another volunteer whose contribution lies on every page. During these last months, the patient dedication of Sergio Klafke to this project was exemplary. Sergio has worked full-time for several months on the final library confirmation of the entries, on the spelling, the proofing of the contributors' submissions, the correction of the typing, and on the design and layout of the pages.

INTRODUCTION

The many diverse countries of Spanish America have a history of women's literature that is full, varied, and for the most part, undocumented in English. The relatively recent "boom" in Latin American literature and the growth of women's studies and women's literature courses in particular have dramatically increased the interest in Spanish-American women writers in high schools, colleges and universities, and even in non-academic settings such as women's centers and community libraries. Women Writers of Spanish America: An Annotated Bio-Bibliographical Guide is designed to serve this diverse new readership as well as the scholar or librarian who has long maintained an interest in the region. The high school or college student who is beginning to study Spanish-American literature, the interested reader looking for a good book, the aspiring expert who may have never studied women writers in graduate school, the literature professor who would like to answer students' questions about women's literary production, the sociologist looking for cultural expressions of a certain reality, the professional bibliographer and the translator: anyone in fact who would like to know more about a certain writer or women writers in general, it is hoped, will find some guidance in this book.

Some knowledge of both English and Spanish is assumed, although the guide will still be useful for those who know only one of the two languages. For those who know no English, the extensive bibliographical descriptions of the annotated books and the simple skeleton of authors and titles, with accompanying indexes, will be one of the most thorough sources available; for those who know no Spanish, the final index of translations and bilingual editions will be particularly relevant.

In many ways, Women Writers of Spanish America is designed to serve as a manual for intellectual affirmative action: to compensate for past sexism in the study of Spanish-American literature as well as to celebrate the wealth of exciting works which Spanish-American women have written. I hope that American publishers will read the annotations and consider commissioning or publishing more translations of women who write in Spanish. Jean Graham's List of Dramatists will help to convince those who doubt that Spanish-American women have produced theater and perhaps encourage the production of the works on stage or the publication of their plays. As part of Greenwood's series of bibliographies in womens' studies, Women Writers of Spanish America is the American companion to Women Writers of Spain, edited by Carolyn Galerstein.

Bibliographies perform a unique type of literary criticism: they measure the quantity of items available within a specialized area of study. Selected, annotated bibliographies evaluate and judge more than the unannotated variety, but then this expanded type is a sort of hybrid, a cross between a collection of short critical notes and a simple enumeration of items. By displaying the number and range of its entries, even the most Spartan of bibliographies discourses about texts. That is one of the reasons why I, as a literary critic and not a bibliographer, have undertaken the task of compiling, editing, and contributing to this annotated bio-bibliography. My hope is that the works in Women Writers of Spanish America will be studied more often, translated into more languages, and reprinted in Spanish more frequently as a result of the efforts of all of us who have made this book possible.

This bibliography began in 1976 as an idea of the Modern Language Association's Division of Women's Studies in Language and Literature; the project was developed and given shape during annual panels over several years at MLA conventions, finally culminating in Women Writers in Translation: An Annotated Bibliography, 1945-1982, edited by Margery Resnick and Isabelle de Courtivron (1984). Women Writers in Translation should be consulted for the annotations of most translations of Spanish-American works, since the same book is rarely annotated both in Women Writers in Translation and in the present volume.

In my introduction to the Spanish-American section of Women Writers in Translation, I discussed some of the characteristics of Spanish-American women's writings and the processes used to develop the list of writers on which both translations in that volume and the entries in the present volume are based. Although much more can be said about the nature of the works included in both these books, I am going to leave such discussions for another, more appropriate time. I am preparing another volume for Greenwood Press on Spanish-American women writers, a collection of essays, on selected writers with an introductory analysis in which I will comment more fully on the body of literature this present bibliography records.

Here I want to limit myself to a brief discussion of my method of editing this volume. As I had for the bibliography of translations, I conceived my task as that of finding the maximum number of published Spanish-American women authors to include and the maximum number of contributors willing to annotate them. This constituted the first several years of my work on Women Writers of Spanish America. At first I gleaned the precious names of authors and, in some cases, titles by perusing published histories, bibliographies, anthologies, and critical articles too numerous to cite here. The inclusion of popular authors, and not merely those with high literary aspirations and attainments, has been a conscious decision. The importance today of the study of popular literature cannot be denied. Additionally, children's literature has been included whenever possible; although academic study of infantile, young children's and juvenile works, like that of popular literature, is relatively new, it too is an important area for women writers and feminist critics. Finally, I tried to make sure that all Spanish-American countries were represented by some authors and that feminists and earlier writers were included.

Soon, however, the sheer number of countries and authors complicated the process by making the number of titles too great. Significantly, the inclusion of twenty countries and several centuries of literature quickly made it impossible to give bibliographical information for the books that were not annotated. Therefore, during the last few years of this project, I have concentrated on finding contributors for specific authors I felt should be annotated, either because they were earlier writers, were from an under-represented country or race or wrote in a less-popular genre, or because they had been translated into English.

What was Included. Once the first thousand titles were culled, I began to consult and verify names and titles with my colleagues and with the Library of Congress's National Union Catalogue. I sent a survey to as many people as possible, asking the respondents to name the most important writers to be translated. Through this process, I initiated a correspondence together in various capacities for different periods of time; as I reflect on the process of working with the more than 100 possible annotators, over 70 of whom eventually contributed, some interesting characteristics appear. In general, the contributors are an energetic group of young women researchers, willing to cooperate, patient with my requests for more information or for clarifications, and as idealistic about the project as I. A few of them are professors who specialize in women writers, and their names will be recognizable in the list of contributors. The majority of the participants live in the United States and are working as teachers in a college/university environment: lecturers, adjuncts, teaching assistant/graduate students, beginning assistant professors, and others who are active professionally, but who are at the very beginning of their careers. In addition, there are a few professors who do not live in the United States, a few male graduate students and professors, occasional undergraduate students, and professionals of various types: translators, publishers, bibliographers and government employees.

Indeed, I believe they are an unusual group of dedicated volunteers. Their cooperation was exemplary. In one case, two contributors worked together on annotations of the same books; in other cases, several groups of contributors, including one married couple, worked together on prolific authors by each annotating some of the books. Certain individual contributors: M.S. Arrington, Jr., Teresa Arrington, Naomi Lindstrom, Stacey Schlau, Betty Tyree Osiek, Susana Hernández-Araico, Erica Frouman-Smith, Ivette López Jiménez, Gabriela Mora, Patricia Rubio de Lértora, and Arlene Schrade, among them, each annotated large numbers of books, in some cases more than fifty works. Many other contributors, particularly those from UCLA, helped during the final stages at very short notice. In summary, this extensive network of collaboration has functioned well in bringing together some of our collective knowledge. For me, it has made editing this book a pleasure. Whereas the experience of compiling a bibliography such as this has required unpleasant repetitive tasks and excruciating attention to detail, my compensation has been the warm experience of the mutual exchange of information and of working together with so many generous individuals.

Suggestions for Further Reading. Women Writers in Translation and Women in Spanish America, as mentioned above, need to be consulted in conjunction with this volume to complete the information in the appendix lists of translations and anthologies. An important early bibliography of criticism is the Bibliography of Hispanic Women Writers, eds. Norma Alarcón and Sylvia Kossnar (Bloomington, Ind: Chicano-Riqueño Studies Bibliography Series, No. 1, 1980). For more information about translations and criticism in English, see Graciela N. V. Corvalán, Latin American Women Writers in English Translation: A Bibliography (Latin American Bibliography Series, 9. Los Angeles: California State University Latin American Studies Center, 1980) and Naomi Lindstrom's "Feminist Criticism of Latin American Literature: Bibliographic Notes" in Latin American Research Review 1980 (Vol. 15, No. 1), pp. 151-159. For more information about bibliographies and anthologies, see Hensley C. Woodbridge, Spanish and Spanish-American Literature: An Annotated Guide to Selected Bibliographies (New York: Modern Language Association, 1983). For a general overview of research in the field of Spanish-American women writers, see "Opportunities for Women's Studies in the Hispanic Field," by Jean Franco in Women in Print I, Opportunities for Women's Studies Research in Language and Literature, eds. Joan Hartman and Ellen Messer-Davidow (New York: Modern Language Association, 1982).

with hundreds of scholars. The tedious process of consulting the many volumes of the National Union Catalogue was one that took many more hundreds of hours. A computer search was not possible for me when I began this project. Today, with the computerization of bibliographic information, the compilation of bibliographies such as this one has been much simplified. Because these titles were searched manually, the information from the printed volumes of the National Union Catalogue was the most important source for the spelling of names and titles for authors listed in the present volume but who are not annotated. For annotated authors, whenever the information compiled by the contributor disagreed with the Library of Congress's bibliographic description or birthdate (and was not an obvious error), I have utilized the contributor's information. In many cases, contributors were in direct contact with the authors themselves; the National Union Catalogue can always be consulted for further information or confirmation of the information found here.

There are two important implications of having used the National Union Catalogue so extensively. First, works published after 1980 are not likely to appear, in most cases, because of the time lag between the publication of a work and its appearance in the reference guide, although a few books listed in this bibliography were published as late as 1985. Annotations of some writers were completed as early as 1982, and meantime the author has continued to write and to publish. Second, this bibliography for the most part is restricted to books held by North American libraries.

Two kinds of works, however, are listed but intentionally were not annotated: (1) translations that were annotated in Women Writers in Translation 1945-1980: An Annotated Bibliography (New York: Garland, 1984); and (2) bibliographies and anthologies annotated in Meri Knaster's invaluable section, "Literature, Mass Media, and Folklore," in her Women in Spanish America: An Annotated Bibliography from Pre-Conquest to Contemporary Times (Boston: G. K. Hall, 1977). Both of these exclusions primarily affect two appendixes in the present volume, the list of "Translations and Bilingual Editions" and the "Partially Annotated List of Anthologies", and were motivated by the desire not to duplicate previous efforts.

As the list of works grew and grew, it became necessary to define just exactly which authors and then which works by each author were going to be included. The first restriction was geographical: only those authors who were either born in Spanish America or lived there most of their lives or those of Spanish-American background who were born or lived in the United States were included. Second, authors must have written principally in Spanish. Chicanas and other Hispanic women writers who write principally in English were not included. Third, they must have produced a published book of creative literature. This means that writers whose works have only been published in magazines, journals, and anthologies were not included. Additionally, writers of non-fiction, travel literature, journalism, etc., would not appear unless they also published other types of works that qualify for inclusion.

This last restriction, however, touches upon a very complex problem in Spanish-American literature, which this bibliography is not intended to resolve. Much contemporary literature today is on the margin between fiction and non-fiction, journalism and creative literature, historical document and historical fiction. How can one not include many of the documentary works of the Mexican writer Elena Poniatowska? Her works are part of a literary movement called the "New Journalism," which is an important Spanish-American contribution to world literature. Indeed, the decision to include Poniatowska's La noche de Tlaltelolco or María Esther Gilio's Los guerrillas tupamaros was based on the belief that they are works that need to be discussed in terms of literature today, as well as in terms of the realities they discuss. On the other hand, Gabriela Mistral's journalism, Victoria Ocampo's cultural commentaries, and Marta Traba's art criticism were not listed because they are not part of this discussion on the nature of fiction, even though they are important in the broader world of writing by women. Therefore, both non-fiction writers and non-fiction works by included writers were excluded unless some argument could be made (or was made by a contributor) in favor of making an exception.

There were a few additional exceptions made which, like the above, affect a relatively small number of entries. First, when an author qualified for inclusion and that author had written a non-fiction work about women, women's studies, or women's literature, then that specific non-fiction work was included. The assumption is that users of this guide are particularly interested in these topics. Second, there are a few dramatists and one film director whose works are written but which appeared in a form other than a printed book (i.e., performances and a film), whose works appear in annotated form. The number of these "writers" is so small and the difficulties of publishing a play or a script in Spanish America are so great that whether or not to include such an author was decided case by case.

Organization and Lists. The decision to organize the entries in alphabetical order by the authors' names, rather than by countries or dates, was motivated by the desire to help those less familiar with Spanish-American women's writing. The chronological list which follows the main bibliography is designed to conform very generally to the MLA Bibliography's division of Spanish-American literature into literature before and after 1930; hence, the demarcation was made of authors born on or before 1900. The "Classified List of Authors by Country" should help those primarily interested in one country or region. Jean Graham's list of "Dramatists" helps one to locate authors who write in this less common genre. Finally, several bibliographies and anthologies have appeared over the years; as many as possible of them are listed or annotated in the "Partially Annotated List of Anthologies".

Entries and Annotations. Each entry begins with the author's full name (see "How to Use This Guide"), the country of origin and primary residence, and as much information as possible about her life dates. When an author's country was not known, the country in which she published is indicated. If information was available about an annotated author's life, it immediately follows the parentheses, within the same paragraph. In the biographical description, mention is made of non-fiction books the author has written (which normally are not annotated), and information about her literary production in general, especially her professional and other work, is given. Although personally I do not consider an author's marital status or number of children to be the most important kind of information to include in this brief paragraph, I have not deleted such information when supplied by a contributor.

The indented paragraphs that follow the biographical information each describe one book: usually other editions are noted within the same paragraph, especially when there are no or only slight differences between the editions listed. The first edition mentioned is generally the one reviewed by the contributor. If, however, there are significant differences between editions, such as deletions of texts or additions of critical materials, there may be two or even three paragraphs, on the book, each treating a major edition or group of editions. In the case of collected works, anthologies, and selections, normally the annotation contains only the list of what is included and a description of the ancillary material. The description of the works themselves is contained in the annotation of each individual work. The International Standard Book Number (ISBN) is not available for all but the most recent of these books, but it has been included when available. In many cases, some comment has been made about the availability of the works during the time they were annotated, that is, sometime between 1982 and 1986.

The Contributors. Large bibliographic enterprises profit from large-scale cooperation. This bibliography is the result of over 150 people working

HOW TO USE THIS BOOK

There is no single way to use this book. The acquisitions librarian and the undergraduate looking for a topic for a research paper will have different goals and therefore will, of necessity, use this book in different ways. However, there are a few points that may help all who wish to take advantage of the information contained here.

1. <u>Alphabetical order follows the English alphabet</u>. This implies that the Spanish letters "ch," "ll," and "rr" are treated as pairs of separate letters, and that "ñ" is treated as "n." Titles of books are alphabetized ignoring the equivalents of the English words "a," "an" and "the," that is, disregarding: "un," "uno," "una," "unos," "unas," "el," "la," "las," and "los."

2. <u>Use the most complete form of the author's name</u>. While the pseudonyms and most common forms of the authors' names are cross-referenced whenever they are known, the list of titles is placed under the complete name of an author. For those unfamiliar with the Spanish naming system, which uses the patronym as well as the matronym, this means that the annotated works of Gabriela Mistral, the pseudonym of Lucila Godoy Alcayaga, are listed under GODOY ALCAYAGA, Lucila. In addition, a second last name will follow all the forms of a single last name, i.e., "LA TORRE" precedes "LATORRE" and GODOY, Elizabeth precedes GODOY ALCAYAGA, Lucila. Please note also that, with very few exceptions, authors are not alphabetized by the "de" in the middle of other names but rather by the name following or preceding it.

This system has been adopted for the sake of consistency, although it has led to the inclusion of married names even when the author herself does not regularly use her husband's name. Quite simply, it proved impossible to find out the preference of the author in every case. The cross-referencing should help anyone to locate an author when she is listed under a name different from the one by which she is known. In the case of nuns, such as Sor Juana Inés de la Cruz, the entry is to be found under the form used by the Library of Congress, i.e., JUANA INES DE LA CRUZ, sor. The consistency and clarity that were achieved following these rules will compensate, it is hoped, for the loss to some individuals of their personal form of expression in their name or pseudonym.

3. <u>The initials of the contributor appear either immediately following each paragraph in an annotation (if done by several contributors) or following all the paragraph annotations of a particular author (if done by a single contributor)</u>.

4. <u>Use the appendix lists only in conjunction with the body of the annotated bibliography</u>. The various lists are only intended to serve as a guide to the body of the bibliography and not as a substitute for it. For

example, if you are interested in a list of Colombian women authors, after examining the Classified List of Authors by Country under Colombia, you should then check the annotated bibliography itself for the most common form of an author's name. Do not assume that Teresa de la Parra was not included; she will be found under PARRA SANOJO, Ana Teresa de la. The chronological list, "Authors Born Before 1900," may not include some authors who indeed are from an earlier period if their birthdates are not listed in the body of the bibliography.

    5.   If an author's works are not listed or annotated, do not assume that is a judgment of their quality. The annotations themselves are for the purpose of making an assessment of the works. The lack of an annotation may well indicate lack of information about an author in the United States, or the difficulty in obtaining works from a certain country due to political circumstances, or, at times, the lack of people willing or available to annotate an author. The lack of annotations for Juana Manuela Gorriti and Sara Gallardo, as well as the incomplete annotation for Marta Brunet, are only a few examples. Women Writers of Spanish America represents in a certain brute form the state of our knowledge of Spanish-American women authors in the United States in the 1980s, but there is still much research to be done.

    Furthermore, one of the purposes of a feminist project such as this one is to examine with a critical eye both literary works and the previous criticism of those works. This is a difficult and controversial process which needs to continue, with you the users, beyond the annotations included herein. Most of these annotations are excellent; we must not forget, however, that they represent widely different opinions about the nature of feminism, feminist literary criticism, and about literature itself. To my knowledge this is the largest collective research project on Spanish-American women writers to date; not only the individual reviews of books but also the information as a whole remains this bibliography's contribution.

A

ABADIA, Herminia Gómez de (see **GOMEZ DE ABADIA, Herminia**)

ABADIA EGUI, María de Jesús (Peru, twentieth century)

Diez cuentos

ABALOS, Carmen (Chile, b. 1921)

Azogue para un espejo, poemas en prosa

Confidencias, poemas en prosa

El dedo en la llaga, cuentos

Exilio 65, poemas en prosa

Libertad condicional, cuentos

Las manos libres, poemas

Noche transfigurada, poemas en prosa

Oratorio menos, en prosa

La semilla de Adán, cuentos

Sencillamente, poemas en prosa

ABELLA CAPRILE, Margarita (Argentina, 1901-1960)

El árbol derribado

Cincuenta poesías

Lo miré con lágrimas

Nieve, poesía

Perfiles de niebla, poesía

Sombras y el mar

Sonetos

ABSATZ, Cecilia (Argentina, twentieth century)

Feiguele y otros cuentos

ACEVEDO, Inés Anchorena de (see **ANCHORENA DE ACEVEDO, Inés**)

ACEVEDO DE CASTILLO, Olga (Chile, 1895-1970)

El árbol solo, poemas

Las cábalas del sueño, poemas

Los cantos de la montaña, poemas

Donde crece el záfiro, poemas

Los himnos, poemas

Isis, poemas

La rosa en el hemisferio, poemas

Siete palabras de una canción ausente, poemas

La violeta y su vértigo, poemas

La víspera irresistible, poemas

ACEVEDO DE GOMEZ, Josefa (Colombia, 1803-1861)

Poesías de una granadina

ACOSTA, Cruz María Salmerón (see **SALMERON ACOSTA, Cruz María**)

ACOSTA, Eloísa Ferraría (see **FERRARIA ACOSTA, Eloísa**)

ACOSTA, Ernestina (Cuba, twentieth century)

En un tiempo de niños, poemas

ACOSTA, Helia d' (pseudonym: see **ACOSTA ANGELES, Helia Diana**)

ACOSTA, Ofelia Rodríguez (see **RODRIGUEZ ACOSTA, Ofelia**)

ACOSTA, Sofia A. (Peru, twentieth century)

La máscara del tiempo, poemas con Francisco Ponce

Omega, poemas

Poemas del agua

ACOSTA ANGELES, Helia Diana (Mexico, twentieth century; pseudonym: Acosta, Helia d')

Nuevo arte de amar

Veinte mujeres

ACOSTA ARCE, Conchita (Colombia, twentieth century)

Fertilidad, poemas

ACOSTA DE BERNAL, Catalina (Mexico, twentieth century)

Griselda la desconocida

ACOSTA DE SAMPER, Soledad (Colombia, 1833-1903)

El descubridor y el fundador

La mujer en la sociedad moderna

Novelas y cuadros de la vida sudamericana

Los piratas en Cartagena, ficción

ACOSTA DE SANCHEZ, Azulina (Uruguay, twentieth century)

La leyenda de Hylas, teatro

Los seis peregrinos, teatro

ACUÑA, Angelina (Guatemala, twentieth century)

Canto de amor en latitud marina

Fiesta de luciérnagas, poemas

La gavilla de Ruth

El llamado de la cumbre, prosa, selección mínima

Madre América, poemas, selección mínima

ACUÑA, Beatriz (Chile, b. 1935)

Aquellos días, cuentos

Búscame, Amor, poesía

Tu amor me lo lleva el viento, poemas

Ven a mi pena, si quieres, poemas

ADAMS, Caridad Bravo (see **BRAVO ADAMS, Caridad**)

ADLER, Raquel (Argentina, b. 1901)

Cánticos de Raquel

De Israel a Cristo

La divina tortura

El libro de siete sellos, visión apocalíptica

Llave de cielo, liras, sonetos y versos de arte menor

Místicas, poemas

Pan bajado del cielo

Sonetos de Dios

Veneración, poemas

ADRIAZOLA, Ximena (Chile, b. 1930)

Amarillo, poemas. Santiago: n.p., 1956. Paperback, 65 pp. The poetic voice observes and reflects about its state of solitude and its marginal condition. The poems present a recurrent struggle against this state of abandonment, and an angry expression of loneliness. Bitter verses ("Me saludo con ají de alegría") express the resentment of the poetic voice, due to the absence of happiness and fulfillment. Different verse forms are used, but there is a predominance of free verse.

Un pez en la portada, cuentos. Santiago: Mazorca, 1960. Paperback, 52 pp. Ten short stories dealing with borderline situations where the limits between reality and fantasy ("Un pez," "El zoológico," "Los globos," "Certificado"), the natural and the supernatural ("Dos hombres"), past and present ("La cómoda," "La abuela"), sanity and insanity ("Un pez") are difficult to determine. The stories succeed in creating a phantasmagoric atmosphere.

Tiempo detenido, poemas

El tiempo se reúne, poemas. Santiago: Grupo Fuego, 1958. Paperback, 37 pp. The poetic voice traces various, mostly negative aspects of time; although intangible, it determines every aspect of existence, ultimately defeating it; the awareness of its flow precludes happiness. Stylistically, the frequent juxtaposition of opposite terms denies positive aspects of the world ("sweet death of the sun," "sweet as an old man's sobbing"). Predominance of free verse. PRL

AEDO, Juana Flores (see **FLORES AEDO, Juana**)

AGNER, María del Carmen Casco de (see **CASCO DE AGNER, María del Carmen**)

AGOSIN HALPERN, Marjorie Stela (Chile-United States, b. 1955). Born in Bethesda, Maryland, of Chilean parents, she spent her infancy and adolescence in Chile, returning to the United States to finish high school, after which she earned a B.A. in Philosophy from the University of Georgia, an M.A. in Spanish literature from Indiana University, and from which she will also receive a Ph.D. She is currently a lecturer in Spanish at Wellesley College. Her works often address the cultural differences between North and South America.

Chile: gemidos y cantares. Quillota: El Observador, 1977. Paperback, 38 pp. A collection of twenty-eight poems and four short prose selections that represent this poet's earliest published work. Throughout these writings, Agosín expresses a sense of longing for the Chile she has left behind. As María Luisa Bombal points out in the Prologue, this work is a "song of love" to Chile.

Conchalí. New York: Senda Nueva, 1980. ISBN 0-918454-23-9, paperback, 54 pp. Prologue by Fernando Alegría and critical aside by Norma Alarcón. A collection of thirty poems, the first by Agosín to be published in the United States. She confronts the different realities of North and South American life in a playful yet lyrical manner. She is aware of the inequities that exist, in particular those suffered by the Latin American woman.   GH

AGOSTINI DE DEL RIO, Amelia (Puerto Rico-United States, b. 1896)

A la sombra del arce

En la porche, comedy

Hasta que el sol se muera, poemas

Puertorriqueños en Nueva York, cuentos

Viñetas de Puerto Rico, cuentos

AGÜERO, Omega (Cuba, b. 1940)

La alegre vida campestre, cuentos

AGÜERO VERA, Carmen (Argentina, twentieth century)

Tiempo de ternura, poemas

AGUIAR, Marta (Uruguay, twentieth century)

El espejo azul, poemas

Gaviotas sobre la ciudad, poemas

El mar y la rosa, poemas

Poemas

AGUIAR DE MARIANI, Maruja (Uruguay, twentieth century)

Alas, poemas

Aventuras del gnomo 24 (veinticuatro) horas, cuentos ejemplares

Los paisajes iluminados, poemas

Poemario

Trilogía de la maternidad, poemas de la madre

AGUILERA, Cristina Camacho Fahsen de (see **CAMACHO FAHSEN DE AGUILERA, Cristina**)

AGUILERA DE SANTOS, Luisa Victoria (Panama, twentieth century; also, Luisita)

El secreto de Antaturá, novela

AGUILERA DOMINGUEZ, Mirta (Uruguay, twentieth century)

Ritmos de la voz desnuda

AGUILILLA, Araceli de (see **CAPOTE DE AGUILILLA, Araceli**)

AGUIRRE, Ana María Chouchy (see **CHOUCHY AGUIRRE, Ana María**)

AGUIRRE, Berta (see **AGUIRRE VIGOUROUX, Berta**)

AGUIRRE, Dora de (Argentina, twentieth century)

El estanque, novela

AGUIRRE, Ingrid Dolores (Mexico, twentieth century)

Para ti, poemas

AGUIRRE, Isidora (Chile, b. 1919)

Anacleto Chin Chin, teatro

Carolina, teatro

La dama del Canasto

Dos y dos son cinco, teatro

Entre dos trenes, teatro

Los que van quedando en el camino, teatro

Los Macabeos

La micro

Pacto de medianoche, teatro

Los papeleros

Pascuales, teatro

La pérgola de las flores, teatro musical

Población Esperanza, teatro

Las sardinas o la supresión de Amanda, teatro

AGUIRRE, Lily (Guatemala, twentieth century)

Estigma, novela

AGUIRRE, Magdalena Mondragón (see **MONDRAGON AGUIRRE, Magdalena**)

AGUIRRE, Margarita (Chile, b. 1925)

Cuadernos de una muchacha muda. Illus. by Emilio Piera. Santiago: Nascimento, 1951. Paperback, 32 pp. Separata de la Revista Atenea, vol. CLLL, noviembre-diciembre 1951. Written in fragments, the short story is the diary of a mute girl who struggles to achieve some kind of communication with those who, like her but for different reasons, are secluded in an institution. Also included in La oveja roja.

La culpa, novela. Santiago: Zig-Zag, 1963. Paperback, 347 pp. Illegitimacy in its various manifestations is the theme prevalent in the lifestories of three members of a Chilean family of landowners. Illegitimacy is a stigma deserving estrangement, when it is the product of rape and the victim is a member of the upper class; a sign of class superiority, when the mother, as opposed to the father, belongs to the working class; and always a symbol of rebellion against the decadence, hypocrisy and immorality of the bourgeoisie.

El huésped. Buenos Aires: Emecé, 1958. Paperback, 157 pp. The novel of an orphan who has been abandoned by his father in the hands of his crazy and religious-fanatic aunt. The boy is unable to rid himself of the oppression victimizing him, not only precluding his development, education and integration in society, but also greatly affecting his physical and mental well-being. Emecé Prize, 1958.

La oveja roja, cuentos. Buenos Aires: Sudamericana, 1974. Paperback, 193 pp. Both "El nieto" and "La oveja roja," return to characters and themes developed, respectively, in El huésped and La culpa. Prevalent topics in the other stories are those of loneliness ("El desalojo," "La visita," "Arreglar el ropero"), the presence of the imaginary in everyday reality ("El abrigo gris," "El cazador") and the need of each individual to find her- or himself ("Final," "Un día como hoy").

El residente, novela. Buenos Aires: Emecé, 1967. Paperback, 183 pp. The alienated youngster of El huésped emigrates to Argentina, where he experiences the process of integration into the world. Buenos Aires provides him with a new atmosphere, the opportunity to learn about friendship, love and solidarity.   PRL

AGUIRRE, Mirta (Cuba, b. 1912)

Ayer de hoy, incluye Presencia interior

Del encausto a la sangre, Sor Juana Inés de la Cruz, biografía

Influencia de la mujer en Iberoamérica

Juegos y otros poemas

Ofrenda lírica de Cuba a la Unión Soviética

Presencia interior, verso

AGUIRRE VIGOUROUX, Berta (Chile, 1919-1977; known as Aguirre, Berta)

Afrodita. Santiago: Grupo Fuego de la Poesía, 1977. Paperback, 57 pp. Forty poems. The first half, "Afrodita," presents twenty poems dealing with the theme of love: eroticism, love as refuge, the longing for love. The second part, "Otros poemas," explores the themes of loneliness, the relationship between the individual and nature, maternal love and friendship. The author uses different metric forms, ranging from sonnets to free verse.

Anillos en la alfombra, novela. Santiago: Arancibia Hermanos, 1967. Paperback, 254 pp. Thematically, structurally and stylistically of little interest. Although it deals with a potentially interesting problem, that of male/female relationships both within and outside of marriage, the topic is superficially and naively treated. Stylistically, the discourse of the characters is incongruent with their characterization usually superseding it, thus unintentionally caricaturizing them.

Ardiente sinfonía, novela. Santiago: Nascimento, 1969. Paperback, 203 pp. Received the "Luis Tello Prize." The protagonist is a twenty-year-old woman, a victim of the patriarchal structures prevalent in the Chilean lower-middle class. In spite of her sensitivity, she is unable to rebel or to develop a critical attitude against the state of affairs oppressing her. The novel fails mainly because the author does not succeed in creating characters whose discourse and actions are congruent.

El círculo tornasol, novela. Santiago: Nascimento, 1973. Paperback, 230 pp. A conscious rejection of the established bourgeois values of the Chilean middle class, and a constant search for authenticity through love and artistic expression, characterize the quest for identity of the young woman protagonist. The novel is unfortunately stylistically flawed, and the characters fall too easily into stereotypes.

Muelles viejos, poemas. Santiago: Pacífico, 1959. Paperback, 35 pp. Seventeen poems. The most relevant themes developed are: the individual's orphan condition in a materialistic and decadent society; the possibility of escaping from it only through love, love as a refuge; a constant questioning of the reasons of life and death; the individual's relationship with nature, especially the sea. There is a predominance of free verse. PRL

AGURTO MONTESINO, Claudina (Chile, b. 1897)

Cuentos chilenos

Pétalos al viento, poemas

Ramillete, poesías y adivinanzas infantiles

AGUSTINI, Delmira (Uruguay, 1886-1914). An active participant in the intellectual life of her time, and a member of the post-modernista generation of poets which included Juana de Ibarbourou, Gabriela Mistral, and Alfonsina Storni, Agustini produced a limited body of work because of her early death at the hands of her husband of a few months. Critics have generally chosen to describe her writing as "erotic" and have dismissed or missed its existential content. An extraordinarily gifted child, she participated as an adult in the intellectual life of her time. Frequently misunderstood as superficial and an innocent whose poetry in no way reflects her bourgeois life, Agustini's work needs re-evaluation. SS

Antología. Selection and Prologue by Esther de Cáceres. 2nd ed. Colección de Clásicos Uruguayos, #69, Biblioteca Artigas. Montevideo: Departamento de Investigaciones de la Biblioteca Nacional, Ministerio de Instrucción Pública y Previsión Social, 1965. Paperback, xlv & 65 pp. The Prologue treats the relation between María Eugenia Vaz Ferreira and Agustini, the various editions of her work (calling this one "more limited, more severe"), and the major critical commentaries, lamenting the overly biographical tendencies of most of them. The formal analysis of several poems distinguishes this edition despite the small number of poems included, almost all of which are from Los cálices vacíos (Ed. by Bertani, 1913). Six additional poems (sources given in the "Criterio de la edición") are included. DEM

Los astros del abismo. Los poetas, 2a serie, vol. 10. Buenos Aires: Claridad, 19??. 85 pp.

Los astros del abismo. Obras Completas de Delmira Agustini, vol. II. Barcelona: Máximo García, 1924. Illus., 174 pp. "Juicio" by Fernando Maristany. Includes photographs and the essay "Delmira Agustini" by Alberto Zum Felde taken from his "Crítica de la Literatura Uruguaya." Includes the following sections from previously published collections: "Otros cantos de la mañana," "Pequeños motivos" (three short prose poems), "El libro blanco," and her juvenile poems collected by her family after her death, the first and second part of "La alborada." The section "Opiniones" includes short comments by Darío, Nervo, Unamuno, Storni, and many others. Among even the earliest poems, written when she was ten to fifteen years old, the theme of writing poetry appears. SS

Los cálices vacíos. Siete Poetas Hispanoamericanos. Montevideo: O.M. Bertani, 1913. 135 pp. Another edition: (Montevideo: Populares, 1963), 49 pp. Dedicated to Eros, this volume contains some of Agustini's most powerfully erotic poems. The poet rhapsodizes about her lover's body. The setting is usually nocturnal; the language frequently modernista. Metrical and rhyme schemes are irregular as is the length of the stanzas. Exclamation points and question marks recur. In "Nocturno," however, she uses the swan persona to shock; it is the poetic voice which leaves a trail of blood behind. In "El cisne," the erotic rhetoric and imagery disguise an important theme: writing poetry. SS

Los cálices vacíos por Delmira Agustini. La isla de los cánticos por María Eugenia Vaz Ferreira. Biblioteca Uruguaya Fundamental, #14. Montevideo: Centro Editor de América Latina, 1968. 72 pp. Includes only the first section of poems published as Los cálices vacíos in the 1924 Obras completas. The twelve poems, including "Nocturno," "Otra estirpe," and other primarily erotic verses, are reproduced faithfully. No prologue or introduction. SS

Cantos de la mañana. Prologue by Pérez y Curis. Montevideo: O.M. Bertani, 1910. 48 pp. Existential themes of anguish and death assert themselves in this collection. It contains Agustini's best-known poem, "Lo inefable," which falls within this category, and love poems. The modernista influence is still somewhat apparent through preciosista metaphors like "el abanico de oro de su risa se abría." Such images serve Agustini's lyrical expression of anguish and other emotions, more than a Parnassian search for formal perfection. Contains "Opiniones sobre la poetisa." SS

Correspondencia íntima y tres versiones de "Lo inefable." Ed. Arturo Sergio Visca. 2nd ed. Montevideo: Biblioteca Nacional, 1978. 88 pp. 1st ed.: Correspondencia íntima (Montevideo: Publicaciones del Departmento de Investigaciones, 1969), 58 pp. This volume includes an extensive introductory essay by the editor, and letters (some of which include poems) between Agustini and five men: Enrique Job Reyes, Manuel Ugarte, Alberto Zum Felde, N. Manino, and Ricardo Más de Ayala. Also included are three abstracted versions of "Lo inefable" from the wealth of materials still relatively unstudied in Montevideo. SS

Delmira Agustini: Exposición en su homenaje de documentación y objetos pertenecientes al "Instituto Nacional de Investigaciones y Archivos Literarios" al cumplirse el aniversario cincuenta de la publicación de "Los cálices vacíos." Montevideo: Amigos del Arte, 1963. 12 pp. SS

El libro blanco. Prologue by Manuel Medina Betancourt. Montevideo: O. M. Bertani, 1907. Illus., 100 pp. Although the imagery and motifs of Agustini's first volume of poetry demonstrate a strong influence from modernismo (marble, rubies, gold, fairies, and diamonds recur), its themes (God, beauty, love, and poetry itself) reveal the poet's intent to define her voice. Capitalized abstractions, such as Thought, Idea, Natura, and Extravagance, contrast with discordant imagery. Length and metrical schemes vary with occasional rhymes, particularly in the sonnets. SS

Obras completas de Delmira Agustini. 2 vols., 2nd ed. Montevideo: M. García, 1924. See annotation under separate volumes: vol. I: El rosario de eros; vol. II: Los astros del abismo. SS

Obras poéticas. Official ed. Montevideo: Institutos Penales, 1940. 307 pp. The poems are presented as follows: published books (in chronological order) and the two sections of early poems (1896-1900 and 1901-1910) that appeared under the same name, "La alborada," in the 1924 Obras completas authorized by Agustini's family. Neither the prologue nor the short biography contribute much not already written before. SS

Poesías. 2nd expanded ed. Las Mejores Poesías de los Mejores Poetas, #193. Barcelona: Cervantes, 70 pp. 1st ed. 1923. SS

Poesías. Biblioteca Rodó, Autores Uruguayos #45-47. Montevideo: Claudio García, La Bolsa de los libros, n.d. [1941]. Paperback, 245 pp. Contains essay, "Perfil" de Ovidio Fernández Ríos, a drawing of Agustini, a "Ficha Biográfica," and "Elogio" (1912) by Ruben Darío. Some poems show dates; included are the prose pieces "Ana" and "6 de enero." Contains all poems known to be written by her except "Variaciones," an early version of "Ave, ¡envidia!" The books of poetry are in chronological order, except that the "Poemas de Infancia" are at the end. DEM

Poesías. 2nd ed. With a study by Luisa Luisi. Biblioteca Rodó. Montevideo: Claudio García, 1944. 255 pp. The "Nota del editor" says that this volume attempts to be her complete works. The purpose of any corrections made is to protect her authenticity. Contains all of first edition (see above) plus "La poesía de Delmira Agustini" by Luisa Luisi (1925), which calls her the best poetess of America, perhaps the best poet. Discusses her poetry as a psychological outlet because she lived so intensely, with discipline, and without intellectual training. Sexuality is often her topic, exalted and excessive; her poetry reveals enigmatic images, the hermeticism of symbolist verses, sexual realism and metaphysical mystery. DEM

Poesías completas. Prologue and notes by editor Manuel Alvar. Textos Hispánicos Modernos, #11. Barcelona: Labor, 1971. 253 pp. This edition includes only that poetry which Agustini herself published in her lifetime. It contains a scholarly introduction which classifies her writing as modernista and critical comments contemporaneous with her poetry. While the volume includes poems missing from the Zum Felde edition, the posthumous poems from Rosario de eros and Los astros del abismo, do not appear. Nevertheless, Alvar has given us the only edition that can claim the adjective "critical," although it is flawed by his unconscious sexism in his unquestioning acceptance of clichés about her life and work. SS

Poesías completas. Prologue and selection by Alberto Zum Felde. Poetas de España y America. Buenos Aires: Losada, 1944. Paperback, 197 pp. 4th ed. 166 pp. The most readily available edition of Agustini's poetry. Zum Felde's judgment of her poetry is primarily based on themes and demonstrates a bias toward the erotic poems. Contains an initial selection of poems preferred by Zum Felde, followed by others arranged by book title. Agustini's poetic originality lies partly in her exploration of erotic and emotional landscapes framed in nocturnal scenes. Other themes in her writing are: writing poetry, existential torment, and nature. A strongly dramatic quality is evident, frequently characterized by the poetic voice's addressing herself to a "tú," who may be lover, muse, or object. SS

Por campos de ensueño. Colección Apolo. Barcelona: B. Bauzá, 1927. Illus. vi & 229 pp. A fragile and rare edition which differs from Poesías (Rodó edition) in that it is missing the short prose poems ("Pequeños motivos," "6 de enero," and "Ana"). A few footnotes contain publication histories for the poems. DEM

El rosario de Eros. Las Grandes Poetisas de América, Colección Estudio. Montevideo: M. García, 1924. 110 pp. Collected after Agustini's death, these poems contain all the characteristic elements of her previous poetry, including erotic themes, the modernista stylistic influence, and existential anguish. Nevertheless, there is a strong sense of self-assurance, gradually developed throughout Agustini's poetic production, but most apparent here. The poems are tightly constructed, suggestive, and complex. SS

El rosario de Eros. Vol. I, Obras Completas de Delmira Agustini. Montevideo: M. García, 1924. Illus., 174 pp. Contains the poems and short prose pieces which had remained unpublished upon Agustini's sudden death. A large edition whose publication was carefully supervised by her family, with several photographs and line drawings. Contains an unsigned introduction, "Rumbo," probably written by the editor, praising her family and talents and providing some biographical details. Also contains "Elogio," Darío's letter to Agustini, and "Opiniones." DEM

El rosario de Eros. Los Poetas, #59. Buenos Aires: Claridad, 19??. 62 pp. SS

Selección de poesías. Santiago de Chile: Luz, 1923. 89 pp. Contains forty-six poems from El libro blanco, Los cálices vacíos, and Cantos de la mañana, but none from El rosario de Eros. Poems are arranged without chronology or separation into sections. No prologue or other indication of the editor appears.   SS

ALARCON DE FOLGAR, Romelia (Guatemala, twentieth century)

Astros y cauces, y Casa de pájaros, libros de poemas

Claridad, poemas

Clima verde en dimensión de angustia, poemas

Cuentos de la abuelita

Día vegetal, poemas

El gusano de luz, cuentos infantiles

Isla de novilunios, poemas

Llamaradas y libelundios

Más allá de la voz, poemas

Pasos sobre la yerba, poemas

Plataformas de cristal, poemas

Poemas de la vida simple

Sin brújula, cuentos de misterio

Tiempo inmóvil

El vendedor de trinos, cuentos de misterio

Viento de colores, poemas en prosa

Vigilia blanca, poemas

ALARDIN, Carmen (Mexico, twentieth century)

El canto frágil, poemas

Canto para un amor sin fe, poemas

Celda de viento, poemas

Después del sueño, poemas

Pórtico labriego

Todo se deja así, poemas

ALATORRE, María de los Angeles Mendieta (see **MENDIETA ALATORRE, María de los Angeles**)

ALBA, Carlos Enrique de (pseudonym: see **ESPEDES DE ESCAÑAVERINO, Ursula**)

ALBA, María Luisa Aldunate de (see **ALDUNATE DE ALBA, María Luisa**)

ALBALA, Eliana (Chile, twentieth century)

Los ríos, por ejemplo, poemas

ALBIÑANA, Asunción Izquierdo (see **IZQUIERDO ALBIÑANA, Asunción**)

ALBORNOZ DE VIDELA, Graciela (Argentina, twentieth century)

Chiqui, Chiqui y Capachito, cuentos

Los cuentos de tía Graciela

Mi tío Alejandro, novela

El milagro

Teatritos de mi barrio, teatro

Valle encantado, relato

Veinte cuentos para niños

ALCAYAGA, Lucila Godoy (see **GODOY ALCAYAGA, Lucila**)

ALCORTA, Gloria (France-Argentina, twentieth century)

En la casa muerta, novela

El hotel de la luna y otras imposturas, novela

Noches de nadie, cuentos

La pareja de Núñez, novela

ALDUNATE, María Elena (Chile, b. 1925; also Elena)

Angélica y el delfín. Colección Mistral. Preface by Arturo Aldunate Philipps. Santiago: Aconcagua, 1977. Paperback, 130 pp. Ten short stories belonging either to the genre of the fantastic ("Angélica y el delfín," "Un señor don Luis," "Marea alta," "Ventana," "El carrusel," "Diez centímetros de sol," "El niño") or to science fiction ("Ela y los terrícolas," "El ingenio," "La bella durmiente"). The themes of loneliness and of the search for love prevail. The preface deals briefly with the significance of science fiction.

Candia, novela

Del cosmos las quieren vírgenes. Santiago: Zig-Zag, 1977. Paperback, 91 pp. Science fiction novel. Extraterrestrial forces intend to renew the human species by giving life to seven thousand girls, born from maidens around the world. Their task is to impose new feminine values over dominating and decaying male ones. The novel develops the life of one of these exceptional beings, from the time of inception until she finds her male counterpart.

Francisca y el otro. Santiago: Pomaire, 1981. Paperback, 217 pp. A novel which portrays -- in a rather naive manner-- the degradation of the Chilean upper class, whose principal aim is enrichment and the pursuit of immediate pleasure. Its main thematic concerns are the hypocrisy of marriage and the marginal and alienating circumstances of the bourgeois woman who accepts the prevalent androcentric social structures.

Juana y la cibernética, cuento. Colección El Viento en la Llama. Santiago: Arancibia Hnos., 1963. Paperback, 43 pp. Accidentally locked for three days in the factory where she works, a single, middle-aged woman reviews her lonely and meaningless life; she hallucinates about a relationship -- at one point with erotic connotations -- with the cutting machine she usually operates. Her careless handling of the machine causes an accident and her ultimate death.

María y el mar, novela. Santiago: Pacífico, 1953. Paperback, 85 pp. A young fisherman's daughter, a victim of the double standards prevalent in the Chilean androcentric society which allow sexual freedom in men but condemn it in women, attempts to find consolation in her relationship with nature -- the sea. This, however, does not offer a valid escape and, in desperation, the young woman kills herself. Outstanding poetic prose.

El señor de las mariposas, cuentos. Santiago: Zig-Zag, 1967. Paperback, 167 pp. Eleven short stories dealing with the themes of loneliness ("Juana y la cibernética," "El hulahoop," "Navidad"), the quest for a fulfilling love ("Candia," "Golo," "La otra," "A imagen de Dios los creó"), and of the magical present in everyday life ("El señor de las mariposas," "El mecano verde," "Candia").

Ventana adentro, novela. Letter-prologue by Eduardo Anguita. Santiago: Alfa, 1961. Paperback, 79 pp. At the verge of suicide, the protagonist plunges into introspection. Her interior monologue explores her loneliness, a consequence of her desperate inability to communicate and to establish meaningful links with other individuals.

PRL

ALDUNATE DE ALBA, María Luisa (Peru, twentieth century)

Songoipi t'idachisgay (Floreció en mi corazón), poemas en kechua

ALEGRIA, Claribel (Nicaragua-El Salvador, b. 1924). Actually born in Nicaragua, Alegría considers herself to be Salvadoran, having gone there as a child. She has been publishing poetry since 1948, but her most recent work has taken on a more political tone as her country further entrenches itself in violence. Her present home is in Mallorca, but she has also lived in the United States. She was the editor of New Voices of Hispanic America, a 1962 anthology which included early works of those who have become major figures in Latin American literature. In 1978, she received the Casa de las Américas poetry award for her book Sobrevivo.

Acuario

Angustia y soledad

Anillo de silencio. Mexico: Botas, 1948. 90 pp. Her primicias: not much to notice in these early poems written between 1944 and 1948. Some are included in Aprendizaje.

Aprendizaje. San Salvador: Universitaria de El Salvador, 1970. 94 pp. Available only in libraries. Anthology of poems from Alegría's major books (which, for the most part, are not available) including: Anillo de silencio (1944-1948), Vigilias (1950-1953), Acuario (1953-1955), Huésped de mi tiempo (1958-1961), Vía única (also containing Auto de fe [1962-1965], and Comunicación a larga distancia [1966-1969]). Her more youthful endeavors give way to a continued preoccupation with women, especially in "Datos personales," "Carta al tiempo" and "Minuto adentro." As she approached the seventies, the themes of politics and death intermingle in "Se hace tarde, doctor" and "The American Way of Death." Good for class use, especially in conjunction with Sobrevivo.

Flores del volcán. Flowers from the Volcano. Trans. Carolyn Forché, bilingual edition. Pittsburgh: Univ. of Pittsburgh Press, 1982. ISBN 0-8229-3469-8, ISBN 0-8229-5344-7. Paperback, 87 pp. A bilingual edition of Alegría's nine major poems with translations by poet Carolyn Forché. Traces her childhood memories of her home, El Salvador, to the cemetery she now considers herself to be, remembering her dead who are "too many to bury." Forché's moving preface as well as Alegría's poetry are a testimony to a reality incomprehensible to most of us. One woman's poetic/political account of a homeland ravaged by war. Would be perfect for class use since a paperback edition is available.

Cenizas de Izalco. With Darwin J. Flakoll. Barcelona: Seix Barral, 1966. 175 pp. A novel in which some of the major themes of Alegría's later work begin to appear: mother/daughter relationships; female insatisfaction with and rebellion against married sexuality; political repression as reality and metaphor; United States intervention in Central America; revolution as the eruption of a volcano. Narrated in the first person by a Salvadoran woman married to the "perfect organization man" and interwoven with fragments of an old diary which constantly makes the narrator/protagonist alter her perspective about her home, her mother's death (and life), and herself. As a woman who is about to erupt like the volcano itself, she is also the symbol and metaphor for the sleepy tropical village underneath whose veneer lies the passion, longing, violence, and the desire for freedom. Would be ideal for a class. Predates much contemporary writing on Central America, giving it (and the reader) an historical perspective.

El detén. Barcelona: Lumen, 1977. ISBN 84-264-2949-1, 76 pp. A novella which takes place simultaneously at a Catholic girls' boarding school and in Key West, contrasting the repressive sexuality of the school with the freedom of Key West. The story of a latina girl raised in the United States in which the narrator explores the ways the cross-cultural experience is subverted to the protagonist's advantage. What might have been a run-of-the-mill story is converted into one which deals with major feminist themes of the American way of life as seen by foreign eyes. Good for class use, especially if used in conjunction with other women's novels about boarding schools and Catholicism.

Huésped de mi tiempo. Buenos Aires: Americalee, 1961. 61 pp. A collection of twenty-two poems written between 1958 and 1961, which deals principally with death, travel, identity and leaving one's past behind. "Bajo relieve" begins to show woman-identified themes with its concern with the poetic persona as "una cadena de madres."

Pagaré a cobrar y otros poemas. Barcelona: Libros de Sinera, 1973.

Suite de amor

Suma y sigue, poesía

Tres cuentos. San Salvador: Ministerio de Cultura, 1958. 40 pp. A collection of three very short stories which can best be described as children's literature. In all three, "El niño que buscaba ayer," "La historia del sauce informe," and "Beni," flora and fauna communicate with children revealing a special fantasy world. Thus, the impossible becomes the possible as the weeping willow is converted into a child and the fine line between dreams and reality is temporarily banished. While this may be useful for an intermediate class (or even an advanced beginning group), there is little feminist orientation in these short texts.

Vía única, Auto de fe. Montevideo: Alfa, 1965. 62 pp. Two separate books of poetry combined into one edition and representing Alegría's production from 1962-1965. The beginning of her assertion as a woman and as a poet. Contains some of the poems which would later be included in Flores del volcán. Of interest for either their feminist or political consciousness are her poems "Prisionera" and "Documental" as well as her long poem to her America, "Mis adioses." NSS

Vigilias

ALEMAN DE QUIJANO, Laura Elena (Mexico, twentieth century)

Seis poemas

Vida y sueño, poesías 1945-1951

ALEMANY, Ofelia (Mexico, twentieth century)

Alarido infernal

La condesa de Reus

ALFEREZ, la monja (see **ERAUSO, Catalina**)

ALLAMAND, Maité (Chile, b. 1911). Allamand was born in Santiago to French parents. She received little formal education but spoke and wrote both English and French as is apparent in her delicate prose. While raising five children and helping her husband in his sucessful medical career, she has written prolifically: novels, poems, and children's stories. Stylistically, she falls midway between the lyricism of the Romantics and the realism of the Costumbristas, without the affectation of the first nor the political concern of the latter.

Alamito el largo, novela para niños

Cosas de campo. Santiago de Chile: Cultural, 1935. Hardback, 114 pp. These fourteen short stories are sketches of the people and daily events which comprise the life of the Chilean countryside, told in a delicate language of precise images. There is an overwhelming sense of fatality: Man's helplessness against nature and death gives a pessimistic, haunting quality to the stories. The author's own voice speaks in the Epilogue where, like Unamuno, she meets with her characters. Good classroom material; occasional colloquialisms.

El funeral del diablo, cuentos

Huellas de la ciudad. Santiago de Chile: Pacifico, 1966. Hardcover, 162 pp. A first-person narrative in journal form without chapters, with headings of the days of the week. A semi-autobiographical novel portraying a young woman's evolving consciousness. This spirited and original twenty-year-old records her aspirations, frustration and experiences as she supports her family after her father's death. Forced to play a male role, she confronts the restrictions of her traditional role, poverty, and social status to define her own values. For the first time, Allamand portrays a woman who can achieve her goals because of her education, social background, and urban setting.

La niña de las trenzas de lana, cuentos para niños

Parvas viejas. Illus. by Miguel Allamand. Santiago de Chile: Cultura, 1936. Paperback, 136 pp. Limited availability. Allamand's second collection of short stories exhibits characteristically delicate language to portray the harsh, poverty-stricken reality of the Chilean countryside. "Las tres leyes" tells of the limited options available to poor women and the subsequent suffering of men, women, and children. Other stories spotlight one character against a richly described background. "Mi tío León" is a traditional folktale.

Renovales. Colección Amura. Santiago de Chile: Cultura, 1946. Hardback, 120 pp. Renovales portrays a poor peasant woman's efforts to transcend the constraints placed upon her by her sex, social status, and environment. Her reality defeats her before she begins: poverty, a useless husband, numerous childbirths, and natural disaster. Like a beast of burden, she rallies against each defeat until an earthquake kills her husband and favorite child. Allamand reveals an acute perception of the futility of poor women's position in Latin American society. The language is delicate with images of nature. Dialogue is rendered colloquially. NE

El sueño y la lumbre, cuentos

ALLENDE, Isabel (Chile-Venezuela, b. 1942). Allende is considered the most widely read woman writer in Latin American today. She is the niece of the late Chilean president, Salvador Allende Gossens, who was assassinated during the military coup of 1973. Following his death, Allende and her family moved to Caracas, Venezuela, where she presently resides. Before writing fiction, Allende was a popular journalist in Chile, who scandalized her public with her articles on such topics as marital infidelity and machismo. Her literary style is characterized by a powerful blend of the real and the fantastic, reminiscent of the magical realism of García Márquez.

La casa de los espíritus, novela. Barcelona: Plaza & Janés, 1982. ISBN 84-01-38011-1, 380 pp. Allende's first novel, translated into more than fifteen languages, is a compelling tale of the Trueba-del-Valle family, set against the backdrop of contemporary Latin American politics. Allende artfully combines the sordid realities of recent Chilean history with the magical world of the imagination as she depicts four generations of women, sharing their legacy of creativity, clairvoyancy and political activism in a social structure first controlled by the family patriarch, Esteban Trueba, and subsequently by Pinochet's military regime. Based in part on real events from the author's life, this novel was initially banned in Chile.

De amor y de sombra. Barcelona: Plaza & Janés, 1984. ISBN 84-01-38034-0, 282 pp. Allende's second novel takes place in an unnamed country of Latin America, which the reader soon recognizes as Pinochet's Chile. It is a fascinating tale of a political awakening, as seen through the eyes of a young woman journalist who inadvertently discovers the mutilated bodies of the "disappeared" buried in a sealed-up mine. Allende creates a climate of suspense as she carefully reveals the individual dramas of the characters engulfed in the killings, either as victims, victimizers or denouncers. The novel is based in part on actual events which occurred in the Chilean mine of Lonquén. LGL

The House of the Spirits. Trans. Magda Bogin. New York: Alfred A. Knopf, 1985. ISBN 0-394-53907-9, 368 pp.

ALLOÜIS, Hilda Morales de (see **MORALES DE ALLOÜIS, Hilda**)

ALMADA, María Inés (pseudonym: see **ALMADA DE ZILVETTI VALDIVIESO, Irma**)

ALMADA DE ZILVETTI VALDIVIESO, Irma (Argentina, twentieth century; pseudonym: Almada, María Inés)

A ti, mujer, poesía

Canto de juventud, poesía

Juventud heroica, poesía

Maternal, poesía

Mensaje, poesía

Unos versos de amor para el recuerdo, poesía

ALMAZAN DE PEREZ BARRERA, María Helena (Mexico, twentieth century)

Caminando, poemas

Clamor de tierra

Los hombres tienen sed, novela

Perfil sociológico de la mujer que trabaja a domicilio

El sol camina de noche y otros cuentos

3 (Tres) horas

ALOMA, Mariblanca Sabás (see **SABAS ALOMA, Mariblanca**)

ALONDRA (pseudonym: see **LAMAS DE SAENZ, María**)

ALONSO, Carmen de (pseudonym: see **CARRASCO, Margarita**)

ALONSO, Dora (Cuba, b. 1910). Born in a small town in the province of Matanzas, Alonso has had little formal education. She nevertheless began publishing articles and engaging in political activity at twenty. She has written stories, a novel, essays, and plays (unavailable here and mostly unpublished). Since the 1959 revolution, she has dedicated herself primarily to writing children's stories whose themes uphold ideals of racial, social, and economic equality for all Cubans. Her earlier works include similar themes and preoccupations.

Agua pasada. Ciudad de la Habana: Girón, 1981. 51 pp. In this series of brief sketches dedicated to her mother, Alonso invokes the people, animals, objects, places and feelings of her childhood. The tone is nostalgic, the language lyrical. Her prose poems as easily capture the grief of a starving, over-worked laundress whose infant child has just died, as the unalloyed joy of the little girl nestled in a tamarind tree, who feels that she rules everything.

Arbol de navidad

Aventuras de Guille, en busca de la gaviota negra, literatura para jóvenes. La Habana: Juvenil, 1966. Paperback, illus., 143 pp. Other editions: En busca de la gaviota negra (La Habana: Juvenil, 1966), paperback, illus., 143 pp.; Aventuras de Guille (La Habana: Instituto del Libro (Gente Nueva), 1969), paperback, illus., 143 pp. The protagonist is a curious, eager twelve-year-old boy with a scientific bent. His guardian aunt fits the stereotype of a fearful, unadventurous, over-protective mother. In contrast, the scientist whom Guille accompanies on an expedition and the fisherman he befriends both have idealized male traits. The story's background highlights the benefits of the Revolution: the fight to save Cuba's fauna, the literacy campaign and new roads. Includes a vocabulary list.

Bombón y Cascabel

La casa de los sueños

El cochero azul. Illus. by Félix Rodríguez. La Habana: Gente Nueva, Instituto Cubano del Libro, 1975. 93 pp.

Cómo el trompo aprendió a bailar

Cuba, ayer y hoy: dos novelas. Buenos Aires: Ambos Mundos, 1965. Paperback, 296 pp. This volume contains Tierra inerme and a novel by a young writer, Daura Olema, La maestra voluntaria. Alonso's text is reproduced unchanged from the 1961 version, and without introduction or any other ancillary materials.

Cuentos/Dora Alonso. Prologue by editor Gustavo Eguren. Illus. by Ricardo Raymena. 1st ed. La Habana: Unión de Escritores y Artistas de Cuba, Bolsilibros Unión, 1976. Paperback, 243 pp. This collection contains the majority of Alonso's stories for adults up to 1976. Several of Alonso's favorite motifs recur: animal characters, old women protagonists, and pre-revolutionary injustice -- especially racism and poverty. An included shorter volume, Once caballos, takes place at the zoo, and best exemplifies Alonso's extraordinary sense of fantasy. Female characters here, including the animals, are particularly poignant and complex. They point to a new, non-stereotyped direction in female characterization in Latin American narrative fiction.

Doñita Abeja y doñita Bella. La Habana: Gente Nueva, 1976. Illus., 43 pp.

Espantajo yo los pájaros

La flauta de chocolate. Ciudad de la Habana: Gente Nueva, 1980. Illus., 101 pp. A collection of poems for young children written in 1974-1975. This volume is divided into four sections entitled: "Nanas y tonaditas," "Nidal," "Vaqueras y marineras," and "La tierra mía." Political poems with themes ranging from Playa Girón to the children of Chile and Vietnam are included, as well as those using more traditional themes and characters, such as one recounting Pinocchio's search for a piece of his nose. Fanciful color drawings add to the book's charm.

Gente de mar. La Habana: Gente Nueva, 1977. Paperback, illus., 96 pp. The author's "words to the reader" which preface this illustrated book for pre-adolescent children about Cuba's fishermen maintain that the stories are true, and are told in the people's own words. Alonso's stamp is nevertheless apparent in the polished language and style of the adventures narrated. The book's didactic purpose is to contrast the fishermen's miserable conditions before the Revolution with those after. No female characters.

El grillo caminante

Kiri Kiriko

Letras. Selection, Prologue and Notes by Imeldo Alvarez García. Ed. Ana María Muñoz. La Habana: Letras Cubanas, 1980. 509 pp. The first section of this, the most complete one-volume anthology of Alonso's narrative fiction available, contains a selection of stories from 1936 to 1979. Tierra inerme, Gente de mar, Once caballos, and Ponolani are reproduced in full with some new section titles added to the end.

El libro de Camilín

El mago Cachucho

Once caballos. 1st ed. La Habana: UNEAC (Unión de Escritores y Artistas de Cuba), 1970. Paperback, illus., 198 pp. All the stories take place at the zoo, are written for adults, and include the famous "Algodón de azúcar," which has been translated into English. (It appeared in: Naomi Katz and Nancy Milton, eds. Fragments from a Lost Diary and Other Stories: Women of Asia, Africa, and Latin America. Boston: Beacon Press, 1973, 1975.) Alonso's concern with those separate from male society at large is again exemplified in her sympathetic and complex portrayal of old women and female animals. The title story focuses poignantly on a mare condemned to be fodder for carnivorous animals. Oblivious to external circumstances, she delivers a foal in the cage of her death.

Pelusín y los pájaros

Ponolani, cuentos. Serie del Dragón. La Habana: Granma, 1966. Paperback, illus., 132 pp. The protagonist of this volume of stories is an African slave brought to Cuba and renamed Florentina. The first part of the book tells her story, while the second recounts the African stories she tells in slavery. The lyrical style is also reminiscent of the folk sense of Afro-Antillian literature. Written to fulfill the political purpose of exposing Cuba's historical evils of racism and slavery, this work also suggests an interesting response to the societal silencing of women. Ponolani at the same time rescues her African culture and her own female identity, through the act of telling tales.

Saltarín

El sueño de Pelusín

Tierra inerme, novela. 1st ed. Habana: Casa de las Américas, 1961. Paperback, 202 pp. Habana: Bolsilibros Unión, 1961[?]. Paperback, 237 pp. An early example of Alonso's social realism, originally written in 1944, this novel portrays the miserable conditions under which Cuba's peasants lived before the Revolution. Alonso's lived experience in the campo where she grew up infuses vitality and concreteness into an otherwise conventional criollista narrative. Two female characters are contrasted -- a maid doomed through ignorance and misery, and a young woman brought up in the city, who unsuccessfully fights ignorance and disease among the peasants.

Tierra inerme. Prologue by Imeldo Garcia. La Habana: Arte y Literatura, Huracán, 1977. 234 pp. Alonso slightly expanded and revised the 1961 text for this edition. The prologue characterizes the novel as uniquely 1940's criollismo.

Tin Tin Pirulero

Una. Serie Mínima Narrativa, #9. La Habana: Arte y Literatura, 1977. Paperback, illus., 60 pp. Eight stories for adults of which only two -- "Cristobal y el año nuevo" and "El traje de novia" -- are not found in Cuentos. The collection's title is taken from the short story of the same name, about a woman (mother and widow) who demonstrates extraordinary strength on learning of her husband's death. The same able handling of fantasy within a realistic setting that characterized Cuentos may be discerned in the two additional stories. SS

ALONSO, Josefina Estrella (see ESTRELLA ALONSO, Josefina)

ALVARADO DE RICORD, Elsie (Panama, twentieth century)

Entre materia y sueño, poemas

Holocausto de rosa, poemas

Pasajeros en tránsito, poemas

ALVARADO RIVERA, María J. (Peru, twentieth century)

Abriendo nuevas sendas, teatro

Amor y gloria, novela histórica

Ante los hijos, teatro

Evolución femenina, ensayo

El feminismo reclamando para la mujer educación superior y derechos conculcados, ensayo

La gesta heroica de la libertad, teatro

El imperativo de la sangre, teatro

El martir José Olaya, teatro

Nuevas cumbres, novela

La Perricholi, novela histórica

El puñal del abuelo, teatro

ALVAREZ, Ada Borja (see **BORJA ALVAREZ, Ada**)

ALVAREZ, Consuelo (Cuba, twentieth century)

La ciudad de los muertos

Hombres-dioses

Sara, novela

ALVAREZ, Gloria de (Mexico, twentieth century)

Es cuestión de alas, poemas

ALVAREZ, Griselda (Mexico, twentieth century)

Anatomía superficial, sonetos

Cementerio de pájaros, poemas

Desierta compañía

10 (Diez) mujeres en la poesía mexicana del siglo XX, antología

Dos cantos, poemas

Estación sin nombre, poemas

Letanía erótica para la paz

La sombra niña

ALVAREZ, Luisa María (Mexico, twentieth century)

México, troquel y escenario, narraciones históricas

ALVAREZ, Mariela (Venezuela, b. 1947)

Cuestión de tiempo

ALVAREZ, Marta (Argentina, twentieth century)

Como quien calza dos pájaros, poemas

ALVAREZ, Mercedes Hurtado de (see **HURTADO DE ALVAREZ, Mercedes**)

ALVAREZ, Mercedes Valenzuela (see **VALENZUELA ALVAREZ, Mercedes**)

ALVAREZ, Rosa Elvira (United States, twentieth century)

El alba perdurable, poesía

Nostalgia, poemas

ALVAREZ CABUTO, María Angélica (Uruguay, twentieth century; pseudonym: Valle, María del)

Alma viajera, poesías

Inquietudes, poesías

Lluvia de pétalos, poesías

Susurros, poesías

ALVAREZ DAVILA, Nadya (Ecuador, twentieth century)

Tierra renovada, poemas

ALVAREZ DE CAÑAS, Dulce María Loynaz de (see **LOYNAZ DE ALVAREZ DE CAÑAS, Dulce María**)

ALVAREZ DE TOLEDO, Adelaida (Uruguay, twentieth century)

La pared de cristal, prosa y poemas

ALVAREZ DE TOLEDO, Luisa Isabel (Argentina, b. 1936; also la Duquesa de Medina Sidonia)

La base, novela

Colores, poemas

La huelga, novela

The strike, translation of La huelga

ALVAREZ DEL CASTILLO DE CHACON, Graciana (Mexico, twentieth century)

Ana y Gracia, prosa

En el jardín de la luna, poesía

Opalo, poesía

Rincón de recuerdos, relato autobiográfico

ALVAREZ REYNOLDS, Mercedes (Argentina, twentieth century)

El hilo de un fantástico sentido, poemas

ALVAREZ RIOS, María (Cuba, b. 1919)

La víctima, teatro

ALVEAR, Elvira de (Argentina, twentieth century)

Reposo

ALVES PEREIRA, Teresinha (Brazil-United States, b. 1934; also Pereira, Teresinka) [Pereira assures me that these are not translations but works written in Spanish. -- Editor]

La alegría está de huelga, poesía

El alma en un hilo, teatro

El amor de los narcisos, poesía

Andale, Rosana, teatro

Help, I'm Drowning, translation

Hetaira, teatro

¡Hey, Mex!, teatro

... Más entramos en la noche, poesía

Mientras duerme la primavera, poemas

Peligro, los ángeles se caen, cuento

Tienda de rondas, poesía

Torre de mitos

AMAT Y LEON DE BOGGIO, Consuelo (Peru, twentieth century)

Hojas, poesía

Novelas, cuentos y otros poemas, poesía

AMOR, Guadalupe (Mexico, b. 1920; also: Amor, Pita)

Las amargas lágrimas de Beatriz Sheridan

Antología poética

Círculo de angustia, poemas

Como reina de baraja, poema

Décimas a Dios, poemas

Fuga de negras

Galería de títeres, cuentos

Letanías

Más allá de lo oscuro

Otro libro de amor, poemas

Polvo

Puerta obstinada

Sirviéndole a Dios de Hoguera, poemas

Todos los siglos del mundo

Yo soy mi casa, poemas

El zoológico de Pita Amor, ciento sesenta décimas

AMOR, Pita (see **AMOR, Guadalupe**)

AMORES, Carmen Blanco (see **BLANCO AMORES, Carmen**)

AMORES DE PAGELLA, Angela Blanco (see **BLANCO AMORES DE PAGELLA, Angela**)

AMPARO DAVILA, María (see **DAVILA, Amparo**)

AMUNATEGUI, Amanda (Chile, twentieth century)

Espejos del éxtasis, poemario

Umbral girante, poemas

Velero de tréboles, poemas

ANABALON, Luisa (Chile, 1892-1951; pseudonym: Rokha, Winet de)

Cantoral

Formas del sueño

Lo que me dijo el silencio, poemas

Oniromancia

Suma y destino

El valle pierde su atmósfera, poemas

ANAYA DE URQUIDI, Mercedes (Bolivia, b. 1885)

Evocaciones de mi vida y de mi tierra

Paso en silencio, novela

ANCHORENA DE ACEVEDO, Inés (Argentina, twentieth century)

Costa romántica, relatos

La mujer errante y otros cuentos

ANDA, María Elena de (Mexico, twentieth century)

Canto a Ibero-América, poesía

Claroscuro, poesía

Maribel, cuentos

Poema castellano a Miguel de Cervantes Saavedra, poesía

Trotamundos, cuentos

ANDRION DE MEJIA ROBLEDO, Rita (Colombia, twentieth century)

Mis recuerdos de colegio

ANGEL, Albalucía (Colombia, b. 1939). Angel studied the history of art in Bogotá, Rome and Paris. In the sixties, she earned her living as a folk singer in Europe. Interested in films and journalism, she has made several successful documentaries about Colombia and written many articles on art. Her narrative fiction, feminist in perspective, uses difficult structures and a poetic language filled with Colombian idioms that demand an attentive reader. An outstanding writer who deserves to be studied and translated, she has won important literary prizes in her country.

Las andariegas

Dos veces Alicia. Barcelona: Barral, 1972. Paperback, 161 pp. Twenty-two untitled fragments that use sudden changes of narrator, characters and chronology, comprise this novel set in London in the sixties. Humor and suspense draw the reader through the metaliterary games of the narrator/author in a biting satire about power and aggression in the conventional bourgeois family and society. Freedom in form, language, and as an ideal, is the trademark of this remarkable novel.

Estaba la pájara pinta sentada en el verde limón. Bogotá: Instituto Colombiano de Cultura, 1975. Paperback, 396 pp. Another edition: (Colombia: Plaza y Janés, 1981), hardbound, 325 pp. A *bildungsroman*, this is the story of growing up female in Colombia in one of that country's most violent periods (1948-1957). Contemporary in structure, i.e., employing shifts in narrators, chronologies, and themes, the core of the narrative centers on the erotic and the political awakening of its protagonist. The novel uses historical documents and innumerable voices of different ages and classes to witness the individual and collective lives of the period. One of the best examples of *la novela de la Violencia* in Colombia.

Los girasoles en invierno. Bogotá: Bolívar, 1970. Paperback, 208 pp. A first novel that reveals the author's dexterity with language. A female voice narrates her memories of loving and travelling in Europe in the sixties. The core of the scanty plot is the relationship of the young narrator with a novice painter. Both are trying to find themselves through the art and the beauty of their surroundings.

Misiá Señora. Barcelona: Argos Vergara, 1982. Paperback, 308 pp. The difficult structure of this novel demands alertness in following the life of the female protagonist from childhood to disenchanted old age. Feminist in conception, the story permits the reader to see four generations of women suffering under male power. Critics have praised the poetic style of the book in which regional idioms are used with a keen musical ear.

¡Oh gloria inmarcesible!. Bogotá: Instituto Colombiano de Cultura, 1979. Paperback, 186 pp. Thirty-five fragments conceived as film 'flashes' about Colombian landscapes and people. Most of them are narrated by humble, uneducated men and women whose speech is characterized by colorful idioms and humor. The total effect of these pieces is a razor-sharp condemnation of those in power who benefit from the socio-economic injustices from which the majority of people suffer.

GM

ANGELES, Helia Diana Acosta (see **ACOSTA ANGELES, Helia Diana**)

ANGELES, I. Orfelinda Herrera de (see **HERRERA DE ANGELES, I. Orfelinda**)

ANGELES, Isabel de los (Mexico, twentieth century)

Cariátides, poemas

ANTIGUA, Madre María de la (see **MARIA DE LA ANTIGUA, Madre**)

ANTUÑA, Rosario (Cuba, b. 1935)

Son de otros, versos

APAIKAN (pseudonym: see **FERNANDEZ DE TINOCO, María**)

ARAMBURU LECAROS, Helena (Peru, twentieth century)

Cartas rosas, autobiografía

Como árbol milenario, poesía

Ideas que cantaron, poesía

El infiel y tres, teatro

Lo que piensan las mujeres, ensayo

Pirito con Lucema y Ajolí, cuento

Vida, mundo, religión y sueño, novela

ARANGO, Esther (Colombia, twentieth century)

Espumas, cuentos

ARAUJO, Carmen Hernández de (see **HERNANDEZ DE ARAUJO, Carmen**)

ARCE, Conchita Acosta (see **ACOSTA ARCE, Conchita**)

ARCINIEGA, Rosa (Peru, b. 1909)

Engranajes, novela

Jaque Mate, novela

Mosko-strom, novela

Playa de vidas, cuentos

Vidas de celuloide, novela

ARELLANO, Diana Ramírez de (see **RAMIREZ DE ARELLANO, Diana**)

ARELLANO DE NOLLA, Olga Ramírez de (see **RAMIREZ DE ARELLANO DE NOLLA, Olga**)

ARENAS RUIZ, Maruja Uribe de (see **URIBE DE ARENAS RUIZ, Maruja**)

AREVALO, Teresa (Guatemala, twentieth century)

Emilia, novela

ARGÜELLES, Emma Vargas Flórez de (see **VARGAS FLOREZ DE ARGÜELLES, Emma**)

ARGÜELLES DE MOLLOY, Lucila Castellanos (see **CASTELLANOS ARGÜELLES DE MOLLOY, Lucila**)

ARIAS, Gloria Nieto de (see **NIETO DE ARIAS, Gloria**)

ARIAS, Irene Zapata (see **ZAPATA ARIAS, Irene**)

ARIAS, María Velasco y (see **VELASCO Y ARIAS, María**)

ARIAS, Olga (Mexico, twentieth century)

A Durango, poesía

Acusación, poesía

Canción laudatoria, poema

Canciones para Natacha, poesía

Canto al maestro rural, poesía

El cornetín de los sueños

Cuatro preludios para una ciudad, poesía

Deliaiza, cuento

Dos estados medulares y un momento de transición, poesía

Elegías en tu ausencia

El elegido, poemas

En la espiga del viento, poemas

Espirales, cuentos

Felipe pescador, poesía

Fragmentario, poemas

Francisco Villa, poesía

El grito, poesía

El héroe de Silex, poesía

Homenaje, poesía

La que todos amaron, poesía

Libro de espejos, poemas

La mansión

Metamórficos

Mínima galaxia, poemas

Nocturnos

Nostalgia en el otoño, poemas

Paisajes, poesía

Poemas de mayo, 1963

El portillo

Los preludios

Preludios fáciles, poesía

Las pupilas, poesía

La sequía y nosotros, poesía

Sobreviviente, poemas

Toribio, literatura para niños

Tres poemas

Trilogía, poemas

ARIAS DE CABALLERO, Blanca Graciela (Venezuela, b. 1921)

Canta una madre, poesía

Chicharras en el bambú, poemas para niños

Pasitos de luz, poesías infantiles

Puente del jazmín viajero, poesía

ARMSTRONG, Ana Inés Bonnin (see **BONNIN ARMSTRONG, Ana Inés**)

ARNAO, Luz Machado de (see MACHADO DE ARNAO, Luz)

AROCHA, Mercedes Carvajal de (see CARVAJAL DE AROCHA, Mercedes)

AROSEMENA, Olga Elena Mattei de (see MATTEI DE AROSEMENA, Olga Elena)

ARRATIA, Olga (Chile, twentieth century)

Makoe, cuento

Zona de sombras, cuentos

ARREDONDO, Inés (Mexico, twentieth century)

La señal

ARREDONDO, Isabel Machado de (see MACHADO DE ARREDONDO, Isabel)

ARRILLAGA, Josefina Perezcano de Jiménez (see PEREZCANO DE JIMENEZ ARRILLAGA, Josefina)

ARRILLAGA, María (Puerto Rico, b. 1940). A teacher at the University of Puerto Rico and a writer by profession, Arrillaga was awarded first prize in the poetry contest of the Ateneo Puertorriqueño (1972) for her first book of poetry, Vida en el tiempo. Besides poetry, her literary work includes essays and short stories. Her life and work are the testimonial expression of her struggle for the affirmation of women's individuality. She is married and has one daughter.

Cascada de sol. Serie Literatura Hoy. San Juan: Instituto de Cultura Puertorriqueña, 1977. 92 pp. Written at the same time as Poemas 747, it is again the poetry of a woman who is alone. These are poems of love or, more specifically, they are poems of disaffection (desamor). A melancholic tone characterizes the remembrances of unfulfilled love. The woman poet has learned that the reality of love has nothing to do with the false image that a bourgeois tradition and education has given her. Love is a creation, a creation of self and of love itself.

Frescura 1981. The poet joyfully sings of fulfillment, in a mature poetic affirmation. There is a clear consciousness of feminine identity and of the oppressed situation of womanhood. Erotism as a subject or as erotic language has traditionally been forbidden grounds for feminine expression. It is for this reason that, as a would-be participant in what ironically was supposed to be a congress of feminine creativity, her contribution was censored by the congress organizers. One of the censored works appears on page 33.

Poemas 747. These are poems of the affirmation of woman's life alone. The poems become intimate in the feminine space of the home, the child, the garden and its flowers. The number in the title refers to this intimacy as it is, literally, the number of the poet's home. But 747 is also a metaphor for the "supersonic" intensity and spiritual vigor of these poems.

Taller de poesía

Vida en el tiempo, poemas. San Juan de Puerto Rico: Instituto de Cultura Puertorriqueña, 1974. 134 pp. Characterized by the critics as a young woman's vibrant and daring testimony of her time, this extense book with its sincere and direct language of frequent and intentional prosaic quality, is the expression of the poet's search for cultural identity. It is the painful process of the rediscovery of her Hispanic identity after many years away. IV

ARVELLO, Clotilde C. de (see **C. DE ARVELLO, Clotilde**)

ARVELO LARRIVA, Enriqueta (Venezuela, twentieth century)

El cristal nervioso

Mandato del canto, poemas 1944-1946

Poemas perseverantes

Voz aislada

ARZARELLO DE FONTANA, Sofía (Uruguay, twentieth century)

Oro y sombra, versos

ARZOLA, Marina (Puerto Rico-Spain, 1939-1976). In the Puerto Rican literary milieu of the early sixties, Arzola was one of the few women poets. She was part of a literary group which published a periodical called Guajana. Bright and eccentric, Arzola left Puerto Rico and lived in Spain. She returned in the seventies and commited suicide in 1976. Only one of her books was published during her lifetime. Her poetry is obscure and dense; time, death and nature are the main themes. Her style is highly metaphorical and lyric.

Palabras vivas, poemas de 1961, 1962, 1963. Barcelona: Rumbos, 1968. Hardbound, 159 pp. The author includes a note at the beginning of the book in which she relates poetry to the geography of the southern part of the island where she grew up. The poems are hermetic and very abstract, full of obscure metaphors, chaotic in meaning. Several themes are constant: being, death and nature. Short verse forms predominate, as well as traditional ones like the sonnet.

El niño de cristal y los olvidados. Serie Literatura Hoy. San Juan: Instituto de Cultura Puertorriqueña, 1977. Paperback. Award-winning book at the contest sponsored by the Ateneo Puertorriqueño in 1966. These poems present reality as a multiple entity, as something chaotic and full of contradictions. The creation of new words, complexity of syntax and an abundance of images characterize this book. The crystal child is a sign of innocence and hope amidst constant destruction. ILJ

ARZON, Anadela (Argentina, twentieth century)

Reportaje al paraíso, poemas

ASBAJE, Juana de (see **JUANA INES DE LA CRUZ, sor**)

ASTORGA, Irma Isabel (Chile, b. 1920)

Ceniza quebrada, poemas

La compuerta mágica; el mundo del huaso contado por el mismo, novela

La muerte desnuda

Tríptico

Viaje a la garganta de la luz

ASTRADA, Etelvina (Argentina, b. 1930). Primarily a poet, Astrada has also authored short stories and several critical articles. While her works display a social concern for humanity's circumstances (both in her homeland and in the world at large), she projects as her central theme an interest in death in all its various aspects and ramifications. Sensitive to humanity's existential dilemma, in the Heideggerian sense, and conscious of the inevitability of death, she eschews in her poetry sentimentality, verbosity, formality, nonessential description and complicated imagery. TR

Autobiografía con gatillo. Madrid: Ayuso, 1980. ISBN 84-336-0175-X, paperback, 72 pp. Introductory poem and art work by Rafael Alberti. Dominated by a first-person speaker, the fifty-three poems comprise the anticipated themes of an "autobiography" (birth, life, death, love, hope, despair, etc.). By eschewing narrative description, sentimentality, and trite rhetoric, the poetic voice finds its inspiration in the commonplace and in the world of physical and psychic pain. Alienation and solitude surface as the paradox of life is fully explored and the reader becomes involved in the need to relate to a poetic reality that is both therapeutic and challenging. The reader is thus drawn into the tension that emerges from the enigmas of life itself. TR

Autobiography at the Trigger. York, S. Carolina: Spanish Literature, 1983. ISBN 0-938972-04-9, hardback, 146 pp. Bilingual edition. Introd., biographical information, and trans. by editor Timothy J. Rogers. This work reflects an inner spirit laden with a sense of alienation, solitude, and skepticism, written in an imagery that eschews narrative description and sentimentality. Shows awareness of her plight of "existing for death" and her need to "get accustomed to the possible." Clear, accurate and excellent translations. Introductory poem and cover design by Rafael Alberti. JZ

Muerte arrebatada, poesía. Preface by Carlos Edmundo de Ory. Madrid: Ambito Literario, 1981. ISBN 84-7457-115-4, Paperback, 99 pp. The volume presents a sorrowful lament over humanity's awesome power to destroy the world with the neutron bomb. The poetic voice (speaking on behalf of all humanity) reflects a preoccupation and concern over the potentiality of world annihilation brought on by insensitive world leaders and scientists gone amuck. The voice, fully cognizant of the inexorable presence of death, pleads that if the end must come, let it at least be through natural causes. The language is uncluttered, direct, and, at times, poignant. TR

ASTRADA, María Nélida (Argentina, twentieth century)

Cantos para mi ciudad, poemas

AVELLANEDA, Gertrudis (see GOMEZ DE AVELLANEDA Y ARTEAGA, Gertrudis)

AVELLANEDA Y ARTEAGA, Gertrudis Gómez de (see **GOMEZ DE AVELLANEDA Y ARTEAGA, Gertrudis**)

AZEVEDO, Idilia (Uruguay, twentieth century)

Lo que yo he visto, autobiografía

B

BABIN, María Teresa (Puerto Rico, b. 1910). Having taught at the university level both in Puerto Rico and the United States, Babín is best known as a major literary critic, professor and creative writer. At Lehman College, 1969-1972, she founded and headed the Department of Puerto Rican Studies. Her literary studies give insight into the personality, culture and soul of Puerto Rico and her people. Not only does she approach Puerto Rican literature regionally, but also in the context of Latin American literature.

La barca varada, poesía

Fantasía boricua: estampas de mi tierra. Colección Símbolo. New York: Las Américas, 1956. 122 pp. This short biography begins with the lethargic rhythms of life and brief descriptions of a woman's fantasies and images or estampas of her native land. Gradually, the story becomes more culturally intertwined with major events, such as the celebration of Christmas in Puerto Rico, Saint Ciriaco, the great hurricane of 1899, and the importance of fishing and harvesting sugar cane. However, the most interesting characters, memories, and thought-provoking points are revealed at the end of the book. Family memories and dreams for her country show her deep-felt ties to the motherland. The women portrayed are socially oppressed, reduced to the traditional sedate roles of housewives, childbearers, and religious worshippers. CK

La hora colmada, fábula teatral

Las voces de tu voz, poemas

BACELO, Nancy (Uruguay, twentieth century)

Barajando, poemas

Cantares, poemas

Cielo solo, poemas

Círculo nocturno, poemas

El pan de cada día, poesía

Razón de la existencia, poemas

Tránsito de fuego, poemas

BAENA, Lilia Senior de (see **SENIOR DE BAENA, Lilia**)

BAEZA, Astencia Cid (see **CID BAEZA, Astensia**)

BAEZA, Leticia Repetto (see **REPETTO BAEZA, Leticia**)

BALMACEDA, Virginia Cox (see **COX BALMACEDA, Virginia**)

BALUARTE, Amparo (Peru, twentieth century)

Alma cancionera, poesía

Amor: luz y sombra, poesía

Breviario pasional, poesía

Cáliz de amor, poesía

Luminosa, poesía

Paz sobre la tierra y la ruta

Romancero místico, poesía

BANDA FARFAN, Raquel (Mexico, b. 1928)

Amapola, cuentos

La cinta, cuentos

Escenas de la vida, relato

Cuesta abajo, novela

La luna de Ronda, cuentos

Un pedazo de la vida rural, cuentos

El secreto, cuentos

La tierra de los geránios

Valle verde, novela

BARBAT DE MUÑOZ XIMENEZ, María del Carmen Izcua (see **IZCUA BARBAT DE MUÑOZ XIMENEZ, María del Carmen**)

BARBE, María López de Victoria y (see **LOPEZ DE VICTORIA Y BARBE, María**)

BARBITTA COLOMBO, Adela (Argentina-Uruguay, twentieth century)

Yo te quise, teatro

BARCO DE VALDERRAMA, Lucy (Colombia, twentieth century)

La picua ceba

BARRA, Emma de la (Argentina, nineteenth century; pseudonym: Duayen, César)

Eleonora, novela

Graziella

El manantial

Mecha Iturbe, novela

Stella, novela de costumbres argentinas

BARRA DE LOS LLANOS, Emma (see: **BARRA, Emma de la**)

BARRAGAN, Lida (Argentina, twentieth century)

Poemas radioactivas, con Raúl Fortin y Omar Gancedo

BARRAGAN DE TOSCANO, Refugio (Mexico, 1846-1916)

Celajes de occidente, composiciones líricas y dramáticas

Las cuatro estaciones, zarzuela de fantasía

Diálogos, monólogos, y comedias para niños

La hija de Nazareth, poema

La hija del bandido, o los subterráneos del Nevado, novela

Luciérnagas, cuentos

Poesías

Premio del bien y castigo del mal, novela

BARRANTES, Olga Marta (Costa Rica, twentieth century)

La familia Mora, teatro

BARRIOS, María Esther Llana (see **LLANA BARRIOS, María Esther**)

BARRIOS DE CHUNGARA, Domitila (Bolivia, b. 1937)

Let me speak! Testimony of Domitila, a Woman of the Bolivian Mines, translation

BARROS, Silvia (Cuba, b. 1939)

Teatro infantil

Veintisiete pulgadas de vacío, poemas

BASTOS, Laura Carreras de (see **CARRERAS DE BASTOS, Laura**)

BASURTO GARCIA, Carmen (Mexico, b. 1904)

Alborada, poesía

Asambleas escolares, literatura para niños

En torno al amor, poesía y prosa

Festejando a Mamá, teatro

Madre bien aventurada, poesía

La mujer, proletaria, poesía

Musa popular, poesía

La patria del futuro, república de trabajadores, poemas

Teatro infantil, poesía

Vida ascendente, poemas en prosa

BATIZA, Sarah (Mexico, twentieth century)

Eso que se llama un niño, novela

Mis "yos" y Larry, comedia de buen humor

Vosotras las taquígrafas, novela

BAZAN DE CAMARA, Rosa (Argentina, b. 1895)

Collar de momentos, cuentos

Espirales de humo, poesía

Extraño delirio, novela

Norte América-Brasil-México, poesía

El pozo del balde, novela

Prados de oro

Soledad, novela

Sombra, novela

Sueños y verdades de una gran pensadora; cuentos, reflexiones, pensamientos de Rosa Bazán de Cámara, antología

BECERRIL, Dominga Cruz de (see **CRUZ DE BECERRIL, Dominga**)

BEDREGAL DE CONITZER, Yolanda (Bolivia, b. 1916)

Alemán

Almadía

Bajo el oscuro sol

Del mar y la ceniza

Ecos, poemas (alemán-castellano, castellano)

Nadir, poemas

Naufragio

Poemar

Primera antología de Yolanda Bedregal

BELEVAN, Enriqueta (Peru, twentieth century)

Poemas al estilo de una pintura ingenua

BELINZON, Concepción Silva (see **SILVA BELINZON, Concepción**)

BELLI, Gioconda (Nicaragua, b. 1948). Born in Managua, Belli began writing poetry in 1970 and was soon published in various Latin American revues, including La Prensa Literaria, El Gallo Ilustrado, and Nicarauac. In 1972, she was awarded the Mariano Fiallos Gil prize for poetry. Her first book, Sobre la grama, revealed a strong mastery of her art and a true poetic gift, whether dealing with female concerns and experience or artistic creation and its demands. Línea de fuego represents a complete departure in tone and subject matter. Winner of the Casa de las Américas prize for poetry, this anthology is devoted to Belli's deep involvement in the Revolution, the suffering and dedication of her comrades, her voluntary exile in Costa Rica and her longing for her home and family.

Sobre la grama. [Nicaragua:] n.p., n.d. [1974], n. pag. [77 pp.] The poet's first book, containing an extensive introductory essay by José Coronel Urtecho, and illustrated with sketches of Belli, Sobre la grama significantly establishes the young poet as an important voice in Latin American literature. Despite the preponderance of love poems in the collection, Belli does not wallow in sentimentality but rather imbues her lyrical statements with a strong sense of self. The pieces to her young daughters are exceptionally tender, documenting their birth and early years, her sense of joy and fulfillment, as well as the realistic demands of motherhood. She exults in being a woman: "Y Dios me hizo mujer" -- the leading piece in the anthology, which was later combined with "Tengo," a shorter work, to make an extraordinary statement about the female condition. Suitable as college text.

Línea de fuego. Ed. Dominica Diez. Ciudad de La Habana: Casa de las Américas, 1978. 89 pp. Winner of the 1978 Casa de las Américas prize for poetry, the fifty-five poems are divided into three sections, "Patria o Muerte," "Acero," and "A Sergio," reflecting the themes of revolutionary fervor, pervading nostalgia for Nicaragua, and frank expressions of sexual desire and fulfillment. Added stylistic interest is provided by eight prose-poems and one work combining both genres. The most incisive pieces deal with new roles for revolutionary women, as well as the traditional ones in new guises which they must play. An admixture of real and surreal, powerful imagery, inventive metaphor and true poetic vision create incisive statements. Suitable for college classes in women's studies, literature and Latin American studies.

ME & ED

Truenos y arco iris

BELLO, Ana Luisa Prats (see **PRATS BELLO, Ana Luisa**)

BELTRAN NUÑEZ, Rosario (Argentina, b. 1908)

Gualicho, teatro

La llama en éxtasis, poesía

Poemas de la Arcilla y el ala, poesía

Psicología de la mujer moderna, ensayo

Raíz india, novela

Rascacielos, poesía

El retablo de Satanás, cuento

Sol de amanecer, poemas en prosa

Tierra brava, cuentos

El vuelo de Kakuy, cuentos

BEMBERG, María Luisa (Argentina, twentieth century). Bemberg is the director and one of the screenwriters of the 1984 film, Camila, based on the true story of the nineteenth-century young Argentinian bourgeoise who eloped with the parish priest, only to be executed, pregnant and with her lover, by order of Rosas. Camila (Susu Pecoraro) and Ladislao (Imanol Arias) are presented as romantic victims of their passion, which unfolded in one of the darkest and bloodiest moments of Argentinian history. One is urged to read the screenplay (and film) as the protagonist and other young women read French novels of the epoch, as a "readerly" reader, immersed in the romantic tragedy. Bemberg was unable to make the film until the occurrence of the free elections in Argentina in 1983.

Camila, guión. Written with Beda Docampo Feijoo and Juan Bautista Stagnaro, GEA Cinematográfica, SRL (an Argentinian-Spanish production), 1984. BM

BENCOMO, Carmen Delia (Venezuela, twentieth century)

El burrito retozón, teatro

Cocuyos de cristal, relatos para niños

Los luceros cuentan niños, poesía

Mientras crece la hierba, novela

Muñequitos de aserrín, poesía

Rostro de soledad, poesía

BENITEZ, Eloísa Celi de (see **CELI DE BENITEZ, Eloísa**)

BENITEZ, María Bibiana (Puerto Rico, 1783-1873)

    A la vejez

    La cruz del morro

    Diálogo alegórico

    La ninfa de Puerto Rico

    Soneto

BENNET, Daisy (Chile, twentieth century)

    La paloma encendida

    Sólo recuerdos, poesía

    Vértigo, poesía

BENVENUTA, Ofelia Machado Bonet de (see **MACHADO BONET DE BENVENUTA, Ofelia**)

BERENGUER, Amanda (see **BERENGUER BELLAN, Amanda**)

BERENGUER BELLAN, Amanda (Uruguay, b. 1924; known as Berenguer, Amanda)

    A través de los tiempos que llevan a la gran calma, poemas

    Contracanto, poemas

    Declaración conjunta, poesía

    La invitación, poemas

    Materia prima, poesía y prosa

    Quehaceres e invenciones

BERIO, Blanca Teresa (Puerto Rico, twentieth century)

    De 13 (trece) a 19 (diecinueve)

    El paso, poemas

BERMUDEZ, María Elvira (Mexico, b. 1916)

    Alegoría presuntuosa y otros cuentos

    La vida familiar del mexicano

    Diferentes razones tiene la muerte

BERNAL, Catalina Acosta de (see **ACOSTA DE BERNAL, Catalina**)

BERNAL, Emilia (see **BERNAL Y AGÜERO, Emilia**)

BERNAL DE SAMAYOA, Ligia (Guatemala, twentieth century)

Canción de los dos caminos

Su majestad el miedo, teatro

La piedra en el pozo y tus alas, teatro

Tus alas, Ariel, teatro

BERNAL JIMENEZ, Lucía Cock de (see **COCK DE BERNAL JIMENEZ, Lucía**)

BERNAL Y AGÜERO, Emilia (Cuba, b. 1884; known as Bernal, Emilia)

Alma errante, poemas

América, poemas

¡Como los pájaros!

Exaltación, poema sinfónico

Lagka frogka, novela

Mayorca, prosa y verso

Negro, poemas

Los nuevos motivos

Poesías: Vida

Sentido, prosas

Sonetos

BERTHELY JIMENEZ, Lylia C. (Mexico, twentieth century)

Copal, poesía

Opalo, poesía

Remanso, poesía

Vida de Zancos, cuento

Vórtice, poesía

BERTOLE, Emilia (Argentina, b. 1903)

Espejo en sombra

Estrella de humo

BERTOLE DE CANE, Cora María (Argentina, twentieth century)

El amor

La ciudad distante, poemas

Después de Clarisa, novela

Jubilación en trámite, teatro

Sendero de piedra, poesía

BETANCOURT DE BETANCOURT, Isabel Esperanza (Cuba, b. 1868)

Demasiado bella, teatro

Poesías

BETANCOURT FIGUEREDO, María de (Venezuela, b. 1876)

¿Castigo o redención?, novelita

Manojo de flores, comedia infantil

El cuarto mandamiento, comedia infantil

BETONA, Salvadora Medina Onrubia de (see **MEDINA ONRUBIA DE BETONA, Salvadora**)

BIAGONI, Amelia (Argentina, b. 1916)

Las cacerías

El humo, poemas

La llave, poemas

Sonata de la soledad, poemas

BIANCHI DE ECHEVERRIA, María Flora Yáñez (see **YAÑEZ BIANCHI DE ECHEVERRIA, María Flora**)

BIDART ZANZI, Blanca (Uruguay, twentieth century)

Una mujer está bordando

Nacarina, tragedia

BLANCO, María Teresa (Colombia-United States, twentieth century)

Clave trémula, poesía

BLANCO, Marta (Chile, b. 1938)

La generación de las hojas, novela

Todo es mentira, cuentos

BLANCO AMORES, Carmen (Argentina, twentieth century)

Raíz desnuda, poemas

La voz bajo el ciprés, poemas

BLANCO AMORES DE PAGELLA, Angela (Argentina, twentieth century)

Hombres con su dolor

Para tu soledad, poesías

El retrato, cuentos

Silencio entero, poesías

BLANCO VILLALTA, Manuela de (Argentina, twentieth century)

Las horas en el tiempo, poemas

La senda incesante, poemas

Un tiempo en la eternidad

BLOCH, Olga Bruzzone de (see **BRUZZONE DE BLOCH, Olga**)

BOBES ORTEGA, Evelina (Mexico, twentieth century)

La ciudad y la música, novela

Otoño estéril, novela

El viento de noviembre, novela

BOCCALANDRO, Ada Pérez Guevara de (see **PEREZ GUEVARA DE BOCCALANDRO, Ada**)

BODMER, Helvia García de (see **GARCIA DE BODMER, Helvia**)

BOGGIO, Consuelo Amat y León de (see **AMAT Y LEON DE BOGGIO, Consuelo**)

BOHORQUEZ, Abigael (Mexico, twentieth century; pseudonym: Vidal, Marzo)

Acta de confirmación, poemas

Las amarras terrestres, poemas

Canción de amor y muerte por Rubén Jaramillo y otros poemas civiles

La madrugada del centauro, poema dramático

Nocturno del alquilado y la tórtola, poema dramático

Poesía y teatro por Marzo Vidal

BOLIO DE PEON, Dolores (Mexico, b. 1880)

A tu oído, poemas y prosa

Aromas de antaño, novela

La cruz del maya

Días de verano, novela

El dolor de la vida

En silencio, poemas

Una hoja del pasado, novela

Intimidad, poesía y prosa

Mamá grande cuenta que . . . , balada

Un solo amor, novela

Wilfredo el velloso, novela

Yerbas de olor, poemas

BOLLO, Sarah (Uruguay, b. 1904). Known mainly as a poet, Bollo is also the author of several volumes of literary criticism and one verse-play. Her play treats an historical heroine from Bolívar's time, but the majority of her poetry is contemporary, the exceptions being her re-telling of the myth of the goddess Diana and the story of Ariel. In contrast to other better-known women writers of her day, Bollo's work is less obviously erotic, much more spiritual in tone. Her early works are tinged with Modernist vocabulary (flowers, gems, rare woods, etc.), and at times a Neo-Barroque flood of emotion, imagery, and expression. The later volumes are calmer, more introspective, and often times treat Bollo's increasing awareness of her own mortality.

Antología lírica. Buenos Aires: Nova, 1948. 180 pp. This volume contains the complete works of Bollo published through 1944, reprinted here in the following order: Diálogo de las luces perdidas (1927), Las voces ancladas (1933), Los nocturnos del fuego (1931), Regreso (1934), Baladas del corazón cercano y otros poemas (1935), Gozosos destierros (1935) (which was included as a part of Baladas), Ciprés de púrpura (1944), as well as two scenes from Acto III, Cuadro II of Bollo's verse tragedy, Pola Salavarrieta.

Ariel prisionero, Ariel libertado. Montevideo: Uruguaya, 1948. 66 pp. This short work opens with quotes from Shakespeare, Goethe, and Rodó, then details, through narrative poems, aspects of the story of the mythic character Ariel. Like her Diana transfigurada, this work is an extended technical exercise for Bollo. The author takes great pains to use learned forms of words (for example, creatura instead of criatura) as if pointing to an earlier age in time, thus reenforcing the antiquity of her topic. However, the epic tone of these poems is similar to that of Bollo's religious works, as she uses exclamations, contrasting extremes and the glorification of nature. As in most of Bollo's other works, this book has two main sections which contrast despair and pain on the one hand and triumph and restitution on the other.

Baladas del corazón cercano y otros poemas. Montevideo: Rosgal-Hilario Rosillo, 1935. 142 pp. Bollo divides this series of poems into two thematic units: the ecstasy of passion followed by the pain of lost love. The baladas of the opening part have short lines which quicken the tempo, and words such as dulce, gozo, sonrisa, luz, ardiente, and diamante are used over and over again to express the poet's joy in the presence of or contemplation of the lover. In the somber second half, the tempo slows with longer lines and a combination of quatrains and sestets. These poems cry out to God for salvation from the pain of separation from the lover. Most revealing of this shift is the use of the word diamante. In the first half of the book the jewel is warm, catching the light of love and spreading its joy. In the second half, the jewel is cold and hard, like a piece of ice. As in many of Bollo's early works, there is no middle ground, only agony or ecstasy.

Ciprés de púrpura, poesía. Montevideo: Uruguaya, 1944. 147 pp. Although his prologue to this work contains several now suspect generalizations about the nature of women's poetry vs. men's poetry, Américo Castro is correct in his assessment of Bollo's work as "una poesía tan cálida y tan bellamente angustiada." The book contains a variety of poetic forms all treating anguish. Death is several times addressed as a desired friend who will end the pain of existence. "Sombras ardientes: Elegías" deals with the death of Bollo's father. The preceding poem, "Jardín secreto," reveals an angel's vision who cannot answer the poet's questions as if to suggest that even God cannot assuage her grief this time. Several later poems reflect Bollo's more traditional dependence on God or Christ as the savior from earthly pain, although this volume is unique in Bollo's work for its treatment of a single theme rather than a contrasting mixture.

Delmira Agustini: espíritu de su obra

Diálogos de las luces perdidas, poemas. Montevideo: Casa A. Barreiro y Ramos, 1927. 123 pp. This volume is historically important for its preface by Juana de Ibarbourou commenting not only on Bollo's book but on the field of Latin American poetry in general. Ibarbourou sees Delmira Agustini and María Eugenia Vaz Ferreira as the older generation, with Bollo in the younger group about whom Ibarbourou says "la vida pasa por sus versos como una llamarada." As she also notes, there is a distinct oriental flavor to these poems as if Bollo had discovered Modernism after the movement itself had died out. Bollo's persona is always crying out to a lost or absent lover, sometimes revealed as God, at other times as a physical, human lover. Recurring symbols are metals, such as bronze, and long-stemmed flowers such as lilies, in accordance with Modernism.

Diana transfigurada, poemas. Montevideo: Rosgal-Hilario Rosillo, 1964. 30 pp. This slender volume of poetry, divided into two sections, "Despertar" and "Encuentro y transfiguración," is composed of hendecasyllabic octets. These stanzas tell of the goddess Diana's passion for Endymion, from her first encounter with him as he sleeps to the blazing culmination of their sexual desire. Bollo's style and vocabulary are highly stylized. Although the work is beautifully lyrical at times, it represents an exercise in classical style for Bollo and thus is not characteristic of the main body of her poetic work. Typical of Bollo in this work is her finely detailed description of nature, a recurrent theme throughout her poetic career.

Espirituales, poesías. Montevideo: Rosgal-Hilario Rosillo, 1963. 125 pp. This volume contains a wide variety of traditional verse forms (rhymed couplets, simple quatrains, sonnets, etc.). The numerous elegies that comprise Part I are dedicated to friends, other women writers, Bollo's mother, as well as to incidents of national tragedy and outrage. In Part II, "Mensajes a mi Madre," Bollo expresses her feelings for her mother in terms used previously for the lost lover. "Canciones íntimas" presents topics as disparate as Mary, the Mother of Christ; unrequited love; and dawn. A short poem in this section sums up, perhaps, Bollo's motivation in writing: "El vuelo libre de la mente/es la sublime libertad" ("El vuelo"). The closing section which gives the volume its title is more somber than even some of the elegies, complaining of lost loves and of mortality. The majority of these poems are more introspective and philosophical than 'spiritual' in the religious sense.

Mundo secreto. Montevideo: La Paz, 1977. 44 pp. Bollo's poetry here has lost the fire of her earlier works and the tone of her anguish has softened a little. Now Bollo deals with the anguish of separation between mother and adult child or of lost opportunities in life which can never be realized in the face of death. There is still a religious flavor to some poems, but on the whole they are more philosophical than her other works. For example, in "Elegía del cercano otoño" death is seen as an accepted part of Nature's cycle and is much less horrifying than in earlier works. In the second section of poems (which are like haiku in form and content), the end of life is seen as a natural call to another world; leave-taking is calm and resigned. Truly the most mature of her works.

Los nocturnos del fuego, poemas. 2nd ed. N.p.: n.p., 1933. 78 pp. The theme of the title section is anguish over the persona's abandonment by her lover and her resultant solitude. In the second section, "Himnos al Cántaro del Amanecer," the theme turns to rejoicing over the newly found love of God or man, tempered by the remembered pain of despair. This work is the most feminist of all Bollo's works in the sense that poems deal with female characters; several poems deal with her relationship with her mother, one is addressed to her deceased sister, and one to an unnamed 'fallen woman' about whom she says "Tú no tenías quien te dijera: 'Hermana mía'." Since Bollo's other works deal either with the contemplation of Nature or with her own pain or exaltation, it is noteworthy to find poems where she deals with another's pain.

Pola Salvarrieta, tragedia. Montevideo: Claudio García, 1945. 114 pp. This three-act verse tragedy takes place in Bogotá in 1817, during the wars for Spanish American independence. In Act I, Pola (who is engaged to the rebel Alejo) gets secret documents from a rebel sympathizer among the Royalist troops. The rebels meet at Alejo's house in Act II, and he is later captured. Pola surrenders herself to be with him. In Act III Pola refuses to identify the Spanish officer who gave her the secret papers. Both she and Alejo meet on their way to execution and they proclaim their love and patriotism. Pola's many ecstatic patriotic and political speeches are reminiscent of the fervor of Bollo's romantic or religious poems of the previous decade of her career. This edition contains critical and journalistic commentaries published when the play opened.

Regreso: poesías religiosas. Mercedes, Uruguay: Victorio S. Bartesaghi, 1934. 36 pp. This early volume of religious poems treats two basic themes: the suffering and loneliness of the abandoned lover for whom Christ provides solace, and the wonders of nature as God's handiwork. Several of the poems appear also in French (as translated by Enrique Legrand), and the entire work was motivated by the Eucharistic Congress held in Buenos Aires in 1934. Each poem picks up an image from the preceding one as its focus, lending unity to an otherwise heterogeneous group of poetic forms, from sonnets to free verse to school songs. The poem "Escuadra celeste" is noteworthy for its novel imagery comparing airplanes and angels. Tierra y cielo, poemas. Montevideo: Rosgal-Hilario Rosillo, 1964. 158 pp. Divided into nine sections comprising from two to seventeen lyric poems each. Most poems treat aspects of nature such as the moon, forest creatures, the sea, and rain, although there is a section of poems on silence and another on loneliness. The section "Sueños y llamados" is a mixture of nature poems and lyrics of love couched in religious or nature metaphors, as well as one purely religious poem. Earlier in her career Bollo probably would have published some of the longer sections as separate volumes, since there is little thematic unity among the sections. In one poem, "Llamada a la ardilla recordada," Bollo mentions having visited the United States ("tierras y selvas de Walt") as a teenager, one of the few times she specifies the autobiographical incident which inspired the poem.

Las voces ancladas: poemas en prosa. Montevideo: Germano Uruguayo, 1933. 38 pp. In the title section, each poem tells part of a slowly unfolding description of nature, by contrasting two points of view on the same event which demonstrate the mutual interdependence of all elements of nature. In the other section entitled "Los regresos" the scene shifts to the city and depression sets in. From the opening "Ciudad de ceniza" to the final poem, "Lluvia," the mood is one of increasing sadness and emptiness in the absence of Nature as God intended it. Although the themes and images used in these early poems recur in Bollo's work, this is her only experiment with prose poetry, as in general she favors more traditional poetic forms. TA

BOMBAL, María Luisa (Chile, 1910-1980). Although Bombal was born in Chile, she spent most of her life abroad: first in Paris (1920-1931), then in Buenos Aires (1933-1940), and in the United States (1940-1973). She only lived in Chile during her last years. In the context of Chilean literature, her work is unique. Her vision of reality as a complex conglomerate of the real, the fantastic, and the oneiric expressed in her works through revolutionary techniques makes of her one of the most outstanding representatives of the avant-garde in Latin America. On the other hand, the themes of erotic frustration, social marginality, and cosmic trascendence must be considered as a profound expression of women's predicament presented through a feminine perspective. LGC

La amortajada, novela. Buenos Aires: Sur, 1938. Paperback. In counterpoint to a journey to the depths of the earth that expresses a magic and teluric vision of death, the protagonist of this novel evaluates her life -- which starts free and instinctive and ends as a surrender to social conventions. Cinematic montage and perspectivism destroy the rational limits between life and death and in this fluid reality, women are conceived as an integral part of nature. LGC

La historia de María Griselda, novela. Quillota, Chile: El Observador, 1976. Paperback, also includes "Las trenzas." In this nouvelle structured as an inverted fairy tale, the author presents the tragic dilemma of women whose essential bond to cosmic harmony has been destroyed by the rational regulations of men who attempt to control nature in the name of civilization. The main conflict of this work lies in the confrontation between the magic and the pragmatic which, in turn, represents the opposition between the feminine and the masculine. The triumph of the rational in contemporary society produces the defeat and the degradation of the Mother-Earth archetype. LGC

House of mist, translation. New York: Farrar, Straus, 1947.

New Islands. Trans. Richard and Lucía Cunningham. New York: Farrar, Straus & Giroux, 1982. 112 pp. New translation of "Trenzas" and all the stories in La última niebla. Includes very brief Preface by Jorge Luis Borges and a Translator's Note. DEM

The Shrouded Woman, translation. New York: Farrar, Straus, 1948.

La última niebla, novela. Buenos Aires: Sur, 1935. Available in a paperback edition which also includes the short stories "El árbol," "Islas nuevas," and "Lo secreto." In this short novel, the subjectivity of the protagonist permeates concrete reality, creating an ambiguous atmosphere where the identity of the love fluctuates between the real and the fantastic. The mist motif simultaneously underlines ambiguity and symbolizes the oppressing forces of social convention which have led women to a no-exit situation. One of the most important works of the avant-garde movement, it is also a strong testimony to the tragic predicament of Latin American women. LGC

BOMBAL, Susana (Argentina, twentieth century)

El cuadro de Anneke Loors, cuentos

Los lagares

Morna

La predicción de Bethsabé

Tres domingos

BONET, Ofelia Machado (see **MACHADO BONET DE BENVENUTA, Ofelia**)

BONNIN ARMSTRONG, Ana Inés (Puerto Rico, b. 1902)

Fuga 1944-1948

Un hombre, dos corbatas y un perro

Luz de blanco, poemas

El mendigo y otros diálogos

Poemas de las tres voces y otros poemas

BORDES, Inés (Chile, twentieth century)

Canté, amé, viví, biografía novelada

BORJA ALVAREZ, Aída (Ecuador, twentieth century)

Nautilo, versos

Sinfonía heroica, poemas

BORJA DE YCAZA, Rosa (Ecuador, twentieth century)

Aspectos de mi sendero

Hacia la vida

Libertad, poema

Ritmo espiritual, poesías

Teatro

BORJA MARTINEZ, Luz Elisa (Ecuador, d. 1927)

La bella durmiente musita sus cantos ocultos, dispersos perdidos

Cofre romántico

BORNEMANN, Elsa Isabel (Argentina, twentieth century)

El cazador con caricias, cuento infantil

Cuento con caricia, cuento infantil

BORRERO, Juana (Cuba, 1877-1896)

Epistolario

Poesías

Rimas

BORRERO DE LUJAN, Dulce María (Cuba, 1883-1945)

Como las águilas, poemas

Dos discursos: el magisterio y el porvenir de Cuba; la fiesta internacional de la mujer

Horas de mi vida

BOSCO, María Angélica (Argentina, b. 1917)

El arte de amar: el hombre

Carta abierta a Judás, novela

Cartas de mujeres, cuentos y ensayos

El comedor de diario, novela

¿Dónde está el cordero?, novela

En la estela de un secuestro, novela

En la piel del otro

Historia privada, novela

La muerte baja en el ascensor, cuentos

La muerte en la costa del río, novela

La muerte soborna a Pandora

La muerte vino de afuera

La negra Vélez y su ángel

La trampa, novela

BOTTINI, Clara (Argentina, twentieth century)

Caza mayor, cuentos

Los árboles del San Matías, novela

BRANDT DE RICARDO, Blanca (Venezuela, twentieth century)

Después, novela

Mi dolor, poesías

BRANNON DE SAMAYOA, Carmen (El Salvador, 1899-1974; pseudonym: Claudia Lars). With a desire to awaken a love for literature in children, Lars wrote a great deal of poetry and short stories especially for them and published an anthology of children's poetry. Lars directed a publishing house and the magazine Cultura for the Salvadorian ministry of culture and education.

Canciones, poesía. San Salvador: Ministerio de Cultura, 1960. 28 pp. From its opening themes (such as the night's enchanting qualities) which appeal to the young child's imagination until its closing themes related to the Christ child's birth, the work reflects a simplicity and clarity of rhymed verse. Half of the work's poems appear in other collections of Lars such as Escuela de pájaros and Estrellas en el pozo which also closes with the Nativity theme.

Canción redonda, poesía. San José, Costa Rica: Convivio, 1937. Over 100 pp. With clarity and beautiful simplicity, this early work exalts the beauty of nature as the ideal poetic subject. In addition, the pains and joys of love are presented in a moving manner. Many of the poems contain dedications to such friends and colleagues of Lars as the poet Alberto Velázquez and the artist Salarrue.

La casa de vidrio, poesía. Santiago, Chile: Zig-Zag, 1942. 82 pp. Dedicated to Lars' son Roy and beginning with a Preface by Lars' friend, the artist Salarrue, the work resembles a large glass house that encases the beauty and magic of a child's world in a delicate and transparent showcase containing rhymed poems of varying lengths. The poems present such delightful themes of childhood as blowing giant iridescent soap bubbles which drift gently away in the breeze.

Donde llegan los pasos, poesía. San Salvador: Ministerio de Cultura, 1953. 82 pp. Dedicated to Alberto Guerra Trigueros and to Lars' husband Carlos Samayoa Chinchilla, a Guatemalan short story writer, the work traces the poet's journey through life and her attempt to find herself. The work is divided into seven sections of long complex poems which deal with such major themes as love, death, and religion. Six of the sections have themes which revolve around introductory quotes by such poets as Emily Dickinson and Christina Rossetti.

Escuela de pájaros, poemas. San Salvador: Ministerio de Educación, 1955. 98 pp. Introductory poem by David Escobar Galindo and Preface by Lars. Like a little woodland school, the collection of simple poems of rhymed verse is divided into sections with the majority focusing on a specific forest creature. Many of these children's poems appear in her other works.

Estrellas en el pozo, poemas. San José, Costa Rica: Convivio, 1934. Over 100 pp. Belonging to the early stages of Lars' literary development, the work consists largely of sonnets and poems divided into quatrains. While the first section deals with the essence of poetry, the second and more famous treats the theme of motherhood from the moment of conception until the child becomes an independent adult.

Fábula de una verdad, colección de poesía. San Salvador: Ministerio de Cultura, 1959. 92 pp. Dedicated to Lars' friend and fellow poet, Alberto Velázquez, this poetic biography of Lars' life is divided into various sections which deal with some aspect of Lars' family history or the history of her beloved El Salvador. In the section entitled "Cantora y su tierra," Lars expresses her deep love for El Salvador.

Girasol, antología de poesía infantil

Nuestro pulsante mundo

Obras escogidas. Vol. I. San Salvador: Universitario, 1973. 311 pp. This volume begins with a prologue and extensive notes on Lars' individual works by Dr. Maltilde Elena López. In this volume appear selected poems from each of the following collections of poetry: Estrellas en el pozo; La canción redonda; La casa de vidrio; Romances de norte y sur; Sonetos; Ciudad bajo mi voz; and Donde llegan los pasos.

Obras escogidas. Vol. II. San Salvador: Universitario, 1974. 450 pp. Once again Dr. Maltide Elena López opens the work with a preface dealing with Lars' poetry. The volume ends with the manuscripts of Lars' correspondence with fellow poets. Moreover, included in this volume are selected poems from the following collections: Fábula de una verdad; Sobre el ángel y el hombre; Del fino amanecer; Nuestro pulsante mundo; Apuntes; and Cartas escritas cuando crece la noche.

Poemas de Claudia Lars

Poesía última, 1970-1973

Presencia en el tiempo, antología poética por Claudia Lars

Romances de norte y sur, poesía. Preface by Alberto Velázquez. San Salvador: Funes, 1946. 38 pp. Reminiscent of the ballad form employed by Lorca in his Romancero gitano, these ballads not only speak of Lars' North and South American roots, but are dedicated to the memory of her Irish American father and her native El Salvador. The work ends with ballads which sing the praises of each Central American country.

Sobre el ángel y el hombre, poesía. San Salvador: Ministerio de Educación, 1962. 82 pp. An explanation of the 1961 Certamen Nacional de Cultura begins this work which won second place in that contest. Yehuda Haley introduces the work's theme of humanity's continual struggle with the demands and temptations of the physical world in opposition to the restrictions and needs of the spiritual world. While the theme is presented with more complex poetic forms than those used in Lars' children's poetry, it is still presented with the same clarity of style.

Sonetos. El Salvador: Estrella, 1974. 49 pp. The first section contains poems which are not only dedicated to such poets as Gabriela Mistral, Christina Rossetti, and Sor Juana Inés de la Cruz, but reflect their philosophies in regard to life, love, and death, as well. The latter section entitled "Sonetos del arcángel," which speaks of the beauty of God's world and man's unending attempts at earthly perfection, won the Central American Literary Contest of 1941.

Sueños de diciembre, poesía

Tierra de infancia, poesía. Prologue by Eduardo Mayora. San Salvador: Ministerio de Educación, 1969. 215 pp. Lars' first work in prose, this collection of short stories presents Lars' childhood memories of growing up in El Salvador. This work puts much emphasis on the local color and customs of El Salvador. In addition, the work concludes with a glossary of native terms. AP

BRAVO ADAMS, Caridad (Mexico, twentieth century)

Agueda, novela

Aguilas frente al sol, novela

Agustina Ramírez, teatro

Alma en la sombra, novela

Alma y carne, novela

Bodas de odio, novela

Cantos de juventud, poesía

Cita con la muerte, novela

Corazón salvaje, novela

Cristina, novela

Déborah, novela

La desconocida, novela

El destino de un patriota, novela (continuación de Aguilas frente al sol)

El enemigo, novela

Estafa de amor, novela

Flor salvaje, novela

Infierno azul, novela

La intrusa, novela

Juan del diablo, novela

Laura, novela

Lo que tú callaste, novela

Marejada, poesía

María Eugenia, novela

Más fuerte que el odio, novela

La mentira, novela

Mónica, novela

Otras seis cartas de amor, teatro

El otro, novela

Paraíso maldito, novela

Pasión y fe, novela (continuación de Yo no creo en los hombres)

Patricia, alma rebelde, novela

Al pie del altar, novela

Los poemas de ayer, poesía

El precio de un hombre

Reina sin corona, novela

Reverberación, poesía

Un rostro en el espejo, teatro

Seis cartas de amor, teatro

Senda de rencor, novela

Soledad, novela

Una sombra entre los dos, novela

Trágica revelación, novela

Tormenta de pasiones

13 (Trece) novelas cortas

Trópico, poesía

Trópico de fuego

Tzintsuntzan, la noche de los muertos

Veinte historias de amor

Yo no creo en los hombres

BRICEÑO, Clara Vivas (see **VIVAS BRICEÑO, Clara**)

BRIGE, Carmen (Venezuela, twentieth century)

Carmen

BRINDIS DE SALAS, Virginia (Uruguay, twentieth century)

Cien cárceles de amor, poemas

Pregón de Marimorena, poemas

BRITO DE DONOSO, Tilda (Chile, 1899-1936; pseudonym: Monvel, María)

Fue así, poesía

El marido gringo

Poesías

Remansos del ensueño, poesía

Sus mejores poemas

Ultimos poemas

BRITO SUMARRAGA, Sahara (Mexico, twentieth century)

A través de una vida

Desolación

Manojo de cuentos y dramatizaciones escolares para el segundo ciclo

BROOK, Paulita (Mexico, twentieth century)

Cartas a Platero

Entre cuatro paredes, teatro

La espiga y el racimo

Los jóvenes, pieza en tres actos

BRUM, Blanca Luz (Uruguay, twentieth century)

Atmósfera arriba, veinte poemas

Cancionero de Frutos Rivera, versos

Cantos de la América del Sur

Un documento humano, penitenciaría niño perdido, epistolario

Levante, poesía

Las llaves ardientes

BRUMANA, Herminia (Argentina, 1901-1954)

Cabezas de mujeres, cuentos

Cartas a las mujeres argentinas, ensayos

Esclava en el día de libertad, cuentos

La grúa, cuentos

Me llamo Niebla, cuentos

Mosaico, cuentos

Obras completas

Palabritas, poesía

Tizas de colores, poesía

BRUNER, Carmen (Chile, 1906-1927)

Herida, poemas

BRUNET, Marta (Chile, 1897-1967). Born in Chillán of a Chilean father and Spanish mother, Brunet was educated privately until she was fourteen, then spent three years traveling in Spain, Italy, Switzerland, France, Belgium, England, Germany, Portugal, Argentina, Uruguay and Brazil. She then joined a literary group and wrote poetry. She sent a sample to "Alone," the critic of La Nación. He encouraged her, and in 1923 she wrote her first novel, Montaña adentro. She then moved to Santiago where she won prizes for a story and a novel. In 1934 Brunet became editor of Zig-Zag, and in 1939 was named consul in Buenos Aires. From 1948 to 1952 she was involved in diplomatic work, then was removed from her post. In 1961 she traveled again and in 1963 published Obras completas.

Aguas abajo, cuentos. Santiago, Chile: Cruz del Sur, 1943. Includes "Piedra Callada" and "Soledad de la Sangre."

Aleluyas para los más chiquitos

Amasijo, novela. Santiago de Chile: Zig-Zag, 1962. 182 pp.

Antología de cuentos. Selection, Prologue, Notes and Bibliography by Nicomedes Guzmán. Santiago de Chile: Zig-Zag, 1962. 237 pp.

La ballena, cuento

Bestia dañina, novela. Santiago, Chile: Nascimiento, 1926. Reprinted: (Buenos Aires: Losada, 1953).

Bienvenido, novela. Santiago, Concepción, Chile: Nascimiento, 1929.

Cuentos para Mari-Sol, para niños. 4th ed. Santiago de Chile: Zig-Zag, 1966. (The original may have been published in 1938). Moralizing fables about birds, frogs, cats, rabbits, rats, mice and other animals found in Chile. Includes three versions of why cats and dogs hate each other. These children's stories have been very popular and there have been several editions of the book.

Don Florisondo, cuentos

Humo hacia el sur, novela. Buenos Aires: Losada, 1946. 255 pp.

La mampara, novela. Buenos Aires: Emecé, 1950. 80 pp.

María Nadie, novela. Santiago de Chile: Zig-Zag, 1957. 159 pp.

María Rosa, la flor del Quillén, novela. Santiago de Chile: La Novela Nueva, 1929. Reprinted: (Buenos Aires: Losada, 1953).

Montaña adentro, novela. 1923. Reprinted: (Buenos Aires: Losada, 1953).

Novia del aire, poesía

Obras completas. Prologue by Alone. Santiago de Chile: Zig-Zag, 1963. 870 pp.and l. pp.

Raíz del sueño, cuentos. Santiago de Chile: Zig-Zag, 1949. 144 pp. Descriptive and realistic stories of people in unfortunate circumstances. Women protagonists play an important role, but the viewpoint is feminine rather than feminist. The characters exhibit a fatalistic attitude and submit to whatever happens. There is anthropomorphism with talking flowers, rivers, trees and stars. One story is particularly good as an example of a strong woman able to cope in spite of age and lack of beauty: "Doña Santitos." She hangs on to the man she lives with not because she needs support, but because she enjoys having a man around. AMA

Reloj del sol, cuentos

Soledad de la sangre, cuentos. Prologue by Angel Rama. Montevideo: Arca, 1967.

BRUZUAL, Narcisa (Venezuela, twentieth century)

Bettina Sierra, historia de una provinciana, novela

La causa del mal, comedia

Las cuatro estaciones, novela

Horas sentimentales, poesías

La leyenda del estanque, novela

Los naufragios, drama

Veneno del pecado, drama

BRUZZONE DE BLOCH, Olga (Bolivia, twentieth century)

Hondo muy hondo, poemas

Trás la cortina del incienso, novela

BUCETA, María Villar (see VILLAR BUCETA, María)

BUITRAGO, Fanny (Colombia, b. 1940). Although born in Barranquilla, Buitrago considers Cali her literary birthplace, having won her first literary prize there. She spent her childhood at boarding school where she cultivated her imagination to escape from the tedium of her environment. The theme of the abandoned girl child runs throughout her work, in her prize-winning play and in her novels and short stories. Other common motifs are true lovers separated by marriage (to unloving spouses); a child who destroys her parents' marriage through real or suspected seduction of the father; an almost Naturalistic view of climate or locale as determining the character or actions of the protagonists, as well as curses or racial or genetic memory affecting the outcome of interpersonal relationships. She has succeeded admirably in drama, the short story, and the novel, and is also author of the libretto for an award-winning ballet, La garza sucia.

Los amores de Afrodita. Bogotá: Plaza y Janés, 1983. 276 pp. This volume contains four short stories and one novelette dealing with different aspects of love: parent-child, husband-wife, between friends who are betrayed for money or power. The first, "¡Anhelante, oh anhelante!", is told in the second person as a mother addresses her son who abandons his first wife to marry someone she thinks is inappropriate. The novelette, "Legado de Corín Tellado," shows the triumph of an unattractive girl whose only boyfriend is (unknown to her at first) paid to assume that role. Their sham marriage vindicates her in society after his suicide, although the reader views with horror the tragedy she has caused to her husband's true love.

Bahia Sonora, relatos de la isla. Bogotá: Almanaques Supremo, 1976. 159 pp. This collection contains thirteen short stories, an opening "historical" note and a closing note. In the latter, Buitrago explains the principal epithet of the island. The island is the setting for these stories as well as her later novel, Los pañamanes. Topics here include a couple whose perfect marriage survives his affair but is shattered by her past as a madam; the depth of responsibility of paternity; a man whose marvelous talent for making love leads to his suicide since the women he makes happy never consider his feelings. Buitrago has created a marvelous world in her island, peopled with an infinite variety of characters to reflect her obsession with love/betrayal, parents/children, and reality/dreams.

La casa del abuelo. Illus. by Mario Duarte. Bogotá: Voluntad UNESCO, 1979. ISBN 84-8270-406-0 and ISBN 0-8325-0235-9, 47 pp. This delightfully illustrated children's book won Second Prize in the Primer Concurso Latinoamericano de Literatura Infantil. The stories revolve around the adventures of three children who, with their mother, visit their grandfather's house while their father is away on business. The stories depict the simple, everyday pleasures of young children, culminating in the unexpected return of their father at Christmas. Buitrago is innovative even in this restricted type of discourse; for example, in the third story, "La casa" liked to be painted different colors so it wouldn't be bored. The stories are charming vignettes of a loving, happy childhood, in sharp contrast to Buitrago's view of childhood in her adult works.

Cola de zorro, novela. Bogotá: Monolito, 1970. 257 pp. Buitrago deals with some of her favorite themes here: love/hate relationships between men and women; sterility/fecundity; biological and/or adoptive parents and their relations with their children. The tripartite novel utilizes a confusing blend of flashbacks, flashforwards, and time-line plot developments to tell the stories of Ana, Emmanuel, and Malinda, who are all interconnected through the mythically disappearing and reappearing character Benito. This novel seems to be more consciously feminist than her earlier novel, El hostigante verano de los dioses. Women are treated more cruelly here, but they also suffer more common female ailments than her earlier characters did, as if to make them more universal or more acceptable to the average reader.

"Las distancias doradas" in El hombre de paja y Las distancias doradas. Six short stories comprise this section of Buitrago's double volume (see bibliographical information below). The themes and plot devices here are very similar to the longer treatments in her later collection, Los amores de Afrodita: a daughter who usurps her mother's place with her step-father; narration in the second person; betrayal and death; the relation between love and (in)sanity; the relationship between parent and child. These stories depend more on mood and atmosphere than those of the later collection (which use either action or interior monologue to reveal character).

"El hombre de paja," in El hombre de paja y Las distancias doradas (see bibligraphical information below). This three-act play opens Buitrago's only double publication. Most of the characters have generic names: la maestra, el pastor, el extraño, la niña. The plot revolves around Jafet, a writer, and Berta, his girlfriend, who is jealous of his affection for la niña, apparently a refugee from a nearby village destroyed by the revolution. The figure of the scare-crow, doubled by el extraño, another refugee, seems to represent the townspeople's fear of the unknown (perhaps new or "revolutionary" ideas). Jafet tries to get the townspeople to take care of la niña, but all abandon their professions as well as this chance for compassion. After the sombras perform a Dance of Death with Jafet he is next seen hanging from a tree, without an explanation of suicide or execution. La maestra reads from her papers "Alguien escribía sobre una niña, un árbol, un extraño" as one wonders what has triumphed here.

El hombre de paja y Las distancias doradas. Bogotá: Espiral, 1964. 139 pp.

El hostigante verano de los dioses, novela. Bogotá: Tercer Mundo, 1963. 346 pp. This long first novel tells of a young female reporter who comes to a town to investigate a best-seller that turns out to be a literary hoax. The perpetrators are a group of friends who call themselves "los dioses." Each chapter is narrated in the first person by individual female members of that group alternating with the reporter, called "una forastera." Couples fall in and out of love passionately, marry other people in apathy, all against a background of natural disaster (a major flood), death, suicide, and revolution. The reporter, Marina, has a child by one man, whom she later marries. Eleven years afterward a reunion of the survivors is covered by another young female reporter and the reader finds that still no one has admitted writing the literary hoax that Marina came to investigate during that previous hostigante verano. Buitrago's use of the asphyxiating summer weather as an image of the contagious apathy felt by los dioses is beautifully developed throughout.

La otra gente, cuentos. Bogotá: Instituto Colombiano de Cultura, 1973. 192 pp. This is a collection of fourteen short stories, many dealing with ghosts, family curses, the bad luck of abused and abandoned children, and the often tortured relationships husbands and wives have. Several are traditional horror stories of the Alfred Hitchcock genre with an unexpected or subtle twist to the denouement. The final story, "Mammy deja el oficio," deals with an upper-class woman whose abominable taste in clothing leads people to suspect she is a prostitute; therefore she becomes one, leaving her husband and children who were already ashamed of her. Her husband is more loving and kind to her when she is his "kept woman" than when she acts as his legitimate wife, much to the surprise of the traditional (in this case, lower-class) prostitutes.

Los pañamanes, novela. Barcelona: Plaza y Janés, 1979. 415 pp. Like Cien años de soledad by García Márquez, this is a pseudo-historical novel involving a panorama of characters interconnected by love, hate, marriage, and treachery. The mythic elements include characters in disguise, the abandoned child growing up to claim his/her inheritance, and a curse of thirty years' bad luck. Buitrago artfully fleshes out the problems inherent in a culture based on rape and pillage by Spanish conquistadores, where legitimacy derives from marriages which are often loveless, and real love can more often by found in back-street affairs. TA

BULLRICH PALENQUE, Silvina (Argentina, b. 1915; known as Silvina Bullrich after 1946). Bullrich is an important name in the history of the development of female writers in Argentina. Although primarily a novelist, Bullrich has written short stories, essays, one book of poems, literary and film criticism and has been a journalist for most of her career. Her literary themes center around the evolving drama of the contemporary Argentinean woman and the political/sociological situation of Argentina. Her work always contains strong elements of irony, satire and criticism while presenting perceptive insights into her country and its people, especially women. Bullrich belongs to the individualistic "Generación intermedia" and can also take her place among the small but significant group of Argentinean women writers whose work during the first half of this century paved the way for a large and important group of women writers who followed. The author divides her work into three literary periods: época juvenil (1935-1949); novelas sentimentales (1951-1961); and obras de madurez (1964 to present).
EFS

Abnegación

La aventura interior

Bodas de cristal, novela. 6th ed. Buenos Aires: Sudamericana, 1973. Paperback, 177 pp. Available commercially and in major research libraries. Deals with the secondary status of women, adultery, and contrasting temperaments of men and women. One of the author's most commercially successful novels. It is the first time the principal character is also the narrator, a technique which will become typical of Bullrich's most popular novels. Bodas de cristal (of the period of the novelas sentimentales) marks the starting point of a long phase of commercially successful bestsellers that capture the essence of the upper middle-class Argentinean woman's preoccupation with love, marriage, children, career and society. Reprinted many times and translated into several languages. EFS

Los burgueses, novela. Colección Novelistas Latinoamericanos. 18th ed. Buenos Aires: Sudamericana, 1975. Paperback, 133 pp. Available commercially and in major research libraries. The decline of Argentina as detailed in the study of four generations of a once aristocratic family. The author's most important political novel and most critically acclaimed work. Traditional and innovative techniques are skillfully combined to create a formally original work. The first novel of a trilogy that examines the decadence and deterioration of Argentina, all of which are obras de madurez. Expresses the author's growing pessimism over the present and future of the nation. Despite its critical success, Bullrich was disappointed that it did not bring her the international renown she has wanted for so long. EFS

Calles de Buenos Aires, novela. Escritores Argentinos. Buenos Aires: Emecé, 1979. Paperback, 237 pp. Available commercially. Bullrich's first novel, written in 1939 (during the época juvenil), explores the empty lives of the inhabitants of the wealthy barrio norte section of Buenos Aires. Considering the era in which it was written, it represents a perceptive and novel awareness of the problems of women trapped in the limited roles society has designated for them. The implication is that the inability of women to fulfill themselves contributes to the failure of Argentina as a nation. The streets of Buenos Aires reflect what is wrong on the national level: hypocrisy, superficial values and goals. EFS

El calor humano, novelas. Colección Tiempos Modernos. 3rd ed. Buenos Aires: Merlín, 1970. 95 pp. Available in major research libraries. A minor, short novel written in 1969 that strongly criticizes Argentineans' personal values that place primary importance on money and appearances instead of love and sincerity. The work does not add anything that is new in either content or style to previous works. The preoccupations are similar to the ones expressed in the novels of the sixties and seventies except that here the protagonist is male. Irony is characteristically a strong element underscoring the paucity of human warmth, a virtue most Argentineans profess to have in abundance.
EFS

Carta a un joven cuentista

Carta abierta a los hijos, novela

El compadrito, su destino, sus barrios, su música, verso en prosa

La creciente. Colección El Espejo. 5th ed. Buenos Aires: Sudamericana, 1970. 320 pp. Available commercially and in major research libraries. An allegory of contemporary Argentina and other Latin American nations where the only constants are chaos, revolution, corruption and the inability of people to confront reality. A continuation of the socio-political novels begun in 1964 with Los burgueses (obras de madurez). The fate of the nation is secondary to the selfish, petty needs of government officials and pragmatic villains. The sole optimistic note revolves around a couple who deeply love one another and work for the good of the nation but who are ultimately overwhelmed by the corruption surrounding them. Despite the tragic ending, their love stands as a sign of hope that there is a way out of the national despair. For this reason La creciente is less pessimistic than Los burgueses. EFS

Los despiadados, novela. Escritores Argentinos. Buenos Aires: Emecé, 1978. Paperback, 228 pp. Available commercially. This novel deals with the problems of the modern woman in combining career and marriage, the significance of family and upbringing in determining one's values and marriage as friendship. In addition to being suspenseful, the first-person narration jumps back and forth from past to present and underscores the changing values of contemporary Argentines. The past is evoked in positive terms whereas the present is viewed with suspicion and ambivalence. The author sees marriage as, most importantly, a friendship. Bullrich continues to comment and to criticize the evolution of her country. She reaffirms the importance of the pareja as the only way of surviving happily during today's difficult times. EFS

Entre mis veinte y treinta años. Buenos Aires: Emecé, 1970. 621 pp. An anthology that contains mostly novels, one novella, one biography and a short autobiographical essay. The works include: Calles de Buenos Aires, Saloma, La redoma del primer ángel, La tercera versión, George Sand, Historia de un silencio, Hágase justicia and "Nota autobiográfica." Unites works from Bullrich's earlier period, some of which had been out of print until recently. Also contains some important autobiographical information that had been unavailable until the publication of Mis memorias in 1980. EFS

Escándalo bancario. Escritores Argentinos. Buenos Aires: Emecé, 1980. Paperback, 263 pp. Available commercially. This novel is a cautionary tale about the insidious effects of greed and unethical conduct and its implications for the nation. The contrast of good and evil is paralleled by the campo / ciudad theme. The image of the newly arrived Italian family, sent by a Mafia-linked patriarch, results in the portrayal of Argentina as the victim of those who use and abuse her. The work is a commentary on a society whose valuing of fame and fortune can only lead to adverse consequences. By innundating the reader with details of purposeless spending, the tragedy that follows becomes inevitable. EFS

George Sand, biografía

Hágase justicia. (See annotation under Será justicia.)

El hechicero, novela. Colección Tiempos Modernos. Buenos Aires: Goyanarte, 1961. 79 pp. Another edition: (Buenos Aires: E. Merlín, 1971). Limited availability in major research libraries. In this novel written during the same period as Un momento muy largo (novelas sentimentales), the major theme is illusion vs. reality. The heroine is typical of the major Bullrich protagonists: women who devise their own unhappy situation by creating and living in a world of illusions. Thus the title refers to the heroine's willingness to be bewitched by lies. Neither a commercial nor a critical success. EFS

Historia de un silencio. 1st ed. Buenos Aires: Medina del Río: Folia, 1949. 80 pp. Another edition: Colección Continentes (Caracas: Monte Avila, 1976),Paperback, 210 pp. Available commercially and in research libraries. A collection of short stories from different periods of the author's life. The tone, themes and styles are quite diverse. Contains revealing statements about Bullrich and her attitude toward life, literature and love. The title story is filled with subtle, evocative and sensual details. Its ambiguous ending adds to the aura of mystery and interest surrounding the protagonist, a prototype of later Bullrich heroines. The book is highly regarded by both literary critics and the author. EFS

Historias inmorales, cuentos. 8th ed. Buenos Aires: Sudamericana, 1973. Paperback, 109 pp. Available commercially and in major research libraries. Stories thematically united by the issue of morality/immorality in contemporary Argentinean society. The overwhelming tone of irony, emphasized by each narrator's lack of both self-awareness and the implications of his/her personal situation further serve to unify the stories. The work is significant in pointing to Bullrich's talent for writing in this genre, although she has concentrated principally on novels. EFS

Un hombre con historia, cuentitos. Colección Tiempos Modernos. Buenos Aires: Merlín, 1973. 77 pp. Not available. This work consists of two short stories: the title story plus "Lo demás es mentira." These stories are included in a later collection, Historia de un silencio. The title work deals with the significance and value of true love that increases in importance as the nature of a relationship is finally understood by a young observer. Once disdainful of love because of its bourgeois nature, he now becomes aware of its value. The purpose of "Lo demás es mentira," the author's only fairy tale, is to inform us that reality is a lie and that fantasy makes us happier. EFS

Mal don, novela. Novelistas Contemporáneos. Buenos Aires: Emecé, 1973. Paperback. 263 pp. Available commercially. The work (one of the obras de madurez) presents the problem of social inequities in Latin American society and the extent to which any individual controls his or her own future. The novel continues certain preoccupations evident since the beginning of Bullrich's career: social injustice and the betrayal of one's youthful ideals upon reaching maturity. The theme of the questioning of violence as a means to solving social inequities is in obvious response to the actual situation of Latin America. EFS

Mañana digo basta, novela. 10th ed. Buenos Aires: Sudamericana, 1971. Paperback, 247 pp. Available in major research libraries and commercially. This novel presents a woman's mid-life crisis Latin American style as she grapples with problems of loneliness, men, the generation gap and friendship. The work is effective in presenting the issues of a Latin American woman trying to come to terms with herself in a society that challenges everything she is: female, middle-aged, independent and rebellious. Written in the form of a diary and filled with typical Bullrich irony, Mañana is part of the literary phase, las novelas de madurez, in which Bullrich continues her saga of the situation of the contemporary Argentinean woman while intensifying her focus on the sociological/political condition of Argentina. EFS

Mientras los demás viven. Colección Novelistas Hispanoamericanos. Buenos Aires: Sudamericana, 1958. Paperback, 114 pp. Available commercially and in major research libraries. One of the novelas sentimentales, this novel was written after the death of her second husband, and deals with the significance of love between a man and a woman and between parent and child and the tragic results when this love is destroyed. The gloomy themes and tone are characteristic of the autobiographical nature of the novel. The issue of the generation gap will become more prominent in later novels. The author's growing pessimism over the state of the nation is expressed through the dichotomy of ciudad/campo, the former being a malevolent influence, the latter soothing and tranquil. It is pessimistic in terms of people's ability to love and to communicate. EFS

Mis memorias. Buenos Aires: Emecé, 1980. 394 pp. This autobiography is of primary importance to scholars of Bullrich's works. The author's major reason for writing it is to give testimony to the personal struggles she overcame in order to survive as a woman alone and to establish herself as a writer. Bullrich emphasizes the significance of the love and affection she received growing up in a closely knit, upper-class family, the horror of seeing most of them die prematurely, one by one, and the loss of the one great love of her life, Marcelo, all resulting in an even greater devotion to her career which serves as an escape from her loneliness. She describes the importance of travels and friends in later years. Little discussion is given to writing or her philosophy as a writer, making this principally a personal work.

EFS

Un momento muy largo. Colección El Espejo. 7th ed. Buenos Aires: Sudamericana, 1976. Paperback, 155 pp. Available commercially and in major research libraries. The story of an obsessive love affair that has tragic consequences for both partners. Belonging to the novelas sentimentales, the novel is significant in dealing frankly with a woman's sexuality. The female protagonist reverses the style of her independent, career-oriented life to become the victim of her female destiny. Love strikes in all of its fury, leaving her helpless and completely dependent on the whims of an egotistical and insensitive lover. The lyrical style is significant to the novel's critical success. EFS

Los monstruos sagrados. Colección El Espejo. Buenos Aires: Sudamericana, 1971. Paperback, 211 pp. Available commercially. The loneliness and frustration of being a writer in a society that does not value the profession or the product but prefers to view the author as a media personality. The third novel of the trilogy that began with Los burgueses and was followed by Los salvadores de la patria (both obras de madurez). This third and final book does not pursue the political/sociological orientation of the first two and thus does not seem like a logical sequel. It expresses the author's frustrations about the writing profession: being interviewed and harassed by the press and public who care more about the author's lifestyle than the quality of his/her writing. EFS

La mujer argentina en la literatura, ensayo. Buenos Aires: Centro Nacional de Documentación e Información Educativa, 1972. Unavailable. The author traces the development of women's growing contribution in Argentina, especially in literature. Bullrich demonstrates a clear concern for women. She notes that World War II was the turning point for Argentinean women writers who finally began making an important contribution in presenting women realistically. The author sees Argentinean women as the backbone of the boom of the Argentinean novel without having received appropriate recognition.

EFS

El mundo que yo vi

Páginas de Silvina Bullrich, seleccionadas por la autora. Preliminary study by Nicolás Cócaro. Buenos Aires: Celtia, 1983. ISBN 950-0106-07-8. Another edition: (Barcelona: Gedisa, 1983), ISBN 84-7432-165-4, 189 pp. Cócaro's introduction situates Bullrich's family, life and works with the Argentinean historical context, emphasizing: her bourgeois background, early French cultural influence, social conscience, interest in women's issues, her autobiographical tone and mature emphasis on lo argentino. Short excerpts from fifteen different books (her most famous novels and Mis memorias) are included. Fourteen articles are reprinted, including "La mujer, eterna postergada: ¿por qué?," on the refusal to recognize women writers in Argentina; and "Condiciones esenciales para ser feminista," an angry response to requests from women's groups for her to speak without pay. Contains "Cronología," "Bibliografía," and "Juicios críticos." DEM

Los pasajeros del jardín. Novelistas Argentinos Contemporáneos. 5th ed. Buenos Aires: Emecé, 1971. Paperback, 185 pp. Available commercially. The author's most idyllic and optimistic view of a couple. A major portion of the novel, one of the obras de madurez, deals with the narrator's reaction to her lover's death. The work was praised by critics for its lyricism, complex simplicity and insights into the psychology of the pareja. It was written many years after the death of Bullrich's second husband, when she was ready to come to terms with the loss.
EFS

La redoma del primer ángel, crónica de los años 40 (cuarenta), novela. Escritores Argentinos. Buenos Aires: Emecé, 1943. Another edition: Colección Mundial Rueda (Buenos Aires: S. Rueda, 1967), 224 pp. Available commercially and in major research libraries. This novel received the Premio Municipal de la Ciudad de Buenos Aires in 1943. The theme of "yo soy yo y mis circumstancias" reflects the author's receptivity to the influences of European literature and philosophy of the period. Bullrich uses Unamuno's technique of a fictional author as a main character who responds directly to her creations. The novel represents the philosophy of the literatura comprometida in that the character of the Author in the novel suffers with her own characters and feels responsible for them. Belonging to the época juvenil, it contains an important prologue by Bullrich commenting on the background of the work. EFS

Reunión de directorio. Escritores Argentinos. 1st ed. Buenos Aires: Sudamericana, 1977. Paperback, 216 pp. Available commercially. This novel (one of the obras de madurez) represents the culmination of the author's use of satire, irony, caricature and black humor. Argentina is conceived of as a tropical island paradise, underscoring the author's view of the country as totally alienated from the rest of Latin America. The principal female character plays a secondary role to the fierce satire of Argentina's economic, political and moral problems. A courageous novel written during a time when censorship and political reprisals were common. EFS

Saloma, novela. Buenos Aires: A. Contreras, 1940. Paperback. Available commercially. Saloma links the unfulfilled lives of upper-class Argentineans to the national crisis. Similar in form and content to Calles de Buenos Aires, it belongs to the época juvenil phase since it was published one year after Bullrich's first novel. Rarely an object of study, the work is most notable for its use of narrated monologue resulting in a more fluid narration. Bullrich demonstrates the influence of Argentinean essayists of the period by focusing on the contribution that individual citizens can make by devoting themselves to nationalistic values. EFS

Los salvadores de la patria. Colección Novelistas Latinoamericanos. 9th ed. Buenos Aires: Sudamericana, 1975. Paperback, 147 pp. Available commercially and in major research libraries. The work deals with the immorality of the private and public lives of government officials as a fundamental cause of national corruption. Published immediately after Los burgueses (one of the obras de madurez), it is the second part of the trilogy that studies the decline of Argentina, as a satire of the Argentinean government where dishonesty and corruption are the norm. Although it was not as successful critically or commercially as Los burgueses, it is an important novel for its critical and ironic view of Argentinean politics. EFS

Será justicia, novela. Colección El Espejo. 5th ed. Buenos Aires: Sudamericana, 1976. Paperback, 159 pp. Available commercially. Originally written in 1949 as Hágase justicia, it was not published until 1970. A novel of suspense that centers around Bullrich's major concerns: the inability of men and women to be successful in relationships because of personal self-deception and illusion vs. reality. Written in the form of four letters, each addressed to the same person to clarify a crime, the novel is a secondary work and is of interest principally to scholars of Bullrich's works. EFS

Su excelencia envió el informe. Novelistas Contemporáneos. 1st ed. Buenos Aires: Emecé, 1974. Paperback, 226 pp. Available commercially. The author returns to the literary technique of narrated monologue used in earlier novels to present a conflict between two generations of mothers and daughters. It reiterates ideas suggested in previous works: people as a product of their past, their environment and their upbringing. The ending narrates the revolutionary activities of the young daughter and her boyfriend and does not seem in keeping with the original tone and intent of the work. Belongs to the literary phase of the obras de madurez. EFS

Su vida y yo, novela. Buenos Aires: Espasa-Calpe Argentina, 1941. 253 pp. Available in some research libraries. A novel that deals with the frivolous and unhappy life of an upper-class Argentinean woman whose lack of an early and proper education prevents her from obtaining peace and self-fulfillment. For the first time Bullrich uses the first person character-narrator which later becomes her favorite technique. Also for the first time she focuses on a woman as the central character. The work calls attention to the inadequate guidance and education women receive which result in a focus on superficial preoccupations. Belongs to the época juvenil. EFS

Te acordorás de Taormina. Novelistas Contemporáneos. 1st ed. Buenos Aires: Emecé, 1975. Paperback, 253 pp. Available commercially. The generation gap is lyrically detailed in monologue form by an elderly mother to her youngest daughter whom she simultaneously resents and admires. The novel, one of the obras de madurez, is a striking portrayal of the clash of two worlds, each with its own valid point of view. Culmination of the author's representation of the drama of the contemporary alienated woman who suffers by either accepting her traditional destiny or by trying to assume new values in a changing world. EFS

Teléfono ocupado. Buenos Aires: Goyanarte, 1955. 108 pp. Novelistas Contemporáneos. 4th ed. corrected by the author: (Buenos Aires: Emecé, 1971), paperback, 108 pp. Available commercially and in some research libraries. This work presents the superficial lifestyle of an upper-class porteña in a society characterized by alienation. A psychological portrait written during one of the happiest periods of Bullrich's life, when she was married to Marcelo. An indictment of the trivial lifestyle of upper-class Buenos Aires and the only novel published during the period 1951-1958 when, as Bullrich indicates, she was too wrapped up in her personal happiness to care about writing. One of the novelas sentimentales. EFS

Teléfono ocupado. El hechicero. Buenos Aires: Selectas, 1969. 239 pp. (See annotations under individual titles.)

La tercera versión, novela. Novelistas Argentinos Contemporáneos. Buenos Aires: Emecé, 1944. 153 pp. Another edition: Colección Mundial (Buenos Aires: S. Rueda, 1969), 142 pp. Available commercially and in major research libraries. This novel deals with the themes of the relativity of reality, love vs. art and obsessive love. It uses the limited point of view of a first-person narrator and introduces the important element of ambiguity which will reappear significantly in later works. An example of her psychological period (época juvenil), the work represents a change from naturalism to the individual and his or her inner world. EFS

Tres novelas: Bodas de cristal, Mientras los demás viven, Un momento muy largo. Colección Piragua, 105. 1st ed. Buenos Aires: Sudamericana, 1966. 292 pp. Limited availability in research libraries. This collection is a logical and also chronological presentation of three novels that belong to the author's second literary phase (novelas sentimentales). Bodas and Un momento met with great commercial success and deal with women in the roles of wife and lover. Mientras presents woman in the additional role of mother and broadens the scope by adding sociological and political issues. It is interesting to note that the three novels become increasingly pessimistic in outlook, setting a tone that will dominate later novels. That alienation and lack of communication characterize the three works underscores how the limited options available to women damage all involved. EFS

Vibraciones. Buenos Aires: By the Author, 1935. 137 pp.

BULNES, María Villanueva de (see **VILLANUEVA DE BULNES, Marta**)

BURGOS, Elizabeth (Guatemala, twentieth century)

Me llamo Roberta Menchu, historia contada a Elizabeth Burgos

BURGOS, Julia de (Puerto Rico, 1915-1952). Burgos started writing in the thirties; one of the few women writers at the time. She left for Cuba in the early forties and later settled in New York, where she died, ill and poor. Love, death and solitude are the main themes of her poems, death becoming the prevalent one in her last works. Burgos' poetry represents a departure from the conventional, idealized view of love and nature. Some poems are lyrical and metaphorical; others, more direct. The poetic subject presents itself as a writer and as an assertive, active being. She has become a legend in Puerto Rico, influencing other poets.

Antología poética. San Juan: Coquí, 1975. Paperback, 133 pp. This collection of poems is preceded by a critical essay by Ivette Jiménez de Báez. It includes poems from Burgos' work but the selections are not divided according to the different books. Burgos' complete works have not been published since 1961, so this anthology has had five editions. It was originally produced for students. Burgos' sister, Consuelo Burgos, helped in the process of selecting the poems.

Canción de la verdad sencilla. Río Piedras: Huracán, 1982. ISBN 0-940238-66-7, paperback, 60 pp. Previously published in 1939, this book has been published again with illustrations by artist José A. Torres Martinó. There is no index or prologue.

Julia de Burgos, poesía

El mar y tú. Río Piedras: Huracán, 1981. ISBN 0-940238-46-2, paperback, 92 pp. Published originally in 1954 after Burgos' death, El mar y tú has been published again by Huracán with graphics by J.A. Peláez. The book is divided in three parts: The first one, "Velas sobre el pecho del mar," the second, "Poemas para un naufragio," and the third, "Otros poemas."

Obras poéticas. Preliminary study by José Emilio González. Compiled by Consuelo Burgos and Juan Bautista Pagán. San Juan: Instituto de Cultura Puertorriqueña, 1961. Hardbound, 332 pp. Includes Poema en veinte surcos (1938), Canción de la verdad sencilla (1939) and El mar y tú (published posthumously in 1954). The recurrent themes are love and death; the poems present a view of the world as something conflictive, not harmonious. The best poems are those in which the tensions between the poetic subject and the false values imposed by society are incorporated in the textual processes and the poetic voice struggles against solitude and death. The texts recognize the oppresive nature of a world in which death has become the only alternative. She uses mostly long verse forms and symbols taken from nature; the sea as an image of death is an important motif in El mar y tú. ILJ

Poema en veinte surcos

BUSTAMANTE, Cecilia (Peru, twentieth century)

Altas hojas

Discernimiento: (1971-1979)

El nombre de las cosas

Nuevos poemas y audiencia

Poesía

Símbolos del corazón

BUSTAMANTE, María Teresa de (Chile, b. 1907; pseudonym: Victoria, Alejandra)

El alero de las lechuzas mojadas, narraciones

Bajo el templo del sol, sonetos

En la tierra de los indios, narraciones

El huache, novela

Lenguas del siglo, poesía

La prisión de los cóndores, poemas

C

C. DE ARVELLO, Clotilde (Venezuela, twentieth century)

Flores de invernadero

Por opuestos senderos

CABALLERO, Blanca Graciela Arias de (see **ARIAS DE CABALLERO, Blanca Graciela**)

CABALLERO, Pepita (Puerto Rico, twentieth century)

Bajo el vuelo de los alcatraces

CABALLERO, Teresa (Argentina, twentieth century)

9 (Nueve) cuentos y una invitación

La telaraña, cuentos

CABELLO DE CARBONERA, Mercedes (Peru, 1845-1909). Often credited with introducing Naturalism to Peru, this novelist was unable to free herself completely from the trappings of Romanticism. Her misfortune and that of her friend Clorinda Matto de Turner was that they lived in a time when outspoken, educated women were not easily accepted by society. The moralizing tone and the didacticism of her novels reflect the positivism of the day. Her aim as a novelist was to expose the hypocrisy and vices of society while preserving traditional moral values. The extravagance and pretense of society along with political corruption, gambling, and prostitution are depicted in her works. She died in a mental institution.

Los amores de Hortensia. (See annotation under Las consecuencias.)

Blanca Sol, novela social. Lima: Universo de Carlos Prince, 1889. 189 pp. A naturalistic novel in the tradition of Zola and her best-known work. She condemns the vanity, ostentation, and hypocrisy of Lima society in the latter part of the nineteenth century. Blanca, the principal character, is a self-centered young woman who mingles in high society and feels little compassion for the poor. She marries for money rather than love, gambles, and has an overall disdain for domestic life and for her role as a mother. Pride causes her downfall, and following her bankruptcy, she turns to alcohol and becomes a prostitute. In a prologue the author discusses the value of the social novel in combatting society's defects and vices. She compares the art of writing novels to a science and stresses the importance of the factors of heredity and environment.

Las consecuencias. Lima: Torres Aguirre, 1889. 245 pp. This novel points out the evils of gambling. First appearing with the title Los amores de Hortensia, it was later modified and published as Eleodora and then reworked and given its final form along with the new title, Las consecuencias. The plot concerns the self-sacrifice of a young mother in order to preserve the honor of her family. In a prefatory letter to Ricardo Palma, Cabello de Carbonera acknowledges her debt for the story to his tradición, "Amor de madre."

El conspirador: autobiografía de un hombre público. Lima: E. Sequi, 1892. 290 pp. Her last novel takes the form of memoirs of a jailed political leader who writes to confess his mistakes and to help pass the time while he is in prison. This character, Jorge Bello, is considered to be a fictionalized portrait of the well-known Peruvian political figure, Nicolás de Piérola. Bello recounts his revolutionary activities and his rise to become head of the party, and warns against involvement in political intrigue and conspiracy, a habit-forming vice which he finds more addictive than liquor or gambling.

Eleodora. (See annotation under Las consecuencias.)

Sacrificio y recompensa. Lima: Torres Aguirre, 1886. 369 pp. The sentimentalism, exaggerated emotions, faintings, references to fate, and improbable plot of this novel indicate the strong ties it has with Romanticism. Overcoming innumerable obstacles, the young lovers are finally united in marriage at the end. In the preface, Cabello de Carbonera comments on the nature of realism, the literary vogue in her day. She expresses her preference for the beautiful and noble aspects of reality over its ugly side. MSA

CABRERA, Lydia (Cuba, b. 1900). Cabrera was born in Havana of a distinguished and well-to-do family. Her father was one of the patriots of the Cuban War of Independence. She was raised by a black "nanny" who used to entertain her with stories of African origin. Her parents' household was full of black servants, many of them ex-slaves. She lived in Paris (1922-1939) where she studied art, religion, literature and oriental civilizations. She returned to Cuba in 1939 and after the Cuban Revolution moved to Miami where she now lives. She studies Afrocuban society, takes material from Afrocuban folklore and elaborates it in a literary fashion. Her style is poetic and humorous and she always shows a profound respect for the material she presents in her works.

Anaforuana

Anagó, vocabulario lucumí (El yoruba que se habla en Cuba). La Habana: C.R., 1957. Yoruba is proven to be still spoken in the island. Although Lydia Cabrera admits her lack of knowledge of linguistics, her work is still invaluable due to her ability to transfer her deep knowledge and genuine understanding of the Afrocuban culture.

Ayapá, cuentos de Jicotea. Miami: Universal, 1971. Presents nineteen short stories about the symbol of intelligence, the turtle. It was written in the same manner as her two previous collections of short stories, namely Cuentos negros de Cuba and ¿Por qué?.

Cuentos negros de Cuba. Prologue by Fernando Ortiz. La Habana: La Verónica, 1940. 279 pp. This work, which she began around 1930, is a collection of twenty-two short stories on African themes. The book was originally written in Spanish and was translated into French by Francis de Miomandre. The first edition was also in French, in 1936. This work is an artistic elaboration of the material she remembered from her infancy and also that which she obtained during her short visits to the island.

La laguna sagrada de San Joaquín

El monte, igbo finda, ewe orisha, vititi nfinda, notas de los negros criollos y del pueblo de Cuba. La Habana: C.R., 1954. A compilation of Cabrera's notes about religion, magic, superstition and Afrocuban folklore. The information is sometimes presented as a literal transcription of her informant's testimony. It has won the respect of the santeros, who consider it the most important compilation of their knowledge. In this work one can find a description of the Afrocuban Gods and the stories of their adventures, a section on religious rituals and folk medicine and another on miraculous legends. It also includes a long list of the plants used by the santeros on their rituals and medical practices.

Otán iyebiyé: las piedras preciosas. Miami: Universal, 1970. A brief study of precious stones and metals, their magical powers and legends about them. The work is unpretentious and easy to read, and the investigation is always mixed with the recollections of stories and anecdotes told in a light and poetic style.

¿Por qué? Cuentos negros de Cuba. La Habana: C.R., 1948. 2nd ed. Madrid: Ramos, Colección de Chicherukú en el exilio, 1972. 256 pp. A continuation of Cuentos negros de Cuba written in the same manner. It is comprised of twenty-eight short stories from the material collected after her first publication, and, as her previous work, portrays the magic reality born out of the experience of the new environment by the people brought as slaves to the island, together with the traditions of the African culture. Explanatory footnotes.

Refranes de negros viejos. La Habana: C.R., 1955. A collection of Yoruba and Abakuá proverbs. The latter were published both in the original language and also in its Spanish translation. She presents a number of Spanish proverbs that underwent African influence. The importance of this work lies in the presentation of the philosophy and the psychology of the Afrocuban people during slavery and the first generations after the liberation.

La sociedad secreta Abakuá narrada por negros adeptos. La Habana: C.R., 1959. Cabrera studies the origins, beliefs and rites of the secret Ñañigo societies in this book. It helped change the belief that the secret Ñañigo societies were exclusively made of criminals, and gives emphasis to the Ñañigo contributions to the Cuban culture. The book is difficult to read due to its erudition.

Yemayá y Ochún. Miami: Universal, 1974. This is also a collection of stories about the two most important goddesses of the Afrocuban pantheon. The second part is a study of the different santero rites. JP

CABRERA DE GOMEZ REYES, Adriana (Bolivia, twentieth century)

Aleteos y chispazos, poesía

Bolivia, poesía

Canto a la ciudad de los cuatro nombres, teatro

Remanso nativo, poesía

Rocío, poesía

Sueños o latidos, versos

Voces de ayer y de hoy, poesía

CABRERO, Berta Lastarria (see **LASTARRIA CABRERO, Berta**)

CABUTO, María Angélica Alvarez (see **ALVAREZ CABUTO, María Angélica**)

CACERES, Esther de (Uruguay, twentieth century)

El alma y el ángel, poemas

Antología, 1929-1945, poemas

Canción de Esther de Cáceres, poesía

Los cantos de destierro

Los cielos, poemas

Concierto de amor y otros poemas

Espejo sin muerte, poemas

Evocación de Lanxar, tiempo y abismo

Las ínsulas extrañas

Libro de la soledad, poemas

Mar en el mar: madrigales, trances, saetas

Paso de la noche, poemas

CADILLA, Carmen Alicia (see **CADILLA DE RUIBAL, Carmen Alicia**)

CADILLA DE MARTINEZ, María (Puerto Rico, 1886-1951)

Cazadora en el alba y otros poemas

Cuentos a Lillian

Hitos de la raza, cuentos tradicionales y folklóricos

CADILLA DE RUIBAL, Carmen Alicia (Puerto Rico, b. 1908)

Ala y ancla, poemas

Alfabeto del sueño, poesía niña

Antología poética

Canciones en flauta blanca, poemas

Cien sinrazones, poemas

Entre el silencio y Dios, poemas

Litoral del sueño, poemas

Lo que tú y yo sentimos, poemas

Mundo sin geografía, monólogos de un muchacho campesino

Raíces azules, poemas

Los silencios diáfanos, poesía

Tierras del alma, poemas de amor

Voz de las islas íntimas, poemas

Zafra amarga

CAIÑAS PONZOA, Angeles (Cuba, b. 1898)

Agonías, poesía

Confesión a José Martí, poesía

De mis soledades, poesía

Desnudez, poemas

Destierro, poesía

Elegía en azul, poemas

En fuga, poesía

Esclavitud y agravio, poesía

Filiales, poesía

Gritos sin ecos, poesía

Manantial amargo, poesía

Ultimos tiempos, poesía

Versos

CALANDRELLI, Susana (Argentina, b. 1904)

A la sombra del gran templo, novela

Al trasluz de las horas, poesía

Allá por el novecientos, novela

El chango del altiplano

Cuentos alucinados

Cuentos y baladas, poesía

El dios desconocido, historia novelada

El manuscrito de Silvia Gallus, novela

El otro sol, cuento

La palabra que no se pronuncia, cuento

El reloj de ébano

La señal de Caín, novela

La verdad y el sueño, poemas

CALCAGNO DE CIONE, Catita (Uruguay, twentieth century)

Aguas amargas, poesía

Azabaches, poesía

Cantos de los asphodelos, poesía

La danza de mis llamas, poesía

La muerte azul, teatro

Ojo clínico, cuento

Renovación, novela

Rosas rojas, novela

Trampas de zorros para pájaros de barro, teatro

CALDERON, Ana Gutiérrez (see **GUTIERREZ CALDERON, Ana**)

CALDERON, Gloria Salas (see **SALAS CALDERON, Gloria**)

CALLEJAS, Mariana (Chile, b. 1922)

La larga noche, cuentos

CALLER IBERICO, Clorinda (Peru, twentieth century; pseudonym: Juanacha)

Ayahuasca, novela

Doña Shabi, novela

CALNY, Eugenia (Argentina, twentieth century)

El agua y la sed, cuentos

Clara al amanecer, novela

La madriguera, teatro

Las mujeres virtuosas, cuentos

La tarde de los ocres dorados, cuentos

CALVO, Deyanira Urzúa de (see **URZUA DE CALVO, Deyanira**)

CAMACHO DE FIGUEREDO, Pomiana (Colombia, 1841-1889)

Escenas de nuestra vida, novela

CAMACHO DE SALAZAR PEREZ, Isabel (Mexico, twentieth century)

Hojas secas, poesías

CAMACHO FAHSEN DE AGUILERA, Cristina (Guatemala, twentieth century)

Siderales, poesía

CAMARANO DE SUCRE, Yolanda (Panama, twentieth century)

Los Capelli

La doña del Paz

CAMARILLO DE PEREYRA, María Enriqueta (Mexico, b. 1875; pseudonym: Enriqueta, María)

Album sentimental, poesía

El arca de colores, novela

Brujas, Lisboa, Madrid

El consejo del buho, novela

Cuentecillos de cristal

Del tapiz de mi vida

Dos enemigos

Enigma y símbolo

Entre el polvo de un castillo, cuentos infantiles

Fantasía y realidad

Hojas dispersas

Jirón del mundo, novela

Lo irremediable, novela

Mirlitón, el compañero de Juan, cuentos

El misterio de su muerte, novela

Poemas del campo

Rincones románticos, poemas

Rosas para la infancia

Rumores de mi huerto, poesía

El secreto

Sorpresas de la vida, novelas cortas

CAMELINO VEDOYA, Mercedes Pujato Crespo de (see **PUJATO CRESPO DE CAMELINO VEDOYA, Mercedes**)

CAMPO, Margarita del (Argentina, twentieth century)

La niña y su sorpresa, novela

La voz de las manos, poemas de la mujer y el hombre, poemas en prosa

CAMPO Y PLATA, Graciela del (Peru, twentieth century)

Hontanares, poesía

Y ahora es el silencio, poesía

CAMPOBELLO, Nellie Francisca Ernestina (Mexico, b. 1912). Best known as a chronicler of the Mexican Revolution, Campobello utilizes a hybrid form of fictionalized autobiography to great advantage. Campobello also forged her artistic life through dance; she and her sister Gloria founded and oversaw the National School of Dance. A protagonist of her narratives is her mother, whose strength and serenity seemed to have shielded the author from the insanities of war. Campobello has also devoted a large part of her life to the defense and vindication of Francisco Villa. Both her mother and Villa are portrayed as idealized figures in Campobello's works.

Abra en la roca. (See annotation under Mis libros.)

Cartucho; relatos de la lucha en el norte de México. 1st ed. México: Integrales, 1931. 143 pp. These relatos are drawn from Campobello's childhood experience of the Mexican Revolution, and therefore are both historically and literarily interesting. The young, female narrator observes the violence and bloodshed around her. Her recounting of executions she witnesses and other incidents that form a disturbing picture of a bloody civil war, provides the volume's unifying thread. Her mother appears as a stabilizing force in these vignettes. Other characters include famous historical figures (such as Francisco Villa), various common soldiers, and other people whose destinies were changed by the war.

Cartucho; relatos de la lucha en el norte de México. 2nd ed. México: Iberoamericana de Publicaciones, 1940. 211 pp. This edition of Cartucho is dedicated to the author's mother. It contains some changed section titles and several retratos and vignettes not included in the first. A vignette called "Villa" from the first edition which describes an exchange between the general and Campobello's mother, for example, is replaced in the second by one called "Las cintareadas de Antonio Silva," containing anecdotes about a general of Villa's; when he dies, her mother cries.

Las manos de mamá. 2nd ed. Illus. by José Clemente Orozco. México: Villa Ocampo, 1949. 77 pp. 1st ed.: (México: Juventudes de Izquierda, 1937), 89 pp. The idealized portrait of the narrator's mother depicts a self-sacrificing, strong, capable, beautiful, loving woman. Her hands symbolize all these qualities. The entire narrative is devoted to lengthy descriptions of mamá, from her skirt to her heroic exploits during the war. In the name of her children she allows herself to be drawn into the army's activities. The writing is tinged with nostalgia; Mamá becomes the earthly Mexican symbol of the Virgin Mary, mother par excellence.

Mis libros. 1st ed. Prologue by Nellie Campobello. Colección Ideas, Letras y Vida. México: Compañía General de Ediciones, 1960. 514 pp. This is the most complete compendium of Campobello's work available. She authorized its publication, and wrote a lengthy and revealing prologue describing her literary, political, and personal concerns. Works available in other editions appear here with minor changes. Such is the case of Apuntes sobre la vida militar de Francisco Villa; the author has added a final sentence to this version. Also included are: Yo, por Francisca, a very early work of fifteen short unadorned poems whose most consistent and recurrent themes are fantasy loves, dreams, and the poet's relationship with her sister; and Abra en la roca, whose generally unembellished poems contain Campobello's recurring themes, but also others about love, the sea, and the past.

Tres poemas. México: Compañía General de Ediciones, 1957. 37 pp. "Ella" is a nostalgic narrative poem whose idealized portrait of the author's mother includes description of her skirt, hands, and grace. The last part of the poem poses a series of questions about its subject. In "Río florido," the poetic voice speaks to the river, calling it padre mío. Although the old (pre-revolutionary) Mexico is gone, she says, one remains to bring life. Using as a motif the cities in which she has danced publicly, the author provides a portrait of the people, history, and feelings of Mexico. The colors red and green dominate. SS

Yo, por Francisca. (See annotation under Mis libros.)

CAMPOS, Alicia (Argentina, twentieth century)

Mañana, novela

CAMPOS, Grama de los (pseudonym: see CELI DE BENITEZ, Eloísa)

CAMPOS, Julieta (Cuba-Mexico, b. 1932). Since 1955, Campos has lived in Mexico where most of her fiction and literary criticism have been published. Her novels are among the most accomplished Latin American examples of the "open work" structure, defined by Umberto Eco. Highly articulate in Western culture, her fiction is "the invention of the world and of man, constant invention and perpetual challenge" designed to fill a void or the irreproachable silence caused by two existential fatalities: love and death. Self-reflexive writing about the creative process, desire, the obsessive usury of time, and the eternal search for a utopia are major themes. Author of La imagen en el espejo and Oficio de leer, both collections of essays.

Celina o los gatos, cuentos. Mexico: Siglo XXI, 1968. Paperback, 119 pp. Three short stories, two lyrical narrative texts and an introductory selection about feline cultural history mark this volume. The protagonists are usually women; the focus is generally sensual and obsessive; the plots are purposefully ambiguous and mysterious with character "doubles" and hints of insanity and illness. The intrusive flow of time undermines memories in narratives that resemble "tone poems" of a descriptive, sensitive nature. There is a tendency here and in other works to merge genres.

La herencia obstinada

El miedo de perder a Eurídice. Mexico: Joaquín Mortiz, 1979. ISBN 968-27-0076-0, 169 pp. This lyrical novel, with extensive collage citations in the margins that form a text alongside a text, is an attempt to recover eros in its ideal form from thanatos. Campos spins a tale of constant literary representations of the primordial utopia, of the original paradisiacal love between Eve and Adam, isolated from time on an island of desire -- the novel itself. Campos once again links three constant themes -- desire, writing and time or death. The first two are linked against the third; thus the title, as Campos explains: "Faithful to the urgent need to bring to light the obscure object of that desire, Orpheus reclaims Eurydice every time a text emerges from silence."

Muerte por agua, novela. Mexico: Fondo de Cultura Económica, 1965. Paperback, 142 pp. A reaction to her mother's bout with cancer, this novel established several constants in Campos' fiction: intimacy and detail; a minimal plot; imperceptible physical motion; the paralysis of any will to action; sensitivity and maximum receptivity to internal voices of conscience; banal conversations; a self-reflexive nature; a limited physical setting; illogical relationships between situations that force reader participation; and time as a physically corrosive phenomenon.

Tiene los cabellos rojizos y se llama Sabina, novela. Mexico: Joaquín Mortiz, 1974. ISBN 968-27-0027-2, paperback, 179 pp. In this "open structure" novel, Campos captures a work in gestation, a self-reflexive artistic theme she has dealt with in her literary criticism. Theme and structure fuse in a defiant challenge to the inexorable flow of time in both plot and novelistic process of writing. Neither concludes definitively in the text. Simultaneity, ambiguity, multiplicity, contingencies, inconsistencies, contradictions and negations abound in this kaleidoscopic and metamorphic narrative. EPG

CANDEGABE, Nelly (Argentina, b. 1927)

En el linde de los espejos, poemas

El pan de ceniza

La piel distante

CANE, Cora María Bertolé de (see BERTOLE DE CANE, Cora María)

CANO, Isabel Farfán (see FARFAN CANO, Isabel)

CANTO, Estela (Argentina, b. 1920). A prolific novelist and short story writer, who has been working steadily for almost forty years. She deals mostly with characters drawn from the Argentinean upper classes, whose manners and morés she seems to know intimately. Her works usually include a touch of the fantastic, even against an ordinary background. In general she has remained within the traditional mold of the Argentinean woman writer both in regard to subject matter and to style. Her language is simple, direct, and highly effective.

Las ciencias ocultas

Los espejos de la noche, cuentos. Buenos Aires: Claridad, 1945. Paperback, 166 pp. Available only in libraries. Interesting collection of short stories illustrated by the author, and told in a straightforward style. Stories included: "El destino," "El disparo," "La calesita," "La huida," "La muñeca de porcelana," "La ventana," "La linterna," "Una estrella," "El retorno," "El sepulcro," "El cangrejo," and "Los espejos de la sombra."

El estanque, novela. Buenos Aires: Goyanarte, 1956. Paperback, 141 pp. Available in research libraries only. Atmospheric tale of the effect that an old country house and a mysterious pool, half-hidden by wild vegetation, have on eleven-year-old Jacinta. The pool is a mirror that reflects the mood of those who reside in the house. The social milieu is the upper-middle class. Characters are somewhat diffused and show no development or psychological insight. The novel does not have social or political significance.

El hombre del crepúsculo. Buenos Aires: Sudamericana, 1953. Paperback, 142 pp. Available only in libraries. The story of an obscure, old bachelor office worker, Evaristo Lérida, whose life suffers a drastic change on the beaches of Uruguay. Interesting, well-developed plot which ends in tragedy.

La hora detenida, novela. Buenos Aires: Emecé, 1976. Paperback, 256 pp. Available only in libraries. Semi-fantastic background. Minor personal incidents in the life of a schoolteacher who goes through an unexpected adventure in the winter of Buenos Aires. Entertaining, good structure. Background is the last days of Eva Perón.

Isabel entre las plantas. Buenos Aires: Falbo, 1966.

El jazmín negro, novela. Buenos Aires: Emecé, 1978. Paperback. Available only in libraries. A fine novel in autobiographical form; well-written, excellent character studies. Narration by a sixteen-year-old girl who leads an objectionable lifestyle from a moral standpoint. She is partly the willing victim of men's sexual appetites. The title symbolizes her moral curruption. The story is told in a straightforward manner, with no evidence of feminist consciousness.

El muro de mármol, novela. Buenos Aires: Losada, 1945. Paperback, 227 pp. Available only in libraries. Life among the Argentine upper classes. Idle rich with no clear purpose in life. Their only concern is their own immediate personal relationships. Good portrait of a class of people. Straight narration with no obvious critical intention. Won first prize organized by Imprenta López, with celebrated Victoria Ocampo as one of the judges.

La noche y el barro, novela. Bueno Aires: E. Platina, 1961. Paperback, 164 pp. Available only in research libraries. Well-structured novel that explores the depths of good and evil. Plot concerns the efforts of an Argentine politician, his mistress, and two American entrepreneurs to create a favorable climate for United States investments in Argentina. How they proceed to achieve their aim is perhaps far-fetched but not entirely improbable. Canto's characters are believable and appealing. One of her best works.

Los otros, las máscaras, novela. Buenos Aires: Losada, 1973. Paperback, 224 pp. Available only in libraries. Novel in three parts, one of Canto's best works. Interesting and absorbing portrait of a decaying segment of Argentine society: the very rich and their dolce vita. Contrast with the life of a young man from a modest family who is marked by his contact with affluence. Overtones of a detective story, good character delineation. Suspense is well-maintained. Narrated in the first person. Solid structure and highly polished style. AT

El retrato y la imagen, novela. Buenos Aires: Losada, 1950.

Ronda nocturna

CAÑAS, Dulce María Loynaz de Alvarez de (see LOYNAZ DE ALVAREZ DE CAÑAS, Dulce María)

CAPMANY PUCCIO, Mireyra (Argentina, twentieth century)

Cuentos del monte desamparo

CAPOTE, Renee Méndez (see MENDEZ CAPOTE, Renee)

CAPOTE DE AGUILILLA, Araceli (Cuba, b. 1920; also Aguililla, Araceli de)

Asamblea, poesía

De por llanos y montañas, cuentos

Las madres en la Revolución, cuento

Primeros recuerdos, novela

CAPRILE, Fifa Cruz de (see CRUZ DE CAPRILE, Fifa)

CAPRILE, Margarita Abella (see ABELLA CAPRILE, Margarita)

CARBONERA, Mercedes Cabello de (see CABELLO DE CARBONERA, Mercedes)

CARDENAS, Margarita Cota- (see COTA-CARDENAS, Margarita)

CARDENAS, Nancy (Mexico, twentieth century)

El cántaro seco, pieza en un acto

CARDONA, Adylia (Honduras, twentieth century)

Auras campesinas, poemas regionales

CARDONA TORRICO, Alcira (Bolivia, b. 1926)

Carcajada de estaño

De paso por la tierra, cuento

Rayo y simiente, poemas

Tormenta en los Andes, cuentos

CARIMATI, Victorina Malharro de (see **MALHARRO DE CARIMATI, Victorina**)

CARLO, Adelia di (Argentina, twentieth century)

Astillas de sándalo, novela

La canción de la aguja, cuentos

Cuentos para niños

En espera de la hora, novela

El hijo del Guarabosque, cuento

Maternidad, ensayo

La mujer ante la ley, ensayo

La mujer en el periodismo nacional, ensayo

CARMEN, María del (Mexico, twentieth century)

Lilia Montero, novela

CARMEN ORTEGA, María del (see **ORTEGA, María del Carmen**)

CARMEN RODRIGUEZ, Clotilde del (see **RODRIGUEZ, Clotilde del Carmen**)

CARNELLI, María Luisa (Argentina, b. 1900)

Poemas para la ventana del pobre

Rama frágil, poesías

Versos de una mujer

CARNELLI DESPOSITO, María Cristina (Argentina, twentieth century)

El mal destino

Segunda conversación

CARO, Rosa Marrero y (see **MARRERO Y CARO, Rosa**)

CARRANZA, Celia Treviño (see **TREVIÑO CARRANZA, Celia**)

CARRANZA, Maríamercedes (Colombia, twentieth century)

Vainas y otros poemas (1968-1972)**CARRASCO, Margarita** (Chile, b. 1909; pseudonym: Alonso, Carmen de)

Anclas en la ciudad, novela

La brecha, novela

Cantaritos, leyendas

La casita de cristal, cuentos

La cita, cuentos

Erase una Amapolita, leyenda

Gleba, cuentos

Medallones de luna, cuentos

Medallones de sol, cuentos

Provena, cuentos

Y había luz de estrellas, cuentos

CARRASCO, Ofelia Judith (Argentina, twentieth century)

Poemas de cobre y ochavos

CARRASCO DE BUSTAMANTE, Catalina (Chile, b. 1903). Teacher who graduated from the Chilean Escuela Normal de Profesoras. In 1930-1931, she published the children's magazines Pasitos and Abejita. She was a poet laureate in the "Fiestas Primaverales" in 1936, 1943, 1944 and 1945. She has published extensively and continues publishing in the newspapers and journals of her country. Tenderness, human suffering, and the love of country and children are the sentiments that predominate in her works. She has four unpublished books.

Antología. Santiago, Chile: Carabineros, 1980. Paperback, 66 pp. A selection of poems in which the fundamental human sentiments are expressed in tender, smooth and delicate tones. The language is colloquial, but always maintained at an artistic level. Deeply-felt poems dedicated to her Spanish ancestry and to the suffering of Spanish children after the Civil War are also included. The poet follows the example of Gabriela Mistral in exalting spiritual values.

Canto a la vida, poemas. Santiago, Chile: Carabineros, 1967. Paperback, 119 pp. Presents the anguish of modern man without strong protest, but rather with a generous feeling of hope for human solidarity and a better world. A message of tenderness and love is expressed in transparent and musical verses of captivating naturalness. A clear vision of the Southern landscape of Chile predominates in this song to life.

Canto entre lágrimas, poemas. Santiago, Chile: Carabineros, 1973. Paperback, 48 pp. The first two poems deal with themes of maternal and filial love expressed with deep tenderness. The other eight poems evoke the poet's bitterness and sorrow over the loss of her husband. The poet expresses her anguish in the face of solitude in a touching manner, but without denying life, and with hope for a new springtime. Her language is delicate, clear, transparent. RI

CARREÑO, Mada (Mexico, twentieth century)

Los diablos sueltos

Poesía abierta

CARREÑO, Virginia (Argentina, twentieth century)

María de los Angeles, novela histórica con Constanza de Menezes

Subterráneo, pieza en tres actos

CARREÑO FERNANDEZ, Yolanda (Chile, twentieth century; pseudonym: Condal, Lucía)

Presencia del otoño, poemas

República celeste, poemas

CARREÑO-MALLARINO, Isabel Pinzón Castilla de (see **PINZON CASTILLA DE CARREÑO-MALLARINO, Isabel**)

CARREON GUTIERREZ, María Luisa (Mexico, twentieth century)

El aparador, cuentos

Solito, cuentos

Tríptico mexicano, teatro

CARRERAS DE BASTOS, Laura (Uruguay, b. 1872; pseudonym: Gioconda)

Tránsito de Mercurio, comedia

CARRILLO, Sonia Luz (Peru, b. 1948). Born in Callao and raised in the Rimac district of Lima, in a poverty-stricken family, she attended Catholic school before her teenage years. Her formal lay education includes secretarial school and literature courses at a private university. Her poetry has appeared in Peruvian and foreign journals since 1967. She is a columnist for several Lima newspapers and teaches at various institutions. She has two sons from her marriage to the poet Ricardo Falla.

La realidad en cámara oscura. N.p.: Capuli, 1981. Paperback, 31 pp. This edition of twenty-one very brief poems comprises sixteen from . . . y el corazón ardiendo and five previously unpublished. The book forms part of the series on "Peruvian Feminine Poetry" directed by Cecilia

Bustamante. The title apparently originates from one of several poems criticizing mass media for their technological distortion of human values. The poem "Frutos" identifies the author with Sor Juana for her unrecalcitrant rationalism. Some poems about Lima or Peru recall Vallejo's restrained sadness. Technically, Carrillo continues her free-verse haiku-like form, with precise and explosive adjectives, and frequent incomplete sentences.

Sin nombre propio, poesía. Lima: Causachun, 1973. Paperback, 42 pp. Collection of thirty-three concise poems. The title stems from the threat, through marriage, of losing her own last name, Carrillo. The poems are written in free verse, a haiku-like form for which the author has shown a decisive preference, and a restrained tone deliberately lacking in sentimentalism. With biting sarcasm towards the social order that manipulates women and the poor, her poetry nevertheless expresses hope in the renewal that children and uncompromising poets offer.

. . . y el corazón ardiendo. Prologue by Alejandro Romualdo. Lima: Poesía, 1979. Paperback, 64 pp. Available in research libraries. Some poems in this collection of thirty-two recall Vallejo's restrained sadness; those about mass media express disdain for the technological distortion of human values. The three addressed to her children are a superb aesthetic expression of pregnancy, an infant's death, and the relationship between childbearing and her own country. The book is divided into nine sections; two longer poems (most are in haiku-like form) prove Carrillo' descriptive skills and her ability to sustain a calm distance from potentially sentimental topics. SHA

CARRIZOSA, Zita Serrano de (see **SERRANO DE CARRIZOSA, Zita**)

CARTAGENA PORTALATIN, Aída (Dominican Republic, twentieth century)

Del sueño al mundo

Escalera para Electra

Una mujer está sola

Mi mundo el mar, poema

La tierra está escrita, elegías

Víspera del sueño, poemas para un atardecer

CARTOSIO, Emma de (Argentina, b. 1924)

El arenal perdido

Criaturas sin muerte

Cuando el sol selle las bocas

Cuentos del ángel que bien guarda, para chicos, y uno final para profesores de filosofía

En la luz de París

Elegías analfabetas

La familia, poesía

La lenta mirada

Madura soledad, poemas

Tonticanciones para Grillito, poemas

CARVAJAL, María Isabel (Costa Rica-Mexico, 1888-1949; pseudonym: Lyra, Carmen). Known affectionately as "Chabela," Lyra, an illegitimate orphan, wished to join her convent, the Sisters of Charity. Due to her social status, however, she was refused. Her literary life included journalism, fantasy and children's stories; she was well-known as one of the most important women writers in Latin America and an educator. Her writing style was heavily influenced by Flaubert and other French writers. Always concerned with social injustice and political repression, she became a libertarian and a member of the communist party, and was expelled from Costa Rica. She died in Mexico in exile. Lyra's style is ironic, employing simple, popular language filled with barbarismos; she writes of illusions, dreams, fantasies, with childlike tenderness, and uses classical, Biblical and mythological themes.

Los cuentos de mi tía Panchita. San José, Costa Rica: Las Américas, 1956. 210 pp. Similar to María Leal de Noguera's Cuentos Viejos, Tía Panchita ingeniously recreates didactic children's tales, some well known, like Cinderella and Snow White, others not found in books, but in the imagination born in America--tales taken from the Old World and given the flavor of the New. Tía Panchita introduces the stories, telling the stories in Costa Rican regionalisms to her nephews and nieces at twilight in the garden. Unlike logical, ethical Tío Jesús, sharp, cigarette-smoking Tía Panchita was beloved by the children for her ability to make them laugh and dream.

En una silla de ruedas. San José, Costa Rica: Editorial Pl, 1973. In Lyra's early, romantic novel (which was later changed), she treats the theme of a human being in the depths of misery, unimportant in the total scheme of things. Sergio is a two-year-old, paralyzed boy, confined to a wheelchair. Life for him is cruel and Sergio remains with his pain, although a happy ending displays the joy of life as well. Lyra was criticized for her sentimental portrayal.

Las fantasías de Juan Silvestre. Introd. by Francisco Soler. San José, Costa Rica: Falcó y Bórrase, n.d. 80 pp. Lyra's narrator and alter-ego, writing in first person, presents a world of fantasies in diary form. An old man smoking a pipe, a vagabond, an observer, taciturnly he tells stories of his idealistic vision of human misery and social problems. Influenced by the French naturalists (Flaubert, France and Monnier), Lyra satirizes society in "Madama Bovary," employing less fantasy and more social criticism.

Obras completas de María Isabel Carvajal, "Carmen Lyra," Vol. 1. 1st ed. Prologue by Ricardo Quesada López-Calleja. San José, Costa Rica: Patria Libre, 1972. Paperback, photographs, 354 pp. An important collection of Lyra's work and a resource tool. The entire Obras contains En una silla de ruedas, Juan Silvestre and many works written for journals and newspapers, but unpublished elsewhere. The author's prologue tells of memories awakened by an old trunk.

Relatos escogidos is a collection of Lyra's works published in magazines and newspapers, with some excerpts from Juan Silvestre, essays and conversations. With an important, extensive prologue by Alfonso Chase, the volume also contains a chronological synthesis of the author's life, a general bibliography and many photographs. Along with Obras completas, this is an important collection of otherwise unpublished works, and a valuable resource tool. AS

CARVAJAL DE AROCHA, Mercedes (Venezuela, twentieth century; pseudonym: Palacios, Lucila)

Ayer violento, cuentos

Los buzos, novela

Cinco cuentos del sur

El corcel de las crines albas, novela

Cubil, novela

El día de Caín, novela

La gran serpiente, teatro

Juan se durmió en la torre, teatro

Mundo en miniatura, cuentos breves

Niebla, teatro

Orquídeas azules, teatro

La piedra en el vacío, novela

Poemas de noche y de silencio, poesía

Rebeldía, novela

Reducto de soledad, novela

Signos en el tiempo

Tiempo de siega, novela

Tres palabras y una mujer, novela

Trozos de vida, cuentos

CARVALLO DE NUÑEZ, Carlota (Peru, twentieth century)

El árbolito, cuentos

Cuentos fantásticos, cuentos para niños

El niño de Cristal, teatro infantil

El pájaro niño, cuentos

Rutsí, el pequeño alucinado, novela

La tacita de plata, teatro infantil

CASAL, Selva (Uruguay, twentieth century)

Han asesinado el viento, poesía

No vivimos en vano

Poemas de las cuatro de la tarde

Poemas 65 (sesenta y cinco)

CASAL DE SANCHEZ, Marynés (Uruguay, twentieth century)

Bosque pequeño, poesía

Crisol, poesía

Cuna de río, poesía

Rosa ceñida, poesía

CASANOVA, Cecilia (Chile, b. 1926)

Como lo más solo, poesía

De acertijos y premoniciones, poemas

De cada día, poemas

Los juegos del sol, poemas

El paraguas, cuentos

CASANOVA-SANCHEZ, Olga (Puerto Rico, b. 1947)

Raíz al aire

CASANUEVA, Inelia Uribe (see **URIBE CASANUEVA, Inelia**)

CASAS, Myrna (Puerto Rico, b. 1934). Playwright and director who studied at Harvard and in Boston. Since 1955 she has taught in the Drama Department of the University of Puerto Rico, directing and writing. All of her plays have been published. Her plays always present women who live alone, rejected by society, struggling on their own. They have not been performed very frequently.

Absurdos en soledad, teatro. Opened in the theater el Ateneo Puertorriqueño in San Juan, Puerto Rico, on February 22, 1963.

Cristal roto en el tiempo, pp. 267-349, in Teatro Puertorriqueño, Tercer Festival de Teatro. San Juan: Instituto de Cultura Puertorriqueña,

1961. Hardcover, 613 pp. Described by the author as a "painful pause in two acts and a voice," the drama is a psychological study of three women in a run-down brothel. Sorrow and regret for their lives are evident in the main characters. The play uses an omniscient narrator identified as the "voice" of the house. Each woman is lighted with a particular color on stage. Psychological drama was introduced in Puerto Rico by René Marqués, but it is not a tradition in Puerto Rican literature.

Eugenia Victoria Herrera. Opened on January 31, 1964, performed by Producciones Cisne.

La trampa. El impromptu de San Juan, Río Piedras: Universitaria, 1974. Paperback, 178 pp. ILJ

CASCO DE AGNER, María del Carmen (Argentina, twentieth century)

Corona lírica, poesía

Mi terruño, poesía

Siembra de esperanza, poesía

CASO, María Lombardo de (see **LOMBARDO DE CASO, María**)

CASTAÑEDA DE MACHADO, Elvia (Honduras, twentieth century)

Anteros, cuentos

Canto inicial, poesía

La lección de Sofía Seyers, teatro

CASTAÑEDO, Angelina Acuña de (see **ACUÑA DE CASTAÑEDO, Angelina**)

CASTAÑEIRA, Josefina Guevara (see **GUEVARA CASTAÑEIRA, Josefina**)

CASTAÑO, Rosa de (Mexico, twentieth century)

El coyote

Fruto de sangre

La gaviota verde

Rancho estradeño

La sequía, novela

El torrente negro

Transición

CASTEJON DE MENENDEZ, Luz (Guatemala, b. 1916)

Por ese olor de azucena, poemas

CASTELLANOS, Carmelina de (Argentina, twentieth century)

La puerta colorada, cuentos

CASTELLANOS, Colombina de (Dominican Republic, twentieth century)

Inquietud prenatal, poema

Vibraciones de un alma

CASTELLANOS, Dora (Colombia, twentieth century)

Clamor, poemas

Escrito está, poemas

Eterna huella, poemas

Luz sedienta

Verdad de amor, poemas

CASTELLANOS, Esther de Tapia (see **TAPIA DE CASTELLANOS, Esther**)

CASTELLANOS, Rosario (Mexico, 1925-1974). The most important Mexican spokeswoman for the twentieth century feminist revival, Castellanos was also a skilled poet, prose writer, and a sharp observer of interracial relations (white-Native American). Her childhood in rural Chiapas provided her with an insider's knowledge of tzotzil tribal culture, learned from her nanny; the experience of the largely failed reform period of 1935-1945; and a satirical revulsion against the constraining male/female patterns of traditional society.

> Album de familia. Mexico: Joaquín Mortiz, 1971. ISBN 70-868577, paperback, 155 pp. Two of the four short stories contained here are virtual models of feminist principles in literary elaboration. "Lección de cocina" is a sardonic look at a woman moving from the independence of student days into the strictly delimited and banalized housewife role. The longest story presents a variety of types of intellectual women, brings them through the horrors of stereotyped "cattiness," and on to a recognition of sisterhood.

> Apuntes para una declaración de fe

> Balún-Canán, novela. Mexico: Fondo de Cultura Económica, 1957. Paper/hardback, 292 pp. The difficulties of the effort to institute land reform in rural Chiapas province (1935-1945) and the confusing intercultural relations between Indian and white are treated. Much of the narration is in the voice of a small girl who, though white, identifies with the indigenous mind and political interests because of her intimate association with an Indian nanny.

> Ciudad Real, cuentos. Mexico: Novaro, 1974. Paperback, 198 pp. Difficult to obtain. The setting of these interrelated stories is named the Royal City; but in fact it is an obscure provincial town. Several explore the unstable relations between Indians, always excluded from the town's decision-making and wealth, and precariously wealthy whites, fearful of any reform that might upset their advantage. Under these

conditions, altruistic attempts to assist the indigenous population prove self-defeating. The dour subject does not prevent Castellanos from exercising wit and ironic precision in her depiction of the confusion produced by any disturbance in rigidly observed social rules.

Los convidados de agosto, cuentos. Mexico: Era, 1964. Paperback, 169 pp. Difficult to obtain. The interrelated stories in this volume share a small-town setting and a concern for showing the hierarchical and closed structure of power in backwoods Chiapas. The constraints placed on the behavior of men and women in their rigidly defined roles are held up to examination. The title story is excellent in showing the joy, panic and distress that result from a rupture of these norms.

La corrupción

De la vigilia esteril

Dos poemas

El eterno femenino, farsa. Mexico: Fondo de Cultura Económica, 1975. Paperback, 204 pp. This amusing and eloquent play, published the year after Castellano's death, expresses the feminist concerns so prominent in her last works. A beauty-parlor customer undergoes a profoundly transforming experience. The salon's equipment indirectly causes the women to develop an awareness of woman's historical and contemporary problems. The means of consciousness-raising, and the amazing rapidity of the transformation, provide humor. Yet the insights the women reach through this curious stimulation are serious and valid ones.

Juicios sumarios, ensayos. Xalapa, Mexico: Universidad Veracruzana, 1966. Paperback, 434 pp. Not generally accessible. Written before Castellanos' more overtly feminist criticism, these essays are notable for a determination to keep social concerns in focus while examining the structural features of the text. Castellanos argues that innovatively constructed texts--those of the Latin American "boom," especially-- should not be examined without regard to their meaning for society. Her sex-role analysis of Choderlos de Laclos' Les liaisons dangereuses is a model for feminist studies.

El mar y sus pescaditos, crítica. Mexico: Secretaría de Educación Pública, 1968. Paperback, 198 pp. Not generally accessible. Without elaborate terminology, Castellanos offers a literate person's guide to modern Latin American writing and the critical approach to that writing. Hers is a Third World voice with special emphasis on dictatorship, the indigenous component of modern culture, and the oppressed and marginal subpopulations. She makes an excellent case for an approach that will not reduce literature to sociology, but rather appreciate the social meaning conveyed by literary structures.

Meditación en el umbral, antología poética. Compiled by Julián Palley. Serie Colección Popular. Mexico: Fondo de Cultura Económica, 1985.

Mujer que sabe latín, crítica. Mexico: Secretaría de Educación Pública, 1973. Paperback, 313 pp. Unavailable. The best of Castellanos' literary feminism is found in this collection of reviews and short essays. For Castellanos, feminist literary analysis is no simplistic matter of identifying "images of woman in..." She insists that the study of sex roles can be combined with close study of the specifically literary features, including narrative voice or point of view, time and space factors, and the representation of various registers of speech.

The Nine Guardians, translation of Balún Canán.   Trans. Irene Nichols. New York: Vanguard, 1960. Hardback, 213 pp.

Oficio de tinieblas, novela. Mexico: Fondo de Cultura Económica, 1962. Hardback, 368 pp. Generally considered Castellanos' great triumph in the novelistic form, this work examines troubled Indian-white relations during the period of agitation caused by the attempted implementation of land reform (1935-1945). Part of the interest of the work is its extremely vivid and detailed rendering of the experience of Indians, not from an outsider's perspective, but with an ability to go inside the tribal mind and the non-Western organization of perceptions.

Poesía no eres tú; obra poética: 1948-1971. Mexico: Fondo de Cultura Económica, 1972. 347 pp. Includes: Al pie de la letra, Lívida luz, Materia memorable, Salomé y Judith. This carefully prepared collection of Castellanos' poetic production makes available her early, rather classical and solemn works as well as her ironic, sharply observant later manner. She mimics and thus deconstructs the clichés that limit both women and men. Many of the strongest poems are placed in the mouths of representative women of the past.

Salomé y Judith, poemas dramáticos. Mexico: Jus, n.d. Paperback, 79 pp. Unavailable. Based on Biblical narratives, these dramatic poems are experiments in letting well-known heroines speak to the reader in their own voices. Both women are limited by tightly constrained roles, yet remain insightful. They are astute observers of such social phenomena as war, interpersonal power struggles and hierarchical "pecking orders." The implication is that women may become first rate analysts of the power system, but their participation is limited to embittered commentary and devious ruses.

Presentación al templo, poemas

El rescate del mundo, poesía

Sobre cultura femenina, ensayo

Tablero de damas. Mexico: Revista América, 1952. 20 pp. Unavailable. This early one-act play presents the stereotypical roles (venomous hypercritic, fluttery poetess, high-priestess) assigned to intellectual women in contemporary Mexico. Women characters embodying each of these role possibilities confront one another; each is capable of seeing through the game-playing and the narrowness of the others' lives much more easily than she can examine her own stereotyped and constrained existence.

Trayectoria del polvo, poesía

El uso de la palabra, artículos. Mexico: Excélsior, 1975. Paperback, 313 pp. Castellanos' journalistic essays originally published in Excélsior and its cultural supplement, are brought together in a posthumous collection. Excellent commentary on Indian-white relations, hierarchical power structures in Mexican society, language as instrument of oppression and liberation, the relations between women and female roles. In autobiographical notes, Castellanos subjects her own life experience to a feminist analysis. NL

CASTELLANOS ARGÜELLES DE MOLLOY, Lucila (Peru, twentieth century)

Burbujas, poemas

CASTELLANOS DE ETCHEPARE, Delia (Uruguay, late nineteenth century)

Mariposas

CASTELLANOS DE GALLINAL, Elina (Uruguay, twentieth century)

Alas en el viento, poesías

Florecillas

Poesías

Viajar, poemas

CASTELLANOS DE RIOS, Ada (Bolivia, twentieth century)

Floración, poemas

CASTELLO, Lucía (Uruguay, twentieth century)

"La edad incierta" y "Confidencias de dos inmigrantes," relatos

CASTILLA DE CARREÑO-MALLARINO, Isabel Pinzón (see PINZON CASTILLA DE CARREÑO-MALLARINO, Isabel)

CASTILLO, Amelia del (United States, twentieth century)

Urdimbre

CASTILLO, Carmen (Chile, b. 1923)

Cantos rebeldes, poesía

Lámpara de Arcilla, poesía

Salada miel

Vivencias, poemas

CASTILLO, Laura del (Ecuador, b. 1927)

Mirar el limonero y morir

CASTILLO, Olga Acevedo de (see ACEVEDO DE CASTILLO, Olga)

CASTILLO, Polita de Lima de (see LIMA DE CASTILLO, Polita de)

CASTILLO, Regina Pía (Venezuela, twentieth century)

Sol y médanos, poemas

CASTILLO DE CHACON, Graciana Alvarez del (see ALVAREZ DEL CASTILLO DE CHACON, Graciana)

CASTILLO DE GONZALEZ, Aurelia (Cuba, 1842-1920)

Cuentos de Aurelia

Fábulas

Trozos guerreros y apoteosis

CASTILLO DE OTERO, Margarita Díaz de (see **DIAZ DE CASTILLO DE OTERO, Margarita**)

CASTILLO LEDON, Amalia de (Mexico, twentieth century)

Bajo el mismo techo, teatro

Coqueta, teatro

Cuando las hojas caen, teatro

Cubos de noria, teatro

La mujer en las Naciones Unidas, conferencia

La verdad escondida, teatro

CASTILLO Y GUEVARA, sor Francisca Josefa (Colombia, 1671-1742; also Castillo, Madre; sor Francisca Josefa de la Concepción de Castillo). The author of a spiritual autobiography and a two-volume account of her mystical life, Madre Castillo's life and work demonstrate one paradigm open to middle- and upper-class women in the late seventeenth and early eighteenth centuries. She spent her life enclosed behind the walls of her family home and--from her eighteenth year until her death -- those of a convent in the provincial city of Tunja. Nevertheless, she managed to forge a unique religious and literary identity from her visionary life.

Afectos espirituales de la venerable madre y observante religiosa Francisca de la Concepción, en el siglo doña Francisca Josefa de Castillo y Toledo, Guevara, Niño y Roxas, escritos por ella misma, de mandado de sus confesores según primera copia hecha por don Antonio María de Castillo y Alarcón, en Santa Fé de Bogotá, año de 1896. 2 vols. Preliminary Study by Darío Achury Valenzuela. Biblioteca de Autores Colombianos #104-105. Bogotá: Ministerio de Educación Nacional, 1956. vol. 1: 357 pp.; vol. 2: 371 pp. These two volumes complement the Vida. Madre Castillo recounts her visions, using Biblical exegesis and other religious authorities to establish her orthodoxy. The visions describe her mystical marriage with Jesus, the Virgin Mary's approval, and self-affirming communications with other saints. They also portray devils and other torments in many shapes. The lyrical language used often borrows directly from the Bible, particularly the Psalms and the Song of Songs. Achury Valenzuela's work on Madre Castillo provides much-needed background scholarship on her life and writings.

Análisis crítico de los afectos espirituales de sor Francisca Josefa de la Concepción de Castillo. Edition, introd. and commentary by Darío Achury Valenzuela. Biblioteca de Cultura Colombiana #1. Bogotá: Ministerio de Educación Nacional, 1962. 427 pp. Achury Valenzuela offers the complete texts of the first forty-five afectos, along with an intensive, line-by-line explication analyzing their structure, linguistic devices, and themes. This book is of interest to scholars concerned with Madre Castillo's theological context as well as her literary style, which borrows heavily from Biblical and other religious sources. Madre Castillo's first forty-five afectos illustrate her skillful use of these sources to re-create, in orthodox terms, her mystical life.

Examen crítico de los afectos espirituales de sor Francisca Josefa del Castillo. Ed. Darío Achury Valenzuela. Separata de la Revista Bolívar, 59-60. 45 pp. Achury Valenzuela here reprints and analyzes the eighth afecto of the first series. The unusually long afecto includes a descriptive poem of the mystical experience, which is possibly the reason Achury Valenzuela chose to explicate it; a parable; and several metaphors typical of Madre Castillo's literary use of her everyday life. The editor relies primarily upon theological interpretations of the Bible for his analysis.

Mi vida. Biblioteca Popular de Cultura Colombiana, #16, Clásicos Colombianos. Bogotá: Imprenta Nacional, 1942. 226 pp. An example of one of the most practiced genres by women in the early modern period, this special form of spiritual autobiography called a Vida achieves fruition in the work of Madre Castillo. She documents life in the convent from the smallest details of daily existence, including the gossip and dissension among the sisters, to ecstatic renderings of her visions. The Vida's style is colloquial; the tone is confessional; the implicit beliefs are orthodox; Madre Castillo nevertheless manages to affirm herself as mystic and writer.

Obras completas de la madre Francisca Josefa de la Concepción de Castillo, según fiel transcripción de los manuscriptos originales que se conservan en la Biblioteca Luis-Angel Arango. 2 vols. Introd., notes and indexes by Darío Achury Valenzuela. Bogotá: Banco de la República, 1968. Vol. 1: 463 pp.; Vol. 2: 620 pp. Introd.: ix-ccxiv. These two volumes include a book-length introduction and several indices by the editor, including a chart of Biblical references and allusions correlated with their place of appearance in Madre Castillo's writings. This critical edition represents the culmination of years of work, and is invaluable to the research scholar for background information, although Achury Valenzuela does not undertake a feminist reading of the texts. He does situate Madre Castillo in her time and place, compare her at length with Santa Teresa and Sor Juana, and offer an orthodox reading of her spirituality.

Su vida, escrita por ella misma, por mandado de sus confesores. Preliminary Study by Darío Achury Valenzuela. Biblioteca de Autores Colombianos, #103, Bogotá; Ministerio de Educación Nacional, Ediciones de la Revista Bolívar, 1956. 414 pp. First published in Philadelphia in 1817 under the title: Vida de la V.M. Francisca Josefa de la Concepción. This was the first critical, scholarly edition of Madre Castillo's Vida to be published. It antedates the Obras completas reprinting of the same text by the same editor. Provides a lengthy, but solid introduction to Madre Castillo and her works. SS

CASTRO, Dolores (see CASTRO DE PEÑALOSA, Dolores)

CASTRO, Esmeralda González (see GONZALEZ CASTRO, Esmeralda)

CASTRO, Margarita Jaramillo de (see JARAMILLO DE CASTRO, MARGARITA)

CASTRO, Rebeca Navarro de (see NAVARRO DE CASTRO, Rebeca)

CASTRO, Tania Díaz (see DIAZ CASTRO, Tania)

CASTRO, Zoila María (Ecuador, b. 1917). Castro has spent a lifetime promoting cultural activities and programs in Ecuador and the United States. In the past, she has worked closely with Ecuador's Casa de la Cultura and while residing in New York, she helped establish the Casa Social-Cultural Ecuatoriana de Nueva York. During the years she has written poetry, short stories, a novel, textbooks for secretaries, and numerous articles for journals and newspapers. Castro is at her best when writing about the suffering and frustrations of the urban poor.

En el norte está "El Dorado," cuentos. Guayaquil: Casa de la Cultura Ecuatoriana, 1981. Paperback, 238 pp. As is suggested by the title, this collection of stories depicts the false hopes and impossible dreams which bring many Hispanics to the United States. Castro is at her best when portraying those characters who are gradually destroyed by their belief that success and happiness are primarily dependent upon the number of consumer products one possesses. In short, the color televisions, the new cars, and the expensive wristwatches do not seem to compensate for the loneliness.

Urbe, cuentos. Guayaquil: Grupo Madrugada, 1949. 43 pp. Available only in libraries. Castro uses this collection of short stories as a kind of mirror that reflects the suffering, the ambitions, the failures, and the successes of Guayaquil's poor and middle-class inhabitants. Unlike much earlier social protest literature, Castro's stories are devoid of overt messages and didacticism.

Verónica: Historia de amor. New York: UNIDA Printing Corporation, 1975. 233 pp. Available only in libraries. This novel centers on a young couple's love which is doomed from the very beginning because of the social and class differences that separate the aristocracy from the rest of society. Frequently melodramatic and somewhat artificial, Verónica is a variation of the Romeo and Juliet theme. MH

CASTRO DE JIMENEZ, Auristela (Costa Rica, twentieth century)

Cantos, poesía

CASTRO DE PEÑALOSA, Dolores (Mexico, b. 1923)

Barcos de papel, poesía

Cantares de vela, poemas

La ciudad y el viento, novela

El corazón transfigurado, poesía

Dos nocturnos, poesía

Siete poemas

La tierra está sonando, poemas

CASTRO LEAL, Paloma (Mexico, twentieth century)

A la sombra de Dios, poemas

CASUSO, Teresa (Cuba, b. 1912; also Casuso, Teté)

Los ausentes, novela

¡Bienvenida la vida!

Canción de cristal sin motivo

Canción frutal

El retorno sencillo

Versos míos de la libreta tuya

CATALINA DE JESUS, sor (Ecuador, seventeenth century)

Secretos entre el alma y Dios, autobiografía

CAZANUEVE DE MANTOVANI, Fryda Schultz (see **SCHULTZ CAZANUEVE DE MANTOVANI, Fryda**)

CEIDE DE LOEWENTHAL, Amelia (Puerto Rico, b. 1908)

Cuando el cielo sonríe, poesía

Interior, poesía

Mi cantar de cantares, prosas

Puertas, poesía

CELI DE BENITEZ, Eloísa (Ecuador, twentieth century)

La hija de nadie

CELIS, Gloria (Chile, twentieth century)

Momentos, poesía

Penetración en la llama

Y al principio era agua

CEPEDA, Cecilia (Colombia, nineteenth century)

Los treinta sonetos, contestación al siglo XX (veinte)

CEPEDA, Josefina de (Cuba, b. 1907)

Grana y armiño, versos

La llama en el mar, poesías

Palabras en soledad, poemas del sanatorio (1938-1939)

Versos

CERDA, Eliana (Chile, b. 1920). Born in Temuco, Chile, Cerda has been active in Chilean literary life since the mid-sixties. As a writer who has imaginatively probed into the realm of childhood and adolescence, Cerda has been well-received by local critics. She has three sons from marriage to a lawyer, and has remarried. Cerda was secretary of the Chilean chapter of P.E.N. Club.

La flauta en el horizonte, novela. Santiago de Chile: Universitaria, 1965. Paperback, 154 pp. Another edition: (Santiago: Zig Zag, 1968), paperback, 155 pp. Includes an insightful preface by Guillermo Blanco. This novel nostalgically evokes, in small yet significant incidents, the lost days of a happy childhood. This almost magical realm is brought forth through the eyes of Alejandra, the narrator. She feels that the source of her maturity and full integration to adult life lies in the tenderness and innocence enveloping her youth. Of interest for Spanish high school and beginning college literature courses. IR

CERDA, Vicenta de la Parra (see **PARRA CERDA, Vicenta de la**)

CERNA GUARDIA, Rosa (Peru, twentieth century)

Desde el alba, poesía

Un día de silencio, poesía

Los días de carbón, literatura infantil

Figuras del tiempo, poesía

Imágenes en el agua, poesía

El mar y las montañas, poesía

Maternidad, poesía

CERVANTES, Lorna (United States, twentieth century)

Emplumada, poesía

CESPEDES DE ESCAÑAVERINO, Ursula (Cuba, 1832-1874; pseudonym: Alba, Carlos Enrique de)

Ecos de la selva, poemas

Poesías

CESPEDES LIARTE, Gioconda (Chile, twentieth century)

Instantes irascibles, poemas

CHABELA (nickname; see **CARVAJAL, María Isabel**)

CHACON, Graciana Alvarez del Castillo de (see **ALVAREZ DEL CASTILLO DE CHACON, Graciana**)

CHACON NARDI, Rafaela (Cuba, b. 1926)

    Homenaje a Conrado y a Manuel, poesía

    36 (Treinta y seis) nuevos poemas

    Viaje al sueño, poesía

CHAMBERS, Nancy (Chile, twentieth century)

    Trasfondo, poesía

CHAMORRO, Bertilda Portocarrero de (see **PORTOCARRERO DE CHAMORRO, Bertilda**)

CHAMS, Olga (Colombia, b. 1922; pseudonym: Delmar, Meira)

    Alba del olvido, poemas

    Huésped sin sombra, poemas

    Los mejores versos

    Secreta isla, verso

    Sitio del amor, versos

    Verdad del sueño

CHAVEZ, Elisa Rodríguez (see **RODRIGUEZ CHAVEZ, Elisa**)

CHAVEZ DE FERREIRO, Ana Iris (Paraguay, b. 1923)

    Historia de una familia, crónica

CHIESA DE PEREZ, Carmen (Puerto Rico, twentieth century)

    Príncipe, autobiografía de un perro, novela corta

    La telaraña, novela

CHINA, la (see **MENDOZA, María Luisa**)

CHOPITEA, María José de (Mexico, twentieth century)

    La dictadora, teatro

    Guieshuba, jazmín del Istmo

    Lazos de infancia, cuentos infantiles

CHOUCHY AGUIRRE, Ana María (Argentina, twentieth century)

    Alba gris, poemas

    Los días perdidos, poemas

CHUMACERO, Rosalía d' (Mexico, twentieth century)

Alma, novela

Breviario de emociones, poesía

Cita en el cementerio, novela

Corazón de cristal, poesía

Floración de pecado, novela

Perfil y pensamiento de la mujer mexicana, biografías

Sacrilegio, novela

Sorpresa, cuentos

El vaso de las siete almas, novela

Vencedores del destino, novela

La visitante de la casa gris, novela

CID BAEZA, Astensia (Chile, 1887-1932)

Corazón de artista, novela

Juramento de los Manquileff, novela

Lucrecia Durney, novela

Reflejos, versos

Ultima lágrima, novela

Variaciones de Carmen, novela

CIONE, Catita Calcagno de (see **CALCAGNO DE CIONE, Catita**)

CISNEROS, Isabel Velasco y (see **VELASCO Y CISNEROS, Isabel**)

CLARO, Ester Huneeus de (see **HUNEEUS DE CLARO, Ester**)

CLAUDIO DE LA TORRE, Josefina A. (Puerto Rico, twentieth century)

Mi sinfonía rosa, poemas

COCK DE BERNAL JIMENEZ, Lucía (Colombia, twentieth century)

La hora propicia, poemas

CODINA DE GIANNONI, Iverna (Chile-Argentina, b. 1928). Regarded as an Argentine writer because she has lived in Mendoza, Argentina, since childhood, Codina de Giannoni has published novels, short stories, poems, and literary critiques. She was awarded the International Prize for Best Novelist (1961) by Editorial Losada. Concerned with living conditions of the poor on both sides of the Andes (Argentina and Chile). Strong psychological insight and political content. Situations described are now somewhat outdated as a result of progress and education, but basic passions remain unchanged. An outstanding, forceful, unique woman writer.

Canción de lluvia, poemas

Después del llanto, poemas

Detrás del grito. Colección Novelistas de Nuestra Epoca. Buenos Aires: Losada, 1962. Paperback, 165 pp. Available in libraries. Subhuman environment, set in the Andes between Chile and Argentina. Characters are miners, smugglers, landowners. Primitive instincts prevail: appeasing hunger, sexual drives, men and women coupling like animals. Lack of idealism and tenderness in human relations; fatalism, all-devouring poverty. Excessive machismo and crude language. Of interest to both literary scholars and social historians, but shows no evidence of political or social protest.

La enlutada, cuentos. Buenos Aires: Losada, 1966. Paperback, 142 pp. Available in libraries. Short stories set against the Andean mountains. Smugglers, miners, bandits, muleteers, and their miserable lives, cunning ways, superstition, as well as occasional glimpses of wisdom. Human beings obscured by majestic landscape. Strong determinism, language of the region. Of interest to both literary and social scholars. The title of the collection is taken from the story by the same name.

Los guerrilleros, novela. Buenos Aires: Flor, 1968. Paperback, 213 pp. Available in libraries. Novel dealing with guerrilla fighting in Argentina in the early seventies. Idealistic students, pseudo-communists, workers, and others struggling against the "establishment." Interplay of numerous lives held together by a common conflict. Crude language; mixes straight narration with monologues and dialogues. Lively action. Of interest to literary scholars, sociologists, and political historians.

La luna ha muerto, novela. Buenos Aires: La Reja, 1957. Paperback, 148 pp. Available in research libraries. Uneven story which may be divided into two parts: the first one is a tale of marital infidelities among characters of the upper-middle class. Dialogue is stilted and pedantic. In the second half Codina proves once more her thorough knowledge of the Andean area. Urban characters are now transported to a cruel, inhospitable terrain, and, for one character at least, the encounter with the awesome mountains results in death. Just this second part would have made a story of great merit.

Más allá de las horas, poemas

Siempre amanece, novela. Won First Prize from the city of Mendoza, Argentina, in 1954. No copy is available for review since it was never published commercially. AT

COLL, Isabel Cuchi (see CUCHI COLL, Isabel)

COLLAZO, Paula (Puerto Rico, b. 1917; pseudonym: Poliana)

Forma clara

Versos del amor amargo

COLLAZO COLLAZO, Eulalia Nila (Cuba, twentieth century)

Arte misa, poesía

COLLAZO G., Josefina (United States, twentieth century)

Simplemente . . . Cartas

COLMENARES DE FIOCCO, Delia (Peru, b. 1901)

Con el fusil al hombro, epistolario del soldado desconocido 1879-1883, ficción

Confesiones de Doris Dau, novela

Conjunción de yoes, teatro

Las cuatro de la mañana, teatro

Cuentos infantiles

Cuentos peruanos

Delirio, teatro

De los caminos, poesía

El drama del monje, teatro

En medio del mundo, poemas

La extraña, teatro

La hermana del Cardenal, teatro

Iniciación, versos

Locura, teatro

Una mujer equivocada, novela

Náufragos, teatro

Panales de oro, poesía

Poemas marinos

Quince colapsos, poemas

Una sesión de espiritismo, teatro

Teatro: El drama del monje, Delirio, La extraña, Conjunción de yoes, Una sesión de espiritismo

Vendaval, teatro

COLOMBO, Adela Barbitta (see **BARBITTA COLOMBO, Adela**)

CONCEPCION, sor Francisca Josefa de la (see CASTILLO Y GUEVARA, Madre Francisca Josefa)

CONCHA, Graciela Sotomayor de (see SOTOMAYOR DE CONCHA, Graciela)

CONDAL, Lucía (pseudonym: see CARREÑO FERNANDEZ, Yolanda)

CONITZER, Yolanda Bedregal de (see BEDREGAL DE CONITZER, Yolanda)

CONTRERAS, Hilma (Dominican Republic, twentieth century)

Cuatro cuentos

El ojo de Dios, cuentos de la clandestinidad

CONTRERAS FALCON, Victoria (Chile, twentieth century)

Diapasón sin sonidos, poemas

Trompo dormido, poemas para niños

CORBO FAURE, Estela (Mexico, twentieth century)

Ellos conmigo, poemas

CORDERO, Carmen (Cuba, twentieth century)

Agraz, poesías

La ciudad sin riberas, poesías

Paralelas, poesías

Presencia negra, versos afro-cubanos

CORDERO DE ROMERO, Aurelia (Ecuador, d. 1922)

Poemas de anemia

CORDERO Y LEON, Ramona María (Ecuador, b. 1901; pseudonym: Corylé, Mary)

Aguafuertes

Antología mínima

Canta la vida, poesía

Cenit en mi cumbre, poemas

El cóndor del Aconcaqua

Doctora Santa Teresa, versos

Gleba, cuentos

El mío romancero

Mundo pequeño

Nuestra Cuenca de los Andes, romancero escrito

Padre

Romancero de Bolívar, escripto

Romances, fechos laureles

Rubén Darío, poemario

CORDOVA, Olivia Fernández de (see **FERNANDEZ DE CORDOVA, Olivia**)

CORNEJO, María Isabel Eloísa (Mexico, twentieth century; pseudonym: Hipalia, Hada)

Bouquet de Papillons, poesía

Flores de angustias del jardín de un alma, poesía

Rosas enfermas de colores pálidos, poesía

CORON PELLOT, Carmen (Puerto Rico, twentieth century)

Ambar mulato, poesía

CORPI, Lucha (Mexico, b. 1945). Corpi was born in Jaltiplan, Veracruz, a coastal state in Mexico. Her family moved north to San Luis Potosí when she was nine. At the age of nineteen she married and with her husband emigrated to the San Francisco Bay Area. They settled in Berkeley,California, where she obtained a B.A. from the University of California-Berkeley. She also holds an M.A. from San Francisco State University in Comparative Literature. She has been a recipient of the National Endowment for the Arts fellowship for creative writing. Corpi views herself as a Chicana, even though she was born in Mexico, because of her socialization and living in the United States. She has served on the board of Aztlán Cultural, a Chicano Organization in Oakland. She lives in Oakland, California, where she has taught ESL in the Oakland Public Neighborhood Centers since 1973.

Palabras de Mediodia, Noon Words. Berkeley, California: El Fuego de Aztlán, 1980. ISBN 0-936470-00-3; ISBN 0-936470-01-1, paperback, 169 pp. The English translation by Catherine Rodriguez-Nieto is in the same book. The English translation appears on the opposite side of the page. YGR

CORREA, Nina Donoso (see **DONOSO CORREA, Nina**)

CORREA, Wally de Gómez- (see **GOMEZ-CORREA, Wally de**)

CORREA DE RINCON SOLER, Evangelina (Colombia, nineteenth century)

Los emigrados, leyenda histórica

CORREA LUNA, Delia Orgaz de (see **ORGAZ DE CORREA LUNA, Delia**)

CORREA MORANDE, María (Chile, twentieth century)

La guerra de las mujeres

Inés . . . y las raíces en la tierra, novela

CORREA ZAPATA, Dolores (Mexico, nineteenth century)

Estelas y bosquejos, poesía

Mis liras, poesía

CORTAZAR, Mercedes (Cuba, b. 1940)

Dos poemas de Mercedes Cortázar, poesía

Largo canto, poemario

CORTINA, María Teresa (Argentina, twentieth century)

Lo que importa, poesía

Momentos de un itinerario, poesía

Paréntesis de sol, poesía

CORTINAS, Laura (Argentina, twentieth century)

Como el mundo quiere, teatralización de la novela Mujer

El hombre nuevo, novela

Mujer, novela

La niña de las trenzas negras, novela

Teatro de amor

La vidente

CORVALAN POSSE, Stella (Chile, twentieth century)

Alma, poesía

Amphion, poesía

Geografía azul, poesía

La luna rota, poesía

Nocuentos

Palabras, poesía

Responso de mi sangre

Rostros del mar, poesía

Sinfonía de la angustia, poesía

Sinfonía de viento, poesía

Sombra en el aire, poesía

CORYLE, Mary (pseudonym: see **CORDERO Y LEON, Ramona María**)

COSSIO, Alicia Yáñez (see **YAÑEZ COSSIO, Alicia**)

COSTA, Rosa García (see **GARCIA COSTA, Rosa**)

COTA-CARDENAS, Margarita (United States, twentieth century). Cota-Cárdenas was born in the small border town of Heber, California, in the Imperial Valley. Her father was from Sonora, Mexico, and her mother from New Mexico. Cota-Cárdenas received her B.A. from Stanislaus State College in 1966, her M.A. in 1968 from University of California, Davis, and the Ph.D. in 1980 from the University of Arizona. She is currently a professor of Chicano and Mexican literature at Arizona State University. She is about to publish two collections of poems: Antimitos y contraleyendas and Marchitas de mayo: sones pa'al pueblo. Puppet is her first novel. Cota-Cárdenas was co-founder of Scorpion Press where she has published poetry by bilingual women.

Noches despertando inConciencias, poemas

Puppet. Petra García and Juan Rodríguez. Austin, TX: Relámpago Books, 1965. ISBN 0-9614-964-2-8, paperback, 135 pp. The brutal shooting of a young man, Puppet, arouses the suspicions of the community and Pat Leyva, a Chicana writer, struggles to write his story. The litany of "No lo vites en las news?" runs throughout the novel as the need to know the causes and circumstances of the events becomes more and more crucial. As Pat attempts to write Puppet's story, questions about her own life's choices, her political commitment and her commitment to the community, reach crisis proportions. "Puppet" (so nicknamed because of a congenital disease that deforms his legs and makes him walk like a puppet) becomes a metaphor for a community that is manipulated and controlled by the dominant society. We are told the story mainly through one-sided dialogues (telephone conversations), second-person narration (tú), stream of consciousness. Popular speech is beautifully captured and reflects the different societal and educational levels of its speakers. The language (both English and Spanish), in all its combinations and wordplays, is rich with irony, humor, tragedy, and is itself a metaphor for the struggle between two cultures. HP

COX, Patricia (Mexico, twentieth century)

Amanecer, novela

El batallón de San Patricio, novela

Cuahtémoc, semblanza de un héroe, ficción

El enemigo está adentro, novela

Ese pequeño mundo, novela

Maximiana, novela

Por los dominios del hierro

Pueblo olvidado, novela

Umbral, novela

COX BALMACEDA, Virginia (Chile, b. 1905)

Desvuelo impaciente, cuentos

Los muñecos no sangran, cuentos

COX STUVEN, Mariana (Chile, 1882-1914; pseudonym: Shade)

Un remordimiento, novela corta

La vida íntima de Marie Goetz, novela

COYA, Mercedes García Tudurí de (see **GARCIA TUDURI DE COYA, Mercedes**)

CRESPO, Iris de López (see **LOPEZ CRESPO, Iris de**)

CRESPO DE CAMELINO VEDOYA, Mercedes Pujato (see **PUJATO CRESPO DE CAMELINO VEDOYA, Mercedes**)

CRESTA DE LEGUIZAMON, María Luisa (Argentina, b. 192?). Born in Paraná, Entre Rios, she did postgraduate work, has taught in high schools and universities, and has published in journals both in other Argentinean provinces and abroad. Córdoba has been the center of her literary and academic activities. At the National University there, she has held the chair of Spanish American Literature for twenty years. Her numerous publications include poetry, literary criticism, children's books and editions of Spanish American literature.

De todo un poco, poemas. Paraná, Argentina: Dirección Cultural Entre Ríos, 1972. Paperback, 64 pp. This collection of twenty-three poems received first prize in the "Fray Mocho" 1971 contest in the Argentinean province of Entre Ríos. Most poems are written in free verse; a few are sonnets; a few are particularly musical. In the name of love, some exhibit a delightful irony towards literature and daily routine. Others evoke the history and geography of Entre Ríos. Solitude and sensuality stand out as themes; flowers, trees and water as images. One poem is especially note-worthy for its lyrically concise criticism of nuclear war.
SHA

CROSS, Elsa (Mexico, twentieth century)

La dama de la torre, poemas

Naxos

Peach Melba, poemas

CRUCHAGA DE WALKER, Rosa (Chile, b. 1931)

Bajo la piel del aire

Descendimiento

Después de tanto mar, poemas

Ramas sin fondo, poemas

Raudal

CRUZ, Josefina (Argentina, twentieth century)

Los caballos de don Pedro de Mendoza, novela

La condoresa, novela

El conquistador conquistado: Juan de Garay, novela

Doña Mencía la adelantada, novela

Inés Suárez, la Condoresa, ficción

El viento sobre el río, novela

CRUZ, María (Guatemala, 1876-1915)

María Cruz a través de su poesía, compilación

CRUZ, María de la Luz Lafarja de (see **LAFARJA DE CRUZ, María de la Luz**)

CRUZ, María de Santa (see **SANTA CRUZ, María de**)

CRUZ, sor Juana Inés de la (see **JUANA INES DE LA CRUZ, sor**)

CRUZ DE BECERRIL, Dominga (Puerto Rico, twentieth century)

Mi larga espera, poemas

CRUZ DE CAPRILE, Fifa (Argentina, twentieth century)

El chúcaro

La niña del mar

CRUZ DE MORENO, María de la (Mexico, twentieth century)

Oro blanco, poesía

Veinticinco poemas para declamar

CRUZ Y OSSA, Elvira Santa (see SANTA CRUZ Y OSSA, Elvira)

CUCHI COLL, Isabel (Puerto Rico, b. 1904)

La familia de Justo Malgenio, puertorriqueños en Nueva York, teatro

Frutos de mi pensamiento

Historia de la esclavitud en Puerto Rico

Mujer

La novia del estudiante, drama

El seminarista, comedia

The student's sweetheart (a drama in three acts), translation

Trece novelas cortas

CUELLAR, Aída (Argentina, b. 1942)

Diálogo con el ausente, versos 1959-1961

CUELLAR, Francisca Carlota (Mexico, b. 1861)

Antología, poesía

CUELLAR DE TORRICO, Yolanda (Bolivia, twentieth century)

Prisma, poesía

CUENCA, Laura Méndez de (see MENDEZ DE CUENCA, Laura)

CUEVAS, Raquel García Santos de (see GARCIA SANTOS DE CUEVAS, Raquel)

CUTANDA, María Concepción (Argentina, twentieth century)

Cajita de música, poesía

Cien coplas marineras

Confesión, poesía

Copias e imágenes de Catamarca y la Rioja, poesía

Rama quebrada

CUVI, Victoria Vásconez (see VASCONEZ CUVI, Victoria)

CUZA MALE, Belkis (Cuba-United States, b. 1942). Cuza was born in Oriente. Her first two books of poetry won honorable mentions in the Casa de las Américas literary competition. She later moved to Havana and worked as a journalist for the newspaper Granma. In 1981 she left Cuba and currently lives in the United States. Her poems have been included in several anthologies of Cuban poetry. Her style is lyric and her best known poems deal with literary figures like Rimbaud and Virginia Woolf. ILJ

Los alucinados

Cartas a Ana Frank. Habana: Unión, 1966. Paperback, 48 pp. This book, the third published by Cuza Malé, encompasses a vision of a strange, hallucinating world. The poems are structured as a series of letters to Ann Frank (a Jewish victim of Nazism, author of a diary). Life, death and self-discovery constitute its main themes. More recent poems follow the format of dialogues with other women writers like Virginia Woolf and Juana de Asbaje. Her style has the intimacy of letter writing; verses are long, in free forms. The poetic voice is identified with the author, since each letter (poem) is signed by "belkis."
                                                                                    ILJ

El clavel y la rosa

Juego de damas

Tiempo de sol, poesía. La Habana: El Puente, 1963. Paperback, 91 pp. Received Honorable Mention in the III Concurso Literario Latinoamericano de la Casa de las Américas. Written near the end of 1961, this long poem is divided into fifty-nine short sections of unequal length. Each section/poem stands alone in terms of rhythm and imagery but all are thematically related to the idea of the passing of time; the praise of physical labor, children and nature; foreign intervention and greed; and especially death by war and living in fear of war. The imagery is tropical and the optimism Romantic. DEM

El viento en la pared. Colección Poesía. Santiago: Universidad de Oriente, 1962. Paperback, 55 pp.

D

DALL, Gloria (Colombia, twentieth century)

Una catedral de sal y silencio

A la orilla del ensueño, selección poética

DALMAU DE SANTESTEBAN, Emma Teresa (Argentina, twentieth century)

Canto al trigo, poesía

El instante y la vida, poesía

Juana de Arco, poesía

La palabra y el tiempo, poesía

Peregrinación y la Tierra del Pan, cuento

DALTON, Margarita (Mexico, b. 1943)

Al calor de la semilla

Larga sinfonía en D y había una vez, novelas

DANIEL (pseudonym: see **MANSILLA DE GARCIA, Eduarda**)

DARLEE, Irina Rukavishnikova (see **RUKAVISHNIKOVA-DARLEE, Irina**)

DAVILA, Amparo (Mexico, b. 1928). She started her career as a writer by publishing three books of poetry. Although she won two prizes in poetry, the recognition of her literary talents started with her short stories in which she revealed herself as a master of the genre. She won the 1977 "Benito Juárez" and the 1980 "Ayuntamiento de Guadalajara" prizes for short stories. Arboles petrificados won the Villaurrutia short story prize in 1978. Dávila's texts deal with universal themes such as solitude, sorrow, art, insanity, and death. They occur on two levels: daily reality and the human mind. For the high quality of her works, Dávila could easily belong to the so-called "Boom Generation."

Arboles petrificados, cuentos. México: Joaquín Mortiz, 1977. Paperback, 130 pp. Available in bookstores. This volume of twelve short stories confirmed her place as one of the best women writers in Mexico and in Latin America. A sense of unity in Dávila's texts stems from the psychological insights of the characters, from the poetic prose, from the dream-like world which sometimes seems to be the projection of the reader's mind, from the themes, and from the existentialist nuances blended harmoniously with surrealistic effects. The interest in women's world barely apparent in the previous books has been significantly intensified. "La rueda," "Griselda," "El último verano," etc., deal with the tragedy of women as the main theme.

Meditaciones a la orilla del sueño, poesía. San Luis Potosí: El Troquel, 1954. Paperback, 57 pp. Available in the main Hispanic libraries. Meditaciones is a book of very short poems in which sensations of nature are harmoniously blended with the poet's emotions. Dávila's Neo-Romanticism becomes diluted by the presence of oneiric surrealistic images. An existencialist tendency enhances the pessimistic tone of Dávila's previous book. This pessimism embraces also the Baroque Hispanic tradition. In these poems, an harmonious unity in which the theme of futility stands out against the themes of "bitter solitude," "remote love," and others.

Música concreta, cuentos. México: Fondo de Cultura Económica, 1964. Hardbound, 150 pp. Dávila's talent as a narrator had been widely recognized by the time that she published these eight short stories. The narrative voices unfold once more a dreadful and distressing world. For example, by getting away from his daily routine, a serious and methodical clerk experiences a regression back to his childhood in "Arthur Smith." The man who knows that he is going to die soon carries out his last wish to abandon his bed, only to face in the street his own burial in "El entierro," and so on. Frustration, loneliness, pain and fear become the characters' constant feelings and the usual themes of Dávila's short stories.

Perfil de soledades, poesía. San Luis Potosí; El Troquel, 1954. Paperback, 55 pp. Unavailable. The thirteen poems in this book are in the line of a moderate literary avant-garde. Speaking in the first person, the poetic voice expresses the main theme of solitude in free verse and with surrealistic images. Dávila's Neo-Romantic poetry enhances other themes such as death, sorrow, oblivion, and the end of love. The pessimistic tone that characterizes Dávila's lyric texts is already manifested through key words, such as: fog, silence, obscurity, bones, emptiness, desolation, corpse, and broken dreams.

Salmos bajo la luna, poemas. San Luis Potosí; El Troquel, 1950. Paperback, 65 pp. Available only in libraries. These fourteen poems in prose have a remarkable poetic rhythm obtained by the constant use of repetition, alliteration, and euphonic discourse. The poems have reminiscences of the Biblical psalms. The real landscapes depicted become spiritual ones from the force of the images and the lyric emotion. Universal themes like solitude, emptiness, anguish, sorrow, do not set aside Mexican and/or Hispanic settings. The presence of the autochthonous blended with universal themes is a peculiarity of Dávila's texts, especially those in prose.

Tiempo destrozado, cuentos. México: Fondo de Cultura Económica, 1959. Hardbound, 128 pp. This first collection of twelve short stories by Amparo Dávila reveals an unusual maturity. The daily life of common people is used as background. "Tiempo destrozado," the story that gives the book its title, sets the example for the undefined plots: the reader is confronted with an ubiquitous being and with an elusive experience of death which maintain suspense. Death, fear, hate, eerie companionship and insanity are the main themes. Open structures, a rich variety of narrative modes, surrealistic motives, symbols and the extraordinary ability to play tricks on the reader by means of language and the manipulation of narrative time characterize Dávila's literary craftsmanship.

Tiempo destrozado y Música concreta, cuentos. México: Fondo de Cultura Económica, 1978. ISBN #968-16-0154-8, paperback, 248 pp. This volume is composed of Dávila's first two volumes of short stories, Tiempo destrozado and Música concreta, without any changes. RRV

DAVILA, Angela María (Puerto Rico, b. 1945). At present, Dávila is one of the most outstanding Puerto Rican poets. She also sings her own compositions and has taken part in readings with other writers of her generation. During the sixties, she was a member of a significant group of young poets known by the name of its journal, Guajana. She was the only woman poet included in the Antología de jóvenes poetas published by the Institute of Puerto Rican Culture in 1965.

Animal fiero y tierno, poesía. Río Piedras: Huracán, 1977. ISBN 0-940238-50-0, paperback, 74 pp. The book is dedicated to three outstanding Puerto Rican women: the poet, Julia de Burgos; a singer and composer, Sylvia Rexach; and patriot, Lolita Lebrón. The poems explore the dialectic of personal and social experiences. Some deal with personal relationships (mother/daughter, mother/child, woman/man); others treat solitude versus solidarity; objects -- in reference to human work -- and the exploration of poetic language. The style is lyric; the verses are mostly long. Even though forms tend to be traditional, the poetic language is innovative. ILJ

DAVILA, María Amparo (see **DAVILA, Amparo**)

DAVILA, Nadya Alvarez (see **ALVAREZ DAVILA, Nadya**)

DAVILA DE PONCE DE LEON, Waldina (Colombia, nineteenth century)

Poesías

Serie de novelas, tomo primero

El trabajo, novela

Zuma, drama

DAVIU, Matilde (Venezuela - United States, b. 1942). Daviu studied literature at the Universidad Central de Caracas. She lived in India and Europe and resides in New York, where she teaches at Hunter College. In 1973 she received the Prize for Short Stories from "La Casa de la Cultura" de Maracay and in 1977 the Prize "Dirección de Cultura" from the Universidad de Carabobo. She collaborates in the literary section of El Nacional de Caracas.

Barbazucar y otros relatos

Maithuna, cuentos. Colección Donaire. Caracas: Monte Avila. Venezuela, 1978. Paperback, 152 pp. This book is a compilation of fourteen short stories. The themes are the struggle to survive, love, sex, violence and hatred. Searching for her own way of expression, the author relates myth and reality. She uses a rich and strong language, very innovative in Venezuelan literature. FO

DELALKE, Gemma (Mexico, twentieth century)

Que hiele en verano, mininovela

DELAVAL, Alicia (Mexico, twentieth century)

Hablemos de amor, poemas

Las vírgenes terrestres, novela

DELGADO, Edna Licelott (see **LICELOTT DELGADO, Edna**)

DELGADO, María Isabel Sañudo de (see **SAÑUDO DE DELGADO, María Isabel**)

DELMAR, Meira (pseudonym: see **CHAMS, Olga**)

DEL RIO, Ana María (Chile, b. 1942)

Entre paréntesis, cuentos

DEL RIO, Marcela (pseudonym: see **REYES, Mara**)

DEMAR, Carmen (Puerto Rico, twentieth century)

Alas plegadas, poesía

Alturas del silencio, poesía

Derrumbe, poesía

Lucideces de angustia, poemas

Mar del Sargazo, poesía

Puerto Rico, poemas

Vuelo íntimo, poesía

DEMITROPOLOUS, Libertad (Argentina, b. 1922). Born in Ledesma, Jujuy, she has been a teacher since 1942. Although her first publication was a book of poems, her writing has been devoted thereafter to writing novels with a historical background, especially on the Argentinean Northwest where she was born and raised. She is married to the renowned poet J. O. Giannuzzi with whom she lives in Buenos Aires and has two daughters.

Angeles violentos y ángeles de visillo. Buenos Aires: n.p., 1974.

Los comensales, novela. Buenos Aires: Testimonio, 1967. Paperback, 94 pp. Set in the aridness of Salta and Jujuy, the novel depicts the inertia of the poor, uneducated and illegitimate living at the mercy of the powerful ("los comensales satisfechos"). A foreword provides the colonial background of the novelized region, where political unrest on the eve of Irigoyen's rise momentarily offers a glimmer of hope for improvement. A jump in time bypasses this leader's rule altogether to indicate that no changes have taken place in the province. The third person narration is interspersed with vivid regional dialogue, references to chronicles, ballads, sayings, and one long folk tale.

La flor de hierro, novela. San Antonio de Padua, Buenos Aires: Castañeda, 1978. Paperback, 113 pp. This novel centers on the northwestern Argentinean town of Medinas in an undefined present juxtaposed with its historical origin in the warring factions of the colonial Lima - Santiago - Chacras authorities versus the rebellious governor Francisco de Aguirre and his supporters, the Medina family. The key element is the passing of time and its symbolic repetition. Medina is a waterless community dependent for its livelihood on the burial of the neighboring town's dead. It is as sterile as Diego de Medina's wife who lyrically laments her husband's prolonged absence in seemingly unending battles. The dynamism of the Spanish conquerors is wasted in useless fighting and the futile search for Eldorado, which only yields a "steel flower," blood on their swords' blades, death.

Muerte, animal y perfume. Buenos Aires: n.p., 1951. Paperback.

Río de las congojas, novela. Buenos Aires: Sudamericana, 1981. Paperback, 173 pp. The title refers to the Paraná River as the means by which Juan de Garay misled the narrator and his fellow "bastard" mestizos from Asunción in order to found Santa Fe, but only as a stepping stone to his reestablishment of Buenos Aires. The river functions as the classical metaphor for time and accounts for the coming and going of the characters during the first hundred hopeless years of Santa Fe. One of Garay's lovers, María Muratore emerges as a heroic and tragic protagonist. Colloquial and regional language. This story received the municipality of Buenos Aires' first prize for an unpublished novel in 1980. SHA

DENIS DE ICAZA, Amelia (Panama - Guatemala - Nicaragua, d. 1911). Icaza was of French and Panamanian heritage. She was a lyrical, sentimental poet, known as "the Panamanian lark." Because of duties to husband and children, she lived in Guatemala and Nicaragua, but always missed her beloved Panama. Denis de Icaza's themes are of mother and family love, patriotism, religion, concern for humanity, and particularly, her family and admired friends. In her work, flowers are a symbol of peace, giving a mystical perfume of intimate sadness. She was well-loved and understood as an intelligent, sentimental, passionate and patriotic singer of songs.

Hojas secas. León, Nicaragua: Robelo, 1975. 187 pp. The edition contains sections of patriotic poems, those dealing with friends and family, and with poor, suffering common people. Her most famous poem, "Al Cerro Ancón," tells of her deep love for Panama and of her sadness at what political madness has done to it. "Cansancio," typical of her maternal, sentimental poetry, reveals the weariness the poet feels from life's demands, and she asks for God's help to strengthen her mother's heart. Accompanied by biographical notes and a short criticism of her work by Zoraida Díaz de Escobar. Poems list dates. This edition is old, valuable and contains a photograph of the poet. AS

D'ERZELL DULCHE, Catalina (pseudonym: see **DULCHE ESCALANTE, Catalina**)

DESANDOVAL, Hylda Pino (see **PINO DESANDOVAL, Hylda**)

DE VALLS, Julia A. (Argentina, twentieth century)

Vibraciones

DEVETACH, Laura (Argentina, twentieth century)

Los desnudos, narrativa

La torre de cubos, libro para niños

DHIALMA TIBERTI, María (Argentina, twentieth century)

Cielo recto

Las sombras amarillas

Tierra de amapolas

Los títeres

DI CARLO, Adelia (see **CARLO, Adelia di**)

DIAZ, Anita (Colombia, twentieth century)

Arbol de luceros, poemas

Las espigas de Ruth, poesías

Evangelios de la mujer en el sueño, poesías

El jardín de la palabra iluminada, poemas

Vuelo de mariposas, versos

DIAZ, Susana Rubio de (see **RUBIO DE DIAZ, Susana**)

DIAZ CASTRO, Tania (Cuba, b. 1939)

Agua de felicidad, poesías

Apuntes para el tiempo, poesías

De frente a la esperanza

Todos me van a tener que oír

DIAZ DE CASTILLO DE OTERO, Margarita (Colombia, b. 1903; pseudonym: Río, Berta del)

Otra nave en el puerto

Sentires y cantares

Trenos

DIAZ DE RODRIGUEZ, Albertina (Cuba, b. 1895)

Mis versos

DIAZ DE SCHTRONN, Zoraida (Panama, b. 1881)

Nieblas del alma

DIAZ-DIOCARETZ, Myriam (Chile - Netherlands, b. 1951). This young poet, translator, and critic was educated in Chile and the United States and currently resides in the Netherlands. She has translated into Spanish and written extensively on the poetry of Adrienne Rich and black North American women poets and has also edited and contributed to several volumes on literary theory and collections of feminist writings. Her poetry has appeared in numerous journals and anthologies. To date, she has published one collection of poems, Que no se pueden decir, with two more volumes, Cantos de la Albendera and Paquilorilos, about to go to press. Her work incorporates feminist themes and is a testimony to the liberating power of poetry.

> Que no se pueden decir, poemas. New York: Peninsula, 1982. ISBN 0-916312-10-0, 71 pp. The thirty-seven poems gathered here signify a reaction to the limitations imposed upon people, especially women and poets, by society and language. The inability to express thoughts and feelings adequately with words, one of the underlying motifs of the collection, is set forth in a prefatory epigraph taken from Sor Juana's Respuesta a Sor Filotea. Díaz-Diocaretz affirms her womanhood and her solidarity with victimized women. Problems created by exile and lack of communication can be overcome by looking within oneself and forging one's own destiny. Her poetry, characterized by verbal play and freedom from metrical inhibitions, breaks down the linguistic barriers emblematic of restrictive societal codes. It is, therefore, both a tool to instigate change and an end in itself. MSA

DIAZ LOZANO, Argentina (Honduras, b. 1909)

And We Have to Live, translation

Aquel año rojo, novela

Cuarenta y nueve días en la vida de una mujer, novela histórica

Enriqueta and I, translation

Enriqueta y yo, autobiografía

Fuego en la ciudad, novela histórica

Luz en la senda, novela

Mansión en la bruma, novela

Mayapán, novela histórica

Peregrinaje, autobiografía

Perlas en mi rosario, cuentos

Topacios, cuentos

Y tenemos que vivir, novela

DIAZ VARIN, Stella (Chile, b. 1926)

Razón de mi ser, poesía

Sinfonía del hombre fósil y otros poemas

Tiempo, medida imaginaria, poesía

DIEGO, Celia de (Argentina, twentieth century)

La arena del reloj

Bosquejo bárbaro

Camino de luz y sombra, teatro

El escollo, novela

La exigencia infinita, novela

El forastero

La fuerza oscura, novela

Gramilla serrana

Un grillo entre los juncos

Más allá de mañana, drama

La tierra llama

DIEZ, Catalina Nieto de (see **NIETO DE DIEZ, Catalina**)

DIEZ DE RAMOS, Nena (United States, twentieth century)

Hojas sueltas

DIOCARETZ, Myriam Diaz- (see **DIAZ-DIOCARETZ, Myriam**)

DOBLES YZAGUIRRE, Julieta (Costa Rica, b. 1943)

El peso vivo, poesía

DOLUJANOFF, Emma (Mexico, b. 1922)

Adiós, Job, novela

La calle del fuego, novela

Cuentos del desierto

DOMINGUEZ, Delia (Chile b. 1932). Domínguez is perhaps the most well-known woman poet living in Chile today. She belongs to the generation of writers that began publishing their works in the 1950's. Domínguez is presently editor of the journal <u>Paula</u>. She often gives readings at the universities throughout the country. Her poetry deals with the life and hardships of the peasant workers of southern Chile.

<u>Obertura siglo XX</u>, poemas

<u>Parlamentos del hombre claro</u>, poemas

<u>Pido que vuelva mi Angel</u>

<u>Simbólico retorno</u>

<u>El sol mira para atrás</u>, poemas. Santiago de Chile: Lord Cochrane, 1977. Paperback, 92 pp. Poems marked by a ragged landscape, the presence of the forest and monotonous rainfall are the frame of reference for this intensely lyrical book that depicts the ways of life of the rural people of Chile, particularly the women. Domínguez' poems have very powerful images mostly when describing the marginal position of the peasants in relation to the city dwellers. The language of this book tries to re-capture the spoken idiom of Chileans living in the south of Chile. MA

<u>La tierra nace al canto</u>

DOMINGUEZ, María Alicia (Argentina, b. 1904)

<u>El aire de tu vuelo</u>, poemas

<u>Las alas de metal</u>, poesía

<u>Campo de luna</u>

<u>Canciones de la niña Andersen</u>, poesía

<u>Crepúsculos de oro</u>, poesía

<u>La cruz de la espada</u>, novela

<u>Francisco de la tierra</u>

<u>El hermano ausente</u>, poesía

<u>Idolos de bronce</u>, novela

<u>Mar de retorno</u>, cuentos

<u>Mariquita Sánchez</u>, prosa

<u>El ministro de los pájaros</u>, poesía

<u>Las muchas aguas</u>

<u>Música de siglos</u>, poesía

<u>El nombre inefable</u>, poesía

<u>Redención</u>, prosa

<u>Romanzas del lucero y el pesebre</u>, poesía

Rosas en la nieve, poesía

La rueca, poesía

Siete espadas, poesía

Vida y ensueño, prosa

Vidas de una calle, novela

DOMINGUEZ, Mirta Aguilera (see **AGUILERA DOMINGUEZ, Mirta**)

DOMINGUEZ ROLDEN, María Luisa (Cuba, twentieth century)

Entre amor y música, novela

25 (Veinticinco) cuentos

DONOSO, Tilda Brito de (see **BRITO DE DONOSO, Tilda**)

DONOSO CORREA, Nina (Chile, b. 1920)

El destino de la niña, teatro

Entre el pan y la estrella, poesía

Poemas

Poemas para un difícil olvido

DORYAN, Victoria Garrón de (see **GARRON DE DORYAN, Victoria**)

DOS SANTOS, Estela (Argentina, b. 1940)

Las despedidas, cuentos

DOUMERC, Beatriz (Argentina, b. 1928)

Un cuento muy blanco, libro para niños

La línea, con Ayax Barnes

El pueblo que no quería ser gris, libro para niños

DROZ, Vanessa (Puerto Rico, b. 1952). Studied comparative literature at the University of Puerto Rico and has worked as a teacher, journalist and graphic designer. She has been a member of the editorial board of important literary journals of the seventies, such as Penélope o el otro mundo. In 1980 Droz and other women writers founded the journal Reintegro. Her poetry has been published in various journals and anthologies. Since 1982 she has written a weekly literary column for a local newspaper.

La cicatriz a medias. Colección El Trabajo Gustoso. Río Piedras: Cultural, 1982. Paperback, 80 pp. The poems, written between 1974 and 1979, are ordered chronologically. The book is divided in four sections: the first one, "Poemas," does not show thematic unity; "Vasos" uses the image of the vase as a form in which something (love, death, woman's body) is held; the four poems of "Payasos" focus on the idea of masks; "Inicio del mapa," the last section, uses the image of the scar, sign of the mark or inscription of poetry, of knowledge, of acts. This scar is present in the body and is also the possibility of a "map," a "forest" of scars, hence the title of the book. Droz's poetry reveals a search for formal perfection and is highly metaphorical. ILJ

DRUMOND, Liliana Echeverría (see **ECHEVERRIA DRUMOND, Lilia**)

DUARTE, Nieves Xenes y (see **XENES Y DUARTE, Nieves**)

DUARTE DE PERON, Eva María (Argentina, 1919-1952)

Evita; Eva Duarte de Perón Tells Her Own Story, translation

El libro de mi vida

DUAYEN, César (see **BARRA, Emma de la**)

DUEÑAS, Guadalupe (Mexico, b. 1920). Born in Guadalajara, her early stories were in the Colegio Teresiano de México, D.F., and in Morelia, Michoacán. Some independent literary studies followed. Her first writings were poems, but she refused to have them published. She became associated with the literary and cultural journal Abside, where she came into contact with other prominent writers, such as Emma Godoy, published her first collection of short stories, and worked as colaboradora de planta. She received a fellowship from the Centro Mexicano de Escritores to work on her first novel. Some individual stories have appeared in journals or anthologies in the United States, Germany, France, Italy and England.

Imaginaciones

Máscara para un ídolo

No moriré del todo. México, D.F.: Joaquín Mortiz, 1976. Paperback, 128 pp. A collection of twenty-four short stories in which the author frequently employs a poetic style. Themes of mystery and magic predominate, as in her entire production, but there also are some more realistic examples based on observation. At times, the author leans to criticism of Mexican institutions, particularly the Church, but such criticism is generally light and revelatory of the author's middle-class origins. Of interest to scholars dealing with Mexican life, science fiction and imaginative subject matter.

Pasos en la escalera, La extraña visita, Girándula, con Angeles Mendieta Alatorre, et al. (See Partially Annotated List of Anthologies.)

Las ratas y otros cuentos. Mexico: Abside, 1954. Paperback. A short story collection that gathers the best of her early stories that had appeared in various Mexican magazines, literary journals, and anthologies. She establishes the themes and tone developed in her later works, particularly her love for the small things of life, often considered repulsive by many, as seen in the title story. Magic, fantasy and the unexpected are a predominant threat, and she displays a good balance of observation and creativity in these pieces.

Semblanzas imaginarias

Tiene la noche un árbol, cuentos. Mexico, D.F.; Fondo de Cultura Económica, 1958. Other editions: 2nd ed. 1968; 3rd ed. 1973.

Hardback, Colección Letras Mexicanas, #41; paperback, Colección Popular, 124 pp. Winner of the Premio José María Vigil (Guadalajara, 1959), this collection of twenty-five short stories represents the best of her literary production to date. In it, she demonstrates the qualities which have established her reputation: the pursuit of the imaginative, a fine sense of observation, an inclusion of the smaller things of life and of beings normally considered repulsive in a sympathetic setting. She displays remarkable ability in making skillful transitions from the real world to a world of horror and the unknown. Of interest to scholars dealing with Mexican life, imaginative subject matter, poetic prose, and the fantastic, as well as the general reader of Latin American literature. EE

DUENDE, Damita (pseudonym: see **MORVAN, Henriette**)

DUHART, Sara María (Argentina, twentieth century)

En la ciudad de los hombres, poemas

Lo que el diluvio perdona, poemas

Monadas

Santa María de los Buenos Sueños, poemas

DULCHE ESCALANTE, Catalina (Mexico, b. 1897; pseudonym: Erzell, Catalina d')

Apasionadamente, novelas cortas

Chanito, teatro

La ciénega, teatro

Cumbres de nieve, drama

"El," poesías

¡Esos hombres!, comedia dramática

Los hijos de la otra, teatro

La inmaculada, novela

La sin honor, comedia

Lo que sólo el hombre puede sufrir, teatro

Maternidad, teatro

El pecado de las mujeres, comedia en tres actos

La razón de la culpa, alta comedia

El rebozo azul, drama

El último charro, sainete

Xulitl, ópera

DUPREY, Ana Roqué de (see **ROQUE DE DUPREY, Ana**)

DURAN, Ana Luisa (Puerto Rico-United States, twentieth century)

Prometeo y el estreno, cuentos

Toro de minos, cuentos

DURAND, Luz María (Mexico, twentieth century)

Ante la vida, cuentos

Caminos de América, prosa y verso

En busca del espíritu, novela

Ideas femeninas, 13 (trece) semblanzas

Intensidad, poemas

Lo que no puede callar

Luz y sombra, poemas

Mi alma y yo, poemas

Perfiles

Pétalos 1938

Poemas de México

Ráfagas, cuentos y poemas

DURAND, Mercedes (El Salvador, twentieth century)

Espacios, poema

Juego de ouija

Las manos en el fuego, poesía

Las manos y los siglos, poesía

Sonetos elementales, poesía

Todos los vientos, antología poética

E

E. DE GUTIERREZ SUAREZ, Emma (see **GUTIERREZ SUAREZ,** **Emma E. de**)

EASLEY, Marina (Colombia, twentieth century)

    Rosas para Rosa, novela

EASTMAN, María (Colombia, b. 1901)

    El conejo viajero, cuentos para niños

ECHEVARRIA DE LARRAIN, Inés (Chile, 1869-1949; pseudonym: Iris)

    Emociones teatrales, recopilación

    Entre dos siglos, diario

    Hojas caídas, autobiográfico

    La hora de queda, cuentos

ECHEVARRIA DE LOBATO MULLE, Felisa Carmen (Argentina, twentieth century)

    Romancero de la villa de Luján

ECHEVERRIA, María Flora Yáñez Bianchi de (see **YAÑEZ BIANCHI DE ECHEVERRIA, María Flora**)

ECHEVERRIA DRUMOND, Liliana (Chile, twentieth century)

    De mi huerto en sombras, novela

    Murmullos del alma, novela

ECHEVERRIA LOPEZ, Maruja (Ecuador, twentieth century)

    Motivos del cristal, poemas

ECHEVERS, Malin d' (Guatemala, twentieth century)

El canto perdido, versos, año 1934

Galope de astros, poesía

Mago pequeño, 1949-1950), poemas

Mah rap, novela

Metal noble, novela

Mieses líricas

EGUI, María de Jesús Abadía (see **ABADIA EGUI, María de Jesús**)

EGUZA, Tirso de (pseudonym: see **GUTIERREZ ISAZA, Elvira**)

ELDELBERG, Betina (Argentina, b. 1930)

Ciudad a solas, poemas

Crónica menor, poemas

Imposturas

Mutaciones, poemas

Para la red

ELFLEIN, Ada María (Argentina, 1881-1919)

Biblioteca infantil argentina

De tierra adentro

Leyendas argentinas

ELGUERA DE MACPARLIN, Alida (Peru, twentieth century)

Coplas de las calles de Lima, poesía

Cruces del camino, poesía

Juguetes, cuentos

Romance, intriga e incienso, novela

ELGUL DE PARIS, Marta (Argentina, twentieth century)

Con sabor a tierra

ELIM, Miriam (Chile, twentieth century)

Ojos extasiados

ELIZONDO, Hortensia (Mexico, twentieth century)

Mi amigo azul, cuento

ELORZA DE ORTI, Ana Manuela (Argentina, twentieth century)

Copitos de nieve, poesía

Palomas de paz, poesía

Salve América, poesía

EMILIANI IMITOLA NINFA, María (Colombia, b. 1882; pseudonym: Mery, Fanny)

Hojas de acacio, prosas y versos

ENGEL, Lya (Mexico, twentieth century)

Juegos dramáticos

ENRIQUE DE ALBA, Carlos (pseudonym: see **CESPEDES DE ESCAÑAVERINO,** Ursula)

ENRIQUETA, María (pseudonym: see **CAMARILLO DE PEREYRA, María Enriqueta**)

ERAUSO, Catalina (Spain - Mexico, 1592-1650?; also la Monja Alférez). Born in San Sebastián de Guipúzcoa to a family of noble ancestry, she entered a convent at four and escaped when she was fifteen, before professing as a nun. Disguised in a man's outfit, she wandered from one city to another serving different masters like the pícaros did. Afterwards, she embarked for the New World where she spent nineteen years under the name of Alonso Díaz Ramírez de Guzmán. Later she revealed her female identity, and went to New Spain (Mexico), where she died and was buried. Although historically documented, the authenticity of her Vida y sucesos has been questioned. See details in the annotations that follow.

Historia de la Monja Alférez Doña Catalina de Erauso, escrita por ella misma. Ed. Joaquín María Ferrer. Paris: Didot, 1829. Hardbound, 213 pp. Available in research libraries. Follows closely the manuscript Vida y sucesos de la Monja Alférez deposited after 1784 in the Real Academia de la Historia in Madrid by Juan Bautista Muñoz. Because of the obvious novelistic extrapolations in the original manuscript, it is considered autobiographical fiction. The life of Erauso is essentially incredible: disguised as a man, she fought against the Araucanians, gambled, killed, was sentenced to death. In short, this text portrays the image of a woman who, possessed by Renaissance restlessness, broke with the conventions of her times. Some critics consider this text an important forerunner of the Spanish American novel.

Historia de la Monja Alférez Doña Catalina de Erauso, escrita por ella misma. Ed. J.[oaquín] M.[aría] F[errer], 2nd ed. Barcelona: José Tauló, 1838. Hardbound, 155 pp. Available in research libraries. This second edition differs from the first only in the prologue: the forty-six pages have been reduced to ten. In this prologue, Ferrer is somewhat more cautious in making categorical affirmations than in the first edition. In the nine years between the two texts, critics had stated that the text was a literary fraud "because of the many errors in it." However, after a careful revision of such errors and thorough documentation, recent studies have proven that they are only few mistakes, which do not constitute a reason to reject the text. Editora Nacional from Madrid is preparing a new critical edition for 1984.

Historia de la Monja Alférez Doña Catalina de Erauso, escrita por ella misma. Ed. José Berruezo. Pamplona: Gómez, 1959. Paperback, 154 pp. This contemporary edition follows closely Ferrer's editions without any of its valuable footnotes. Of interest are: 1) a picture in black and white of Catalina de Erauso's portrait painted in 1630 by Francisco Pacheco; 2) new historical documents transcribed in the prologue by Berruezo and related to the real life of Catalina de Erauso; and 3) a reproduction of the "Ultima y tercera relación" published in Mexico in 1653 about the last days of her life.

Memorias de la Monja Alférez. Madrid: Felmar, 1974. ISBN 84-379-0011-5, paperback, 154 pp. Reproduces with footnotes and some of the historical documents contained in the "Appendix" of the edition by Ferrer. It only changes the distribution of chapters, showing that the editor followed the original manuscript instead of subsequent reproductions. Of interest is the short "Preface" in Spanish that José María Heredia wrote to his French translation of the text published in 1894 in Paris. RRV

ERZELL, Catalina d' (pseudonym: see DULCHE ESCALANTE, Catalina)

ESCANDELL, Noemí (Cuba - United States, b. 1936). Escandell was born and raised in Havana, where she received her primary and secondary education. She came to Georgia on a scholarship where she met and married an American. After several years of travel, they settled in the United States. She received her B.A. from Queens College in 1968, her M.A. and Ph.D. from Harvard University and taught at Bard College. Her publications include books of poetry and translations in several magazines. Escandell was an artist-in-residence at the Millay Colony for the Arts. She teaches at Westfield State University (1984).*

Ciclos, poesía. Colección Juglar. Madrid: Gahe, 1982. ISBN 84-7076-081-5, paperback, 45 pp. This collection of thirty-five poems reveals the poet in a more personal dimension than her first book. In poems which speak of physical cycles, she tells of personal evolution, of return and rebirth. This is the mature reflective poetry of a woman who has seen and experienced the harshness life offers and yet savors it and appreciates its beauty.

Cuadros, poesía. Somerville, New Jersey: SLUSA, 1982. ISBN 0-9606758-0-9, paperback, 49 pp. A collection of thirty-three poems. Introd. by Isaac Goldemberg. Short poems written in blank, alliterative verse. Delicate and sensual language paints brief insightful portraits (cuadros) of people and places. The poet achieves a universal and intimate portrayal of her subjects. Her concern with humanity, with the human dimension of politics and suffering and, above all, a personal search for the simple but profound truths to be found in human interaction and natural images is evident. TF

ESCAÑAVERINO, Ursula Cespedes de (see CESPEDES DE ESCAÑAVERINO, Ursula)

---

*Noemí Escandell is also an annotator for this volume. -- Editor.

ESCANDON PREVOWSOIR, Gemma Violeta (Mexico, twentieth century)

Gemas, poesía

Mujer, prosa

ESCOBAR THORBURN, Elizabeth (Guatemala, twentieth century)

7 x 4 (Siete por cuatro) poemas

El río lila, novela

ESPEJO, Beatriz (Mexico, twentieth century)

La otra hermana

ESPINDOLA, Lourdes (Paraguay-United States, twentieth century; also Lourdespínola)

Almenas del silencio

Monocorde amarillo, poesía

Visión del arcángel en once puertas, poesía

Womanhood and Other Misfortunes, tr. Naomi Lindstrom and Lourdes Espíndola. Prologue by Sharon Keefe Ugalde. Fort Worth: Latitudes, 1985.

ESPINDOLA DE PASCUAL ROMERO, Sofía (Argentina, b. 1904)

Almas sedientes, novela

Ansias en fuga, poesía

El azote en la llaga, novela

Elegía para un destino angustiado, poesía

El ídolo de luz y barro, poemas

Luján, novela

Márgenes de sombras, cuentos

Un momento de extravío

Sombras en llamas, novela

Sombras y luces del camino, poesía

ESPINEL, Ileana (Ecuador, b. 1933). Since the age of sixteen, Espinel has written poetry, and since the age of twenty-one, she has been a journalist. As one of Ecuador's best-known female poets, she has had many of her works appear in numerous anthologies and has had many others translated and published abroad. In addition, she was a cofounder of the "Club 7 de Poesía" in Guayaquil. For many years she has written cultural columns for such

Ecuadorian newspapers as El Universo and El Telégrafo. She currently has a daily column in El Telégrafo entitled "Artes y Letras."

Arpa salobre, poesía. Caracas: Poesía de Venezuela, 1966. 18 pp. Composed mainly of sonnets, the work is slightly autobiographical in nature with some poems reflecting the pain and solitude of Espinel's life while others eulogize her dear friend and fellow poet David Ledezma who committed suicide.

Diríase que canto, 1950-1968, poemas. Guayaquil, Ecuador: Casa de la Cultura Ecuatoriana, 1969. Over 100 pp. The opening poem is a homage to Espinel by the famous Ecuadorian poet, César David Andrade. In addition to containing a wide range of poetic forms -- from the sonnet to short poems of free verse, the work has a variety of themes dealing mainly with the poet's family, friends, and loves. The majority of the poems are from Espinel's other collections: Arpa salobre, La estatua luminosa, and Piezas líricas. Several poems are accompanied by black and white sketches.

La estatua luminosa, y poemas escogidos. Ecuador: Lírica Hispana, 1959. 61 pp. Conie Lobell and Jean Aristeguieta, two friends and associates of Espinel from the Casa de la Cultura Ecuatoriana of Guayaquil, contribute the introduction. Mainly in free verse and ranging from very short concentrated forms to longer more complex ones, the poems are often personal in nature, speaking of Espinel's parents, her unhappy love affairs, and the creative artists whom she admires. A biographical section on Espinel's life and a poem by the Ecuadorian poet, Mary Corylé, praising Espinel's poetry, follow the poetry.

Poemas escogidos (1954-1978). Guayaquil, Ecuador: Cultura Ecuatoriana, 1978. Paperback, 145 pp. This vast sampling of Espinel's poetry begins with a biographical discussion of her life and poetry. The poems were selected from all of her previous volumes. The book is truly representative of Espinel's work, and it concludes with a section of critical opinions.

Piezas líricas

Tan solo 13 (trece), poemas. Guayaquil, Ecuador: Casa de la Cultura Ecuatoriana, 1972. 23 pp. Despite its small size, the collection reflects an intensity of theme and form. In spite of their brevity, the poems possess a profound social consciousness in presenting themes that range from the violence and suffering of the Vietnam War to modern man's desolation and complete loneliness. The Ecuadorian critic Ignacio Carvallo Castillo provides a discussion following the poetry. AP

ESPINOSA DE CUSAN, Cecilia (Colombia, twentieth century)

Tengo las manos en la piel de la tierra

ESPINOSA DE MENENDEZ, Leonor (Peru, twentieth century)

Zarela, novela feminista

ESPINOSA DE PEREZ, Matilde (Colombia, twentieth century)

Afuera, las estrellas, versos

Pasa el viento, poemas

Por todos los silencios, poemas

ESPINOSA DE RENDON, Silveria (Colombia, 1815-1886)

El día de reyes

El divino modelo de las almas cristianas

Consejos a Angélica

Lágrimas y recuerdos

Pesares y consuelos

Poesías

ESPINOSA, Juana Mélendez de (see **MELENDEZ DE ESPINOSA, Juana**)

ESTENSSORO, María Virginia (Bolivia, twentieth century)

Ego inútil, poemas

El occiso, cuentos

ESTENSSORO, Quica (see **ESTENSSORO MACHICADO, Angélica**)

ESTENSSORO MACHICADO, Angélica (Bolivia, b. 1908)

Violeta de oro, cuentos

ESTEVEZ Y VALES DE RODRIGUEZ, Sofía (Cuba, b. 1848)

Alberto el trovador, novela

Lágrimas y sonrisas, poemas

María, novela

ESTHER DE MIGUEL, María (see **MIGUEL, María Esther de**)

ESTIGARRIBIA DE FERNANDEZ, Graciela (Paraguay, twentieth century)

Los derechos civiles de la mujer, ensayo

Influencia francesa en la evolución cultural de la mujer, ensayo

La mujer y su mundo, ensayo

ESTRADA, María Helena Uribe de (see **URIBE DE ESTRADA, María Helena**)

ESTRADA DE RAMIREZ PEREZ, Aurora (Ecuador, 1902-1967). In 1952 Estrada began her fight for the rights of women and children. She was president of the feminist organization, Unión de Mujeres del Guayas, and in 1954 she was Ecuador's representative to the first Latin American conference of women. In addition, she has directed several educational institutions. As a poet, she was greatly influenced by the poetry of Delmira Agustini. However, the majority of her poetic works, like her few prose works, are unpublished.

Como el incienso. Guayaquil: Biblioteca Ecuatoriana, 1982. Paperback, 78 pp. One of Estrada's few published works, the poems reflect Delmira Agustini's influence upon Estrada's poetry. Estrada, like Agustini, is a dreamer whose search for a godlike lover to fulfill her is presented through very sensuous imagery with naturalistic and religious overtones. AP

ESTRADA MEDINILLA, María (Mexico, seventeenth century)

Relación escrita por Doña María de Estrada Medinilla a una Religiosa prima suya

ESTRELLA, María del Mar (Argentina, twentieth century)

El poblador, poemas

Pueblo de Caín y otros poemas

ESTRELLA, Susana Tampieri de (see **TAMPIERI DE ESTRELLA, Susana**)

ESTRELLA ALONSO, Josefina (Argentina, twentieth century)

Cara o cruz

ETCHEPARE, Delia Castellanos de (see **CASTELLANOS DE ETCHEPARE, Delia**)

ETCHEPARE DE HENESTROSA, Armonía (Uruguay, b. 1920; pseudonym: Somers, Armonía). Somers has carefully separated her vocations as a school teacher and librarian from her career as a writer. In 1963, the noted Uruguayan critic, Angel Rama, described the unusual nature and importance of her fiction: "Everything is uncanny, strange, disconcerting, repulsive and, at once incredibly fascinating in the most unusual prose that the history of our literature has known: Armonía Somers' books." (Marcha [Montevideo], 27 dic., p. 30) Her fiction fuses reality and imagination, this world and the beyond where living and dead share a common sense of emptiness and lack of communication. Her dense prose style and expressionistic imagery formed by the unconventional confluence of a visceral or repulsive or violent realism and a lyrical metaphysics is a unique accomplishment.

La calle del viento norte, cuentos. Montevideo: Narradores de Arca, 1963. Out-of-print, 76 pp. Somers adds to her repertoire of short stories, a bizarre murder mystery, sibling rivalry over a dead brother, a suspense thriller that uncovers the private lives of the rich and the hatred for them sustained by the poor, and life's impressions rendered allegorically from the other side, i.e. death. Female eroticism is superbly described in passages like the following: "Suddenly while the elevator door opened automatically like a well-lubricated vagina, the greasy stairway banister winked at me again with the guile of a faun from behind the trees. The exact amount of time for the door to close again. And there I was losing myself, astride the banister, just as someone must have invented them for incipient orgasms that later on overpower the ripe sex in bloom until it ends up contracting like a burnt rag in old age." Some stories have been collected in Muerte por alacrán.

De miedo en miedo. (Los manuscritos del río), novela. Montevideo: Narradores de Arca, 1965. Out-of-print, 102 pp. Somers' creativity is painful; it is a disembowling, a dismemberment. She seems to sympathize with her antiheroes, like the young man in this short novel. Irreverent irony is balanced with tenderness, oneiric imagery is coupled with defiance of taboos. For example, the male protagonist experiences birth, the birth of fear -- "The night I gave birth, I was a man" -- and, also senses the oppression of morality -- "Then I decided to buckle under to custom like any old man riding a bus, tight-lipped though his thoughts keep tugging away like a dog who found a tree, held back by his master, yet free to pee on the conventions of a morality chock full of rules, of a language prickling with barbs that martyr the mind of those who have to write or speak for the rest of the slaves...."

El derrubamiento, cuentos. Montevideo: Salamanca, 1953. Out-of-print, 138 pp. Death and female/male relationships emerge as important constants in this first collection of short stories: the sensations of sexuality, the unusually unencumbered naming of the body's humors -- sweat, saliva, milk, blood, semen -- the taste of mother's milk, of abortions, of intercourse. In most sexual relations, indifference and pernicious eroticism prevail in Somers' explorations of misogynist aggression. Furthermore, Somers tests the taboos of her society in the unique desacralization of cultural stereotypes, both sexual and racial, in her characterization of the Virgin Mary and a Black man- "marianismo" and "machismo." Some stories have been collected in Muerte por alacrán.

Muerte por alacrán, cuentos. Buenos Aires: Calicanto, 1978. Paperback, 187 pp. To eleven earlier short stories, largely out-of-print, Somers adds one new text. Includes some of her best fiction: the suspense thriller, "La calle del viento norte;" the macabre and humorous, "El entierro;" the poignant, "La inmigrante;" the sensual, "El hombre del túnel." Unfortunately, her outstanding desacralization of the cult of Mary ("marianismo") and the powerful and violently misogynous, "El despojo," have been excluded.

La mujer desnuda, novela. Montevideo: Clima, 1950. Other editions: 2nd ed. 1951; 3rd ed. (Montevideo: Tauro, 1967). Paperback, 111 pp. This short novel, allegorical in nature, scandalized provincial Montevideo of the 1950's, whose critics condemned the author as a "gifted and pathological erotic," a "misguided pedagogue" and a "cryptomaniac recidivist." This work marked the start of a continuous and frank treatment of the problems of sexuality and eroticism in Somers' fiction, a narrative that challenges the hypocrisy of social and religious morality and portrays man as a solitary and cruel beast.

Un retrato para Dickens, novela. Motevideo: Arca, 1969. Paperback, 130 pp. This brief novel attests to the literary importance of the Bible -- passages called Documents from the Book of Tobias are interspersed throughout the text -- for Somers who considers the Old Testament to be "the greatest novel ever written, a serialized novel. In it there is poetry, drama, inconceivable massacres that today we call terrorism; we've forgotten that terrorism is nothing new." Somers names a parrot, kept in the patio of a tenement building, Asmodeo (the devil in the Book of Tobias) and allows him to be one of the three narrative voices to describe the rape of a young orphan girl by an idiot.

Sólo los elefantes encuentran mandrágora. Buenos Aires: Legasa, 1983. Paperback. This latest novel, links the universal with the regional, the intimate and psychological with the social, the scholarly with the empirical, and the historical with the fictitious. Different genres and styles also communicate with each other: the serialized story and the romantic atmosphere, occult hermeticism and popular superstitions, pure naturalism and magical realism.

Tríptico darwiniano, cuentos. Illus. Montevideo: Torre, 1982. Paperback, 55 pp. This special limited edition of three new stories is dedicated "To Charles on the Centennial of his death. For what he thought and said, for what he was unable to say although they attributed it to him anyway, and in any case for what he must have suffered." A brief introduction by Jean Andreu situates these simian tales within their literary context (Poe, Quiroga, Lugones, Flaubert). This special issue was designed and executed under the supervision of Rodolfo A. Henestrosa, Somers' late husband.

Todos los cuentos 1953-1967. Two volumes. Montevideo: Arca, 1967. Paperback, I, 127 pp.; II, 127 pp. Vol. II out-of-print. To the women, men and children of previous volumes, Somers adds more marginal characters: assasins, rapists, madmen, vagabonds, prostitutes, lesbians, drunkards, orphans and malcontents. Others are merely shells of the dead living out of the last grotesque, ironic moments of life. Somers' narratives continue to be a unique, lyrical yet unabashed rendering of issues considered taboo in her society, such as a lesbian relationship sympathetically recorded by the curious son of one of the women. Death is always present, at times personified, and dealt with, in only one exceptional short story, in a "tour de force" of black humor with an almost "Poesque" ending. Some stories have been collected in Muerte por alacrán. EPG

EULATE SANJURJO, Carmen (Puerto Rico, 1871-1961)

Marqués y marquesa, novela

La mujer en la historia

La mujer moderna

La muñeca, perfil de mujer, novela

Perfiles de mujeres

EZEIZA GALLO, Carmen N. de (Argentina, twentieth century)

Atardecer, poesía

Breviario de amor perfecto, poesía

Cantos y romances, poesía

La insólita búsqueda

Oasis, poesía

Timón de incertidumbre, poesía

F

FARFAN CANO, Isabel (Mexico, twentieth century)

    Pasos, poesía

    Proyección, poemas

FARIAS DE ISSASI, Teresa (Mexico, b. 1878)

    Ante el gran enigma, obra filosófica

    Como las aves, alta comedia

    Nupcial

    Páginas de la vida, teatro

FELICIANO MENDOZA, Esther (Puerto Rico, b. 1917)

    Arco iris

    Cajita de música, cuentos

    Coqui

    Nanas, poesía de la navidad

    Nanas de la adolescencia

    Nanas de la Navidad

    Sinfonía de Puerto Rico, mitos y leyendas

    Voz de mi tierra

FERGUSON, Gloria (Guatemala, twentieth century)

    La herencia del abuelo, novela

FERIA, Lina de (Cuba, b. 1945). Born in Santiago de Cuba, Feria moved to Havana in 1963 and studied at the School of Drama. She went on to study language and literature at the University of Havana and worked with the journal Juventud Rebelde. In 1966 she was awarded the Rubén Martínez Villena prize and in 1967 she shared the David poetry award with Luis Rogelio Nogueras. She is usually included in the group of poets called the "novísimos" or "second generation of the Revolution." This group changed Cuban poetry through the creation of a new poetic language.

Casa que no existía. Habana: Cuadernos Unión, 1917. Paperback, 52 pp. The non-existent house -- a construction of the imagination -- is inhabited by images of childhood. A vivid evocation of characters, experiences and places is expressed in a colloquial language. The texts articulate the visions of the adolescent coming into the world. Feria's style is highly lyrical; the poems are short and free verse forms are preferred. ILJ

FERNANDEZ, Abigaíl Mejía de (see **MEJIA DE FERNANDEZ, Abigaíl**)

FERNANDEZ, Janina (see **FERNANDEZ PACHECO, Janina**)

FERNANDEZ, Magda López de Victoria y (see **LOPEZ DE VICTORIA Y FERNANDEZ, Magda**)

FERNANDEZ, Zoila Amable (Mexico, twentieth century)

Iradiaciones, poesía

FERNANDEZ DE CORDOVA, Olivia (Mexico, twentieth century)

Amor sublime, cuento

María Luisa, teatro

Rosas y espinas, poesía

FERNANDEZ DE GIL, Zeneida (Costa Rica, twentieth century)

Retorno, novela

FERNANDEZ DE LEWIS, Carmen Pilar (Puerto Rico, b. 1925)

De tanto caminar, teatro

FERNANDEZ DE LOMELI JAUREGUI, Emma (Mexico, twentieth century)

Poemas para declamar

FERNANDEZ DE TINOCO, María (Costa Rica, b. 1877; pseudonym: Apaikán)

Yonta

Zulai

FERNANDEZ PACHECO, Janina. (Costa Rica, b. 1947). Sociologist, former professor, adviser to the Ministry of Culture, Youth and Sport, Vice-Consul of Costa Rica in Havana, Cuba; researcher and dancer, Fernández is also a young, contemporary poet. She writes with perfectly precisioned language, using her poetry as a scalpel-sharp weapon against contemporary issues facing women. In her first book, her poetry is mature, with well-developed images. Her work shows her discouragement as a woman of outstanding intellect.

Biografía de una mujer, poema. San José, Costa Rica: Costa Rica, 1978. 58 pp. This biographical poem, dedicated to Francisco, is both confessional and questioning. Fernández believes woman is trapped, caught by what is considered proper at the expense of herself. Woman has been historically cheated by the male system; she has suffered; she lacks a center. In questioning who woman is, Fernández decides she exists somewhere beneath the surface of ordinary things (upper-middle-class Diors and Max Factors). Fernández, the poet/woman, discovers that the saddest thing is that tradition has isolated woman from love, from man. The poet has lost Francisco, but she knows her search must proceed in order to secure a balanced life with man. The poem is personal. AS

FERRARI DE PLAZA, Angélica (Uruguay, twentieth century)

Canción para el marino iluminado, poesía

La cigarra y el don, poesía

Emociones tendidas al sol, poesía

La gota en el río, poesía

El grito y la eternidad

Hacia la isla poesía

Horas, poesía

Hormiga y estrella

La tierra ilimitada, teatro

Trompo de colores, poesía

FERRARIA ACOSTA, Eloísa (Argentina, twentieth century)

Alas, poemas

La sonrisa de Monna Lisa, fábulas, poemas

Yo y lo mío, novela

FERRAZ DE GADEA, María Julieta (Uruguay, twentieth century)

Alforja de limosnas, poesía

Canción de cuna, poesía

Culpable, novela

Huelga, cuento

Josefina, teatro

Mala suerte, cuento

El milagro, teatro

La querencia, cuento

Perdón, Madre mía, teatro

Primavera, teatro

Ritmo, poesía

Ronda infantil, poesía

FERRE, Patricia (Argentina, twentieth century)

De repente, hoy, poemas

FERRE, Rosario (Puerto Rico, twentieth century). Born in Ponce, Puerto Rico, she specialized in English and Latin American literature in universities in the United States and in Puerto Rico. Her work has been published in numerous journals and her stories have been honored with awards. She founded and directed one of the most important literary journals in Latin America, Zona de carga y descarga, dedicated to the new Puerto Rican literature.

Los cuentos de Juan Bobo. Rio Piedras, Puerto Rico: Huracán, 1981. ISBN: 0-940238-62-4, paperback, 31 pp. This collection of five short stories has a childlike flavor apparent in the simplicity of the situations enacted by the main character and in the language of nursery rhymes and children's stories interspersed in the narration. The primitive quality of the drawings by José Rosa reinforces the link with children's literature. Yet the author dedicates the book to adults and using violent, even monstrous terms, injects each story with a strong moral lesson that reflects Ferré's feminist commitment. The character of Juan Bobo, borrowed from Puerto Rican oral tradition, represents women's desires to overcome the economic and political power structures and to subvert the tyranny of the Church and the family.

Fábulas de la garza desangrada. Serie Las Dos Orillas. Mexico: Joaquín Mortiz, 1982. ISBN #968-27-0131-7, paperback, 75 pp. The dedicatory poem in this collection introduces the theme of the essential duality of woman, a theme traced throughout the work in the coupling of poems and prose "letters" which head each section; in the allusions to mirrors and reflections; and in poems which are meant to serve as counterpoint to each other. The heron of the title embraces the duality of mother and maiden, unified by the image of blood which represents the passion of love. Ferré invokes a procession of archetypes, including Desdemona and Mary Magdalene: not the accepted version of those figures but their doubles, created by Ferré to subvert our expectations and to reinvent in turn their own destinies.

La mano que le pisaron la cola

La muñeca menor/The youngest doll, cuento y traducción. Trans. by Rosario Ferré. De Orilla a Orilla/From Shore to Shore Series. Puerto Rico: Huracán, n.d., n. pag. [2 sheets, 18 pp.] This short story appeared originally as the first in Ferré's collection, Papeles de Pandora, and Ediciones Huracán has presented it bilingually in its own booklet-like package, accompanied by exquisite paper-doll illustrations by Antonio Martorell. The story deals with the exploitation of the maiden aunt and the youngest daughter in an old landed family and the revenge which they take against their male victimizers. The two characters ultimately fuse into a single identity, that of the last doll made by the aunt as a wedding gift for her niece. Ferré reincarnates the myth of Frankenstein rebelling against his master and, on an historical level, represents the confrontation of Puerto Rico's declining plantation aristocracy and the greedy new merchant-consumer class.

Papeles de Pandora, cuentos y poemas. Serie Nueva Narrativa Hispánica. México: Joaquín Mortiz, 1976. Paperback, 207 pp. This collection, Ferré's first book, is composed of fourteen short stories and six poems, all unified by the central theme of the multiplicity of the feminine image, especially as manifested in the roles historically assigned to her by a patriarchal culture. Among those roles are Mary and Eve, mother and whore, Medea, and Sleeping Beauty. Ferré nonetheless rejects these images and seeks to supplant them with that of an autonomous, emancipated new woman. Alternating between male and female voices, between a language charged with cultural and mythological allusions and a language flavored by clichés, colloquialisms, even advertising jingles, Ferré creates an atmosphere which is dream-like, mysterious, malevolent, at times violent.

Sitio a Eros: trece ensayos literarios. Serie Confrontaciones. México: Joaquín Mortiz, 1980. ISBN #968-27-0121-X, paperback, 164 pp. This collection of thirteen essays dealing with the life and work of women writers forms a striking complement to Ferré's imaginative work. The first two pieces, which provide the theoretical underpinning to the rest of the collection, outline Ferré's belief that those women who have followed a literary vocation, typically deprived of economic and political power, have of necessity confronted obstacles unknown to their male counterparts. What spiritually links such diverse writers as Mary Shelley and George Sand, Anaïs Nin and Julia de Burgos, is a consuming passion which has impelled each in turn to overcome her limitations and to transform herself in art and life into a complete, authentic being of almost mythic stature. SSO

FERRER, Surama (Cuba, b. 1923)

El girasol enfermo

Romelia Vargas

FIGUERAS DE WALLS, Isabel (Argentina, b. 1895)

El arte de seducir, novela

Fontana lírica, poesía

Páginas dispersas, prosa

Sombras en relieve, novela

FIGUEREDO, Amalia de (Uruguay, twentieth century)

Te apagarás como las lámparas, poemas

FIGUEROA, Esperanza (Cuba, b. 1913)

Anaxarites, poesía

La luna, poesía

Las manos, poesía

FIGUEROA, Loida (Puerto Rico, twentieth century)

Agridulce, poemas

Arenales, novela

FINKEL, Berta (Argentina, twentieth century)

Mientras voy creciendo, libro para niños

Yasam, el loco espectador, drama

FIRPO, Sylvia Lago de (see **LAGO DE FIRPO, Sylvia**)

FLERIDA (pseudonym: see **MACHADO DE ARREDONDO, Isabel**)

FLOR DE TE (pseudonym: see **HIDALGO DE CHIRIBOGA, Alicia**)

FLORES AEDO, Juana (Chile, twentieth century)

Versos para mi escuela, poesía para niños

FLOREZ, Magdalena (Colombia, twentieth century)

Profanación

FLOREZ DE RIZZOLO, María Esther (Argentina, twentieth century)

Setenta versos y ningún amor

FLOREZ FERNANDEZ DE SERPA, Paz (Colombia, twentieth century)

Extasis de Santa Teresa

Santander, tierra querida

FONSALBA, Pablo María (pseudonym: see **IZQUIERDO ALBIÑANA, Asunción**)

FONSECA, Carlos A. (pseudonym: see **FONSECA RECAVARREN, Nelly**)

FONSECA RECAVARREN, Nelly (Peru, twentieth century; pseudonym: Fonseca, Carlos A.)

Bethmoora, la que mira al mar, teatro en verso

Carlos en el sendero, poemas

Espigas de cristal, poesía

Heraldo del porvenir, poesía

Herodes, teatro

Juan Carlos Crohare, poesía

Luz en el sendero, poesía

Poema de América, poesía

Raíz del sueño, poesía

Río de pájaros, poesía

Rosas matinales, poesía

Sembrador de estrellas, poesía

El velero alucinado, poesía

Voces de América, poesía

FOPPA, Alaíde (Mexico, twentieth century)

Aunque es de noche

Los dedos de la noche, poemas

Guirnalda de primavera

La sin ventura, poemas

FORMOSO DE OBREGON SANTACILLA, Adela (Mexico, twentieth century)

La mujer mexicana en la organización social del país, ensayo

Yanalté, libro sagrado, teatro

FOX, Lucía (see **FOX-LOCKERT, Lucía**)

FOX-LOCKERT, Lucía (Peru-United States, b. 1930; also Ungaro de Fox, Lucía; Ungaro, Lucía; Sol, Lucía; Fox, Lucía). Now resides in the United States and teaches at Michigan State University. Author of more than twenty books of poetry, essays, short stories and plays. Her main scholarly work, entitled Women Novelists in Spain and Spanish America, examines the literature and social trends of developing self-awareness in Hispanic women. Her plays also reveal her feminist perspective.

Aceleración múltiple, poesía. Buenos Aires: Dead Weight, 1969. 26 pp. Seven poems constitute this volume that in a philosophical manner explores the human struggle for truth and human development. "The Second Coming," the longest poem of the collection reveals striking points of conflict in human evolution. Freedom and survival seem to be the most relevant themes in the poems which with clear symbolism deepen the nature and meaning of human existence. Other poems like "Objects without Identification" link man and his cosmic lineage with other interplanetary space travelers.

El aullido de los Magos

Ayer es nunca jamás, dramas. Lima: Salesiana, 1980. 254 pp. Eight three-act plays appear in this volume: "La Santa Comunidad," "Metamorfosis," "El perfil desnudo," "Mujerísima," "Ayer es nunca jamás," "El hombre que ríe," "El loco inquisidor," and "Escalas." There is also a Prologue and a Bibliography. Conflict emerges between strong-willed individuals and their traditional and oppressive society. A search for alternatives in most of the plays does not bring a happy denouement. Although the psychological, approach applies to most of the plays, there is a surrealistic approach to "El hombre que ríe," "El loco inquisidor," and "Escalas." Most of the leading characters are women.

Un cierto lugar, cuentos. Lima: Salesiana, 1980. 92 pp. The following short stories appear in this volume: "Detrás del telón," "Mitomano," "Eco," "El jefe supremo," "Cómplices," "Réquiem de la Locura," "Falsa alarma," "Cuestionario sentimental," "Premonición" y "Maria." The Prologue by Flora Werner affirms that Latin America is that "certain place." The psychological approach predominates in all the stories. Parody and tragedy converge to unmask the characters and leave them naked to the reader. One perceives that many broken dreams are the beginning of a new cultural perception of that "certain place."

Constelación. East Lansing, Michigan: Shamballa, 1978. 12 pp. Fantasy. Fifteen short stories constitute this volume: "La mujer pájaro," "Estrella," "Exit," "Dios creó a los osos polares," "Amelia Hearth desaparece," "Cycrogenic," "La dama vienesa," "Holographs," "The Old Movie," "Tlazoltl," "La señal luminosa," "Orbita," "Réquiem por una princesa muerta," "Transferencia," "El templo de Wizbal." Although the plots begin in the ordinary world, their development carries the characters to another level of reality where their immediate experience achieves full realization. Though the stories remain on the border line of the plausible, there is a tendency to create a significant symbolism through compelling suggestions.

Imágenes de Caracas, poesía. Caracas: H. García e Hijo, 1965. 31 pp. This volume is divided in three sections: 1) "Poemas del regreso," 2) "Poemas del vacío" and 3) "Imágenes de Caracas." The narrator, a woman returning to Latin America, sees a world of change while the reader experiences her explosion of feeling. The contrast between the concise style and the demolishing picture forces the reader to think. Representing three levels of awareness, the sections reveal the soul of the poet. The title has its origins in section number three which captures numerous impressions of a big city moving in chaotic rythm.

Latinoamérica en evolución, poemas. E. Lansing, Michigan: Superspace, 1974. 25 pp. Twenty poems trace Spanish American development. Saints, rebels and intellectuals appear next to aboriginal Indians, humble women and starved crowds. The poet replaces stereotypes with a sensitive gallery of people and their motivations. A fluid world appears and we perceive the dynamics of a new land perceived by a sensitive eye. The poems are long and present historical anecdotes next to reflexive sketches of significant realities. A deep emotional awareness gives a forceful portrait of Latin America.

Leyendas de una princesa india. E. Lansing, Michigan: Shamballa, 1979. 11 pp. Poetry.

Mónstruos aéreos, terrestres y submarinos encontrados en ruinas indias. E. Lansing, Michigan: Superspace, 1974. 8 pp. This small volume has only seven poems with their corresponding illustrations taken from ancient Indian art. The illustrations are meant to be more than a decorative element, and thus we perceive an exchange of meanings between the eyes and the mind. Indian gods, rituals, and mythological creatures move in a continual flow. The poetic persona speaks in order to reinstate the universality of the human soul throughout millenia.

Mosaicos. E. Lansing, Michigan: Old Marble, 1974. 10 pp. 126 epigrammatic poems.

Múltiples, poesía. E. Lansing, Michigan: Ghost Dance, 1969. 16 pp.

La odisea del pájaro o El sol brilla en todas partes. Bilbao, Spain: Comunicación Literaria de Autores, 1972. 55 pp. The book is structured in thirty-seven poems that describe the odyssey of the Bird-Poet from one extreme of the continent to the other. Essentially a journey of self-discovery which illuminates all kinds of experiences from sadness to ecstasy. Each moment in time of the bird's legendary itinerary becomes a possibility for parable. The book is rich in images and symbolism.

El perfil desnudo. E. Lansing, Michigan: Shamballa, 1979. 22 pp.

Preludios íntimos. Lima: Condor, 1945. 76 pp. This is her first book of poems, introduced in a "Prologue" by the Principal of her High School in Lima who gives biographical information concerning her early poetical development. Most of the poems, forty in the book, constitute a radiant discovery of the world in a journey through dreams, thoughts and experiences of her adolescent years. It is an important book to begin research on the poet.

Redes, poema. Barcelona: Carabela, 1967. 55 pp. Twenty-five poems appear in this volume which redirects our attention to the basic choices of our lives. Two worlds appear in a simultaneous counterpoint: that of the Spanish and of the Anglo. The poems bring up an interplay of images and a continuous stream of metaphors to illustrate the undercurrents of the two worlds. The poet places Don Juan, El Greco, Saint Teresa, and Felipe II in contemporary Los Angeles, California. The poetic persona sees the world that surrounds her in a double vision which often is unbearable and painful.

Tiempo atonal, poesía. E. Lansing: Ghost Dance, 1969. 26 pp. This book is divided in three sections: 1) "Thematic inversions;" 2) "Tonal Groups;" and 3) "Tonal Variations." The three sections are linked only by a very personal sense of time. The first section gives a philosophical insight into personal destiny and human history. Columbus, Montezuma, Enriquillo, Tamaracunga symbolize change in cultural consciousness; the second, an excursion into strategic places in cities located in Ecuador, Peru, Bolivia and Chile. Colloquial language and forceful characterization of peoples and their environments predominate here. In the third section the poet goes back to Lima in her adolescent years on a trip. A world of wonder, dreams and yearnings emerge.

Tragaluz, poema. Los Angeles, California: Frontera, 1967. xxiv pp. Seven portraits appear in this volume: "Rosita," "Alfredo," "Blondina," "Ivan," "Marieta," "Beatriz," and "G.M." The author explains in a short prologue that the portraits are successive foci of a reality which in another time was hers. Four women and three men constitute this gallery that comes to life with incisive precision and unsuspected depth. The style captures idiomatic expressions and details which characterize each individual. Peruvian ways of life as well as subtle existential quests are revealed through the characters. SC

Women Novelists in Spain and Spanish America, biographies and criticism. (See Partially Annotated List of Anthologies.)

FRAIRE, Isabel (Mexico, b. 1936). Fraire has taught and lectured frequently in the United States and Britain and has translated and anthologized a great deal of modern English-language poetry, particularly the work of Pound, e.e. cummings and William Carlos Williams. Her own poetry shows an intense preoccupation with perception. She strives to capture the exact "feel" of a moment of perception and uses as her themes the philosophical problems associated with sensory information and its processing.

En el regazo de la muerte, poesía

Isabel Fraire, poems, translation

Un poema de navidad para Alaíde Foppa

Quince poemas de Isabel Fraire

Sólo esta luz, poesía. Mexico: Era, 1969. Paperback, 78 pp. Perception -- the impressions of sensory data, the problem of reconstructing reality through this input -- is the overwhelming concern of these poems. Images of light and meditations on the paradoxical nature of optics provide substantial poetic matter. Fraire is fascinated with the power of the poetic word to synthesize fragmented impressions and thoughts into a discourse that forms a whole. NL

FRANCIS SORIANO DE SOTRES, Susana (Mexico, twentieth century)

Desde la cárcel de mi piel, poemas

Momentos, poemas

FRANCISCA JOSEFA DE LA CONCEPCION, sor (see CASTILLO Y GUEVARA, Madre Francisca Josefa)

FRANCISCA JOSEFA DEL CASTILLO Y GUEVARA, sor (see CASTILLO Y GUEVARA, Madre Francisca Josefa)

FRUCTUOSO DE SHVARTS, Josefa A. (Argentina, twentieth century)

Claudia López, teatro

Fue una noche inolvidable, teatro

La isla de la felicidad, teatro

Morir un poco, teatro

Los muñecos gigantes, teatro

Nuestro reencuentro, teatro

La reina y su zapatero, teatro

FRUNIZ PAZ, Martha Noemí (Argentina, twentieth century; known as Paz, Noemí)

El circo

Los días que habitamos

La muerte en el espejo

Muy al sur del viento

FUENTE, Carmen de la (Mexico, twentieth century)

Las ánforas de abril

Anhelos interiores, poemas

Canto a Lázaro Cárdenas, poesía

Canto al hombre, poesía

De la llama sedienta, poemas

Entre combate y tregua (1968), poemas

Nueva epístola a Fabio, grandeza y ruina de la ciudad de México, poema

FUENTE, María Angélica de la (Uruguay, twentieth century)

Andante lírico

Las voces de la sol

FUENTES MOLINA, Perla (Argentina, twentieth century)

Versos de sol y luna

La voz de la tierra

FUSELLI, Angélica (Argentina, twentieth century)

A cuántos . . . , poesía

A las mujeres de mi país, ensayo

Actuación internacional de la mujer americana, ensayo

Albores patrios, teatro

Arrayanes, poesía

Azimos, teatro

La campana de San Ignacio, teatro

Cruz del sur, poesía

Ensayo general, teatro

El evangelio y la mujer, ensayo

Evocación porteña, teatro

Itinerario del alma que despierta y anda, poesía

Itinerario hacia el Rubí, 1929-1969, poemas

Nahuel Huapi, poesía

El parador azul

La posguerra y la mujer, ensayo

Venga a nos el tu Reino, teatro

El voto de la mujer en Argentina, ensayo

FUTORANSKY, Luisa (Argentina, b. 1939)

Babel, Babel

El diván de la puerta dorada, poesía

Lo regado por lo seco, poemas y prosa

Trago fuerte, poesía

G

G. DE VAZQUEZ GOMEZ, Esperanza (see **GUERRERO DE VAZQUEZ GOMEZ, Esperanza**)

GAETE NIETO DEL RIO, Carmen (Chile, b. 1938)

En estado de gracias, poesía

El pan nuestro, poesía

Resultado de brumas, poesía

Valparaíso y otras almas, poesía

GALAZ, Alicia (Chile, twentieth century)

Jaula gruesa para el animal hembra

GALLARDO, Delia María (Peru, b. 1907)

Engrandeciendo la patria, biografías de mujeres en el Perú

La madre, teatro

GALLARDO, Sara (Argentina, twentieth century)

Eisejuaz

Enero

Los galgos, los galgos

Historia de los galgos

El país del humo

Pantalones azules

La rosa en el viento

El secreto claro: diálogos

GALLARDO DE ORDOÑEZ, Beatrix (Argentina, twentieth century)

Criollo, relato para chicos

El dueño, relato

Indiana

GALLARDO DE SALAZAR PRINGLES, Justa Beatriz (Argentina, twentieth century)

Canto a la fe, poesía

Etapas, poesía

Misión de la mujer en la plasmación de la conducta humana, ensayo

Negro ... ¡El cero! ..., cuentos

Presencia de la mujer en el proceso histórico-social argentino, ensayo

Prosas raras, poesía

GALLEGO, Laura (Puerto Rico, b. 1924)

Celajes, 1951-1953

Laura Gallego, obra póetica

Lecturas puertorriqueñas, poesía

Presencia, poesía

GAMBARO, Griselda (Argentina, b. 1928)

El campo, drama

La cola mágica

Conversaciones con chicos: sobre la sociedad

Cuentos

El desatino, teatro. Includes: "Las paredes," "El desatino," "Los siameses"

Dios no nos quiere contentos, ficción

Una felicidad con menos pena, novela

Ganarse la muerte, novela

Lo impenetrable

Madrigal en ciudad, cuentos. Buenos Aires: Goyanarte. 106 pp. The title of this collection of three stories comes from a line by Quasimodo: "Quasi un madrigale." The title of the first story, "La infancia feliz de Petra," is ironic as Petra is an orphan shunted among relatives unwilling to keep her, hardly a "happy childhood." "El nacimiento postergado" is about Ana who runs off with Antonio. She is forty and he is eighteen and the liaison doesn't last, but the implication is that it's better to do that than to die a virgin. "Madrigal en ciudad" implies that life goes on no matter what. Roberto's nagging wife Elisa deserts him and their unprepossessing son, Yiyi, but the family carries on without her. AMA

Nada que ver con otra historia, novela

Las paredes, teatro

Los siameses, drama

GAMERO DE MEDINA, Lucila (Honduras, 1896-1970; also Gamero Moncada, Lucila). Wife, mother, physician and women's rights advocate, she was born in Danlí, Department of El Paraíso, Honduras. Member of the Honduran Academy of Languages. Delegate to the First Interamerican Women's Congress, in Guatemala, 1947. Delegate of the Popular Mandate Committee of Washington, D.C. to the Chapultepec, Mexico, conference, 1945. Member of the International Women's League for Peace and Freedom. Her works reflect her preoccupation with the condition of women in Honduras as well as the Americas.

Adriana y Margarita, novela

Aída, novela. Tegucigalpa: Nacionales, 1914. 334 pp. Regional vs. cosmopolitan conflicts are reflected in this novel. A young teacher returns to her country after a lengthy period abroad; she faces provincial attitudes which plunge women into a drudgery, challenged by no one other than herself. The novel follows an epistolary form interspersed with the narrative, manifesting Aída's inner self with much more depth. Lengthy narration describes minute details of the social and natural atmosphere in which Aída lives. The use of the "vos" form to depict the uneducated, cruel provincial citizens of the small town contrast with Aída's invariable use of the formal "usted." The theme of social prejudice is strongly advanced as Aída marries "out" of the Danlí societal structure. Short vignette-like stories are told throughout the novel as a manner of giving a complete socio-historical picture of the milieu.

Amalia Montiel

Amor exótico, novela. Tegucigalpa: Nacionales, 1924. 240 pp. A novel developed through an interesting play of mythological figures of dual character, i.e., Juno and Venus, Hercules, Brahma, Vishnu and Shiva. Lillian's relationship with Carlos is of a dual character. The author associates Carlos with Hercules. Carlos' binary character makes him serve both Virtue and Pleasure. The Lillian who fascinates him is not the real, virtuous Lillian he chooses. Education for the sake of knowledge is contrasted with diplomas filled with meaningless titles. Rich language depicts the complex characters, and though the work is linear, theme and characters are skillfully molded. Long, traditional descriptions are used only initially. Once the groundwork is set, the plot develops naturally, strongly.

Betina, novela. Tegucigalpa: Nacionales, 1941. 212 pp. A novel in which the question of social inequality between a man and a woman is resolved through informed intelligence. Both characters are highly cultured. Local color is strongly present in the novel, and it weighs heavily on the characters, who are influenced by their milieu. The young, unexperienced feminine character begins to learn, while the powerful male character learns the strength of being different from her. Much local history -- both factual and folk -- is woven into this novel, set in Peru. This technique supports the mysterious young woman with the tragic love of her dead parents. Much narration and scarce dialogue.

Blanca Olmedo, novela. Tegucigalpa: Nacionales, 1954. 387 pp. A novel in the third person telling of the struggles of a mature young woman. Her position as governess in the home of a wealthy but uneducated family causes her to question false values in society as well as in the Church. Her death is not due to illness but to the constant clash which exists between her and those who surround her. Once her lover, Gustavo, is transformed, death is the only way he sees he can be authentic. This novel is filled with Schopenhauerian influence; the main characters constantly read and discuss these ideas. As intent as Gamero is on her ideals of women's liberation, she portrays it as a complex process which entails existential questionings in Blanca and Gustavo. There is some use of interior monologue. Narration and dialogue are balanced; language is used to a precise purpose, and there are no excesses of description.

El dolor de amar, novela regional y psicológica

Páginas del corazón, novela

Pétalos sueltos

Prosas diversas

La secretaria, novela. Tegucigalpa: Nacionales, 1930. 196 pp. A novel treating the love triangle of Lillian Midence, Rodolfo Lainfiesta and Harry Derby. Recurring themes of the novel are that both Latin American and Anglo-Saxon men must learn to treat women as persons and not objects of either protection or adoration, based on physical characteristics and that professional and social position are secondary to sincerity and maturity. As urgent as the themes, the sentence structure is short, incisive and to the point. Language is clear, but not descriptive. The social theme outweighs other considerations. MQG

GAMERO MONCADA, Lucila (see **GAMERO DE MEDINA, Lucila**)

GANDARA, Ana (Argentina, twentieth century)

Génesis, tres cuentos

La semilla muerta

Tierra apenas tocada, poemas

GANDARA, Carmen (Argentina, b. 1905). Gándara, one of a generation of Argentine authors born in the early part of the century, writes of psychological and metaphysical themes. In quiet, mysterious stories and novels, reality mixes with dream and memories. Gándara's major themes are the mysterious, indefinable quality of reality, the influence of memory on motivativation and present life, solitude, the child's view of reality and the character of Argentine reality. Her writing was influenced by Europeans such as Kafka and Proust as well as by some Argentinians of her own generation.

Los espejos, novela. Buenos Aires: Sudamericana, 1951. 264 pp. Los espejos, set in the Lake Region near Bariloche, Argentina, explores the psychological demands of marriage and friendship. During the disintegration of a marriage, the reader is given insight into both the husband's and the wife's emotions, sometimes through dialogue, but more often through the narrator's report of their thoughts. The novel treats many of Gandara's frequent themes such as memories and morality as motives for action, and the relationship of love and hate. Effective descriptions of isolation and nature at Lake Nahuel Huapi add to the psychological and solitary atmosphere.

La figura del mundo, cuentos. Buenos Aires: Emecé, 1958. 110 pp. The short stories in this collection explore emotions associated with death, solitude, and evil. Simply told, sometimes in first and sometimes in third person, the stories include some from a child's perspective. As is characteristic of Gándara, one image, sound or aspect of nature is repeated and developed as a symbol of emotion or a catalyst to memory.

La habitada, novela. Buenos Aires: Emecé, 1947. 53 pp. La habitada, a novelette also included in the collection El lugar del diablo, concerns a young Argentinean's rejection of the inauthenticity of Argentinean character and his preference for life in New York. However upon inheriting a farm where he reads his grandmother's letters, he rediscovers the authentic Argentina of the pampas. A study of his gradual change of opinion through memories of his childhood, the story is narrated in the third person with frequent excerpts from his grandmother's letters as well as evocative descriptions of the countryside of the pampas.

El lugar del diablo, cuentos. Buenos Aires: Sudamericana, 1948. 181 pp. El lugar del diablo, which includes La habitada, is unified by a style characterized by psychological investigation expressed mainly through third-person narration, and displaying restrained use of surrealistic images. While the stories do not concentrate on a general theme they reveal certain repeated preoccupations: the complementarity of life and death, the subjectivity of time, solitude, memory as motive, the Argentinean immigrant's desire to succeed, and the Argentinean's inauthenticity and rediscovery of authenticity in the traditional life of the pampas. ST

GARAY, María Consuelo (Argentina, twentieth century)

Anterior a la imagen de la rosa, poemario

Locura de cien distancias, poemas

GARAY, Nicole (Panama, 1873-1928)

Versos y prosas

GARAY MUÑIZ, María del Carmen (Argentina, twentieth century)

Cartas, diez poemas

GARCIA, Soledad (Mexico, twentieth century)

La promesa, novela

Protesta, novela

Rebeldes con causa, novela

GARCIA COSTA, Rosa (Argentina, b. 1892)

Esencia, poesía

Poesía, selección de Esencia, La ronda de las horas, y La simple canción

La ronda de las horas, poesía

La simple canción, poesía

GARCIA DE BODMER, Helvia (Colombia, twentieth century)

Campanas sumergidas, poesías

Vitral de bruma, poesías

GARCIA DE LA MATA, Helena (Argentina, twentieth century)

Abraxas, poemas

El tiempo y el fuego, poemas

GARCIA DE PERALTA, María López (see **LOPEZ GARCIA DE PERALTA, María**)

GARCIA IGLESIAS, Sara (Mexico, twentieth century)

Exilio

Isabel Moctezuma, la última princesa azteca

El jaguey de las ruinas

GARCIA MARRUZ, Josefina (Cuba, b. 1923; also Fina)

Lo exterior en la poesía

Las miradas perdidas

Orígenes

Transfiguración de Jesús en el monte

Visitaciones

GARCIA RAMIS, Magali (Puerto Rico, b. 1946). Studied history, journalism and linguistics. She worked for several Puerto Rican journals and later started teaching at the School of Communication (University of Puerto Rico). In 1971 García Ramis received the literary prize given by the Ateneo Puertorriqueño and in 1974 she was awarded an honorary mention by Casa de las Américas. Has published a book of short stories and is working on a novel. Her short stories present a variety of themes, all related to situations of women that belong to different social strata.

La familia de todos nosotros, cuentos. Serie Literatura Hoy. San Juan: Instituto de Cultura Puertorriqueña, 1976. Paperback, 100 pp. Working within a new literary realism, García Ramis incorporates humor and poetry in her short stories, which present a wide spectrum of Puerto Rican life: the poor, the suburban middle class, the almost extinct class of landowners. The main characters are women, seen in a variety of functions: the young student who awakens to sexuality; the single woman in boring suburbia; the revolutionary devoted to her commitment. The book is one of the first to mark the emergence of a new group of short story writers of the seventies. ILJ

GARCIA ROEL, Adriana (Mexico, twentieth century)

Apuntes ribereños

El hombre de barro

GARCIA SALABERRY, Adela (Argentina, 1889-1965). Writer, journalist and teacher. She held important administrative positions and was very active in feminist organizations. In 1961 she was awarded the Silver Medal by the Association of Writers of Buenos Aires. Her nonfiction includes: El momento, 2 vols. (1930, 1949); Vidas, 4 vols. (1938, 1940, 1943, 1950); Florencio Parravicini íntimo (1945); Angelita Vélez, sus danzas y su vida (1950); and Por televisión, 2 vols. (1958). LK

Bruma y hiedra, poesía

La gloria del corazón, ficción

Luz y sombra, ficción

Momentos sentimentales, ficción

GARCIA SANTOS DE CUEVAS, Raquel (Mexico, twentieth century)

Chiripa, novela

Ecos de mi lira, poesía

Juanacho el minero, cuentos

Una mujer en conflicto, cuentos

Myrna, teatro

Sucedió como en cuentos, cuentos

GARCIA TUDURI DE COYA, Mercedes (Cuba, b. 1904)

Alas, poemas

Arcadia, poemas

Arcano, poesía

Ausencia, poemas

Busa, poesía

Inquietud, poesía

Va al alma, poesía

GARDON FRANCESCHI, Margarita (Puerto Rico, twentieth century)

La alondra se fue con la tarde

Con ojos de mochuelo enloquecido, poesía

Tres cánticos en la aurora

GARFIAS, Mimi (Chile, b. 1925)

Monólogo de Pan y Pina, cuentos

GARRASTEGUI, Anagilda (Puerto Rico, twentieth century)

Abril en mi sangre

Desnudez, poemas

Leche de la virgen azul, novela

Niña íntima, poemas

Shizaad, poemas

Siete poemas a Hugo Margenat

GARRO, Elena (Mexico, b. 1917). Studied literature, theatre and ballet in Mexico. As a journalist she published several political articles defending Indian land rights. She has lived in Spain since 1974. Garro's imaginative dramas and fiction show her remarkable ability to derive lyrical and playfully satirical or tragic tones from popular expressions. Some of her work, such as the fine plays "La dama boba" or "La mudanza," remains dispersed in magazines. GM

> Andamos huyendo Lola. México: Joaquín Mortiz, 1980. Paperback, 263 pp. In the majority of these ten short stories, two female characters a mother and a daughter plus Lola the cat, encounter different perils as they escape from unspecified enemies. "El niño perdido," "La primera vez que me vi," "El mentiroso" and "Las cuatro moscas" show Garro's skill in recreating Mexican folk motifs and speech in a language of effective poetic quality. Some stories set in Spain or New York are not so successful. GM

El árbol, teatro

El canto, tendajón mixto

La casa junto al río

Un hogar sólido y otras piezas en un acto, drama. Xalapa, México: Universidad Veracruzana, 1958. Paperback, 150 pp. Six one-act plays, most of them non-realistic farces, where humor and poetic language are key elements. Children, peasants, the dead acting as the living are among the characters who provide critical insights on human follies. Scholars have praised these pieces as "magic," "poetic" and of "high literary quality." The play entitled "Andarse por las ramas" is outstanding as a feminist statement embodied in a very original form.

GM

El hombre, teatro

La muerte de Felipa Angeles, teatro

Parada empresa, teatro

Los perros, novela

Los pilares de doña Blanca, teatro

Recollections of Things to Come, translation of Los recuerdos del porvenir

Los recuerdos del porvenir, novela. México: Joaquín Mortiz, 1963. Hardbound, 295 pp. 2nd ed.: (México: Mortiz, 1980?). A fine early example of the new Latin American novel, the book exposes the cruelty and violence that the greedy Mexican landlords and the soldiers who protect them direct against women and Indians. The story, narrated by the collective voice of a small town, mixes historical facts of the 1920's with magical happenings in a highly poetic language. As suggested by the title, time is significant as a theme in the circular structure of the novel and the characters' perceptions of the invariability of their fates.

GM

Reencuentro de personajes

El rey mago, teatro

La semana de colores, cuentos.   Xalapa, México: Universidad Veracruzana, 1964. Paperback, 217 pp. Whether these eleven short stories deal with the actualization of the make-believe lives of children, the desires of unhappily married women or the superstitions of peasants, the real and the unreal are inseparably fused in the texts. The poetic quality of the language derives mainly from the artistic recreation of children's and Indians' modes of speech. "¿Qué hora es?" and "La culpa es de los tlaxcaltecas," fine examples of the fantastic, depict a woman's longings and fears. GM

Testimonios sobre Mariana. Mexico: Grijalbo, 1981. ISBN 968-419-182-0, 353 pp. The themes of love/seduction, alienation/rebellion and violence/death characterize the story of Mariana as told by three different narrators or witnesses, hence the title. Under the influences of the surrealist Benjamin Peret and his contemporary Henri Michaux, Garro creates a narrative of mythological significance with references to both European and Aztec mythology. Awarded the Premio Novela Juan Grijalbo in 1980. JM

La señora en su balcón, teatro

Ventura Allende, teatro

GARRON DE DORYAN, Victoria (Peru, twentieth century)

El agua, el aire, y el árbol, poesía

. . . Para que exista la llama, poemas

GARZA RAMOS, Corina (Mexico, twentieth century)

María; o, Entre las viñas, novela

Víctimas

GAYA DE GARCIA, María Cristina (Puerto Rico, twentieth century)

Desde la hacienda

Raíz y cielo, poemario

GEADA, Rita (Cuba, b. 1937)

Cuando cantan las pisadas

Desvelado silencio

Mascarada, poesía

Poemas escogidos

Vertizonte

GEEL, María Carolina (Chile, b. 1913)

Cárcel de mujeres, novela

Extraño estío, novela

Huida, novela

El mundo dormido de Yenia, novela

El pequeño arquitecto, novela

Soñaba y amaba el adolescente Perces, novela

GENTA, Estrella (Uruguay, twentieth century)

Cantos de la palabra iluminada

Constelación del sueño, poemas

Elegía del tránsito, poemas

Juana Inés de la Cruz, poema dramático

El Mesías, ficción

Poesías

La sombra en el cristal, poesías

Los vencidos, evocación dramática

GERTNER, María Elena (Chile, b. 1927)

La derrota, novela. Santiago de Chile: ZigZag, 1965. Paperback, 221 pp. First part of the trilogy El hueco en la guitarra. The protagonist is an impoverished member of the Chilean upper bourgeoisie who is unable to confront her poverty. In order to escape from an increasingly deteriorating economic and social situation, she alienates herself from the lower-middle class to which she now belongs, and seeks to perpetuate her past glories in her daughter, who rejects her attempt.

Después del desierto, novela. Santiago: Orbe, 1961. Paperback, 195 pp. The plot develops the tortuous human relationships between characters belonging to the bourgeoisie. There are those who recognize and denounce the debasement and falseness of bourgeois values, and painfully search for their own identity. The rest knowingly succumb to the empty comforts, the security and the pleasures of a meaningless bourgeois life.

El hueco en la guitarra, novela

Homenaje al miedo, poemario. Illus. by Enrique Lihn Carrasco. Santiago: Amistad, 1950. 21 pp. Narrative poem, describing the search (voyage) of the poetic voice for meaningful levels of reality. The fear of the unknown, however, has to be overcome. Next the voice questions the past, the establishment, the unjust social order, the meaning of life confronted by death. The infinite, however, is beyond the reach of the individual, who is an imperfect creature unable to overcome material reality. Different verse forms are used; the metaphors are simple but effective and the language almost colloquial.

El invencible sueño del coronel, cuentos

Islas en la ciudad, novela. Santiago de Chile: Nuevo Extremo, 1958. Paperback, 190 pp. Like most of her later works, Islas is a critique of the Chilean bourgeoisie. The characters yearn for a more meaningful existence, but are blind to the real causes of their discontent, and consequently engage in empty relationships. A pampered woman, unable to understand her husband's rejection of bourgeois pseudo-values, alienates him; a lonely teenager seeks security in a love affair with a successful executive; his wife in turn, kills her boredom with alcohol and the friendship of pseudo-artists, interested in taking advantage of her social position.

Un juego de salón, cuentos

La mujer de sal, novela. Santiago: ZigZag, 1964. Paperback, 308 pp. The protagonist's neurotic experience ending in suicide is developed through the juxtaposition of two time sequences: her past in Chile, in her memoirs which explain the cause of her malaise; her present in Paris, where she unsuccessfully attempts to exorcise her past both by writing her memoirs and by forcing herself into degrading heterosexual relationships. One of Gertner's most ambitious and successful works.

La mujer que trajo la lluvia, novela

Páramo salvaje, novela. Santiago: ZigZag, 1962. Paperback, 205 pp. A farm, located in the rugged Chilean Andes, provides the setting for the passionate and lustful relationship between its owner and his sister by adoption. His desire for a "normal" life leads him to marriage, which however, does not placate his love for his sister, to whom he returns when about to die. The female protagonist has elements in common with such literary figures as Doña Bárbara and La Quintrala. PRL

La risa perdida, novela

GEVERT, Lucía (Chile, twentieth century)

El puma, cuentos juveniles

GIL, Marta Nélida (Argentina, twentieth century)

Raíz en primavera, poemas

GIL, Minerva Alicia (Mexico, twentieth century)

Cantares del alma, poesía

Es un eco infinito, poesía

Renglones descalzos, poesía

GILIO, María Esther (Uruguay, b. 1928). Gilio is a politically committed journalist whose work has been published in Crisis [Buenos Aires] and Marcha [Montevideo]. Her reporting technique incorporates background and critical information to probing questioning, and results in essayistic interviews reflecting the personal experience of both author and interviewees. While the more provocative interviews are those that illustrate her commitment to raising consciousnesses, Gilio is also adept at interviewing well-known figures without sensationalizing them. Very little biographical information is available, but Gilio's persona as a journalist is clearly presented in her work.

La guerrilla tupamara, reportajes, narración. Havana: Casa de las Américas, 1970. 247 pp.

Personas y personajes, entrevistas. Buenos Aires: Ediciones de la Flor, 1974. Paperback, 205 pp. This collection of eighteen interviews contains eleven previously published in Protagonistas y sobrevivientes. The range is again wide, from the famous (Borges) to the mundane (a macumba medium). The most dynamic are those that portray people trying to make sense out of the "chaos in which we live." Gilio excels in presenting a point of view which questions the justice of social reality in Latin America. Where this attitude is not present, her questioning urges people to see the incompatibility of what they are told by society (Church, government, consumerism) and their own reality. Would be useful to have all twenty-six essays from both collections in one volume.

Protagonistas y sobrevivientes, entrevistas. Montevideo: Arca, 1968. Paperback, 158 pp. The nineteen interviews present such varied figures as a conceited boxer, the Russian poet Ievtushenko, a bullfighter, an evangelist, Neruda and Onetti. Outstanding for an informative and

provocative treatment of prostitution in Montevideo are two pieces
originally published in Marcha, "¿Esclavas blancas sin alma y sin
amor?" and a follow-up, "Gotán." The first penetrates stereotypes
society has of prostitutes, and, at the insistence of Gilio, women discuss
their work, the capacity to love, and feelings of social rejection, self-
disgrace, and fear. The other treats responses to this article:
corroborations, denials and additions.

The Tupamaro Guerrillas, translation. Tr. Anne Edmondson. Introd.
by Robert J. Alexander. New York: Ballantine, 1973. Paperback,
ISBN 0436175304, 242 pp.

The Tupamaros, translation. Tr. Anne Edmondson. London: Secker
and Warburg, 1972. Hardbound, 198 pp. CW

GIMENEZ PASTOR, Martha (Argentina, twentieth century)

Cosas de la vida

La pancita del gato, literatura para niños

Selección poética femenina, 1940-1960, antología de varias escritoras

GIOCONDA (pseudonym: see **CARRERA DE BASTOS, Laura**)

GLANTZ, Margo (Mexico, b. 1930). Born in Mexico City, studied for her
doctorate at the Sorbonne, Paris. Professor of literature at the University of
Mexico. Has taught in the United States (e.g., La Jolla, Ca.) Writes for
several Mexican daily newspapers and weekly magazines (Unomásuno,
Sábado, Revista de la Universidad). Founder and director of Punto de
Partida published by the University of Mexico, President together with Elena
Urrutia of the IV Interamerican Congress of Women Writers, June, 1981,
Mexico City. International lecturer.

El día de tu boda

Doscientas ballenas azules, cuentos y poema. México: La Máquina de
Escribir, 1979. Paperback second edition easily available.
Representative of the author's wit, playful eroticism and word play.
Follows contemporary literary trends in Latin America. Sense of humor
and poetic mood combined with vivid imagination. Of great value in the
classroom for intermediate and advanced language levels, and women's
studies.

Las geneologías

Intervención y protesta

Las mil y una calorías (novela dietética), México: Premiá 1978. This
book, made up of short texts, many autobiographical, vignettes,
fabulous, and reduced to their minimal but very substantial expression,
illustrates the author's life-long experimentation with word games, the
reader as creator and the writer as reader. Talks about the two creative
mouths of women, the mouth which speaks and the mouth which gives
birth. With insight and humor, she explores the process of intellectual
digestion which gives birth to ideas through the use of illicit
associations and subversive speech aimed at destroying the patriarchal
order.

No pronunciarás. México: Premiá 1980. ISBN 968-434-149-0. This book contains a series of vignettes dealing with surnames and first names (historical, philosophical, literary, religious). The author, while searching for "the name" plays with words, makes up legends, becomes serious, vicious, innocent and ironic. She makes us experience chaos while reading a list which turns out to be a parody of history as retold by means of recognizable proper names. ML

Síndrome de naufragios

GODOY, Emma (Mexico, b. 1920)

Caín, el hombre misterio trágico, teatro

Del torrente; Pausas y arena, poesía

Erase un hombre pentafásico, novela y algo más

Sombras de magia, poesía y plástica, ensayos

Vive tu vida y sé un genio: hombre, tú eres un dios escondido

GODOY, Tamara (Chile, twentieth century)

Copayapu, poemas

GODOY ALCAYAGA, Lucila (Chile, 1889-1957; pseudonym: Mistral, Gabriela). First published in newspapers, magazines, anthologies and readers for elementary schools. Her many prose pieces on literature, education and contemporary events still have not all been collected. In 1914 she became famous after she won a Chilean national prize for her three famous "Sonnets of Death," about her love for Romelio Ureta and her desolation at his suicide. A primary school teacher and administrator without a degree, 1910-1922, she rose to become a well-known authority on the education of children. 1945 winner of the first Nobel Prize awarded to a Latin American writer. From 1922 until her death in New York, she experienced a long series of moves in her roving life as consul and often official as well as ex-officio representative in various capacities of her country and of Latin America.

Antología de Gabriela Mistral. Prologue and selection by Emma Godoy. Colección "Pensamiento de América," Segunda Serie, Vol. V. México: B. Costa-Amic, 1967. 17 pp. 2nd ed.: 1978, 17 pp. Poetry from Desolación, Lagar and Ternura. Prose from Recados: Contando a Chile and Motivos de San Francisco. Last selection included is a letter by Mistral to Father Dussuel explaining her personal religious beliefs. The prologue by Godoy was later published under the title "Momentos de Su Vida y de Su Obra," in Abside (32:2, April/June, 1968), but it is mainly sentimental, profferring the idea that Mistral's poetry is not intellectual, but on the contrary displays her deep intuition.

Antología de Gabriela Mistral; Momentos de su vida y de su obra. Colección Crítica Literaria, 4. México: Jus, 1967. 170 pp. 2nd ed.: 1978, 170 pp. These two editions are exactly the same as the first and second editions by Costa-Amic, apparently using the same plates for all but the title page and colophon.

Antología general de Gabriela Mistral. Homage by Orfeo, Nos. 23, 24, 25, 26, 27. Santiago, Chile: Comité de Homenaje a Gabriela Mistral,

1973. lxxxviii and 256 pp. Excellent collaboration but on poor quality paper. Contains poems and prose selected from all her volumes. Has four poems from Poema de Chile, five unpublished poems furnished by Doris Dana, five poems in prose from (the unpublished) "Elogio de la Materia," around fifty essays and prose pieces from different prose collections and periodicals where they were published, letters from her to several persons, including Eugenio Labarca. Following her work are thirty-six pages of criticism about her, necrology, poems of homage and an eighty-nine page photo-essay. Unfortunately, it lacks a bibliography and the five unpublished poems are disappointing for their overly sentimental, solipsistic vision and the lack of lyric power as compared with her earlier poems.

Antología poética de Gabriela Mistral. Selection and Prologue ("Entrevista Póstuma de Gabriela Mistral") by Alfonso Calderón. Colección Letras de América. Santiago: Universitaria, 1974. 171 pp. Selection of poems presented in attractive type in the order of appearance of the books from which they are selected: Twenty-one from Desolación, thirty-seven from Tala, twenty-five from Ternura, twelve from Lagar and eight from the posthumous Poema de Chile. Poems subjectively chosen to reflect her principal themes and her best creative talent as poet. Excellent presentation of the gamut of her work. Surprisingly effective fifteen-page interview consists of thirty-seven questions about Mistral's life and her art, with the answers taken from her essays.

Antología: Selección de la autora. Prologue by Ismael Edwards Matte. Colección Poesías. Santiago: ZigZag, 1941. 318 pp. Other editions: 2nd ed. 1946; 3rd ed. Prologue by Hernán Díaz Arrieta (Alone), title shortened to Antología, 1953, 269 pp.; 4th ed. same as 1953 ed., 1955; and Antología, Biblioteca Cultura, Prologue by Alone, 1957, 147 pp.; and 2nd ed. Prologue by Alone, 1969, 173 pp. In the first edition, a twenty-page prologue by Edwards Matte mainly contains biographical data, plus quotations from some of the critics who analyzed her work. The ninety-nine poems, chosen by Mistral for the edition, are mainly from Desolación and Tala with a dozen or so from Ternura. They are certainly among her best, but she elected to leave out some poems such as the three famous "Sonetos de la Muerte" which made her famous. Because of that and the large number of poems, about half, on children or themes centering on children and motherhood, the general impression is more joyous in tone than anthologies of her work usually are. The same poems appear in all the succeeding editions, but in the 1947 edition, an article by Alone becomes a twenty-four page prologue. He has more anecdotical information on her life and production and he is more critical of her, reflecting the usual attitude toward Mistral by her Chilean contemporaries.

Cartas de amor de Gabriela Mistral. Introd. and notes by ed. Sergio Fernández Larrain. Santiago: Andrés Bello, 1978. 243 pp. This book is proof that Mistral loved other men than the one to whom she dedicated some of the most popular and deeply-felt poetry ever written in Spanish. First, there are five letters to the fortyish rancher, Alfredo Videla Pineda, all from 1905, when she was fifteen, a year before Romelio Ureta Carvajal entered into her life. The other man she loved, poet Manuel Magellanes Moure, although married, engaged in a passionate relationship, mainly by letter, with Gabriela, between 1914 and 1931. Their thirty-eight letters paint for us the seven-year romance, its stormy beginnings of deep and chaste passion, their disillusionment and three final years of chary friendship. Excellent introduction, many photographs clarifying notes.

Cartas de Gabriela Mistral a Juan Ramón Jiménez. Prologue by Julio Rodríguez Luis. Publicaciones de la Sala Zenobia-Juan Ramón de la Universidad de Puerto Rico, Serie B, No. 5. San Juan, Puerto Rico: Torre, 1961. 19 pp. Fascinating view of the interplay of personalities of two of the major poets of the period.

Crickets and frogs, a fable, translation

Croquis mexicanos; Gabriela Mistral en México. Colección Panoramas, Vol. 9. México: B. Costa-Amic, 195?. 79 pp. Contains nine of Mistral's prose pieces, all previously published in Lecturas para mujeres, and five poems from Tala and Ternura. Written during various visits to a country which the author deeply appreciated. Final part is "Imagen y Palabra en la Educación," a lecture given by the author at Columbia University (Congreso del Bicentenario), giving her views on the best pedagogical methods.

Dame la mano. Illus. by Miriam González Giménez. Habana: Gente Nueva, 1976. 12 pp. Edition of the poem by the same name with the poem from Ternura, stanza by stanza, on heavy paper with background water colors of flowers and geometric motifs.

Desolación, poesía y prosa. "Nota Preliminar" provided by the Instituto de las Españas. New York: Instituto de las Españas, 1922. 242 pp. Other similar editions: 2nd ed. augmented by the author, Prologues by Instituto de las Españas and by Pedro Prado, "Al Pueblo de México," (Santiago, Chile: Nascimento, 1923), 357 pp.; 3rd ed. revised, Prologues by Hernán Diaz Arrieta (Alone) and by Pedro Prado (Santiago: Nascimento, 1926), 344 pp. Indifferent toward preparing her poetry and prose for publication in book form, Mistral's Desolación has suffered many changes. After the first New York edition, published at the instigation of Federico de Onís, Director of the Instituto de las Españas, two Chilean editions were published. In the second, one poem was substituted, sixteen were added, plus a prologue by Prado. Some corrections were done for the third edition, approximately twenty were added, others removed, and a third prologue prepared by Alone, one of the Chile's leading literary critics, leaving out the Instituto's prologue. The work's title, Desolación reflects the pain of the three "Sonetos de la Muerte." Placed in the section called "Dolor," they treat her despair at the death of the young man she loved. A stability is given by her absolute acceptance of fate and of her own emotions. Rural phraseology, austere and harsh, with a dramatic Biblical accent. The final part is an extension of her pedagogical vocation with stories for and about children.

Desolación. Prologues by Instituto de las Españas and by Pedro Prado, "Al Pueblo de México." Santiago: Pacifico, 1954. 259 pp. Other editions: 2nd ed. 1957, 263 pp.; 3rd ed. Hernán Diaz Arrieta (Alone), "Prólogo a la Tercera Edición," 1960, 263 pp. These editions contain mainly the poems from the first edition of Desolación, but there are at least eight poems included in "Infantiles" from Ternura. Four or five poems were added to other sections of the book and some were left out. At times there were poems which did not fit aptly under the headings, but the author should have been the one to make such changes. Too many liberties were taken by others, especially with her first two volumes of verse.

Desolación. Colección Austral, No. 1002. Buenos Aires: Espasa-Calpe Argentina, 1951. 239 pp. 4th ed.: 1972, 230 pp. This edition, although not repudiated by Mistral, and still entitled Desolación, retains most of the same section titles, but "Infantiles" is cut from twenty-one to two, and a few other poems are left out of the sections. Without any indication to the reader, fourteen poems (sixteen in the original) of the section from Ternura, entitled "Canciones de Cuna" are inserted under the same rubric. Although Gabriela did not prepare the manuscript of this work for publication, her later works were more carefully controlled.

Desolación; Poesía, prosa, prosa escolar, cuentos. Prologues by Pedro Prado and "Nota Preliminar" by the Instituto de las Españas. Buenos Aires: Biblioteca las Grandes Obras, 1945. 192 pp. Popular edition on cheap paper, essentially the same as the 1923 publication in Chile of Desolación.

Desolación; Poesía, prosa escolar, cuentos. Prologues by Pedro Prado and Note by the Instituto de las Españas. Buenos Aires: Tor, 1945. 190 pp.

Desolación, Ternura, Tala, Lagar. Introd. by Palma Guillén de Nicolau. Colección Sepan Cuantos, No. 250. México: Porrúa, 1976. ix-xlviiii and 251 pp. Thirty-one page introduction by Mistral's friend, confidante and her first amanuensis, Palma Guillén de Nicolau. Delicately points out Mistral's excessively hyperbolic language and overly passionate tone, which in Guillén's opinion, lend unevenness to the poetry. Surprisingly objective yet laudatory analysis of her mentor, both as human being and poet, and of the relation between those two planes in her work. Exceptionally complete nine-page biographical resumé by a person who obviously knew and understood the vicissitudes of her life. The volume contains the same poems in the same form and order as in the 1958 Aguilar edition.

The Elephant and His Secret: Based on a Fable by Gabriela Mistral, translation

Epistolario

Gabriela Mistral reading her poetry, at the Library of Congress, Dec. 12, 1950, for the Archive of Hispanic Literature on Tape, phonodisc

Lagar, obras selectas, poesía. Vol. VI. Santiago: Pacífico, 1954. 188 pp. 2nd ed.: 1961, 188 pp. More objective work in a terse style with greater emotion and anguished sensuality. Biblical in tone with a much more obvious social preoccupation and solidarity with humble working people. In one section, "Locas Mujeres," she defines her feminine figures through specific gestures or attitudes. Fewer mystical dark "nights of the soul," fewer interior voices of wild and inebriated genius. Recollections of childhood, poems on the theme of her mother's death, hymns to the tropics and the Andes and poetic prose "recados," messages in conversational style to her friends on various occasions.

Lecturas para mujeres. México: Secretaría de Educación, 1923. 395 pp. Prepared by Mistral at the request of José Vasconcelos, the Minister of Education of Mexico, for use by the girl students in the school named for the Chilean author. (Schools were not coeducational then.) A marvelous didactic selection in Spanish of two hundred and eleven entries by authors from Horace to Mistral (only nineteen are by her) from various Spanish American, European and other sources. They are writings aimed at the formation of a moral and religious conscience and an aesthetic sensitivity. Mistral's six-page introduction explains the criteria and the organization of the work.

Lecturas para mujeres. 3rd ed. San Salvador, El Salvador: Ministerio de Educación, 1961. 523 pp. The third edition, authorized by Doris Dana, has a four-page prologue by Claudia Lars, commenting on Mistral's skillful collection. The sources are given both at the beginning of the selection and in the index, and dates have been added. Fine paper and excellent type.

Lecturas para mujeres. 4th ed. Colección Sepan Cuantos. Ed. Palma Guillén de Nicolau. México: Porrúa, 1967. 267 pp. The fourth edition has the same items and the same full information, both at the head of each entry and in the index as in the third edition. Prologue by Mistral appears plus a six-page apology by Guillén de Nicolau who discusses Mistral's invitation to Mexico by José Vasconcelos, the origin of the anthology in his request, her personality and artistic talent, and finally, the resentment against the visit of Mistral as a pedagogical authority when she held no diploma.

Lecturas para mujeres, destinadas a la enseñanza del lenguaje. 2nd ed. Madrid: Tipografía Moderna, 1924. 450 pp. The second edition has the same selections, the same preface by Mistral and the sources preceding each selection. There are a few corrections of errata and vocabulary changes here and there. Proper noun index added.

Las mejores poesías (líricas) de los mejores poetas. Vol. xlv. Prologue by Manuel de Montoliú. Barcelona: Cervantes, 1923. 2nd ed.: revised [1938]. The second edition has an excellent prologue partly by the publishing house and partly by Manuel de Montoliú which characterizes Mistral as one of those writers of solid spiritual substance in her varied, yet harmonious production. An addition to the prologue, thirteen years after the first edition, comments on the changes in her life and her poetic production since then. He indicates that many changes were made in the second edition: some poems were removed which had been chosen from Desolación, at least half of the forty-eight poems of the second edition were added from Ternura (1924), and many poems were from Tala, unpublished in book form until 1938. Not a good edition, but it shows the early interest in Mistral's work, causing the book publishers of little, inexpensive editions to anthologize her.

Los mejores versos. Prologue by Simón Latino. Cuadernillos de Poesía, No. 17. Buenos Aires: Nuestra América, [1957]. 41 pp. A two-page prologue gives a short biography and adds the news about her death and the loss for America. Inexpensive booklet for popular consumption. The prose "Decálogo del Artista," is followed by forty of her most universally known and loved poems, with at least half on children or motherhood and the other half on anguished loss of love. At the end there are the poems in prose entitled: "Poemas de las madres," "Poemas de las madres más tristes," and last "La oración de la maestra." (Title on inside pages of the booklet changes to: Sus mejores versos.)

Motivos de San Francisco [de Asís]. Selection and Prologue by ed. César Díaz-Muñoz Cormatches. Santiago: Pacífico, 1965. 150 pp. Poems in prose inspired by the famous "little flowers," a history of Saint

Francis' life and other writers' interpretation of the saint's hagiography. Mistral published these in various periodicals between 1923 and 1926, as the editor explains in his five-page Prologue. Mistral begins with lyrical praise of the saint's mother in a familiar, conversational tone, and each one or two-page section which follows treats his life and the legends and facts about him. The poetess portrays his feelings by speaking to him familiarly concerning various themes in his teachings, such as charity, roses and death. In the last section, she engages in a dialogue with him where she laments her inability to truly learn his way of accepting loss.

The Mystery: Five Songs of Motherhood, translation

El niño en la poesía de Gabriela Mistral. Selection by Roque Esteban Scarpa. Fondo de las Naciones Unidas para la Infancia. Santiago: Antártica. 1978. 32 pp. 2nd ed.: 1979. A beautiful edition for children, with heavy paper and excellent drawings. The oil painting, "Amanecer," by Loreto Alessandri Morande is reproduced on the front cover. Has twenty poems from among Mistral's most beautiful ones dedicated to the themes of children and childhood. Begins with her two-page "Recado de las Voces Infantiles," one of her many prose pieces on such themes.

Nubes blancas (poesías) y la oración de la maestra. Colección Apolo. Barcelona: Bauzá, [1925]. v and 215 pp. Two-page unsigned Prologue gives biographical data, and then comments on the first and second editions of Desolación; presented without explanation, and without division into the original sections, the majority of poems are from Desolación, twenty from Ternura, and the prose "Oración de la Maestra." In the Antología of compositions chosen by Mistral in a note on one of the final pages, she repudiates this volume as clandestine. Most of the poems are those reflecting the depths of the writer's personal feelings, ranging from violent passion to tender and sentimental emotion.

Pequeña antología. Santiago, Chile: Escuela Nacional de Artes Gráficas, 1950. 153 pp. Selection of poetry and prose.

Poema de Chile. Texts revised and foreword, "Al Lector," by Doris Dana. Barcelona: Pomaire, 1967. 244 pp. Seventy-seven poems written during the final twenty years of Mistral's life and published posthumously by her heir and executrix, Doris Dana. In a brief commentary, Dana tells of her efforts to put in order the unrevised and in many cases unfinished poems. A tender and didactic description of a voyage after her death, where her spirit travels the length and breadth of Chile in the company of a little Indian boy and an extremely rare Andean deer which is gentle toward humans. The poem relates a sentimental return to her childhood, and through the description of the plants, animals and geography, she makes visible the yearning love of an exile and expatriate for Chile and for the people of the rural areas of her country. Usually evaluated in an uncomplimentary manner by the critics. Two printings of the same edition with the same pagination were made. The large edition has no foreword by Doris Dana and the title was changed to Poemas de Chile.

Poemas de las madres. Epilogue by Antonio R. Romero. Drawings by André Racz. Colección de Artes Plásticas, Cuadernos del Pacífico, vol. 3. Santiago: Pacífico, 1950. 60 pp. Didactic selection for a reading public and on a theme not often addressed in poetry during the time in which Mistral wrote these poems. Contains nineteen deeply emotional poems in prose on the feelings of mothers-to-be, with the last two on the bitter-sweet emotions of an unmarried pregnant girl ejected by her father yet nevertheless welcoming the unborn child. Nineteen-page study by Antonio R. Romero of the Rumanian artist, André Racz, who illustrated the book.

Poesías. Colección Literatura Latinoamericana. Prologue by ed. Eliseo Diego. La Habana: Casa de las Américas, 1967. xix and 295 pp. 2nd ed.: 1975, xix and 291 pp. Collection of those most distinctively Mistralian poems which appear so often in anthologies of her poems. Chosen from Desolación, Tenura, Tala, Lagar, plus three other poems. Thirteen-page analysis by the editor of her poetry as that of a typical woman writer of passionate and suffering expression of love of things, people and nature, fierce and tender, American and Hispanic, terrible and serious. For him, the essence of her poetry is the talent of breathing new life into words, rhythms and themes in her poems. The volume terminates with ten notes by Gabriela explaining poems from Tala as well as a chronology of her life and the cultural and historical events of her time. Excellent student edition, readily available in the Spanish-speaking world.

Poesías completas. Definitive edition established by Margaret Bates, in collaboration with the author. Prologues: "Gabriela Mistral: Su Vida y su Obra," by Julio Saavedra Molina; "Gabriela y Lucila," by Dulce María Loynaz. Biblioteca Premio Nobel. Madrid: Aguilar, 1958. cxliii and 836 pp. Other editions: 2nd ed., 1962; 3rd and 4th eds. Prologue by Esther de Cáceres, "Alma y Poesía de Gabriela Mistral" (Madrid: Aguilar, 1966, 1968), xci and 836 pp. Contains all the poems published by Gabriela during her life (and a few others) in book form, usually in the order of the appearance of the four volumes. However, changes were made in the placement of the poems in the four books as they were being prepared for inclusion. Mistral moved the third section in Desolación, "Infantiles," to the sixth section in Ternura and renamed it "Casi Infantiles." She added sixteen poems to the "Canciones de Cuna," seven of them from Tala, and she placed the whole section at the end of the sections which previously comprised Ternura. Some poems have lines recast or titles changed, but modifications were principally that of moving poems around. She consolidated sections to avoid repetition, added and subtracted some, but very few poems were removed from Tala and Lagar; changes in these two books are minimal, reflecting her maturity and mastery of her poetic art. She did include three poems which had not been published in book form before, from the then unpublished Poema de Chile. In the first and second editions Julio Saavedra Molina's excellent ninety-six page critical study of the life and works of Mistral, and a three-page annotated bibliography of a few of her works precede the poems. A twenty-five page subjective meditation on "Gabriela and Lucila" also appears by Dulce María Loynaz. In the 3rd and 4th editions, the prologue by Esther de Cáceres is confusing due to incorrect page numbering, pages out of place and some blank leaves, marring the seventy-nine page affectionate and laudatory essay on her friend's character and art. Eight pages of notes by Mistral conclude the volume. A critical edition remains to be published which would incorporate all of her poetry.

Producción de Gabriela Mistral de 1912 a 1918. Ed. Raúl Silva Castro. Serie Roja, Letras, No. 11. Santiago: Anales de la Universidad de

Chile, 1957. 181 pp. One hundred and three poems, letters and prose pieces, gathered by Silva Castro, with a good part of them unpublished in book form previous to 1957. Most have dates and ample bibliographical information. Others were published in later versions of Desolación. Good start on a critical edition, since Silva Castro points out variants in some of the poems and he gives information in his commentary about them as well.

Selección de poesías. La Bolsa de los Libros. Montevideo: Claudio García, 1924. 60 pp. Twenty-nine of those poems most often anthologized from Desolación and Ternura in an undistinguished popular edition. No introduction, notes or bibliography. In the Antología of compositions chosen by Mistral, in a note on one of the final pages, she repudiates this collection as clandestine.

Selección de poesías. Vol. 43. Buenos Aires: Claridad, n.d. 80 pp. Thirty-eight poems in an inexpensive, popular booklet, chosen mainly on childhood themes from Desolación and Ternura. These little editions have made Mistral a household word known by people in all walks of life.

Selected Poems of Gabriela Mistral, trans. Doris Dona

Selected Poems of Gabriela Mistral, trans. Langston Hughes

"Los sonetos de la muerte" y otros poemas elegíacos. Colección Bibliófilos Musa Musae, 1. Santiago: Phlobiblión [sic], 1952. xlviii pp.

Sus mejores versos. (See annotation under Los mejores versos.)

Tala, poemas. Biblioteca Clásica y Contemporánea, 184. Buenos Aires: Losada, 1946. 163 pp. Other editions: 2nd ed. 1947, 187 pp.; 3rd ed. 1953, 158 pp.; 4th ed. 1968, 167 pp.; 5th ed. 1972, 167 pp. Same divisions as in the Sur edition, but lacks four sections of poems and prose pieces found there: "Canciones de Cuna," "La Cuenta-Mundo," "Albricias," and two poems in a section entitled: "Dos Cuentos." The final section of "Recados" is followed by her explanatory notes just as in the Sur volume.

Tala, poemas. Buenos Aires: Sur, 1938. 286 pp. Eighty-nine poems divided into thirteen sections: "Muerte de Mi Madre," "Alucinación," "Historia de Loca," "Materias," "América," "Saudade," "La Ola Muerta," "Criaturas," "Canciones de Cuna," "Albricias," "Dos Cuentos," and "Recados." A final section by the author explains her dedication of the royalties of the book to the Basque and Catalonian children scattered by the Spanish Civil War in refugee camps such as Pedralbes. More sophisticated poems, with a controlled, understated emotional power. Presents a new attitude of faith and hope for the future. Themes are similar to those in previous volumes: communion with nature, children, her constant quest for religious harmony, brotherhood and spiritual acceptance. Often her poems are musical but without any apparent effort toward elegance of form.

Ternura: Canciones de niños. Madrid: Saturnino Calleja, 1924. 105 pp. Contains forty-six poems, five of which had already been published in Desolación. Sections of the book given on the title page are: "Rondas," "Canciones de la Tierra," "Estaciones," "Religiosas," "Otras Canciones," and "Canciones de Cuna." Themes include the joys of motherhood, the marvel of infants and the world of nature. Moral and didactic verse which exalts children and their sense of fair play as well as their innocence and idealistic dreams of the future. Not their rhythms, but their sense of profound tenderness makes these poems for children and for those who love children memorable.

Ternura: Canciones de niños. Montevideo: Claudio García, 1925. 74 pp. Same as the Saturnino Calleja edition with forty-six poems in the same order. However, on one of the final pages of the Antología prepared by Mistral, she disavows one anthology of her work by Claudio García as clandestine. This book apparently did not arouse her antipathy, however, since the copy used for this annotation was dedicated and signed by the Chilean poet.

Ternura: Canciones de niños. 1st ed. Colección Austral, No. 508. Buenos Aires: Espasa Calpe, 1945. 190 pp. Other editions: 2nd ed. 1945, 190 pp.; 3rd ed. 1946, 145 pp.; 4th ed. 1949; 5th ed. 1952, 190 pp.; 6th ed. 1955; 7th ed. 1959; 8th ed. 1965, 190 pp. Augmented to reach a total of ninety-seven poems, encompassing most of the children's poems written up to 1945, and some not published previously in book form. All these editions have her nine-page "Colofón con Cara de Excusa," written in the same year as the first edition. In it the author explains how she writes them and her particular use of nursery rhymes, rondas and other children's poems.

Ternura: Canciones de niños. Montevideo: ZigZag, 1953. 191 pp.

Todas íbamos a ser reinas, poemas. Prologue by Gabriela Mistral. Santiago: Nacional Quimantu, 1971. 170 pp. 2nd ed.: Editora Nacional Gabriela Mistral, 1975. 170 pp. These two popular editions of selected poems by Mistral are exactly the same although there was a change of name of the publishing house. Without notes to indicate criteria of choice, nevertheless defensible as a group of her most famous and best-loved poems. Divided into five untitled sections with a total of eighty-seven poems. Includes her "Sonetos de la Muerte," as well as her more positive, didactic poems and those on children and childhood from Desolación, Ternura and Tala. "Como Escribo," three-page explanation of her method of writing serves as prologue. BTO

GODOY GODOY, Eliana (Chile, twentieth century)

Amarente, poesía

Anfora de quietud, poesía

Campanas de sol y lluvia, poesía

Cascada lírica, poesía

Delirio de amor, poesía

Encaje sutil, poesía

Estero de alondras, poesía

Fuego eterno, poesía

Fulgores y sombras, poesía

Hojas de otoño, poesía

Látigo y néctar, prosa

Luz de estrellas, poesía

Milagro por un lazo de amor, relato

Pétalos de brevedad, poesía

Pinceladas y palabras, poesía

Simplemente nada, poesía

Sol y bruma, poesía

Surco tenue, poesía

Taladro de espuma, prosa

Telaraña poética, poesía

Tres horas de ilusión, relato

GOMARA, Susana López de (see **LOPEZ DE GOMARA, Susana**)

GOMEZ-CORREA, Wally de (Chile, twentieth century)

Sólo poemas

GOMEZ DE ABADIA, Herminina (Colombia, b. 1861)

Bajo la bandera

Del colegio al hogar, novela

Dos religiones, o Mario y Frinea, novela

GOMEZ DE AVELLANEDA Y ARTEAGA, Gertrudis (Cuba, 1814-1873; also la Avellaneda; Tula; la Peregrina). Educated by her parents, she writes from an early age. In 1836 she travelled to Europe and in 1840 went to Madrid. In the latter, she entered the literary circles, having already acquired a literary reputation. In 1844, she was recommended as a candidate for a chair in the Spanish Royal Academy but because she was a woman, she did not enter the Academy. Writing at a time in which her country was conscious of the need for independence, she opted not to talk about this issue in her works. Her strong literary personality is better reflected in her erotic poetry, her letters and plays. She wrote novels, short stories, newspaper articles and an autobiography, in addition. RA

Alfonso Múnio, tragedia

Antología de la poesía religiosa de la Avellaneda. Eds. Florinda Alzaga and Ana Rosa Nuñez. Miami: Universal, 1975. Paperback, 47 pp. A selection of fifteen poems from her Devocionario, together with a prologue by the editors and Tula's introduction "Dos palabras sobre la oración y sobre este libro." Reproduces the cover of the 1867 edition of the Devocionario and includes a selected bibliography. EE

Antología (Poesías y cartas amorosas). Ed. and Prologue by Ramón Gómez de la Serna. Colección Austral. Buenos Aires and Mexico: Espasa-Calpe Argentina, 1945. Paperback, 149 pp. A collection of twenty-five lyric poems, principally of romantic themes (nature, poetry, her homeland) or dedicated to individuals (her mother, Napoleon, Washington, Heredia) and a selection of twelve of her love letters to Ignacio de Cepeda. Includes a prologue, "La Divina Tula" by Ramón Gómez de la Serna. EE

El artista barquero; o, Los cuatro cinco de junio. 2 vols. Biblioteca Selecta Habanera. Habana: "El Pilar" de Manuel de Armas, 1890. Hardback, 290 pp. Available in Hispanic Society Library. Written in romantic style. Set in mid-eighteenth century France and Cuba. The life of a well-to-do Cuban family transported to Marseilles. The Platonic love of the daughter for a poor young French fellow who wants to become a painter. Socio-historical importance because of descriptions of the Cuban and the French landscapes, in the setting of eighteenth century courtly life. Significant for its rich vocabulary and perfect control of expression. Writer's cosmopolitism is shown; she uses some French in the Spanish text. LP

El aura blanca, leyenda. Notes by Israel M. Molina. 2nd ed. Cuadernos de Historia Matancera, VII. Matanzas, Cuba: Museo de Matanzas, 1963. 23 pp.

Autobiografía y cartas (Hasta ahora inéditas de la ilustre poetisa). Prologue and Necrology by Lorenzo Cruz de Fuentes. 2nd ed. corrected and augmented. Madrid: Helénica, 1914. Paperback, 301 pp. Includes her Autobiografía and fifty-three letters to Ignacio de Cepeda. Accompanying materials include a portrait of the author; "Al que leyere," "Informe de la Real Academia Española," Prologue to the first edition, Necrology of Ignacio de Cepeda, with his portrait by Lorenzo Cruz de Fuentes, and notes. EE

La aventurera, teatro

Baltasar. La Habana: Consejo Nacional de Cultura, 1962. 139 pp. This play in four acts and in verse was written by Avellaneda in 1858 and had a great acceptance at that time. It is based on the fall of the Babylonian Empire. It shows a deep Biblical meaning and reverence. It lists the cast that performed during the debut in April 1858. A rather small volume not too practical to use. Of special interest to those who investigate the publications of Cuba after the revolution. AA

Baltasar. Ed. Carmen Bravo-Villasante. Colección Biblioteca Anaya #105. Salamanca: Anaya, 1973. ISBN 84-207-1004-0. Paperback, 155 pp. The last of her plays to be produced, the work recreates the story of Belshazzar's feast from the Biblical books of Daniel. The protagonist shares many characteristics of the Romantic hero in his dual qualities of potential greatness and decadent, satanic corruptness. Daniel's niece Elda is an example of dignity under duress, a slave who was violated by the king yet dares to predict downfall even though she is going insane. The Biblical tragedy ends with the downfall of Babylon. The play enjoyed critical praise and a long run in its day but has been little explored by contemporary criticism. Contains introduction and bibliography. EE

"La baronesa de Joux" (in Colección de novelas) recreates a folk legend found in a poem by the French poet Demesnay. Forced into an unwanted marriage although betrothed to another man she truly loves, Berta becomes ill while her husband is a participant in the Second Crusade. A troubadour, who is her former fiancé in disguise, comes to care for her. Upon her husband's return, his servant informs him of the breach of his honor and the troubadour's head is presented to his wife. Berta is said to die, but is actually imprisoned in the castle's dungeons while the headless ghost haunts the castle and fills it with lamentations. EE

Belshazzar. Trans. by William Freeman Burbank. London: B.F. Stevens & Brown, 1914. 44 pp. This edition has two sonnets in translation by Avellaneda in the front page. The translator, in the Preface, states that the "dramatic excellence of this work" led him to put it into English. It is somewhat an older translation, yet it reflects the theme of this play written by Avellaneda in 1858. Of interest to scholars wishing to investigate Avellaneda's impact during the beginning of this century. AA

Cartas inéditas existentes en el Museo del Ejército. Ed. by José Priego Fernández del Campo. Madrid: Fundación Universitaria Española, 1975. ISBN 84-7-392-055-4, 88 pp. This book is a collection of fifty-five letters attributed to Avellaneda and kept by the Secretary of Justice, D. Antonio Romero Ruíz. The majority of these letters are filled with the frustrated passion that tormented the life of Avellaneda and expressed the love she could never admit publicly to anyone. A few are just ordinary letters but even they are written in a careful style and show absolute dominion over the language. AA

Cartas inéditas y documentos relativos a su vida en Cuba de 1859 a 1864. Illus. by José Augusto Escoto. Matanzas: Pluma de Oro, 1911. Hardcover, 258 pp. Available in N. Y. Public Library. Seven letters. The first three letters were her correspondence with Da. Dolores de la Cruz during the last years of Avellaneda's stay in Cuba. They point to her acclimation to Spain, and show her poor state of health due to Cuba's climate. Two other letters are her correspondence with the writer Emilio Blanchet for the publication of El artista barquero. The last two letters are her correspondence with the writer D. Gonzalo Peoli in which she asks him to collaborate for her Album cubano. Documents point to the difficulties that some Cuban writers created for Avellaneda considering her to be a Spanish writer, not Cuban. The book contains notes to the letters, and other documents related to her stay in Cuba. Avellaneda's husband's death certificate. LP

Catilina, drama

Colección de novelas. Havana: Prensa, 1844. Hardback, 424 pp. Contains "La baronesa de Joux" and "Espatolino," together with two novels by other authors. [See individual annotations.] EE

Cuauhtemoc

Devocionario nuevo y completísimo en prosa y verso. Sevilla: D.A. Izquierdo, 1867. Hardback, 503 pp.

Diario de amor. Prologue, ordering and notes by Alberto Ghiraldo. Madrid: Aguilar, 1928. 222 pp. Contains her Autobiografía and thirty-one love letters to Ignacio de Cepeda. Both are important for their insight into Tula's emotions and for their relationship to her other writings. The former also details her evolution as a child prodigy and her growing awareness of the inadequacy of the social role for women as well as her first disappointments. The latter chronicles the stages of the most important relationship in her life. EE

Dolores, novela histórica

El donativo del diablo, drama en tres actos y en prosa. Círculo Literario Comercial, No. 195. Madrid: C. González, 1852. Hardcover, 69 pp. Available in N. Y. Public Library. A variation of the theme of Faust, a man who sold himself to the devil in exchange for the love of a woman, is used as the backbone of this drama. The love of Arnoldo for Ida is not accepted by her family; the solution is to go to a place where the devil is said to be seen and make a pact with him to make Arnoldo rich so he can marry Ida. The devil does not ask for his soul, but points to certain documents that show that Arnoldo is a noble man. The devil is used here to do justice. LP

Dos mujeres, teatro

Egilona, drama trágico en tres actos y cuatro cuadros. Colección de las Mejores Obras del Teatro Antiguo y Moderno. Madrid: D. José Repullés, 1845. Hardcover, 81 pp. Available in N. Y. Public Library and Hispanic Society. Drama written in verse; dedicated to the actress Da. Bárbara Lamadrid de Salas. Takes place in the year 715 A.D. in Seville, under the rule of the Arabic Caliphate. The Emir has taken a wife, Egilona, the wife of King Rodrigo whom he has now put in prison. The plot involves the discontent of the Arab Moslems with the Emir, who has not only taken a Christian woman for his wife, but is now professing that religion. The play is significant for its depiction of the struggle between Spaniards and Arabs over religion and possessions in early medieval times. LP

Ensayo de diccionario del pensamiento vivo de la Avellaneda. Eds. Florinda Alzaga and Ana Rosa Núñez. Miami: Universal, 1975. ISBN #84-399-3090-9. Paperback, 88 pp. This anthology, based on twenty-two works of poetry, drama and fiction as well as her autobiography and letters to Ignacio Cepeda, presents, through quotations, her ideas on a wide variety of subjects, ranging from love, beauty, God, men, happiness, death, passion to vanity and will (seventy-nine topics in all). It provides a useful overview of her ideas and the range of her thought.
EE

Errores del corazón, drama en tres actos y en prosa. Galería Dramática. Madrid: Don José María Repullés, 1852. Hardcover, 60 pp. Available in N. Y. Public Libraries. Contains a prefatory letter to Sr. Don Luis José Sartorius, Conde de San Luis, who had undertaken the creation of a Spanish theatre. The plot is based on the idea of love feigned for the sake of money. The characters in the play have all fallen in love with the wrong persons and their love is not reciprocated. The play abounds in poetic disquisitions about what true love is. Finally, they all realize the beauty in the heart of the person in love with them. In the end they conclude that love rarely has strong reasons to prevail if only the blind instincts of the heart are followed. LP

"Espatolino" (in Colección de novelas) presents another Romantic figure, a bandit chief based on an historical figure in Italy, who is bitter and mistrustful of everything but his wife Anunciata. While Espatolino personifies the rebellion of the oppressed, his wife represents the excessive trust and naiveté that leads to their downfall. Themes of betrayal on all levels and the inadequacy of social institutions (the Church, the criminal justice system, the monarchy, and the social classes) predominate. Anunciata follows the pattern of other female characters, going insane upon realizing the truth. The novel presents similarities with ideas expressed in other novels and dramatic works and was praised for its vivid portrayal of the Italian setting. EE

Flavio Recaredo, drama en tres actos y en variedad de metros. Galería Dramática de Delgado Hermanos. Madrid: Don José María Repullés, 1851. Hardcover, 74 pp. Available in N. Y. Public Library. The action takes place in the sixth century in Mérida and Toledo. A time when both Swabians and Goths were living together in Spain and of the Frank invasion. Bada, the Swabian princess, will marry whoever brings the Church of Rome to its desired height and grandeur, and whoever frees the peoples from ancient tyranny. The enemy is Recaredo, who, later on, frees Spain from the Franks, joins the different peoples (Spaniards, Goths, Swabians) under the Catholic faith; and marries Bada. Much historical data and strong religious message.   LP

Guatimozín, último emperador de Méjico, novela histórica

La hija de las flores; o, Todos están locos, drama en tres actos y en verso. 2nd ed. Galería Dramática. Madrid: C. González, 1859. Hardback, 117 pp. Dedicated to José Zorrilla. The setting is the Valencian countryside around 1810 or 1820. The play is significant for the underlying theme of family union evident at the end. It is a typical comedia de enredos much used in the Siglo de Oro in which partners change, and hidden family relationships are discovered. Contains a list of actors who performed it for the first time in 1852. LP

La hija del rey René, teatro

Leoncia, teatro. Madrid: Rev. de Arch., Bibl. y Museos, 1917. xiii and 104 pp. Madrid is the setting for this five-act drama which deals with the disastrous results of events set in motion by unbridled passion. The play concerns a love triangle and is typified by numerous elements of Romanticism, the reigning literary impulse of the period. Melodramatic language and excessive display of emotions abound. Leoncia, the female protagonist, is a figure shrouded in mystery. She suffers fainting spells and moments of insanity and regards her seducer as an agent from Hell. Believing themselves cursed and pursued by adverse fortune, the characters have premonitions and view ordinary incidents as ill omens. The drama concludes with a revelation of the close kinship between the would-be bride and groom, followed by Leoncia's suicide. A prologue, signed by "C." (not identified), adds relevant biographical data and commentary on the text. MSA

Leyendas, novelas y artículos literarios. Madrid: Leocadio López, 1877. 437 pp. In this volume, Avellaneda includes two novels, "El Artista Barquero," "Espatolino" and a chronicle of a family entitled "Dolores." As always, she is preoccupied with the legends of her time. It is of special interest to note that the first and last novels were written in Cuba during her return for a few years. The plots of both, nevertheless, take place in Italy. Avellaneda calls "Dolores" a little novel written to please the request of the director of a renowned newspaper in Cuba. She states that the purpose of "Dolores" was to entertain. AA

The Love Letters of Gertrudis Gómez de Avellaneda. Trans. Dorrey
Malcolm. Prol. by José Antonio Portuondo. Havana, Cuba: Talleres
Gráficos de Juan Fernández Burgos, 1956. Translation of Autobiografía
y cartas (hasta ahora inéditas).

Memorias inéditas de la Avellaneda. Ed. Domingo Figarola-Caneda.
Habana: Imprenta de la Biblioteca Nacional, 1914. vii and 42 pp. These
memoirs, penned in Seville in 1838, contain la Avellaneda's candid
descriptions and personal impressions of the places she visited on her
journey from her beloved Cuba to Andalusia (1836-38). She comments
on quaint customs, describes local cemeteries, and reflects on the beauty
and historical significance of famous landmarks. Her observations are
often accompanied by emotional outbursts. Other aspects of this work
include her idiosyncratic spellings and her penchant for quoting fellow
Cuban poet, José María Heredia. Originally composed in notebooks as
correspondence to her cousin Heloysa de Arteaga y Loinaz, these
writings remained unpublished until the hundredth anniversary of
Avellaneda's birth. The editor has provided useful ancillary material in
the form of an introduction, notes, index, and a portrait of the author.
MSA

El millonario y la maleta

Obras, vol. I. Ed. and Introd. by José María Castro y Calvo. Biblioteca
de Autores Españoles, #272. Madrid: Atlas, 1974. ISBN 384-363-0486-
1. Hardbound, 358 pp. Contains a lengthy "Estudio Preliminar" on her
life letters; a list of editions; bibliography and "Poesías líricas" (texts),
based on the 1914 centenary edition (Havana, Cuba). EE

Obras de doña Gertrudis Gómez de Avellaneda, vol. II. Ed. and
preliminary study by José María Castro y Calvo. Biblioteca de Autores
Españoles, #278. Madrid: Atlas, 1978. ISBN 84-363-0499-3, 325 pp.
Contains: "Munio Alfonso," "El príncipe de Viana," "Recaredo," "Saúl,"
"Baltasar," and "Catilina." DEM

Obras de doña Gertrudis Gómez de Avellaneda, vol. III. Ed. and
preliminary study by José María Castro y Calvo. Biblioteca de Autores
Españoles, #279. Madrid: Atlas, 1979. ISBN 84-363-0506-X. 325 pp.
Contains: "Egilona," "El donativo del diablo," "La hija de las flores," "La
aventurera," "Oráculos de Talia." DEM

Obras de doña Gertrudis Gómez de Avellaneda, vol. IV. Ed. and
preliminary study by José María Castro y Calvo. Biblioteca de Autores
Españoles, #287. Madrid: Atlas, 1981. 325 pp. Contains: "La hija del
rey René," "El millonario y la maleta," "La verdad vence apariencias,"
"Tres amores," "Leoncia," and "El artista barquero o los cuatro cinco de
junio." DEM

Obras de doña Gertrudis Gómez de Avellaneda, vol. V. Novelas y
Leyendas. Ed. and Preliminary Study by José María Castro y Calvo.
Biblioteca de Autores Españoles, #288. Madrid: Atlas, 1981. 287 pp.
ISBN 84-363-0544-2. Contains: "Espatolino," "Dolores," "La velada del
helecho o el donativo del diablo," "La bella toda y los doce jabalíes," "La
montaña maldita," "La flor del ángel," "La ondina del lago azul," "La
dama de Amboto," "Una anecdota de la vida de Cortés," "El aura
blanca," "La baronesa de Joux," "El cacique de Turmeque," and "La
mujer." DEM

Obras dramáticas. Madrid: Leocadio López, 1877. 408 pp. Includes: "Munio Alfonso," "El príncipe de Viana," "Recaredo," "Saúl," "Baltasar," and "Catilina." Avellaneda was a great play writer and this volume contains the first one written by her. They are all written in verse, a genre very well known and used by the author. She touches different subjects and mixes Biblical topics with profane matters. In most cases she dedicates the plays to people who had strong ties with her. Some of them lack a final correction, but she wrote a lot and followed her inspiration in a very natural way. AA

Obras dramáticas. Madrid: Leocadio López, 1877. 615 pp. Includes: "La hija de las flores," "La aventurera," "Oráculos de Talia," "La hija del rey René," "El millonario y la maleta," "La verdad vence apariencia" and "Tres amores." In this volume the author compiles her most festive plays, although everything written by Avellaneda has serious elements. These plays are, probably, the easiest ones to stage. Of special interest to those who are engaged in studying the style and the way of reasoning of Avellaneda. They are close to the reality of the everyday life. "Tres amores" is a comedy written in prose. Some of them are very short. Of special interest because of the prologues and "words" from the author to the public. AA

Obras literarias de la señora doña Gertrudis Gómez de Avellaneda. 5 vols. Madrid: M. Rivadeneyra, 1868-1871. Hardback. Contents: Vol. I) Poesía Lírica; II) Obras Dramáticas (Munio Alfonso, El príncipe de Viana, Recaredo, Saúl, Baltasar, Catilina) 501 pp.; III) Obras Dramáticas (La hija de las flores o todos están locos, La aventurera, Oráculos de Talia o los duendes en el paraíso, La hija del rey René, El millonario y la maleta, La verdad vence apariencias, Tres amores) 619 pp.; IV) Novelas y leyendas (El artista barquero, Espatolino, Dolores) 439 pp.; V) Novelas y leyendas (La velada del helecho o el donativo del Diablo, La bella toda y los doce jabalíes, La montaña maldita, La flor del ángel, La ondina del lago azul, La dama de amboto, Una anécdota de la vida de Cortés, El aura blanca, La baronesa de Joux, El cacique de Turmeque, La mujer, Artículos, Apéndice) 423 pp. EE

Oráculos de Talia; o, Los duendes de Palacio, comedia en cinco actos y en verso. Madrid: José Rodríguez, 1855. Hardcover, 133 pp. Available in Hispanic Society and N. Y. Public Library. Dedicated to Da. Casta Barredo de León, a friend. The setting is the last years of the reign of King Charles II under the Queen Da. Mariana de Austria. Deals with the schemes and plots of some courtisans to overthrow the Queen, and put D. Juan de Austria in her place with Charles II as his right-hand man. Two underlying sub-themes are love and the usefulness of poetry as a profession. Shows the corruption of the Court at the time. Critique of appointments to high office of persons without qualifications which contribute to decadence of government. Contains a prologue and a list of actors on opening night in 1855. LP

Poesías. 1st ed. Mexico: Juan R. Navarro, 1852. Hardback, 317 pp. A collection of ninety-five poems, fifty-four previously unpublished, that includes various types: sonnets, romances, cuartetos, elegies, and the like. Many poems were inspired by or are in the style of European Romantic poets (Byron, Hugo), and personal dedications include Queen Isabel II (to whom the entire book is dedicated), her mother, Juan Nicasio Gallego (who contributed a Prologue), Washington, and the Duque de Frias. Themes include love, poetry, nature, some funereal subjects, friendship, and other Romantic topics. EE

Poesías. 2nd ed. Mexico: Juan R. Navarro, 1852. Hardback, 532 pp. The book contains poems which are organized around different themes. The first and second editions contain a prologue by Juan Nicasio Gallego with a preface by the author. Some of the poems appeared in the first edition, others were unpublished ones. The second edition is an expanded one. This edition has a dedication to Isabel II of Spain and a good biography. RA

Poesías escogidas. Paris: Franco-Ibero-Americana, n.d. Paperback, 156 pp. The book contains a selection of poems, some of which were published in 1841. The preface was written by Ventura García Calderón. This edition contains some notes from the Madrid edition of 1869. This book has most of her known poems. The selection is varied and not according to a specific theme. Of interest to those who want a general knowledge of Avellaneda's poetry. RA

Poesías selectas. Ed. and Introd. by Benito Varela Jacomé. Barcelona: Brugera, 1968. Colección Libro Clásico. Paperback, 223 pp. The book contains a serious and complete critical study of the life and works of Avellaneda. It is divided in six different parts according to the type of poetry. Analyzes Avellaneda's feminine ideas in Dos mujeres and social ideas in Sab. Includes a bibliography and critical notes. RA

El príncipe de Viana, drama trágico en cuatro actos y en verso. Galería Dramática. Madrid: Don José Repullés, 1844. Hardback, 99 pp. Available in N.Y. Public Library and Hispanic Society. Drama dedicated to Manuel José Quintana. Takes place in the court of Catalonia in 1460. Prince Don Carlos has been exiled for having fought against his father, the King of Aragón and Navarra. The marriage of D. Carlos, son of the King of Spain, to Isabel of Castille will prevent the civil war between Castille, and Catalonia and Aragon--who favor Carlos to be their King--and will bring Spain together again. Portugal also seeks an alliance with D. Carlos and offers him the hand of Catalina. The Queen of Spain also wants power and lands for her real son Fernando, and plots against Carlos. Intrigues and historical ambiance surrounding the death of the Prince of Viana. LP

El príncipe de Viana, drama trágico en cuatro actos y en verso. 2nd ed. México: J.R. Navarro, 1851. Hardcover, 112 pp. There are approximately four pages missing towards the end of the play; these correspond to pages 96-99 of the 1st edition. The 2nd ed. must have had up to 116 pp. Text is incomplete. This edition is found only at the University of Indiana. The plots and texts of the first and second editions are almost identical. Second text is corrected as far as modern accentuation, punctuation, spelling, and capitalization, for ex: "ora" (2nd) instead of "hora" (1st); "Cataluña" (2nd) instead of "Gataluña" (1st); "pardiez" (2nd) instead of "par diez" (1st); "arrostraron" (2nd) instead of "arrastraron" (1st). Also some word changes in Act IV such as "rica habitación" (2nd p. 87) for "honda..." (1st, p. 75). Changes are of interest to scholars for the evolution of the Spanish language. LP

Sab, novela. Ed. Carmen Bravo-Villasante. Colección Biblioteca Anaya, #16. Salamanca: Anaya, 1970. Paperback, 234 pp. Tula's first novel, with an abolitionist theme and Romantic in style. It has memorable portraits of various female characters as well as of the protagonist, the mulatto slave Sab. Avellaneda suggests parallels between slaves' and women's condition in nineteenth century Cuba and anticipated themes found in the Realistic novel through her critique of a society where materialism and crass interests prevail. The edition contains an Introduction, Bibliography and "Dos palabras al lector."

EE

Saúl, tragedia bíblica en cuatro actos. Author's Prologue. Galería Dramática. Madrid: Don José María Repullés, 1849. Hardbound, 80 pp. Available in N.Y. Public Library. In the prologue Avellaneda explains that this drama has been written to portray the power of the passion of excessive pride in the soul of man. The tragedy is based on the Sauls of Alfieri and Soumet. Love represents a secondary theme. We see the wars between Saul of the Israelites and Amalec; the historic fight between Goliath and David takes place as well as the end of the line of Saul by his own hand (he kills his own son thinking he was David). Drama was begun in 1846, and finished in 1849 after many revisions. LP

Selección poética

Simpatía y antipatía, comedia en un acto y en verso. Colección de Obras Dramáticas y Líricas. Madrid: José Rodríguez, 1855. Hardback, 40 pp. Available in N.Y. Public Library and Hispanic Society. The play takes place during the last years of the reign of Fernando VII. It is a very light comedy with no politico-historical implications. Its plot revolves around the concept that the world is organized around the notions of simpatía and antipatía that is, that there are forces that pull things together, and other forces that separate them. These notions are applied to marriage and separation, and to finding the right person and remarrying again, as in the case with the main characters; the Count and Isabel. Antithesis and paradox are used to illustrate better these notions. LP

El teatro. Madrid: José Rodríguez, 1858. (See annotation under Los tres amores.)

Teatro. Prologue by José A. Echeverría. La Habana: Consejo Nacional de Cultura, 1965. 464 pp. This collection contains four plays and a page with the places and dates in which all Avellaneda's plays were put on stage. "Munio Alfonso" and "Saúl" were written within neoclassicism but tinted by the incipient romanticism. The last two plays here are comedies written in a joyful mood. In the prologue, Echeverría includes a succint biography of Avellaneda, narrated by herself. Also, the prologue serves as a critical guide to the plays and somewhat prepares the reader historically. AA

Los tres amores, drama en tres actos, precedidos de un prólogo. Madrid: José Rodríguez, 1858. Hardcover, 84 pp. (On cover El teatro). Available in N.Y. Public Library. The setting is at the time of Charles III. The plot deals with the love triangle of Antonio, a peasant, for Matilde, and of Matilde for Victor, a poet. She has become dazzled with Victor's knowledge of poetry, but Victor leaves for Madrid. In time Matilde becomes a famous actress representing one of Victor's dramas. He falls in love with her. She recognizes that her love for him was a love of his glory, and that the real love is that of Antonio, patient, pure, firm, persevering. LP

La velada del helecho o el donativo del diablo

La verdad vence apariencias, drama en verso, en dos actos y un prólogo. Galería Dramática.   Madrid: Don José María Repullés, 1852. Hardcover, 96 pp. Available in N.Y. Public Library. Drama inspired by Lord Byron's drama Werner. The play takes place in the fourteenth century in Castroviejo, near Soria. The plot is similar to that of Werner's in which Alvaro's lost son, disguised as a soldier escaping, kills Don Tello, Alvaro's brother. The prologue is used by Avellaneda to present the facts of the play and the main plot, which will unfold and be solved in the next two acts; the latter occurs in a different place, and some of the characters are also different. Fine character study of Rodrigo as he tries to convince people that Alvaro is not his step-brother, but that he is the criminal, when in fact Rodrigo is the killer.

LP

GOMEZ DE READ, Ernestina (Dominican Republic, twentieth century)

Poemario de luna y sueños

Versos de una vida

GOMEZ MAYORGA, Ana de (Mexico, b. 1878)

Aprovecha tus días, breviario

Cruz de amor

El divino mendigo

Entreabriendo la puerta

Minutos del tiempo

El mundo mejor

Primeras y últimas rosas, poemas

Río de las horas

GOMEZ MEJIA, Carmen de (Colombia, twentieth century)

Altos muros, poemas

La casa de los espejos

Estación del ritmo, poemas

La sombra de los rostros, poemas

La voz sobre la nada, poesía

GOMEZ PAZ, Julieta (Argentina, twentieth century)

Canciones de tierra y sol

GOMEZ REINA, Irene (Mexico, twentieth century)

Ofrendas, poemas

GOMEZ RUL, Ana María (Mexico, twentieth century)

Lol-há, cuento maya

GOMEZ SANCHEZ, Enriqueta (Paraguay, b. 1900)

Ofrendas, poemas

Oro y acero, poemas

GONTOVNIK, Mónica (Colombia, twentieth century)

Ojos de ternura, novela

GONZALEZ, Edelmira (Costa Rica-United States, 1914-1966)

Alma llanera, cuentos

En gris mayor

Mansión de mis amores

GONZALEZ, Luisa (Costa Rica, twentieth century)

A ras del suelo, autobiografía novelada

GONZALEZ, María Rosa (Africa-Chile, b. 1905)

Arco-iris

Azul violento

Extasis, poemas

Una mujer

Samarita, poemas

GONZALEZ CASTRO, Esmeralda (Peru, twentieth century; pseudonym: Quinteras, Serafina)

Así habla Zarapastro, poesía humorística

Las mujeres de mi canto en el año internacional de la mujer, 1975: igualdad, desarrollo, y paz, poesía

El torrente, novela

GONZALEZ CASTRO, Lida (see **GONZALEZ CASTRO, Esmeralda**)

GONZALEZ DE LEON, Ulalume (Uruguay - Mexico, b. 1931). Born in Montevideo, Uruguay, she studied Humanities at the Sorbonne, Paris. Married a Mexican architect. Has resided in Mexico for many years. Author of critical essays, poems and short stories. Translator. Publishes in several literary magazines (Marcha, Revista de la Universidad de México, Diálogos, La Cultura en México and Vuelta of whose editorial board she has been a member from the start.) A scholar specializing in the works of Camoëns.

A cada rato lunes, cuentos. México: Joaquín Mortiz, 1970. Twelve short stories which remind us of some of Cortázar. A mixture of fantasy and reality which demands the reader's active participation. Understatements and word play help to create a style where humor, desire and intellectual intensity are found between the lines. The stories partake of a search for the foundations of human existence somewhere between the realm of mathematics and the world of dreams.

Plagio I, poemas. México: Joaquín Mortiz, 1973. A book containing poems previously published under the titles of Juegos (1968-1969), Comentarios (1969-1971), Descripciones (1969-1971) and Plagios (1970-1971). The author explains how there are several orders present in the book: a chronological order, one that reflects the seemingly progressive disappearance of the ego and one which, inversely, progressively affirms it, to conclude that "All is plagiarism. All has been said before."

Plagio II, poemas. México: Joaquín Mortiz, 1980. A sequel to poems in Plagio I. Author moves in the realm of literature as play. Word games contribute to exactness of form. Humor. Poems reveal a passionate and complex personality. Facility and sentimentalism are avoided while unveiling a transparent world made up of nuances. As the title indicates, the poems show the author's vast culture. Riddles and nonsense rhymes abound. Love is the ultimate puzzle. ML

GONZALEZ DE MOSCOSO, Mercedes (Ecuador, d. 1911)

Abuela, teatro

Cantos del hogar

En el nido

Rosas de otoño

GONZALEZ DE RAGGI, Ana Hilda (United States, twentieth century)

La sombra invitada, poesías

GONZALEZ MALDONADO, Edelmira (Puerto Rico, b. 1923)

Crisis

Soledumbre

GONZALEZ MALDONADO, Rosario (Mexico, twentieth century)

La jirafa fantástica y otros cuentos, cuentos para niños

GONZALEZ VILLEGAS, Maruja (Uruguay, twentieth century)

Amor callado, poesía

Las manos, novela

Mar demorado, poesía

Tiempo de claridad, poesía

Universidad de Illinois, mi sombra en su luz, relato

Volando sobre los Andes tendidos, memorias

Yo insólito, novela

GORODISCHER, Angélica (Argentina, b. 1930)

Casta luna electrónica, cuentos

Cuentos con soldados, cuentos

Opus dos, novela

Las pelucas, cuentos

Trafalgar, cuentos

GORRITI, Juana Manuela (Argentina, 1819-1892)

Las escritoras

Guemes

La hija de Mashorquero

Oasis en la vida

Páginas literarias, leyendas, cuentos, narraciones

Panoramas de la vida, poesía

El pozo de Yocci, novela

Sueños y realidades

La tierra natal

Veladas literarias de Lima, 1876-1877

GRAMA DE LOS CAMPOS (see **CELI BENITEZ, Eloísa**)

GRAMCKO, Ida (Venezuela, b. 1925)

La andanza y el hallazgo, antología

Cámara de cristal, poemas

Cero grados norte franco

La dama y el oso

Este canto rodado, prosa y poemas

Los estetas, los mendigos, los héroes, poemas 1958

El jinete de la brisa

Juan sin miedo

Lo máximo murmura, poemas

Magia y amor del pueblo

María Lionza, tres actos

Poemas de una psicótica

Poemas: la vara mágica

Poemas 1947-1952

Sol y soledades, poemas

Sonetos del origen

Umbral, poemas

GRANATA, María (Argentina, b. 1923)

Corazón cavado

Derechos justiciales del trabajador, de la familia, de la anciandad, de la educación y la cultura, de la mujer

El gallo embrujado

El jubiloso exterminio, novela

Muerte del adolescente, poemas

El niño en la pintura

Los tumultos, novela

Umbral de tierra, poemas

Los viernes de la eternidad, poemas

GRAVINA TELECHEA, María F. (Uruguay, twentieth century)

Lázaro vuela rojo, poesía

GREENBERG S., Paulina (Mexico, twentieth century)

El silencio, poemas

GREVE, Escilda (Chile, twentieth century)

Alma al desnudo, poesía

De silencio a silencio, poesía

Espejo en el aire, poesía

Guijarros de color, poesía

Imán verde, poesía

La rebelde cosecha, poesía

Las venas de la sal, poesía

GRILLO DE SALGADO, Rosario (Colombia, b. 1856)

Cuentos reales

GUADALUPE, María de Luján Reyes de (see **LUJAN REYES DE GUADALUPE, María de**)

GUARDIA, Gloria (see **GUARDIA DE ALFARO, Gloria**)

GUARDIA, Lilly (Costa Rica, twentieth century)

Contraste, poemas

GUARDIA DE ALFARO, Gloria (Panama, twentieth century)

Tiniebla blanca, novela

El último juego, novela

GUARDIA ZELEDON, Gloria (Panama, twentieth century)

Sed en Sevilla, cuento

GUERRA, Ana María (Argentina, twentieth century)

Las visitas

GUERRA, Dora (El Salvador, b. 1925)

Signo menos, poesía

GUERRA, Hilda (Argentina, twentieth century)

En la fuente de los bailarines

GUERRA, Rosa (Argentina, b. early 19th century - d. 1894; pseudonym Cecilia). She was primarily known for her work as educator and journalist. In 1854 she founded the journal La Educación, to which she contributed articles under the pseudonym "Cecilia." She also published articles in La Tribuna, La Nación Argentina and El Nacional. Her novels, poetry and drama in verse belong to the second period of romanticism, and her style reflects the traits of the times: vivid and dramatic descriptions of landscapes that are premonitions of tragedy, a super-abundance of exclamation marks. Today, her name is little known in Argentina.

La camelia, novela

Clemencia, drama. Buenos Aires: Bernheim y Boneo, 1862. 90 pp. Available in libraries in Buenos Aires. This romantic drama in three acts and in verse has a major plot: the protagonist's personal tragedies, which include a love triangle; and a sub-plot: the historical events in Argentina during the first decades of the nineteenth century. The sub-plot is linked, in part, to the major plot because it is due to the political situation in her country that the protagonist has suffered some of her misfortunes, such as her brother's death, her father's long exile, and their present destitution. There is lack of verisimilitude in the protagonist's actions and in the denouement of the play.

Julia o la educación, novela

Lucía Miranda, novela. Preface by José María Monner Sans (1956) and a letter by Miguel Cané (1858). Buenos Aires: Facultad de Filosofía y Letras de la Universidad de Buenos Aires, 1956. 79 pp. Available in major research libraries. This was the first novel published in Argentina (1860) on the historical or legendary Lucía Miranda. The novel is based on the chronicles of colonial times, but Guerra adapts the historical episode of the foundation and destruction of the Fort of Sancti Spíritu to the nineteenth century, and places the protagonists in a romantic milieu where love, loyalty, and primitive passions lead to tragedy. NG

GUERRERO DE VAZQUEZ GOMEZ, Esperanza (Mexico, twentieth century)

Ana María, novela

Bajo los cedros, teatro

Cardos, poesía

La luz roja, cuentos

Las que no somos madres, novela

El misterio del estanque, cuentos

Un nuevo amanecer, teatro

La quinta de las dalias, novela

Tres corazones y una melodía, novela

GUEVARA, Matilde Ladrón de (see **LADRON DE GUEVARA, Matilde**)

GUEVARA CASTAÑEIRA, Josefina (Puerto Rico, twentieth century)

Los encadenados, novela

La otra voz, novela

Siembra, poemas

GUIDO, Beatriz (Argentina, b. 1928). Well-known inside Argentina, Guido became known internationally as one of the "angry" writers of the generation of 1955. Yet her depiction of a decadent ruling class is not purely one of social denunciation; she includes elements of the Gothic, amorous intrigues and the creation of redundant, personable, if corrupt, men and women. Much of her fame was won through her extensive collaboration with her now-deceased filmmaker husband, Leopoldo Torre Nilsson; they combined social statement with absorbing narrative in successful films.

Apasionados

La caída, novela. Buenos Aires: Losada. 1956. 136 pp. Guido's second novel is in her most Gothic strain, involving a strange old house full of family secrets. The heroine comes to stay with the sinister family in all innocence; the novel relates her steady deterioration under the influence of the disorganized and corrupt household. Sociopolitical commentary, a constant factor in many Guido works, is here held in abeyance in favor of story-telling.

La casa del ángel, novela. Buenos Aires: Emecé, 1956. Paperback, 174 pp. This novel created considerable excitement upon its appearance for its revelations of personal and financial corruption as part of upper-class life. Particular attention goes to the intricate moral code of the wealthy, which permits both the excesses of Puritanism and those of profligacy without allowing for communicative and reciprocally pleasurable relations between partners. The novel has an involving plot and allows identification with the understandably confused young heroine.

End of a day. Tr. A.D. Towers. N.Y.: Scribners, 1966. Translation of El incendio y las vísperas.

Escándalos y soledades, novela. Buenos Aires: Losada, 1970. Paperback, 306 pp. Among Guido's works, this mixed-genre text stands out for its innovative approach. Segments of narrative, descriptive and lyrically evocative writing appear in juxtaposition. The work's system of signs includes graphics. The subject matter is typically Guido's: the corrupt, but fascinating, upper class; gothically mysterious happenings; the disruption of recent decades of Argentina history. Plot continuity is minimal.

Estar en el mundo

Fin de fiesta, novela. Buenos Aires: Losada, 1960. Paperback, 236 pp. Another edition: (Barcelona: Planeta, 1971), paperback, 315 pp. Barcelona edition unavailable. The corruption prevalent among the ruling class is examined while, at the same time, the novel offers a human-interest plot concerning particular members of this stratum. The elegance and wit of the wealthy protagonists is balanced against their involvement in unsavory dealings, their use of deviant sexuality to fend off boredom, and their frequent lack of social awareness. These features become more patent as the wealthy face the loss of their holdings and privileges under populist Peronism (1946-1955).

The House of the Angel. Tr. Joan Coyner MacLean. London: Deutsch, 1957. 172 pp. Translation of La casa del ángel.

El incendio y las vísperas, novela. Buenos Aires: Losada, 1965. Paperback, 192 pp. Treats the rise of populist Peronism (1946-1955) and the consequent despoilment of the goods and status of the monied class. Members of the governing group are portrayed in a manner that is both appealing and repellent -- they have considerable personal charm and style while scandalous power arrangements and private decadence are rampant. This fundamental ambivalence gives the book a certain muddled quality in its portrayal of society.

Los insomnes, cuentos. Buenos Aires: Corregidor, 1973. Paperback, 91 pp. The title story in this collection of short fiction deals with the theme of underground and terrorist political action in early-1970's Buenos Aires -- a departure from her typical fascination with the Peronist period. The interview with the author that prefaces the work includes material on her political outlook and her response to attacks on her writing as privatized, ambiguous in its politics, and covertly supportive of the monied class it appears to denounce.

La invitación. Buenos Aires: Losada, 1979. Paperback, 197 pp. The principal new feature of this novel is the time period (1973 rather than the first Peronist period of 1946-1955). The complex relations between hunting -- a virtual fetish among the rural aristocracy -- and sexuality and sex roles receive considerable attention. Despite a certain amount of "best-seller" type writing and luridness, the novel does offer a commentary on conventions of masculinity and femininity among a certain class.

Una madre, novela

La mano en la trampa, cuentos. Buenos Aires: Losada, 1961. Paperback, 138 pp. Guido's more Gothic and elegant fictional modes are foregrounded in this collection of short fiction, which provided source material for successful films by Torre Nilsson. The treatment of the complex sexual arrangements of the leisured class is not so much denunciatory as Gothic, with much emphasis on either hidden pasts and secret agreements or jet-set cosmopolitan values in a mode reminiscent of Françoise Sagan.

Mujeres cuentan

El ojo único de la ballena, cuentos. Buenos Aires: Merlín, 1971. Paperback, 188 pp. Not available. This collection of previously published texts includes short fiction, short plays and fragmentary prose writings, allowing the reader to form a good overall idea of her themes and approaches; but it also becomes apparent how frequently the same subject matter is given re-elaboration. The most frequent topic is the life of the Argentine ruling class, with suspenseful stories of sinister, Gothic events a secondary current.

El Pibe Cabeza, crónica cinematográfica

Piedra libre. Buenos Aires: Galerna, 1976. Paperback, 203 pp. The title novella is a prose-narrative version of the successful film by Leopoldo Torre Nilsson. It involves such typically Gothic elements as a bride who mysteriously vanishes. Beyond this conventional Gothicism there is an implicit statement about the Argentine landed aristocracy, as a young woman seeks to invade the system of old families. This long story is supplemented with miscellaneous briefer ones.

Regreso a los hilos, novela

Todos los cuentos, el cuento. Buenos Aires: Planeta Argentina, 1979. Paperback, 189 pp. This collection of Guido's stories is not intended to present new material, but to bring together her most typical work. Many of the plots have been utilized in films directed by Leopoldo Torre Nilsson. Gothic plots and stories of the intimate lives of the Argentinean aristocracy predominate. NL

GUILLEN DE RODRIGUEZ, Maribel (Honduras, twentieth century; also Marisabel)

Fantasías teatrales, teatro

Floresta, teatro

Relicario, poesía

GUTIERREZ DE CALDERON, Ana (Bolivia, twentieth century)

Jazmín del oriente, novela

GUTIERREZ ISAZA, Elvira (Colombia, twentieth century; pseudonym: Eguza, Tirso de)

Caos y tiranía

Historia heroica de las mujeres próceres de Colombia

GUTIERREZ KAHN, Asela (Cuba, twentieth century)

Las pirañas y otros cuentos cubanos

GUTIERREZ SUAREZ, Emma E. de (Mexico, twentieth century)

Cuento sobre un perro, cuentos

La madre, cuentos

El mejor amigo del hombre, cuentos

La ranita que no sabía saltar, cuentos

GUZMAN E., Julia (Mexico, twentieth century)

Divorciadas

Nuestros maridos, ficción

¡Quiero vivir mi vida!, comedia

H

HAEDO, Carmelinda Pacheco de (see PACHECO DE HAEDO, Carmelinda)

HALL DE FERNANDEZ, Elisa (Guatemala, b. 1892)

> Mostaza
>
> Semilla de mostaza

HAMEL, Teresa (Chile, b. 1918)

> Las causas ocultas, cuentos
>
> El contramaestre, cuentos
>
> Gente sencilla, cuentos
>
> Negro, cuento
>
> La noche de rebelde
>
> Raquel devastada, cuentos

HARRIAGUE, Magdalena (Argentina, b. 1924). Harriague was born in Buenos Aires, of an English father (Tomkinson) and a Hispanic mother (Martínez). She studied painting and languages. Her literary career has been essentially devoted to poetry. She has published eight books since 1953, six of them with the prestigious Emecé firm; most of them have received outstanding awards. Her latest collection of poems Traslaciones has gone to press. Harriague is a regular contributor to several Latin American and Spanish newspapers and serves on the editorial board of Letras de Buenos Aires. From her marriage to the successful business lawyer Pedro María Harriague Castex, she has two sons and three daughters.

> Criaturas en los siglos, poemas. Cover Illus. by Reinaldo Monclús. Buenos Aires: Emecé, 1960. Paperback, 60 pp. Available in major research libraries. This collection of twenty-eight poems written in free verse continues Harriague's placid contemplation of the destiny of nature and mankind through concretely descriptive imagery. Some

poems focus on country characters and various animals. At least three touch on the inequities and turbulence of life in the city. Others poeticize the author's mother, her children and adolescence in general.

La mano y su viaje, poemas. Buenos Aires: Emecé, 1964. Paperback, 82 pp. Index, available in major research libraries. Illus. by José Bononi, this collection of thirty-five poems received a prize from Argentina's National Fund for the Arts which subsidized its publication. Written in free verse and dedicated to the poet's brother and sister, these poems touch on an all-encompassing deity, unison with a self-mirroring nature and existence as a repetitive cycle from time immemorial. "The hand and its journey" refers to the poetic mind shaping words as it sojourns on earth, separated from an infinite totality.

Oír la tierra, poemas. Buenos Aires: Emecé, 1956. Paperback, 68 pp. Illus. by José Bononi, index, available in major research libraries. Divided into two sections of thirteen poems each, this volume received an honorable mention from Argentina's Society of Writers (S.A.D.E.) Written in free verse, these poems are inter-related by the principal motif of "experiences in the countryside," in Harriague's own words. They constitute a tranquil contemplation of the divine origin, temporal evolution and the ultimate meaning of specific landscapes of the poet, her loved ones and man in general. The psycholinguistic struggle to express immutable philosophical tenets counterbalances the poet's spiritual serenity.

Poemas de evasión. Buenos Aires: Pellegrini, 1953. Paperback, 144 pp. The author herself describes it in the following manner: "Published in paperback, the introductory pages are lilac with titles printed in blue. It is divided into three parts -- the first titled 'Oraciones' contains twenty-one poems; the second titled 'Poemas Enamorados' contains twenty; the third, titled 'Cantos de Noche y Alba' contains twenty-four." Fall 1953 reviews in Buenos Aires newspapers note Harriague's free verse style, her interest in landscape, and her firmly serene expression buttressed by a spiritual disquiet comparable to Santa Teresa and Gabriela Mistral.

Pruebas en descargo, poemas. Buenos Aires: Troquel, 1967. 100 pp. Index, available in major research libraries. Illus. by Horacio Butler. Dedicated to two of her grandchildren, this collection of forty-three poems written in free verse was awarded third prize by the city of Buenos Aires. Of the ten poems entitled "Scenes," several deal with insects as symbols of human existence. Six others written in the second person are addressed to the Deity; and three very short ones, entitled "Prisons," refer to the imprisonment of life by death -- or vice versa -- as an obedient freedom on the part of the poet. In several poems, life is seen a Platonic cave. Images that recur in Harriague's subsequent books include "the hand," "the tower," and "the watchman."

Ronda para un cuerpo, poemas. Buenos Aires: Emecé, 1958. Paperback, 64 pp. Index, available in major research libraries. This collection of thirteen free-verse poems appeared in a very special Emecé format, print arranged by hand with Garamond characters, and one color illustration by M. Ernesto Caldentey. The edition was very limited: twenty copies in "Whatmann" paper signed by the author, plus one-hundred and thirty in "extra strong" paper. Although described by the author as "love poems," only four actually focus on love in a dispassionate manner. The rest, mostly written in second person, deal movingly with the meaning of death for the living as well as the effects of time on the lifeless body.

Sucede en los mundos, poemas. Buenos Aires: Emecé, 1971. Paperback, illus. by José Bonomi, 78 pp. Available in major research libraries. This collection of thirty-three free-verse poems received the Silver Pen Prize from the International Pen Club. Dedicated to a grandaughter, the poems are all untitled but are identified in the index by first lines. The title apparently refers to the various types of creatures experiencing the earth and outerspace, as well as to some geographical areas, e.g., Avila, Patmos and the countryside outside Buenos Aires where the author grew up. In general, the poems deal with the many facets of the passing of time and existence, together with the human attempt to understand it by the untrue-to-life means of reason.

Vigía en la torre, poemas. Buenos Aires: Emecé, 1974. Paperback, 57 pp. Available in major research libraries. This collection of twenty-five untitled poems dedicated to two of her grandchildren continues Harriague's concise free-verse style and her mystic epistemological approach. Several poems deal with the observation of the outer world by an inner spirit through which the poet becomes one with the environment in self-contemplation. The totality of experience takes refuge in her and seeks to reproduce itself through words or poetry. The poet thus sees herself as inseparably integrated into a continuum of life and/or death. The last poem possibly explains Harriague's subsequent restraint from publishing as a silent awareness that her transcendence, firmly grounded on the earth as "the watchman on the tower," suffices for her to understand the world. SHA

HECKER, Liliana (Argentina, b. 1943)

Acuario, cuentos

Cuentos

Los que vieron la zarza, cuentos

Un resplandor que se apagó en el mundo, novela

HELFGOTT, Sarina (Peru, twentieth century)

Hoy no, mañana tampoco, teatro

Libro de los muertos, poema

La luz pródiga, poema

Teatro (La jaula; La sentencia; La señorita Canario)

HENESTROSA, Armonía Etchepare de (see **ETCHEPARE DE HENESTROSA, Armonía**)

HENRIQUEZ, Salomé Ureña de (see **UREÑA DE HENRIQUEZ, Salomé**)

HEREDIA, María Luisa Ocampo (see **OCAMPO HEREDIA, María Luisa**)

HERMINIA (pseudonym: see **UREÑA DE HENRIQUEZ, Salomé**)

HERMOSO, Fernanda (Argentina, twentieth century)

Poemas del árbol fiel

HERNANDEZ, Luisa Josefina (Mexico, b. 1928)

Agonía, pieza en un acto

Aguardiente de caña, teatro

Apocalipsis cum figuras

Apostasía

Botica modelo, teatro

La calle de la gran ocasión, díalogos, ficción

Clemencia, teatro

La cólera secreta, novela

Danza de urogallos múltiples, teatro

Los frutos caídos, teatro

Las fuentes ocultas

Los huéspedes reales, teatro

El lugar donde crece la hierba, novela

La memoria de Amadís

La nave mágica. La bicicleta de Quinque

La noche exquisita, novela

Nostalgia de Troya, novela

Los palacios desiertos, novela

La paz ficticia, teatro

La plaza de Puerto Santo

Popol Vuh y la paz ficticia, teatro

La primera batalla, novela

Quetzalcoátl, teatro

Los sordomudos, pieza en dos actos

Los trovadores

El valle que elegimos, novela

HERNANDEZ, María de Lourdes (Mexico, twentieth century)

En el Nuevo Aztlán

HERNANDEZ DE ARAUJO, Carmen (Puerto Rico, 1832-1877)

Amor ideal, teatro

Los deudos rivales, teatro

Hacer bien al enemigo es imponerle el mayor castigo, teatro

HERNANDEZ DIAZ, Celia de (Mexico, twentieth century)

Porque son hijos no deseados, poema

Señor, tú me probaste, poemas

HERRERA, Carmela Nieto de (see **NIETO DE HERRERA, Carmela**)

HERRERA, Luz María Umpierre- (see **UMPIERRE-HERRERA, Luz María**)

HERRERA, Marta Josefina (Guatemala, twentieth century)

Espada de remordimiento, novela

HERRERA, Sara (Chile, b. 1925)

Ajenjo y almíbar, cuadros satíricos

Cascada de plata, poesía

Pétalos de un girasol, poesía

Pleamar, poemas

Réquiem para un hijo, poesía

Rosal de espinas, cuadros satíricos

HERRERA, Silvia (Uruguay, twentieth century)

Ayer y azul, poemas

Cinco reinos, poemas

Ziegelrot, poemas

HERRERA DE ANGELES, I. Orfelinda (Peru, twentieth century)

Dimensión sencilla, poemas

Gracia de amor, poemas

Infinitud horizontal, poemas

Poemas de mayo

Sinfonía de la sangre

Voz para mi hija, poemas

HERRERA DE RODRIGUEZ URIBE, Leonor (Colombia, twentieth century)

Duelo poético, con Gabriel Echeverri Márquez

Rincón de luz

Sonatina, poemas

Ventana al sol, poemario

HERRERA DE WARNKEN, Marta (Chile, 1902-1978; pseudonym: Morgán, Patricia)

Búscame entre las estrellas, teatro

Fata morgana, poemas

Inquietud de silencio, poemas

Una puerta a la luz, poesía

La tarde llega callada, teatro

Torrente inmóvil, poemas

Viaje de luz, poemas

HIDALGO, María Luisa (Mexico, b. 1918)

El ángel angustioso, poesía

Cuentas de cuentos

Inquietudes, versos

Presagio a la muerte, poesía

Prisión distante, poesía

Renato Camaleón y otros

Retorno amargo, poesía

HIDALGO DE CHIRIBOGA, Alicia (Ecuador, twentieth century; pseudonym: Flor de Te)

Hojas y brotes

HIJA DEL CARIBE, la (pseudonym: see **PADILLA DE SANZ, Trinidad**)

HIPALIA, Hada (pseudonym: see CORNEJO, María Isabel Eloísa)

HUBERTSON, Amanda Labarca (see LABARCA HUBERTSON, Amanda)

HUNEEUS DE CLARO, Ester (Chile, b. 1904; pseudonym: Paz, Marcela)

Caramelos de luz

Diario secreto de Papelucho y el marciano

Mi hermano Ji

Papelucho, cuentos infantiles

Papelucho casi huérfano

Papelucho detective

Papelucho en la clínica

Papelucho historiador

Papelucho, mi hermano Hippie

Papelucho misionero

Papelucho perdido

Soy colorina, cuentos

Tiempo, papel, y lápiz, cuentos

La vuelta de Sebastián

HURTADO DE ALVAREZ, Mercedes (Colombia, d. 1890)

Alfonso, cuadros de costumbres

I

IBAÑEZ, Sara de (Uruguay, 1909-1971). Born in the town of Chamberlain, she married Roberto Ibáñez (also a writer) in 1928 and had three daughters. All of the eight books published before her death were awarded prizes in Uruguay. Publication of Canto póstumo was overseen by her husband who also wrote the introduction and notes. She was accustomed to working alternately on two books at the same time. Mexico's National University recorded a reading by her of selected poems in the Voz Viva de la América Latina series (1968). She also made a recording for the Library of Congress Archive of Hispanic Literature on Tape. The critic Supervielle called her body of work "an immense anthology." Her poetic technique ran the gamut from sonnets to blank verse.

Apocalipsis XX. Caracas: Monte Avila, 1970. Reflects the expansion of technique and artistic control that come with maturity. More use of assonance and blank verse, as well as innovative variations on traditional forms, than in earlier work. Although her intent was for it to stand on its own artistic merit without any explanation, the work can be more fully appreciated if the reader is aware that it represents an apocalyptic vision of the results of a nuclear holocaust. Contemporary and prophetic, it is an example of the poet as seer.

Artigas, poema. Official ed. Montevideo: Uruguaya, 1952. Epic poem exalting Artigas, a hero of the struggle for independence from Spain, whose United States equivalent would be George Washington. Emphasizes the heroism and charisma of the man, epic grandeur of the battle, and strength of the nation and its people. Parts have been anthologized.

La batalla, poesía. Buenos Aires: Losada, 1967. Rich in chromatic and sensory images. Operates on various levels -- the battle of war, the internal moral struggle of the individual, the conflicts of duality in the universe, and the poet's grappling with obstacles to true artistic expression. More accessible than some of her other poetry because meaning can be found on both the obvious and the symbolic levels, and the poems are expressive and complete in either sense.

Canto. Prologue by Pablo Neruda. Buenos Aires: Losada, 1940. 2nd ed. 1954. 112 pp. Made up of several sections: "Islands" (sonnets), "Liras" (poems of six five-line stanzas, rhyming ababb), "Of the Living" (sonnets), "Of the Dead" (sonnets) and "Itinerary" (love poems to her husband, Roberto). Many images from nature, especially the sea: fish, waves, coral, seaweed, ships, islands, etc. Rather hermetic symbolism, reminiscences of modernism. Imbued with sadness and repression, such as the stanza, "I'm going to escape. . . . But no . . . I retreat, frowning, bitter and mute." Laudatory but uninformative prologue.

Canto a Montevideo, poema. Official ed. Montevideo: Uruguaya, 1941. Poem in praise of Montevideo. Of socio-historical interest as an example of patriotic occasional verse. Typical of the genre. Would be appealing mainly to Uruguayans.

Canto póstumo. Poets of Yesterday and Today series. Buenos Aires: Losada, 1973. 209 pp. plus 55 pp. biographical/critical notes. Lovingly edited by her husband, Roberto, this collection is the only one that contains biographical and critical notes on Ibáñez, including commentaries on previously-published work. The first of the three sections, "Diario de la muerte," is her last book and the most varied in technique, more fluid, more inventive, mature and powerful. A major aspect is the duality of death seen from life and life viewed from death. The second part, "Baladas y canciones," includes a beautiful homage to Rubén Darío. The third and last section, "Gavilla," contains a variety of verses.

Las estaciones y otros, poemas. Mexico: Fondo de Cultura Económica, 1957. 228 pp. The title poem is in four sections, Spring, Summer, Fall and Winter: lyrical, symbolic descriptions of the changing moods of nature with which the poet identifies. Also includes selections from Canto, Canto a Montevideo, Hora ciega, Pastoral and Artigas.

Hora ciega, poema. Buenos Aires: Losada, 1943. Written in 1941-1942, these poems reflect the horror of war, such as the one that begins, "I said to my brother, bare your chest," and ends "I come to strip you of clouds and children/and drain forever your full heart." The sections include "Soliloquies of the Soldier," "Caín," "The Pale Ones," and "Passion and Death of the Light," dedicated to her husband.

Pastoral, poesía. Mexico: Cuadernos Americanos, 1948. Divided into three time periods representing three ages of man: infancy, youth and maturity. "Tiempo I" and "III" are made up of fifteen sections each, with fifteen hendecasyllable lines per section, arranged in the sequence: two tercets, a quatrain, a tercet, and two lines completing the rhyme. "Tiempo II" consists of ten sections of thirty-two lines each, divided into four octets. According to the author, it represents "the history of man and his disoriented place in the universe . . . above all, the living history of a poet," identified in the symbol of the shepherd.

Poemas escogidos. Mexico: Siglo Veintiuno, 1974. 175 pp. Published posthumously, this edition contains selections from all of Ibáñez' books: Canto, Apocalipsis XX, Canto a Montevideo, Hora ciega, Pastoral, Artigas, Las estaciones, La batalla and Canto póstumo. However, it does not include the extensive notes from Canto póstumo. AMA

IBARBOUROU, Juana de (Uruguay, 1895-1979). With little formal education, her talent as versifier and story-teller blossomed early and she began publishing poems and short stories. After her marriage to the career military man, Lucas Ibarbourou, she continued writing while living at various military posts. After early happiness, tragic occurrences, especially the loss of her husband, plunged her into depression. In 1919 her first book of poetry, Las lenguas de diamante established her reputation as an excellent young poet. Her first three books were exceedingly popular and they outshone anything that she produced afterwards. Her ceremonial consecration in August of 1929 as "Juana de América" resulted in some silent disapproval of her identification with the establishment. In later years she became a recluse and considered herself to have been totally abandoned in her solitude. She did develop some degree of profundity, but she failed in many instances to reach a universal plane.

Angor Dei, poema. Washington, D. C.: Pan American Union, 1963. 7 pp. Long, religious poem published in a bilingual version. Luis Gianneo, Argentine composer, wrote music for it to be transformed into a cantata for soprano and orchestra. It was incorporated into a section entitled "La Pasajera" in the final edition of the complete works.

Antología de poemas y prosas. Eds. Arturo Sergio Visca and Julio C. da Rosa. Montevideo: Ministerio de Educación y Cultura del Uruguay, Organización de los Estados Americanos, 1980. 199 pp. Excellent prose and poetry anthology, choosing from her most representative works through 1968. The table of contents lists all the sources and their dates. Criterion used to select compositions was to search out those which reflected her creative development. They decided not to use poems from "Dualismo," nor "Romances del Destino," both never published in book form except in her Obras completas. The first four were Las lenguas de diamante, Raíz salvaje, La rosa de los vientos and Perdida. The fifth poetry section combined poems from Azor, "Mensajes del escriba." The prose was mainly from El cántaro fresco, Estampas de la Biblia, Chico Carlo, "Destino," and "Angeles Pintados," (alternate title: Juan Soldado). In Notes preceding the selections from each source, the editors give an excellent short introduction with full bibliographical information.

Antología de poesía y prosa 1919-1971. Prologue by Ed. Jorge Arbeleche. Buenos Aires: Losada, 1972. 215 pp. Collection prepared on the fiftieth anniversary of the publication of Raíz salvaje. The choice was made keeping in mind the popularity of her poems as well as the aesthetic qualities. Long prologue of profound insight by the editor, in which he analyzes the silent negative current directed toward Ibarbourou because of her recognition by a government which was not widely respected. He considered especially damaging her title Juana de América since it created a myth around her work. Both poems and prose are included chronologically from her fifteen books, and they are listed in the index beneath the title of the source and its date.

Antología poética. Prologue by Alberto Zum Felde. Colección Poesías. Santiago: ZigZag, 1940. 134 pp. Nine-page prologue by Alberto Zum Felde compares Ibarbourou, Delmira Agustini and the French writer, Ana de Noailles. He analyzes her conception of the world as reflected in her poetry: to enjoy life and love to the fullest, directly and physically. Points out her move in La rosa de los vientos from musicality toward a concentration on imagery and toward more subjective, and thus more subtle language. Contains fifty-five poems from Las lenguas de diamante, Raíz salvaje and La rosa de los vientos. The Uruguayan Zum Felde has chosen the poems most characteristic of the qualities he has discussed.

Antología poética. Prologue by ed., Dora Isella Russell. Madrid: Cultura Hispánica, 1970. 349 pp. Prepared on the fiftieth anniversary of the publication of <u>Las lenguas de diamante</u> as homage to the author. Russell has chosen with perspicacity poems from across the fifty-year span on the themes which are most representative of her poetic art. They are: love, nature, poetry, solitude and night, time and melancholy, death, maternity and finally, war and peace. Each has the date of first publication beside the title but there was no effort to place them chronologically. The editor's method permits the reader to appreciate the variation in point of view as the years pass. Sentiment and concept become more profound as themes pass from girlish gaiety to mature anguish at the approach of death. For the usual reader, such a work gives a panoramic view of the development of the poet without having to read fifteen volumes. Both distinctive print and fine quality paper add to the attractiveness of this anthology.

<u>Azor</u>. Poetas de España y América. Buenos Aires: Losada, 1953. 108 pp. According to Ibarbourou's "Autobiografía lírica," these poems were from an epoch of constant poetic creation, and for her they represented a renewal of rebellious and combative spirit. She expresses docility and resignation, however, and her retreat from an active life in the world into her artistic task as poet is in certain ways an escape. In her four-line verse preamble she expresses her desire to express her ideas with "lenguas de diamante." Yet the brilliance of earlier works is absent as she writes in muted tones about how absence and growing forgetfulness dominate her while at the same time acceptance comes. Divided into two sections: "Divino Amor," and "Amor Divino," with fifty-three and eight poems, respectively. Varied forms: rhymed, unrhymed and also rhymed in assonance; line length uneven, some sonnets of technical mastery.

<u>El cántaro fresco</u>. Montevideo: La Uruguaya, 1920. 144 pp. Prose work of lyrical meditations, legends from her infancy, descriptions of scenes from her childhood and from later years as well. Contains fifty narratives divided into forty-three in the untitled first part, and seven in "Otras Narraciones." Several are poems in prose and most of them are less than two pages. Optimistic in tone but with nostalgic melancholy and adult sadness. Reminiscences of scenes from nature with plants and animals and other manifestations. Several are on the subject of nature, home, motherhood, her son and children in general. Dialogues with nature and some evocative as well as narrative pieces. Often uses everyday expressions as well as simple metaphors. Exclamatory phrases and reiteration stimulate memories and sentiments.

<u>El cántaro fresco</u>. San José, Costa Rica: J. García Monge, 1922. 56 pp. This popular edition contains only thirty-two of the original fifty short narratives. No visible difference in criteria of choice since here as well as in the first edition the majority of them treat nature or other themes connected with meditations on nature.

<u>El cántaro fresco</u>. Montevideo: A. Monteverde, 1927. 143 pp. 2nd ed.: 1931, 143 pp. The same fifty narratives as the first edition of 1920.

<u>El cántaro fresco</u>. Santiago, Chile: ZigZag, 1943. 118 pp. Exactly the same edition as the first with the exception of the three page impressionistic introduction by Angel Cruchaga, S.M.

<u>El cántaro fresco</u>. Foreward by José Radamés Lamas. Colección Poesías. Montevideo: Acacia, 1958. 61 pp. 2nd ed.:1969, 63 pp. Two-

page biographical note followed by four paragraphs on the work. Contains only the first section of forty-three compositions.

Chico Carlo, cuentos. Prologue and Notes by editor, José Pereira Rodríguez. Montevideo: Barreiro y Ramos, 1944. 130 pp. 2nd ed. [194?]. One of her most inspired books of short stories and narratives about her rural childhood. Although most are longer and several are more structured with a well-developed plot, the ideas are presented with the same spontaneous simplicity as in El cántaro fresco. The first story, "Las Coronas," is about a nostalgic memory of Susana, Juana's alter ego, and the pact of her and a little friend to buy for each other a beautiful funeral wreath of which they were enamoured if either of them were to die. The title story and one other treat the poor, mischievous and unruly boy of the neighborhood who enchanted Susana because of his unpredictability, but whose apparent gruffness and cruelty hid gentleness and affection, especially toward her. Seventeen narrations of nostalgia and innocence, which would be good for children from six to twelve or even to eighty.

Chico Carlo, cuentos. Buenos Aires: Sudamericana, 1944. 132 pp. Attractive popular edition of the same seventeen stories in the original order of the first edition.

Chico Carlo, cuentos. Prologue and Notes by editor, José Pereira Rodríguez. Buenos Aires: Kapelusz, 1953. 118 pp. 2nd ed.: 1954, 118 pp. Edition prepared for the use of students as a reader. Three-page chronological resumé of Ibarbourou's life and "Había una vez," eight-page note which catalogues her other works and characterizes briefly her poems and especially her short stories. Notes on each page clarify vocabulary and an occasional literary reference. Two pages at the end of the first edition only, "Algunos Juicios Críticos sobre Chico Carlo" quotes Dora Isella Russell and a literary manual.

El dulce milagro. Prologue by editor, Dora Isella Russell. Buenos Aires: Universitaria de Buenos Aires, 1964. 76 pp. Another of the various anthologies by Ibarbourou's friend Russell.

Ejemplario. Montevideo: A. Monteverde, 1925. 108 pp. Other editions: 2nd ed. 1927; 3rd ed. 1928. Poetic prose anthology adopted for use as a textbook by Uruguay's National Council of Primary Education.

Elegía. Palma de Mallorca: Ayuntamiento de la Ciudad de Palma de Mallorca, 1967. 55 pp. Same edition published in San Juan: Universidad de Puerto Rico, 1968, 55 pp. She sufficiently distances herself from the pain resulting from the loss of her husband to cause the reader to empathize with her. Deep nostalgia for her lost love in metrically free verse and varied verse forms, with a final sonnet of compressed anguish. Rhymes mostly in assonance. Alliteration increases musicality. Some metaphors are striking, as "el alzán liviano de la lluvia." A fitting tribute to the man who inspired some of the most fervent love poems in the Spanish language.

Estampas de la Biblia. Prologue by Gustavo Gallinal. Illus. by Antonio Pena. Montevideo: Barreiro y Ramos, 1934. 140 pp. Forty dramatic portraits, told in first person, of some of the main Biblical figures such as Job, Ruth and many lesser-known ones. In a simple conversational style she gives warm and expressive feeling to their personalities and their life stories. Ibarbourou was an assiduous reader of the Bible, and talented at capturing the main theme or central idea of each person's story. Four-page eulogistic prologue. All portraits are less than four pages in length.

Juan Soldado. Biblioteca Clásica y Contemporánea, 370. Buenos Aires: Losada, 1971. 163 pp. Seven narratives in one part and eleven in another. Included earlier in her Obras completas, 2nd ed., minus three of the stories, and with the less felicitous title: "Angeles Pintados I, II." The weak title story was removed in this volume. The narratives evoke her childhood, returning to her past as an antidote to a less magic present. She captures sights, sounds, smells of nature, plus the personality and speech of the people from her past, as for example, the Blacks on her family's ranch. Themes such as ghosts, death, nature, diabolical forces, magic, childish escapades, her love of Montevideo, and the title story's theme of the evil stepmother. Wicked and murderous, the stepmother's plan is foiled by virtuous persons aided by animals and a witch-doctor, who brings the victims back to life. For children from six to twelve.

Juana de Ibarbourou: sus mejores poemas

Las lenguas de diamante, poesías. Prologue by Manuel Gálvez. Buenos Aires: Agencia General de Librerías y Publicaciones, 1919. 174 pp. Seven-page prologue by Manuel Gálvez gives a critical introduction to her work. Five-hundred copy edition contains sixty-five poems of intimate tone, where poetry is created from sexual sublimation, dramatizing female desire for satisfaction. Melodic verse, fresh and semi-pagan, with impressionistic images of nature. A delicate natural sensuality and vital spontaneity lend delicacy to her main theme of heterosexual love without limits, and the glory of total surrender to it. Emotional and sentimental in her ardent invitation to take her, before youth and beauty have flown, to enjoy to the fullest life's pleasures. Sixty-five poems in three sections: "La Luz Interior," "Anforas Negras," and "La Clara Cisterna." Sonnets predominate in parts one and three. The rhyme in all the poems is mainly in consonance, and cesuras, interior rhyme and alliteration make them even more rhythmical.

Las lenguas de diamante, poesías. Montevideo: Maximino García, 1919. 174 pp. The same as the Buenos Aires edition of 1919, except that there is no prologue nor dedication of the work to her fiancée, Lucas Ibarbourou.

Las lenguas de diamante, poesías. 2nd ed., augmented and corrected. Colección Estudio. Montevideo: Maximino García, 1923. 183 pp. 2nd and 3rd eds.: 1923, 183 pp. Without introduction, dedication or notes, these two editions have the same three sections and the same poems as the first edition. The additions are nine new poems in the final section. Some minor emendations were made in a few poems. The third edition is the same as the second.

Las lenguas de diamante, poesías. Montevideo: A. Monteverde, 1927. 208 pp. On good paper and with attractive type, but without introduction, notes or other information. This edition contains the same poems as in the 1923 Maximino García edition.

Las lenguas de diamante, poesías. Prologue by José Periera Rodríguez. Colección de Clásicos Uruguayos, Vol. 42. Biblioteca Artigas. Montevideo: Uruguaya, 1963. xxvii and 141 pp. Nineteen-page Prologue gives brief biographical and bibliographical information and discusses Periera's judgement of her poetic talent. One-page "Criterio de la Edición" explains that he has used the same contents as the 1927 edition but has added five poems. Ibarbourou later removes those five to a later section called "Dualismo" in her Poesías completas.

Las lenguas de diamante, poesías. Drawings by Raúl Soldi. Buenos Aires: Losada, 1969. 147 pp. Contains the same poems as the 1927 Montevideo edition. Especially prepared with fifteen excellent illustrations to commemorate the fiftieth anniversary date of the book's first publication. Very attractive.

Loores de Nuestra Señora. Montevideo: Barreiro y Ramos, 1934. 85 pp. Forty-one prayerful, poetic commentaries, or expanded versions of tributes to the Virgin in the Litany. She uses the Latin titles for each and explains in a two-page introduction that she always held the Virgen del Perpetuo Socorro in high esteem and offers her compositions as tribute of her faith and devotion. Some like "Virgo potens," are lyrical poems in prose on the power, on the beauty and other characteristics of the Virgin.

Los más bellos versos. Ed. F. Santelso. Los Angeles, México, Habana: Art, 1936. 66 pp. Small, unattractive and inexpensive folleto of fifty-six poems chosen from among those of Las lenguas de diamante, Perdida, La rosa de los vientos and "Dualismo," which was never published separately, but formed a part of her Obras completas. The majority of the poems are from her earlier works and are an indication of her popularity only seven years after the publication of her first work. Others of the poems had not been published in any form at that time, but no information was given on where they were found.

Los mejores poemas. Prologue by Angel Rama. Ed. Jorge Arbaleche. Colección Bolsilibros. Montevideo: Arca, 1968. 93 pp. Nine-page prologue by Angel Rama categorizes Ibarbourou as prisoner of her own legend, and more so, of her own early poetry. According to him, she had no route open to her after her first wild and free eroticism. But for him, even that was an existential mask and at the mature age of seventy she was still unable to express her human truth in poetry, although experiencing solitude and rapidly approaching death. Thirty-three poems with from three to ten out of each book, listed chronologically in the table of contents under the works from which they came: Las lenguas de diamante, Raíz salvaje, La rosa de los vientos, Perdida and Azor. Poems chosen to illustrate his thesis.

Las mejores poesías (líricas) de los mejores poetas. Barcelona: Cervantes, 1921. 67 pp. 2nd augmented ed.: Vol. xxiv, 1930, xvii and 84 pp. (The first 1921 edition of sixty-seven pages had the same title and publisher.) Only second edition available. Nine-page prologue signed "Editorial Cervantes," followed by reproduction of short speech of thanks by Ibarbourou on receiving the title "Juana de América" (1929). Fifty-five poems, all from Las lenguas de diamante except "Suprema Ofrenda," and "Un Día." Popular inexpensive edition especially of interest because it indicates her popularity, which had even reached Spain early in her career. The Prologue indicates that the second edition was augmented, and the editions were in all likelihood from Raíz salvaje (1924) and La rosa de los vientos (1930).

Obras completas. Compilation, notes and biographical information by editor, Dora Isella Russell. Foreward by Ventura García Calderón. Madrid: Aguilar, 1953. lxvii and 1088 pp. 2nd ed.: 1960, lxvii and 1088 pp. Excellent edition worthy of accolades for Aguilar. "Palabras

Liminares," by Ventura García Calderón, are lyric praise for the poet. Dora Isella Russell's long "Noticia Biográfica" is exceptionally complete and provides an intimate view of her personality as well as an analysis of her works with the keen critical sense of a longtime reader and editor of her poems. Four-page chronology. Well-prepared and chronologically ordered volume with few changes from her separate publications, since she usually published her manuscripts with great care. Some poems were added to sections, such as nine to Las lenguas de diamante. Several sections appear which had not previously been published in separate volumes: "Dualismo," "Puck" (a work of short children's dramas), "Perdida," "Destino," "Azor," and "Mensajes del Escriba" (the latter composed of a kind of automatic writing). In most of the additions her themes and attitudes become more sedate and sober as she experienced the vicissitudes of mature life.

Obras completas. 3rd ed. Compilation, notes and biographical information by editor, Dora Isella Russell. Forward by Ventura García Calderón. Madrid: Aguilar, 1968. lxvii and 1497 pp. Substantial changes from the first and second edition. The editor has moved some poems around, removed several and added others, as in "Azor," which exhibits a new title: "Otras Poesías." In four hundred additional pages of poetry and prose, the following are included: "Romances del Destino," "Angeles Pintados" (This book-length section of short narrations was later published as Juan Soldado), "Elegía," "La Pasajera" and "Oro y Tormenta," the last three later were published separately. Other sections were "Diario de una Isleña" (poems in prose), "Dilidiums" (named for a type of autochthonous orchid), "La Ofrenda," "Mis Amados Recuerdos," with additional addresses and speeches by the author. On the whole all these continue the currents in her poems visible after 1930; coming to terms with the limitations to life and love, suffering due to the inevitability of loss and pain, the inexorable passing of loved ones, and the fear and dislike of growing old. Her style has become more mature and sober, with less spontaneity, matching the increased thematic complexity.

Oro y tormenta. Santiago: Zig-Zag, 1956. 92 pp. Collection of seventy sonnets of eleven-syllable verse exemplifying her facile and technically excellent command of the form, but lacking her earlier depth of emotion. Languid and melancholy in tone upon remembering her golden past. Tormenting memories ask the anguished question, ubi sunt? Poems with simple, direct imagery, mainly from nature and material things around her, described with sound, smell and color. Sometimes repeats her phraseology in earlier poems, but here and there are touches of her early brilliance in metaphors like that of the title poem: "diálogo con mi ayer, oro y tormenta," or "olvidada entre un pliegue de la vida." Divided into four sections but apparently not grouped thematically since all four sections have numerous poems about the loss of her beloved husband, her pain, sorrow and solitary suffering.

La pasajera, diario de una isleña. Elegía. Poetas de Ayer y de Hoy. Buenos Aires: Losada, 1967. 94 pp. The first section contains thirty sentimental and melancholy poems of luminous imagery which is mainly as direct and natural as in her first book. However, there are fewer moments of that early strength of expression and spontaneity of image and metaphor. Fifteen poems in prose in the second part portray the life of self-imposed solitude of the later years of her life. She felt as though she were alone on an island. Ibarbourou contemplates the death of her husband and the repercussions of his loss in her life in the fourteen-page elegy which terminates the book. Poems vary in form, some with irregular syllabification and rhymed in assonance or not at all, others rhymed and regular; a few are in sonnet form.

Perdida. Poetas de España y América. Buenos Aires: Losada, 1950. 116 pp. "Perdida," which to Ibarbourou meant "lost" in the sense of distraught by grief rather than gone astray morally, as the title has been interpreted by some, was the production of an anguished and desperate period in her life. Her father, mother and husband had died in a seventeen-year span, and their loss was weighing heavily upon her, in spite of the honors she received as a writer during the same period. There is in her verse a conscious melancholy introspection into life's servitude and a sad acceptance of passing time. Her poetic voice, toned by those tragedies, became more like her simple, straight-forward expression in her early books, but with less lyric power. Longer poems with varied types of rhyme, many in assonance, and some unrhymed. Alliteration and internal rhyme. Images of sadness prevail: "Muertos ya los neblíes de la sangre," and "Ya en mi garganta se ha cuajado la sangre."

Poemas. Colección Austral, No. 265. Buenos Aires: Espasa-Calpe, 1942. 152 pp. Other editions: 2nd ed. 1942, 152 pp.; 3rd ed. 1944, 151 pp.; 4th ed. 1945, 151 pp.; 5th ed. 1946, 152 pp.; 6th ed. 1947, 152 pp.; 7th ed. 1950, 147 pp.; 8th ed. 1952, 147 pp.; 9th ed. 1961, 145 pp.; 10th ed. 1968, 145 pp. Eighty-eight poems with a short prologue by Ibarbourou entitled "Ruth," comparing her behavior in gleaning poems to that of the Biblical figure. Chosen in honor of the thirteenth anniversary of her declaration as Juana de América. Not divided into sections. The first twelve poems correspond to the months of the year, but a few were taken from her previous publications and retitled for this collection. The remainder were chosen, seemingly at random, from the rest of her work. Many are surely her favorites, as they are for her reading public, such as "Rebelde," "Vida-garfio," "Angustia," "Una enredadera," and "Raíz salvaje."

Poemas de Juana de Ibarbourou. El Arco y la Lira, 45. Medellín: Horizonte, n.d. 40 pp. Booklet on inexpensive paper. No introduction or notes and the table of contents lists the titles of seventy-two poems. Same content as the Espasa-Calpe edition of Poemas (1st ed. 1942) with the exception of the last poem: "Romance de Don Juan Zorilla de San Martín." One-page analysis of her work on the back cover.

Raíz salvaje. Montevideo: Maximino García, 1922. 102 pp. Other editions: 2nd ed. 1924, 102 pp.; 3rd ed. 1930, 102 pp. One of her works of most spontaneous expression and freedom of form. She choses personal sensorial images which capture the world of nature of her youth with all its smells, colors and sounds. A marvellous world of pure and quintessential images and pagan joy that carried little sense of guilt, yet sadness and disillusionment at the process of living threaten to calm the eroticism of young love. A rebellious work of yearning for the wild, free life of nature, to accompany her eroticism in fulfilling her sensual desires with her young husband. Resentment of the sheltered city life, far from her country childhood and girlhood roots. Various verse forms: free verse common, longer lines, irregular syllable-count, alliteration and use of rhythmical groups. In general less regular sound. Forty-eight poems without division into sections.

Raíz salvaje. Los Poetas: Biblioteca de Grandes Poetas Clásicos y Modernos, Vol. 54. Buenos Aires: Claridad, n.d. 64 pp. In addition to the poems from Raíz salvaje, this popular, inexpensive edition contains seven poems from Las lenguas de diamante.

Romances del destino. Colección La Encina y el Mar, Poesía de España y América, 21. Madrid: Instituto de Cultura Hispánica, 1955. 148 pp. Agile mastery of the romance on themes from Ibarbourou's life as well as others of romantic tone and inspiration. Includes eighteen in the "Romances" section, five in "Coplas y Otros Romances." Four-page chronology of her life through 1945. Titles range from "Autorromance de Juanita Fernández," (her maiden name) through "Romance de la Salud Quebrada," and to the final "Relato del Beso de San Francisco." The influence of García Lorca is visible, but while his poems are passionately lyrical, hers are over-sentimental. The romance flows smoothly with rhyme, at times in assonance, others in consonance. Plagiarizing herself, she over-dramatizes her suffering. Not nearly so effective in treating sad themes as the happy ones.

La rosa de los vientos. Montevideo: Palacio del Libro, 1930. 127 pp. As subjective in tone as in previous works but with more enigmatic, hidden meanings. Less direct and more cerebral with more elaborated metaphor. Some avant-garde tendencies visible. Serious and taciturn, at times joyous solely in an obvious effort to fall into despair. In the first section: "Los Días y las Noches," she rails at fate in poems of sorrow for her husband's death, for the difficult days of becoming accustomed to his absence, with less stress on her youthful dreams of fulfillment of hopes and desires. In the second section, "Claros Caminos de América," she shows her love of the continent, but at the same time her desire to have experienced other worlds, and her resentful tone displaces chauvinism. She desires the "rose of the winds" from gigantic and varied America. Treatment, in a more mature, sober way, of themes such as nature, solitude, implacably fleeting time, night, childhood, mother love and death. No sonnets, more free verse. Rhyme in assonance with long meters, at times lines are as long as twenty-one syllables.

San Francisco de Asís. Introd. by J.N. Quagliotti. Montevideo: Rosgal, 1935. 32 pp. Narrative on St. Francis including the episode of kissing the leper.

Los sueños de Natacha, cinco obras de teatro para niños. Montevideo: Liceo, 1945. 147 pp. Contains five delicate, lyrical prose dramas for children up to ten or twelve. Poems are interspersed occasionally as songs and lullabies. Preceded by a two-page lyrical meditation by Ibarbourou on the imaginative and fantastic reality of childhood. The title play is a one-act bedtime scene where the main characters are Natacha and her mother, who puts her to bed. Then her toys, animals and her guardian angel chat, play, dance and sing, leaving at midnight. "La Mirada Maléfica," is a recasting in three acts of a loveable Bluebeard; "Caperucita Roja" is an idealistic interpretation of the wolf reformed by the protagonist. "El Dulce Milagro" is three acts of Cinderella. The final one-act scene is of the dancing "silfos" of nature and their queen. Abundant diminutives and a flowing, poetical but natural language whether used by children, animals or adults. Written for the daughter of Pedro Henríquez Ureña but several became very popular and were presented many times in children's theatres.

Tiempo. Prologue by Hugo Petraglia Aguirre. Selecciones Poesía Española. Barcelona: Plaza y Janés, 1962. 199 pp. No table of contents. The editor points out that Ibarbourou herself chose the poems, limiting them to the period from the date of Perdida in 1950 until the date of the edition. In a twenty-eight page prologue, Petraglia Aguirre gives a warm and affectionate introduction to the events of the life and the most important works of his long-time friend. The poems are from Perdida, Oro y tormenta, Azor, La rosa de los vientos and two never printed in book form until Obras completas, "Mensajes del Escriba," and "Dualismo." Nevertheless, Ibarbourou does put in a few poems from La lenguas de diamante, La rosa de los vientos, which are earlier than 1950. In a section called "Tiempo," she has ninety poems from several different epochs, most of them previously unpublished. In the majority of these poems she has returned to her early images of simpler type, but there is less lyric power and the emotions are less vigorous. She no longer uses diamond-like, precisely chiseled and original words or images as in her early poems. Longer lines with mainly rhyme in assonance.

Verso y prosa. Selection and notes by ed. María Hortensia Lacau. Prologue by Leonilde León de Tedesco. Buenos Aires: Kapelusz, 1968. 124 pp. One of the most attractive as well as scholarly collections of her verse and prose. Includes a four-page selection of critics who wrote about Ibarbourou and a two-page annotated bibliography of works on her. The chronology is equally complete and the twenty-one page study is mainly dedicated to Ibarbourou's work, treating it and her themes with excellent knowledge. It analyzes her style and techniques in both poetry and prose and her meter in poetry. Limited to seven of Ibarbourou's books of poetry and to Estampas de la Biblia in prose. Unfortunately, León de Tedesco considers in depth in her study only Las lenguas de diamante, El cántaro fresco and Raíz salvaje. The selection is preceded by Ibarbourou's "Casi en Pantuflas," concerning her poetic conception, and the poems are listed under the titles of the seven works from which they were extracted. Notes are given on vocabulary and style, making the work a superior student edition. BTO

IBARRA, Graciela Patero de (see **PATERO DE IBARRA, Graciela**)

IBARRA, María de la Selva de (see **SELVA DE IBARRA, María de la**)

IBERICO, Clorinda Caller (see **CALLER IBERICO, Clorinda**)

ICAZA, Amelia Denis de (see **DENIS DE ICAZA, Amelia**)

IDOBRO, María Angélica (Ecuador, twentieth century)

　　Homenaje a la madre

　　Taita Imbabura, leyenda

IGLESIAS, Sara García (see **GARCIA IGLESIAS, Sara**)

IMITOLA NINFA, María Emiliani (see **EMILIANI IMITOLA NINFA, María**)

INES DE LA CRUZ, sor Juana (see **JUANA INES DE LA CRUZ, sor**)

IÑIQUEZ, Dalia (Cuba, twentieth century)

　　Ofrenda al hijo soñado, doce poemas de ternura

IRIS (pseudonym: see **ECHEVARRIA DE LARRAIN, Inés**)

ISAZA, Elvira Gutiérrez (see GUTIERREZ ISAZA, Elvira)

ISAZA DE JARAMILLO MEZA, Blanca (Colombia, b. 1898)

Al margen de las horas

Alma, poesías

La antigua canción

Claridad, poesía

Cuentos de la montaña

Del lejano ayer, autobiográfico

Itinerario breve

Itinerarios de emoción, ensayos

Obras completas

Páginas escogidas

Romances y sonetos

Selva florida

ISLAS, Maya (pseudonym: see VALDIVIA, Omara)

ISRAEL DE PORTELA, Luisa (Argentina, twentieth century)

Vidas tristes, cuentos

ISSASI, Teresa Farías de (see FARIAS DE ISSASI, TERESA)

ITURBIDE DE LARIS RUBIO, Sara (Mexico, twentieth century)

Tres almas de mujer

IZA, Ana María (Ecuador, b. 1947)

La casa de tía Berta

Pedazo de nada, poesía

Poemas

IZAGUIRRE, Ester de (Paraguay - Argentina, b. 1923). Born in Paraguay, Argentinian through naturalization, she graduated from the National University of Buenos Aires with degrees in secondary teaching, education and literature. She has taught at the National University and various high schools, also at the University of California, Irvine, and the California State University of San Diego. She has published at least eight volumes of poetry since 1960. Her poems and short stories have received several awards. Her work often appears in La Nación, La Prensa and other important newspapers throughout Argentina. She has participated in international symposia, has lectured extensively in Europe and the Western Hemisphere, has served on juries for important literary contests, has frequently appeared on radio and television and serves on the editorial board of Letras de Buenos Aires.

Girar en descubierto, poemas. Buenos Aires: Ismael B. Colombo, 1975. Paperback, 59 pp. This collection of thirty-two poems received the "Gran Premio Dupuytren," under the auspices of Argentina's National Fund for the Arts in 1975. Except for six sonnets, most poems have variable rhyme and rhythm, as well as length. Most deal with the passing of time, the blending the poet's reminiscences with her hopes and longings. The title of the book is taken from a line in the poem "Libre," which strikes the reader as the lyrics to a tango. Fourteen of the poems reappear in an identical manner in Judas y los demás, except for the accomplished sonnet "Todo," whose title is changed quite suitably to "Tiempo." Index; recommended for any Latin American literature course.

Judas y los demás. Buenos Aires: Carra, 1981. Paperback, 78 pp. Winner of the PEN Club's Silver Pen Award, this book contains fifty-six of Izaguirre's poems selected by Enrique Anderson Imbert, who also wrote the prologue. At least thirteen poems are from Girar en descubierto, seven from No está vedado el grito, and two from El país que llaman vida; three others appeared in the May 28, 1981, issue of Clarín (p. 5). All of them exemplify Izaguirre's poetic accomplishments: her mastery of the sonnet, her rhythmic subtlety, her philosophical depth and her profound psychological sensitivity. Index; strongly recommended for a Latin American literature course.

No está vedado el grito, poemas. Buenos Aires: F.A. Colombo, 1967. Paperback, 61 pp. This book of twenty-five poems with no index contains a prologue by Antonio Pages Larraya and three original drawings by Carlos Diamond Hartz. All, except one, are dedicated to a particular individual, including Ernesto Sábato and Syria Poletti. They are written in free verse and the first person, varying in length from twelve to thirty lines. They express the poet's search for her own identity in terms of her past experiences and her present relationships with other people and Buenos Aires. The monotone rhythm and the unobtrusive vocabulary tone down yet add profundity to plaintive self-revelations.

El país que llaman vida, poemas. Buenos Aires: Ismael B. Colombo, 1964. Paperback, 50 pp. Izaguirre's second book received an award from the National Fund for the Arts. Jorge Luis Borges' congratulatory remarks and two illustrations by Antonio Mazza precede its twenty-two poems, which are divided into four sections. The title of the book as well as of its first section composed of ten poems originates in the Austrian poet Rilke's reference to an after life. A few other poems express a Christian faith. Most notable, however, is the development of a profound awareness of time as a human experience. The sonnet continues to be a frequent form handled with subtle dexterity. Index; recommended for any course which includes contemporary poetry.

Para nombrar mis límites

Qué importa si anochece

Trémolo, poemas. Buenos Aires: La Mandrágora, 1960. Paperback, 73 pp. Izaguirre's first book contains twenty-nine poems preceded by a note of two errata and followed by an index. Illus. by both Federico Berghini and the author herself. Thirteen poems are sonnets. Besides love, death and time, the poems also deal with the frustration of writing, memories of childhood, adolescence and motherhood, disdain for an unimaginative male and a professor's endearment with her students. One poem is based on Unamuno's idealization of Don Quijote. Some poems displaying a fundamentally feminine perspective may be of interest in Women Studies' courses.

Las últimas cabalas

Yo soy el tiempo, cuentos. Buenos Aires: Guadalupe, 1973. Paperback, 99 pp. Winner of the 1970 municipal first prize for unpublished short stories, this collection with a prologue by María Granata comprises thirteen very concise narratives. Written mostly in first person, the stories present various unusual experiences of time as a simultaneous past and present. The seemingly fantastic gains credence through vivid descriptions of various psychological states. The book has an index; its title is also that of one of the stories. These brief and stimulating stories are recommended for any contemporary Latin American literature course -- including an intermediate reading class -- that would include Borges. SHA

IZCUA BARBAT DE MUÑOZ XIMENEZ, María del Carmen (Uruguay, twentieth century)

Alma, poesías

Atena de pájaros, poemas

Fábulas

Frutal, poesías

IZQUIERDO ALBIÑANA, Asunción (Mexico, twentieth century; pseudonyms: Fonsalba, Pablo María ; Sandoiz, Alba)

Andréida, el tercer sexo

Caos

La ciudad sobre el lago

La selva encantada

Taetzani, relato novelado de El Gran Nayar

J

JAMILIS, Amalia (Argentina, b. 1936)

    Detrás de las columnas, cuentos

    Los días sin suerte, cuentos

    Los trabajos nocturnos, cuentos

JARA, Marta (Chile, 1922-1972)

    La camarera, cuentos

    Surazo, cuentos

    El vaquero de dios, cuentos

JARAMILLO DE CASTRO, Margarita (Colombia, twentieth century; pseudonym: Perdomo, Susana)

    Campanas de pagoda

JARAMILLO GAITAN, Uva (Colombia, b. 1893)

    Hojas dispersas, cuentos

    Infierno en el alba

    Maldición, novela

JARAMILLO MEZA, Blanca Isaza de (see **ISAZA DE JARAMILLO MEZA, Blanca**)

JARQUE, Delia (Argentina, twentieth century)

    Susurros del alma, versos

JAUME, Adela (Cuba, twentieth century)

Dádiva

Génesis, versos 1937-1941

Mi muerte para tu amor, versos

Viaje a través de una emoción lírica, conferencia y poesía

JAUCH, Emma (Chile, b. 1915)

Los hermanos versos

Noticia de Papa-Nui, poemas

JAUREGUI, Emma Fernández de Lomelí (see **FERNANDEZ DE LOMELI JAUREGUI, Emma**)

JAUREGUI MONTES, Rosa (Guatemala, twentieth century)

Vida en azul, poemas

JESUS, sor Catalina de (see **CATALINA DE JESUS, sor**)

JESUS, Teresa de (Chile, twentieth century; pseudonym)

De repente / All of a sudden, bilingual edition, poetry

JIMENEZ, Auristela Castro de (see **CASTRO DE JIMENEZ, Auristela**)

JIMENEZ, Lucía Cock de Bernal (see **COCK DE BERNAL JIMENEZ, Lucía**)

JIMENEZ, Lylia C. Berthely (see **BERTHELY JIMENEZ, Lylia C.**)

JIMENEZ ARRILLAGA, Josefina Perezcano de (see **PEREZCANO DE JIMENEZ ARRILLAGA, Josefina**)

JODOROWSKY, Raquel (Chile, b. 1927)

Ajy Tojen, bilingual edition, poetry

Alguien llama, poesía

Alnico y Kemita, cantata del espacio

Aposento y época, poesía

La ciudad inclemente, poesía

Cuentos para cerebros detenidos: con licencia de los superiores

Dimensión de los días, poesía

En la pared de los sueños

Ensentidoinverso, poesía

JOFFRE DE RAMON, Sara (Peru, b. 1935). Joffré became involved in theatre in her teens. In 1963, she founded "Homero, Teatro de Grillos," theatre group for children, for which she wrote and directed close to fifty plays, which perhaps explains her abundance of unpublished manuscripts. Belonging to the third generation of Peruvian postwar dramatists, she writes simple and poetic verse on universal themes. Joffré dramatizes fantasy, social injustice and the human condition. Concerned with the development of national theatre, she is one of a handful of women playwrights to see her works published in Peru.

Cuento alrededor de un círculo de espuma, teatro

Embargo, teatro

En el jardín de Mónica, teatro

Teatro Peruano. Vol. II. 1st ed. Lima: Homero, Teatro de Grillos, 1978. 138 pp. A collection of eight Peruvian plays, half by Sara Joffré and the other four by César de María. Not available in United States libraries, obtainable by writing to Joffré at Pedro Peralta 221, Urbanización San Joaquín, Bellavista, Callao 2 Peru. The first of Joffré's works, "Pre-Texto," was performed in 1968 and treats isolation, violence and power. Clever plays on words and grammar in a conversation between three nameless characters. "Se administra justicia," later called "Embudo de la ley," and "Se consigue madera" were based on short news clips which appeared in the Lima press. Each poignantly show lower-class Peruvian life and offer commentary on the nepotism, corruption, discrimination and shortcomings of the Peruvian judicial system. Finally, "Los tocadores de tambor o parábola sobre el servilismo" is a delightful parody on truth and justice, innocence and guilt. As in her other plays in this collection, Joffré adeptly criticizes the society in which she lives. VB

Tríptico del Boom, teatro

JUANA INES DE LA CRUZ, sor (Mexico, 1648-1695; also Asbaje, Juana de). The main Mexican Baroque poet of her time, she not only used the conceptista and other contemporary modes, but also held an ideal of attaining clarity of knowledge. Her writings were her instrument for achieving this knowledge. She chose the only life that would permit her to be a scholar and an intellectual, that of a nun. In brilliant poems scattered among her many circumstantial works written for or in honor of particular persons or occasions, she expressed ideas which were often more apropos for a feminist scholar and writer of the twentieth century than for a religious one of the seventeenth. Her best-known works are her more personal poems expressing a conscious intellectual examination of human emotions. But like her alter ego, Icarus, in Primero sueño, her rise to fame ended in a swift fall to anonymity in her personal life. Fortunately, various works had already permanently consecrated her literary and intellectual reputation.

Amor es más laberinto, comedia

Antología. Ed. Elías L. Rivers. Salamanca: Anaya, 1965; 2nd ed. 1971. Twelve-page Introduction gives a succinct biographical resumé a brief analysis of her work and a one-page survey of her critics. Contains a three-page bibliography with one-page discussion of colonial editions and forty-six critical studies and a chronology of her life followed by her best known poems: four romances, her famous redondillas on men, one

villancico, thirteen sonnets, one lira, her long allegorical poem "El
Sueño," and "Respuesta a la Muy Ilustre Sor Filotea de la Cruz."
Annotations in large part are from the Méndez Plancarte's edition of her
works.

Autos sacramentales: El cetro de San José; El divino Narciso; San
Hermenegildo. México: Viuda de Calderón, 1690, 32 pp. The auto
converts Ovid's fable to an allegory of Christ as a heavenly Narcissus,
and also interprets in that light the institution of the Eucharist. The
poet uses various sources of both sacred and profane inspiration,
forming a literary collage of exceptional interpretations of Christ's
redemption of man, his death and resurrection and the final incarnation
in Corpus Christi.

Carta atenagórica (Respuesta a sor Filotea de la Cruz), religiosa profesa
de velo y coro en el muy religioso Convento de San Jerónimo de la
Ciudad de México, cabeza de la Nueva España. Puebla: Diego
Fernández de León, 1690. 46 pp. Bishop Manuel Fernández de
Santacruz y Sahagún of Puebla explains in an introductory letter,
written under the pseudonym of Sor Filotea de la Cruz, that he has
decided to assume the costs of publication of the prose piece by Sor
Juana. His analysis delineates the points made by her about a sermon
by the Portuguese Jesuit orator, Antonio de Vieyra, in a private
conversation. Sor Juana refutes Vieyra's negation of the view of the
most marvellous favors given by Christ, as taught in the writings of the
three church fathers: St. Augustine, Thomas of Aquinas and St.
Chrysostom. Not only does she criticize Vieyra's affrontery in denying
their consecrated interpretations, but she chastizes the Jesuit father for
his pride and arrogance. The Bishop praises the nun's intellectual
talent and urges her to cease writing on profane themes which are
dangerous to the soul.

Carta de sor Filotea de la Cruz; Respuesta a sor Filotea de la Cruz.
Notes by ed. Ermilo Abreu Gómez. México: La Voz Nueva, 1929. 47 pp.
2nd ed. : (México: Botas, 1934). After a three-month silence, Sor Juana
answers the Bishop's letter of introduction to her exegesis of the sermon
of Antonio de Vieyra. First she shows her desire to obey him and to
follow his orders, and then she defends her reasons for not having done
so previously. She presents her intellectual and poetic activities, in
essence, her life, for the Bishop's criticism and judgment. She tells the
story of her natural inclination toward study, admitting that it may be
sinful but that God gave her the overwhelming desire. She argues for
poetry and knowledge as a perfecting process and a way to gradually
reach union with God. But her talent has provoked the worry of friends
and the envy of her enemies. She ends vowing to submit anything she
writes to the Bishop, but she defends herself and all women in their
right to be educated so they can solve their societal dilemmas. Included
in the majority of the collections of her work.

Los empeños de una casa. Prologue by Julio Jiménez Rueda. Biblioteca
del Estudiante Universitario, 14. México: Universidad Autónoma,
1940. 190 pp. 2nd ed.: 1952, 194 pp. An eighteen-page prologue begins
with a brief biographical sketch, followed by a consideration of Sor
Juana's dramatic production and its probable Spanish sources. It is a
typical cape and dagger drama with a very complicated plot of
infatuated young people who form involved, convoluted triangles of
mistaken identity. It centers on a frivolous love involvement of Doña
Leonor, a young woman actually enamoured of knowledge. The
characters include Leonor's father, a gracioso disguised as a woman

whom for a short time a youth loves, one galán with whom Leonor is in love, and another who loves her in spite of her disdain. The title is a reminder of Calderón's Los empeños de un acaso. Sor Juana showed her command of the genre in this drama written for a celebration in honor of the new Archbishop of México, Francisco de Aguiar y Seijas.

Endechas. Ed. Xavier Villarrutia. México: Taller, 1940. 37 pp. Ten endechas, increased to fourteen by Méndez Plancarte in his Volume I, which Villarrutia collected from one of each of the three early volumes of Sor Juana's complete works. They are ordered chronologically, following Abreu Gómez' Bibliografía. Some occasional poems, but they are mainly on themes such as the loss or absence of a loved one. A final page of notes clarifies the editor's method and some historical allusions.

Fama y obras póstumas, tomo tercero, del fénix de México, y décima musa, poetisa de la América, sor Juana Inés de la Cruz. Ed. Juan Antonio Castorena y Ursúa. Madrid: Manuel Ruiz y Murga, 1700. 210 pp. Other editions: 2nd ed. (Barcelona: Rafael Figueró, 1701), 212 pp.; 3rd ed. (Lisboa: Miguel Deslandes, 1701), 212 pp.; 4th ed. (Madrid: Rodríguez y Escobar, 1714), 335 pp.; 5th ed. (Madrid: A. Pascual Rubio, 1725), 325 pp. This work, which forms Volume III of Sor Juana's works, was published posthumously. It contains her famous "Respuesta a la Muy Ilustre Sor Filotea de la Cruz," some romances and other lyric poems mainly on religious themes and in prose, and religious meditations and prayers. Included are various documents abjuring her previous profane interests, renewing her vows, confessing and rededicating herself to her religious vocation. Most of the latter were at the time of her abandonment of her literary pursuits to enter into the quest for perfect virtue, as her spiritual advisors had urged her to do. To be found here is her biography written by the Jesuit Father, Diego Calleja. There are several elegiac poems on her death.

Inundación castálida de la única poetisa, musa décima, soror Juana Inés de la Cruz . . . en varios metros, idiomas y estilos, fertiliza varios asuntos, con elegantes, sutiles, claros, ingeniosos, utiles versos. Ed. Juan Camacho Gayna. Madrid: Juan García Infanzón, 1689. 328 pp. Other editions: 2nd ed. re-edited, corrected and augmented by the author, with the title changed to Poemas de la única poetisa americana, musa décima (Madrid: Juan García Infanzón, 1690), 338 pp.; 3rd ed., title same as 2nd ed. (Barcelona: Joseph Llopis, 1691), 406 pp. (There are two other so-called 3rd eds. [Zaragoza: Manuel Román, 1692], 336 pp. and [Valencia: A. Bordazar, 1700], 351 pp.); 4th ed. (Madrid: Escobar, 1714), 334 pp.; 5th ed. (Madrid: Pascual Rubio, 1725), 374 pp. This first volume of the works of Sor Juana was collected, copied and sent to Spain by the author, assisted by her mentor and patron, the Condesa de Paredes, recently returned to Spain where she directed the publication. Juan Camacho Gayna was in charge of editing the edition, as well as most of the ones which followed, including the 3rd edition, to which Sor Juana added El Divino Narciso, both the loa and the auto sacramental. Some of her most engaging and authentic lyric poems in this work are on themes such as divine love, human love, loving friendships and various philosophical aspects of them. Sor Juana spoke out in her poetry against the moral double standard and she defended everyone's right to learn, both males and females. With Gongoristic, conceptista techniques she analyzed such ideas as carpe diem, vanitas vanitatum, desengaño, decepción, and time and its fleeing impermanence. Some of these rare colonial editions are to be found on film, positive and negative, at the Brown University Library, the

Library of Congress, the Biblioteca Nacional de Chile, the Hispanic
Society in New York and the Biblioteca Nacional of Madrid.

Liras

Neptuno alegórico, océano de colores, simulacro político, que erigió la
muy esclarecida, sacra y augusta iglesia metropolitana de México, en
las lucidas alegóricas ideas de un arco triunfal, que consagró obsequiosa
y dedicó amante a la feliz entrada del excelentísimo señor don Tomás
Antonio Lorenzo Manuel de la Cerda [. . .], conde de Paredes, marqués
de la Laguna [. . .]. México: Juan de Ribera en el Empedradillo, 1680.
Description in prose and verse, which Sor Juana was charged with
writing, of a triumphal arch in honor of the Marqués de la Laguna,
Conde de Paredes, new Viceroy, upon his taking office. Not of great
interest today, this piece nevertheless presents a clear idea of Sor
Juana's literary and mythological background and the authorities
whom she uses as sources. An exaggerated, hyperbolical, allegorical
presentation of the Count and of his wife.

Obras completas. Prologue by Francisco Monterde. México: Porrúa,
1969. 941 pp. 2nd ed.: 1972, 941 pp. This edition is an authorized
reproduction of four volumes in one of the Fondo de Cultura
Económica's Obras completas omitting completely all the critical
apparatus.

Obras completas, autos y loas. Biblioteca Americana. Serie de
Literatura Colonial, Vol. III. Prologue and notes by editor, Alfonso
Méndez Plancarte. México: Fondo de Cultura Económica, 1955. 736 +
xcviii pp. This volume contains Sor Juana's three religious autos as
well as her eighteen loas, three religious and fifteen non-religious.
Father Méndez Plancarte correctly judges that Sor Juana was equal to
Calderón in her autos. But it is obvious that the remainder, while they
show her talent as versifier, are constrained because of being written on
demand for specific occasions.

Obras completas, comedias, sainetes y prosa. Biblioteca Americana.
Serie de Literatura Colonial, Vol. IV. Prologue and notes by ed. Alberto
G. Salceda. México: Fondo de Cultura Económica, 1957. 720 + xlviii
pp. The last volume was prepared after the death of Alfonso Méndez
Plancarte by his collaborator on a small scale from the very beginning,
Alberto G. Salceda. It contains all the remainder of the literary works
of which the editor was aware, which was not all of them to be sure. It
contains her comedias and the short dramatic pieces which accompanied
them; almost certainly these complete her secular theater. Within the
final section of the volume is her entire extant production in prose.
While the volume is not on a par with the three prepared by the
ambitious former editor, its quality is nevertheless quite acceptable.

Obras completas, lírica personal. Biblioteca Americana. Serie de
Literatura Colonial, Vol. I. Prologue and notes by editor, Alfonso
Méndez Plancarte. México: Fondo de Cultura Económica, 1951. 638 +
lxviii pp. Although several of various individual works and collections
of selected works appeared in the nineteenth and twentieth centuries, it
was not until this volume and the succeeding three were published by
the Fondo de Cultura Económica that Sor Juana's work became almost
completely accessible, arranged in sections by metrical categories with
chronological, thematic subdivisions, and with the added feature of
having sound scholarly information. Ample notes accompany the text of
this and the other three volumes and they are usually divided into

textual, bibliographical and illustrative notes. In the section of
Illustrative Notes a prose version of Primero sueño is given. The prose
version also appears in Méndez Plancarte's 1951 edition of the work.
(See El sueño.)

Obras completas, villancicos y letras sacras. Biblioteca Americana.
Serie de Literatura Colonial. Vol. II. Prologue and notes by editor
Alfonso Méndez Plancarte. México: Fondo de Cultura Económica, 1952.
550 + lxxxviii pp. The editor projected this volume as a collection of the
works which he classified as "Lírica Colectiva." But in the prologue to
Vol. II, Méndez Plancarte admits that these poems, although choral and
collective poetry, are nevertheless just as sincere and personal as that in
Volume I, but in a different manner. While many of these poems were
written on request, there is a considerable amount of originality. These
also prove to Méndez Plancarte's satisfaction that quite a bit of Sor
Juana's poetry was on religious themes. However, at least half of the
volume is composed of religious carols and songs that the editor
attributes to her, without absolute proof that she wrote them.

Obras escogidas. Ed. Pedro Henríquez Ureña. Colección Austral, 13.
Buenos Aires, México: Espasa-Calpe, [1938]. 177 pp. Other editions:
2nd ed. [1939], 187 pp.; 3rd ed. [1941], 187 pp.; 4th and 5th eds. [1943],
184 pp.; 6th ed. [1944], 184 pp.; 7th ed. [1946], 184 pp. The anonymous
prologue was authored by one of the most preeminent critics among
those who at the time were interested in a revival of Sor Juana and her
works. It points out the need for partial editions like this one as well as
critical ones. Various editions followed with the same content. In the
seventh edition the editor who prepared the work was named, Pedro
Henríquez Ureña, along with his collaborator, Patricio Canto.

Obras selectas. Prologue, Selection and Notes by Georgina Sabat de
Rivers and Elías L. Rivers. Barcelona: Noguer, 1976. 812 pp. Excellent
and informative study of Sor Juana's work precedes a collection of all
the lyric poetry, "Carta Atenagórica," "Carta de Sor Filotea de la Cruz,"
and "Respuesta," a selection of villancicos, El divino narciso, Los
empeños de una casa and Sueño with a more logical division into
stanzas, which are in turn grouped into three main sections. A
perceptive modern prose version follows with a one-page thematic
outline of the contents. Although the editors use Méndez Plancarte's
prose version as a source, theirs is lucid, clarifying some previously
obscure meanings. Good explanatory notes are given for the lyric
poetry, both for historical references and for some vocabulary and
usage. While the one-page preface admits their debt to Alfonso Méndez
Plancarte, it states that they had to make corrections. Their thirty-
page study of her life and works contains a penetrating four-part
analysis of Sor Juana's Villancicos, Teatro religioso, Teatro profano,
and Poesía lírica which deftly characterizes the fundamental opposition
in her lyric poetry of the spiritual and the material, the problem of
knowledge in El sueño, her personal, ironical use of the comedia de capa
y espada and her revelation in "Respuesta" of the tragedy of an
intellectual woman imprisoned by the culture of her epoch.

Obras selectas de la célebre monja de México, sor Juana Inés de la Cruz.
Ed. Juan León Mera. Quito: Nacional, 1873. 402 + lxxxvi pp. The
edition was tastefully and perceptively done. The prologue by Juan
León Mera indicates the renewed modern interest in Sor Juana. His
remarks are biographical and critical and he considers her complete
production.

Páginas escogidas

The Pathless Grove, A Collection of Seventeenth Century Mexican Sonnets of Sor Juana Inés de la Cruz, translation.

Poemas de la única americana musa décima. (See annotation under Inundación castálida. . . .)

Poesías completas. "Advertencia" by ed. Ermilo Abreu Gómez. México: Botas, 1941. 538 pp. 2nd ed.: 1948, 538 pp. One-page preface by editor explains his use as main source of the editions of the three volumes of her work published in Madrid, Valencia, Zaragoza and Barcelona, 1689-1725. Adds to the collection from those volumes the poems inserted in her non-poetic works. Includes a small number of her villancicos and seven letras profanas as well. Index is alphabetical, listing first lines and section titles. Admirable effort but quite incomplete compared to the poetry in Méndez Plancarte's imposing edition of her works.

Poesías (selectas). Prologue and Notes by ed. Ermilo Abreu Gómez. México: Botas, 1940. 300 pp. Although Abreu Gómez was sometimes considered to produce slipshod work, he nevertheless was a major figure in the stimulation of interest which culminated in the edition of Alfonso Méndez Plancarte, a work unsurpassed until the present time. To the credit of Abreu Gómez are this work and his competent bibliographical production on Sor Juana and the first modern editions of Primero Sueño, "Carta atenagórica," and the "Respuesta a sor Filotea de la Cruz."

"Primero sueño" in Obras completas, vol. II. (See prose version under El sueño.) A hermetic but exceedingly original and profound exploration of epistomology, accepted recently by some as her main work. It is a 975-verse poem in silva form which presents an allegorical confrontation of one of Sor Juana's main concerns, the search for knowledge. Phaeton and Icarus are symbols for the human intellect and their failure illustrates the futility of the individual's daring attempt to achieve an intellectual understanding of reality. Failure and punishment come from excessive faith in the self and from the narcissistic effort to succeed intellectually. Nevertheless, the effort is not in vain since humans develop compensating virtues through courage and persistence in the quest.

Prosas selectas de la célebre monja de México. Precedidas de su biografía y juicio crítico sobre todas sus producciones. Ed. Juan León Mera. Quito: Nacional, 1873. 402 + lxxxvi pp. Edition tastefully but subjectively done with the basis of selection that of the author's opinion of the most beautiful poems or fragments of poems. A complete rearrangement of their order to coincide with his own poetic aesthetic. As Méndez Plancarte points out, Mera's edition takes various other liberties with her poems, such as classifying as a silva one of her ovillejos. Also included are "Los empeños de una casa," "Carta atenagórica," and "Respuesta," plus the letter from Sor Filotea (pseudonym of the Archbishop Manuel Fernández de la Cruz y Sahagún), whose identity was unknown to Mera.

Segundo volumen de las obras de sor Juana Inés de la Cruz. Ed. Juan de Orve y Arbieto. Sevilla: Tomás López de Haro, 1692. 542 pp. Other editions: 2nd ed. title changed to Segundo tomo de las obras de sor Juana Inés de la Cruz (Barcelona: Joseph Llopis, 1693), 467 pp.; 3rd ed. (Madrid: Real, Joseph Rodríguez de Escobar, 1715); 4th ed. (Madrid:

Angel Pascual Rubio, 1725), 438 pp. Available in New York Public and Brown Univ. libraries. This volume, like the first, was collected and prepared by Sor Juana. In the dedication Sor Juana defends her intellectual being, explains the disadvantages of her sex, her lack of formal education, her inordinate love of knowledge and the difficulties she faced because of it. At least one-third of the work contains approving articles, critical panegyrics, and compositions both in prose and verse lauding and defending Sor Juana for some of the things for which she was censured by her colleagues, religious advisors, censors and confessors. This is the most important volume of the first edition of her works, containing her most remarkable production. The "Carta Atenagórica," the long poetic work, "Primero sueño," her three <u>autos</u> <u>sacramentales</u>, two comedias and short dramatic pieces, plus <u>El mártir</u> <u>del Sacramento</u>, <u>San Hermenegildo</u>, and several lyric <u>villancicos</u> are included.

<u>Sainetes</u>

<u>Sonetos</u>. Notes by ed. Xavier Villarrutia. Colección de Clásicos Agotados, 2. México: La Razón, 1931. 173 pp. Collection of sixty-five sonnets is introduced by a one-page indication by Villarrutia of his sources for the poems, which he has arranged according to themes. His main source was <u>Inundación castálida</u>, but he also collated with three editions each of the colonial Volumes I, II and III. Variant readings of fifteen of the sonnets are given very briefly in his notes. Four which were attributed to her but never published in her books are included. An appendix lists the order of appearance of the sonnets in the original works.

<u>Sonetos y endechas</u>. Notes and Prologue by ed. Xavier Villarrutia. México: Nueva Cultura, 1941. 153 pp. 2nd ed.: prepared by Manuel Arellano Z. and Felipe Remolina Roqueñi (México: Libros, 1976), 167 pp. Sixty-three sonnets grouped in thematic order and with both spelling and punctuation modernized. The distinguished editor chose what he believed to be the best variants as he collated several of the editions of the first three volumes. Four additional sonnets attributed to her accompany the others. The ten <u>endechas</u> also were prepared just as carefully but are presented in chronological order. The major part of the poems are those of intimate tone and on intellectual, philosophical and amorous themes. Among the sonnets are some of her most famous poems.

<u>Sor Juana Inés de la Cruz, Poems</u>, a bilingual anthology. Tr. Margaret Sayers Peden. Binghamton, N.Y.: Bilingual Press / Editorial Bilingüe, 1985?

<u>El sueño</u>. Prose version, introduction and notes by editor, Alfonso Méndez Plancarte. Textos de Literatura Mexicana. México: Imprenta Universitaria, 1951. lxxxiv + 126 pp. (See annotation under "Primero sueño.")

<u>Villancicos</u>

<u>A Woman of Genius, The Intellectual Autobiography of Sor Juana Inés</u> <u>de la Cruz</u>. Tr. and Introd. by Margaret Sayers Peden. Salisbury, Ct.: Lime Rock, 1982. Bilingual. ISBN 0-915998-15-7 and 0-915998-14-9, 105 pp. BTO

JUANACHA (pseudonym: see **CALLER IBERICO, Clorinda**)

JURADO, Alicia (Argentina, twentieth century)

La cárcel y los hierros, novela

En soledad vivía, novela

Lenguas de polvo y sueño, relatos

Los rastros del engaño, cuentos

K

KAHN, Asela Gutiérrez (see **GUTIERREZ KAHN, Asela**)

KAMENSZAIN, Tamara (Argentina, b. 1947). Simultaneously critic and prose poet, Kamenszain is as freely irrational as an imaginative writer but shows the theoretic concerns of contemporary criticism (deconstruction, the esthetics of silence, de-centered writing). She resembles French-language feminist theorists of literary language (e.g., Hélène Cixous) in her efforts to evade the internal censor and write unconstrainedly of the indecorous and the irrational.

De este lado del Mediterráneo. Buenos Aires: Noé, 1973. 79 pp. These fragmentary prose pieces show a strong interest in creating alternatives to the dominant model of writing, a model that is essentially European (hence the title), male and rational linear. Irrational and mythic discourse is preferred in order to move toward a literary language for those outside the dominant structures: Third World persons, women, others with an outsider perspective.

Los no. Buenos Aires: Sudamericana, 1977. 67 pp. The artistic structuring of silence, a characteristic preoccupation of contemporary innovators, is explored in this book composed equally of blank and print-bearing pages. Kamenszain seeks a form of writing that will demand of the reader a maximum effort of involvement to make a coherent and readable text out of her provocative fragments. She works with the themes of saying and not saying, repression of language and its possibilities of liberation. NL

KATZ, Elsa (Ecuador, twentieth century)

Eran dos hermanos

La vida en escena, drama

KNEER, Luisa (Chile, twentieth century)

Andando Patita

Cuando los ángeles crecen

De los Andes a los Epeninos

Poesía del Norte Verde

Por los caminos de los sueños

Sed infinito

La serena y el Valle de Elqui

Sonetos en mis recuerdos inolvidables

Upita Papito

KOCIANCICH, Vlady (Argentina, b. 1941)

Coraje, cuentos

La octava maravilla, novela

KRAPKIN, Ilka (Argentina, twentieth century)

La batalla, poema épico

El buey blanco; El dique, cuentos

Gudruna Trogstad, capitana

El hombre que perdío el sueño, novela

La taza de chocolate, cuentos

Tres cantatas al mar

Las tres manos, un poema para ballet

L

LABARCA HUBERTSON, Amanda (Chile, 188?-194?). In her own words
Labarca's two greatest life goals were pedagogy and feminism. As the first
woman catedrática of her country, she combines both. As delegate to
innumerable feminist conferences during the twenties, thirties and forties,
she chronicles Chilean and Latin American feminism in contrast to her
Nordic and/or North American sisters, which she has the tendency to
idealize. Her careful eye can frequently put the finger on the specific problem
in Latin America, a socialization process which she herself does not entirely
escape. Her feminist essays are particularly interesting as are some of her
short stories. González Vera, who wrote the introduction of her Desvelos en
el alba, says of her: "She writes for newspapers, directs women of the radical
party, does the script of a movie, uses the telephone as if it were her own
invention, and sewing is not unknown to her."

¿Adónde va la mujer?, ensayos. Santiago de Chile: Letras, 1934.
266 pp. Collection of approximately twenty-five essays dealing with
Chilean feminism in the earlier part of the century. Although there is
some naiveté and exaggeration as to the freedom of American and
Scandinavian women, as well as some concessions to the Latin male, the
series of essays is useful from a historical perspective. Recommended
for its documentation, insights into feminist literary criticism and the
problems and advances for Latin American feminism from the point of
view of the first woman catedrática of Chile.

Actividades femeninas en los Estados Unidos. Santiago de Chile:
Universitaria, 1914, 178 pp. Also available in History of Women
microfilm series.

Al amor de la tierra

Desvelos en el alba, ensayos. Santiago de Chile: Cruz del Sur, 1945.
131 pp. Series of short essays supposedly written in the wee hours of
Labarca's insomnia during the twenties and thirties. Unlike some of
her later feminist writings, she still laments the fate of "ugly women"
who are past their youthful prime. More interesting than the actual
essays is the biographical introduction by José Santos González Vera
which is rich in details of the life of the indefatigable Labarca
Hubertson.

En tierras extrañas, novela. Santiago de Chile: Universitaria, 1915. 329 pp. The Library of Congress owns the only copy available of this book and is unwilling to lend it for review because of the brittle condition of the pages of this 1915 edition.

Feminismo contemporáneo, ensayos. Santiago de Chile: Zig-Zag, 1947. 242 pp. Collection of essays written immediately following the Second World War which focuses on the role of women in various nations. Would be of interest primarily to the historian interested in documenting the history of Latin American feminism. There are some short biographies of outstanding Chilean women and her minutes of International Congresses on Women show great enthusiasm. She has lost some of the naiveté which characterizes ¿A dónde va la mujer? and can and does focus on major feminist issues.

Impresiones de juventud

La lámpara maravillosa, cuentos. Santiago de Chile: Minerva, 1921. 187 pp. Collection of short stories written in the first quarter of this century, reflecting the trials and tribulations of the upper classes without money and the dreams and fantasies of adolescents, but especially focuses on girls. Some of the stories reveal Labarca's pedagogical background, and certain ones would be excellent for use in the classroom as they are short and fairly easy to understand. Recommended especially are "La lámpara maravillosa" and "Los cuatro." NSS

Lecturas de Juan y Juanita. Serie destinada a la enseñanza del idioma materno en los cursos primarios

La sombra inquieta, cuentos

LA BARRA, Emma de (see **BARRA, Emma de la**)

LACAU, María Hortensia Palisa Mujica de (see **PALISA MUJICA DE LACAU, María Hortensia**)

LADRON DE GUEVARA, Matilde (Chile, b. 1908)

Adiós al cañaveral

Amarras de luz, poesía

Celda 13 (trece), novela

Che, poesía

Desnudo, sonetos

En Isla de Pascua "Los Moai están de pie," novela

Madre soltera, novela

Muchachos de siempre, novela

Pórtico de Iberia, poesía

Testamento de Matilde Ladrón de Guevara, prosa y poesía

LAFARJA DE CRUZ, María de la Luz (Mexico, b. 1902; pseudonym: Melduí, Lázara)

Nacu-Xanat, novela

LAFAURIE, Juana Sánchez (see **SANCHEZ LAFAURIE, Juana**)

LAGO DE FIRPO, Sylvia (Uruguay, b. 1932)

Detrás del rojo, cuentos

Las flores conjuradas

Tan solos en el balneario

Trajano, novela

La última razón

LAGOS, Aída Morena (see **MORENA LAGOS, Aída**)

LAGOS GARAY, Yolanda (Chile, twentieth century)

Preludio para las sombras

LAHITTE, Ana Emilia (Argentina, b. 1930)

La alcoba sin puertas, teatro

Madero y transparencias, poemas

El muro de cristal, poemas

La noche y otros poemas

Raíces desnudas

Sueño sin eco, poemas

LAIR, Clara (pseudonym: see **NEGRON MUÑOZ, Mercedes**)

LAMARCHE, Martha María (Dominican Republic, twentieth century)

Cauce hondo

Retozos de luz, poemas

LAMAS DE SAENZ, María Luisa (Uruguay, twentieth century; pseudonym: Alondra)

Pitangas y Sina-Sina, versos

Sinfonía en rosa y azul, poemas

Voz y silencio, con Raquel Sáenz

LANDAZURI, Isabel A. Prieto de (see **PRIETO DE LANDAZURI, Isabel A.**)

LANDIVAR, Zoila Ugarte de (see **UGARTE DE LANDIVAR, Zoila**)

LANDRON, Iris (Puerto Rico, b. 1940). Landrón is a poet who also writes feature articles for the Puerto Rican daily newspaper, El Nuevo Día. Her poetic voice alternates violent and lyrical images dealing with the pain of self discovery, the limits of emotional endurance, and the search for communion with others. Her poet's sensitivity makes her a perfect listener, while her apparent fragility masks her resemblance to the resistant Puerto Rican tree, the ausubo.

Cucubanos, poesía. Río Piedras, Puerto Rico: Cultural, 1983. ISBN: 84-499-6659-0, 116 pp. Cucubanos, or "fireflies," contains over one hundred poetic flashes, haiku-like in nature, loving bullets that always hit the mark. Landrón has also created the whimsical pen and ink drawings that accompany the cucubanos; boats, flowers, fish, shells, trees, birds and the famous coquí, the typically Puerto Rican diminutive frog with its distinctive sound, an echo of its own name. These deceptively simple verses include plays on words and Zen-like reminders to live in the here and now, while they offer the reader profound messages.

Víspera y día, poesía. San Juan de Puerto Rico: Instituto de Cultura Puertorriqueña, 1977. 95 pp. In this representative volume, Landrón refers to language, to the word in poetry, and to the difficulty of capturing its magic and authenticity. The word is a corner where "sun and saliva, verse and sweat, pain and silence meet." In her poem "Moments," written in the tradition of César Vallejo and the Neruda of the Spanish Civil War poems, she catalogs life's blows and stoically suggests that these losses often lead its victims to unexpected gains in maturity and personal growth. She also documents, in "The Search," the quest for communion and oneness we feel as "We search for an endless aurora to confirm us, a single word to explain what we are and an ample horizon where, though still different, we become one." GFW

LANGE, Norah (Argentina, b. 1906). Born in Argentina and of Norwegian descent, Lange published her first volume of poetry, La calle de la tarde (preface by Jorge Luis Borges) at the age of fifteen. Active in the Buenos Aires literary scene of the 1920's and 1930's, Lange contributed to avant-garde journals like Revista Mural, Martin Fierro and Proa. Married to the ultraist poet Oliverio Girondo, her home became a center of Argentinean avant-garde activity. Received city's literary prize in 1937 for Cuadernos de Infancia.

Antes que mueran, novela. Buenos Aires: Losada, 1944. Paperback, 205 pp. In this short novel the inner world of the narrator is evoked through the objects that make up her external existence. Portraying inner confusion and fear through fantasy, Lange skillfully enriches the confessional tone which dominates the bulk of her work.

La calle de la tarde, poemas

Cuadernos de infancia, novela. Buenos Aires: Losada, 1957. Paperback, 178 pp. The fanciful world of childhood and adolescence is evoked in this confessional narrative. The novel is built around episodes of the narrator's early life in Mendoza and her subsequent move to Buenos Aires, where the family is confronted with sudden death and economic distress. The story comes to life through the eyes of the young narrator interacting with her sisters, parent, and British governess. The sparse, imagistic prose skillfully depicts the inner changes undergone by the narrator as she gradually comes to terms with adulthood. Of interest to scholars.

45 (Cuarenta y cinco) días y 30 (treinta) marineros, novela. Buenos Aires: Tor, 1933. Paperback, 187 pp. This short novel tells the story of a determined young woman who is the sole female passenger on a ship bound from Argentina to Norway. In this humorous and essentially anecdotal work, Lange subtly critiques the traditional roles assigned to women.

Los días y las noches, verso

Los dos retratos, novela. Buenos Aires: Losada, 1956. Paperback, 196 pp. Here Lange explores the mysteries of memory by telling the story of two older women who attempt to reconstruct their past through an old family portrait. In simple, sometimes lyrical language, and through an intermingling of the characters' evocations and detailed descriptions of rooms, Lange explores the intricacies of consciousness.

Estimados congéneres

Páginas escogidas de Norah Lange

Palabras con Norah Lange

Personas en la sala, novela. Buenos Aires: Sudamericana, 1950. Paperback, 214 pp. This novel revolves around the impressions and recollections of an adolescent girl striving to probe into the inner secrets of the adults that surround her. Permeated with subjectivism, the narrative focuses primarily on the protagonists' fears and aspirations. To a greater degree than in other works, the external world becomes an insignificant frame of reference.

El rumbo de la rosa, poemas. Buenos Aires: Proa, 1930. Paperback, 103 pp. Short, lyrical poems which sing of love's agonies, the loss of a beloved one and the incapacity to resign oneself to solitude. Written in free verse, with an imagistic touch. IR

Voz de la vida

LARDE DE VENTURINO, Alice (Argentina, b. 1915)

Alma viril, poemas

Belleza salvaje, poesía

El nuevo mundo polar, poesía

Pétalos del alma, poemas

Sangre del trópico, ensayo

LARIS RUBIO, Sara Iturbide de (see ITURBIDE DE LARIS RUBIO, Sara)

LARRAIN, Inés Echevarría de (see ECHEVARRIA DE LARRAIN, Inés)

LARRIVA, Enriqueta Arvelo (see **ARVELO LARRIVA, Enriqueta**)

LARS, Claudia (pseudonym: see **BRANNON DE SAMAYOA, Carmen**)

LASCARRO MENDOZA, Elvira (Colombia, 1930-1950)

Poemas selectos

Roble y clavel, poemas

LASTARRIA CABRERO, Berta (Chile, 1883-1945)

Cuadros de Oriente, viñetas

Cuentos del nano

Escaramuzas mundanas, cuentos

Historia del árbol viejo, cuentos

Lo que cuentan las hojas, cuentos

Lo que cuentan las nubes, cuentos

Lo que cuentan las olas, cuentos

LA TORRE, Josefina Muriel de (Mexico, twentieth century)

Los recogimientos de mujeres, ensayo

Versos y estampas

LATORRE, Marina (Chile, b. 1935)

Fauna austral, poesía

Galería clausurada, cuentos

El monumento, cuento

El regalo, cuentos

Soy una mujer, testimonio

LAURA, Victoria (pseudonym: see **PEÑUELA DE SEGURA, Gertrudis**)

LAZO, Loreley (Uruguay, twentieth century)

Bajo la piel, poemas

LEAL, Paloma Castro (see **CASTRO LEAL, Paloma**)

LEAL DE NOGUERA, María (Costa Rica, b. 1890). Writer and former educator. Like Carmen Lyra, she is guardian and weaver of popular folk stories, meant for children. Rich in imagination, her stories, like much children's folk literature, are moral, humorous and magical. In Leal's work, the outstanding characteristic is the representation of the customs, language and ideals of Guanacaste, her native province of Costa Rica.

Cuentos viejos. San José, Costa Rica: Costa Rica, 1978. 168 pp. Cuentos viejos is a collection of folk stories and legends that have survived through generations from remote corners of the world. Here, however, they have taken the fresh form of the culture and language of the hot, guanacastecan (northwest Costa Rican) savannas. Picaresque Tío Conejo is the most well-known character, a character in the tradition of Uncle Remus. The stories are told simply, as a mother and teacher would tell them. AS

LEBRON, Lolita (Puerto Rico, b. 1919). Lebrón is a living symbol. She has spent twenty-five years in the Women's Penitentiary in Alderson, West Virginia, for leading and participating in a desperate act of national affirmation, the attack against the House of Representatives in 1954. Her charisma, at once mystical and political, is communicated through her poetry, collected in the volume Sándalo en la celda. She writes passionately and frankly about her sister inmates, her loneliness, her homeland, and her deep religious faith. Since her release from prison in 1979, she has resided in Puerto Rico.

Sándalo en la celda, poesía. Cataño, Puerto Rico: Betances, 1974. 209 pp. Available from the author, Cooperative Ciudad Universitaria, Edificio A, Apt. 309, Trujillo Alto, Puerto Rico 00760; or Dr. Gloria F. Waldman, 315 Ave. C, New York, New York 10009. Lebrón's poetry reflects the traditional Latin American fusion of patria and religion, not unlike Joan of Arc, to whom the poet, Francisco Matos Paoli compares Lolita in his Introduction to Sándalo en la celda. Just as the women's movement speaks of women giving birth to ourselves, so Lolita speaks of "Puerto Rico giving birth to itself, with the tenderness of a mother, with the courage of a soldier." In the poem "The Unwritable Book," she evokes the solitude all women share, and which was intensified by her singular role as a political prisoner serving one of the longest terms in the continent. Until she writes her own autobiography, her poetry is the only vehicle we have to experience her personal joys, triumphs, and struggles as well as her doubts, conflicts, and sorrows in the historical context of her country's struggle for independence. GFW

LECAROS, Helena Aramburú (see **ARAMBURU LECAROS, Helena**)

LEDON, Amalia de Castillo (see **CASTILLO LEDON, Amalia de**)

LEIGHTON, Marcela (Chile, twentieth century)

  Vendimia en diciembre

LEON, Esmeralda Zenteno de (see **ZENTENO DE LEON, Esmeralda**)

LEON, Margarita de (Uruguay, twentieth century)

  ¡Mar . . . !, poesías

LEON, Ramona María Cordero y (see **CORDERO Y LEON, Ramona María**)

LEON, Rosario Rexach de (see **REXACH DE LEON, Rosario**)

LEON, Ulalume González de (see **GONZALEZ DE LEON, Ulalume**)

LEON DE BOGGIO, Consuelo Amat y (see **AMAT Y LEON DE BOGGIO, Consuelo**)

LE QUESNE, María Antonieta (Chile, 1895-1921)

Recodo azul, poemas

LERGIER, Clara Luz S. de (see **S. DE LERGIER, Clara Luz**)

LERNER, Elisa (Venezuela, b. ca. 1934). Lerner is probably the only published, female, Jewish, Venezuelan playwright in history. By training and profession, she is an attorney who from an early age felt the stirrings of a writer. Without exception, her plays are about unmarried women, who, despite success in their professional lives, feel emotionally unfulfilled. They suffer from feelings of loneliness and alienation and define themselves by the absence of men in their lives. She has also published two collections of essays.

Carriel número cinco (Un homenaje al costumbrismo). El Libro Menor. Caracas: Academia Nacional de la Historia, 1983. 156 pp. A variety of monologues, dialogue, and remembrances, the book is composed of the following sections: "Las voces de costumbre" (six monologues), "Solitario" (cassette), "Entre viejas y nuevas costumbres" (three fantasies), "Carriel número 5" (three dialogues), "Carriel sanjuanero" (eight memories of infancy). These short works contain Lerner's favorite topics: womanhood (single, and, here, married); her mother; the changing face of Caracas; Hollywood movie stars, obese women, and in this book some comments on Jewish women.

"Conversaciones de café en torno a la envidia . . . o casi." In Los siete pecados capitales. Caracas: Monte Avila, 1974. 131 pp. Each of seven Venezuelan dramatists wrote a one-act play on a mortal sin: Lerner's is on that of envy. The play is different from most of her others in that there is a male character in it. According to Mujer, envy is the only original contribution that womankind has made to the world. Like the other female characters in Lerner's plays, she suffers from feelings of loneliness and helplessness; she also suffers from jealousy. An additional theme is that of nostalgia, as in Vida con mamá.

Crónicas ginecológicas

En el vasto silencio de Manhattan. In Carlos Miguel Suárez Radillo, ed., 13 (Trece) autores del nuevo teatro venezolano. Caracas: Monte Avila, 1971. 537 pp. A play in twelve scenes, included in a book which contains one play each by thirteen Venezuelan playwrights who belong to the movement known as the "Nuevo Teatro." The 1964 play treats the theme of the loneliness and alienation of an unmarried woman working in New York City. It incorporates Lerner's most sophisticated dramatic techniques and won top honors in the Concurso del Ateneo de Caracas. It is preceded by a brief biographical sketch of the playwright and a few bibliografical references.

Una sonrisa detrás de la metáfora, crónicas

"Vida con mamá," "Una entrevista de prensa o la Bella de inteligencia," "El país odontológico," "La mujer del periódico de la tarde." Caracas: Monte Avila, 1976. 103 pp. "Vida con mamá" is a play in two acts and with two characters, Madre and Hija. It consists of conversations between mother and daughter on the subjects of change and the passing of time, and on the perceived need of the daughter to find a husband in order to give meaning to her life. The larger issue is the search for happiness in the future: In that search, time is the culprit; woman is the victim. The play won the Premio del Consejo Municipal del Distrito Federal al "Nuevo Grupo" the first time that the prize was awarded. It was the most successful Venezuelan play of 1975. The same volume contains three one-scene plays. All of these demonstrate preoccupations with loneliness, womanhood, sex, as well as the subject of authors. DK

LESQUERRE, Lola Tapia de (see **TAPIA DE LESQUERRE, Lola**)

LEVINSON, Luisa Mercedes (Argentina, b. 1912). Worked as a newspaper reporter. Writes mostly short stories. Themes: people vs. the land, fantasy, human relations. Her approach sometimes resembles the style of Jorge Luis Borges, with whom she collaborated on at least one occasion. She is regarded as a serious writer in that she has broken away from the traditional role of the Argentine woman writer, by transcending her own intimate experiences and projecting them into the world of ideas.

A la sombra del buho, novela. Buenos Aires: Losada, 1972. Paperback, available only in libraries. Novel set in three stages, each identified by a different time period: the 1800's, 1970's and the 1980's. Common theme in all three is the search for a hero, who in each case symbolizes the values and the ideas prevailing in his time.

La casa de los Felipes, novela

Concierto en mí. Santa Fe, Argentina: Castellví, 1956. Paperback, available in libraries. Tone is pedantic and affected, typical of the Argentine rich. Contrast between their behavior in Buenos Aires and the force of their passions when they are face to face with nature. Characters are superficial and not fully developed.

El estigma del tiempo, cuentos. Barcelona: Seix Barral, 1977. Paperback, available in libraries. Short stories, including some from previous collections. Of excellent quality, enigmatic, intellectual, to be read and savored more than once. There is fantasy, violence, and myth: "El laberinto del tiempo," "La familia de Adam Schlager," "La muchacha de los guantes," "El mito," "La isla," "Con pasión," "Miedo a Valparaíso," "El chico que vio las lágrimas de Dios," "El pesador del tiempo," "El castillo," "El pintor," "Mas allá del Gran Cañón," "Los dos hermanos," "La isleta," "La telaraña de los lunas."

La hermana de Eloísa. Buenos Aires: E.N.E., 1955. 71 pp. Available only in libraries. Four short stories, two by Jorge Luis Borges -- "La escritura de Dios" and "El fin" -- and two by Levinson: "El doctor Sotiropoulos" and "El abra," a brilliant tour de force regarded as her best work. A fifth story, "La hermana de Eloísa," was written by both Jorge Luis Borges and Luisa Mercedes Levinson, and provides the title for the collection. A work of high caliber, mixture of the grotesque, the fantastic, and the real.

La isla de los organilleros, novela. Buenos Aires: Losada, 1964. Paperback, 151 pp. Available only in libraries. Short stories ranging from the real to the grotesque, the sensuous to the fantastic or exotic. Of interest to students of the short story because of their novel approach and the powerful imagination displayed by their sophisticated author. A wide range of subjects with no common theme.

La pálida rosa de Soho, cuentos. Buenos Aires: Claridad, 1959. Paperback, 136 pp. Available in libraries only. Collection of short stories: "La pálida rosa del Soho," "Del 33 al 24," "El abra," "Los dos hermanos," "En la otra orilla," "La isla," "La niña Panchita," "La familia de Adam Schlager," "En un cuaderno cuadriculado," "La represa," "Remanente," "El muchacho," "Una pareja singular," "Entre el bosque y el mar," "El minuet," "Los otros zapatos," "El sueño violado," and "El ángel." A series of very ingenuous stories covering a wide range of subjects and situations. Most outstanding of all is "El abra."

Las tejedoras sin hombre, cuentos. Buenos Aires: Losada, 1967. Paperback, 123 pp. Available only in libraries. Short stories which show a possible influence from Borges. The author displays a powerful imagination, touching the immediate reality, the fantastic, the nightmarish, the force of Latin American landscapes, and the refined versus the brutal.

Tiempo de Federica; Julio Riestra ha muerto, teatro. Buenos Aires: Nueva Visión, 1963. Paperback, 90 pp. Available only in libraries. Two dramas in one volume. Levinson's first attempt to write drama. "Tiempo," based on her 1959 story "Los dos hermanos," takes place in a semi-jungle atmosphere. It is the tale of two German landowners, brother and sister. "Julio" is set in the Argentine pampas and is a tale of passion. Of interest as a different facet of Levinson's work. Were not performed on the stage. AT

LEWIS, Carmen Pilar Fernández de (see **FERNANDEZ DE LEWIS, Carmen Pilar**)

LEZAETA, Gabriela (Chile, b. 1927)

Color Hollín, novela

Incendiaron la escuela, novela

Quién es quién, autoretrato

LIARTE, Gioconda Céspedes (see **CESPEDES LIARTE, Gioconda**)

LICELOTT DELGADO, Edna (Puerto Rico, twentieth century)

Y cuando digo todos, poema

LIMA DE CASTILLO, Polita de (Venezuela, nineteenth century)

Anatolia, comedia

Atomas, poemas

Sueños rítmicos, poemas

Ladrón de sal

LLACH, Leonor (Mexico, twentieth century)

Cuadros conocidos, cuentos

Retratos de almas, cuentos

LLANA, María Elena (Cuba, b. 1936)

La reja

LLANA BARRIOS, María Esther (Uruguay, twentieth century)

Cielo en el agua, poemas

La montaña horizontal

Rondas de muerte y vida

Tierra y sol

LLARENA, Elsa de (Mexico, twentieth century)

Ayotzin, cuentos para ninos

Catorce mujeres escriben cuentos, cuentos de varias autoras.   (See
annotation in the List of Anthologies.)

Cuentos cortos

Durero, maestro grabador

Prosas

LLEONART, Yolanda (Cuba, twentieth century)

Los duendes de cristal, poemas

Hora-luz, poemas

Rondas escolares para los grandes primarios, con Andrés de Piedra-
Bueno

Rueda-Rueda, poemas

LLERAS RESTREPO, Isabel (Colombia, twentieth century)

Sonetos

LLONA, María Teresa (Colombia, twentieth century)

Celajes, poemas

Encrucijada

Encrucijada/Intersection, translation

Nuestra casona era así

LLORENS TORRES, Soledad (Puerto Rico, 1880-1968)

Antares mío, poesía

Entre las azucenas olvidado, poesía

LOBATO MULLE, Felisa Carmen Echevarría de (see **ECHEVARRIA DE LOBATO MULLE, Felisa Carmen**)

LOEWENTHAL, Amelia Ceide de (see **CEIDE DE LOEWENTHAL, Amelia**)

LOHENGRIN (pseudonym: see **SOTOMAYOR DE CONCHA, Graciela**)

LOMAR, Martha (pseudonym: see **LOPEZ DE VICTORIA Y BARBE, María**)

LOMBARDO DE CASO, María (Mexico, 1905-1964)

La culebra tapó el río

Una luz en la otra orilla

Muñecos de niebla

LOMELI JUAREGUI, Emma Fernández de (see **FERNANDEZ DE LOMELI JUAREGUI, Emma**)

LOPEZ, Maruja Echeverría (see **ECHEVERRIA LOPEZ, Maruja**)

LOPEZ, Margarita Mendoza (see **MENDOZA LOPEZ, Margarita**)

LOPEZ, Moravia Ochoa (see **OCHOA LOPEZ, Moravia**)

LOPEZ CRESPO, Iris de (Uruguay, twentieth century)

Acero y nardo

Teatro

Yo lo viví, acuarelas del campo

LOPEZ DE GOMARA, Susana (Argentina, twentieth century)

Las lunas de Juan Luna, novela de adolescencia

LOPEZ DE VICTORIA DE REUS, María (see **LOPEZ DE VICTORIA Y BARBE, María**)

LOPEZ DE VICTORIA Y BARBE, María (Puerto Rico, b. 1893; pseudonym: Lomar, Martha)

La canción de la hora, poemas

He vuelto a buscarla, teatro

La hormiguela

Por aquí pasa un hombre

Silbario de espumas

Vejez sonora

LOPEZ DE VICTORIA Y FERNANDEZ, Magda (Puerto Rico, b. 1900)

Amor, poesía

Clarindas en tiempos de mi isla, poemas

De mi templo interior, poemas

De Puerto Rico al corazón de América, poemas

Hijos, poemas para las madres

¡Tú, hombre!, poemas

LOPEZ GARCIA DE PERALTA, María (Argentina, twentieth century)

Vendimias poéticas

LOPEZ PORTILLO, Margarita (Mexico, twentieth century)

Los días de la voz

Toña Machetes

LOPEZ PUELMA, Lucía (Chile, b. 1928)

Algunos curiosos cuentos, poemas en prosa

No. 13, número trece, poemas

Reflejos, poesía

Sonetos del mar

LOPEZ SURIA, Violeta (Puerto Rico, b. 1926)

Amorosamente, poemas

Antología poética

Unas cuantas estrellas en mi cuarto

Diluvio

En un trigal de ausencia

Gotas en mayo, poemas y cuentos

Hubo unos pinos claros

Me va la vida

Las nubes dejan sombras

Obsesión de heliotropo

La piel pegada al alma

Poema de la yerma virgen

Poemas a la Cáncora

Resurrección de Eurídice

Riverside

Sentimiento de un viaje

LOS LLANOS, Emma de (see **BARRA, Emma de la**)

LOSADA, Amalia Puga de (see **PUGA DE LOSADA, Amalia**)

LOUBET, Jorgelina (Argentina, b. 1918). Novelist, short-story writer. She graduated in mathematics from the National Institute of Professors and holds a degree with honors from the Facultad de Filosofía y Letras, Universidad de Buenos Aires. She is a constant contributor to La Nación and Revista Criterio of Buenos Aires.

El biombo, novela. Prize from Municipality of Necochea, Province of Buenos Aires. Buenos Aires: Losada, 1963. The Spanish Civil War impinges on the life of an Argentinean who fights for the Republic, a circumstance which determines a future devoid of confidence in success. He desires to destroy the abyss into which he is falling.

La breve curva, novela. Buenos Aires: Losada, 1961. Second Prize from the Municipality of Buenos Aires. Received the "Faja de Honor" of the Society of Argentine Writers and was selected for Fondo Nacional de las Artes. The title alludes to the trajectory of human life. Is it the arc of a perfect circumference or a minor portion of another curve? It posits the intellectual siege of the unknown, laid by characters condemned by the barriers of the flesh, but who aspire to an unreachable transcendence. The novel is set during the dictatorship of Perón.

Los caminos, novela. Barcelona: Plaza y Janés, 1981. First prize for Argentinean novel of the year 1980. The political situation of the seventies, a dark period in the history of the country in which Argentineans became either pursuers or the pursued, forms the backdrop of this narrative sequence. The writer does not choose sides: the complicity of the terrorist, the union leader and the repressive military commander are all part of the situation. The clash between city and country surfaces in the path of the unforgettable character Julia who through her love for the country retrieves the best of human virtues and is able to add the burdens of others to her own and to remain steadfast in her faith.

La complicidad, novela. Buenos Aires: Losada, 1969. In a novel set in the streets and among the people of Buenos Aires, the author's existential focus allows her to transcend regional parameters and to approach crises common to all people of our time. An avowed atheist, Irene suffers from an intellectual pride which pushes her to reject life's mysteries and the "complicity" of becoming a mother and perpetrating the human species. She refuses to create a being whose future is a world of absurdities. Hope is suggested symbolically in the final scene where the protagonist, having been abandoned by her husband and having rejected suicide, understands that she needs to join humbly the world's awakening and begin a new life cycle.

Mi barrio, mi país, el mundo, cuentos. Buenos Aires: Corregidor, 1978. Prize from Dupuytren Foundation. Nineteen brief stories which in concentric circles cover three human and geographical areas: the neighborhood; with beings who can be recognized and whose intimacy can be approached by the writer; the country with abstractions which erase individuality and replace it with multitudes; the world which exists beyond the here and now of individuals and where survival in and of itself is a major feat. Yet the author does not project pessimism, but offers alternatives for new beginnings.

Penélope aguarda, teatro. In collaboration with Rodolfo Modern. Buenos Aires: Carro de Tespis, 1970. Prize from Municipality of Buenos Aires, Fondo Nacional de las Artes and Argentores.

La victoria, novela corta. Buenos Aires: International P.E.N. Club, 1974. First prize from Municipality of Buenos Aires. The relationship between a daughter and her mother marks the central theme of this subtle and tender story. The impending birth of a grandchild elicits memories in the mind of the prospective grandmother who in a lucid monologue synthesizes in her mind a collage of her life with her daughter which incorporates pressures, strategies conceived by love, feelings damaged by reproach, incomprehension, severity, and moments of true communication. With the birth of a healthy child, a future of hope and love is augured. EA

LOURDESPINDOLA (see **ESPINDOLA, Lourdes**)

LOYNAZ, Dulce María (see **LOYNAZ DE ALVAREZ DE CAÑAS, Dulce María**)

LOYNAZ DE ALVAREZ DE CAÑAS, Dulce María (Cuba, b. 1901)

La Avellaneda

Del día de las artes y las letras

Jardín, novela lírica

Juegos de agua, versos del agua y del amor

Poemas sin nombre

Obra lírica

Un verano en Tenerife

Versos 1920-1938

LOYOLA, Adriana (Chile, twentieth century)

Transpariencias, relatos y prosa lírica

LOZANO, Abigaíl (Venezuela, 1821-1866)

Colección de poesías originales

Poesías selectas

Tristezas del alma

LOZANO, Argentina Díaz (see **DIAZ LOZANO, Argentina**)

LUGO FILIPPI, Carmen (Puerto Rico, twentieth century). Studied in Puerto Rico and in France; teaches French language and literature at the University of Puerto Rico. She started writing short stories in the seventies and won prizes in several literary contests. Many of her stories deal with the image of women in the mass media and the images women have of themselves. A sense of irony is constant in her writing. ILJ

Vírgenes y mártires. Río Piedras: Antillana, 1981. ISBN 84-499-4932-7, paperback, 139 pp. (See VEGA, Ana Lydia for annotation.)

LUISI, Luisa (Uruguay, twentieth century)

Inquietud, poemas

Poemas de la inmovilidad y canciones de sol

Poesías

Polvo de días, poemas

Sentir, poemas

LUJAN, Dulce María Borrero de (see **BORRERO DE LUJAN, Dulce María**)

LUJAN, María Diana (Argentina, twentieth century)

Inicial de asombro, poemas

LUJAN, Mónica (Chile, twentieth century)

"Tipuani," el camino del infierno

La vereda del sol, novela

LUJAN REYES DE GUADALUPE, María de (Uruguay, twentieth century)

Cariño, poesías

Vida, poesía y amor

LUNA, Delia Orgaz de Correa (see **ORGAZ DE CORREA LUNA, Delia**)

LUNA, Violeta (Ecuador, b. 1943). One of Ecuador's best-known women poets and prose writers, Luna has won numerous literary prizes for her poetry which is mostly social in nature and reflects a strength and force of expression lacking in the social poetry of Ecuador's earlier female poets. She has a Master's degree in Spanish and literature from the Universidad Central de Ecuador and a Ph.D. in education. Furthermore, she has held teaching positions in high schools of Ecuador. AP

Los pasos amarillos, cuentos. Quito: Casa de la Cultura Ecuatoriana, 1969. 113 pp. This collection of short stories reflects Luna's deep concern over the social injustices which the poor and uneducated continue to suffer. Women characters and their problems are of particular interest to Luna. Modern man's search for moral and ethical values in a world of automation and cybernetics along with the ever-widening gap between the rich and the poor are predominant themes in Luna's work. MH

Posiblemente el aire, poesía. Guayaquil, Ecuador: Casa de la Cultura Ecuatoriana, 1970. 91 pp. The first section, "Cantos de temor y de blasfemia," won third place in the Ismael Pérez Pazmino Contest in 1969. Here the poet narrates the constraints society places upon mankind in general and on women in particular. In this regard, she longs to be free-spirited without any shame in experiencing her own sexuality. The second half, "Una espina en la raíz de la azucena," continues the search for happiness and freedom. While she wants to be free to experience her passion, she does not want to be enslaved by it.
AP

La sortija de la lluvia, poesía. Guayaquil, Ecuador: Casa de la Cultura Ecuatoriana, 1980. Paperback, 103 pp. Introd. by Juan Manuel Rodríguez; short biographical sketch of author. The work's first section contains poems which speak of man's enslavement to the concept of time and his own passions. The second section, "Ayer me llamaba primavera," won first place in the national poetry contest held by channel 8 of Ecuadorian television in 1973. In both sections of the work, Luna employs free verse in a direct style to show her empathy for the suffering of this world and her belief that the past was a better age. AP

El ventanal del agua, poemas. Quito, Ecuador: Universitaria, 1965. 63 pp. Water imagery dominates this collection of poetry; the first poem begins with a quotation from Ibarbourou concerning water and ends with a line in which Luna expresses her own feelings towards water. While for Ibarbourou water is a life-giving and soothing force, for Luna it is an impotent force unable to quench the thirst of modern man. The water theme appears repeatedly in free verse which tells of an earlier age of innocence when water flowed freely and nourished all. Only in our age has water become dammed up and stagnant, flowing freely now only as uncontrollable and destructive rain. AP

Y con el sol me cubro, poemas. Quito, Ecuador: Casa de la Cultura Ecuatoriana, 1967. 86 pp. Introd. by G. Humberto Mata. With directness and clarity of style, Luna once again employs free verse to project the problems of modern man. These problems consist mainly of man's inability to love not only a member of the opposite sex, but his fellow man. In regard to his inability, the poems are very pessimistic and reflect little hope for mankind. AP

LUSIGNAN, Marzia de (pseudonym: see SANCHEZ LAFAURIE, Juana)

LUSZCZYNSKA, Laura Riesco Malpartida (see RIESCO MALPARTIDA LUSZCZYNSKA, Laura)

LUZ, Alba (Argentina, twentieth century)

Cumbres y abismos, poesías

El grito alucinante

LUZ PEREA, María (Mexico, twentieth century)

Bodas trágicas

Un gran señor

Incertidumbre

Mar de pasiones, novela

Prisionero

LYNCH, Marta (Argentina, b. 1929). Lynch is Argentina's most widely esteemed woman writer. As well as producing excellent works of fiction, she is active in various media, speaking out regularly on panels, in interviews, and in journalistic writing. She has become especially concerned with the relation between the mature woman and her family, with the difficulties of reconciling woman's new activities in the work world with her traditional wife and mother roles and with woman's problems in efficaciously communicating her vital needs and problems.

Al vencedor, novela. Buenos Aires: Losada, 1965. Paperback, 168 pp. Difficult to obtain. Written in a fairly conventional mode of denunciatory realism, this novel follows two young men recently released from military service. The fundamental tension is between Argentina's official "land of opportunity" rhetoric, initially believed by the young men, and the barren, closed and hierarchical nature of the society they encounter.

La alfombra roja, novela. Buenos Aires: Fabril, 1962. Paperback, 237 pp. Difficult to obtain. Treats charismatic leadership in Argentine politics. A group portrait of a man who attracts mass adulation, together with the variously motivated members of his entourage. Each of those who describe him speaks in his or her own voice, bringing to the fore the personal-experiential side of politics. The style is, in each chapter, created to correspond to the character narrating. It ranges from the delicate and sensitive expression of the candidate's thoughtful mistress to the crude, blunt talk of his henchmen.

Los años de fuego, cuentos. Buenos Aires: Losada, 1980. Paperback, 262 pp. The short stories show less concern with events of political life than early collections. Instead, she concentrates on everyday, especially amorous, experience. A favored theme is a love affair made up of occasional encounters over a period of time. This arrangement allows the female narrator to reflect articulately upon nuances of change in the relationship, her lover, herself and their circumstances.

Apuntes para un libro de viaje, crítica social. Buenos Aires: Cástor y Póllux, 1978. Paperback, 78 pp. The only book collecting her cultural and social criticism which often appears in newspapers and magazines. A trip through Europe and Latin America is merely the pretext for Lynch to analyze aspects of contemporary society including the relations of young adults to the generation of their parents and, most significantly, the role of women. She is especially concerned with young European women who have discarded the traditional constraints of decorum, and reacts ambivalently to their rebellious dress and grooming, rejection of ladylike ways, and frankness in sexual matters.

Un árbol lleno de manzanas, novela. Buenos Aires: Sudamericana, 1974. Paperback, 203 pp. Essentially a love story, this novel brings together a self-assured married woman, part of international artistic culture, with a frequently bewildered Argentine professor. The political chaos and violence of mid-seventies Argentina is present principally as a backdrop of disturbance and disruption, remaining less developed than the personal element of the plot. The most striking technical feature is the inclusion of events that may be characters' fantasies, dreams or actual occurrences.

Crónicas de la burguesía

El cruce del río, novela. Buenos Aires: Sudamericana, 1972. Paperback, 313 pp. Treats guerrilla warfare as personal life experience. The figure of the guerrilla fighter's mother has won special critical praise. The reader watches the uneducated but clear-thinking woman evolve from a traditional household role to assume, after her son's death, an active part in the liberation struggle. Stylistically, the mother's interior monologues are especially impressive. Her inner voice is poetic and eloquent yet simple and befitting a woman of her limited experience.

Los cuentos de colores. Buenos Aires: Sudamericana, 1971. Paperback, 208 pp. Much more well-developed than the stories of Los cuentos tristes, these short narratives contain a careful fictional examination of mass media acculturation, the imposition of norms through family pressure and other factors leading to restrictive male/female roles. The beauty-pageant contestant Gladys is perhaps the most impressively realized figure. Her own words, full of a commercialized, clichéd language communicate her loss of autonomous thought and expression in pursuit of a fixed ideal of glamor.

Los cuentos tristes. Buenos Aires: Centro Editor de América Latina, 1967. Paperback, 139 pp. Buenos Aires: Merlín, 1971. Paperback, 152 pp. Neither edition is currently accessible and Centro Editor has closed down. Uneven early stories whose themes are: the mechanisms of conventional female passivity and the male's felt obligation to dominate along with the nature of the mother-child bond. Still, one can see evidence of Lynch's growing concern for woman in an untenable position and the social forces that create such oppressive female roles.

Los dedos de la mano, cuentos. Buenos Aires: Sudamericana, 1976. Paperback, 235 pp. Another edition: (Madrid: Alfaguara, 1977), 258 pp. Several stories treat the situation of upper-middle-class women, particularly those suffering from boredom and frustration. Lynch obtains especially good results by placing the narration in the voices of these women. The contrast between the well-educated heroines' ability to understand their difficulties and their inability to speak out or to take decisive action is striking and indicative of widespread cultural problems.

Informe bajo llave

Madame Bovary Siglo XX

La penúltima versión de la Colorada Villanueva, novela. Buenos Aires: Sudamericana, 1978. Paperback, 365 pp. Treats the older woman who must move out of her accustomed wife-and-mother role. Amid the confusing violence of the seventies in Argentina, the heroine attempts a number of strategies for reorganizing her identity and daily life. Notions prevalent in her culture -- particularly the idealization of the romantic couple -- cause her added conflict and distress. In a rapidly changing society, she has lost her traditional identity without finding a new supportive system.

La señora Ordóñez, novela. Buenos Aires: Jorge Alvarez, 1967. Paperback, 375 pp. Another edition: (Buenos Aires: Sudamericana, 1968), paperback, 401 pp. 1967 edition not available. Lynch's best-regarded work, the novel presents a woman in two cultural milieux: immigrant-lower-middle-class (her childhood) and upper-middle-class (her marriage). The heroine narrates only half the chapters: an effective way of showing her subtle distortions in contrast to a reliable third-person account. The woman tries politics, art, and an autonomous career; yet her basic concerns are her physical attractiveness and her liaisons with men. NL

LYRA, Carmen (pseudonym: see **CARVAJAL, María Isabel**)

M

MCDONALD, Sonia Rincón de (see **RINCON DE MCDONALD, Sonia**)

MACEDO C., María Rosa (Peru, b. 1912)

Hombres de tierra adentro

Ranchos de caña

Rastrojo

MACHADO, Elvia Castañeda de (see **CASTAÑEDA DE MACHADO, Elvia**)

MACHADO BONET, Ofelia (see **MACHADO BONET DE BENVENUTA, Ofelia**)

MACHADO BONET DE BENVENUTA, Ofelia (Uruguay, twentieth century)

Allegro scherzando, poesía y prosa

Andante, poemas

Un ángel del bolsillo

Circunstanciales, poemas

La emboscada del sueño, novela

Hacia la revolución del siglo, ensayo

Mujeres de nadie, novela

Salir de la fila

MACHADO DE ARNAO, Luz (Venezuela, b. 1916)

Canto al Orinoco

Cartas al señor tiempo

La casa por dentro 1946-1965, poemas

La ciudad instantánea

La espiga amarga, poemas

Luz Machado de Arnao

Palabra de honor (1962-1970), poesía

Retratos y tormentos, poemas 1960-1972

Ronda, poemas

Soneterío 1966-1972

Vaso de esplandor, poemas

MACHADO DE ARREDONDO, Isabel (Cuba, 1838-1919; pseudonym: Flérida)

Ecos del bélico

MACHICADO, Angélica Estenssoro (see **ELGUERA DE MACPARLIN, Alida**)

MACIAS, Elva (Mexico, b. 1944)

El paso del que viene, poesía

MACPARLIN, Alida Elguera de (see **ELGUERA DE MACPARLIN, Alida**)

MADRE CASTILLO (see **CASTILLO Y GUEVARA, Madre Francisca Josefa**)

MADRID, Antonieta (Venezuela, twentieth century). Studied at the Universidad Central in Caracas. Attended the Writers Workshop at the University of Iowa in the late sixties. A book of poems, Nomenclatura cotidiana, was her first publication. Her narratives deal with problems of contemporary life and Venezuelan politics. Her No es tiempo para rosas rojas won the Municipal Prize for Prose in 1974.

Feeling, relatos

Naming day-by-day/nomenclatura cotidiana, poesía, translation

No es tiempo para rosas rojas, novela. Caracas: Monte Avila, 1975. Paperback, 184 pp. The narrator of this novel is a young female university student involved in politics, rock music and drugs. Written as fragments broken in chronologies, places and characters, the book is equally critical of the consumerist high bourgeoisie and the leftist pseudo-revolutionaries. Actively political and with open views on sexual pleasure and abortion, the female characters show that new experiences coexist with the repression of women in a macho-dominated society.

Reliquias de trapo, cuentos. Caracas: Monte Avila, 1972. Paperback, 192 pp. Fourteen short stories, many of them about police brutality against young political activists. In satirical views of the family and capitalist society, the author uses innumerable local idioms to recreate the speech of young 'sophisticated' people. GM

MADRID, María Cristina (Chile, twentieth century)

Mar adentro, poemas

MADRIGAL, Carmen Nieto de (see **NIETO DE MADRIGAL, Carmen**)

MAGGI, Marinés Silva de (see **SILVA DE MAGGI, Marinés**)

MAIA, Circe (Uruguay, twentieth century)

En el tiempo, poesía

Presencia diaria, poesía

El puente, poemas

MAIRENA, Ana (Mexico, twentieth century)

El apóstol regresa, farsa

El cántaro a la puerta

Los extraordinarios

Majakuagymoukeia, literatura cora, bilingual edition

MALDONADO, Edelmira González (see **GONZALEZ MALDONADO, Edelmira**)

MALDONADO, Rosario González (see **GONZALEZ MALDONADO, Rosario**)

MALE, Belkis Cuza (see **CUZA MALE, Belkis**)

MALHARRO DE CARIMATI, Victorina (Argentina, twentieth century)

Amor y meteorología, cuentos

De amor y de dolor, novela y cuentos

In memoriam

Verax

MALINOW, Inés (Argentina, b. 1922). Born in Argentina of Russian-Jewish background, Malinow is a resident of Buenos Aires. Journalist, teacher, author of more than two hundred children's books, Malinow has won literary prizes for her prose and poetry. Her first five books, all poetry, were published between 1949 and 1961. In her novels and short stories, Malinow emphasizes the psychological and poetic dimensions of human relationships, often adopting a style that shows the influence of magical realism's master prose writers: Borges, Cortázar, S. Ocampo and Rulfo. Her prose and poetry tend toward a brevity and purity of style which heightens their dramatic impact.

¡Buena suerte, Inosito!, cuento para niños

Las canciones de Anna'Sao

Canciones para mis nenas llenas de sol, poesía juvenil. Buenos Aires: Plus Ultra, 1958, 1981. A richly illustrated book of verses for very young children. Written in a popular style of lines of six syllables or less, these short poems convey a child's view of nature, games, daily life -- all with the apparent end of entertaining and building vocabulary. Malinow originally wrote this volume, her favorite of all her children's books, for her own daughters.

Cuentos elegidos

Distancia fija, cuentos. Buenos Aires: Taller, 1973. Paperback, 108 pp. A collection of nine short stories with contemporary settings incorporating supernatural elements. Its preferred themes include alienation and the lack of communication between men and women, and between parents and children. The stories frequently focus on the psychological dimensions of time and space with narrative techniques that recall Cortázar's early stories and Silvina Ocampo's fey qualities. The title story and "La esquina del sueño" have been translated by this annotator.

Entrada libre, novela. Buenos Aires: Emecé, 1978. Paperback, 238 pp. A groundbreaking novel of mythopoetic dimensions, Entrada libre is the story of a mother and daughter's journey to Cuzco -- an experience with autobiographical origins which Malinow fictionalized. The two women explore their environs, including the famous Incan ruins nearby, and, in their mysterious lodgings in Nueva Alta, come to understand their own female identities more fully. A powerful poetic style, akin to Rulfo in its sparseness and incorporation of otherworldly elements. Deserves to be translated.

Lunes mi enemigo, novela. Buenos Aires: Nueve 64, 1965. Paperback, 175 pp. A novel of contemporary, middle-class Argentina, set in Buenos Aires, dealing with a series of encounters and relationships one Sunday, an election day. The novel is presented in ten chapters using the traditional third-person narrative voice. Less successful as a novel than Malinow's later work, Entrada libre, but still well written and faithful to its locale.

Máscara y transparencia, poesía. Buenos Aires: Fundación Argentina para la Poesía, 1981. Paperback, 75 pp. A book of poetry organized in two parts: "El Ojo, El Oído, Nosotros," a collection of poems in prose; and "Solapadamente Intimo," short poems in modern verse form, mainly of an erotic, personal nature. Intimate probings into the nature of relationships -- primarily addressed to a tú of a past encounter -- these poems are expressions of the ambiguities of love. As the title indicates, the games of love are many while the pain of love is their most transparent reminder. This brief volume is richly illustrated with drawings by noted Argentinean artists. DM

Páramo intemperie

Poemas de estrellas y vientos

Tal vez el amor

La tercera mitad

Versitos para caramelos

MALLARINO, Isabel Pinzón Castilla de Carreño- (see **PINZON CASTILLA DE CARREÑO-MALLARINO, Isabel)**

MALPARTIDA LUSZCZYNSKA, Laura Riesco (see **RIESCO MALPARTIDA LUSZCZYNSKA)**

MANSILLA DE GARCIA, Eduarda (Argentina, 1838-1892; pseudonym Daniel). Author of various collections of fantastic short stories and novels, originally published under the pseudonym Daniel, that reached considerable success in her country and abroad in the second half of the nineteenth century. She also wrote a drama in three acts, essays about her travels in Europe and in the United States, journalistic articles and a novel in French: Pablo ou la vie dans les Pampas (Paris, 1869). She possessed great talent, erudition, and imagination. She is considered one of the major female writers of the literary generation of 1880, to which her brother Lucio V. Mansilla also belonged.

Creaciones, cuentos y teatro. Buenos Aires: Juan A. Alsina, 1883. 297 pp. Available in libraries in Buenos Aires. A collection of six stories and a one-act play treating various themes. Some belong to the genre of the fantastic, others incorporate elements of dreams and premonitions that had already appeared in the author's earlier works and that characterized the literature of the times. They are open-ended stories, narrated with great skill and imagination. A recurrent theme is complication in love and in other personal relationships. The protagonists and their social milieux are also varied: Russian aristocrats in Paris, poor Italian immigrants in New York City, middle-class families in Buenos Aires or in Rhode Island.

Cuentos, para niños. Buenos Aires: República, 1880. 180 pp. Available in major research libraries. A delightful collection of short stories for children that can be enjoyed by readers of any age. In the preface, the author states that she wanted to produce in Spanish something that, as far as she knew, did not exist in that language: "Anderson's literary genre." The major themes are arrogance and ingratitude, jealousy, cruelty and generosity. Although the stories contain fantastic elements, the action takes place in a concrete socio-historical milieu, nineteenth century Argentina, and the protagonists are vivid examples of the society and the times in which they lived.

Lucía, novela. Buenos Aires: Tribuna, 1860. 110 pp. Available in libraries in Buenos Aires. A novel based on the historical episode of Sancti Spíritu, on the Paraná River, during the first years of the Conquest in the sixteenth century, as told by Ruy Díaz de Guzmán in his Argentina, 1612. The action of the novel centers on Lucía Miranda, the historical or legendary heroine of colonial times. Part I shows her early life in Spain till the moment of her marriage to Captain Hurtado. Part II recreates her voyage to the New World with Cabot's expedition, and the tragedy that followed when her beauty and tenderness aroused the deepest passion in the twin brothers Mangorá and Siripo, of the Timbú tribe.

Lucía Miranda. Buenos Aires: Juan A. Alsina, 1882. 386 pp. Available in libraries in Buenos Aires. This is a reprint of Lucía (1860). The author has changed the title of the novel, and has added a preface explaining that she had hidden her true identity under the pseudonym "Daniel" (the name of one of her children) to publish her earlier works. She adds that she decided to leave the novel exactly as it was originally published in her youth, with all its merits and defects. Included is a laudatory letter written by the American critic Caleb Cushing in 1870, in which he tells her that he is reviewing the English translation of her novel.

El médico de San Luis, novela. Buenos Aires: Universitaria de Buenos Aires, 1962. 156 pp. Available in major research libraries. Originally published in 1860 under the pseudonym "Daniel," this novel gives an excellent picture of the creole customs and the socio-historical milieu of a remote town in the Argentine province of San Luis in the mid-nineteenth century. The author skillfully combines moments of intense violence, which she attributes to the barbaric milieu and corruption in those who ruled the town, with idyllic scenes of love and family life. In the accompanying preface to the 1962 edition, Antonio Pagés Larraya points out that this was the author's first novel, and one of the first novels written by a woman in Argentina. NG

MANSO DE NORONHA, Juana Paula (Argentina, 1819-1875)

Los misterios del Plata

MANTOVANI, Fryda Schultz Cazanueve de (see **SCHULTZ CAZANUEVE DE MANTOVANI, Fryda**)

MAR ESTRELLA, María del (see **ESTRELLA, María del Mar**)

MAR, María del (Mexico, b. 1903)

El alma desnuda, poesía

Atmósfera sellada, poemas

Cántico del amor que perdura

Cántico panorámico de la revolución, poemas

La corola invertida, novela

En ti, sólo distante, poesía

Fiel trayectoria, poemas

Horizonte de sueños

Luna en zozobra, poesía

Sombra de flor en el agua, poesía

Vida de mi muerte

MARCHAND, Lilianne Pérez (see **PEREZ MARCHAND, Lilianne**)

MAREA, Eva C. Verbel y (see **VERBEL Y MAREA, Eva C.**)

MARIA DE LA ANTIGUA, Madre (Mexico, 1566-1617)

Estaciones de la pasión del señor

MARIA DE LAS ESTRELLAS (see **ESTRELLAS, María de las**)

MARIANELA (pseudonym: see **PALMA Y ROMAN, Angélica**)

MARIANI, Maruja Aguiar de (see **AGUIAR DE MARIANI, Maruja**)

MARIN, Guadalupe (Mexico, twentieth century)

Un día patrio

La única, novela

MARIN DEL SOLAR, Mercedes (Chile, 1804-1866)

Poesías de la señora doña Mercedes Marín del Solar

MARMOL, Adelaida del (Cuba, 1840-1857)

Ecos de mi arpa

MARPONS, Josefina (Argentina, twentieth century)

44 (Cuarenta y cuatro) horas semanales

Mamá Noé, teatro

La mujer en el trabajo

La mujer y su lucha con el ambiente

Rouge

Satanás y otros cuentos

MARRERO, Carmen (Puerto Rico-United States, b. 1907)

Fémina, poesía

Mujer sin isla, poemas

¿Por qué no se casa, señor Senador?, comedia

Sonetos de la verdad

Tierra y folklore

MARRERO Y CARO, Rosa (Cuba, d. 1868)

Poesías de Rosa Marrero y Caro

MARROQUIN, Clemencia Morales Tinoco de (see **MORALES TINOCO DE MARROQUIN, Clemencia**)

MARRUZ, Fina García (see **GARCIA MARRUZ, Josefina**)

MARTI, Ana Selva (see **SELVA MARTI, Ana**)

MARTINEZ, Angela (Cuba, twentieth century)

Memorias de un decapitado

MARTINEZ, Celina (Honduras, twentieth century)

Poemas del amor y del olvido

MARTINEZ, Luz Elisa Borja (see **BORJA MARTINEZ, Luz Elisa**)

MARTINEZ, María Cadilla de (see **CADILLA DE MARTINEZ, María**)

MARTINEZ, Rosa Restrepo de (see **RESTREPO DE MARTINEZ, Rosa**)

MARTINEZ DE TINAJERO, Blanca (Ecuador, twentieth century)

En la paz del campo, novela

Luz en la noche, novela

Poemas camperos

Prosas camperas

Purificación, novela

MATA, América Villanueva (see **VILLANUEVA MATA, América**)

MATA, Helena García de la (see **GARCIA DE LA MATA, Helena**)

MATAMOROS, Mercedes (Cuba, 1858-1906). Born in Cienfuegos, she moved to Havana with her father after her mother's death. At age fourteen she published perceptive artículos de costumbres in various newspapers. Following the end of the first war of independence, she published again in newspapers for a few years until her father lost his job, his money and eventually his health. From then on (1884), she lived in obscurity until her benefactors succeeded in raising money for the publication of Poesías completas. She then published other poems, including El último amor de Safo, which appeared in book form in 1902. Matamoros' somberly erotic tone in the latter, very different from the melancholy and restrained one of earlier poems, and her audacity of expression bring her closer to such Latin American poets as Ibarbourou and Storni than to other women poets of her own generation.

Poesías completas. Havana: La Moderna, 1892. Hardcover, 295 pp. Biographical and critical prologue by Aurelia Castillo de González. Divided into five parts, the volume includes "Sensitivas;" translations grouped under the headings "Melodías Hebreas de Byron," "Cantos y Baladas de Moore;" "Traducciones e Imitaciones de Diferentes Autores;" and "Primeras Poesías." The forty-eight sensitivas are short lyric compositions in the manner of Bécquer's rimas. The translations, more or less faithful to the originals, reveal Matamoros' facility with traditional form. "Primeras Poesías," eighteen miscellaneous poems, include the romantic ballad "Caonabo," said to be the author's favorite as well as several lyric poems held in high esteem by her contemporaries.

Sonetos

El último amor de Safo. Introd. by Manuel Márquez Sterling. La Habana: n.p., 1902. Twenty sonnets. NE

MATTE ALESSANDRI, Ester (Chile, b. 1932). Matte Alessandri has occupied a central role in the promotion of Chilean writers, especially young people. She has been a judge of several literary contests and for a number of years she was in the board of directors of the Society of Chilean writers. The themes of her poetry vary; she writes about motherhood, friendship and love, but above all she is interested in a pantheistic mysticism that impregnates most of her work. In her poetry we see constant associations with primitive Christianity and eastern religions.

Desde el abismo, cuentos

Entre la vigilia y el sueño, poemas. Santiago de Chile: Nascimento, 1980. Paperback, 81 pp. These poems are connected by the strong longing for unification with the spirit of the divine in order to tie and achieve an inner state of calm and general well-being. The poems in this collection bear a strong resemblance to the works of Santa Teresa de Jesús and therefore are interesting for those who study mysticism in Hispanic literature. Throughout the collection, there are several graphic images such as the ones dealing with a personal and pantheistic communion with nature and linked with the idea of ascending towards heaven in search of a magic union with the divine -- a theme that appears in almost every poem. MA

La hiedra, cuentos

Las leyes del viento, poesía

Otro capítulo, cuentos

El rodeo y otros cuentos

MATTEI DE AROSEMENA, Olga Elena (Puerto Rico - Colombia, b. 1933). Although born in Puerto Rico, Mattei has lived in Colombia for most of her life. Her three published volumes encompass a diversity of styles which reflects the poet's interest in the form and function of art. Sílabas is a first effort that includes conventional sentimental pieces, as well as more socially-oriented works. Pentafonía, a dramatic poem with solo and choral parts, deals with cosmic and religious questions, while La gente, conversational, informal, sometimes almost casual in tone, contains wry social and philosophical commentary beneath the deceptively simple surface.

La gente. Biblioteca Colombiana de Cultura, Colección Popular, 152. Bogotá: Instituto Colombiano de Cultura, 1974.   184 pp. Includes many of the poet's unpublished works, written between 1965 and 1973, and planned for other books. The best pieces are grouped under the general title of "La Gente" and they deal with Mattei's travels in Europe, the Near East, and the United States, during which she deftly sketched distinctive experiences and the people encountered on her tour. In a natural tone, she captures specific elements and traits which characterize and differentiate cities and individuals. Of particular interest are the poems about Greece. Other well-conceived works deal with poetic creation and frustration, and with the juggling of household duties, family, and the need to write. The final portion of the book is of less impact than the "Gente" pieces. Suitable for college-level courses.

Pentafonía, poema. Colección Rojo y Negro. Medellín: Universidad Pontífica Bolivariana, 1964. 64 pp. Pentafonía is a long symphonic poem in five parts, each titled "Visión" (I to V). A bilingual edition of the poem (Spanish-French) was printed in Medellín, Colombia, to coincide with the premiere (December 4, 1975) of a cantata written by Marc Carles, based on the work. The poem is a majestic interpretation and re-elaboration of the creation of the universe and the history of mankind. It is inspired by the Book of Genesis, the New Testament, and the cosmogonies and religious mythologies of the pre-Columbian Indian cultures. Although the poem has deep religious and mystical overtones, it can be favorably compared with the best pieces dealing with the New World by Mistral, Neruda, and Cardoza y Aragón. Suitable for civilization and literature courses on the college level.

Sílabas de arena. Tertulia, vol. 2. Medellín: Imprenta Departmental de Antioquia, 1962. A collection of poems, divided into five sections, and containing a prologue by René Uribe Ferrer, Sílabas de arena (1964) also includes a prose poem by Mattei, entitled "Invocación," which serves as a poetic introduction to the volume and sets the tone for many of the pieces, particularly those dealing with social topics. The first part of the book, "Cantos fraternales," is the most successful of the five groups. Mattei sets aside personal and sentimental involvements and deals with more universal and socially related concerns. Some of the works in this part, "Juan Pedro," "El viento ajeno," "Violencia," reflect the conversational and deliberately prosaic style which characterizes the best pieces of La gente. Sílabas de arena is a first attempt by an obviously gifted poet but lacks the quality of a major work. ED & ME

MATTO, Mabel (Argentina, twentieth century)

Poesía

MATTO DE TURNER, Clorinda (Peru, 1852-1909). Born and educated in Cuzco, Matto married at seventeen years of age an English businessman, José Turner, and lived in a small Andean town (the setting of her most famous novel, Aves sin nido) until after his death in 1881. She was a prolific writer of articles and short tales based upon local traditions and legends, a playwright, novelist, essayist, educator, translator into Quechua, lecturer and publisher. She lived in Buenos Aires after 1895, and died there in 1909.

Aves sin nido, novela peruana. Lima: Universo, de Carlos Prince, 1889. 300 pp. Other editions: (Buenos Aires: Félix Lajouane, 1889), 279 pp.; Preface by Emilio Gutiérrez de Quintanilla (Valencia: F. Sempere, 1908), 285 pp.; Prefaces by Emilio Gutiérrez de Quintanilla, Eulogio Tapia Olarte and Alfredo Yépez Miranda (Cuzco: Universidad Nacional del Cuzco, 1948), 269 pp.; (Cuzco: H.G. Rozas, 1958), in 2 volumes.; Preliminary study by Fryda Schultz de Mantovani (Buenos Aires: Solar-Hachette, 1968), 214 pp.; (Lima: Peisa, 1973), 186 pp.; Prologue by Antonio Cornejo Polar (Havana: Casa de las Américas, 1974), 264 pp. Famed as the first "Indianist" novel in Peruvian fiction, the first exposé of the cruel exploitation of Andean Indian villagers and peasants by landlords, priests and officials of Spanish descent, Aves sin nido is also a description of Andean village life and a romantic love story. It denounces corruption caused by greed, lust, ignorance and alcoholic excess. It portrays strong, compassionate, loyal women who are often victimized but ultimately triumph over depravity.

Birds Without a Nest: A Story of Indian Life and Priestly Oppression in Peru. Translated by J.G. Hudson. Preface by Andrew M. Milne. London, Charles J. Thynne, 1904. 236 pp. An eloquent translation of Aves sin nido which could be reprinted. Andrew M. Milne's preface describes how the novel is "under the ban of the Roman Catholic Church. For this and like offenses the writer has been excommunicated and practically exiled from her own country."

Boreales, miniaturas y porcelanas. Buenos Aires: Juan A. Alsina, 1902. 320 pp. Divided into three sections. The first is a chronicle of the 1894 revolution in Peru and a description of the author's 1895 visit to Chile and Argentina. The second is a series of short descriptive essays about Peruvian writers and public figures. The third section is a collection of other essays; for example: "Las obreras del pensamiento en la América del Sud," "Espíritu y materia." The last section would be of interest to anyone studying Matto de Turner as a feminist or literary activist.

Cuatro conferencias sobre América del Sur. Buenos Aires: Juan A. Alsina, 1909. 58 pp. Texts of lectures given in Madrid and Buenos Aires between 1904 and 1908: "República Argentina," "El Perú: tres etapas históricas, su presente," "El Perú: Imperio, Virreinato, República" and "La obrera y la mujer."

Elementos de literatura según el Reglamento de Instrucción Pública para uso del bello sexo. Arequipa: 1889. 68 pp.

Herencia, novela peruana. Lima: Masías, 1895. 343 pp. Another edition: Prologue by Antonio Cornejo Polar (Lima: Instituto Nacional de Cultura, 1974), 247 pp. The main characters of Aves sin nido appear again in Herencia and their stories are continued. Set in Lima, the book describes the pleasures and criticizes the hypocrisies and injustices of city life. The plot centers on two love stories, one happy and one corrupt; the importance of inherited family character traits is stressed. Matto de Turner provides a detailed and lively description of the customs, dress, speech, recipes and prejudices of the late nineteenth century.

Hima-Súmac o El Secreto de los Incas. Drama en tres actos y en prosa. Lima: La Equitativa, 1892. 84 pp. Another edition: Hima Súmac (Lima: Servicio de Publicaciones del Teatro Universitario, 1959), 33 pp., mimeographed. First performed in Arequipa, Peru, on Oct. 16, 1884, Hima Súmac is a play based upon the legend that a great part of the Inca gold treasure was hidden from the Spaniards and its location kept secret for centuries. Hima Súmac, fiancée of the rebel Tupac Amaru, inherits the secret but nearly betrays it. The play contrasts Indian sincerity and loyalty with Spanish hypocrisy and greed.

Indole, novela peruana. Lima: Bacigalupi, 1891. 225 pp. Another edition: Indole, Prologue by Antonio Cornejo Polar, (Lima: Instituto Nacional de Cultura, 1974), 275 pp. The "índole" of the title is the basic goodness, rectitude and strength of the heroine who contends with a weak and jealous husband, a lecherous priest and duplicitous friends. The book describes life in the Andean countryside and contrasts Indian honesty and joyfulness with the more troubled lives of the landowners, but it is primarily a denunciation of a corrupt priest and the system which fostered his immorality and undeserved power.

Leyendas y recortes. Includes commentaries by Joaquín Lemoine and Nicanor Bolet Peraza. Lima: La Equitativa, 1893. 204 pp.

Tradiciones cuzqueñas. Prologue by Ricardo Palma. Biographical notes by Julio F. Sandoval. Arequipa, Peru: La Bolsa, 1884. 252 pp.

Tradiciones cuzqueñas. Vol. II. Prologues by José Antonio de Lavalle and Ricardo Palma. Lima: Torres Aguirre, 1886. 198 pp.

Tradiciones cuzqueñas. Cuzco: H.G. Rozas, 1958. 128 pp. Includes thirty-seven of the fifty-four "tradiciones."

Tradiciones cuzqueñas completas. Prologue and selection by Estuardo Núñez. Lima: Peisa, 1976. 205 pp. Includes all the "tradiciones" and additional texts but omits the "leyendas," "recortes" and "hojas sueltas" of previous editions.

Tradiciones cuzqueñas. Leyendas, biografías y hojas sueltas. Includes prologues by Ricardo Palma, José Gabriel Cosio, Abelardo Gamarra, Manuel Rafael Valdivia and Julio F. Sandoval. Cuzco: H.G. Rozas, 1955. 273 pp.

Tradiciones cuzqueñas y Leyendas. New edition. Prologue by José Gabriel Cosio. Biographical notes by Julio F. Sandoval. Cuzco: H.G. Rozas, 1917. MB

MATURO, Graciela (Argentina, b. 1928; married name: Solá, Graciela de)

Habita entre nosotros

El mar que en mí resuena

El rostro, poemas

Un viento hecho de pájaros, poesía

MAURA, María Elena (Argentina, twentieth century)

Brisas y pamperos, poemas

Canto llano

Conciencia en albor

Crepúsculos y ocasos, versos y prosa

Malena

Pulpo gigantesco

MAURIES, Blanca B. (Mexico, twentieth century)

La vida y yo

MAYORGA, Ana de Gómez (see **GOMEZ MAYORGA, Ana de**)

MEDEIROS, María Paulina (Uruguay, twentieth century)

Bosque sin dueño, extraordinaria historia de una recién casada

Corazón de agua, novela

El faetón de los Almeida

Fronda sumergida, poesía

Un jardín para la muerte

Las que llegaron después

Miedo, su servidor, cuentos

Otros iracundos

Párpados de piedra, versos

El posadero que hospedaba sueños sin cobrarles nada

Río de lanzas, novela romántica

MEDINA, Lucila Gamero de (see **GAMERO DE MEDINA, Lucila**)

MEDINA ONRUBIA DE BETONA, Salvadora (Argentina, twentieth century)

Akasha

Alma fuerte, teatro

Cuentos

Lo que estaba escrito, teatro

Una mujer que pecó

La rueca milagrosa, versos

La solución, teatro

El vaso intacto y otros cuentos

MEDINILLA, María Estrada (see **ESTRADA MEDINILLA, María**)

MEJIA DE FERNANDEZ, Abigaíl (Dominican Republic, twentieth century)

Brotes de la raza

Ideario feminista y algún aparte para la historia del feminismo dominicano

Sueña, Pilarín, novela

MEJIA, Carmen de Gómez (see **GOMEZ MEJIA, Carmen de**)

MEJIA, Gloria Paúl (see **PAUL MEJIA, Gloria**)

MEJIA ROBLEDO, Rita Andrión de (see **ANDRION DE MEJIA ROBLEDO, Rita**)

MELDIU, Lázara (pseudonym: see **LAFARJA DE CRUZ, María de la Luz**)

MELENDEZ, Concha (Puerto Rico, b. 1895; also Conchita)

Psiquis doliente, poemas

MELENDEZ DE ESPINOSA, Juana (Mexico, twentieth century)

En el cauce del sueño

Esta dura nostalgia . . . , poemas

Mirando bajo el árbol donde los astros cantan

Río sin orillas

Voces del hombre

MELO DE REMES, María Luisa (Mexico, twentieth century)

Brazos que se van, cuentos

Castillos en el aire, ficción

Lejanías

Mi amigo el mar, escenario de vidas

MENARES, María Cristina (Chile, b. 1914)

Antología, poesía

Cuentos de patria o muerte, poesía social

La estrella en el agua, poesía

Lunita nueva, poesía para niños

Pluma de Nidal Lejano, poesía

Raíz eterna, poesía

La rosa libre, poesía

MENDEZ, Concha (Mexico, twentieth century)

El carbón y la rosa, teatro infantil

Lluvias enlazadas, poemas

Niño y sombras, poemas

Poemas, sombras y sueños

El solitario, misterio en un acto, teatro

Vida a vida

Villancicos de Navidad

MENDEZ CAPOTE, Renée (Cuba, b. 1901)

Apuntes

Cuatro conspiraciones, para niños

Un héroe de once años

Memorias de una cubanita que nació con el siglo

MENDEZ, Dolores Montenegro de (see **MONTENEGRO DE MENDEZ, Dolores**)

MENDEZ DE CUENCA, Laura (Mexico, b. 1853)

Mariposas fugitivas

Simplezas

MENDIETA ALATORRE, María de los Angeles (Mexico, twentieth century)

Cumbre de niebla, novelas cortas

Margarita Maza de Juárez: la dama de la República

Margarita Maza de Juárez: epistolario, antología, iconografía y efemérides

La mujer en la revolución mexicana

Mundos cerrados, relatos

MENDOZA, Elvira Lascarro (see **LASCARRO MENDOZA, Elvira**)

MENDOZA, Esther Feliciano (see **FELICIANO MENDOZA, Esther**)

MENDOZA, María Luisa (Mexico, b. 1928; also la China). With her exuberant and wildly personalized prose manner, Mendoza is Mexico's best exponent of a subjective New Journalism. Despite her apparent frenzied eccentricity, she reveals herself to be a lucid feminist analyst of consumer society. She is particularly disturbed by the way in which women are trivialized by the model of the perfect housewife, by the tyranny of fashion, and by the banalizing effects of a mass-media-drenched, technologized society.

Con él, conmigo, con nosotros tres: cronovela. Mexico: Joaquín Mortiz, 1971. 187 pp. Part of the literary response to the 1968 massacre of students at Tlatelolco Esplanade, Mexico City, this novel goes beyond the immediate circumstance of the killings and imprisonments to look at the background of Mexican culture and society in 1968. The countercultural student movement receives attention as an alternative to the hierarchical, stagnant status quo. The language is inventive and, despite the grim topic, often playful and exuberant.

Las cosas. Mexico: Joaquín Mortiz, 1976. Paperback, 188 pp. Short, fragmentary texts are juxtaposed with the author's own collages of mail-order catalogue images. Both refer to the work's overall theme: concrete things (consumer products, household objects, etc.) and how they are emblematic of the alienated, trivialized state of modern woman. In her eccentric, effusive prose, Mendoza conveys a critique of the technologized consumer culture as well as of the traditional angel-of-the-hearth female role. She skillfully coordinates social analysis and whimsy.

De Ausencia, novela. Mexico: Joaquín Mortiz, 1974. 211 pp. Nostalgia, capricious innovation and moments of the absurd are here successfully integrated with a serious examination of woman's role. Ausencia, first encountered as an early twentieth-century belle, enters the rapidly technologizing modern period and tests her strength and independence against the constraints imposed by womanly norms of decorum and "virtue." Plot is subsumed to a series of intensely described and telling situations.

Dos palabras dos, crónica de un informe, con Edmundo Domínguez Aragonés. Mexico: Era, 1972. 139 pp. Experimentalism in political journalism is the animating force behind this text, comparable perhaps to Hunter Thompson's "Gonzo Journalism" on United States electoral activity. The two journalists at an elaborate government party for the press, let their thoughts wander to encompass the entire culture of official politics and reportage. Mendoza is accurate and ironic as an observer of official styles, manners and decor.

¡Oiga usted!

La O por lo redondo

El perro de la escribana o Las piedecasas. México: Joaquín Mortiz, 1982. ISBN #968-27-0448-0, paperback, 137 pp. This novel has a fluid, lyrical arrangement of material, organized into casas. Each of these segments contains evocations of scenes from childhood or adult years with a great deal of precise evocation of sensorial detail. Notable for its unusual organization, strong and vivid recreation of experience, and efforts to realize an erotic language for women. NL

Retrato de mi gente

Tris de sol, Carmen Serdán, biografía

MENDOZA, Mercedes Valdés (see **VALDES MENDOZA, Mercedes**)

MENDOZA LOPEZ, Margarita (Mexico, twentieth century)

Una voz alada y ... de un país inexistente

MENDOZA SAGARZAZU, Beatriz (Venezuela, twentieth century)

Al sexto día

Concierto sin música

Viaje en un barco de papel

MENENDEZ, Josefa (Chile, 1890-1923)

Un llamamiento al amor

MENENDEZ, Leonor Espinosa de (see **ESPINOSA DE MENENDEZ, Leonor**)

MENENDEZ, Luz Castejón de (see **CASTEJON DE MENENDEZ, Luz**)

MENENGHETTI, Cristina (Uruguay, twentieth century)

Juego abierto, poesía

MERANI, María (Chile, b. 1919)

La dama que prefirió volver, cuentos de la otra realidad

El diario de Tatiana, novela

El violín enjaulado, cuentos

MERCADER, Martha (Argentina, twentieth century). Teacher and translator, Mercader studied English in London (1949-1950). She became known as a researcher for a very popular television program. Has written narratives and theatre for children. Her novel Juana Manuela, mucha mujer was an instant best seller reaching a fifth edition by late 1980. Her narrative offers harsh political criticism of the contemporary Argentinean military and the economic system it protects.

Belisario en son de guerra

La chuña de los huevos de oro. Madrid: Legasa, 1982. Paperback, 145 pp. These narratives follow the tradition of using the fable to analyze society critically. The narrator, a capybara, uses a funny colloquial speech to talk about events and the defects -- greed, stupidity, vanity, cruelty -- of its animal companions. All the actions and characters are closely patterned after events and personalities in Argentinean politics.

De mil amores

Decir que no

Juana Manuela, mucha mujer. Buenos Aires: Sudamericana, 1980. Paperback, 450 pp. A historical novel based on the life of the early Argentinean writer J.M. Gorriti (1817-1892), a witness of important events and a practicing feminist. Invented dialogue mixed with excerpts of Gorriti's letters and historical documents recreate a fascinating personality and a past era. Although some critics find the novel's length excessive and others are not convinced of its literary merits, the book deserves more careful study.

Los que viven por sus manos. Buenos Aires: Sudamericana, 1973, 1974, 1980. Paperback, 253 pp. This novel is designed to reveal in a realistic manner the mechanisms by which international corporations in collusion with some national authorities rob the Argentinean people of their land and wealth. Although narrated by an impersonal, unobstrusive third person, characters speak in abundant dialogues and interior monologues. An 'ugly' American is the moving force of this story of greed and corruption.

Octubre en el espejo, cuentos

¿Quién de nosotros?

¿Solamente ella? Buenos Aires: Plus Ultra, 1975. Paperback, 141 pp. This novel centers on Paloma, a tango singer in a Buenos Aires night club in search of love and authenticity. Feminist in perspective, the book shows the struggles of a working woman trapped by social repression and the corruption of business interests. The many idioms and tango lyrics -- the title is one of them -- challenge the reader who wants to understand fully the novel. GM

MERCHAN, Isabel María Muñoz de (see **MUÑOZ DE MERCHAN, Isabel María**)

MERINO, Adriana (Mexico, twentieth century)

Crisol de lejana memoria, poemas

MERINO GONZALEZ, Laura (Chile, b. 1928: pseudonym: Solar, Ximena)

Multitud sin nadie, poesía

Rebeldía en la cima, poesía

MERY, Fanny (pseudonym: see **NINFA, María Emiliani Imitola**)

MEZA, Blanca Isaza de Jaramillo (see **ISAZA DE JARAMILLO MEZA, Blanca**)

MEZA, Otilia (Mexico, twentieth century)

Borrasca, novela

Leyendas aztecas

La venenosa, novela

MICHELENA, Margarita (Mexico, b. 1917)

Laurel del ángel, poesía

Paraíso y nostalgia, poemas

Reuniones de imágenes, poemas

La tragedia en rosa

Tres poemas y una nota autobiográfica

La tristeza terrestre, poemas

MIERS, Reyna (Uruguay, twentieth century)

El despertar

Grito, poesías

Universal amor, poesías

MIGUEL, María Esther de (Argentina, b. 1930). Miguel has made her living as a legal secretary and doing fairly routine journalistic tasks. At the same time, she has developed a fictional mode capable of expressing her own radical concerns. She has a strong interest in preserving the traditional, communitarian strain in Argentine rural culture while opening up that culture through more democratic and participatory social structures. Her Third World consciousness is both revolutionary and deeply traditional.

Calamares en su tinta, novela. Buenos Aires: Losada, 1968. Paperback, 141 pp. The love story presented in this short novel coordinates the painful past experiences of two lovers with parallel experiences. He is a Holocaust survivor; she, the victim of small-town narrow-mindedness. The very careful symmetries and contrasts worked out around this small nucleus of plot make this work a model of successful minimalism in narrative form.

En el campo, las espinas. Introductory essay by Héctor Izaguirre, "María Esther de Miguel: Aproximación a su Obra." Buenos Aires: Pleamar, 1980. Paperback, 220 pp. The series of short texts contained in this volume functions to present a picture of the first days of contact between Europeans and indigenous peoples in Argentina. There is a special emphasis on conveying the Indians' experience of the Conquest as well as those of common soldiers and crewmen -- the individuals whose participation in the events of the Conquest is typically omitted from official histories due to a concentration on famous figures.

En el otro tablero, cuentos. Buenos Aires: Fabril, 1972. Paperback, 168 pp. In these short stories, Miguel simultaneously works two productive veins in her fictional repertoire. One is the fantastic, magical element that links her to the so-called "mythical realism" in Latin American narrative. The other is her strong desire to show the home-bred strengths of traditional, rural Argentine culture; even in its most attenuated and modernized manifestations, this culture cannot be altogether squelched by European modes of thought and behavior.

Espejos y daguerrotipos. Buenos Aires: Emecé, 1978. 280 pp. Treats the return to cultural roots and respect for traditional rural society -- although not for its conventional system of land tenure. The heroine's efforts to effect a spiritual homecoming are hampered by her urbanite friends, who accompany her back to her ancestral town but cannot appreciate non-Europeanized local ways. Lyrical evocations of the historical rural past alternate with a modern mystery and love story.

La hora undécima. Buenos Aires: Emecé, 1961. Paperback, 206 pp. This short novel develops a theme of longstanding interest to the author: the reformulation of traditional Catholic notions of morality to make them more flexible and more responsive to the variety of situations presented in the modern world. She has succeeded in utilizing a very slender plot to support considerations about sin and spirituality that stress the persistence of irrational sources of psychic and spiritual strength.

Jaque a Paysandú

Los que comimos a Solís. Buenos Aires: Losada, 1965. 113 pp. These short, evocative texts impress upon the reader the strong cultural continuity still maintained in the harsh arid stretches of Argentina. A positive value is given to those elements of Indian and Gaucho culture that have survived despite extensive emigration out of rural areas and the incursions of modern Europeanized culture. Suiting the almost mystical faith in grass-roots traditions is the lyrical, yet plain-spoken, language of the sketches. Second place winner of a Municipal Prize.

Puebloamérica. Buenos Aires: Pleamar, 1974. Paperback, 199 pp. The currents of the search for roots and cultural identity, the theology of liberation and Third World struggle come together in this novel of guerrilla activity. A Camilo Torres-like priest is the most articulate character, effectively voicing a concern for cultural and economic autonomy of Third World and tribal peoples. The format is varied, including interviews of characters, field reports, transcribed dialogue and even combat diagramming and maps. NL

MILAN, Elena (United States?, twentieth century)

Circuitos amores y anexas

MILLA, Mercedes Tejada (see TEJADA MILLA, Mercedes)

MILLAN, Isabel Santos (see SANTOS MILLAN, Isabel)

MILLER, Jeanette (Dominican Republic, b. 1945). One of the few women who published poetry in the Dominican Republic during the seventies. Miller teaches at the Universidad Autónoma de Santo Domingo and is also an architect and art critic, with a recent book on the history of Dominican art. She belongs to the new generation of poets that began publishing early in the sixties after Trujillo's death. The lyric quality of her poetry distinguishes it from the language of political referentiality characteristic of her generation.

Fórmulas para combatir el miedo, poesía. Santo Domingo: Taller, 1972. Paperback, 59 pp. The poems perceive life as a constant struggle between love, death and hate. Poetic "formulas" or the act of writing serves as a tool for rebelling against the absurdity of time and death. The language is close to surrealism and proposes the representation of a violent, chaotic world. Death is an obsession with variations in the text. The poems use free verse and are lyric in style; the tone is pessimistic, since the poetic 'I' sees herself as constantly followed by the possibility of death. ILJ

MIRALLES, Cecilia (United States?, twentieth century)

Fragmentos del alma, versos

MIRANDA, Marta Elba (Chile, b. 1911)

Aposentos de brujas, cuentos

La heredad, novela

Mujeres chilenas, reportaje

MIRANDA, Paula (Uruguay, twentieth century)

Cerro pelado, sólo para chicos

MISTRAL, Gabriela (pseudonym: see GODOY ALCAYAGA, Lucila)

MOLINA, Marina (Puerto Rico, twentieth century)

Jardín de las emociones, prosa y versos

MOLINA, Paz (Chile, b. 1945)

Memorias de un pájaro asustado, poemas

MOLINA, Perla Fuentes (see **FUENTES MOLINA, Perla**)

MOLINA, Silvia (Mexico, b. 1946). Molina studied anthropology at Mexico's National Institute of Anthropology and History, and Spanish literature at the National University of Mexico. She won the prestigious national Villaurrutia Prize in 1977 for her first novel, La mañana debe seguir gris. In addition, she was a fellow at the Mexican Center for Writers in 1979-1980, during which time she wrote her second novel, Ascensión Tun. Molina is a member of the most recent generation of Mexican novelists, who tend to focus in their writings on concrete episodes of Mexican history as filtered through personal experience.

Ascensión Tun, novela. Serie La Invención. Cuernavaca, Mexico: Martín Casillas, 1981. Paperback, 154 pp. Molina's second novel is set in the city poorhouse in Campeche during 1889-1890. It focuses on the arrival of Ascensión Tun, an eleven-year-old Mayan orphan, at the house and his growing friendships with two other inmates: an elderly Mayan man who tells the boy about his participation in the Caste Wars of Yucatán during 1847-1855, and a schizophrenic mestiza woman whose madness was brought on by the Caste Wars. The novel is based on historical figures and events, and is noteworthy as the first indigenista novel to be published in Mexico in twenty years. Accompanied by an index of characters and a chronology.

Leyendo en la tortuga

La mañana debe seguir gris, novela. Serie Nueva Narrativa Hispánica. Mexico City: Joaquín Mortiz, 1977. Paperback, 116 pp. This novel tells of the love affair between the Mexican poet José Carlos Becerra and a young Mexican woman (the author?), beginning in London in November of 1969, and ending with Becerra's death in Italy in May of 1970. The first section of the novel is written in the form of a diary, and the rest, in the form of an autobiographical narrative. La mañana debe seguir gris is noteworthy for combining autobiography with fiction, traditional prose narrative with nonfictional elements. CS

MOLINA DE RODRIGUEZ, Blanca Luz (Guatemala, twentieth century)

Azul cuarenta, novela

Los brutos, novela

Sabor a justicia, novela

MOLLA, Rosana (Uruguay, twentieth century)

Este tiempo largo 1967-1971, poesía

MOLLOY, Lucila Castellanos Argüelles de (see **CASTELLANOS ARGÜELLES DE MOLLOY, Lucila**)

MOLLOY, Sylvia (Argentina, twentieth century)

En breve cárcel, novela

MONCADA, Lucila Gamero (see **GAMERO DE MEDINO, Lucila**)

MONDRAGON AGUIRRE, Magdalena (México, b. 1913; pseudonym: Seminoreff, Vera). Born in Torreón, she attended elementary and secondary schools in San Antonio, Texas, completing a business degree in Torreón and an M.A. in Letters at the National Autonomous University of México. She has worked as a journalist/correspondent for many periodicals in México. She was the first female director of a daily newspaper in Mexico (Prensa Gráfica) and has also directed Sólo para Ellas and Boletín Cultural Mexicano. She founded the "Centro Cultural Vito Alessio Robles" providing children with free education. In 1983, she was living in Mexico, having retired from writing.

Cuando Eva se vuelve Adán, teatro

El choque de los justos, teatro. México: Instituto Nacional de la Juventud Mexicana: 1962.

El día no llega, novela. México: Juan Pablos, 1950.

Dos obras de teatro. México: Colonia México Grupo América, 1951. Contains: El mundo perdido and La sirena que llevaba el mar.

Dos obras de teatro. México: Enciclopedia Popular de la Secretaria de Educación Pública, 1947. Contains: Cuando Eva se vuelve Adán and Torbellino (originally entitled La tarántula).

Habla un espía. México: Prensa, 1962. Documentary novel about espionage in Latin America.

Lo divino no es humano. México: Juego de Pasiones, n.d. Novela.

Más allá existe la tierra, novela. México: Cortés, 1947.

México pelado ¡pero sabroso! Recopilación de Magdalena Mondragón

Mi corazón es la tierra, novela. México: Prensa, 1968.

El mundo perdido, teatro

No debemos morir, teatro

Norte bárbaro, novela. Baja California, México: Marco J. Lara, 1944.

¡Porque me da la gana!, teatro. México: Universitaria, 1953. Alta comedia.

Puede que'l otro año, novela. Prologue by Eutiquio Aragonés. México: Alrededor de América, 1937.

Los presidentes dan risa

Que crezcan los hombres, novela

Saludo a la vida, crónica de un viaje

La sirena que llevaba el mar, teatro

Si mis alas nacieran, poemas. México: Alfredo del Bosque, 1960.

Someday the Dream. Trans. Samuel Putnam. New York: The Dial Press, 1947. Hardback, 240 pp. A very dated translation of Yo como pobre, a novel which merits a more vibrant contemporary translation.

Souvenir, poemas. México: Angel Chápero, 1938.

Tenemos sed, novela. México: Revista Mexicana de Cultura, 1954. Premio Nacional de novela.

Torbellino, teatro

Yo como pobre, novela. México: Ariel, 1944. Hardback, 323 pp. Set in Mexico City's garbage dumps, Mondragón's third novel treats the miserable reality and dreams of the poor with respect yet without liberal pity. This very strong, lively and tersely narrated novel indicts corruption and praises the human spirit. It was the first translation of a Mexican novel to win a "Book of the Month" award in the United States. (The original edition has a cover by José Clemente Orozco, entitled Los pepenadores.) JG

MONSERRATE, Isabel de (pseudonym: see **PINZON CASTILLA DE CARREÑO-MALLARINO, Isabel**)

MONTENEGRO, Blanca de Sánchez (see **SANCHEZ MONTENEGRO, Blanca de**)

MONTENEGRO, Dolores (see **MONTENEGRO DE MENDEZ, Dolores**)

MONTENEGRO DE MENDEZ, Dolores (Guatemala, 1857-1933; also Lola)

Antología de Lola Montenegro

Flores y espinas

Versos de Lola Montenegro

MONTES, Rosa Jáuregui (see **JAUREGUI MONTES, Rosa**)

MONTES DE OCA, Julia Luisa Pérez (see **PEREZ MONTES DE OCA, Julia Luisa**)

MONTES DEL VALLE, Agripina (Colombia, 1844-1915)

A la América del sur

Poesías originales

MONTESINO, Claudina Agurto (see **AGURTO MONTESINO, Claudina**)

MONTI, Luisa María Pérez de (see **PEREZ DE MONTI, Luisa María**)

MONTSERRAT, María de (Venezuela, twentieth century)

Arriates en flor, poesías

Con motivo de vivir, novela

Cuentos mínimos

Los habitantes, novela

Los lugares, relatos

El país secreto, novela

MONTT, Teresa Wilms (see **WILMS MONTT, Teresa**)

MONVEL, María (pseudonym: see **BRITO DE DONOSO, Tilda**)

MORA, Antonia (Mexico, twentieth century)

Los cuarenta chatos, ficción

Del oficio

MORA, Carmen de (Mexico, twentieth century)

Ciudadela del sueño, poemas

Mi voz y el agua, poemas

Río abierto, poesía

Sonetos 1968-1973

MORA Y RIERA, Argentina (Ecuador, twentieth century)

Adolescencia triste

MORALES, Violeta (Chile, b. 1918)

Canto del silencio, poesía

La noche robada, poesía

Raudal, poesía

MORALES DE ALLOUIS, Hilda (Cuba, twentieth century)

La senda perdida, novela

MORALES TINOCO DE MARROQUIN, Clemencia (Guatemala, twentieth century)

Balcón de ensueños, poemas

Jugando y cantando, poemas para niños

Manojo de rimas

MORANDEYRA, Mary (Cuba, b. 1905)

Antagonismos, novela cubana

Apreciaciones de mujer

Aurora

Estremecimientos, poemas en prosa

El hombre a través del corazón de una mujer

La que fue su otro yo, novela

Plenilunios, versos

Poema del amor eterno

La pureza no está en los códigos

El sueño roto, novela

MORANDI, María Correa (see **CORREA MORANDI, María**)

MOREJON, Nancy (Cuba, b. 1944). Born in Havana, Morejón has a degree in French literature and has worked as an editor in the journal Gaceta de Cuba and at UNEAC. She has published articles in the journal Casa de las Américas, edited a book on Nicolás Guillén and translated Césaire, Roumain and Depestre, among other poets. She belongs to the "second generation" of new poets of the Revolution. Her style searches for simplicity; poems are predominantly narrative, particularly in Parajes. ILJ

Amor, ciudad atribuída, poemas. La Habana: El Puente, 1964. Paperback, 43 pp. Original poetry influenced by Césaire. DEM

Mutismos y amor

Parajes de una época, poemas. La Habana: Letras Cubanas, 1979. Paperback, 27 pp. The poems included give symbolic representations of fundamental moments in the history of Latin America. Its heroes, struggles and victories -- the historical referents -- constitute the mythology of these poems. "Black woman" synthetizes the history of a slave; the economic situation, race and sex give the poetic subject a political consciousness. The poems are short, in free verse forms; language is mostly colloquial. ILJ

Parque central, poesía

Poemas. Mexico City, Mexico: Universidad Nacional Autónoma de México, 1980. Paperback, 62 pp. Available in libraries. This is a collection of eighteen poems which had been previously published in other volumes. Among the themes represented here are: memories of childhood and her family; criticism of the United States and its involvement in Vietnam; slavery and its part in Cuba's history; and her love of Cuba and faith in its revolutionary ideals. "Adonde iremos, viaje," one of her most peaceful poems, concerns two lovers spending a night wandering together, feeling themselves part of the sea and of the people they encounter. PF

Richard trajo su flauta y otros argumentos, poemas. La Habana: Cuadernos UNEAC, 1967. Paperback, 81 pp. Available in libraries. This is a collection of twenty-eight poems of varying lengths. The style is also varied: she makes use of free verse forms, sometimes with punctuation, sometimes with none. The poems also present varying degrees of difficulty. Some, particularly those concerning childhood memories of her family, are written in a childlike tone. Other themes presented are love between man and woman, and love for Cuba, especially Havana. The title poem consists of eight sections and covers several pages. On the surface it is a description of a family gathering; however, there are subtle, disquieting undertones. "Freedom now" is highly critical of racism in the United States. PF

MOREL, Alicia (Chile, twentieth century)

Como una raíz de agua, 1939-1951, poemas

El increíble mundo de Llanca

El jardín de Dionisio, cuentos

Juanilla, Juanillo y la abuela, literatura para niños

MORENO, Inés (Chile, twentieth century)

Al umbral de la luz, poemas

Llegará un día, obra teatral

Mi mano en su mano, poemas

MORENO, María de la Cruz de (see **CRUZ DE MORENO, María de la**)

MORENO LAGOS, Aída (Chile, twentieth century)

Dolidamente, versos

MORGAN, Patricia (pseudonym: see **HERRERA DE WARNKEN, Marta**)

MORVAN, Henriette (Chile, b. 1900)

Boomerang, novela

Doce cuentos de animales, cuentos para niños

Doce cuentos de juguetes, cuentos para niños

Sume, cuentos

MOSCOSO, Mercedes Gonzalez de (see **GONZALEZ DE MOSCOSO, Mercedes**)

MUJICA, Elisa (Colombia, b. 1918)

Angela y el diablo, cuentos

Arbol de ruedas, cuentos

Catalina

Los dos tiempos, novela

MUJICA DE LACAU, María Hortensia Palisa (see **PALISA MUJICA DE LACAU, María Hortensia**)

MULLE, Felisa Carmen Echevarría de Lobato (see **ECHEVARRIA DE LOBATO MULLE, Felisa Carmen**)

MUNITA, Marta de (Chile, b. 1930)

Arbol de sangre, poesía

Arbol de silencio, poesía

MUÑIZ, Angelina (Spain - Mexico, b. 1936). Muñiz was born in Spain and came to Mexico with her parents during the Spanish Civil War. After writing poetry, drama and literary criticism, Muñiz turned to the novel. Her novels are rooted in religions: Jewish, Christian and Moslem. Her protagonists seek religious identity within the framework of an ancient or a modern world. Muñiz describes their spiritual conflicts with deep sensitivity.

La guerra del unicornio

Huerto cerrado, cuentos

Morada interior, novela. México: Joaquín Mortiz, 1972. 113 pp. The novel which won the Magda Donato prize of 1972 recalls Las moradas of the sixteenth century Spanish mystic, Santa Teresa. Written in the first person, it describes the anguish of a neophyte nun of Jewish ancestry trying to reconcile her beliefs. There is no chronology of time as the protagonist's mind leaps from the barbarities of one century to those of another. Muñiz profoundly explores the existentialist agony of free choice.

Tierra adentro, novela. México: Joaquín Mortiz, 1977. 177 pp. Muñiz' second novel is set in sixteenth century Spain during the time of the Inquisition. A young Jewish boy trudges to Madrid to prepare for the traditional confirmation of his faith. He then decides to walk to the Holy Land, crossing Europe and Turkey before reaching Jerusalem. The lineal narrative provides Muñiz with a broad canvas for a learned study of general sixteenth century history, society and religion. GB

MUÑIZ, María del Garay (see **GARAY MUÑIZ, María del**)

MUÑOZ, Carmen (Chile, twentieth century)

Un poco de amor, novela

MUÑOZ, Mercedes Negrón (see **NEGRON MUÑOZ, Mercedes**)

MUÑOZ, Rosita Silva de (see **SILVA DE MUÑOZ, Rosita**)

MUÑOZ XIMENEZ, María del Carmen Izcua Barbat de (see **IZCUA BARBAT DE MUÑOZ XIMENEZ, María del**)

MUÑOZ DE MERCHAN, Isabel María (Ecuador, b. 1910)

Auroras de eternidad, poemas

MURIEL DE LA TORRE, Josefina (see **LA TORRE, Josefina Muriel de**)

MURILLO, Josefa (Mexico, 1860-1898)

Poesías

N

NAJERA, Indiana E. (Mexico, twentieth century)

A media voz

Barbas y melenas célebres, y uno que otro rasurado

Carne viva

El chulo

El cielo eres tú

Cruz Roja

Páginas íntimas, novela

Pasajeros de segunda

Pifias

Poza negra

Tierra seca, novela

NAJLIS, Michèle (Nicaragua, b. 1946). Born in Granada, Nicaragua, Najlis' early works were published in La Prensa Literaria. Her one volume of collected works, El viento armado, reveals the strong revolutionary tone which informs her most successful pieces. Najlis has taught courses in literature at the National University in Managua. She shows promise as one of the group of young Nicaraguan poets writing today.

El viento armado, poemas. Colección Los Ultimos, vol. 3. Guatemala: Universidad de San Carlos, 1969. 79 pp. The principal themes of these politically militant poems are love of life and revulsion for injustice, hunger, suffering, and repression of personal freedom. Social protest and anti-dictatorial expression are evident in the central portion of the anthology, which includes the best pieces of the collection, their primary value residing in the poet's forceful language. The final section of the book is devoted to rather sentimental love poems whose quality does not match that of the political works. Somewhat uneven overall, the volume is of interest to students of testimonial literature of the armed struggle in Central America. A printing of one thousand copies is extant. ED & ME

NARANJO, Carmen (Costa Rica, b. 1930). Former Ambassador to Israel, Minister of Culture, Youth and Sport, and Director of the Social Security System, Naranjo is also a poet, novelist, short-story writer and essayist. Her work is intellectual, original, linguistically innovative, psychological and compassionate. Her poetry is metrically free and structurally lyrical; her narrative exhibits a mixture of fantasy and reality, a preoccupation with the Spanish language, and a search for identity, both individual and cultural. Naranjo remains Costa Rican in her choice of common people as characters; and her use of regionalisms of language (e.g., "vos estés"). In highly metaphorical language, Naranjo is brutally frank and realistic. Her works take place in San José with constant references to its rain, streets, and lost, wandering people. In the narrative part of the poetry, her main characters are symbolic of herself.

Camino al mediodía, novela. San José, Costa Rica: Costa Rica, 1977. 99 pp. Introduction and short critique by Elizabeth Odio. This novel takes place between 7:30 and 12:30 a.m. one rainy day in San José, Costa Rica. The unnamed narrator hears of the death of an old friend on the radio. During his attempts to view the body at the funeral home, his thoughts go back to former times, to memories of Eduardo, his family, and his life. The narrator, a kind of Greek chorus/Everyman, is at times invisible. Time, space and reality are confused, co-mingled. Midday is symbolic of life crises; the style is psychological, symbolical, and metaphorical. The real protagonist, Eddy, is to be pitied as are all Naranjo's characters, fatally doomed to travel through the vicissitudes and travails of life, unable to save himself. The ordinary person's life is boring, humdrum; humanity's struggles are useless and invisible.

Canción de la ternura, poesía. San José, Costa Rica: Elite de Lilia Ramos, 1964. 35 pp. With her linguistic ability and knowledge of language, Naranjo uses images and metaphors, especially of land and sea, to eternalize love in this, her first poetic work. It is a testimony to hope, a voice for brotherhood and friendship. The writer/speaker says to the reader/listener: "I am always here just to speak to you." There is tenderness to relieve discomfort; the hope of one's life is in others. Her poetry is metrically free and lyrical. The poem is divided into eight parts.

Diario de una multitud, novela. San José, Costa Rica: Universitaria Centro Americana (EDUCA), 1974. 267 pp. The novel, Naranjo's mature statement, proceeds alternately in narrative streams of consciousness and dialogue. In a series of unnamed characters, Naranjo develops the theme of the absurdity, the monotony and the absence of motivation in contemporary San José society, a society pursuing luxury and pleasure, a society of exploitation and class consciousness. In an advanced technological world, solidarity and humanism do not exist; spiritual values are absent. Although not optimistic, the novel reveals hope.

Five Women Writers of Costa Rica: Short Stories by Carmen Naranjo, Eunice Odio, Yolanda Oreamuno, Victoria Urbano, and Rima Vallbona. Ed. Victoria Urbano. Beaumont, Tx.: Asociación de Literatura Femenina Hispánica, 1978. Translation.

Hacia tu isla, poema. San José, Costa Rica: n.p., 1966. 37 pp. Hacia tu isla is a poem and a tribute dedicated to the writer's father, Sebastián Naranjo Prida. She speaks to him in a free verse filled with images and metaphors. He lived a simple, pure, good life, helping others. He made a home, had children, planted a garden and loved roses, sowing seeds with a pride in humanity. He represented the good and the hope in humanity in a world filled with wars, blood and insanity. When he died, he found a way to his freedom, his little island, full of the flavor of the sea and where childhood reposes.

Hoy es un largo día, cuentos. San José, Costa Rica: Costa Rica, 1977. 122 pp. Naranjo's only work of short stories (to date) presents thirteen brief, surrealistic, mystical episodes; stories of reality and fantasy, tragedy and insanity, violence and death. In "El de los Cuatro," Irene, a poor, ugly woman, dies in a patio with only dogs for company. "La Condesa" is killed in the Russian revolution. These stories seem a departure from Naranjo's other work.

Idioma del invierno, poemas. San José, Costa Rica: Conciencia Nueva, n.d. 41 pp. Naranjo uses extended metaphor reduplicated into additional internal metaphors about the Costa Rican (meseta) winter, the rainy season. Both specifically Costa Rican in the rain and winter language, and universal in life and death images, Idioma compares rain to humanity's transitory existence. Parts I and II are universal, Parts III and IV are specific. Begun in the rain in the city of rain, the shift is to a love poem, from tears, rumors and jokes to love, life and death. Part V is prose and connects the personal love story and loneliness with the rain and universal love of life. Part VI reveals a lost love, and Part VIII, in clipped style, says that only rain is real.

Memorias de un hombre palabra, novela. Serie La Propia. San José, Costa Rica: Costa Rica, 1968. 172 pp. The anonymous protagonist of this novel tells his own sad story of living without love. Because humans are limited by their "words" (their humanity), they cannot rise above and beyond themselves; they are caught in their own mediocrity. In Memorias the main character does meditate on his circumstances, but does not always arrive at any conclusion. Naranjo captures the seriousness of language taking form and thought in human beings. Her style is curt, filled with single words and phrases.

Mi guerrilla, poema. Colección Séptimo. Notes by Coronel Uetecho. San José, Costa Rica: Universitaria Centro-Americana (EDUCA). 103 pp. The Guerrilla is the dawn and the dawn is hope. A metrically free poem in five parts which restates her major thesis that, even with great technical advances, barbarism still exists in the inability of human beings to consolidate brotherhood. The hypocrisy of contemporary society sacrifices individuals to the system, people to statistics. Naranjo offers a balance between reality and the hope for something better to come. In this work, her language is sharper, with fewer difficult metaphors than in her earlier poetry. Her style is direct, acrid and confessional.

Misa a oscuras, poesía. San José, Costa Rica: Costa Rica, 1967. 51 pp. Accompanied by short criticisms by Echeverría, Chase and Ramos. This poem, a stage in Naranjo's poetic evolution, follows the order, style and content of the Roman Catholic mass. The journey through life that we do not understand, but must endure, is an age-old theme, but here it is treated in an original, brilliant manner. Its beautiful metaphors, words, and emotions penetrate the human soul, the dark and shining world of human intention to reach the viscera of humanity; it exudes a disquieting philosophy and contemporary mysticism.

Los perros no ladraron, novela. San José, Costa Rica: Costa Rica, 1966. 457 pp. Winner of the Premio Nacional de Novela in 1967, Los perros consists entirely of conversation; names are unimportant, and at times it is difficult to know who is speaking to whom. In this, Naranjo's most important early work, all her themes are present: The city of San José, the streets, rain, stereotyped characters, and the relentlessness of life. Loosely connected with a business office, the characters plod like milkhorses from home to work and back again, along the same city streets. Marriage is described as frightful; the wife is a castrating, carping virago; but a love found outside of marriage makes the dreariness and nothingness of life bearable. Death, painted as a visitor who comes without warning when even loyal dogs "do not bark," is the only release.

Responso por el niño Juan Manuel, novela. San José, Costa Rica: Costa Rica: Conciencia Nueva, 1971. 192 pp. Premio de Novela en los Juegos Florales de Guatemala in 1968. Juan Manuel, fifteen years old, dies in an accident. The novel takes the form of a requiem by Juan Manuel's friend, an unnamed narrator, who searches for the truth of the boy's existence. Returning to boyhood times, he talks to others, remembers, and seeks answers to the ultimate questions of life, death and humanity. Juan Manuel's life becomes the metaphor of existence. Juan Manuel, born old, died young because he was somewhat foolish, an original, afraid of shouting and lightning, master of his own life, searching for the natural in experience and impulse, possessing the grace of virginal discoveries without logic. For him, life was a road with neither beginning nor end; time was relative to love and loneliness. Juan Manuel had his day of love and his years of loneliness and abandonment. Naranjo's language is poetic, mystical and metaphoric.

AS

NARDI, Rafaela Chacón (see **CHACON NARDI, Rafaela**)

NAVA, Thelma (Mexico, b. 1930)

Aquí te guardo yo, poemas

Colibrí 50 (cincuenta), 1962-1964, poemas

La orfandad del sueño, poema

NAVARRO, Ada (Argentina, twentieth century)

Después del incendio, novela

NAVARRO, Eliana (Chile, b. 1923)

Antiguas voces llaman, poesía

La ciudad que fue, poesía

La pasión según San Juan, oratoria poética

Tres poemas

NAVARRO, Sofía Ospina de (see **OSPINA DE NAVARRO, Sofía**)

NAVARRO DE CASTRO, Rebeca (Chile, twentieth century)

El alma y la rosa, poesía

Poesía de gatos

Presencia distante, poesía

NEGRON, Delis (United States, twentieth century)

Palabras, poesías

NEGRON MUÑOZ, Mercedes (Puerto Rico, 1895-1973; pseudonym: Lair, Clara). Along with Julia de Burgos, Lair is one of the few women poets writing during the thirties in Puerto Rico. After publishing two books, Lair went into seclusion, living in isolation and shunning literary circles until her death. In 1946 she received a prize for her journalistic work. The high, sustained quality of her poetry, and her treatment of erotic experience make her stand out among the women writing at the time. Her poems are usually long, with long verses and traditional rhyme patterns. ILJ

Arras de cristal, poemas

Clara Lair: Poesías

Cuadernos de poesía. San Juan, Puerto Rico: Instituto de Cultura Puertorriqueña, 1961. Hardcover, 42 pp. Available only in libraries. This book is a selection of fourteen poems from Trópico amargo, prefaced by a brief biographical note about the poet. It features bold and striking black and white illustrations. The editor has chosen some of her lengthier poems for this collection. Among them, "Fantasía del olvido" echoes the sorrow of a lost love. "Angustia" describes her conflicting emotions about Puerto Rico, her homeland. And "Lullaby mayor" is a strangely haunting poem which joins the themes of love and death. PF

Más allá del poniente, poemas

Obra poética. Notes, Prologue by ed. Vicente Géigel Polanco. San Juan, Puerto Rico: Instituto de Cultura Puertorriqueña, 1979. ISBN 84-499-0307-6, hardcover, 110 pp. The book includes two previously published volumes, Arras de cristal (1937) and Trópico amargo (1950), as well as the first poems written by Lair, Un amor en Nueva York (1920-1928). Her poetry can be studied within the context of erotic poetry written by Latin American women at the beginning of the century. The poems reveal an awareness of the use of women as sex objects, and denounce it. The recurrent image of burning flesh represents both desire and frustration. Following the modernistas, Lair writes long poems with rhythmic patterns. ILJ

Trópico amargo. San Juan, Puerto Rico: Biblioteca de Autores Puertorriqueños, 1978. Hardcover, 132 pp. Available in libraries. A collection of twenty-seven poems, which vary in length, style, and substance. Her most common themes are love, death (the two are often intertwined), the poetic vocation, and her love of life and beauty. Her view of male-female relationships is startlingly frank and realistic for her time, and she frequently expresses her view that women should "live for the moment" and accept love as a temporary thing, without hoping too much for the future. She makes frequent use of tropical images (the plants and insects of Puerto Rico). PF

NIETO, Carmen Gaete (see GAETE NIETO, Carmen)

NIETO DE ARIAS, Gloria (Colombia, twentieth century)

Parábola del misterio

NIETO DE DIEZ, Catalina (Mexico, twentieth century)

Sara, la mapuche

NIETO DE HERRERA, Carmela (Cuba, b. 1875)

Aventura de Buchón, cuento para niños

NIETO DE MADRIGAL, Carmen (Costa Rica)

Poesías

NIETO DE SANCHEZ, Rosa (Mexico, twentieth century)

De buena ley, novela

NIGGEMAN, Clara (Cuba - United States, twentieth century)

Canto al apóstol, verso

En la puerta dorada

Remolino de fuego

NILO, Mariela del (Colombia, twentieth century; pseudonym)

Claro acento, poemas

Torre de niebla, poemas

NINFA, María Emiliani Imitola (see EMILIANI IMITOLA NINFA, María)

NIVAR DE PITTALUGA, Amada (Dominican Republic, twentieth century)

Palma real, poesía

Rosa de América, poemas

NOCEDAD, Lucrecia Silva (see SILVA NOCEDAD, Lucrecia)

NOGUERA, María Leal de (see LEAL DE NOGUERA, María)

NOLLA, Olga (Puerto Rico, b. 1938). Although she began writing later than most poets, Nolla has produced a series of important books. She originally studied biology and chemistry and only later pursued literature. She worked as a journalist and was cofounder of a literary review in the early seventies: Zona carga y descarga. Nolla has also been active in the women's movement and was a member of the editorial board of Palabra de mujer, a feminist journal. Her style is colloquial, with a preference for long verses.

Clave de sol. Serie Literatura Hoy. San Juan: Instituto de Cultura Puertorriqueña, 1979. Paperback, 94 pp. A collection of thirty-seven poems and a fable ("La princesa y el juglar") followed by some reflections on the poems. Most of the texts are short and use traditional verse forms, although rhyme is avoided. Love and the search for and definition of womens' identity are the main themes. In "La Verdadera Cenicienta," the poetic subject sees herself enjoying her own body, dancing in the arms of her own happiness. The reflections that follow the poems refer to the authors she read while writing the book. The poems are seen as a process of revelation of her own being.

De lo familiar. Buenos Aires: Dead Weight, 1973. Paperback, 77 pp. Nolla's first book, De lo familiar, is characterized by images of a chaotic world, incoherent in its multiple representations. The "signs" of mass media expose the confusion of this poetic world. The style corresponds to this chaos; the graphic distribution of the verses on the page is fragmented in order to communicate the sense of dispersion. The poetic subject is an observer of everyday, changing reality. The style is full of surrealistic images; free-verse form and long verses are used.

El ojo de la tormenta. San Juan: Palabra de Mujer, 1976. Paperback, 91 pp. The reader encounters in this poem a process of individual and social transformation. The poetic voice is positioned in the "eye of the storm," witnessing and discovering changes of values and social structures. The metaphoric center allows for a critical confrontation between the self, its past and its values, which had subordinated women to dependence. Verses are long; free-verse form is used. The book is structured as a whole in which all the themes converge in the image of the "eye of the storm."

El sombrero de plata. San Juan: Palabra de Mujer, 1976. Paperback, 63 pp. The reconstruction of childhood images, seen within their ideological framework, forms the core of this book of poems. Women's education, sexist and class-biased, is part of the thematic nucleus. The language is prosaic, with importance given to the narrative aspect of the poems. Through direct confrontation with the world of childhood, the poetic subject is able to break with the past, symbolized by the voyage of Sinbad, the sailor. ILJ

NORONHA, Juana Paula Manso de (see **MANSO DE NORONHA, Juana Paula**)

NUÑEZ, Ana Rosa (Cuba-United States, b. 1926)

Un día en el verso 59 (cincuenta y nueve), poesía

Escamas del Caribe, Haikus de Cuba

Loores a la palma real, poemas

Los oficialeros

Las siete lunas de enero, poesía

Viaje al Cazabe

NUÑEZ, Carlota Carvallo de (see **CARVALLO DE NUÑEZ, Carlota**)

NUÑEZ, Serafina (Cuba, b. 1913)

Isla en el suelo, poemas

Mar cautiva, poemas

Vigilia y secreto, poesía juvenil

NUÑEZ, Zulma (Argentina, twentieth century)

Coplas de la soledad

O

OBALDIA, María Olimpia de (Panama, b. 1891). A native of Panama's northern province of Chiriquí, Obaldía is to Panama what Gabriela Mistral is to Chile: National Poet Laureate. Her early life, her province's natural wilderness, and her personal grief are all deeply reflected in her work. She traveled to Panama City, became a celebrated teacher/educator, married, and parented seven children. Her home, Casa Blanca, figures prominently as a theme in her work. Panama honored her extensively with awards and celebrations.

Breviario lírico

Obras completas, poesía. Panama City, Panama: Colección Kiwanis (K.I.), 1975. 575 pp. Photographs. Prologues by Samuel Lewis, Enrique Ruiz Vernacci and Octavio Méndez Pereira; "Parnaso Infantil" has a preface, and the entire work contains a preliminary biographical and critical chapter by Gloria Guardia. The book of the complete poetry of Obaldía contains six sections: "Orquídeas," "Breviario Lírico," "Parnaso Infantil," "Eternas," "Poesías" and "Reflejos." Her poetry is mostly lyrical and part of the post-Modernist generation indebted to Rubén Darío. Obaldía uses a traditional literary style with vosotros. The themes treat her beloved Chiriquí, Panama, the traditional "pollera," poverty, Christianity, and children. As a mother and teacher, she considers all the people of the world her children. In her poem "Salute" (to Gabriela Mistral), she ponders how a woman never having been a mother could be so great, and calls her a "mother of nations." AS

Orquídeas, poesías

Parnaso infantil

Visiones eternas

OBREGON SANTACILLA, Adela Formoso de (see **FORMOSO DE OBREGON SANTACILLA, Adela**)

OCA, Julia Luisa Pérez y Montes de (see **PEREZ Y MONTES DE OCA, Julia Luisa**)

OCAMPO, María Luisa (see **OCAMPO HEREDIA, María Luisa**)

OCAMPO, Silvina (Argentina, b. 1903). Least known member of the Sur generation of Buenos Aires. Ocampo is a younger sister of Sur editor, Victoria Ocampo. She is also the wife of Adolfo Bioy Casares and a life-long friend of Jorge Luis Borges. She studied painting in Paris in her youth and has exhibited her work from time to time; she has published award-winning poetry; but she is best known for her short stories. These latter are characterized by their brevity (most are under five pages in length), frequent use of women and children as protagonists, and the appearance of fantastic and/or grotesque elements. PK

Amarillo celeste, poemas. Buenos Aires: Losada, 1972. Hardbound, approx. 150 pp. Available in major research libraries. This collection of poetry continues to develop Ocampo's poetic themes of love, the ephemeral nature of happiness, the passing of time, and death. The several religious poems have a more personal tone than those of previous collections. Although there are still several poems in traditional meters, principally sonnets and cuartetos, most of the poems are free verse. PK

Arboles de Buenos Aires, poesía con Aldo Sessa. Buenos Aires: Librería de la Ciudad, 1980. Approx. 75 pp. An extremely limited number of this luxury edition was published and it is virtually unavailable. As the title suggests, the photographs and poetry both address the theme of trees and the city of Buenos Aires. PK

Autobiografía de Irene, cuentos y novela corta. Buenos Aires: Sudamericana, 1975. 120 pp. The four short stories and one novelette included here reveal the author's preoccupation with the themes of death and madness. Unusual characters, surrealistic techniques (dreams, nightmares, visions, and disjointed images), and a circular structure predominate. In the title story, Irene's only recollections are of the future; she has no memory. At the conclusion, as she tells the story of her life to a woman who has plans to publish it, she starts her account with the same words that appear at the beginning of the story.
MSA

El caballo alado, literatura juvenil. Buenos Aires: Flor, 1972. n.pag. [26 pp.]. Illus. by Juan Marchesi. A picture book intended for young children. The story concerns the friendship between a little girl named Irene, who lives in a labyrinthine museum with her father, the caretaker, and her favorite piece in the museum, a statue of Pegasus. The sculpture comes to life, and they fly away together. When they return, Irene begs the winged horse not to leave her. MSA

Canto escolar, poesía

El cofre volante. Colección Cuentos Para Seguir Contando. Buenos Aires: Estrada, 1974. Approx. 30 pp. A children's story probably intended to be read to very young children (ages 4-6 yrs.). The language is difficult and the plot extremely disjointed and whimsical. The illustrations aptly capture the dream-like character of the narrative. The main character, El Gato, and his friend, a little boy named Pimpampum, discover a tiny magic trunk. PK

Los días de la noche, cuentos. Buenos Aires: Sudamericana, 1970. 204 pp. A short story collection in which irony and elements of the fantastic play an important role. The plots and themes are varied while the point of view is primarily first person. The content ranges from portraits of a single character to stories about children, lovers, and animals. Many of the characters are eccentric. In two stories she mentions a character named Borges, a reference to her friend, Jorge Luis Borges. MSA

Enumeración de la patria y otros poemas. Buenos Aires: Sur, 1942. Approx. 200 pp. Out of print and practically unavailable. These poems are long, are written in traditional meters (cuarteto, quintilla, sexteto, and sonnet), and are divided into sections according to theme. Many of the longer poems contain extended allusions to Biblical and mythological characters and to historical figures from Classical Greece and Rome. The theme of Argentina itself appears in the title poem and in several others. "Sonetos del jardín" offers a simple style and a more personal tone than the other poems of the volume. PK

Espacios métricos, poesía. Buenos Aires: Sur, 1945. 154 pp. A book of poetry dedicated to her husband, Adolfo Bioy Casares. In these selections Ocampo, for the most part, employs traditional verse forms and treats universal themes, such as love, death, and nature. Several poems open with an epigraph composed of a quotation from a famous English or French writer. Significantly, these sources represent the two countries, England and France, which have exerted the greatest influence on the development of Argentine culture. The espacios are distances which separate the poetic voice from its subject; for example, the poems on historical and legendary figures represent a temporal separation, while the ones in which she longs for her lover depict spatial separation. MSA

La furia y otros cuentos. Buenos Aires: Sur, 1959. 222 pp. A large volume containing thirty-four short stories. This and Las invitadas are Ocampo's major collections. Once again one finds numerous examples of themes and techniques that are a mainstay in her stories: death, abnormal behavior, and the use of common, routine activities as a springboard for the unusual and the irrational. Irony also plays an important role in the collection. One selection, "Informe del cielo y del infierno," becomes the title story in a subsequent anthology. MSA

Informe del cielo y del infierno, cuentos. Introduction by Edgardo Cozarinsky. Caracas: Monte Avila, 1970. 189 pp. A recompilation of short stories from earlier collections, mainly La furia y otros cuentos and Las invitadas. A good sampling which is representative of her work in this genre. "Sábanas de tierra," the only previously uncollected story in this volume, originally appeared in Revista Sur in 1938. MSA

Las invitadas, cuentos. Buenos Aires: Losada, 1961. 184 pp. This volume, Ocampo's largest short story collection, is composed of forty-four selections. The usual stylistic features (use of irony, surreal visions, fantasy, and memorable characterizations of children) are again present here. Especially effective is her use of the fantastic, which serves as a bridge between the child's world and the realm of the adult. In the title story, told from a third-person point of view, a little boy takes his initial step toward manhood when his birthday party is attended by several ill-mannered little girls, who symbolize the seven deadly sins. MSA

Lo amargo por dulce, poesía. Buenos Aires: Emecé, 1962. Approx. 150 pp. Awarded the first prize in the National poetry competition in 1962, this is probably Ocampo's best collection of poetry. Pessimism and pain color the treatment of the theme of love, and a new note of self-loathing is evident in the collection's first poems, "Acto de Contrición" and "El

Pecado." The theme of death is a major preoccupation with moods alternating between bitterness and resignation. The duality of experience is expressed here in images which utilize paradox and oxymoron (note the title). PK

Los que aman, odian, con Adolfo Bioy Casares. Buenos Aires: Emecé 1946. 119 pp. Ocampo and co-author Adolfo Bioy Casares, her husband, follow the standard formula of the detective novel, a genre that is extremely popularly in Argentina. The story concerns a group of people who, while vacationing at a seaside resort, become involved in a murder investigation. Suspicion quickly shifts from one character to another. The reader is constantly kept off-balance by the introduction of false clues at well-timed intervals. Eventually, through a series of plot twists and startling revelations, the mystery is solved. MSA

La naranja maravillosa, cuentos juveniles. Prologue by Enrique Pezzoni. Buenos Aires: Orión, 1977. 154 pp. As indicated by the sub-title, this is a book of short stories for juveniles but it can be enjoyed by anyone who is young at heart. The stories have children as protagonists, abound in elements of fantasy, and deal with the experience of growing up. They are similar to fairy tales in that they offer pure entertainment while incorporating recognizable archetypal patterns. Some are adaptations of stories that previously appeared in collections intended for adult readers. MSA

Los nombres, poemas. Buenos Aires: Emecé, 1953. 106 pp. A collection of primarily first-person lyrical poems of varying lengths in traditional forms characterized by Ocampo's predilection for relating experience to art. Numerous Biblical allusions and references to personages from classical mythology. Various emotions associated with love are treated from a feminine rather than a feminist perspective. Pure art, devoid of political comment and social concerns (a good example is the sonnet "Leda y el cisne"). MSA*

Los nombres, poemas. Awarded the second prize in the National Poetry Contest (of Argentina) in 1953, this volume represents a new direction in Ocampo's poetry in which she experiments with freer forms of verse. Here she abandons exclusive use of traditional verse forms to introduce unrhymed, irregular meter. The most interesting section of poems is dedicated to Ocampo's husband, Bioy Casares, and treats the theme of the creative process itself. The imagination is seen as a source of both beauty and horror, of pleasure and pain. PK*

El pecado mortal, cuentos. Buenos Aires: Universitaria, 1966. 130 pp. An Introduction provides biographical information on Ocampo and comments briefly on some of the stories. All twenty short stories in this volume were previously anthologized (in Las invitadas, La furia y otros cuentos, or Autobiografía de Irene). MSA

Pequeña antología. Buenos Aires: Ene, 1954. 38 pp. A poetry sampler containing selections from three earlier works: Poemas de amor desesperado, Espacios métricos, and Enumeración de la patria. Included in this brief volume (twelve poems) is one previously unpublished poem, "No Siempre." Although there are no selections

---

*These two annotations are of the same book. -- Editor

from Los nombres, a major collection that appeared the previous year, this anthology is otherwise fairly representative of Ocampo's work as a poet up to 1954. MSA

Poemas de amor desesperado. Buenos Aires: Sudamericana, 1949. Approx. 200 pp. The theme of love, always present in Ocampo's poetry, here gains prominence. The first half of the book deals with the title theme of desperate love, love riddled with lies, jealousy and uncertainty. The second half of the volume returns to themes developed in previous collections: narrative poems with subjects from classical antiquity and the Bible; a section of new sonetos del jardín. One new element is a series of poems inspired by the works of French and English writers, such as Pierre de Ronsard, Andrew Marvell, Alexander Pope, and Baudelaire. PK

Poemas escolares

Sonetos del jardín. Illus. by Héctor Basaldúa. Buenos Aires: Colección La Perdiz, 1948. 28 pp. This is a luxury edition, oversized with heavy paper and large print. Only five hundred numbered copies were published. Ocampo combines the two sections of poems of the same title from her first two collections of poetry into a single volume. She maintains the original ordering: the first seven sonnets come from Enumeración de la patria, while the next six are from Espacios métricos. PK

El tobogán. Colección Cuentos Para Seguir Contando. Buenos Aires: Estrada, 1975. Hardbound, approx. 20 pp. Unavailable. This is a continuation of the child's story, El cofre volante. Beautifully illustrated by Beatriz Bolster. PK

Los traidores, drama con J.R. Wilcock. Buenos Aires: Losada, 1956. 80 pp. Los traidores is a drama-in-verse written in collaboration with J.R. Wilcock. The confusing discontinuity of plot, the atmosphere of dream or nightmare, the absence of consistent characters, as well as the interest in poetry and lyrical expression, all identify this work with the Theater of the Absurd and the poetic avante-garde theater, which appeared in the post-war period. Its setting in ancient Rome repeats a thematic strand apparent in Ocampo's early poetry and stories. The strange, experimental dramatic elements, combined with its setting make this a particularly unsatisfying work. PK

Viaje olvidado, cuentos. Buenos Aires: Sur, 1937. 186 pp. Her first published volume of short stories. As in many of her later works of fiction, the main characters are usually children, most often little girls. Ocampo's evocation of childhood is surrealistic, but her characters live in a world that is real rather than a fantasy world. Not surprisingly, many of the stories contain descriptions of houses, enclosed areas which, in the eyes of children, afford protection and, at the same time, offer opportunities for discovery. MSA

OCAMPO, Victoria (Argentina, 1890-1979). Ocampo was born in Buenos Aires, the eldest of six daughters of an aristocratic Argentine family, and educated by governesses in turn-of-the-century European style. After a brief, unhappy marriage without children, she turned to writing subjective essays (Testimonios), biographical studies of Tagore, T.E. Lawrence, Virginia Woolf, and Keyserling as well as numerous translations of French, English and North American authors, all of whom she knew personally through extensive travels. Founder, director and publisher of Sur, an influential literary journal since 1931 and publishing house since 1933, considered the finest in Latin America for several decades. A feminist since her adolescent rebellion against Victorian restrictions, she worked actively for women's rights in Argentina in the thirties and wrote repeatedly on the subject thereafter. Her opposition to Perón brought her a month's imprisonment in 1953. She continued writing essays, her memoirs, translations and publishing Sur until her death.

Autobiografía. 3 vols. Buenos Aires: Sur, 1979-1981. Paperback, 186, 213 and 152 pp., respectively. Posthumously published memoirs of Ocampo's childhood, adolescence, education, early literary experiences, failed marriage and clandestine love affair. Told in the context of Argentine history with emphasis on the repressive effects of a patriarchal environment. Rich in detail and expressive, lyric prose. Ocampo's most intimate writing.

La belle y sus enamorados

De Francesca a Beatrice

Emily Bronte

La laguna de los nenúfares, fábula escénica en doce cuadros

La mujer y su expresión

Soledad sonora, vol. 4 of Testimonios. [See annotation below.]

Testimonios. 10 vol. series. Vol. 1 (Madrid: Revista de Occidente, 1935), out-of-print; Vols. 2-10 (Buenos Aires: Sur, 1941-77). Paperback. Essays written between 1920 and 1977 recording Ocampo's varied experiences in the cultural worlds of South America, Europe and the United States. Includes her impressions of important literary and artistic figures, their works of all genres and media, her recollections of her own early years, the founding of Sur, the Second World War, feminist efforts in Argentina, the Perón years, and other memorabilia. Of interest to general readers and scholars of literature and socio-cultural history. Only a few dozen essays out of several hundred have been translated into English, some by this annotator.

Victoria Ocampo: Against the Wind and the Tide, a biography with a selection of essays. Tr. Doris Meyer. N.Y.: George Braziller, 1979.

Virginia Woolf en su diario. Buenos Aires: Sur, 1954. Paperback, 109 pp. An extended essay written as a personal reaction to A Writer's Diary, posthumously published selections from Woolf's diary. Particularly interesting as a record of a South American woman's testimony of Woolf's influence on her life and work. Also contains a description of her friendship with Woolf in the late thirties. DM

OCAMPO DE ALVAREZ, Inés (Colombia, twentieth century)

Cantos de la tarde, poemas

OCAMPO DE PERA, María Ofelia (Argentina, twentieth century)

La culpable, novela

El mundo de ensueño, reminiscencias

OCAMPO DE SANCHEZ, Natalia (Colombia, twentieth century)

Una mujer, novela

OCAMPO DE VELASCO, Blanca (Colombia, twentieth century)

Manojos, poemas

OCAMPO HEREDIA, María Luisa (Mexico, b. 1905; known as Ocampo, María Luisa). Originally from Cilpancingo, Guerrero, Ocampo has had an active career in Mexico City's theatrical life as well as business and government posts. She is best known as a playwright and translator and adaptor of works by O'Neill, Dostoyevsky and others. Her own drama and fiction is basically realistic with some tendency to abstract declamatory statements by characters. She is especially skilled at rendering the nuances of workplace sexual and status politics.

Atitlayapán, novela

Bajo el fuego, novela. Mexico: Botas, 1947. 246 pp. Availability poor. This novel of the Mexican revolution is presented in the form of first-person and very personal reminiscences of childhood. It is outstanding principally for offering the perspective of an average child attuned to the normal rhythms of small town life. The reader first becomes acquainted with the rituals of undisturbed provincial existence, then gains an understanding of the profound changes that occurred "under the fire" of both revolution and cultural change. It won the Ignacio Manuel Altamirano Prize.

El corrido de Juan Saavedra

Cosas de la vida, comedia

Ha muerto el Dr. Benavides, novela

La maestrita, novela corta

El señor de Altamira, novela. México: Costa-Amic, 1963. 260 pp. Availability poor. A financially pressed marquis is the hero of this novel of government officialdom. As the protagonist must accept a high bureaucratic post in post-revolutionary Mexico, the novel comments both on the dying world of the aristocracy and the modern wheelings and dealings of government circles. The marquis' dilemma in his status and difficulties in adjustment are alternated with a critical novelistic depiction of the politics of the workplace and the abuse of access to power.

Sombras en la arena, novela

Una tarde de agosto

La virgen fuerte, comedia. Mexico: Sociedad General de Autores, 195?. 68 pp. Difficult to obtain. Woman's vulnerability in the workplace provides the tension in this basically realistic, but somewhat declamatory, drama. The doctor-heroine suffers unwanted advances from a colleague, stereotyping, and a melodramatic conflict between her private and professional roles. The work is modern in its treatment of sexual harassment and role conflicts, but offers an old-fashioned solution: a male protector. NL

OCHART, Luz Ivonne (Puerto Rico, b. 1951). Studied literature and painting in Spain and finished a Ph.D. in Romance languages at Stony Brook University with a dissertation on Leopoldo Alas (Clarín). Has published in Zona, Crisis and Alicia la Roja among other journals. Ochart is part of the group of women poets that started writing in the seventies. Her poetry is innovative in form and deals with a variety of themes that vary from self discovery to the poetic representation of Old San Juan.

Este es nuestro paraíso, poemas. San Juan: Instituto de Cultura Puertorriqueña, 1981. Paperback, 88 pp. Illustrated with a series of photographs of the old city. Ochart's second book includes poems written between 1975 and 1980. The author's prologue is directed mostly to literary critics. The unifying theme is the city of San Juan: its people, streets, houses. The poetic subject is always present, observing the city, recognizing herself in its description. The poems are short, except for "La Otra," in which the contradictory nature of the city, its beauty and its ugliness, is exposed. Free verse forms are used throughout.

Rantamplán, poemas. San Juan: Zona, 1975. Paperback, 21 pp. Rantamplán was awarded the first prize in the Ateneo Puertorriqueño's literary contest, 1974. Published in the format of a small folder with loose leaves inside, the poems give the reader the opportunity to order the pages according to chronology or to themes. The author's prologue explains the reason for this type of format and the notion of a book ordered by its themes. Free verse is preferred and most of the poems are short, using colloquial language. There is no single unifying theme. ILJ

OCHOA, Enriqueta (Mexico, twentieth century)

Los himnos del ciego

Las urgencias de un dios

OCHOA, Rosa Margot (Mexico, twentieth century)

Corrientes secretos, novela policíaca

OCHOA LOPEZ, Moravia (Panama, twentieth century)

Donde transan los ríos, sonetos

El espejo

Raíces primordiales

Yesca, cuentos

ODIO, Eunice (Costa Rica - Mexico, 1922-1974). Born in San José, Costa Rica, Odio spent most of her life in various Latin American countries, and wrote her works while in exile until 1969 when she became Mexican citizen. The main themes of her texts deal with creation, love, mankind's fate, the mystery of life, loneliness and the plurality of the creator/poet. Her poetry may be classified as creacionismo, especially that of El tránsito de fuego, her last book. Although recognized by well-known critics (e.g., Juan Liscano) as an outstanding poet, her lyrical texts have not been translated or reprinted. Her prose writings, which include essays, and short stories had been scattered in magazines all over the world until recently collected in La obra en prosa de Eunice Odio.

Antología, Rescate de un gran poeta. Ed. Juan Liscano. Caracas: Monte Avila, 1975. Paperback, 418 pp. The main interest of this anthology lies first in the prologue by Humberto Díaz-Casanova and the literary study made by Juan Liscano. Second, it gathers all the poems published in Zona Franca (Venezuela) until 1974. The lyrical texts in this edition allow the reader to follow, in poetry and in life, Odio's evolution towards a deep, fanatic Catholic faith. "Arcangel Miguel," considered a masterpiece of Spanish American poetry, is one example. Last, but not least, it offers the interesting collection of letters sent by Odio to Liscano from 1965 to 1974. These letters not only give unusual insights into her poetics, psychology, and life, but some are masterpieces in epistolary literature.

Los elementos terrestres, poesía. Guatemala: El Libro de Guatemala, 1948. Paperback, 63 pp. Available in the United States only in research libraries. Odio's first book of lyric poetry, Los elementos terrestres won the prestigious Central American literary prize "15 de Septiembre" in 1947. It is a collection of eight long poems written in free verse, with a mystical-erotic theme and a cosmic conception of reality. The connotative power of the lyric images suggests the cyclic course of nature, of love, and of poetic creation. Theme, tone, metaphors, key words, and rhythmic devices (i.e., repetition, alliteration, stress) are reminiscent of the Song of Songs. At the same time, they remind us of Saint John of the Cross' "Cántico espiritual."

Five Women Writers of Costa Rica: Short Stories by Carmen Naranjo, Eunice Odio, Yolanda Oreamuno, Victoria Urbano, and Rima Vallbona. Ed. Victoria Urbano. Beaumont, Tx.: Asociación de Literatura Femenina Hispánica, 1978.

La obra en prosa de Eunice Odio. San José, Costa Rica: Costa Rica, 1981. Introd., biography, bibliography by editor Rima Rothe de Vallbona. 294 pp.

El rastro de la mariposa, cuento. Mexico: Alejandro Finisterre, n.d. Paperback, 31 pp. This tiny book can be classified as science fiction. Its theme illustrates Odio's concept of the creator who transubstantiates himself/herself into the object of his/her creation. First published in Zona Franca (Venezuela), 58 (June 1968), 7-13. An English translation by Catherine G. Bellver was included in Five Women Writers of Costa Rica. (See above for more information.)

Territorio del alba y otros poemas. Ed. Italo López Vallecillos. San José, Costa Rica: Universidades Centroamericanas (EDUCA), 1974. Paperback, 254 pp. This anthology was prepared by Odio shortly before her death, although it was published posthumously. It contains poems already included in her three most important books of poetry. However, the major interest of this anthology lies in the previously unpublished poems which presumably were to be included in three books never published but which had already received titles: Filo de luna nueva, Pobre calle pobre, and Agua, camina, clara. These new poems mostly adhere to surrealism and contain the same themes as those written before 1948, to which death, solitude and religious faith are added here.

Los trabajos en la catedral, poesía. Mexico: Espacio, n.d. Paperback, 49 pp. Available only in the private collections of Odio's friends. This rare and beautiful book represents only one part of "Proyectos de los Frutos" included as the third part in El tránsito de fuego. Each one of its four parts comprises several lyric sequences which have complete unity and interdependence according to the various themes. Los trabajos deals with the creation of a cathedral as its main theme and is dedicated to all arquitects. In a suggestive and polyvalent language, the cathedral is described as the anatomic parts of the human body.

El tránsito de fuego, poema. San Salvador: Ministerio de Cultura, 1957. Paperback, 456 pp. Available only in research libraries. One of the most extensive poems in Hispanic literature. Written in free verse from 1948 to 1954, Odio's masterpiece is conceived in the form of transcendental dialogue between the Creator Ion (the poet), different mythical beings, and the chorus which transmits to the whole a dramatic and metaphysical quality. It is divided into four parts: "Integración de los Padres;" "Proyecto de Mí Mismo;" "Proyectos de los Frutos;" and "Alegría de los Creadores," representing an allegory of the fate of mankind's Creator. Parts of the poem have been included in anthologies or constitute in themselves separate texts.

Zona en territorio del alba, poesía 1946-1948. San Rafael Mendoza, Argentina: Brigadas Líricas, 1953. Paperback, 34 pp. Available only in the Library of the Congress. A collection of poems written from 1946 until 1948 which are predominantly short, in free verse, and cover a variety of themes related to children, to friendship, and to art expressed through dance. Chosen by the Editorial Brigadas Líricas as the best exponent of contemporary Central American poetry, it was published as part of a series of books representing different Latin American countries and regions. Of interest is the prologue, "Eunice Odio - Sueño y Raíz, Misterio y Poesía," by Alberto Baeza Flores which represents the first complete study of Eunice's poetry. RRV

OFELIA (pseudonym: see **MATAMOROS, Mercedes**)

OLEMA GARCIA, Daura (Cuba, twentieth century)

Maestra voluntaria, novela

OLIMPIA OBALDIA, María (see **OBALDIA, María Olimpia**)

OLIVER, Carilda (Cuba, b. 1923)

Al sur de mi garganta, poesía

OLIVER, María Rosa (Argentina, b. 1904)

Mundo, mi casa, recuerdos de infancia

La vida cotidiana

OLIVIERI, Marta (Argentina, twentieth century)

La primera fuente

O'NEILL, Carlota (Mexico, twentieth century)

Amor, diario de una desintoxicación, novela abstracta

Circe y los cerdos, teatro

Como fue España encadenada, teatro

Cuarta dimensión, teatro

Una mexicana en la guerra de España, novela

Los muertos también hablan, continuación de Una mexicana en la guerra de España

¿Qué sabe usted de Safo? Amó a las mujeres y a los hombres

Romanzas de las rejas, prosa poética

Teatro

Trapped in Spain. Trans. Leando Garza. Toronto: Solidarity Books, 1978. Translation of Una mexicana en la guerra de España

ONRUBIA DE BERTONA, Salvadora Medina (see **MEDINA ONRUBIA DE BETONA, Salvador**)

ONTIVEROS Y HERRERA, María G. (Venezuela, b. 1909)

Destellos, poesía

Primicias, poesía

ORDOÑEZ, Beatrix Gallardo de (see **GALLARDO DE ORDONEZ, Beatrix**)

OREAMUNO, Yolanda (Costa Rica - Mexico, 1916-1956). Like her friend Eunice Odio, Oreamuno was born in Costa Rica and died a Mexican citizen. She wrote only in prose: novels, short stories, and essays. Regional and propaganda narrative were the main concern of her contemporary Costa Rican writers. However, Oreamuno placed herself in the avant-garde with the best writers of her time by turning her back on those trends and by getting involved in techniques like stream-of-consciousness and surrealism. Her themes deal mainly with women's world, i.e., marriage, divorce, machismo, lesbianism, etc. She had an unhappy and tragic life. Unfortunately, her novels, except La ruta de su evasión, have been lost. Efforts to find the manuscripts have been fruitless.

A lo largo del corto camino, cuentos y artículos. Eds. Lilia Ramos, et al. San José: Costa Rica, 1961. Paperback, 384 pp. Available in research libraries. This valuable anthology collects for the first time letters and the short stories and essays by Oreamuno which had been published in Repertorio Americano from 1936 until 1948. Some universal themes in this text are a lack of communication, cultural myths, return to primal instinct in contact with nature, solitude, and existential death. Many short stories exemplify her mastery of stream-of-consciousness techniques, others employ surrealistic, and a few have linear, traditional structures. All have unexpected endings.

De ahora en adelante

Five Women Writers of Costa Rica: Short Stories by Carmen Naranjo, Eunice Odio, Yolanda Oreamuno, Victoria Urbano, and Rima Vallbona.

Ed. Victoria Urbano. Beaumont, Tx.: Asociación de Literatura Femenina Hispánica, 1978.

Relatos escogidos. Ed. Alfonso Chase. San José: Costa Rica, 1977. Paperback, 388 pp. Available commercially. This anthology is a new collection of all the short stories published in Repertorio Americano with the addition of three texts which previously appeared in other Latin American magazines. "Las mareas vuelven de noche" deals with imagination and blends exotism with oneirism. The theme of "Don Juvenico" is the search for the impossible youth conceived as Unamuno's plots. "De su obscura familia" depicts with nihilistic strokes the theme of the immigrant who finds his identity when he becomes integrated with the "obscure family" of Indians in Mexico City. Because of their analytical and psychological qualities, most of the short stories have the length of novelettes, which show that the author was at her best in the novel genre.

La ruta de su evasión, novela. Guatemala: Ministerio de Educación Pública, 1949. Hardbound, 320 pp. 2nd ed.: (San José: Universidades Centroamericanas [EDUCA], 1970), paperback, 368 pp. The second edition is available commercially. This long and rich novel was considered by Abelardo Bonilla "one of the most audacious novelistic adventures in the Spanish language because of its complicated and difficult narrative techniques." The plot of this novel takes place at two levels: the present and the past. The reality of the characters manifests itself through flashbacks, the stream-of-consciousness and oneiric techniques. It is a psychological novel that deals mainly with middle-class women's conflicts with the opposite sex, and with the characters' monotonous, useless, and problematic lives. RRV

Tierra firme

ORGAZ DE CORREA LUNA, Delia (Uruguay, b. 1921)

Calle hacia el mar, poemas intemporales y sonetos al correr del tiempo

Mínimo ciclo, poemas

Parábola de la voz amarga, poemas

ORJIKH, Victoria (Chile, b. 1913)

El agua entre las manos, teatro

Canto a Villa Alegre, poesía

Como las rosas rojas, teatro

Elegía a Borís Orjikh Svetáev, poesía

Manos de mujer, cuentos

Melodía de rosas rojas, teatro

Puertas adentro, teatro

Puesta al sol, novela

Regalo de París, teatro

Regresé al misterio, cuentos

OROZCO, Olga (Argentina, b. 1920)

Desde lejos, poesías

Los juegos peligrosos

Las muertes, poemas

Museo salvaje, poemas

La oscuridad es otro sol, poemas

ORPHEE, Elvira (Argentina, b. 1930). Orphée studied philosophy and letters at the University of Buenos Aires, and took courses in literature at the Sorbonne. Has published novels, short stories and journalism. Orphée's narrative is unusual for the lyrical quality of its language as well as the harsh landscapes and resentful people that inhabit them. An outstanding writer who deserves to be studied and translated, Orphée as won several important literary prizes in Argentina.

Aire tan dulce, novela. Buenos Aires: Sudamericana, 1966. Paperback, 331 pp. 2nd ed.: (Caracas: Monte Avila, 1977), paperback. The most celebrated of the author's novels. It has three narrators: Felix, a bitter adolescent who despises his family and milieu, a twice unhappily married grandmother, and Talita, her grandaughter, suffering from an unnamed disease and pathetic loneliness. Both adolescents are cruel and aggressive out of the need to be loved. Orphée effectively uses poetic language mixed with street, sometimes obscene, talk to reveal the pain of her characters' solitude.

Dos veranos, novela. Buenos Aires: Sudamericana, 1956. Paperback. Orphée offers in this realistic novel a perceptive inner portrait of a would-be criminal. The illiterate, ugly, adolescent Sixto, who dreams of becoming someone someday, hides his sensitivity and fears in aggressive behaviour. His hopeless life is being shaped by the poverty, superstition and needless cruelty and indifference that pervade the northern Argentinean province the book depicts. Orphée's language reaches lyrical pathos when reproducing Sixto's thoughts and desires.

En el fondo, novela. Buenos Aires: Galerna, 1969. 2nd ed.: (Buenos Aires: Fabril, 1969), paperback, 175 pp. The excursion into the past of the woman protagonist of this novel forms a kind of subjective travelling where objective time and place do not matter in comparison to the intensity of the character's feelings and desires. In a progressive descent into insanity, she recovers her childhood days filled with magic and also terror. Memories of love found in more peaceful lands are obliterated by the attraction of the cruelty, disorder and freedom of her early years that she finally regains.

Su demonio preferido, cuentos. Buenos Aires: Emecé, 1973. 2nd ed. 1973. Paperback, 243 pp. Ten short stories in which characters possessed by demons -- envy, jealousy, gossip, pride -- live intense passions behind the façades of 'normal' lives. The stories are more in the realistic mode than others of Orphée's works. However, mysterious acts and the words of hallucinating old women and frightened, imaginative children add fantastic dimensions to several of the narratives.

La última conquista de El Angel, cuentos. Caracas: Monte Avila, 1977. Paperback, 142 pp. Although Orphée classifies her book as a collection of short stories, the same characters and theme throughout make it seem like a novel. The narrator of these eleven pieces set in contemporary Argentina is a professional torturer who, like his colleagues, is so committed to his "craft" that he offers few details about the victims. Without heroes or hopeful ideologies, this unrelenting exploration of the psychology of torturers makes reading the book a searing experience.

Uno, novela. Buenos Aires: Fabril, 1961. Paperback. Difficult to find. Set in Argentina between 1945 and 1955, the novel, considered by its author the closest to her country's reality, is structured with changes in time and places in which people from different social classes share common, unsatisfactory lives. The anguish of the main characters, a frustrated man and a solitary woman who never meet, springs from the inauthenticity of their existence originated in the hypocrisy and false values which corrupt all levels of society.

Las viejas fantasiosas, cuentos. Buenos Aires: Emecé, 1981. Paperback, 205 pp. 2nd ed. 1981. Fourteen short stories united by a common landscape -- domestic life in a small town -- and imaginative, superstitious characters. The language blends effectively the poetic with daily, ordinary expressions. Magic and realistic elements give some of the stories an aura of old mythical tales, modernized by feminist views. "El alma de doña Tilile," "Noche enjoyada," "Aparten de mí a las bestias" remind the reader of the best of Rulfo's or Garro's stories with their poetic recreation of popular language. GM

ORREGO DE URIBE, Rosario (Chile, 1834-1879)

Alberto, el jugador

Sus mejores poemas

Teresa, novela

ORTEGA, Evelina Bobes (see **BOBES ORTEGA, Evelina**)

ORTEGA, María del Carmen (Mexico, twentieth century)

Floración, poemas

El ramo de amapolas

ORTI, Ana Manuela Elorza de (see **ELORZA DE ORTI, Ana Manuela**)

ORTIZ, Marta Reyes (see **REYES ORTIZ, Marta**)

OSPINA DE NAVARRO, Sofía (Colombia, twentieth century)

La abuela cuenta, memorias

Cuentos y crónicas

OSSA, Elvira Santa Cruz y (see **SANTA CRUZ Y OSSA, Elvira**)

OSSA, María Silva (see **SILVA OSSA, María**)

OSSA DE GODOY, Blanca (Chile, twentieth century)

    Páginas infantiles

OSSANDON, Francisca (Chile, b. 1923)

    Díalogo incesante, poesía

    El don oscuro, poesía

    Humo lento, poesía

    La mano abierta la rayo, poesía

    Tiempo de estar, poemas

    Tiempo y destiempo, poesía

OSSES, Ester María (Panama, b. 1916)

    Crece y camina, poesía

    Mensaje, poemas

    La niña y el mar, poemas

    Para el combate y la esperanza, poesía

    Poesía en limpio, poemas

OTERO, Margarita Díaz de Castillo de (see **DIAZ DE CASTILLO DE OTERO, Margarita**)

OTERO JOY, Sarah (?, twentieth century)

    Vivía la alondra en silencio, poesía

OYARZUN, Mila (Chile, b. 1912)

    Cantos a una sombra, novela

    Esquinas del viento

    Estancias de soledad, poesía

    Pausado cielo, poesía

OYENARD, Sylvia Puentes de (see **PUENTES DE OYENARD, Sylvia**)

P

PACHECO, Cristina (Mexico, twentieth century)

Sopita de fideo, relatos

PACHECO DE HAEDO, Carmelinda (Mexico, twentieth century)

El enganchador, novela de costumbres

PADILLA, Lila (Argentina, twentieth century)

Entre sombras y maldades

PADILLA, Martha (Cuba - United States, b. 1934)

La alborada del tigre, poesía

Comitiva al crepúsculo, poesía

El fin del tiempo injusto

PADILLA DE SANZ, Trinidad (Puerto Rico, b. 1868; pseudonym: La Hija del Caribe)

Cálices abiertos

PAGELLA, Angela Blanco Amores de (see **BLANCO AMORES DE PAGELLA, Angela**)

PALACIOS, Adela (Mexico, twentieth century)

Adrián Rubí, novela

El angelito, cuentos

Cuadros escolares

Dulce y Hurañi

El hombre, novela

México, poema

Mi amigo Pablo, relatos

Muchachos

Normalista, tres relatos

Tangente, novela

Yo soy tus alas, poema

PALACIOS, Antonia (Venezuela, twentieth century)

Ana Isabel, una niña decente

Los insulares, relatos 1965-1967

El largo día ya seguro, relatos

PALACIOS, Lucila (pseudonym: see **CARVAJAL DE AROCHA, Mercedes**)

PALACIOS, Matilde Velas (see **VELAS PALACIOS, Matilde**)

PALAVICINI, Laura (Mexico, twentieth century)

Aleteos, poemas

PALENQUE, Silvina Bullrich (see **BULLRICH PALENQUE, Silvina**)

PALISA MUJICA DE LACAU, María Hortensia (Argentina, b. 191?). Born in Buenos Aires, she graduated from the National Institute of Higher Education and taught Spanish language and literature at various schools, including the Universities of Buenos Aires, Ecuador, Mexico, Peru and Puerto Rico. An indefatigable promoter of children's literature, she has written several award-winning books herself for children and currently directs the series for children and young adults with the publisher Plus Ultra. Her literary production for adults includes collections of poetry and short stories, essays on literary criticism and textbooks on language and literature.

El arbolito Serafín, versos para niños

El oficio de vivir, cuentos. Buenos Aires: Instituto Amigos del Libro, 1963. Paperback, 176 pp. Available in major research libraries. This collection of ten short stories narrated mostly in third person revolves around the theme of life as the special "trade" or skill to survive learned through suffering. All the stories are set in Argentina, particularly Buenos Aires; some of them are preceded by epigraphs from Spanish authors. The title and theme were seemingly inspired by Ricardo Molinari, quoted in an introductory epigraph. Also in connection with the title, there is a reference in one story to Cesare Pavese. The entire collection contains frequent references to renowned authors, composers and painters. Index.

País de Silvia, poesías infantiles. Buenos Aires: Kapelusz, 1962. Paperback, 61 pp. Available commercially. An introductory poem dedicates the volume of sixty-one poems to Silvia Benítez, a brown-eyed

five-year-old who, together with her sister Margarita, has made joy
triumph over the author's sadness. The collection contains at least two
illustrations on every page. The title and index pages contain drawings
of an older woman talking to a child; similarly, some poems represent
the author's persona addressed to a little girl. Most of the poems reflect
a child's wonder-filled mentality. They deal with real and toy animals;
they also explain imaginatively or inquire about natural phenomena.
Written with sing-song rhythm and very obvious rhyme, they are
ideally suited for a child's listening enjoyment.

Permanencia de luz, poesía. Illus. by Oscar Capristo. Buenos Aires:
Ciordia y Rodríguez, 1957. Paperback, 58 pp. Available at the New
York Public Library. The twenty-six free-verse poems in this collection
hail the poet's happiness as a child with her family and as a married
woman with her husband. The book's title refers to this joy expressed in
all the poems. The author persists in narrating the reasons for her
ecstasy, instead of suggesting it or evoking a comparable emotion
through original imagery -- hence the overly sentimental tone of the
entire collection.

Poemas con gente. Buenos Aires: F.A. Colombo, 1972. Paperback, 93
pp. This collection consists of nineteen long, free-verse poems, set in
Buenos Aires, imbued with nostalgia. They lack innovative imagery
but are rich in lyricism. The poet addresses specific individuals in her
family, e.g., her dead father, mother and husband as well as her sister
who died very young. Children play an important role in several poems,
particularly her niece Laura, this niece's son, Leo, and an unidentified
Silvia (who could possibly be the same little girl to whom Lacau
dedicates her volume of children's poetry). Lacau also reminisces about
her professor Pedro Henríquez-Ureña, her own students, Alfonsina
Storni and the patriotic image of Sarmiento.

Prisma de siete colores, versos. Prologue by Mary Rega Molina. Buenos
Aires: Juan Perroti, 1940. Paperback, 116 pp. Available in major
research libraries. The poems are divided into seven sections: 1) "Songs
of Simple Joy," consisting of eleven unsuccessful poems; 2) "Four
Ballads about Clear Water and One about a Looking Glass," made up of
five excellent traditional-sounding romances; 3) "Floral Tryptich,"
containing three mediocre poems; 4) "Songs of Fog and Nostalgia,"
seven poems, one of which reminisces about her dead father, another on
her childhood; 5) "Pages from a Multicolored Calendar," made up of
eight poems; 6) "Evening Diptych;" and 7) "Inspirational Triptych."
The five poems in these last two sections are superb modernist
compositions of outstanding musicality, elegant imagery and
mythological allusions, and use the rhythmic patterns preferred by the
Modernists.

La voz innominada, sonetos. Buenos Aires: J. Perreti, 1943.
Paperback, 106 pp. In this collection of forty-eight sonnets, Lacau does
not succeed in expressing her feelings well by means of these clichés and
a monotone rhythm that pauses with syntactic or semantic units at the
end of every line. Original imagery is nowhere to be found;
commonplace adjectives adverbs isolate the author from the
experimental trends of this century and prove soporific for the
contemporary reader. All the sonnets are split into one stanza on one
page and the rest of the poem on another; they are thus deprived of their
classical appearance. The rhyme does not exactly follow the traditional
pattern either.

Yo y Hornerín, cuento para niños. Serie Leer y Comentar. Buenos Aires: Plus Ultra, 1980. Paperback, 128 pp. 1st ed.: (Buenos Aires: Proel, 1965). The first edition received an award from Argentina's National Fund for the Arts. In the message to the child reader included in every book of the series, the director talks about the author. She explains that the little girl and her bird friends in the stories represent her own rural childhood experiences in the province of Buenos Aires.

SHA

PALMA, Marigloria (Puerto Rico, twentieth century)

Agua mansa

Agua suelta

Aire habitado

Amy Kootsky, novela

Arboles míos, sonetos

Canto de los olvidados, poemas

Los cuarenta silencios, burlismo, poemas

Cuentos de la abeja encinta

Entre Francia y Suiza, comedia en tres actos

La herencia, comedia en un acto

La noche y otras flores eléctricas

Palomas frente al eco

La razón del cuadrante

Saludando la noche, tragicomedia

San Juan, entre dos azules, poemas

Teatro para niños

Voz de lo transparente, poemas

PALMA Y ROMAN, Angélica (Peru, 1883-1935; pseudonym: Marianela)

Contando cuentos

Hareus, novela

Por senda propia, novela

La sombra alucinante

Tiempos de la patria vieja

Uno de tantos, novela

Vencida, novela

PANCHECO DE PANCHECO, Carmen (Argentina, twentieth century)

Cuentos de la estancia, cuentos para niños

PARIS, Marta Elgul de (see **ELGUL DE PARIS, Marta**)

PARODI, Enriqueta de (Mexico, twentieth century)

Alcancía, prosas para mis hijos

Cuarto de hora, cuentos

Cuentos y leyendas

Luis es un don Juan, novela

Madre, prosas

Mineros, la huelga de Canacea

Reloj de arena, prosas

Ventana al interior, prosas

PARRA, Teresa de la (see **PARRA SANOJO, Ana Teresa**)

PARRA, Violeta (Chile, 1917-1967). Parra was a folklorist, poet, musician, and graphic artist. Her efforts in the fifties to disseminate awareness of authentic Chilean musical forms resulted in the rediscovery of these forms and the consequent growth of a political expression in music, the Nueva Canción Latinoamericana. Parra's commitment to the Chilean people is evident both in her work as a folklorist and in the urgency of her political compositions. Her style is always colloquial and direct, but never compromises the poetic quality. Parra showed her surrealist tapestries and paintings at the Louvre in April 1964. The vast legacy of this remarkable artist has not received the recognition it deserves among scholars in the United States.

Cantos folklóricos chilenos. Musical Transcriptions by Luis Gastón Soublette. Photographs by Sergio Larrain and Sergio Bravo. Santiago: Nascimento, 1979. Paperback, 134 pp. In this partial documentation of her important work as a folklorist, Parra explains her mission: "Ando buscando el verdadero canto de Chile ... yo tengo la obligación de salvar la música chilena." The work is transcribed from tapes recorded during her travels throughout Chile, and represents fifteen singers, poets, and storytellers who helped in the rediscovery of Chilean folk music. Texts include direct quotations from Parra and the artists, descriptions added for background, some photographs and musical transcriptions, and explanations of popular expressions and musical terms. This is a major work both by and about Parra.

Décimas, autobiografía en versos chilenos. Introd. by Pablo Neruda, Nicanor Parra, and Pablo de Rokha. Santiago de Chile: Nueva Universidad / Pomaire, 1970. Paperback, 213 pp. First edition of Décimas. Ninety-two décimas pieced together by Isabel and Angel Parra document the story of a remarkable woman. The mixture of joy and suffering so characteristic of Parra is simply and poetically rendered in these memoirs. The glossary of chilenismos is useful, since the poems are written as they would be spoken. A special feature is the inclusion of nine color plates featuring five of Parra's imaginatively embroidered tapestries (arpilleras).

Décimas. La Habana: Casa de las Américas, 1971. Paperback, 296 pp. Introd. by Pablo Neruda, Nicanor Parra, and Pablo de Rokha. Santiago de Chile: Pomaire, 1976. ISBN 8428601186, hardcover, 251 pp. The only edition authorized by Parra's estate. Includes a useful glossary of chilenismos and color plates of some of Parra's graphic work -- five arpilleras and an oil painting. To have access to all of Parra's graphic art in one volume would be of great value.

Toda Violeta Parra: Antología de canciones y poemas. Preceded by "Violeta Entera" by Alfonso Alcalde. Buenos Aires: Flor, 1974. Paperback, 137 pp. Features a collection of popular songs of Chile collected by Parra during her travels. Organized by type: a lo divino, a lo humano, tonada, parabién, esquinazo, cueca. Themes treat popular religion and philosophy, love, and a general celebration of life and of Chile. Includes a biobibliographical chronology and an informative, profusely illustrated introduction. However, because this book features only thirteen of Parra's own songs, this is not a particularly noteworthy anthology of her own work. A volume of her complete works would be more useful.

21 (Veintiuno) son los dolores. Antología amorosa, poemas. Introd., selection and notes by Juan Andrés Piña. Santiago: Aconcagua, 1976. Paperback, 174 pp. The seventy-five love poems collected here have various origins: some are original compositions, some popular traditional ones adapted by Parra, others gathered from various regions of Chile. Recurring themes are the absence and loss of love and the difficulties of women in society; throughout, the personal suffering of Parra is clearly expressed. The notes give historical and contextual background: when composed, from which region compiled, whether recorded by Parra or other artists. A discography identifies recorded works, and a glossary points out popular pronunciation and chilenismos.

Violeta del pueblo, poemas. Prologue, selection and notes by Javier Martínez Reverte. Madrid: Visor, 1976. ISBN 8470531638, paperback, 153 pp. The structuring of the book in four sections -- "Canciones Amorosas," "Canciones Políticas," "Canciones de Aire Popular," and "Décimas" -- illustrates the trajectory of Parra's work as a poet, musician, and folklorist. Especially significant are the political compositions which demonstrate a committed voice denouncing colonialization, imperialism, and urbanization, and exalting revolutionary heroes. In several works, the ironic treatment of the contradiction between the teachings of the Gospel and the practices of the Church exemplifies the didactic goal of her political poetry. In the introduction Martínez nicely points out the relationship between folklore and politics in Parra's work, and discusses this tradition in Chilean folklore.

Yo canto la diferencia; Canciones de Violeta Parra. Buenos Aires: Lagos, 1976. Paperback, 36 pp. A songbook of music and lyrics to nineteen musical compositions by Parra, including one of a sonnet by Neruda ("No te quiero sino porque te quiero"). Includes works from Décimas, 21 son los dolores, and political pieces. Since the poems can be found in other sources, this volume will be of primary interest to musicians. CW

PARRA CERDA, Vicenta de la (Guatemala, 1834-1905)

Angel caído, teatro

Hija maldita, teatro

Los lazos del crimen, teatro

PARRA DE GARCIA ROSELL, Elisa Rodríguez (see **RODRIGUEZ PARRA DE GARCIA ROSELL, Elisa**)

PARRA SANOJO, Ana Teresa (Venezuela, 1890-1936; known as Parra, Teresa de la). She has been recently rediscovered by feminists as a tough-minded analyst of female frustration. Her literary reputation won by her novels Ifigenia and Las memorias de Mamá Blanca derives in part from her keen observation of human follies and the liveliness of her style. Scholars praise her gift to recreate voices of different classes and ages of her native land.

Cartas

Ifigenia, diario de una señorita que escribió porque se fastidiaba, novela. Paris: Sociedad Iberoamericana de Publicaciones, 1924. Another edition: Ifigenia (Caracas: Monte Avila, 1972), paperback, 494 pp. Framed first in the epistolar mode and then as a diary, this novel was considered too 'feminine' in the past. Today it is seen as one of the best early feminist works. Psychological realism is used to show a gifted young woman who, motivated by fear of poverty and spinsterhood, follows family pressures to marry a man she detests. Under the playful, sentimental voice of its young heroine, the novel presents a harsh criticism of a sexist and classist society.

Mamá Blanca's Souvenirs. Trans. Harriet de Onis. Washington, D.C. and Mexico: Pan American Union, General Secretariat, O.A.S., 1959.

Las memorias de Mamá Blanca, novela. Caracas: Antártida, Biblioteca Básica de Cultura Venezolana, 1960. Paperback, 111 pp. Available in many paperback editions. With a glossary of Venezuelanisms. This novel nostalgically recreates life on a sugar plantation run by benevolent aristocrats. Because its main characters are young girls, the work has been considered a literary children's book. The author shows here her particular skill to recreate verisimilar voices and gestures of children and peasants.

"Las Memorias de Mamá Blanca, A Translation with Introduction and Notes." Ed. and trans. Dolly Doyle Harrell. M.A. thesis Univ. of Texas at Austin (1949).

Obras completas de Teresa de la Parra. Caracas: Arte, 1965. Hardback, 943 pp. This volume includes: 1) an Introduction with some biographical details by Carlos García Prada; 2) a Prologue by Francis de Miomandre; 3) Ifigenia; 4) two opinions by Parra about criticisms on her Ifigenia which provide an interesting author's exegesis of the novel; 5) Las memorias de Mamá Blanca; 6) "Un evangelio indio, Buda y la leprosa," a short story; 7) three lectures by Parra, showing clearly her feminist ideas, preceded by A. Uslar Pietri's Prologue; and 8) letters from Parra to different personalities. Those letters, addressed to L. Alvarado, Guzmán Esponda and to a third, unknown person, demonstrate that in Ifigenia, Parra wanted to criticize the status of women in Venezuela. GM

Tres conferencias inéditas

PASAMANIK, Luisa (Argentina, twentieth century)

El ángel desterrado, poema

The Exiled Angel, translation

Plegaria grave, poesía

Poemas al hombre de la mañana

Sermón negro, poemas

Sinfonía de las esferas, o sinfonía celeste

Tlaloke, poemas mexicanos

Vacío para cuerdas, poemas

PASCUAL ROMERO, Sofía Espíndola de (see **ESPINDOLA DE PASCUAL ROMERO, Sofía**)

PASTOR, Martha Giménez (see **GIMENEZ PASTOR, Martha**)

PASTORINI, Eloísa Pérez de (see **PEREZ DE PASTORINI, Eloísa**)

PATERO DE IBARRA, Graciela (Uruguay, twentieth century)

Isla verde, comedia infantil

PAUL MEJIA, Gloria (Honduras, twentieth century)

Ansias desatadas, poesía

PAULO, Valería de (Chile, b. 1923)

El alma de lo inmóvil, cuentos

Hoguera del silencio, poesía

Martes de gracia, novela

PAUT, Elisa de (Chile, twentieth century)

ABC, cuentos

Evasión, cuentos

Incierta primavera, poesía

Júbilo por la sombra, poesía

PAZ, Julieta Gómez (see **GOMEZ PAZ, Julieta**)

PAZ, Leonor Paz y (see **PAZ Y PAZ, Leonor**)

PAZ, Marcela (pseudonym: see **HUNEENS DE CLARO, Ester**)

PAZ, Martha Noemí Frúniz (see **FRUNIZ PAZ, Martha Noemí**)

PAZ PAREDES, Margarita (Mexico, twentieth century)

    Andamios de sombra

    El anhelo plural

    Canto a México, poemas

    Casa en la niebla

    Cristal adentro

    Dimensión del silencio, poesía

    La imagen y su espejo

    Lumbre cautiva, poemas

    Presagio en el viento

    Rebelión de ceniza

    Retorno, poemas

    Señales, poemas

    Sonaja, poemas

    Voz de la tierra, poemas

PAZ Y PAZ, Leonor (Guatemala, twentieth century)

    18 (Dieciocho) cuentos cortos

    La mujer de pelo largo

PELLEGRIN, Mariluz (Chile, twentieth century)

    Armar de nuevo el puzzle

    Distancia invertebrada, poesía

    Exorcismo, poesía

PELLOT, Carmen Corón (see **CORON PELLOT, Carmen**)

PEÑALOSA, Dolores Castro de (see **CASTRO DE PEÑALOSA, Dolores**)

PEÑUELA DE SEGURA, Gertrudis (Colombia, b. 1910; pseudonym: Victoria, Laura)

    Cráter sellado

Llamas azules

PEON, Dolores Bolio de (see BOLIO DE PEON, Dolores)

PERA, María Ofelia Ocampo de (see OCAMPO DE PERA, María Ofelia)

PERALTA, Berta Alicia (Panama, b. 1939; also Bertalicia)

Dos poemas de Berta Alicia Peralta

Largo in crescendo, cuentos

Los retornos, poesía

Sendas fugitivas, poemas

PERALTA, María Isabel (Chile, 1904-1926)

Caravana parada, poética

PERDOMO, Susana (pseudonym: see JARAMILLO DE CASTRO, Margarita)

PEREA, María Luz (see LUZ PEREA, María)

PEREIRA, Teresinha Alves (see ALVES PEREIRA, Teresinha)

PEREGRINA, la (see GOMEZ DE AVELLANEDA Y ARTEAGA, Gertrudis)

PERERA SOTO, Hilda (Cuba - United States, b. 1926). A precocious child, Perera learned to read when she was three years old and was only twenty-one when her first book was published. She received a scholarship to study at Western College for Women in Oxford, Ohio, where she obtained her Bachelor of Arts degree in 1948. She has a Ph.D. degree in Philosophy from the University of Havana and a Master of Arts degree from the University of Miami at Coral Gables, Florida. In 1964, disillusioned with Castro's regime, she left Cuba as a political exile and came to Miami where she resides and writes. Perera is the author of many textbooks, as well as of short stories for children and the novel in which she has been successful.

Cuentos de Adli y Luas. La Habana: Lex, Consejo Nacional de Cultura, 1960. A collection of seven short stories for children and young adults. It has a great variety of themes and each story contains a moral. Some characters are human beings and others are animals. The short stories with human characters are examples of the author's themes: human dignity and social justice.

Cuentos de Apolo. 1st ed. La Habana: Lex, 1929. 2nd ed.: (La Habana: Lázaro y Hno., 1960); 3rd ed.: (Miami: Franhil Enterprises, 1970). Available in the United States through Librería Universal (Miami). A collection of short stories whose theme is social injustice and discrimination. Written in a lyrical prose, the author depicts the life of a poor, young Black Cuban victim of social discrimination. The book is considered "a small gem of Cuban literature" and has been translated into six foreign languages. Useful for culture courses.

Cuentos para chicos y grandes. Valladolid: Miñón, 1975. Winner of the 1975 Lazarillo Prize. A collection of eight short stories suitable for adults and children. Most of the characters are animals and the narrative combines fantasy and reality. The style and the language used are simple. The short stories are suitable for reading aloud and commentary. The theme is the search for identity as well as the struggle against injustice and inequality.

Felices pascuas, novela. Barcelona: Planeta, 1975. A finalist for the International Prize for the Novel sponsored by Editorial Planeta in 1975, the novel depicts the life of a Cuban family exiled in Miami and the adjustments they have to make to their new situation, forcing them to compare their own moral values to those of North America. Written in an engaging and loose style, the author uses a colloquial language which includes cubanismos. The touching account is told with tact and human understanding without melodramatic excesses. Useful in particular to those interested in the Cuban community in the United States.

Mañana es 26 (veintiséis), novela. La Habana: Lázaro y Hno., 1960. Written during the author's period of revolutionary fervor, the novel deals with the struggle of the Cuban people to overthrow Batista's dictatorship. The flow of the narrative is agile with easy dialogues. It has historical value as the first novel written on the Cuban Revolution. Useful to those generally interested in the Cuban Revolution and in the contribution of the underground network to the success of Castro's revolution.

Pericopín, cuento juvenil. León: Everest, 1981. A short story appropriate for the first stage of reading, written in a clear, yet poetic style. Useful in the classroom for the development of oral expression and observation of the environment. Appropriate for children from five to eleven years old. Included in the list of honor of the best children's books by the Spanish Catholic Commission for Children's Literature in 1980.

Plantado, novel. Barcelona: Planeta, 1981. The novel denounces the suffering and treatment of the political prisoners in Castro's jails. It is a realistic and appalling chronicle in which the dramatic events speak for themselves. Its sombre tone is enhanced by a sober style devoid of literary trimmings, in harmony with the author's objective of denouncing human suffering more than in the purely technical aspects of the novel. The title alludes to the prisoners who resist disowning their democratic convictions and accepting Castro's ideology. Useful to scholars and others interested in an exposé of an ugly facet of the Cuban revolution.

Podría ser que una vez. León: Everest, 1981. Winner of the Lazarillo prize for 1978. A collection of six short stories of human interest, written in a simple and, at times, poetic style. The theme of personal identity is well portrayed. Suitable for children and young adults.

El sitio de nadie, novela. Barcelona: Planeta, 1972. First runner-up of the International Prize for the Novel sponsored by Editorial Planeta in 1972, the novel is a dramatic account of life under Castro's regime. Written in the characteristic lucid, poetic prose of Perera, the novel tells of four Cuban families and their reactions to drastic social changes over which they have no control. Although the novel has a Cuban background and the dialogue includes some cubanismos, the appeal is universal. SMA

PEREYRA, María Enriqueta Camarillo de (see **CAMARILLO DE PEREYRA, María Enriqueta**)

PEREZ, Aurora Estrada de Ramírez Perez (see **ESTRADA DE RAMIREZ PEREZ, Aurora**)

PEREZ, Carmen Chiesa de (see **CHIESA DE PEREZ, Carmen**)

PEREZ, Cecilia (Colombia, twentieth century)

La casa donde termina el mundo

PEREZ, Emma (Cuba, b. 1901)

Canciones a Stalin

Haz en la niebla

Una mujer canta en su isla, poema

Niña y el viento de mañana, poesía

Poemas de la mujer del preso

PEREZ, Marta Magaly Quiñones (see **QUIÑONES PEREZ, Marta Magaly**)

PEREZ, Matilde Espinosa de (see **ESPINOSA DE PEREZ, Matilde**)

PEREZ BARRERA, María Helena Almazán de (see **ALMAZAN DE PEREZ BARRERA, María Helena**)

PEREZ DE MONTI, Luisa María (Argentina, b. 1942)

Antología 1962-1970

PEREZ DE PASTORINI, Eloísa (Uruguay, twentieth century)

Detente, peregrino

PEREZ DE ZAMBRANA, Luisa (Cuba, 1835 [1837?] - 1922). Born in El Cobre, Pérez spent her childhood in a rural environment. In her early compositions she reveals herself as a gifted and delicate poet of nature. The year following the publication of her first poem and the death of her father (1852), Pérez moved with her family to Santiago de Cuba where she was well received by the young literary circles of the provincial capital. Her first collection of poems (1856) reached Ramón de Zambrana in Havana. After a brief correspondence he proposed and, following their marriage, the couple moved to Havana. Zambrana died eight years later and so did the five Zambrana children within the next thirty years. 1866 marks the beginning of the poet's lyric plenitude. Her family elegies have been considered to be among the best written in Spanish. The poetic individuality and sincerity with which she expresses her suffering, the originality of her imagery and the musicality of her language place Pérez de Zambrana in a unique category among the poets of her generation.

Angélica y Estrella, novela. La Escuela Nueva Havana: P. Fernández,
1957. Paperback, 126 pp. First published in serial form in El Siglo,
from Jan. 10th to Feb. 16, 1864. The novel was reprinted in the
collection Los Zambrana (Vol. XIII). The story of two cousins, Angélica,
the virtuous one, and Estrella, the coquette, who selfishly flirts with
Angélica's fiancé. Virtue triumphs in the end and all major and minor
characters are happily married in a conventional setting. Although
angelic Angélica is, unquestionably, the heroine, it is Estrella who
offers a more interesting character to the present-day reader. It is not
only frivolity that makes her hold back from a serious commitment.
Loving her freedom and having a will of her own, she is reluctant to
submit to an authoritarian husband. Nevertheless, she listens to the
voice of reason (Angélica's) and resigns herself to become a "martyr of
marriage."

Elegías familiares

Poesías completas. Colección Los Zambrana, Vol XI. Ed. Angel Huete.
Havana: P. Fernández, 1957. Hardback, 772 pp. Her complete works,
painstakingly edited by Angel Huete, author of the lengthy
biographical and critical introduction and notes and compiler of the
bibliography. The poems, which are grouped into five chronological
periods, include those published by Pérez de Zambrana in her selections
of 1856, 1860, and 1920 as well as many unpublished ones. Several
versions of some poems are given in the appendix. The lyric trajectory
of Pérez de Zambrana begins with delicately melancholic poems of
bucolic, religious, philosophical, social and domestic themes and
culminates in the desolately moving family elegies in which loss and
sorrow are expressed by the poet in a profound and personal voice that
surpasses the romantic boundaries of her earlier compositions. NE

Poesías de Luisa Pérez de Zambrana

PEREZ GUEVARA DE BOCCALANDRO, Ada (Venezuela, b. 1908)

En ausencia tuya

Horizontes, poemas

Pelusa y otros cuentos

Tierra talada, novela

PEREZ MARCHAND, Lilianne (Puerto Rico, b. 1926)

Tierra indiana, poesía

PEREZ WALKER DE SERRANO, Elisa (Chile, b. 1927; pseudonym: Serrana, Elisa). She has written mostly novels, although she has also
published some short stories. She is one of the first Chilean women writers to
devote her entire work to women's issues.

Chilena, casada, sin profesión, novela. Santiago: ZigZag, 1963.
Paperback, 240 pp. A woman searches in vain for fulfillment in
marriage. Her first husband, a lawyer and victim of an Oedipus
complex, destroys her self-confidence and illusions. Her second, a
diplomat stationed in India, uses her in pursuit of his own professional
ambitions. Final fulfillment only comes in her friendship with a leprous
Buddhist spiritual leader.

En blanco y negro, novela. Santiago: ZigZag, 1968. Paperback, 296 pp. The protagonist-narrator is a blind girl who struggles: first, for a spatial knowledge of the world she inhabits attempting to defeat the loneliness imposed on her by her condition; and second, for a socially meaningful existence. Aided by her cousin, she is able to defeat the stagnation imposed on her by her family, composed of a neurotic mother who neglects her, a crazy aunt, an alcoholic uncle and an alienated grandmother.

Las tres caras de un sello, novela. Santiago: ZigZag, 1960. Paperback, 227 pp. Three women: the wife, a woman of the bourgeoisie; the secretary, belonging to the lower-middle class; and the prostitute-lover all strive for fulfillment in their relationship with one man. A successful engineer uses each one to lead a different facet of his life: that of the honorable married man; the compassionate boss; and the exploitative lover. Good critique of androcentrism.

Una, novela. Santiago: ZigZag, 1964. 211 pp. The protagonist's development is followed from childhood to adulthood. She is a beautiful woman possessed by an immature desire to stand out and to be different; she challenges the bourgeois modes of life and conventions, without questioning its pseudo-values, settling for an empty existence of social glamour. Her final disillusionment, loneliness, and the recognition of her wasted life, lead her to suicide. PRL

PEREZ Y MONTES DE OCA, Julia Luisa (Cuba, 1841-1875)

Poesías de la señorita doña Luisa Pérez y Montes de Oca

PEREZCANO DE JIMENEZ ARRILLAGA, Josefina (Mexico, twentieth century)

Al final del camino, novela sólo para mujeres

Brochazos surrealistas

Mañana el sol será nuestro, novela

PERI ROSSI, Cristina (Uruguay-Spain, b. 1941). Novelist, short story writer, poet and journalist. Peri Rossi taught literature for ten years in Montevideo and wrote for various newspapers and magazines, Marcha among the latter. A member of a coalition of leftist parties, she was persecuted and had to emigrate. She has lived in Barcelona since 1972. Committed to change in literature, politics and sexual mores, her work breaks generic modes and traditional patterns, treating with great imagination erotic, social and artistic subjects. Her prose and poetry -- marked by playfulness, humor and irony -- project an almost apocalyptic vision of the world in the process of desintegration.

Descripción de un naufragio, poesía. Barcelona: Lumen, 1975. Paperback, 99 pp. Poems about love and exile. Imagery and motifs of the sea reveal longing for lost land and home, celebration of woman's body and ingrained opposition to social and political repression. Humor and street language are mixed with dazzling metaphors in the free verse of the poems. The weaving of politics into the dramatic narrative sometimes echoes the poetry of Ernesto Cardenal.

Diáspora, poemas. Barcelona: Lumen, 1976. Paperback, 91 pp. Poems about social revolution, aesthetic creation, loneliness and lesbian love. In a free type of verse, the use of colloquialisms, plays on words and irony result in humorous and ambiguous effects. The book won the Inventarios Provisionales Prize in 1973 in Spain.

Evohé, poemas eróticos

Indicios pánicos. Montevideo: Nuestra América, 1970. Paperback, 141 pp. 2nd ed.: (Barcelona: Bruguera, 1981), paperback, 184 pp. A prologue and forty-six fragments in a book difficult to classify. Many of the pieces are short stories, poems, essays and aphorisms. The common theme running through the work is the evil of misused power in social and private relations. Considered a prediction of the repression to come under dictatorship, the book has been banned in Uruguay since 1973. The humor that lightens the corrosive satires does not diminish the impact of Peri's powerful indictment of fascism.

El libro de mis primos, novela. Montevideo: Biblioteca de Marcha, 1969. Paperback, 173 pp. 2nd ed.: (Barcelona: Planeta y Janés, 1976), hardbound, 236 pp. (The second edition contains errors.) In its first edition, this novel was divided in nineteen fragments, eleven of which are narrated by a male child with a keen, critical eye for the faults of his upper-class family. Adult cousins narrate the remaining chapters thereby providing different perspectives and voices. Mixing chronology, prose and verse, humor and poetic language, the book is a devastating satire of the rich, capitalism, patriarcal institutions, and militarism. Feminist views form part of the revolutionary perspective of the novel.

Lingüística general, poemas. Valencia, Spain: Prometeo, 1979. Paperback, 77 pp. This slender volume of poems is divided into three sections. The first "Lingüística General" is comprised of very brief -- sometimes only two lines -- free verses, with an aphoristic flavor, about poetry and love. The second, "Cuaderno de Navegación," and the third, "Travesía," add the motif of travel and underscore lesbian love. The verses are inventive, playful and humorous.

Los museos abandonados, prosa. Montevideo: Arca, 1969. Paperback, 143 pp. 2nd ed.: (Barcelona: Lumen, 1974). Four narrative pieces portraying a decaying, meaningless culture. Symbolized by empty museums, this culture produces cruel, lonely people. In three of the four stories, a man and a woman play sad erotic games. Closed to the outside world, they are neither able to see the destruction occurring around them nor to communicate with each other. An unusual touch of the fantastic enhances the interest of "Los extraños objetos voladores," the realistic first story of peasants' poverty and powerlessness.

El museo de los esfuerzos inútiles, prosa. Barcelona: Seix Barral, 1983. Paperback, 182 pp. Thirty prose pieces difficult to classify. Some are short stories, others journalistic-like chronicles or vignettes. Loneliness and absurdity dominate the dark humored portrayal of different aspects of contemporary life. Among the pieces, some outrageously funny, are satires against psychoanalysis, artificial beauty, political repression and war. The author's stance against oppression of any kind is as clear as her feminist outlook.

La nave de los locos

La tarde del dinosaurio. Barcelona: Planeta, 1976. Paperback, 149 pp. Eight short stories, several of which have as protagonists children who are wiser and more mature than adults. The author displays great imagination in dealing with incest, eroticism and power non-realistically, set in lunar landscapes, remote spaces and times, but also in contemporary Uruguay. Humor and lyric tones blend to produce a poetic-like prose.

La rebelión de los niños. Caracas: Monte Avila, 1980. Paperback, 117 pp. Eight short stories mainly about children and adolescents growing up under the terror of dictatorship. In an interesting role-reversal, mothers fight with guerrillas, fathers are inept caretakers and children seriously discuss repression and revolution. The author uses humor and effective lyrical language to expose the personal and social ills of contemporary life.

Viviendo. Montevideo: Alfa, 1963. Paperback, 125 pp. Written when the author was only twenty-one, these three realistic stories offer a dark vision of the enclosed world inhabited by women. The unifying theme is loneliness. In "Viviendo," the central character is a thirty-four year-old woman growing aware of her spinsterhood. "El baile" and "No sé qué" discretely suggest lesbian relations. GM

PERON, Evita (see **DUARTE DE PERON, Eva María**)

PETIT, Magdalena (Chile, 1903-1968)

Caleuche, novela

El cumpleaños de Rosita, teatro infantil

Don Diego Portales, el hombre sin concupisciencia, biografía novelada

Un hombre en el universo, novela

Kimeraland, comedia satírica

Una llave y un camino, novela

El patriota Manuel Rodríguez

Los Pincheira, novela

Pulgarcito, novela infantil

La Quintrala, novela y drama de la novela

La Quintrala, translation

PIAGGIO, Edda (Uruguay, twentieth century)

Complementos, poesía

PICHETTI, Leonor (Argentina, twentieth century)

Los pájaros del bosque

PINCHEIRA, Dolores (Chile, b. 1915)

Apología de la tierra, poesía

Canto a Concepción, poesía

Mi cielo derribado, poesía

PINO, Tegualda (Chile, b. 1911)

Corolas de cristal, poesía

Horizontes perdidos, poesía

Poemas

El rostro desolado, poesía

PINO DESANDOVAL, Hylda (Ecuador, b. 1917)

Llanto sin lágrimas, versos

Poemas

Ventana al ocaso, cuentos

PINTO, Julieta (Costa Rica, b. 1921). Born in San José, Pinto studied philosophy and philology at the University of Costa Rica and in France and then travelled extensively in Europe and America. This gave her wide experience and a vision of universality. She had spent her youth on her parents' hacienda which afforded her an intimate knowledge of the land and its people. She founded and is Director and Professor of the School of Languages and Literature at the National University in Heredia, and works with the Instituto Mixto de Ayuda Social promoting the life of the campesinos. Her novels and short stories are not distinguished by action, but by details, characters and depth of psychological penetration. She is a stylist, and a voice of concern for the marginal, socially ignored and mistreated portions of society.

A la vuelta de la esquina. San José, Costa Rica: Costa Rica, 1975. 121 pp. This work is a collection of eighteen short, short stories in the realistic tradition describing the anonymous, marginal people of urban San José. Pinto uses the Costa Rican capitaline dialect in stories featuring a little boy drunk at seven because he was thirsty, a factory girl probably pregnant, prostitutes at a dance, an amateur singing contest with a rude, cruel audience, and a beggar girl at Christmas looking through the window at a doll.

Cuentos de la tierra. Illus. by Francisco Amighetti. San José, Costa Rica: L'Atelier, re-edited by Costa Rica, 1963. 109 pp. In her first book, Pinto achieves a haunting, melancholic, even poetic and musical quality in her sixteen stories. Abandoned children, animals, natural phenomena nostalgically blend together to reveal the author's love and deep understanding of rural Costa Rica, its forgotten people, and of the beauty and relentlessness of nature.

La estación que sigue al verano. San José, Costa Rica: Lehman, 1969. 146 pp. A vivid picture of urban Costa Rican society that rigidly restricts behavior, this novel shows the eternal conflict between human beings of different social and moral conditions ruined by their milieu. The husband, the wife and the other woman are devoured by passion, driven by social and personal success and obsessed with things. The society demoralizes and destroys these anti-heroes, only nostalgia and negation remain. Pinto's style uses inner thoughts, narrative and conversation. Her work is clear, realistic, at times poetic.

Los marginados, cuentos. San José, Costa Rica: Conciencia Nueva, 1970. 131 pp. A collection of eighteen short stories displaying Pinto's deep knowledge of and concern for rural people. Includes the story of a family working diligently on their new farm only to lose it to a large banana company; of a drunken father and his daughter; of a medicine woman who wills a man to death because he deserted the girl who aborted their child; and of a man lying in a tuberculosis hospital who wants to leave in order to kill his children who will otherwise die, even more miserably, from lack of care.

El sermón de lo cotidiano, novela. San José, Costa Rica: Costa Rica, 1977. 105 pp. A psychological novel set against a backdrop of social criticism, El sermón displays, in interior monologue and dialogue, the relationship between its two main characters, a priest and a woman. In a sanitorium, the priest, suffering from internal conflict, a man who was not born for the church, but mean to be a lay-person, talks with a woman, the victim of childhood neglect and men, the mother of an illegitimate daughter. Through their mutual therapy, she becomes free to begin life anew; he, to help himself discover his masculinity, his limitations and his mission. Pinto's style is smoother, her narrative more sophisticated.

Si se oyera el silencio, cuentos. San José, Costa Rica: Costa Rica, 1967. 95 pp. Eleven short stories of middle-class, urban, feminine life. The title refers to the author's intent to reveal what is usually kept silent. Pinto's social concerns here focus on women caught in the traditional roles society forces upon them with tragic results. With exquisite sensitivity she paints stories of marriage, love, motherhood and emotion. Nostalgia, memories, abandonment, sadness, and rural influences permeate the stories. Pinto's style is hard and direct, almost without adornment, sharp, realistic and poetic. AS

PINZON CASTILLA DE CARREÑO-MALLARINO, Isabel (Colombia, twentieth century; pseudonym: Monserrate, Isabel de)

Hados, novela

PITTALUGA, Amada Nivar de (see **NIVAR DE PITTALUGA, Amada**)

PIWONKA, María Elvira (Chile, b. 1915). Born in Santiago, she attended French schools and there began to write poetry in French. She also speaks English, German, Italian and Portuguese. After high-school, her marriage to a diplomat took her to Rio de Janeiro and Buenos Aires. She has since traveled extensively and has given readings in Lima and New York. She was a founding member and one-time director of the Grupo Fuego poetic association. As director of the PEN Club in Chile for several years, she represented her country at the international meeting of the Club in New York in 1966. Her poetry appears in several anthologies and has been translated into English. She has one son from her first husband who left her a widow; she married for the second time to a prestigious politician who was vice-president of the Senate before the fall of Allende. Three grandchildren and the management of a grocery store in Santiago occupy much of her time.

Intima, poesía. Santiago de Chile: Tegualda, 1946. Paperback, 86 pp. Available in major research libraries. This collection of twenty-seven poems is divided into three sections titled "Life," "Pain," and "Love." These are preceded by a thematically interesting composition where, in reply to potential criticism, the author defines her style and its shortcomings as inescapably feminine. Three poems deal with the death of a child and one provides an original dimension to a rhythmic pattern used by Gabriela Mistral. Many establish a sensual bond between nature and the poet; a few are addressed to a lover.

Lazo de arena, poemas. Santiago de Chile: Grupo Fuego, 1957. Paperback, 60 pp. Available in major research libraries. This collection of thirty-eight poems was the seventh published by the Associación "Grupo Fuego" of which Piwonka was a founding member. Most of the poems are constructed traditionally with some form of rhyme scheme and rather conventional love imagery. A few stand out for their bold expression of sensuality and chromatic description of nature at different hours of the day. It contains a portrait of the author by Jorge Delano F., an index and excerpts of reviews of Piwonka's works.

Llamarlo amor, poemas. Illus. Santiago de Chile: Universitaria, 1949. Paperback, 63 pp. Available in major research libraries. This collection of twenty-nine poems is divided into three sections: "Wingless Love," "Interlude," and "Winged Love." The first poems in the first and third section -- "Bad Love" and "Good Love," respectively -- identify the poet's attitude toward her development from a passionate unrequited love to a secure and peaceful relationship. The poems in "Interlude" express disenchantment with the former and outline a search for the latter through consciously limited experiences. With the same title as the book, the last poem reflects the author's hesitation to call her joyful peace by a name that connotes passion and suffering.

Selected poems Tr. Edward Newman Horn. New York: Osmar, 1967. Paperback, 61 pp. SHA

PIZARNIK, Flora Alejandra (Argentina, 1936-1972; known as Pizarnik, Alejandra). Born in Buenos Aires, she lived in both Argentina and France, collaborating on various literary magazines. She was interested in fantastic literature and that interest is reflected in her often mysterious and tragic poetry. She suffered from depression and took her own life on Sept. 25, 1972. Her heterodox poetry reflects her studies: philosophy in 1954; literature from 1955 to 1957; then she dropped out of the university and studied painting. Her style is to transmute reality into revelation.

Alejandra Pizarnik, A Profile. Ed. Frank Graziano. Trans. Suzanne Jill Levine, et al. Colorado: Logbridge - Rhodes, 1986.

El árbol de Diana, poemas. Introd. by Octavio Paz. Buenos Aires: Sur, 1962. 65 pp. Unavailable. Paz writes: "El árbol de Diana es transparente. . . . Tiene luz propia." He describes her as focusing the light from the luminous, mythological tree into a poem whose luminosity is so intense that it "hasta volatiza" unbelievers.

Los árboles y la noche

Las aventuras perdidas. Buenos Aires: 1958. Unavailable. Her third book, published when she was twenty-two. Death, paradoxes and the loss of childhood innocence are portrayed with the intensity of expression that was her trademark. The suicidal tendencies can be seen in lines such as: "Why don't I pull out my veins to make a ladder to flee to the other side of night." There is a bittersweet taste to childhood in: "I remember my childhood when I was old. I remember the black sunny mornings."

La condesa sangrienta

El deseo de la palabra, poemas. Colección OCNOS. Barcelona: Barral, 1975. ISBN 84-211-0652-X, 265 pp. Foreword by Octavio Paz, epilogue by Antonio Beneyto. Contains poems from six collections plus essays: El infierno musical, 1971; Extracción de la piedra de locura, 1968; Los trabajos y las noches, 1965; El árbol de Diana, 1962; Las aventuras perdidas, 1958; and La útima inocencia, 1956. Published posthumously.

Extracción de la piedra de locura, prosa y poesía. Buenos Aires: Sudamericana, 1968. 67 pp. Unavailable. On of her last collections, published when she was in her early thirties. These prose poems are more mature. Sound and rhythm heighten the mesmerizing, surreal effect. She continues her fascination with death: "all night long I listen to the song of death next to the river." The image of herself as a paper doll recurs in different forms. Some of these poems have the same quality of nostalgia for irredeemable love and beauty as Poe's "The Raven" and Coleridge's "Kublai Khan."

El infierno musical. Serie La Creación Literaria. Buenos Aires: Siglo Veinteiuno, 1971. 76 pp. Prose poems: "Endechas" sad songs and lamentations; "Fragmento;" and "Piedra Fundamental." The fragments have the inexplicable quality of a dream. Images from childhood take on a mythic quality as in this fragment: "One night in the circus I recovered a lost language at the moment the horsemen with torches galloped wildly on their black charges." AMA

Nombres y figuras

La tierra más ajena

Los trabajos y las noches

La última inocencia y las aventuras perdidas

PIZARRO DE RAYO, Agueda (United States - Colombia, b. 1941)

Sombraventadora / Shadowinnower. Trans. Barbara Stoler Miller with the poet. New York: Columbia Univ., 1979. ISBN 0-231-04828-9 and 0-231-04829-7, paperback, 103 pp.

PLA, Josefina (Spain-Paraguay, b. 1909)

Al oído del tiempo, poesía

Antología poética. Asunción: Cabildo, 1977. 90 pp. Available from Temple University Library. This selection includes poems from El precio de los sueños (1927-1932), Poemas de 1935-1940, Poemas de 1941-1952, Poemas de 1952-1960, Rostros en el agua (1960-1963), Invención de la muerte (1964), Satélites oscuros (1966), El polvo enamorado (1968), Luz negra (1975), Inéditos (1945-1959), Biografía (1951), Al oído del tiempo (1960-1972). The prologue explores the dialectic of the material and spiritual world, the essence of Plá's poetry, and the search for identity, both personal and for all mankind. The jacket provides a comprehensive listing of Plá's activities as critic and cultural historian of her adopted Paraguay. Contains an index.

Aquí no ha pasado nada, comedia

Biografía

Desnudo día. Asunción: Diálogo, 1968. 21 pp. Available from Cornell University Library. This slim volume contains nineteen poems ranging from 1935-1940, and includes several romances and sonnets. The poems are highly abstract, densely packed with startling images of love, nature and especially the correlation and interpenetration of these two themes.

Fiesta en el río, teatro. Asunción: Siglo Veintiuno, 1977. 112 pp. Available from Yale University Library. Fiesta en el río, a play in three acts, is an overtly feminist play dealing with the bizarre custom of a small, nameless town in an equally nameless country which calls on its young men to severely chastise unwed mothers. The theme is rebellion against this practice by one young female villager. The majority of the characters are allegorical figures. The text is preceded by a reprint of the official announcement of the contest for which this play won first prize and also by an introduction to the three winning plays, all written by Plá. Jacket contains summary of Plá's work in and on the theatre.

Follaje del tiempo, poemas. Asunción: NAPA, 1981. 44 pp. Available from SUNY Buffalo Library and the UCLA Library. The book contains a short biographical sketch and is followed by an index. Six poems serve as an introduction. Following are "Follaje del tiempo (1965-1979)," "El libro de los sueños (1966-1979)" and "El hijo pródigo (1976)" which is one long poem divided into twenty-two parts. The majority of the poems are of a highly personal nature, first-person revelations of various states of being, and a dialogue with a second person. The last long poem is an objective conception of the prodigal son.

Hermano negro, la esclavitud en Paraguay

Invención de la muerte, poemas

La mano en la tierra, cuentos. Asunción: Alcor, 1963. 27 pp. Available from Cornell University Library. This is a collection of four short stories: "La mano en la tierra," "La niñera mágica," "A caacupe" and "Mala idea." The stories focus on peasant men and women, although the plight of the latter is highlighted. Social conditions ranging from colonial to modern times are exposed in an intense, subtle prose which is flavored with Indian dialect. PS

Luz negra, poesía

Obra y aporte femeninos en la literatura nacional

El polvo enamorado, poemas

El precio de los sueños, poemas

La raíz y la aurora, poesía

Rapsodia de Eurídice y Orfeo, poema

Rostros en el agua

Satélites oscuros

Teatro breve

PLATA, Graciela del Campo y (see **CAMPO Y PLATA, Graciela del**)

PLAZA, Angélica Ferrari de (see **FERRARI DE PLAZA, Angélica**)

POLETTI, Syria (Italy-Argentina, b. 1921). Born in Northern Italy, Poletti earned a teacher's degree in Venice in 1943 and emigrated to Argentina in 1945. She earned a degree in Spanish and Italian from the University of Córdoba in 1948, taught Italian in Rosario and later worked in newspaper and radio journalism in Buenos Aires. Her first short stories appeared in La Nación, Vea y Lea, and El Hogar in 1950 and in the anthology, Veinte cuentos infantiles. Poletti's stories have since appeared in at least ten other Spanish, German, and English anthologies. Her novels, short-story collections, and children's books blend the themes of childhood, immigration and artistic creativity as a social mission that transcends personal relationships. Besides the many prizes won by her books, she has received teaching and lecture fellowships in Italy, Germany, Spain and the United States; the Italian government's title of "Gran Caballero de la Estrella de Solidaridad" (1974); special recognition from Argentina's National Department of Immigration; and the title "Woman of the Year" from the Association for International Development (1975).

Amor de alas. Buenos Aires: Arte Gaglianone, 1981. 57 pp. A large-size art book combining Poletti's philosophical poetic fairytale with color prints of thirteen paintings by Raúl Soldi. Poletti's tale focuses on the one-winged angel, Doriel, whose inability to fly leads him to Earth in search of the purpose of his existence. His only human contacts are children and an old woman. Following a mysteriously inquisitive voice, he travels south--after his disappointment in Los Angeles--and finds his other wing in Sigma, a little shepherdess in mountainous La Rioja. This story symbolically summarizes Poletti's constant themes and motifs, and constitutes a positive counterpart to the pessimistic allegory at the end of Extraño oficio.

Cuentos desde el Taller "Leonor Alonso": dirigido por Syria Poletti. (See annotation in the List of Anthologies.)

Extraño oficio, crónicas de una obsesión, novela. 3rd ed. Buenos Aires: Losada, 1974. 266 pp. 2nd ed. 1972. Divided into seven main parts made up of short stories, monologues, chronicles, and an allegory. Together these sections, mostly narrated in the first person, tell the story of a girl who progressively realizes that her destiny is the art of song, i.e., verbal creativity. Most of the sections present the protagonist-narrator as a child or adolescent in Italy discovering her fascination with words, her love for her old grandmother, her attraction for the opposite sex and her disgust for narrow-minded people. Two of the last sections are narrated by the mature protagonist in Buenos Aires sorting out her past and present. The final allegory--a tale told by the grandmother to the child protagonist--is structurally and symbolically the most imaginative part.

La gente. Ed. Catalina Paravati. Buenos Aires: Kapelusz, 1977. 165 pp. This anthology includes excerpts from Gente conmigo and Extraño oficio, three short stories from Línea de fuego, the children's story "El rey que prohibió los globos" and a five-page essay entitled, "Complejidad del escritor argentino." These are preceded by a table of contents, a biobibliography up to 1974 and a thirty-five-page introduction by the editor. Paravati explains briefly the structure and content of the works anthologized, brings out their themes and motifs, and summarizes those sections contained in the anthology.

Gente conmigo, novela. 8th ed. Buenos Aires: Losada, 1976. 201 pp. This novel won the Losada International Contest in 1961. First published in 1962, it has seen nine editions in twenty years. In 1965, J. Masciangioli made it into a movie, directed by J. Darnell, chosen for the Venice Film Festival and awarded honorable mention at the Locarno (Switzerland) Festival. In 1967, the author adapted the novel for television. In 1968, a German translation appeared. The novel's twenty chapters portray a brave young woman who transcends loneliness and romantic disappointment through a commitment of service to her people. The story is narrated in retrospect by the protagonist immigrant Nora Cardiani whose compulsion to write from early childhood alongside her grandmother has mysteriously resulted in her imprisonment in Buenos Aires. The narrative oscillates between past and present as she reads her diary in jail to try to figure out how her assistance to fellow Italian immigrant has brought her to such a low ebb.

Historias en rojo, cuentos. 2nd ed., corrected and augmented. Buenos Aires: Losada, 1973. 211 pp. First published in 1967, the original collection of five mysteries received the First National Prize for Narrative in 1969. This edition features two additional stories: "A largo plazo," and "Las vírgenes prudentes," besides the original five: "Mola suerte," "Pisadas de caballo," "El hombre de las vasijas de barro," "Estampa antigua," and "Rojo en la salina." Marco Denevi prefaces the anthology with a page-and-a-half of remarks entitled "Para leer a Syria Poletti." Index.

Inambú busca novio. Serie Para Leer y Comentar, Colección Tejados Rojos, La Escalerita. Buenos Aires: Plus Ultra, 1983. ISBN 950-21-0558-3, 80 pp. An illustrated children's story first published in 1966 by Ed. Bib. Constancio C. Vigil in Rosario. Inambú is a freedom-loving bird who inexplicably wants to get married. But she does not know or want to learn how to build or care for a nest. She prides herself as particularly gifted with a narrative skill. The story humorously shows the problems Inambú gets into as she looks for a rich and strong mate by pretending to have a brighter plumage. She ends up marrying the simple partridge suitor she had avoided; without giving up her story-telling gift she decides to learn how to build a nest.

El juguete misterioso. Buenos Aires: Sigmar, 1977. N.pag. [21 pp.]. Illustrated by Santos Martínez Koch, this story for young readers blends the theme of creativity with a touch of mystery. The protagonists are the seventeen-year-old Rondino who unsuccessfully tries to sell the fantastic but unagressive toys he invents, and Florinda, grandaughter of a famous toy manufacturer, Mirko Zanka. Rondino's friend, Luzmil, who owns a "workshop of marvels" where he builds imaginative toys, arranges for Rondino to meet with Mr. Zanka. Florinda's grandfather would prefer more ingenious war-like inventions instead of Rondino's colorful but innocent toys which enthrall his daughter. This meeting establishes a bond between the old and the young man; Rondino, advised by Luzmil, builds for Mr. Zanka three toy guns that shoot out iridescent flowers, bubbles and rockets to musical accompaniment. Since Florinda tests them by herself, when one of the guns later turns out to be real, she insists on Rondino's innocence to everyone's disbelief. Once her pet monkey discovers the original toy gun in the manager's drawer, the mystery is solved. Florinda and her grandfather shoot the colorful guns when he welcomes Rondino and Luzmil as his new partners and decides to become a toy inventor again himself.

Línea de fuego, novela. 6th ed. Buenos Aires: Belgrano, 1982. ISBN #950-077-000-8, 185 pp. First published by Losada in 1964, the second edition (1966) of this collection of short stories was nominated for the National Prize in Literature. The sixth edition features her own signed comments on the meaning of these stories in her life on the back cover. The inside front cover provides brief biographic information and a list of her publications. Followed by an index, thirteen short stories make up this edition: "Los caballos," "El tren de medianoche," "Medias para fiestas," "El tren de medianoche," "Medias para fiestas," "El último pecado," "Apenas una planta," "Altavoces," "Un muchacho con suerte," "Unas monedas," "Santidad de almanaque," "Cosquín de noche," "Línea de fuego," "Un carro en la esquina," and "En el principio era la cal."

Marionetas de aserrín. Buenos Aires: Crea, 1980. 63 pp. With colorful illustrations by Clara Urquijo, this children's book forms part of the series "Cuentorregalo" directed by Poletti herself. The first thirty-two pages tell the story of Ninín whose grandmother inspires her to make her own marionette theatre which she eventually stages for the townspeople together with her wealthy cousin Horacio. The second part of the book, entitled "La fuente mágica," is meant to explain to the reader or potential writer -- as the handwritten introduction notes -- how the story's characters were born. "La fuente mágica" refers to the author's childhood memories in Italy and later experiences as an adult emigrée in Argentina. This nineteen-page section includes photographs and closes with a hand-written note of encouragement from Ninín for the young readers-writers to compose their own stories together with their angel. The book ends with a poem signed by Ninín Airys -- that is, Syria's capicúa, to be read the same from right to left or vice versa -- and addressed to her own angel Doriel, her fairy-grandmother, all marionettes including Pinocchio, and all other living characters.

El misterio de las valijas verdes. Serie Para Leer y Comentar, Colección Tejados, El Altillo. 3rd ed. Buenos Aires: Plus Ultra, 1979. 111 pp. A mystery novel for young readers which focuses on a family of puppeteers--an old Italian grandfather, a mother, and four children (three boys and a girl)--who set out from Buenos Aires on a train to give a show. Their green suitcases get mixed up with those of some thieves who had stolen millions from a bank. The suspense builds as the reader wonders whether the thieves will be caught in time for the family to be able to stage its show. Just like the thief-turned-puppeteer, the reader also delights in the resourceful and imaginative world of the adventurous family.

Reportajes supersónicos, literatura para niños. Buenos Aires: Sigmar, 1979. N. pag. [21 pp.]. First published in 1972 with illustrations by Vilar, this children's literature book was recommended for translation into all languages by the UNESCO Research Institute on Children's and Young Readers' Books in Munich. It received an honorary award from the Argentine Society of Writers (SADE) and was adopted as an additional reading text in Argentine schools by the National Council of

Education. It merited for the author an invitation from the Munich Library to the International Children's Book Fair held in Bolonia, Italy. Published a second time in 1974, the book contains four stories: "¡Atención: Lilín llamando!" "La historia del chocolate," "Buenas noches, tortuguita," and "El primer plato volador." The first one introduces the narrator's niece Lilín who, instead of the garden she dreamed of for her fifth birthday, gets a "supersonic" recorder to interview magic characters, just like her newspaper-reporter and story-writer aunt. The next three stories involve Lilín-Sin-Patio first with a Mexican doll who explains the marvelous history of chocolate, then with her pet turtle who explains the process of hibernation, and lastly with a Mandarin who rises up from a Chinese stamp to tell about the invention of kites. This edition is lavishly illustrated by Santos Martínez Koch.

El rey que prohibió los globos. Rosario: Bib. Constancio C. Vigil, 1966. This illustrated children's story was first published in the same year and by the same editor as Inambú busca novio. It was translated into English in 1984 by Norman Di Giovanni, according to a letter from the author, who also indicates (8-28-84) that "'El rey . . .' and 'Enanito siete' just came out," apparently in a new Spanish edition. The story is included in the anthology La gente. The story tells how once upon a time, balloons, kites and fireworks were invented in China and how everyone there lived a joyous and literally colorful life until the Emperor forbade first kites and then balloons because his people were too playful. Soon the secret of making balloons was forgotten. When the Emperor's youngest son became very ill -- with melancholy -- he asked for a balloon which was impossible to find. All attempts to make a balloon were of no avail until the Emperor shed a tear which transformed the silk cloth it fell on into a beautiful balloon. His son was immediately playful and healthy again, and everything in China was happy and bright.

Taller de imaginería, ensayos y cuentos. Buenos Aires: Losada, 1977. 180 pp. This anthology intended for high-school students comprises three previously unpublished stories -- "La pala," "Agua en la boca," and "Taller de imaginería" -- plus five more from Línea de fuego and four excerpts from Extraño oficio. María Granata provides a two-and-a-half-page introduction to the twelve stories. Twenty-six pages of interviews with the author follow. Edited by Dora Fornaciari, this section includes the author's own ideas about her own literary career, in seven subdivisions: "Infancia y literatura," "Preferencias, credo e idioma," "Los éxitos y los premios," "Periodismo, literatura policial e infantil," "Gente conmigo," "Línea de fuego," and "Extraño oficio." A five-page biobibliography up to 1976 and an index end this anthology.
SHA

POLIANA (pseudonym: see **COLLAZO, Paula**)

PONIATOWSKA, Elena (Mexico, b. 1933). Poniatowska emerged from a chicly cosmopolitan upbringing with a determination to re-root herself in real-world Mexican speech and cultural patterns. From adolescence, she developed a practice of fieldwork that enabled her to reproduce, with spirit and precision, the oral expression of Mexicans of the popular classes. She continues to be an active experimenter with the interview format, eliciting revealing and original material from both superstars and women or men in the street. NL

La casa en la tierra

Los cuentos de Lilus Kikus. Veracruz, Mexico: Universidad Veracruzana, 1967. 147 pp. Childhood, with its feelings of great longing, anxiety and excitement, is evoked in these short, sometimes enigmatic sketches. The central character is a rather isolated child, separated from her fellows by her aristocratic, Europeanized background and the intensity of her private mental and emotional life. The child's own version of traditional Catholicism -- saints, wonders, purity -- receives an exceptionally vivid representation. NL

De noche vienes. México: Grijalbo, 1979. ISBN 968-419-102-2, softcover, 231 pp. Fictional narrative in this collection of short stories is the favored form for Poniatowska's continuing effort to represent the experience of women from many social backgrounds. There is a skilled use of many modes, from various types of interior monologue through forms of dialogue and a bemused, ironic, meditative narrator. Especially interesting is "The Green Light," representing the unuttered musings of a woman looking back over her life. Though the life is outwardly unexceptional, access to the woman's thoughts of it reveals her intense sense of living out a privileged, unique experience, emblemized by her ability to perceive a special green light. NL

Fuerte es el silencio. México: Era, 1980. ISBN 968-411-054-5, softcover, 278 pp. This book of reportage and essays shows why Poniatowska is regarded as a renovator of the reporter's form. Her lengthy coverage of the 1968 student movement, a peasant radical-action collective, a hunger strike and disappeared activists moves beyond information and description to constitute analytical social and cultural criticism. While feminism as such is not an overt concern, she focuses on a group of women organized to protest the disappearance of family members. The transformation women undergo in joining in a common cause is strikingly evoked. NL

Domingo

Gaby Brimmer. Mexico: Grijalbo, 1979. ISBN 968-419-101-4, 200 pp. A collaborative work of documentary literature, Gaby Brimmer presents a collective portrait of a cerebral-palsy victim, her mother, her nanny, and Poniatowska herself, who becomes involved with the three. The words of all four are presented in juxtaposed fragments, using the typical "mosaic" of voices Poniatowska has developed as one of her journalistic innovations. Contains a long essay by Poniatowska on disability. NL

Hasta no verte, Jesus mío, novela. Mexico: Era. 1969. Paperback, 315 pp. The highly nuanced and richly expressive voice of a woman of the people is recreated in what might be called a collaborative autobiography. Poniatowska worked extensively with the real-life heroine of this work, learning her characteristic language, her organization of stories and anecdotes, and her life story. Includes valuable material on the role of women in the Mexican Revolution and on popular religiosity. NL

Massacre in Mexico. Trans. Helen R. Lane. N.Y.: Viking, 1975.

Melés y Teleo

La noche de Tlatelolco, testimonios de historia oral, novela. Mexico: Era, 1971. 282 pp. This work is perhaps the most widely read account

of the student massacre that occurred in Mexico City on October 2, 1968. It is a collection of documents and testimonies that bears witness to and passionately denounces governmental repression. Poniatowska's treatment of this incident, however, is not purely journalistic. Indeed, her artistic handling of the evidence collected lends a markedly fictional quality to the finished product. Furthermore, Poniatowska enhances the novelistic tone of the discourse by creating imaginary speakers whose narrations are intermixed with those of her real-life informants.
SSR

Palabras cruzadas, crónicas. Mexico: Era, 1961. 327 pp. Poniatowska takes journalistic reporting and reportage up to the level of deliberately structured essayistic writing. Her interview work is of particular interest where Poniatowska creates a persona for herself: the innocent, unguarded individual who has no fear of asking the most "naive" and therefore fundamental questions. She avoids the conventions of journalism by this apparently simple, but in fact artful and complex, technique. NL

Querido Diego, te abraza Quiela. Mexico: Era, 1978. Paperback, 72 pp. Imaginary letters recreate the affair between the Mexican painter Diego Rivera and his displaced Polish mistress. The woman's point of view as she addresses her absent lover brings home to the reader the difficult situation of woman in a Bohemian culture. Apart from its inherent interest as it communicates the woman's anguish and longing, the work offers an implicit critique of the old ideal of "free love," in which family responsibilities are jettisoned without creating alternative supports. NL

PONCE DE LEON, Waldina Davila de (see **DAVILA DE PONCE DE LEON, Waldina**)

PONZOA, Angeles Caiñas (see **CAIÑAS PONZOA, Angeles**)

PORRO FREIRE, Alicia (Uruguay, b. 1908)

Eva, cuentos

Savia nueva, poesías

PORTAL, Herminia del (Cuba, b. 1909)

Aguas de paz, poemas

PORTAL, Magda (Peru, b. 1901). Deeply committed to the cause of social justice and equal opportunity for all, Portal often used literature for propagandistic purposes. In political tracts and in speeches delivered throughout Latin America she preached the tenets of APRA (Alianza Popular Revolucionaria Americana), the party founded by Victor Raúl Haya de la Torre. During her years of activism she worked closely with another influential political leader, José Carlos Mariátegui. Portal assumed a leading role in the founding of the Partido Aprista Peruano and became its foremost female spokesperson. She broke with the Party in 1949 over women's issues. Her poetry is simple and at times prosaic, but it does reveal her intimate feelings, especially the pain and grief caused by solitude.

El aprismo y la mujer. [See annotation under Hacia la mujer nueva.]

Constancia del ser. Preface by José Carlos Mariátegui. Lima: P. L. Villanueva, 1965. 224 pp. This poetry collection is composed of selections from Portal's various published and unpublished works, including her first poems, which originally appeared in periodicals under the title, Anima absorta. Her collected poems reveal the wide range of her poetic voice from sad lyrics on death, solitude, and the absence of her lover to overtly political ones in which she commits herself to the struggle against injustice and issues a call for action. A reprint of Mariátegui's discussion of Portal and her work, taken from his Siete ensayos de interpretación de la realidad peruana (1928), appears as a preface. The volume concludes with the Chilean critic Ricardo A. Latcham's article on Portal reprinted from La Nación (December 24, 1944).

Costa Sur, poemas. Santiago de Chile: Nueva, 1945. 130 pp. The theme of alienation unites this collection of poems, most of which are private, introspective reflections on solitude. Sadness dominates the tone, and the sea is the focus of much of the imagery. The basic structure centers around a subject/object relationship which is expressed by the longing of the poetess for her lost love, her distant homeland, and personal freedom. In a series of poems at the end of the collection, alienation extends beyond the individual to encompass the masses. Recalling her experiences as a political prisoner, she pays homage to those who have fallen and to those who continue to fight while exalting the Indian, in whom she places her hope for the nation's future.

Una esperanza y el mar, poesía. Lima: Minerva, 1927. 92 pp. Also identified by the title, Varios poemas a la misma distancia, these poems deal with Portal's attempts to cope with frustration. Through abundant images of the sea, which represents freedom and life itself, she expresses her longings for fulfillment and a desire to escape her limitations. One section of the book, called "El Desfile de las Miradas," is dedicated to Serafín Delmar, the pseudonym of Reynaldo Bolaños, who was her lover and the brother of her husband. Portal and Delmar became separated as a result of their political activities and exile. In these poems of frustrated love, she conveys her anguish on being apart from her loved one and alone.

Flora Tristán, precursora. Lima: Páginas Libres, 1945. 34 pp. This pamphlet, which reproduces the entire text of Portal's lecture (October 28, 1944) at the inauguration of the First Congress of Chilean Women, summarizes the life, work, and significance of Flora Tristán (1803-1844), a little-known forerunner in the women's and workers' movements. During the tumultuous life of this early feminist, who was born in Spain, the daughter of a Peruvian father and a French mother, women had few legal rights. At a time when divorce was practically unknown, Tristán sought to dissolve her marriage, used her maiden name, and demanded that her children not be required to bear their father's name. She also petitioned for abolishment of the death penalty and, before Marx and Engels, wrote a pamphlet calling for an international workers' union. Included are a biographical sketch on Portal, a bibliography on Tristán, and a picture of each.

Hacia la mujer nueva. Lima: Cooperativa Aprista Atahualpa, n.d. [1933]. 76 pp. El aprismo y la mujer is the alternate title by which this propagandistic essay is sometimes called. Of Portal's numerous political tracts, all of which are devoid of literary pretensions, this one most clearly focuses on women's concerns. While condemning the

Church for teaching women to be submissive, she does not believe that the terms Christian and Aprista are mutually exclusive. APRA is working to eradicate old prejudices and form a new social conscience. Through its programs women will achieve equality without sacrificing their femininity. The six appendices are, for the most part, documents which condemn the Civilista government and enumerate the goals of Aprista women. Among those goals is their commitment to work not only for their own rights but also for those of the exploited masses.

La trampa, novela. Lima: Andimar Peruana, 1956. 138 pp. Based on real events, this novel reflects Portal's disillusionment with the Party's failure to pursue all of its goals. A young man, Charles Stool, lies abandoned in prison after being used by the Unionist Party (a fictionalized APRA) to eliminate an unsympathetic newspaper publisher. Finally, after all of the other political prisoners have been released, Stool realizes that he has fallen into the Party's trap and they will never let him go free. The story of María de la Luz, a young mother who spends time in prison and later advances in the ranks, eventually becoming the leading woman in the Party, closely parallels events in Portal's life. The novel's interest lies in its political message rather than its literary merit.

Varios poemas a la misma distancia. [See annotation under Una esperanza y el mar.] MSA

PORTALATIN, Aída Cartagena (see **CARTAGENA PORTALATIN, Aída**)

PORTELA, Luisa Israel de (see **ISRAEL DE PORTELA, Luisa**)

PORTILLO, Margarita López (see **LOPEZ PORTILLO, Margarita**)

PORTOCARRERO, Elena (Peru, twentieth century)

La multiplicación de las viejas

La señorita Canario, teatro

PORTOCARRERO DE CHAMORRO, Bertilda (Panama, twentieth century)

Sin dimensión, poemas

POSSE, Stella Corvalán (see **CORVALAN POSSE, Stella**)

POTTS, Renée (Cuba, b. 1908)

Fiesta mayor, poemas

Romancero de la maestrilla, poemas

PRADO, Blanca del (Peru, twentieth century)

Caima, poemas

Los días del sol

Yo no quiero mirar la primavera

PRADO, Pura del (Cuba, b. 1931)

　　Canto a Martí

　　Canto a Santiago de Cuba y otros poemas

　　Color de Orisha, poemas a los Santos Náñigos

　　Idilio del girasol

　　Otoño enamorado, poemas

　　El río con sed

　　Los sábados y Juan

PRATS BELLO, Ana Luisa (Chile, twentieth century)

　　Impresiones y recuerdos

　　Los patronatos de niñas

　　El silbario moderno

　　El teatro de la infancia

PREN, Rosario Sansores (see **SANSORES PREN, Rosario**)

PREVOWSOIR, Gemma Violeta Escandón (see **ESCANDON PREVOWSOIR, Gemma Violeta**)

PRIDA, Dolores (Cuba-United States, b. 1943)

　　Pequeñas prosas

　　Poemas de la sangre

　　Treinta y un poemas

PRIETO DE LANDAZURI, Isabel A. (Mexico, 1833-1876)

　　Las dos flores, teatro

　　Isabel Prieto de Landázuri, poesía escogida

　　Un lirio entre zarzas

　　Obras poéticas

PUCCIO, Mireyra Capmany (see **CAPMANY PUCCIO, Mireyra**)

PUELMA, Lucía López (see **LOPEZ PUELMA, Lucía**)

PUENTES DE OYENARD, Sylvia (Argentina, twentieth century)

　　De Chistera y Bastón, libro para niños

PUEYRREDON, Victoria (Argentina, b. 1920). Born in Argentina, of a historically prestigious family. She is certified as a teacher of Spanish literature as well as a legal secretary, her liberal studies include English and French; she is an interpreter in the latter. Her first book of poems, Sentiments (1940; 1942) was written in French. Her next volume, written in Spanish and based on the traditional stanza known as the copla, appealed to a wider public. Acabo de morir received a coveted award from the Argentinian Society of Writers (S.A.D.E.). Another book of short stories, Destinos, was awarded the silver pen in 1972 by the Argentinian PEN Club. Together with Pablo Neruda, she wrote a preface in 1972 to an edition of one of her famous forebears' memoir, written about his friendship with a Chilean folk hero. In 1980, Pueyrredón founded Letras de Buenos Aires; she has since been editor of this literary quarterly.

Acabo de morir, cuentos. Buenos Aires: Emecé, 1976. Paperback, 162 pp. This collection of seventeen short stories of length ranging from two to ten pages deals with bizarre or fantastic situations where chance functions as the prime mover. Five are narrated in the first person, the rest in the third. Their suspenseful exposition leads to an ironic ending, sometimes of tragic proportions played down through sarcasm. Three have definite political implications; two bring marvellously to life a dog and a player piano as protagonists. These stories make for uncomplicated yet quite stimulating reading, enjoyable even for an intermediate Spanish class.

Coplas para ti, poesía. Buenos Aires: Emecé, 1969. Paperback, 42 pp. This revised and expanded edition, based on the first one of 1942, is divided into three sections with no distinguishable differences among them. The last section comprises twelve coplas previously published at the end of Poemas de soledad in 1966. These, as well as the other forty-four, deal with love; most are written in the first person; some are addressed to the lover. With a constant rhythm and theme, these coplas can easily be put to music. Recommended for a course on popular culture or literature in Latin America.

Destinos, cuentos. Buenos Aires: Noé, 1972. Paperback, 100 pp. Available in major research libraries. This collection of short stories consists of twenty-one very concise mystery tales, all of them dealing with bizarre events. Written in the first and third persons, or in dialogue, they are interconnected by the force of fate that pursues or propels the protagonists. Most of the stories range from one and a half to three pages. The longest one, "Las pantaloneras" is an accomplished piece of morbid intrigue with novelistic potential. Any one of these stories would be of adequate difficulty for intermediate Spanish reading course. The book received the coveted silver pen award from Argentina's P.E.N. Club in 1972.

Poemas de soledad. Buenos Aires: Emecé, 1966. Paperback, 69 pp. Contains thirteen poems, plus twelve coplas which were republished in the revised edition of Coplas para ti. Given the romance rhythm, the entire collection resembles the spoken language. The consonant rhyme in the poems, however, makes them sound quite repetitive. There is no innovation and no imagery to speak of. Easily understood by the unsophisticated reader. The predominant theme is loneliness, particularly in old age, with its regrets, the assurance of approaching death and uncertainty about an afterlife. Index. SHA

PUGA DE LOSADA, Amalia (Peru, twentieth century)

Amalia Puga, poesía

Los Barzúas, novela

El jabón de hiel, cuentos

Tragedia inédita, cuentos

El voto, novela

PUIGDOLLERS, Carmen (Puerto Rico, b. 1924)

Dominio entre alas, poemas

PUJATO CRESPO DE CAMELINO VEDOYA, Mercedes (Argentina, twentieth century)

Albores, poesía

Días de sol

Flores del campo, poemas

Liropeya, poema dramático

PUYHOL, Esther Rodríguez (see **RODRIGUEZ PUYHOL, Esther**)

PUYHOL, Lenica (Mexico, twentieth century)

Entre lo silvestre, cuentos

Maremagnum, poemas

Q

QUESNE, María Antonieta Le (see LE QUESNE, María Antonieta)

QUIJANO, Laura Elena Alemán de (see ALEMAN DE QUIJANO, Laura Elena)

QUIÑONES PEREZ, Marta Magaly (Puerto Rico, b. 1945). Quiñones studied literature and languages at the University of Puerto Rico and has worked as a librarian. Her poems have appeared in various journals. She has also written a book of texts presented as letters from a poet to a poet. Her poetry encompasses a variety of themes including time, cultural identity, and objects.

   Cantándole a la noche misma, poemas. Prologue by the poet Carmen Alicia Cadilla. San Juan: n.p. [Author's edition], 1978. 45 pp. Divided in four sections. In a note, Quiñones writes about the development of her poetry. "Naturalezas," the first section, establishes a relation between self and nature. "Corazón encendido" has longer and more personal poems that refer to the need for structuring a poetic voice. "El reino de los pocos" are poems about poverty and exploitation. In "Destrozos," the idea of destruction is softened by the existence of a poetic voice; language is lyrical and poetic form is traditional.

   Cosas de poetas, cosas nuestras

   En la pequeña Antilla, poemas. San Juan: Mairena, 1982. Paperback, 63 pp. Río Piedras: Puerto Rico, 1982. 63 pp. A series of poems divided into four sections. The first one, "Corazón de mi gota," relies on a central metaphor, water, to reveal intimacy. "Corazón de mi pena" brings together poems about pain and sadness. "Corazón del miedo y de la muerte" deals with the reality of death and time. The last section refers more directly to the title of the book: poems located in the Antilles, poems about war and love in the islands, poems about the process of migration. The tone of the poems is intimate; short verse and traditional verse forms are preferred.

   Entre mi voz y el tiempo, poemas. San Juan: Juan Ponce de León, 1969. Paperback. The book is divided in five sections with five poems included in each. The author sees life as existing between poetic voice and time. The idea that time has lost its meaning is exposed in the first section of the book. In the second section, Puerto Rico and its history are seen within a pessimistic view. The poet compares the island to someone commiting suicide. The third group of poems presents the theme of solitude. The section, "Amaneceres de una Tierra Chica" uses the metaphor of dawn as referring to nature and the beginning of life. In the last section a sense of nostalgia and sadness is exposed. Form and poetic language follow a lyric and traditional context.

Era que el mundo era, poemas. Illus. by Antonio Martorell. Carolina: Nacional, 1974. Paperback, 46 pp. The poems are grouped in four series. The initial part focuses on the poet's relationship with nature. In "Por el Mundo," childhood and its remembrance emerge as important themes. "Del Odio Vivo" describes hatred and its tragedy; "Caminos de Fondo" treats the survival of people in their struggle against solitude and hatred. The illustrations are based on images of shoes, an important motif in the book. The poems are brief, in short lines and free-verse forms.

Zambayllu, poemas. San Juan: n.p. [Author's edition], 1976. Paperback, n.pag. A group of nine poems about a single theme form this book, which can be seen as a single poem. The word "Zumbayllu" comes from Quechua and means "trompo zumbador." The book is dedicated to Chile, Peru and Latin America. The poems avoid the use of metaphors and rely on the sense of rhythm. The poet sees her voice as that of the Zumbayllu, since this object is related to the history of Peru. A sense of admiration for Indian culture and solidarity for its oppression is evident in the poetic voice. The last three poems are short love poems. ILJ

QUIÑONEZ, Delia (Guatemala, twentieth century)

Barro pleno

QUIÑONEZ, Isabel (?, twentieth century)

Alguien maulla, poesía

QUINTANA, Caridad (Cuba, twentieth century)

Cristal de gruta, poemas

QUINTANA, Elvira (Mexico, 1935-1968)

Poesías de Elvira Quintana

QUINTERAS, Serafina (pseudonym: see GONZALEZ CASTRO, Esmeralda)

R

RABELL, Malkah (Mexico, twentieth century)

En el umbral de los ghettos, novela

Tormenta sobre El Plata, novela

RAFFO, Hortensia Margarita (Argentina, b. 1910)

Canciones de sal y cuestas, poesía

Con pan y el ángel, poesía

Cuentos de nochebuena y navidad

En vaso de murano, poesía

Oro y sangre, poesía

El pájaro y la gruta, poesía

La planta en su terrón

Romances fueginos, poesía

RAGGI, Ana Hilda González de (see **GONZALEZ DE RAGGI, Ana Hilda**)

RAMIREZ DE ARELLANO, Diana (Puerto Rico, b. 1919)

Albatros sobre el alma

Angeles de ceniza, poema

Del señalado oficio de la muerte

Privilegio

Relieve y gesto de una poética: Josefina Romo Arregui

Un vuelo casi humano, poesía

Yo soy Ariel

RAMIREZ DE ARELLANO DE NOLLA, Olga (Puerto Rico, b. 1911)

A la luz de Flamboyán, poemas

Amor es como un rezo, el libro de las nanas

Cada ola

Cauce hondo, poemas

Cundeamor

Diario de la montaña 1957-1960

Dos veces retoño

En mis ojos verás todos los mundos

Escucha mi alma un canto

Mar de poesía

Orbe, poema

El rosal fecundo

Te entrego, amor

La tierra de la diafanidad

Traigo un ramillete

RAMIREZ PEREZ, Aurora Estrada de (see **ESTRADA DE RAMIREZ PEREZ, Aurora**)

RAMIS, Magali García (see **GARCIA RAMIS, Magali**)

RAMON, Sara Joffré de (see **JOFFRE DE RAMON, Sara**)

RAMOS, Corina Garza (see **GARZA RAMOS, Corina**)

RAMOS COLLADO, Liliana (Puerto Rico, b. 1954).   Ramos studied comparative literature at the University of Puerto Rico and has worked as a translator.   Her poems, translations and criticism have appeared in several journals.   She is one of the founding editors of Reintegro, which gathers young writers who started publishing in the seventies.   Her book Proemas para despabilar cándidos won the Luis Palés Matos award given by the journal Sin Nombre in 1976. Two years later she received First Prize in the literary contest sponsored by the division of Cultural Activities of the University of Puerto Rico for her unpublished Avión de papel sobre la Isla de Pascua.

Proemas para despabilar cándidos, poesía. San Juan: Reintegro, 1981. Paperback, 68 pp.   Preceded by a quote from Rimbaud about prose and poetry, the poems (called "proemas", too) refer to the need for a new kind of poetry. Ramos' poetic language relies on the unexpected image, constant surprises for the reader and an ironic detachment aimed at revealing the contradictions in modern Puerto Rican society. Her poetry is innovative, experimental and tends toward colloquial expressions; the poems are written in free verse. Sixteen poems form this book, which is beautifully illustrated with photographs. ILJ

READ, Ernestina Gómez de (see **GOMEZ DE READ, Ernestina**)

REINA, Irene Gómez (see **GOMEZ REINA, Irene**)

REINBECK DE VILLANUEVA, Margos (Mexico, b. 1920; also Villanueva, Margos de)

Un destino

La muerte nos visita, comedia policíaca

22 [Veintidós] horas

REMES, María Melo de (see **MELO DE REMES, María**)

RENDIC G., Amalia (Chile, b. 1928)

Cuentos infantiles

Greda tierna, cuentos

Hierro amargo, cuentos

Los pasos sonámbulos, novelas

Pequitas y yo, cuentos infantiles

RENDON, Silveria Espinosa de (see **ESPINOSA DE RENDON, Silveria**)

REPETTO BAEZA, Leticia (Chile, b. 1912)

La cenicienta de jazz

La voz infinita

REQUENA, María Asunción (Chile, b. 1915)

Ayayema, teatro

El camino más largo, teatro

Chiloé, cielos cubiertos, teatro

La Chilota, teatro

Fuerte Bulnes, teatro

Homo chilensis, teatro

Pan caliente, teatro

Teatro

RESTREPO, Isabel Lleras (see **LLERAS RESTREPO, Isabel**)

RESTREPO DE MARTINEZ, Rosa (Colombia, twentieth century)

Momentos, poemas

RESTREPO DE THIEDE, María (Colombia, twentieth century)

A través del velo, novela

Cadenas y silencio, novela

REUS, María López de Victoria de (see **LOPEZ DE VICTORIA Y BARBE, María**)

REXACH DE LEON, Rosario (Cuba-United States, twentieth century)

Rumbo al punto cierto

REYES, Alicia (Mexico, twentieth century; pseudonym: Tikis)

Poesías por Tikis

Y en la sombra viva, poemas

REYES, Aurora (Mexico, twentieth century)

Humanos paisajes

REYES, Chela (Chile, b. 1904). A social worker by profession, Reyes has written short stories, poetry and novels of intimista themes; some of her poetry, especially Elegías, shares characteristics with that of the modernistas. She has received various prizes, including the Premio Atenea, and is the founder of the Chilean P.E.N. Club. She presently resides in Santiago.

A la ronda, ronda, del agua redonda, rondas

Andacollo, teatro. Mimeograph; available only from the author. Dramatic poem. A simple story of love, enchantment and vengeance between Indians and gypsies, allows the presentation of both Indian customs and celebrations, and Christian-pagan festivities, such as the celebration of the Virgin of Andacollo in northern Chile. The value of the play lies in its effort to represent elements of Chilean popular culture. It has never been published, only performed.

Bosque sonoro, cuentos

Las cadencias secretas, cuentos. Santiago: Pacífico, n.d. Paperback, 120 pp. Loneliness as experienced by adults and children, is the prevailing theme of these fifteen short stories. Their most salient aspect, however, lies in the atmosphere they recreate; by means of a poetic prose and the predominance of "telling" over "showing," the author creates enchanted worlds. The protagonists experience levels of reality detached from the material world and where the imaginary and the oneiric prevail.

Elegías, poesía. Santiago: Nascimento, 1962. 53 pp. The book is organized into four sections, each one devoted to a specific meter. Each part explores the mystery of death and presents the intense grief death provokes. The first two sections express pathetically the sense of loss produced by the death of individuals with whom there existed poetic or spiritual communication: Gabriela Mistral and her mother, respectively. The other two sections are songs of mourning: to an abandoned house, the forest, the sea, the sun, etc. All these poems reveal a meditation on human solitude.

Epoca del alma, poemas. Illus. by Meléndez. Santiago: Nascimento, 1937. 59 pp. Available as Poemas in the Library of Congress. Using a variety of meters and themes, these nineteen poems capture forms and sensations associated with vital human experience. Each poem attempts to capture these experiences as an instant, both fugitive and perishable in memory. In spite of the different tones expressed by the poems, the completeness of the vision predominates over the depth of the reflection.

La extranjera, cuentos. Antología Autores Actuales, #4. Santiago: Renovación, 1953. 55 pp.

Historia de una negrita blanca, cuentos

Inquietud, poesía

Mujeres chilenas cuentan, selección por Chela Reyes. (See annotation in the List of Anthologies.)

Ola nocturna, poesía

La paloma paseadora, cuentos y poemas para niños. Illus. by Carlota Godoy. Santiago: Lord Cochrane, 1974. 28 pp. Some of these children's stories and nursery rhymes deal with animal motifs: "La paloma paseadora," "Los amigos," "La lluvia y el sol," "El pescadito" and "El patito perdido;" some are simple adventure stories with clear didactic intentions: "La pequeña casita" and "A la selva."

La pequeña historia de un pececito rojo. La negrita blanca. Santiago: ZigZag, 1967. Paperback, 79 pp. These are two different children's stories published in one volume. "Pececito rojo" develops the theme of the adventurous youngster, the fish, who leaves the security of his home, the fishbowl, in order to explore the world, the fishtank. The "voyage" is a maturing process which makes him appreciate the security of his bowl, to which he finally returns. "La negrita blanca" is disturbing, due to its racist implications. The protagonist is a Black girl who in dreams becomes white and experiences an adventurous existence in a fairy-tale land. There are constant allusions to the black and white elements of her personality and behaviour, the most obvious being the color of her skin and her speech, a deviation from "correct" pronunciation, which should be considered typical of "black speech."

Poemas. Illus. by Meléndez. Santiago de Chile: Nascimento, 1937. 59 pp. [See annotation under Epoca del alma.]

Puertas verdes y caminos blancos, novela. Santiago: Nascimento, 1939. 163 pp. Available in major research libraries. A young woman who, like most of Reyes' protagonists, is in tune with -- almost a part of -- nature, searches for her identity and freedom by trying to come to terms with her feelings toward both her dead father and a prospective husband. The novel focuses exclusively on her psychological and emotional development, subordinating all other elements of the fictive world to this end. Some good poetic prose.

Tía Eulalia, novela. Santiago: Rapa Nui, n.d. Paperback, 373 pp. Tía Eulalia explores the confrontation between two expressions of existence: passion and earthiness versus harmony and beauty, as represented by two sisters belonging to a Chilean family of landowners. Both sisters fall in love with the same men, and although the principle of passion succeeds over harmony, at the end it is harmony which appears as the prevailing principle. The novel is imbued with criollista and romantic elements. PRL

REYES, Clara Silva de (see SILVA DE REYES, Clara)

REYES, Doris (Peru, twentieth century)

Poesía

REYES, Mara (Mexico, twentieth century; pseudonym: Río, Marcela del). Ever since she can remember Marcela del Río has lived in a literary environment. Her father, mother and brothers were all writers. Her great uncle was the famous Alfonso Reyes, who was also her first critic. Although she has written fiction and poetry she is chiefly known for her work in the theatre. From 1972 to 1977 she was the Mexican cultural attaché to Czeckoslovakia. She is married to the violinist Hermilo Novelo with whom she travels on many of his concert tours.

Claudia y Arnot, teatro

Cuentos arcaicos para el año 3000 (tres mil)

El hijo del trapo, teatro

Miralina, teatro

Opus Nueve, teatro. Mexico: UNAM, 1978. 371 pp. Nine previously published plays comprise Río's ninth work. In her prologue she divides them into three categories. She defines her teatro realista as the way different individuals react to different stimuli. She illustrates her teatro documental by an account of the critical moments in the life of President Benito Juárez. She describes her teatro realista as one depicting characters trapped by their circumstances. Her use of the fantastic is most imaginative.

Proceso a Faubritten, novela. Mexico: Aguilar, 1976. 347 pp. Río's first novel boldly enters the area of science fiction. What if man should become immortal? She goes back in time to the real horrors of Hitler's Germany to an imaginative future where death does not exist. An overpopulated earth and endless aging produce practical problems. In the course of describing past, present and inconceivable future events, Río poses many philosophical, social and religious questions as well.

Trece cielos, poemas. Mexico: Menhir, 1968. 94 pp. Trece cielos may be interpreted as thirteen Indian heavens. Winner of the 1968 prize for poetry, the selections take liberties with the myths of the Indian gods, particularly with the metamorphosis of the sun god. Río strictly observes the Indians' reliance on symbolism and numerology. Written in simple narrative form, the poems have an aura of ancient authenticity. GB

REYES, María Esperanza (Chile, twentieth century; pseudonym: Airam, Seyer)

Cántaro de América, poemas

Estampas criollas de mi tierra y mi pueblo, cuadros

Las inadaptas, novela

REYES DE GUADALUPE, María de Luján (see **LUJAN REYES DE GUADALUPE, María de**)

REYES ORTIZ, Marta (Argentina, twentieth century)

Aleteos, primeros poemas

Inquietud, poemas

REYNA, Margot (Ecuador, twentieth century)

Sinfonía en colores, poesía

REYNOLDS, Mercedes Alvarez (see **ALVAREZ REYNOLDS, Mercedes**)

RICO, Carmen de (Mexico, twentieth century)

Amapa

RICO, Dina (Mexico, twentieth century)

Senderos de pasión

RICORD, Elsie Alvarado de (see **ALVARADO DE RICORD, Elsie**)

RIERA, Argentina Mora y (see **MORA Y RIERA, Argentina**)

RIERA, Pepita (Cuba, twentieth century)

El amor que no quisiste, novela

Bajo el hábito

En las garras del pasado

Prodigy, translation of El amor que no quisiste

Tentación

Tu vida y la mía

RIESCO MALPARTIDA LUSZCZYNSKA, Laura (Peru - United States, b. 1940). Although born in La Oroya, in the central Andean region, Riesco's childhood and adolescent years belong to Lima. After graduating from the Colegio María Alvarado, she studied in the United States, receiving her B.A. from Wayne State University, and her M.A. and Ph.D. from the University of

Kentucky. Her doctoral thesis is a critical study of selected poems from Poemas humanos by César Vallejo. Riesco makes her home in Maine, with her husband and three daughters. A professor in the Department of Foreign Languages and Classics of the University of Maine, she teaches literature courses in the contemporary novel.

El truco de los ojos, novela. Lima: Milla Batres, 1978. 188 pp. A Peruvian novel which spins out the workings of the mind of an eight-year-old girl whose consciousness touches the external and internal dimensions of her homelife, her school life, her friends, her neighborhood. A single narrative sequence without separation of paragraphs, the entire novel carries along a flow of moments, impressions and sensations. This interior focus provides access to a feminine childhood world, and to the subtle formative influences that mold a girl's attitudes. The experimental narrative techniques present new perspectives of childhood. An important contribution to the contemporary Latin American novel. PRP

RIESTRA, Gloria (Mexico, twentieth century)

Celeste anhelo

La noche sosegada

Según tus palabras

La soledad sonora, poemas

RIMAC, Flor de (pseudonym: see **VILLARAN, Consuelo María Eufrosina**)

RINCON DE MCDONALD, Sonia (Guatemala, twentieth century)

El destino sonríe, novela

RINCON SOLER, Evangelina Correa de (see **CORREA DE RINCON SOLER, Evangelina**)

RIO, Amelia Agostini de del (see **AGOSTINI DE DEL RIO, Amelia**)

RIO, Berta del (pseudonym: see **DIAZ DE CASTILLO DE OTERO, Margarita**)

RIO, Carmen Gaete Nieto del (see **GAETE NIETO DEL RIO, Carmen**)

RIO, Marcela del (pseudonym: see **REYES, Mara**)

RIOS, Ada Castellanos de (see **CASTELLANOS DE RIOS, Ada**)

RIOS, María Alvarez (see **ALVAREZ RIOS, María**)

RIVERA, Etnairis (Puerto Rico, b. 1949). Rivera began writing during the sixties, publishing in journals like Guajana, Mester and Zona. She studied literature at the University of Puerto Rico and in Spain. Her poetry is influenced by the philosophy of yoga, which gives it a mystic quality uncommon in Puerto Rican literature. A long trip to South America is related in three books, one written in Bolivia, the others (unpublished) in Peru. Her poetic language is full of symbols of rebirth, regeneration and transcendence, especially in her latest books, and uses long, free-verse forms.

El día del polen, poesía. [Unpublished?]. This is a book about life, fertility, and birth. Esotericism, Indian mythology and cosmic mysticism are the recurrent referents. The central metaphor of the journey is associated with the mythic search for the sacred, and with metamorphosis. A real voyage to the Dominican Republic and the Virgin Islands is symbolic of the spiritual voyage to the origin, to transcendence. Language functions within the lyric tradition. Long verse forms are preferred; some textual constructions are analogous to the structure of prayers and hymns.

María Mar Moriviví, poemas. New York: El Libro Viaje, 1976. Paperback, 137 pp. The preface of this book, the poem "A la Tribu," states that each of its poems is part of one poem, which is life in its constant evolution. The poetic subject searches for her origin, which is associated with water, the sea and earth. A parallel search for a name is also constant. The persona of the poems is transformed and in the last texts is identified with the name of "María Mar Moriviví," the "eternal pilgrim." This transformation is part of the recurrent images of movement which define the poetic voice. The poems are a continuous flow of long verses in free form.

Pachamamapa Takín, poemas. Serie Literatura Hoy. Preface by poet Francisco Matos Paoli. San Juan: Instituto de Cultura Puertorriqueña, 1976. Paperback, 11 pp. Written in Bolivia, these long poems constitute a search for a lost time in which the Indian identified with the earth and its rituals. The book is structured as a voyage towards the earth, seen as a mother symbol and as harmonic principle. The geographical setting is a recurrent motif. Glossary of Indian words and religious rituals.

Wydondequiera. Río Piedras: Puerto, 1974. Paperback, 150 pp. This first book of poems is an experimental exercise, innovative in its rhythmic patterns, poetic language, spacing and graphic distribution. Divided in several sections, without a unifying theme, some of its topics are the reconstruction of childhood, the life of Puerto Ricans living in New York, the evocation of Puerto Rico. ILJ

RIVERA, María J. Alvarado (see ALVARADO RIVERA, María J.)

RIVERO, Eliana Suárez- (see SUAREZ-RIVERO, Eliana)

ROBLES, Mireya (Cuba, twentieth century)

En esta aurora, poesía

Los octubres del otoño

Tiempo artesano / Time, the Artesan, bilingual edition

RODAS, Ana María (United States, twentieth century)

Poemas de la izquierda erótica

RODAS, Virginia (Argentina, twentieth century)

Habrá un día, y otros poemas

Hermano siglo XXI, poemas

RODRIGUEZ, Albertina Díaz de (see **DIAZ DE RODRIGUEZ, Albertina**)

RODRIGUEZ, Blanca Luz Molina de (see **MOLINA DE RODRIGUEZ, Blanca Luz**)

RODRIGUEZ, Catalina (Cuba, 1835-1894)

Poesías

RODRIGUEZ, Clotilde del Carmen (Cuba, b. late nineteenth century)

Efusiones del alma

RODRIGUEZ, Maribel Guillén de (see **GUILLEN DE RODRIGUEZ, Maribel**)

RODRIGUEZ, Sofía Estévez y Vales de (see **ESTEVEZ Y VALES DE RODRIGUEZ, Sofía**)

RODRIGUEZ ACOSTA, Ofelia (Cuba, twentieth century)

Algunos cuentos de ayer y de hoy

La dama del arcón, novela

Dolientes, novela

En la noche del mundo

Hágase la luz, novela

Sonata interrumpida, novela

La tragedia social de la mujer

El triunfo de la débil presa, novela

La vida manda, novela

RODRIGUEZ CHAVEZ, Elisa (Guatemala, twentieth century)

Oro de cobre, novela

RODRIGUEZ DE TIO, Lola (Puerto Rico, 1843-1924)

A mi patria en la muerte de Corchado, versos

Claros de sol

Claros y nieblas, poesías

Mi libro de Cuba, poemas

Mis cantares

Noche buena

Ofrendas

Poesías patrióticas, poesías religiosas

RODRIGUEZ PARRA DE GARCIA ROSELL, Elisa (Peru, twentieth century)

Ideas . . . (motivos, recuerdos, comentarios)

RODRIGUEZ PUYHOL, Esther (Mexico, twentieth century)

Naturalezas muertas, poemas

RODRIGUEZ URIBE, Leonor Herrera de (see **HERRERA DE RODRIGUEZ URIBE, Leonor**)

ROEL, Adriana García (see **GARCIA ROEL, Adriana**)

ROEPKE, Gabriela (Chile, b. 1920)

The Dangers of Great Literature, a Lecture in One Act, translation of Los peligros de la Gran Literatura

La invitación, teatro

Jardín sólo, poesía

Juegos silenciosos, teatro

Una mariposa blanca, teatro

Los peligros de la Gran Literatura, teatro

Primeras canciones, poesía

La telaraña, teatro

Three Non-Shakespearean plays in One Act, translations

A white butterfly, translation of La mariposa blanca

ROFFE, Reina (Argentina, b. 1951). Argentinian novelist, representative of the "new narrative" in her country. Her first novel, Llamado al Puf, won the Sixto Pondal Ríos Prize in 1975 for the best novel by a young writer. In 1973, she also published a book on a Mexican writer, Juan Rulfo: Autobiografía armada. Her novel Monte de Venus was unanimously acclaimed by literary critics. She was awarded a Fulbright in 1981, and participated in the International Writing Program at the University of Iowa. Her short stories appear in various national and international magazines and anthologies. Also a journalist, she writes literary criticism and interviews for several newspapers and journals.

Llamado al Puf. Buenos Aires: Pleamar, 1973. Paperback, 142 pp. Story of a middle-class Argentinian family through the vision of an adolescent girl who descends to the depths of the past, and submerges herself into the shambles of her old home in search of the foundations that structure her present. It is the x-ray of a peripheral country, of a social class, of a system of relationships. This novel was written by the author at the age of seventeen.

Monte de Venus, novela. Buenos Aires: Corregidor, 1976. Paperback, 270 pp. The problems of women in contemporary Argentinian society are examined to the minutest details. This is a novel not only about women who question their lives, but of the history that makes or unmakes them as human beings; it is a song of life, of rebellion, of audacity. LK

ROJAS, María Teresa de (Cuba, b. 1902)

Señal en el agua, poemas 1959-1968

ROJAS SUCRE, Graciela (Panama, b. 1904)

Terrañudas de lo chico, cuentos

ROKHA, Winet de (pseudonym: see **ANABALON, Luisa**)

ROLDAN, María Luisa Domínguez (see **DOMINGUEZ ROLDAN, María Luisa**)

ROMAN, Angélica Palma y (see **PALMA Y ROMAN, Angélica**)

ROMERO, Aurelia Cordero de (see **CORDERO DE ROMERO, Aurelia**)

ROMERO, Chita (Uruguay, twentieth century)

Guiños de estrellas, poesía

Luz en la lágrima, poemas

Umbrales del sueño, poemas

ROMERO, Mariela (Venezuela, twentieth century)

El juego, teatro

ROMERO, Sofía Espíndola de Pascual (see **ESPINDOLA DE PASCUAL ROMERO, Sofía**)

ROQUE DE DUPREY, Ana (Puerto Rico, 1853-1933)

Luz y sombra

Novelas y cuentos

Pasatiempos, novelas cortas

Sara la obrera, novela

ROSA, Lilia (Mexico, twentieth century)

La brecha olvidada

Noche sin fin, novela

Vainilla, bronce y morir

ROSELL, Elisa Rodríguez Parra de García (see **RODRIGUEZ PARRA DE GARCIA ROSELL, Elisa**)

ROSENZWEIG V., Carmen (Mexico, b. 1925). She was born in Toluca where there was little opportunity for formal schooling. She simply borrowed books from her neighbors. After her first short stories were published, she received a scholarship to study in Paris. She then served for ten years on the editorial staff of the magazine, El Rehilete. She is a serious philosophical writer who shows deep empathy for her characters. She is also the foster mother of three boys.

Esta cárdena vida. Mexico: Salvador Avelar, 1975. 82 pp. A series of short poems and brief essays sum up Rosenzweig's philosophy of life. While she criticizes sexual discrimination and modern hedonism, she is essentially optimistic. She likes to play with words to the extent of creating bright neologisms. Her style is pungent, her insight is sharp and clear.

Mi pueblo

1956 (Mil novecientos cincuenta y seis), novela. Mexico: Los Presentes, 1958. 140 pp. Rosenzweig treats a difficult subject with skill. Her novel describes the agony of a young woman watching her father dying of cancer. The relationship between the two is tender and touching. The woman finally finds solace in her religious faith which gives her the strength to endure her ordeal. 1956 is a sober, thoughtful study related with economy of style, never slipping into sentimentality.

Los presentes, novela

Recuento para recuerdo, ensayos, cuentos y análisis de crítica literaria

El reloj. Mexico: Los Presentes, 1956. 93 pp. Rosenzweig's bright sense of humor, her compassion and her religious devotion are all evident in a series of sketches based on daily life in Mexico City. She writes sardonically about radio commercials and soap operas. She sympathizes with the driver of a taxi (colectivo) unable to find a fifth passenger for his fare and she shares the grief of a poor woman who has just lost her husband. She shows great empathy with the "little people" of the city as she expresses her solicitude for their problems. GB

ROSS, María Luisa (Mexico, twentieth century)

Cuentos sentimentales

ROSSI, Cristina Peri (see **PERI ROSSI, Cristina**)

ROSTAND, Aura (pseudonym: see **SELVA DE IBARRA, María de la**)

ROTHE DE VALLBONA, Rima Gretel (Costa Rica - United States, b. 1931; known as Rima de Vallbona). A graduate of the University of Costa Rica, the writer has resided for many years in Houston, Texas, where she organized the Spanish Department of St. Thomas University and served as its first Chair, later receiving her doctorate in Modern Languages from Middlebury. She has recently served as a Visiting Professor at Rice University. A specialist in Latin American literature, Vallbona has published studies of Yolanda Oreamuno and Eunice Odio as well as other scholarly works. Her four collections of short stories and two novels reveal her subtle penetration into the world of modern Latin American women and into the world of children. She is married to Dr. Carlos Vallbona of Baylor

College of Medicine and is the mother of four children. She is extremely active in local literary and cultural events.*

Baraja de soledades. Barcelona: Rondas, 1983. 32 pp. Four of Vallbona's previously published stories -- three dealing with "feminist" themes -- comprise this short volume: "Caña hueca" from Polvo del camino; and "Penélope en sus bodas de plata," "Parábola del Edén," and "El arcángel del perdón," from Mujeres y agonías. In the last story, a small girl confuses a theft to which her love of sweets has led her with the cause of a coup d'état and resulting loss of civil order. The child's confusion is heightened by the narrative cacophony of media sounds that have become a norm of twentieth-century life. The four stories are well chosen to demonstrate Vallbona's virtuosity in the realm of the short story.

Five Women Writers of Costa Rica: Short Stories by Carmen Naranjo, Eunice Odio, Yolanda Oreamuno, Victoria Urbano, and Rima Vallbona. Ed. Victoria Urbano. Beaumont, Tx.: Asociación de Literatura Femenina Hispánica, 1978.

Mujeres y agonías. Introd. by Luis Leal Houston, Texas: Arte Público, 1982. ISBN 0-934-77012-3, 99 pp. In "Penélope en sus bodas de plata," a dutiful but dull housewife shocks her son, who is just awakening to sensuality, by announcing the dissolution of her marriage and her imminent elopement with a lover. The son, who has despised his mother's former limitations, now turns against her rejection of this conventional role, thus dramatizing the woman's no-win situation. A follow-up story, "Parábola del Edén," sees the woman regretting her attempt to resolve complex problems through impetuous action. Other stories enter brilliantly into the world of troubled children. The author here demonstrates the total adequacy of her own Costa Rican dialect for literary purposes.

Noche en vela. 1st ed. San José, Costa Rica: Costa Rica, 1968. Other editions: 2nd ed. (San José, Costa Rica: Fernández-Arce, 1976); 3rd ed. (San José, Costa Rica: Universidad Estatal a Distancia, 1982), 237 pp. This first novel deals with the adolescence of Luisa as seen through the girl's own eyes. Physical, intellectual and spiritual awakening is presented in a sequence of flashbacks that reflects Luisa's thoughts during the long and tedious wake of her detested aunt Leonor -- a character with most of the vices and little of the charm of la Celestina. The reader may be deceived by early hints that dramatic tension will hinge melodramatically upon the ultimate disposition of "Tía Leo's" putative fortune. This is not the case at all. The novel's strength lies in its penetration of the intense, painful and sometimes lyrical world of a young Latin American girl searching for meaning. Vallbona's fine intuition and notable expressive talents predominate over form. Winner of the "Aquíleo J. Echeverría" National Novel Prize in Costa Rica in 1968.

Polvo del camino. San José, Costa Rica: Autores Unidos, 1971. 129 pp. The protagonists in most of these ten stories are the victims of societal discrimination. Three stories treat mature themes from unusual

---

*Rima Vallbona is also an annotator for this volume. -- Editor.

perspectives. In "La niña sin amor," a young girl will be denied love from caring adults because of her own father's act of incest. In "La caña hueca," a lonely rural schoolteacher is condemned by priest and villagers alike for a lesbian relationship that has finally brought her love. In "Con los muertos al cinto," a retarded blind girl defends herself before an attorney, tragically revealing the rape and resulting pregnancy she herself was unable even to comprehend. Other stories reflect an implied author in the process of assimilating a foreign (i.e., United States) culture. Each story is also an implicit inquiry into the question of narration itself.

La salamandra rosada. Montevideo, Uruguay: Géminis, 1979. 117 pp. This unusual work blends sketches and photographs by Vallbona, her four children, and Federico González, all of which illustrate stories, "viñetas," and three poems -- all written by the author. A remarkable ability to penetrate the world of the child that is reminiscent of the Spaniard Ana María Matute is evident in many of the stories, which are neither cloying nor overtly moralistic. Rather, along with the eighteen brief vignettes, they explore the child's coming-to-terms with the reality in which he or she must eventually function and, in a number of cases, the mother-narrator's poignant awareness of each step. Originally conceived as an album for the Vallbona family, this text, although somewhat difficult to obtain, offers important insight into Vallbona's process of transforming reality. It also includes an interesting essay of "autocrítica."

Las sombras que perseguimos. San José, Costa Rica: Costa Rica, 1983. ISBN 9977-23-017-X, 183 pp. This novel's narrative structure, its many reflections upon the act of writing, and certain ludic elements, situate it squarely within the pulse of the nueva narrativa hispanoamericana. A trinity of characters explores the shadows of each one's lived reality in Costa Rica. Tata Blas, a patiently enduring peasant, occupies himself with the nature of hope. Pedro, an aspiring author, tells the story of the deportation of Costa Rican Germans during World War II. Pedro also presents Cristina, the victim of an insensitive and brutish husband. While Cristina is initially just a character in Pedro's novel, a process of self-discovery eventually enables her to become her own narrator -- a highly significant step. While Vallbona's characters speak a clearly Costa Rican dialect of Spanish, and while Costa Rican history and reality are explored, the problems probed are universal. LD

ROTZAIT, Perla (Argentina, b. 1923?)

Cuando las sombras

El otro río

La postergación

La seducción

El temerario, poesía

RUBERTINO, María Luisa (Argentina, b. 1929)

Alma y paisaje, poesías

El caballo en el espejo

El cerco

Rebotín: Medio litro y serenita

El rompecabezas

Las señales

El silencio, drama

Tantos muchachos menos un ángel, poemas

RUBIO, Sara Iturbide de Laris (see **ITURBIDE DE LARIS RUBIO, Sara**)

RUBIO DE DIAZ, Susana (Colombia, twentieth century)

Almas cautivas, poemas

Clemencia, poemas

Orquídeas

RUIBAL, Carmen Alicia Cadilla de (see **CADILLA DE RUIBAL, Carmen Alicia**)

RUIZ, Maruja Uribe de Arenas (see **URIBE DE ARENAS RUIZ, Maruja**)

RUKAVISHNIKOVA-DARLEE, Irina (El Salvador, twentieth century)

Al azar de los caminos, relatos

Aunque es de noche, novela

Viaje incluso

RUL, Ana María Gómez (see **GOMEZ RUL, Ana María**)

RUMAZO, Lupe (Ecuador, b. 1935). Considered to be one of Ecuador's most brilliant intellectuals, Rumazo has published three volumes of literary criticism (En el lagar, 1961; Yunques y crisoles americanos, 1967; and Rol beligerante, 1974). Experimentation with diverse literary techniques is prevalent in Rumazo's fiction.

Carta larga sin final. Madrid: EDIME, 1978. ISBN 84-499-2053-1, paperback, 303 pp. Although this novel was originally conceived as a letter written to the author's deceased mother, Rumazo offers the reader a series of reflections on numerous topics such as music, the meaning of life and death, and literary criticism. Some critics, in fact, have referred to this work as an essai-roman.

Sílabas de la tierra, cuentos. 2nd ed. Madrid: EDIME, 1968. 183 pp. The stories which make up this collection are all characterized by Rumazo's deep interest in her characters' psychological development. Interior monologues and first-person narration are frequently used to depict the inner struggles, the anguish, and the fears that beset modern humanity. Of particular interest is Rumazo's portrayal of the women characters who feel trapped in a patriarchal and highly technological world. MH

RUSSELL, Dora Isella (Uruguay, b. 1925)

Los barcos de la noche, poemas

El canto irremediable, poesía

Crónicas andariegas

Del alba al mediodía, poemas

Había una vez una isla

Juana de Ibarbourou

Oleaje, poesía

El otro olvido, poemas

Los sonetos de Simbad

Sonetos, umbral del dr. Alejandro C. Arias

El tiempo del regreso

S

S. DE LERNIER, Clara Luz (Puerto Rico, twentieth century)

    Con los ojos del alma, poemas

SABAS ALOMA, Mariblanca (Cuba, twentieth century)

    Feminismo, poesía

    La rémora, poesía

SAENZ, María Luisa L. de (see **LAMAS DE SAENZ, María Luisa**)

SAENZ, Raquel (Uruguay, twentieth century)

    La almohada de los sueños, poemas

    Bajo el hechizo, poemas

    Estos versos míos, poemas

SAGARZAZU, Beatriz Mendoza (see **MENDOZA SAGARZAZU, Beatriz**)

SAKS, Katia (Peru-United States, b. 1939?)

    La leyenda de todos y de nadie

    La mojigata

    La rifa

    Su majestad el destino, novela

    Los títeres

SALADO, Minerva (Cuba, b. 1954). Poet and journalist. Her poems Al cierre, won the David prize of the UNEAC in 1971; in 1978 she published Temas sobre un paseo which won the Julian del Casal prize. Her poems have appeared in Casa de las Américas.

Al cierre, poemas. La Habana: UNEAC, 1972. 89 pp. This collection of poems should be seen in the context of a new Latin American poetry (Cardenal, Dalton) which incorporates linguistic codes alien to traditional poetic discourse. Here the language of the news media is read and re-created from a poetic, sometimes lyrical perspective. The first part of the book deals with international and national news, information about the weather and sports events, interviews. The mostly humorous second part, "Segunda Emisión" has a section of horoscopes and a debate with Robinson Crusoe, which closes the book.

ILJ

SALAS, Virginia Brindis de (see **BRINDIS DE SALAS, Virginia**)

SALAS CALDERON, Gloria (Mexico, twentieth century)

Cerro de los jumiles, novela

SALAZAR, Ina (Peru, twentieth century)

El tacto del amor, poesía

SALAZAR PRINGLES, Justa Beatriz Gallardo de (see **GALLARDO DE SALAZAR PRINGLES, Justa Beatriz**)

SALGADO, Rosario Grillo de (see **GRILLO DE SALGADO, Rosario**)

SALGADO, Teresina (Puerto Rico, b. 1901)

De mi ayer romántico, poesía

Por los caminos blancos, versos

Rimas del sendero, poesía

SALMERON ACOSTA, Cruz María (Venezuela, 1892-1929)

Fuente de amargura

SALOTTI, Martha (Argentina, twentieth century)

Guaquimina, crónica de una aventura temeraria, ficción juvenil

El patito Coletón, literatura para niños

SALVADOR, Nélida (Argentina, b. 1930). Poet, critic, researcher. Professor of literature at the Facultad de Filosofía y Letras, Universidad de Buenos Aires. She has participated in international congresses in the United States (California), Mexico, Puerto Rico, and Brazil and in national congresses as judge and special guest.

Al acecho, poesía. Buenos Aires: Hachette, 1966. Winner of the 1966 Buenos Aires P.E.N. Club prize. An attitude of hope aspires to tear down the barriers of isolation and to establish a vital equalibrium in human relationships. A more anguished yet more caring perspective on loved ones and things due to her desire to capture them at the moment of their fleeting plenitude.

Las apariencias, poesía. Ed. Carabela. Colección Nudo del Alba, # 48. Barcelona: Campos, 1972. The poet, without resorting to hermeticism, explores herself and her environment in verses which reject formal restrictions in favor of interior rhythm. She is lucidly conscious of her emotional world as she explores with acute perception the mysteries of time and being.

Canto de extramuros, poesía. Buenos Aires: Americalee, 1963. Published under the auspices of the Fondo Nacional de las Artes. Immersed in quotidian reality, the poet searches out strange ties and symbols in everyday things as a result of her transfer to Buenos Aires and emotionally charged memories make themselves heard again.

Las fábulas insomnes, poesía. Mendoza: Azor, 1962. Received the "Faja de Honor" of the Society of Argentinean writers. Themes incorporate memories of childhood and adolescence in Mendoza where she was born. Evocations illuminate the faces of loved ones, "things," papers, furniture, streets, names. The poet reveals the doubts, moments of happiness, and questions of a period in her life when magic and logic are not easily separated.

Tomar distancia, poesía. Buenos Aires: Marymar, 1980. Prize for Poetry from the Municipality of Buenos Aires. The lirical content of this sixth collection of poems is nourished by a questioning spirit which seeks answers through magical histories because the poet has left behind the period of joy and hope and places herself before new enigmas which she faces with a judicious conformity devoid of philosophical declarations.

Tránsito ciego, poesía. Buenos Aires: Cooperativa Impresora Argentina, 1958. In these twenty-six brief poems, the poet initiates a journey into intimacy which is contained yet not hermetic. The works are frequently sustained by anecdotal allusions to rain, old houses, and "el pino desmantelado." The yearning to overcome the emptiness of life predominates. The verses are precise, yet flow smoothly. EA

SAMAYOA, Carmen Brannon de (see **BRANNON DE SAMAYOA, Carmen**)

SAMPER, Soledad Acosta de (see **ACOSTA DE SAMPER, Soledad**)

SANCHEZ, Azulina Acosta de (see **ACOSTA DE SANCHEZ, Azulina**)

SANCHEZ, Enriqueta Gómez (see **GOMEZ SANCHEZ, Enriqueta**)

SANCHEZ, Marynés Casal de (see **CASAL DE SANCHEZ, Marynés**)

SANCHEZ, Natalia Ocampo de (see **OCAMPO DE SANCHEZ, Natalia**)

SANCHEZ, Olga Casanova- (see **CASANOVA-SANCHEZ, Olga**)

SANCHEZ, Rosa Nieto de (see **NIETO DE SANCHEZ, Rosa**)

SANCHEZ, Rosaura (United States, b. 1941)

Una noche, cuento

SANCHEZ DE FUENTES, María (Cuba, twentieth century)

> Polvo de luz, poemas

SANCHEZ LAFAURIE, Juana (Colombia, b. 1902; pseudonym: Lusignan, Marzia de)

> A la sombra de las parábolas, cuentos

> Arco de sándalo, poesías

> Oro y mirra, poemas en prosa

> Viento en el otoño, novela

SANCHEZ MONTENEGRO, Blanca de (Colombia, twentieth century)

> Diafanidad, versos

SANDOIZ, Alba (pseudonym: see **IZQUIERDO ALBIÑANA, Asunción**)

SANDOR, Malena (Argentina, d. 1968)

> Arco en tensión

> Teatro completo

> Tu vida y la mía, comedia

> Y la respuesta fue dada

SANFIORENZO, Carmen (Puerto Rico, twentieth century)

> Adiós póstumo; vida, muerte, eternidad

> ¡Hola, mi gente!

> Optimismo vs. logros, autobiografía

SANHUEZA, Eugenia (Chile, b. 1925)

> Libro

SAN JOAQUIN, sor Tadea de (see **TADEA DE SAN JOAQUIN, sor**)

SANJURJO, Carmen Eulate (see **EULATE SANJURJO, Carmen**)

SANOJO, Ana Teresa Parra (see **PARRA SANOJO, Ana Teresa**)

SANSORES PREN, Rosario (Mexico, b. 1898)

> Breviario de Eros, poesía

> Cantaba el mar azul, poesía

> Los cien mejores poemas

Del país del ensueño, poesías

Diez años de juventud, cuentos

Ensueños y quimeras

Fruta madura, poesía

Las horas pasan, poesía

Mi corazón y yo, poesía

Mientras se va la vida, poesía

La novia del sol, poesía

País del ensueño, poesías

Polvo de olvido, poesía

Rutas de emoción

Sombra en el agua, poemas

SANTA CRUZ, Elvira (see **SANTA CRUZ Y OSSA, Elvira**)

SANTA CRUZ, María de (Cuba, 1843-1923)

Confidencias

Historias campesinas

Un ramo de perlas, cuento

SANTA CRUZ Y OSSA, Elvira (Chile, 1886-1960)

La familia Busquillas, pieza de dos actos

Flor silvestre, novela

Herne, el cazador, para niños

La marcha fúnebre, teatro

Saber vivir, teatro

Tacunga, para niños

El voto femenino, teatro

SANTESTEBAN, Emma Teresa Dalmau de (see **DALMAU DE SANTESTEBAN, Emma Teresa**)

SANTOS, Estela Dos (see **DOS SANTOS, Estela**)

SANTOS, Luisa Victoria Aguilera de (see **AGUILERA DE SANTOS, Luisa Victoria**)

SANTOS DE CUEVAS, Raquel García (see **GARCIA SANTOS DE CUEVAS, Raquel**)

SANTOS MILLAN, Isabel (Colombia, b. 1902)

> Lucha de un alma, novela

SANZ, Trinidad Padilla de (see **PADILLA DE SANZ, Trinidad**)

SAÑUDO DE DELGADO, María Isabel (Colombia, b. 1909)

> Sol y luna

SCHAPIRA FRIDMAN, Flor (Argentina, b. 1935)

> Amor país natal
>
> Memorias de la víspera

SCHÖN, Elizabeth (Venezuela, twentieth century)

> El abuelo, la cesta y el mar
>
> La aldea, teatro
>
> Casi un país
>
> La cisterna insondable, poemas
>
> Es oír la vertiente, poemas
>
> La gruta venidera, poemas

SCHULTZ CAZANUEVE DE MANTOVANI, Fryda (Argentina, 1912-1977)

> El árbol guarda-voces, poesía y teatro para niños
>
> Canto ciego
>
> Fábula del niño en el hombre
>
> Leyendas argentinas
>
> La marioneta que dejó de ser palo
>
> La mujer en la vida nacional
>
> Navegante, poemas
>
> Los títeres de maese Pedro, farsa
>
> Versos a un gran amor

SCHVARTS, Josefa A. Fructuoso de (see **FRUCTUOSO DE SCHVARTS, Josefa A.**)

SEGOVIA, Marily Morales (see **MORALES SEGOVIA, Marily**)

SEGURA, Estrella Soto de (see SOTO DE SEGURA, Estrella)

SEGURA, Gertrudis Peñuela de (see PEÑUELA DE SEGURA, Gertrudis)

SEIBEL, Beatriz (Argentina, b. 1934). Born in Buenos Aires, she has devoted herself exclusively to writing and directing theatre. She has written two works for children ("De gatos y lunas" and "Retablillo para tres") which have received awards at the Children's Theatre Festival of Necochea (1965, 1968). Her works for adults are the product of her own literary and historical research. Often with musical accompaniment, they dramatize poetic and narrative passages by Argentinian writers as well as other Hispanic authors. None of Seibel's dramatic pieces has been published.

"El amor." This unpublished one-act piece premiered at the El Vitral Theatre in 1972 and was also presented at San Telmo and at La Cebolla Café Concert, under the direction of the playwright. With troubadour-like questions and answers, three actors (one woman and two men) and one musician introduce the theme of love, quoting anonymous Medieval Spanish poetry. A provençal love court gives way to Jorge Manrique's Coplas, which lead directly into the twentieth-century treatment of love. Costumes and scenery were designed by Graciela Galán; electric guitar music by Hugo Racca; medieval music arranged by Camaleón Rodríguez.

"Crónicas de mi gente." Premiered in 1972 at the Payró Theatre and on tour through 1973, this unpublished one-act work, directed by the playwright, includes four actors (two males and two females) and two musicians for bandoneón and "criolla guitar." Tangos, songs, poems and dramatic dialogues bring out political issues from the beginning of this century, e.g., child labor, malnutrition, immigration, election fraud, unemployment, women's position. Costumes were designed by Leandro G. Ragucci; the music was directed by Carlos Núñez Cortés.

"De gatos y lunas." This unpublished work for children premiered in 1965 at the Arts and Sciences Theatre in Buenos Aires and was presented in 1966 at the Fifth Children's Theatre Festival in Nicochea, where it received two prizes for best spectacle and best performance. Its two acts involve two magicians and two youths, both male and female, that assume various roles, singing and reciting poetry of different periods, as they revive eighteenth- and nineteenth-century children's games with the audience's participation. Includes music by Jorge Schussheim and slides of original drawings by Carlota Beitía, who also designed the sets and costumes.

"Nací o me hice." This one-act unpublished work premiered in 1971 at the Bar Sur and was presented again in the same year at El Vitral and the Bar del Puerto (Punta del Este) Theatres. Always directed by the playwright, in 1972 it played at the Theatre of San Telmo, the Café Concert El Trovador (Martínez, province of Buenos Aires), and at the Teatro Opera de La Plata; it also went on tour through inland provinces. A single actress-pianist assumes various roles in different historical periods through poems, songs and dramatic monologues. The themes of the woman-actress, love and social issues emerge as excerpts from Góngora, Leon Felipe, Jardiel and Poncela, etc. are contrasted with popular tangos and contemporary Argentinian writers. Original music was composed by Pablo Ziegler; costumes were designed by Amorin, scenery by Graciela Galán.

"Retablillo para tres." Premiered in 1968, this unpublished work, received the award for best performance at the VI Children's Theatre Festival of Necochea. It was restaged twice more in two different Buenos Aires' Theatres, always directed by the playwright herself. Its two acts involve a singer, a mime and an actress in a minstrel game. Through old Hispanic-Argentinian songs, poems and children's stories, the minstrel makes up various participatory games for the children in the audience around a boat. The toys and costumes were designed by Carlota Beitía; the music was arranged by Carlos Waxemberg and the choreography by Eduardo Jorge.

"7 (Siete) veces Eva." Directed by the author, this unpublished play for one actress premiered at the theatre Casa Castagnino, June 20, 1980. It was also presented at the University of Puerto Rico at the Primer Congreso de Creación Femenina in Spanish America. It was invited to appear in October, 1981, at Caracas' Centro de Creación e Investigación Teatral. Also in 1981, it played at the Feria del Libro under the auspices of the Argentinian Society of Writers (S.A.D.E.). The play portrays seven women from various stages of Argentinian history and tradition as well as from an imaginary future. Two of the characters are based on novels by Libertad Demitrópulos and Martha Mercader. The costumes were designed by Carlota Beitía; the music was written by Sergio Aschero. SHA

SELIGSON, Esther (Mexico, b. 1941)

Otros son los sueños, novela

Tras la ventana un árbol, cuentos

SELVA DE IBARRA, María de la (Nicaragua, twentieth century; pseudonym: Rostand, Aura)

Huerto cerrado

SELVA MARTI, Ana (Argentina, twentieth century)

Consagración del alma, poemas

Itinerario de angustia, poesía

Silencio emancipado, poemas

Sinfonía máxima, poemas

La sombra conjurada, poemas

Transeúnte de los días, poemas

SEMINOREFF, Vera (pseudonym: see **MONDRAGON AGUIRRE, Magdalena**)

SENIOR DE BAENA, Lilia (Colombia, b. 1911)

El osito azul, cuentos

SEÑORET, Raquel (Chile, b. 1923)

Sin título, poesía

SEPULVEDA, Ximena (Chile, twentieth century)

Yo, pagana

SERPA, Paz Flórez Fernández de (see **FLOREZ FERNANDEZ DE SERPA, Paz**)

SERRANA, Elisa (pseudonym: see **PEREZ WALKER DE SERRANO, Elisa**)

SERRANO DE CARRIZOSA, Zita (Colombia, twentieth century)

Claroscuro, cuentos

SEYER, Airam (pseudonym: see **REYES, María**)

SHADE (pseudonym: see **COX STUVEN, Mariana**)

SIERRA, Stella (Panama, twentieth century)

Agua dulce, claroscuro de infancia, recuerdos infantiles

Canciones de mar y luna

Libre y cautiva

Poesía

Sinfonía jubilosa en doce sonetos

SIERRA, Tina (Mexico, twentieth century)

Oro negro, novela

SILVA, Clara (Uruguay, 1908 - 1976). Well-known author of poetry in Uruguay. Lesser known are her novels published later in life which express the existencial anguish of a Latin American woman caught in the dychotomy of the soul vs. the body.   Most of her novels explore the social and psychological traps that Latin American women suffer. Her techniques are stream-of-consciousness and interior monologues. There is no doubt that she is very original in her prose. LFL

El alma y los perros, narrativa

Antología

Aviso a la población, novela

Las bodas, poesía

La cabellera oscura, poesía

Los delirios

Las furias del sueño, poemas

Guitarra en sombra, poesía

Habitación testigo

Juicio final, poesía

Memoria de la nada

Pasión y gloria de Delmira Agustini: su vida y su obra

Preludio indiano y otros poemas

Prohibido pasar, cuentos

La sobreviviente, novela

SILVA, Luisa del Valle (see **VALLE SILVA, Luisa del**)

SILVA, Margarita (Puerto Rico, twentieth century)

Los aventureros de los siete mares

SILVA, Teresa de (Mexico, twentieth century)

Cuatro libros, poemas

Niebla, poemas

Nueva primavera, poesías

Ocasos, poesías

Oro y azul, poemas

Sonetos al amor divino

SILVA BELINZON, Concepción (Uruguay, twentieth century)

Amor no amado, poemas

El cordero terrible, poemas

La mano del ángel, poemas

El más justo llamó, poesía

Me espera el mundo entero, poesía

El plantador de pinos, poemas

El regreso de la samaritana, poemas

Los reyes de oro, poemas

Sagrada cantidad, poemas

SILVA DE CAMARGO, Esther (Colombia, twentieth century; pseudonym: Esmeralda)

Horas, cuentos

SILVA DE MAGGI, Marinés (Uruguay, twentieth century; also Silva Vila, María Inés)

Felicidad y otras tristezas; La mano de nieve, prosa

Los rebeldes del 800

SILVA DE MUÑOZ, Rosita (Puerto-Rico, b. 1907)

El cántico de Asís, cuentos

SILVA DE REYES, Clara (Venezuela, twentieth century)

Asesinato en Caracas

Por una mancha de rouge, novela

SILVA NOCEDAD, Lucrecia (Argentina, twentieth century)

El aire y la paloma, poemas

SILVA OSSA, María (Chile, b. 1918)

Aventuras de tres pelos, cuento para niños

La ciudad y los signos, poesía

Cuento y canción, poesía con Carlos Correa

De la tierra y el aire, poesía

En la posada del sueño, poesía

El hombre cabeza de nieve, cuentos para niños

Perejil piedra, cuentos para niños

Raíz, poemas

Vida y muerte del día, poesía

SILVA VILA, María Inés (see **SILVA DE MAGGI, Marinés**)

SIMO, Ana María (Cuba, b. 1943)

Las fábulas, cuentos

SOFOVICH, Luisa (Argentina - Spain, 1905 - 1970). Sofovich lived mostly in Spain as the wife of Ramón Gómez de la Serna. She traveled extensively through Europe with her husband. She excelled in the biographical sketch. She was influenced by the avant-garde style of the twenties, and her work is characterized by a dream-like atmosphere and surrealistic imagery. She is not widely known in her country of origin. Wrote essays, short stories, and novels.

El baile, novela. Buenos Aires: Losada, 1958. Paperback, 124 pp. Available only in libraries. Novel where characters seem to move in a trance, going through motions with no apparent purpose. Personal conflicts are solved, or remain unsolved, during a ball held at a mansion. Life among the well-to-do. Polished language and style. Surprising complexity of style, with surrealistic metaphors that would appeal to students of stylistics.

Biografía de la Gioconda, novela. Colección Austral. Buenos Aires: Espasa-Calpe, 1953. Paperback, 147 pp. Available only in libraries. Fictionalized biography of Mona Lisa from youth to famous portrait. Literature of escapism that has appealed to generations of Argentine women writers. Mona Lisa is portrayed as a pleasant, superficial young woman. Entertaining, with no social significance or particular interest for historians.

La gruta artificial, cuentos. Buenos Aires-Montevideo: Sociedad Amigos del Libro Ríoplatense, 1936. Paperback, 205 pp. Available only in libraries. Collection of short stories with an introduction by Ramón Gómez de la Serna. All female characters. Dream-like sequences in which fantasy is hard to distinguish from reality. No clear plots; surrealistic, difficult to understand. Polished style. Characters seem to float rather than walk. Dialogue consists of disconnected sentences. Each heroine moves within the confines of her own private world. Style more important than content. Of great interest to literary scholars.

Historia de ciervos, cuentos. Buenos Aires: Losada, 1945. Paperback, 161 pp. Available only in libraries. Short stories where deer are used both realistically and symbolically. Pleasant reading. As in the case of other works by this author, content is obscured by brilliant and complex style.

El ramo, novela. Buenos Aires: Huella, 1943. Paperback, 203 pp. Available only in libraries. Novel which explores relations between the members of a rich Argentinian family and their friends. Rather limited atmosphere within the circle of the affluent. Plot is secondary to style. Breaks away from traditional narrative style; unusual metaphors and similes, refined language. Characters without soul, move about just saying things. Author succeeds in giving a glimpse into the aimless life of the rich.

Siluetas en negro

La sonrisa, cuentos. Buenos Aires: La Peña, 1933. Paperback, 179 pp. Available only in libraries. Narrow confines of a woman's world and the idle rich. Worth reading because of early straight style before Sofovich evolved toward surrealism. Small scenes of daily life, human relations. Earned literary prize "La Peña." AT

SOHNTRONN, Zoraida Díaz de (see **DIAZ DE SOHNTRONN, Zoraida**)

SOL, Lucía (see **FOX-LOCKERT, Lucía**)

SOLA, Emma Solá de (see **SOLA DE SOLA, Emma**)

SOLA, Graciela de (see **MATURO, Graciela**)

SOLA DE SOLA, Emma (Argentina, twentieth century)

Esta eterna inquietud, poesías

La madre del viento y otros poemas

Miel de la tierra, poesía

El sendero y la estrella

SOLAR, Adriana (Mexico, twentieth century; pseudonym)

Sueños de mujer

SOLAR, Carmen (Cuba, twentieth century)

Sangre criolla

SOLAR, Mercedes Marín del (see **MARIN DEL SOLAR, Mercedes**)

SOLAR, Ximena (pseudonym: see **MERINO GONZALEZ, Laura**)

SOLARI, Olga (Chile, 1910-1974)

Corazón de hombre, poesía

Donde termina el mar, poesía

Selva, poesía

SOLARI, Zita (Argentina, twentieth century)

Extraño, cuentos

SOLDEVILLA, Loló de (Cuba, twentieth century; also Dolores)

El farol, novela

Ir, venir, volver a ir, crónicas 1952-1957

Versos populares

SOLEDAD (pseudonym: see **SOTOMAYOR DE CONCHA, Graciela**)

SOLIS DE KING, Fabiola (Ecuador, b. 1936). A clinical psychologist by profession, Solís de King has used her professional experiences as a basis for her fiction. As recently as 1978, four of her stories were finalists in a national short story competition.

Al otro lado del muro, cuentos. Quito: Publitécnica, 1978. 110 pp. This is a series of psychological stories which employs the best of contemporary narrative technique. Also, several Goya-like prints and sketches accompany the stories and reflect the frustrations and the tension that have beset Solís de King's characters. MH

Mundo aparte y otros mundos

SOMERS, Armonía (pseudonym: see **ETCHEPARE DE HENESTROSA, Armonía**)

SORAVILLA, Lesbia (Cuba, twentieth century)

Cuando libertan los esclavos, novela

El dolor de vivir, novela

SORIANO DE SOTRES, Susana Francis (see **FRANCIS SORIANO DE SOTRES, Susana**)

SOSA DE NEWTON, Lily (Argentina, b. 192?). Born in the province of Buenos Aires, she published her first work in newspapers and magazines in Santa Fe and the capital. She collaborated with her husband Jorge Newton in several historical studies. Her own non-fiction books include the award-winning Las argentinas, de ayer a hoy, three works on nineteenth-century military leaders and a study of the gauchesco poet Hilario Ascasubi, awarded first prize in the Editorial Universitaria's 1979 contest for its series "Genio y Figura." SHA

Las argentinas, de ayer a hoy. [See List of Anthologies for annotation.]

Diccionario biográfico de mujeres argentinas. [See List of Anthologies for annotation.]

SOTO, Carmelina (Colombia, twentieth century)

Octubre; 1942-1952, poemas

Tiempo inmóvil, selección poética

SOTO, Hilda Perera (see **PERERA SOTO, Hilda**)

SOTO DE SEGURA, Estrella (Cuba, twentieth century)

Flor de sombra, poesía

Soledades, poesía

SOTO Y CALVO, Edelina (Argentina, b. 1844?). Argentinian writer and painter. Afectos, her first book, was edited in Paris. At the age of 85, she published Emociones (1929); Parque vetusto appeared in 1931. LK

Afectos

Emociones

Parque vetusto

SOTOMAYOR, Aurea María (Puerto Rico, b. 1951). Studied comparative literature at the universities of Puerto Rico and Indiana; finished her Ph.D. at Stanford. She teaches at the Inter-American University of Puerto Rico. Was a member of the editorial board of several journals (Penélope, La Sapa Tse-Tsé, Vórtice); at present is working with Reintegro. Her poems have appeared in numerous journals and anthologies. She has also published translations and critical essays.

Aquelarre de una bobina tartamuda. San Juan: Romualdo Real, 1973. Paperback, 65 pp. Sotomayor's first book approaches various themes: the act of writing, the menace of a frightening and absurd reality, the analysis of the poetic self. The latter dominates in the book, as the title suggests: the idea of stuttering ("tartamuda") represents the difficult search for an original voice. Language follows the discoveries of vanguardism, specially in the typographical setting of verses and the idea of writing as an act produced by a machine ("bobina").

Sitios de la memoria, poemas. San Juan: Edición de la Autora, 1983. 72 pp. A book about memory, its process in time and how it recuperates the world: everything is memory, as one of the poems states. Remembrance creates and destroys the past, memory is like a pulp. As in her previous books, language is metaphoric: Sotomayor's poetry is certainly one of beauty, a difficult encounter with the subtleties of language, in the tradition of Eliot and Rilke (both quoted in the opening pages of this book). The poems are divided into four sections, which are presented as four "gestures." The long poem that closes the book is an evocation of family life, seen through a series of photographs. The poetic subject reconstructs its history, that of her own memory.

Velando mi sueño de madera, poemas. San Juan: Instituto de Cultura Puertorriqueña, 1980. Paperback, 69 pp. The poems are divided in four sections: "Adivinanzas," "Línea Viva," "Tropos" and "Jugando a mí." The epigraph by Palés Matos, "En lo que si se nombra se destruye," serves a clue for these poems in which language evokes the destruction of the real. Visual images and references to painting recur. Sotomayor's poetry tends to be hermetic, revealing a sound knowledge of literature. Sentimentality is avoided and the poems are objective, sometimes referring to human figures and movements. Some of the most interesting poems are those that depict theatrical situations, in which the reader encounters characters, their movements and dialogues. ILJ

SOTOMAYOR DE CONCHA, Graciela (Chile, b. nineteenth century).

Luz de atardecer, poesías. Santiago: Casa Nacional del Niño, 1940. 130 pp. Available only in research libraries. The book appears to be her complete poetical production: naive poetry, rooted in the traditional mode, and of little thematic or literary value. Recurrent topics: faith, love, religious figures, historical and nationalistic themes, elements of nature and its relationship with the individual, elements of everyday life. It also includes Malía and Margarita, her "poems of adolescence."

Malía, poema. Santiago: Kirsinger, 1898. 51 pp. Available only in research libraries. Delightful pastoral poem about the aborted love of Malía and Hilario. The young shepherd is called to defend his land; in battle he is blinded and wounded, and decides not to return to Malía. He takes refuge in a nearby shrine, where Malía stricken by grief, is taken to die. Fictive prologue to the reader by Godofredo.

Margarita, leyenda. Santiago: Roma, 1894. 15 pp. Available only in research libraries. Narrative poem treating the pure, unresolved (due to death) love of a couple of adolescent villagers. Pablo and Margarita love each other, but Bernabé, a jealous suitor destroys her worthiness in the eyes of her loved one, by speaking ill of her. He dies at sea but returns in a golden boat to take her with him. Anchored in the classical tradition; of little importance within the development of Chilean literature.

Un recuerdo de amor, poema dramático histórico. Santiago: Nascimento, 192?. 128 pp. Available only in research libraries. Dedicated to King Alfonso XIII of Spain, this historical poem centers the plot around the figure of Bolívar and his visit to Potosí, where the royalists plan to kill him. Bolívar is saved by a young woman who falls in love with him. The play lacks any literary interest, and further exemplifies the author's effort to revitalize traditional literary modes. Followed by press reviews of the staging of the play. PRL

SOTRES, Susana Francis Soriano de (see **FRANCIS SORIANO DE SOTRES, Susana**)

STALK, Gloria (Venezuela, twentieth century)

Angel de piedra, cuentos

STEIMBERG, Alicia (Argentina, b. 1933)

La loca 101 (ciento uno), novela

Músicos y relojeros, novela

STORNI, Alfonsina (Switzerland-Argentina, 1892-1938). Along with Sor Juana Inés de la Cruz, Storni is the most influential feminist precursor among Spanish American women writers. Her life is a paradigm of proto-feminist rebellion; she supported herself and raised a son alone while continuing to write. Best-known as a poet, she also wrote theater (for children as well as adults) and innumerable newspaper articles and columns. The trajectory of Storni's poetry includes early sentimental verse utilizing stock themes and conventions, a transitional more lyrical stage, and a final period of avant-garde exploration of the external world. SS

Alfonsina Storni. Anthology annotated by Carlos A. Andreola. Commemorative edition on the twenty-fifth anniversary of her death. Buenos Aires: Nobis, 1963. Hardcover, 142 pp. This book gathers a selection of poems, most of them unpublished, and ceded to the annotator for this special edition. Also contains prose, photographs and a musical composition with words by Storni. An interesting essay is included proving the birth of the poet in Switzerland and not in Argentina. Also has a Zodiac study of Storni's sign. AA

Alfonsina Storni, antología. Prologue and selection by María de Villarino. Biblioteca de Sesquicentenario, Colección Antologías. Buenos Aires, Argentina: Culturales Argentinas, Ministerio de Educación y Justicia, Dirección General de Cultura, 1961. 99 pp. After a lengthy introduction by María de Villarino which summarizes Storni's life and characterizes each of her books of poetry, this anthology includes selections from all except La inquietud del rosal. This book has been omitted because Storni herself left it out of her own Antología, according to the editor. Also included are: the posthumous sonnet "Voy a dormir," a fragment of a letter from Storni to a friend, and several photographs. SS

Alfonsina Storni: Argentina's Feminist Poet, The Poetry in Spanish with English Translations. Ed. Florence Williams Talamantes. Los Cerrillos, New Mexico: San Marcos, 1975. ISBN 0-88235-027-7, paperback, 67 pp.

El amo del mundo, comedia en tres actos. Buenos Aires: Bambalinas, revista teatral, year IX, no. 470, 1927. 39 pp. Originally called Dos mujeres, this is the most overtly feminist of Storni's plays. Dos mujeres contrasts the life decisions of two women. One opts for security and conventionality, at the expense of her self; the other gives up her husband in the name of truth and principle. After the latter confesses to her husband that the teenager who lives with them is really her illegitimate son, he rejects her and subsequently marries her shrewd, manipulative ward. The action moves more smoothly than in Storni's later plays. SS

Antología poética. Prologue by the author. Buenos Aires: Espasa-Calpe Argentina, 1938. Hardcover, 190 pp. This anthology collects, in its first part, Storni's poems not included in books and written between 1916 and 1921. The selection was done by the poet herself from the five books published by 1934. The last part contains the poems written after 1934. Her versatile style, her mythical and philosophical views are found here. There is a search for the place in which miseries would be abolished. AA

Antología poética. Prologue by the author. 10th ed. Buenos Aires: Espasa-Calpe Argentina, 1951. Paperback, 170 pp. Poems were selected by Storni herself. Includes a short prologue, in which she reiterates her preference for her own later works, and excludes La inquietud del rosal from this volume. The last section contains many poems from a book not yet completed, not even labeled as such -- Mascarilla y trébol. SS

Antología poética. [No edition indicated.] Poetas de Ayer y Hoy. [No prologue.] Buenos Aires: Losada, 1961. Paperback, 221 pp. This anthology is a product of Storni's recollection of her own poems. It is a vast selection in which the reader perceives the tenderness, the passion and the profound ways used by the author to express her feelings. Her pantheism permeates her production. Useful to scholars and students for the amount of poems contained. AA

Antología poética. Selected by Alfredo Veirave. Biblioteca Fundamental Argentina, #34. Buenos Aires: Centro Editor de América Latina, 1968. Paperback, 92 pp. This anthology includes the most representative selections from her seven books published before her death. It touches the themes she used to expose her unconformity with life, her loneliness and desolation. She traveled through the unknown and talked to the heavenly bodies as well as with the mythological deities. Her pantheistic idea arises from the poems. AA

Antología poética. Prologue by Susana Zanetti. Ed. Alberto Zum Felde. 8th ed. Buenos Aires: Losada, 1977. Paperback, 232 pp. Other editions: 1st ed. 1956; 10th ed., Biblioteca Clásica y Contemporánea, 1980. This collection is the 1938 Antología poética that Storni herself put together. She excluded La inquietud del rosal. The prologue by Zanetti briefly describes the trajectory of Storni's life and work. This edition also contains a short bibliography of works by and about Storni. SS

Antología poética. Introd. by Manuel A. Penella. Colección Poesía y Prosa Popular, núm. 9. 2nd ed. Madrid: Busma, 1982. ISBN 84-7520-048-6, paperback, 120 pp. 1st ed.: (Felmar, 1981). The introduction's tone is patronizing. Penella portrays Storni as incurably depressed because her ideal of love is impossible to realize. He prefers her early "innocent" poetry, thinks Ocre is her best work, and considers El mundo de siete pozos faddish. The anthology, which emphasizes the four books before Ocre, included some poems rarely reprinted, of varying quality. Darío's influence is paramount; the poet struggling to define her voice and refine her technique is evident. SS

"Blanco, negro, blanco" in Teatro Infantil. Based on Lugones' "El pierrot negro" in Lunario sentimental, this musical play for elementary school children combines fantastic scenery with a sentimental plot line in which love conquers all obstacles. The silly, frivolous heroine Colombina rejects her lover Pierrot after he accidentally falls into a vat of dye and becomes totally black. The play dramatizes his successful quest to recover his color and love, thus revealing the author's unconscious racism. SS

"Cimbelina en 1900 y pico" in Dos farsas pirotécnicas. A highly experimental, expressionistic, and satiric treatment of Shakespeare's play. There are two parallel sets, side by side on stage, which represent 1500 and 1900. The plot moves jerkily, and at times not at all. Characters are types, serving obviously symbolic purposes. Dialogue is stilted. The action also makes the characters seem wooden. Thus, Hector hammers at a globe to "fix" the world. The theme is nevertheless sentimental; love conquers all. SS

Cinco cartas y una golondrina. Colección del Instituto Amigos del Libro Argentino, vol. III. Buenos Aires: Instituto Amigos del Libro Argentino, 1959. Hardcover, 75 pp. The first page contains a poem signed by Storni, dated, with time and place given. The manuscript, handwritten by the poet, is also included. Three of the five letters are addressed to different men and signed by different women. The other two are not addressed to any man but are signed. The theme in all of them, is passionate and tormented love. "Una golondrina" is the story of a woman involved in love, passion and hatred. AA

"Los degolladores de estatuas: comedia en un acto," in Teatro infantil. The toys in a rich children's room come alive and decide to revolt against their masters. They cut off the heads of all the statues in the house. When the family returns, they call the police, but meanwhile the toys replace the heads, so that the police think the family is playing a practical joke on them. The family quarrels, and the toys are satisfied with their revenge. Written for elementary school children. SS

"El dios de los pájaros: comedia en dos actos, divididos en cuatro cuadros" in Teatro infantil. This elementary school children's play is longer, more complex, and more clearly resolved than the others in this volume. Its themes are mistreatment and slavery. After some children kill birds, the bird god kidnaps two children, and puts them in a cage. The others embark on a journey of purification and sacrifice, seeking their companions, which culminates in their realization that birds are as valuable as people. The god sends them home with a guide, after they promise not to harm birds any longer. SS

Dos farsas pirotécnicas. Buenos Aires: Buenos Aires, 1931. 168 pp. Contains "Cimbelina en 1900 y pico" and "Polixena y la cocinerita." [See annotations under individual titles.]

Dos mujeres. [See annotation under El amo del mundo.]

El dulce daño, poemas. Buenos Aires: Latino Americana, 1964. 91 pp. Other editions: 1st ed. (Buenos Aires: Sociedad Cooperativa Editorial Limitada, 1918); 2nd ed. 1920. This title is a reference to the pain of love and of writing. El dulce daño duplicates the emotional tone of La inquietud del rosal, although the technique is more polished. The first-person-singular poetic voice is used repeatedly, insistently. Storni suffered criticism for the erotic nature of some of these poems. Included is "Tú me quieres blanca," her most famous poem, which anticipates the ironic challenge of later works. Metric schemes of these easy-to-read poems vary greatly. They offer many kinds of rhyme, differing lengths of the lines, and frequent metaphors. SS

Entre un par de maletas a medio abrir y la manecilla del reloj. Ed. and notes by José D. Forgione. Buenos Aires: Católicas Argentinas, 1939. 40 pp.

La inquietud del rosal, poemas. Prologue by Juan Julián Lastra. Buenos Aires: Latino Americana, 1964. 91 pp. 1st ed.: (Buenos Aires: Librería La Facultad, J. Roldán, 1916), 126 pp. Storni's earliest published collection of poetry, this volume reflects the author's youth and sentimentality, but also her consciousness of literary craft. The principal theme is love, expressed in a personalized poetic voice which utilizes generally romantic language and rigid forms. The swans, swallows, and crystal of modernista imagery accompany a highly exaltative emotional tone more characteristic of Romanticism. SS

Irremediablemente, poemas. Buenos Aires: Buenos Aires, 1919. 165 pp. Another edition: (Buenos Aires: Latino Americana, 1964). 91 pp. The poetic voice here is again highly personalized; generally felicitous metaphors and tight rhyme schemes demonstrate improving technical skills. After the initial group of poems, there are two sub-divided sections: "Momentos humildes-amorosos pasionales" and "Momentos amargos-selváticos tempestuosos." Contains the well-known "Hombre pequeñito," as well as several poems illustrating aspects of women's lives and roles, such as "Bien pudiera ser," in which the female poet is the voice of generations of silent women. SS

Irremediablemente (1919). Vol. II of Obras completas. 5th ed. Buenos Aires: Meridion, 1957. 121 pp. The first poem that appears in this volume is entitled "This Book." It serves as an introduction to what Storni is going to express throughout the book. It contains poems appearing in others of her books. The poems are grouped by what the author calls moments, and through them she brings out her anxieties, disillusions, and fears of life. AA

"Jorge y su conciencia: diálogo," in Teatro infantil. A satiric critique of sex-role stereotyped work, this "diálogo" for elementary school children depicts the hero winning praise from his conscience by accomplishing the enormous task of sewing on a button. He wishes never to have to do such terrible work again. SS

Languidez, poemas. Buenos Aires: Buenos Aires, 1920. 156 pp. Buenos Aires: Latino Americana, 1964. 107 pp. In the prologue, Storni divides her poetic production into an earlier, subjective mode and her future, more objective writing. The poetry is characterized by tension between the two modes; it contains a more distanced "I." The sub-divisions are: "Motivos líricos e íntimos" and "Exaltadas." The poems treat themes already developed, such as disillusionment with love ("Rosales de suburbio"), as well as mocking such myths as female chastity ("La ronda de las muchachas"). A long, bleak poem in couplets called "Letanías de la tierra muerta" is dedicated to Gabriela Mistral. SS

Languidez. Vol. III of Obras completas. Buenos Aires: Meridion, 1959. 122 pp. The author dedicates the book to those who, like herself, have never accomplished any of their dreams. The tone of the book is sad and ironic, typical of Storni. The reader sees her soul pouring out all the illusions and hallucinations that at the end deceive the poet. Her poems in this volume are filled with great emotions but expressed as if they were burdens. She grouped the poems in a very arbitrary manner.   AA

Mascarilla y trébol, círculos inmantados, poemas. Buenos Aires: Mercatali, 1938. 222 pp. Other editions: 1st ed. (Buenos Aires: Meridión, 1957), 114 pp.; 4th ed. (Buenos Aires: Meridión, 1959), 114 pp.; (Buenos Aires: Latino Americana, 1964), 75 pp. The most experimental -- and last -- volume of Storni's poetry asks for an "imaginative collaboration" from the reader. New forms and techniques serve the author's growing preoccupation with her approaching death, as well as demarcating her increasing interest in the world, objects and nature, surrounding her. She names these poems "antisonetos"; within the tight structure of the sonnet, she uses irregular rhyme and surrealistic imagery to great effect. Desolate city scenes, nightmarish visions of the river and sea, and microscopic dissection of parts of the human body all contribute to the book's brooding, dream-like quality.
SS

Las mejores poesías (líricas) de los mejores poetas. Vol. XLIII. Note by Editorial Cervantes. Barcelona: Cervantes, n.d. [1923]. Hardcover, 68 pp. The egoism of her poetry is contained within this little hardcover book. The selection was obviously made to show the sensible soul of the poet and her desire to elate her spirit to reach her ideals. In her pantheistical delirium, she wanted to see goodness in everything. The preliminary note introduces the style of Storni to the readers and gives some information about her life. AA

Los mejores versos de Alfonsina Storni. Cuadernillos de Poesía, #21. Buenos Aires: Nuestra América, n.d. [1963]. 40 pp. Contains almost eighty of her most well-known poems plus a short note by Dora Isella Russell, "Alfonsina y la muerte;" "Alfonsina Storni" by Simón Latino; and a biografical and bibliographical note. DEM

Mundo de siete pozos, poemas. 3rd ed. Buenos Aires: Tor, 1935. Other editions: 1st ed., n.d. [1934]; 2nd ed., 1934, 156 pp.; (Buenos Aires: Latino Americana, 1964), 123 pp. Commencing a new, radically different direction in Storni's poetry, this volume's avant-garde forms and themes place its author within the experimental literary trends of her time: surrealistic imagery, experimentation with meter, fragmentation of reality, and themes of urban isolation and desolation. Also, the cycle of sea poems here highlights a recurrent motif in Storni's work: her identification with, and attraction to, the sea's potentially destructive beauty. SS

Obra poética. Illus. by Arturo Gerardo Guastavino. Buenos Aires: Ramón J. Roggero, 1946. Hardcover, 571 pp. 3rd ed.: (Buenos Aires: Roggero-Ronal, 1952). Includes the complete poetic work of Storni, except La inquietud del rosal. Almost a complete compilation, it displays the wide variety of topics and themes this author developed in her works. AA

Obra poética completa. 2nd ed. Buenos Aires: Latino Americana, 1964. 453 pp. Contains: La inquietud del rosal (1916), El dulce daño (1918), Irremediablemente (1919), Languidez (1920), Ocre (1925), Mundo de siete pozos (1934), Mascarilla y trébol (1938), "Poesías no incluídas en libro (1916-1921)," and "Poesías no incluídas en libro (1934-1938)." The seven original volumes of Storni's poetry appear in this volume, followed by two chronologically divided groups of other poems. The majority of the section of poetry from 1916 to 1921 contains love sonnets. The poems of the 1934-1938 period demonstrate her experimental inclination; they include "A Horacio Quiroga" and "Voy a dormir," the sonnet written just before her voluntary death. This volume is fairly easy to obtain. First edition contains a Prologue by Juan Julián Lastra. SS

Obras completas. Vol. 1, Poesías. 3rd ed. Buenos Aires: Latino Americana, 1976. 1st ed. 1964. Includes: La inquietud del rosal (1916), El dulce daño (1918), Irremediablemente (1919), Languidez (1920), Ocre (1925), Mundo de siete pozos (1934), Mascarilla y trébol (1938), and "Poesías sueltas." [See annotations under volume titles.]

Ocre, poemas. 3rd ed. Buenos Aires: Babel, 1927. Other editions: 1st ed. 1925, 140 pp. ; (Buenos Aires: Latino Americana, 1964), 75 pp. Distinctly different in tone from earlier works, Ocre begins to fulfill Storni's promise to write more "objective" poetry made in the Prologue of Languidez. The volume contains several poems in praise of women, such as "Palabras a Delmira Agustini," "Ternura," and "Traición," and a poem about the writing process, "La palabra." The sonnet form predominates; rhyme and meter vary. Modernista language and imagery are transformed into poetry whose voice demonstrates its author's self-assurance and skill. SS

"Pedro y Pedrito: comedia en un acto," in Teatro infantil. This elementary school children's play juggles the concepts of freedom and captivity. All the characters are animals, and include Mickey Mouse. The two heroes are parrots, who lead the overthrow of the animal tamer and his daughter who had kept them locked up. SS

Poemas de amor. Illus. by Gambartes. Buenos Aires: Meridion, 1956. 109 pp. Peculiar edition with appropriate, yet simple illustrations. Divided into four sections: I) "El Ensueño," II) "Plenitud," III) "Agonía;" and IV) "La Noche." The type characters are big, very easy to read and attractive to young readers. The poems are short but sharp, filled with sadness and desperation. Of interest to teachers of high school who want to introduce Spanish American poetry to advanced students. AA

Poesías. Las mejores poesías de los mejores poetas, # XLIII. Barcelona: Cervantes, 1923. 66 pp. [See annotation under Las mejores poesías de los mejores poetas.]

Poesías. Vol. I of Obras completas. Preface by Ramón J. Roggero. Buenos Aires: Latino Americana, 1968. Hardcover, 565 pp. This volume includes the seven books of poems published between 1916 and 1938. The last section contains those never published in books. These poems appeared in magazines and/or newspapers and their titles are arranged chronologically in the back of the book. The names of the publications are also given. This is the first of three volumes that contain Storni's available production. AA

Poesías completas. 6th ed. Buenos Aires: Latino Americana, 1968. 502 pp. Cover title: Obra poética completa. [See annotation under Obra poética completa.]

Poesías (seleccionadas e inéditas). Cuadernos Quincenales de Letras y Ciencias. Buenos Aires: América, 1920. 29 pp. Contains eighteen poems, culled principally from Irremediablemente, El dulce daño, y Languidez. Themes and techniques are typical of Storni's early sentimental verse; the influence of modernismo is also still quite apparent. Two poems not listed as included in one of her books in Obra poética completa appear, as do four others not included elsewhere. SS

Poesías selectas. Los Angeles: Art, 19??. 60 pp.

Poesías sueltas. Vol. VIII of Obras completas. Buenos Aires: Latino Americana, 1964. Hardcover, 91 pp. This selection includes a variety of themes. Her philosophical views of the world are expressed, at times with tenderness and in other instances in a cold tone. It shows her desperation. The poet combined different metrics that reveals her absolute dominion of the verse and the language. Of special interest to the general public for its apparent simplicity. AA

"Polixena y la cocinerita" in Dos farsas pirotécnicas. The stylized sets and props of this play act as reminders that the performance is a farce. Storni's condemnation of men is clear. The heroine is a kitchen maid who decides to end her life in imitation of the Trojan women's tragedy. That is, she chooses death over slavery. The play undermines the dominant dramatic aesthetic by its choice of heroine and its satiric tone, both supposedly inappropriate to tragedy. In an epilogue, Euripides decides to end his own life after death upon learning that an upstart twentieth century Argentinean writer has deformed his play. SS

"Un sueño en el camino: mimodrama," in Teatro infantil. Written for elementary school children, this play is a pantomime in which a poor boy dreams that such celebrities as Charlie Chaplin, Little Red Riding Hood, Cinderella, and others visit him, bringing gifts and merriment. They leave, however, taking the gifts with them. He awakens hungry, and without food. Accompanied by softly sung music, he then falls asleep again in the falling snow. SS

Teatro infantil. Buenos Aires: R. J. Roggero, 1950. 162 pp., illus., music. 2nd ed.: (Buenos Aires: Huemal, 1973), 138 pp. Includes incidental music to "Blanco, negro, blanco" by author. The two published editions of this collection of children's plays are identical. Contains: "Blanco, negro, blanco;" "Pedro y Pedrito: comedia en un acto;" "Jorge y su conciencia: diálogo;" "Un sueño en el camino: mimodrama;" "Los degolladores de estatuas: comedia en un acto;" "El dios de los pájaros: comedia en dos actos, divididos en cuatro cuadros." [See annotations of plays under separate titles.] SS

STUVEN, Mariana Cox (see **COX STUVEN, Mariana**)

SUAREZ, Clementina (Honduras, twentieth century)

    Antología: el poeta y sus señales

    Canto a la encontrada patria y su héroe

    Corazón sangrante, poesía

    Creciendo con la hierba, poemas

    De la desilusión a la esperanza, poemas

    De mis sábados, el último, cuentos

    Engranajes, poesía

    Ronda de niños, poesía

    Templo de fuego

    Veleros, 30 (treinta) poemas

SUAREZ, Emma E. de Gutiérrez (see **GUTIERREZ SUAREZ, Emma E. de**)

SUAREZ, Isabel Estrella de (Argentina, twentieth century)

    Mis pensamientos, poemas

    Pensemos en nuestros hijos

SUAREZ, Josefina (Mexico, twentieth century)

    Poemas

SUAREZ, María (Mexico, twentieth century)

    Azulejos, prosa y poesía

SUAREZ, María del Carmen (Argentina, twentieth century)

    Desde Buenos Aires, poemas

    Los dientes del lobo, poemas

    La noche y los maleficios, poesías

    Los nuevos habitantes, poemas

SUAREZ, María Dolores (Cuba, twentieth century; pseudonym: X., Marilola)

    Cantos de amanecer

    Fruto dorado

SUAREZ, Mariana (Chile, b. 1929)

    La danza de los vendedores, novela

    El mundo de Colombita, para niños

    Los tejados en agosto, novela

SUAREZ, sor Ursula (Chile, 1668-1749)

    Relación de las singulares misericordias que el Señor ha usado con una religiosa indigna esposa suya

SUAREZ-RIVERO, Eliana (Cuba-United States, b. 1929)

    Cuerpos breves

    De cal y arena, poemas

SUCRE, Dolores (Ecuador, d. 1917)

    Poesías

SUCRE, Graciela Rojas (see **ROJAS SUCRE, Graciela**)

SUCRE, Yolanda Camarano de (see **CAMARANO DE SUCRE, Yolanda**)

SUIFFET, Norma (Uruguay, twentieth century)

    Las voces incandescentes, poemas

SUMARRAGA, Sahara Brito (see **BRITO SUMARRAGA, Sahara**)

SURIA, Violeta López (see **LOPEZ SURIA, Violeta**)

T

TADEA DE SAN JOAQUIN, sor (Chile, 1755?-1827)

Romance que narra la inundación del convento San Rafael en 1783. Microfilm, Library of Congress. 10 pp. Narrates the flood suffered by the Monasterio de las Carmelitas (Santiago, Chile) on July 16, 1783. It tells how the nuns were moved to the Casa de Belén, where they stayed for three months until they could return to their own house. Uses the traditional Spanish romance metric form. As the author states, she is not a writer, and was asked by her superior to record the problems they encountered due to the flood. PRL

TAGLE, María (Chile, 1899-1946)

Flautas de sombra

El signo que huye

TAIN DE TRABA, Marta (Argentina - Colombia, 1930-1983; known as Traba, Marta). Born and raised in Argentina, Traba lived many years in Colombia. Known primarily for her controversial essays on contemporary Latin American art (El museo vacío, La pintura nueva en Latinoamérica), Traba first ventured into literature in the early sixties. Concerned with the existential and social dilemmas confronting contemporary Latin Americans, she gained continental recognition with Ceremonias del verano which received the Casa de las Américas fiction award in 1966. Traba contributed regularly to several Latin American art journals, taught modern art at the Universidad de Los Andes and directed the Museum of Modern Art in Bogotá.

Las ceremonias del verano. Introd. by Mario Benedetti. La Habana, Cuba: Casa de las Américas, 1966. Paperback, 145 pp. Four episodes in the life of a young woman who struggles to understand the meaning of love, communication and friendship. The story is built around the incidents of four summers spent in Buenos Aires, Paris, Italy and an unspecified European city. In each instance the protagonist is caught in a seemingly unsolvable dilemma: how to find a middle way between utter detachment and annihilating dependence. The narrative techniques she employs are the most notable aspect of the novel. The effective use of stream of consciousness and cinematic devices render a rich portrait of the protagonist's inner world.

Conversación al sur, novela. Mexico: Siglo Veintiuno, 1981. ISBN 968-23-1029-6, paperback, 175 pp.

La jugada del sexto día, novela. Santiago de Chile: Universitaria, 1970. Paperback, 215 pp. This novel focuses on the despair, boredom and alienation which pervades the lives of young upper-middle-class Latin American couples. Underlying this theme is a strong critique of middle-class life in Latin America, which Traba believes lacks in authenticity and spiritual vigor. As in previous works, the author resorts to the use of cinematic techniques and other modernistic narrative devices.

Historia natural de la alegría, poemas

Homérica Latina

Los laberintos insolados. Barcelona: Seix Barral, 1967. Hardback, 173 pp. This novel is Traba's vision of the fears and obsessions which haunt the minds of contemporary, urban Latin Americans. Like an Odysseus, the protagonist wanders aimlessly through the United States and Europe in a fruitless search for his identity and an existence free of the burdens of society, family and middle-class standards. His quest ends with the realization that the past can't be eluded, that he is inevitably condemned to return home.

Pasó así. Montevideo: Arca, 1968. Paperback, 139 pp. These sixteen short stories portray the spiritual sterility and suffocation that permeates life in a working-class Colombian neighborhood. Peopled with characters whose thoughts and deeds reflect the mediocrity, hopelessness and degradation of their lot, the book probes into the grim social realities of Latin American urban life. More interesting as a social document than as a work of fiction. IR

Poemas en prosa

TAMAYO, Evora (Cuba, b. 1940)

Cuentos para abuelas enfermas

La vieja y el mar, cuentos

TAMPIERI DE ESTRELLA, Susana (Argentina, twentieth century)

Melquisedec

TAPIA DE CASTELLANOS, Esther (Mexico, 1842-1897)

Los cánticos de los niños, poema

Flores silvestres, poemas

Obras poéticas

Rasgos biográficos y algunas de las poesías inéditas

TAPIA DE LESQUERRE, Lola (Argentina, twentieth century)

Pinceladas de gloria, poesía

TARAN, Ana Enriqueta (Venezuela, b. 1920)

Al norte de la sangre, poemas

Presencia terrena, poemas

Verdor secreto, poemas

TAYLHARDAT, Concepción de (Venezuela, nineteenth century)

Arpegios, poesía

Flores del alma, poesía

TEJADA MILLA, Mercedes (Guatemala, twentieth century)

La patria era aquel valle, poesía

Una vida, comedia

TEJEDA, Patricia (Chile, twentieth century)

Algo para romper

TEJERA, Nivaria (Cuba, b. 1933)

El barranco, novela

La gruta, versos

Innumerables voces, poesía

Sonámbulo del sol, novela

TERAN, Ana Enriqueta (Venezuela, b. 1920)

De bosque a bosque, poemas

Libro de los oficios, poemas 1967

TERAN, Cora de (Venezuela, twentieth century)

En sueños de un album rosado

TERRES, María Elodia (Mexico, twentieth century)

Dos salones, crónica

Seis cuentos

TERZAGA, Etelvina Astrada de (see **ASTRADA DE TERZAGA, Etelvina**)

TESTA, Celia (Uruguay, twentieth century)

De los seres, las cosas y la vida

Largos cuentos cortos

THEIN, Gladys (Chile, twentieth century)

<u>Corolas de cristal</u>

<u>Poemas</u>

<u>Poesía, selección</u>

<u>El rostro desolado</u>

<u>Territorio de fuego</u>, poemas

THENON, Susana (Argentina, b. 1937)

<u>De lugares extraños</u>, poemas

<u>Edad sin treguas</u>

<u>Habitante de nada</u>

THIEDE, María Restrepo de (see **RESTREPO DE THIEDE, María**)

THORBURN, Elizabeth Escobar (see **ESCOBAR THORBURN, Elizabeth**)

TIBERTI, María Dhialma (see **DHIALMA TIBERTI, María**)

TIKIS (pseudonym; see **REYES, Alicia**)

TINAJERO, Blanca Martínez de (see **MARTINEZ DE TINAJERO, Blanca**)

TINOCO, María Fernández de (see **FERNANDEZ DE TINOCO, María**)

TINOCO DE MARROQUIN, Clemencia Morales (see **MORALES TINOCO DE MARROQUIN, Clemencia**)

TIO, Elsa (Puerto Rico, b. 1951). Tió is an intense woman, equally passionate about her writing, her poetry workshops for children, and her involvement with artists and humanists who share her dream for a free Puerto Rico. Presently on the Board of Directors of the prestigious Institute of Puerto Rican Culture, she was the recipient of the 1978 Premio Nacional de Literatura. Tió writes of love in all its dimensions, and of solitude, absence and death. One of her most moving poems, "To Arnaldo Torres and Carlos Soto Arriví" recreates, in an angry and lyrical tone, the 1978 assassination of the two young <u>independentistas</u> in Cerro Maravilla, a mountain in Puerto Rico. Her poem is a testimony of her faith in her fellow citizens and an expression of her certainty of a renewal of national commitment, the positive outcome of the tragic deaths.

<u>Detrás de los espejos empañados</u>, poesía. San Juan de Puerto Rico: n.p., 1979. ISBN 84-399-6969-4, 79 pp. Available from the author: Elsa Tió, Calle España 2024, Ocean Park, Puerto Rico 00911. In this collection Tió writes of love. In "Let me be your shadow," she blends the desire to merge with the loved one, to nurture him, to be both mother and lover, while at the same time she delivers an impassioned plea to be herself. Tió also reflects the pain of the commitment to a culturally, spiritually, and politically free Puerto Rico. Her poem "In this Island" links her to the long tradition of Puerto Rican writers who critically explore its

complex reality in verse and prose. Her commitment to her country recalls the militant lyrics of Puerto Rico's national anthem "La Borinqueña," written by her ancestor, the nineteenth century poet, Lola Rodríguez de Tió.

Poesías. San Juan de Puerto Rico: n.p., 1978. ISBN 84-499-0129-4, 91 pp. Available from the author [see previous annotation]. Her first volume, Poesía was published in 1958 when she was scarcely seven years old. The poems were dictated by Tió between the ages of four and seven to her parents. They are gentle poems for adults, as well as children, impressive for the originality of the complex images she invents, reminiscent of Japanese haiku, García Lorca, and nursery rhymes. An example is "The Dove is Sad": "The dove is sad, she cries on her wings caressing the death of her tears." GFW

TIO, Lola Rodríguez de (see **RODRIGUEZ DE TIO, Lola**)

TOLEDO, Adelaida Alvarez de (see **ALVAREZ DE TOLEDO, Adelaida**)

TOLEDO, Luisa Isabel Alvarez de (see **ALVAREZ DE TOLEDO, Luisa Isabel**)

TORRE, Josefina A. Claudio de la (see **CLAUDIO DE LA TORRE, Josefina A.**)

TORRE, Josefina Muriel de La (see **LA TORRE, Josefina Muriel de**)

TORRENS DE GARMENDIA, Mercedes (Cuba, b. 1888)

Esquila en el poniente, versos

La flauta del silencio, versos

Fragua de estrellas, poesía

Fuente sellada, poesía

Jardines del crepúsculo, versos

Jazminero de la sombra, poesía

TORRES, Araceli (Cuba, twentieth century)

Así, poesía

Lámpsana, poesía

TORRES, Eugenia (Mexico, twentieth century)

En torno de la quimera

La hermana, drama

Lo imprevisto

El muñeco roto

TORRES, Maruja (Chile, twentieth century)

Simplemente, poemas

TORRES, Soledad Llorens (see **LLORENS TORRES, Soledad**)

TORRICO, Alcira Cardona (see **CARDONA TORRICO, Alcira**)

TORRICO, Yolanda Cuéllar de (see **CUELLAR DE TORRICO, Yolanda**)

TOSCANO, Carmen (Mexico, b. 1910)

Inalcanzable

Leyendas de México colonial

La llorona

Mío

Trazo incompleto

TOSCANO, Refugio de Barragán (see **BARRAGAN TOSCANO, Refugio de**)

TRABA, Marta (see **TAIN DE TRABA, Marta**)

TREJO, Blanca Lydia (Mexico, b. 1906)

El congreso de los pollitos

Lecturas de juventud

Limones para Mr. Nixon, y otros más, cuentos

Lo que sucedió al nopal

La marimba, cuento

El padrastro, novela

Un país en el fango, novela

Paradojas

El ratón Panchito Roe-libros, cuentos para niños

TREVIÑO CARRANZA, Celia (Mexico, b. 1912)

Mi atormentada vida

Rimas sinfónicas, poemas

TRINIDAD DEL CID, María (see **CID, María Trinidad del**)

TUDURI DE COYA, Mercedes García (see **GARCIA TUDURI DE COYA, Mercedes**)

TULA (see **GOMEZ DE AVELLANEDA Y ARTEAGA, Gertrudis**)

TURINA, Pepita (Chile, b. 1907). Born in Punta Arenas of a Yugoslavian family, Turina first gained literary prestige with her two novels, Un drama de almas (1934) and Zona íntima (1941). Subsequently she devoted herself to literary criticism. She was noted by Fernando Alegría as one of two Hispanics and the only Latin American woman to have written about Walt Whitman; she published an essay on the American poet in 1942. In 1952, she published a book on seven not-too-well-known Chilean poets, among them two women, titled Sombras y entresombras de la poesía chilena. In 1960 she did an edition of six short stories by Chilean writers of Yugoslavian origin. Her last work does not deal with literature per se. Multidiálogos is a collage-like essay which incorporates the views of many authors on various topics. Turina appears in several studies on Chilean literature. Turina is married to the prestigious folklorist and indefatigable promoter of Chilean letters, Oreste Plath.

> Un drama de almas, novela. Santiago de Chile: Ercilla, 1934. Paperback, 128 pp. The author's husband, Oreste Plath, has summarized this novel in the following way: "It is a novel without any major transcendence, written when the author was twenty years old. It was well received and extensively reviewed in the local newspaper of Valdivia, where the author lived at the time. It is a novel about love, the impossible love of a man for a woman. Its technique is that of ordinary novels. It contains a good deal of dialogue."

> Zona íntima, la soltería, novela. Santiago de Chile: La Nación, 1941. Paperback, 230 pp. Available in major research libraries. This novel traces a love affair over a period of twenty months between a man recently separated from his wife and an introspective, self-assertive twenty-five-year-old woman in a coastal provincial town of Chile. Stylistically uninnovative, the third-person narrative shifts to first in minimal dialogue and numerous letters; it analyzes the woman's growing eroticism and apprehensions over the man's passionate persistence yet undecisive intentions. Her final disenchantment with his selfish immaturity, which en passant parallels the nation's political disillusionment, brings on her resignation to a lonely but peaceful existence. SHA

TURNER, Clorinda Matto de (see **MATTO DE TURNER, Clorinda**)

U

UGARTE, María Mercedes Vial de (see VIAL DE UGARTE, María Mercedes)

UGARTE DE LANDIVAR, Zoila (Ecuador, twentieth century)

María

UMPIERRE-HERRERA, Luz María (Puerto Rico, b. 1947; known as Umpierre, Luzma). Puerto Rican poet and critic. Ph.D. from Bryn Mawr College. Winner of creative writing awards from International Publications and Chase Manhattan. Critical works include: Ideología y novela en Puerto Rico (Playor, 1983), Nuevas aproximaciones críticas a la literatura puertorriqueña contemporánea (Cultural, 1983-1984) and articles on Ferré, Soto, Casas, Uslar Pietri, Fuertes, Zavala and others. Editorial Board of Third Woman. National Research Council Fellow (1981-82). Associate professor of Caribbean literature at Rutgers University.

En el país de las maravillas, poesías. Kempis puertorriqueño. Preface by Eliana Rivero. Bloomington, Indiana: Third Woman Press, 1982. 38 pp. Combining Biblical allusion with the theme of Alice in Wonderland, Umpierre's main speaker in this small volume of poems finds herself in symbolic exile, an outsider separated from the North American mainstream by culture, values and language. The skillful fusion and juxtaposition of Spanish and English, street language, cliché and formal diction serves as a mirror to reflect the hypocrisy and inverted values present in North American society. Includes previously published Una puertorriqueña en Penna. Significant work for those interested in poetry, women's studies, and minority studies.

Una puertorriqueña en Penna., poesía. Puerto Rico: 1979. 20 pp. The twelve poems in this, the first published volume of Umpierre's poetry, reflect her initial experience of life in the United States as a student at Bryn Mawr College. Umpierre combines Spanish, English, onomatopeic language and the placement of words on the page to reflect the cultural confrontation she feels as a Puerto Rican student, alone in an elitist, alien environment. All but one of the poems in this collection have been re-published in En el país de las maravillas. NM

UNGARO DE FOX, Lucía (see FOX-LOCKERT, Lucía)

URBANO, Victoria (Costa Rica-United States, d. 1984)

Agar, la esclava, teatro

Esta noche un marido, comedia en un acto

Five Women Writers of Costa Rica: Short Stories by Carmen Naranjo, Eunice Odio, Yolanda Oreamuno, Victoria Urbano and Rima Vallbona. Ed. Victoria Urbano. Beaumont, Tx.: Asociación de Literatura Femenina Hispánica, 1978.

El fornicador, teatro

La hija de Charles Green, teatro

Marfil, cuentos y poesías

Mentiras azules, juguete cómico

La niña de los caracoles

Los nueve círculos

El pájaro negro, teatro

Platero y tú

Y era otra vez hoy y otros cuentos

UREÑA DE HENRIQUEZ, Salomé (Dominican Republic, 1850-1897; pseudonym: Herminia). Ureña de Henríquez, considered an outstanding Dominican poet, was called the "muse of civilization." She studied with her father, a noted literary figure and educator; she attended public school until age fifteen when she began writing. At seventeen she published under the pseudonym of Herminia. Married and the mother of four, she also organized the first institution for secondary education for women on the island, a normal school: the Instituto de Señoritas. Ureña de Henríquez worked with the celebrated Antilles philosopher and educator, Eugenio María de Hostos and was awarded a medal by the Dominican Literary Society.

Poesías completas. Santo Domingo, Dominican Republic: Publication of the Secretary of Education, Fine Arts and Culture, 1975. 338 pp. This volume contains her short poems, the long, narrative poem, "Anacaona," two short speeches for the investitures of the Normal School she founded, and a letter. The poetry is divided into sections: "A la Patria," "Páginas Intimas," "Varia," a few more short poems and "Anacaona." Her short poetry treats three topics: civilization, country and sentimental intimacy. Known as the "muse of art," her best poems include: "Ruinas," a melancholy picture of the destiny of her country; "En la muerte de Espaillat," an elegy; "En defensa de la Sociedad" and "La Gloria de Progreso," odes; and "Las Horas de Angustia," a sensitive poem of motherhood. "Anacaona," an Indian narrative in many cantos, often severely criticized, contains descriptive passages that are fluid, energetic and vivid. Poesía contains a picture of the poet, a fairly extensive bibliography, a prologue and excellent criticism by Joaquín Belaguer, former Dominican president and educator. AS

URIARTE, Chayo (Mexico, twentieth century)

 Cosecha, poemas

 En el final del cuento, poemas

 Musgo, poemas

URIARTE, Yolanda (Mexico, twentieth century)

 Dos ensayos y un cuento, prosas cortas y verso

URIBE, Leonor Herrera de Rodríguez (see **HERRERA DE RODRIGUEZ URIBE, Lenor**)

URIBE, Rebeca (Mexico, twentieth century)

 Poema a modo de un suite

 Poema en 5 (cinco) tiempos

 Poesía

URIBE, Rosario Orrego de (see **ORREGO DE URIBE, Rosario**)

URIBE CASANUEVA, Inelia (Chile, b. 1936)

 Carcajadas a medianoche, poesía

 Mis poemas para ti

 Taberna en la luna, poesía

URIBE DE ARENAS RUIZ, Maruja (Colombia, twentieth century)

 El por qué del dolor

URIBE DE ESTRADA, María Helena (Colombia, twentieth century)

 Polvo y ceniza, cuentos

URQUIDI, Mercedes Anaya de (see **ANAYA DE URQUIDI, Mercedes**)

URQUIZA, Concha (Mexico, 1910-1945)

 Antología; poemas

 México; Concha Urquiza

 Obras, poemas y prosas, retitled Poesías y prosas

 Poemas

URSULA SUAREZ, sor (see **SUAREZ, sor Ursula**)

URUETA, Margarita (see **URUETA DE VILLASEÑOR, Margarita**)

URUETA DE VILLASEÑOR, Margarita (Mexico, b. 1918; known as Urueta, Margarita). She has written novels, short stories and scripts for television and cinema. She is, however, best known for her avant-garde theatre. She takes an active part in the production of her plays which are usually presented in her own theatre named after her father, Jesús Urueta, distinguished for his activities during the Mexican Revolution. Her biography of her father is the work of an accomplished historian.

Almas de perfil

Amor en 13 (trece) dimensiones, cuentos. México: Organización Novaro, 1970. 131 pp. Thirteen episodes illustrate various forms of love such as the love of parents for their children, the love of children for each other, the infatuation of an adolescent, the attraction between man and woman. The object of one's love may be unattainable or foredoomed to failure. Frequently love may change to utter boredom. Related realistically, most of the episodes defy the convention of the happy ending.

Ave de sacrificio

Una conversación sencilla

Espía sin ser

¡Hasta mañana, compadre! Biografía de un presidente, novela. Mexico: B. Costa Amic, 1975. 175 pp. Political powers select an unknown, uncommitted candidate to run as president of the country. He and his family are told what to say and how to behave. As he wins the election his opponent warns him, "Until tomorrow, friend." Intentionally melodromatic, the novel is a harsh indictment of a system that pretends to be democratic.

El mar la distraía

Mediocre, novela. México: Ibero Americano de Publicaciones, 1947. 189 pp. Urueta's protagonist is a colorless, friendless, timid factory worker who has left a journal behind her before disappearing. It reveals the agony of her solitude and the hopelessness of her dreams. The novel is deeply compassionate, a plea for understanding the plight of the lonely. It may be taken as a denunciation of a thoughtless, self-centered society.

Poemas

San Lunes, una hora de vida, mansión para turistas

El señor Perro, teatro

Teatro nuevo. México: Joaquín Mortiz, 1963. 181 pp. Four surrealist plays, typical of Urueta's avant-garde theatre, are closely akin to the theatre of the absurd. In one of them a family's possessions begin to multiply much like the chairs in Ionesco's Les chaises. Each play is a caricature, spiced with irony. Explicit stage directions, music and pantomime contribute to the eerie dreamlike atmosphere. GB

Tierra hermana y otros poemas

URZUA, María (Chile, b. 1916)

Alta marea, cuentos

Altovalsol, poesía

El invitado, cuentos

La isla de los gatos, cuentos

El presidente, novela

Río amargo, novela

También el hombre canta

URZUA DE CALVO, Deyanira (Chile, twentieth century)

El capitán Veneno, comedia

La carta misteriosa, comedia

El concurso literario de Chincolco, sainete

Entre escritores y periodistas, sainete

El necio orgullo, comedia para niños

Patria y hogar, poesías y dramas

Por el escenario de la vida, poesías y comedias

La travesura de Rosario

El trovador del hogar, colección de poesías, diálogos, trílogos, y comedias para la juventud

La verdadera hermosura, comedia

UTRERA, Esther (United States, 1915-1978)

Mensaje a luces, versos

V

VACA DE FLOR, María Natalia (Ecuador, twentieth century)

De mi vida, poema

Pobre María, novela

VALDERRAMA, Lucy Barco de (see **BARCO DE VALDERRAMA, Lucy**)

VALDES MENDOZA, Mercedes (Cuba, 1822-1896)

Poesías

VALDIVIA, Omara (Cuba-United States, b. 1947; pseudonym: Islas, Maya)

Sola, desnuda, sin nombre

VALDIVIESO, Mercedes (pseudonym: see **VALENZUELA ALVAREZ, Mercedes**)

VALENCIA, Angela de (Colombia, twentieth century)

Rumor de frondas, versos

VALENCIA, Tita (Mexico, twentieth century). Valencia began a career as a musician but changed her medium to literature because of the current strong possibilities for the creation of new genres fusing various previously existing modes. Her writing is indeed inter- or cross-generic with features of poetry, prose fiction and women's personal writing (e.g., diary or journals). She has a marked interest in developing an erotic language adequate for a woman's expression.

El hombre negro

Minotauromaquia, crónica de un desencuentro. Mexico: Joaquín Mortiz, 1976. 209 pp. Composed of brief fragments of poetic prose, diary-like fragments, and letters (perhaps only composed in the narrator's mind) to an unresponsive lover, this work presents the experience of a woman suffering loneliness abroad, disturbing and

unaccustomedly strong erotic feelings and a difficult reworking of her ideas about artistic expression and love. Most impressive for the experimental development of an erotic language for woman in Spanish.
NL

VALENTI, Walda (Guatemala, twentieth century)

Azul y roca, novela

VALENZUELA, Luisa (Argentina, b. 1938). Narrator and journalist who has lived in Europe and Mexico, she now resides in New York City where she occasionally teaches. Her work has a kinship with Expressionism and Surrealism. Her main concern centers on Latin American sociopolitical issues. Most of her narrative, feminist in perspective, presents satirical views of the relations between the sexes. Humor, irony, neologisms, clever use of Argentinean slang with sparks of poetry are some of the trademarks of her literary language. GM

Aquí pasan cosas raras, cuentos. Buenos Aires: Flor, 1975. Paperback, 134 pp. Thirty prose pieces, mainly short stories, in which grotesque parodies render a devastating vision of Argentina today. Humor derived from plays on words, political and sexual jokes and Buenos Aires slang do not diminish the impact of the terrorism, censorship, senseless killing, and fear that Valenzuela depicts. GM

Cambio de armas, cuentos. Hanover, N.H.: Norte, 1982. Paperback, 146 pp. In these five narratives women's love is menaced by spies, torturers and the police. Fear increases the intensity of feelings and destroys the traditional goals of stability in love relations. The women, an actress, a writer, guerrilla activists, are directly involved in the political present: they kill or die for their beliefs. "Cambio de armas," the story which gives the book its title, is an extraordinary story dealing with the horror of torture in Argentina today. GM

Clara, Thirteen Short Stories and a Novel. Trans. Hortense Carpentier and J. Jorge Castello. New York: Harcourt Brace Jovanovich, 1976. Translation of Hay que sonreír and stories from Los heréticos. DEM

Cola de lagartija, el brujo hormiga roja señor del Tacurú, novela

Como en la guerra, novela. Buenos Aires: Sudamericana, 1977. Paperback, 195 pp. A novel narrated by a male searching for his identity through metamorphoses, drugs and witchcraft in Spain, Mexico and Argentina. In Buenos Aires, after witnessing poverty and repression, he joins the insurgents. Humorous digressions form part of the loosely structured chapters of the book. Parodies of traditional myths about women evidence the feminist stance of the author. Highly allegorical, the language of this novel is playful, poetic and satirical.
GM

Donde viven las águilas, cuentos. Buenos Aires: Celtia, 1983. ISBN 950-9106-29-1, paperback, 92 pp. Mexico provides the setting, legends and language for many of the ostensibly simple, allegorical stories in this collection which takes us into the world of fantasy, dream, and myth as it reconsiders contemporary society and our own rhetorical, mythic structures. With a playful narrative self-consciousness, the stories comment upon themselves as well as the power of language to create "reality." SMI

El gato eficaz, narrativa. México: Joaquín Mortiz, 1972. Paperback, 120 pp. A metaphoric text that does not fit conventional notions of the novel. Plotless, the different fragments are united by the narrative voice of a female figure whose identity continually changes. She speaks on many subjects but mainly about male/female relations. Sexuality is openly and humorously discussed. Plays on words and irony mark the speech of the narrative voice as it demythifies human relations with humor and irreverency. GM

Hay que sonreír, novela. Buenos Aires: Americalee, 1966. 196 pp. Valenzuela's first novel focuses on an unpretentious, childlike woman who becomes a prostitute to assure economic survival while her simple desires to see the sea and to be somebody by using her head prove fatal. Structured on classic triad of Western religion, the main theme is woman's plight amidst the social expectations that she will be passive, silent, possessed by a male, and continue to smile in spite of all. In the final eloquent act of violence, her head is severed from her body, and she literally becomes a body without a head. The text demonstrates that there is no inherent disjunction between body and mind but rather that we are surrounded by contradictory discourse designed to oppress. SMI

Los heréticos, cuentos. Buenos Aires: Paidos, 1967.

Libro que no muerde. Mexico: UNAM, 1980. 174 pp. This eclectic volume, impossible to label in terms of genre, includes fourteen stories from Aquí pasan cosas raras, four stories from Los heréticos, and the collection of stories, essays, or nuggets of wisdom with this title. Many of the latter are extremely brief, essayistic observations on socio-political identity and/or the act of writing itself as the author once again demonstrates her entertaining linguistic virtuosity. Clearly a search for truth within language or vice versa, the collection offers an interesting, if indeed subtle, examination of language as it creates or converts our reality. SMI

The Lizard's Tail, translation of Cola de lagartija. Trans. by Gregory Rabassa. New York: Farrar, Straus, Giroux, 1983. ISBN #374-18994-3, hardbound, 280 pp. A fascinating flight of fantasy amidst political realities, this is the tale of Minister of Social Well Being, a sorcerer with three testicles, one of whom is her sister, Estrella, to whom he gives birth as he concludes his autobiography. His story alternates with the female narrator's discussion of problems of writing the novel we read, for discourse is not an exclusively masculine domain. The novel is an extended exposé of rhetoric that "re-creates" reality, and writing the novel is a metaphor for writing history and sacred texts, as the male character "plays" at being god and controlling all when he is merely the creation of woman, as biologically he always must be. SMI

Other Weapons, translation of Cambio de armas. Trans. by Deborah Bonner. New Hampshire: Ediciones del Norte, 1985. ISBN 3-1158-01048-2007, paperback, 135 pp. This book of short stories belongs to the genre of literary erotica, yet with a contemporary international background. The female protagonists live for sensual and sexual encounters with men who are frequently unavailable, despicable, or committed to other causes. The translation of "Fourth Version" is occasionally awkward; this could be partially attributed to the deliberate use by the narrator of non sequitor as a rhetorical device, yet the dialogue is often rather stilted and loses the flow of colloquial speech. The other translations are very well-crafted, on the other hand, particularly that of "Other Weapons," the title story of the volume. BM

Sofía, novela histórica

Strange Things Happen Here, Twenty-Six Short Stories and a Novela. New York: Harcourt Brace Jovanovick, 1979. Translation of Aquí pasan cosas raras and other writings. DEM

VALENZUELA ALVAREZ, Mercedes (Chile, 1925-1965; pseudonym: Valdivieso, Mercedes). Valdivieso studied Humanities at the Universidad de Chile in Santiago, taught at the Institute of Foreign Languages in Peking and is presently teaching at Rice University in Texas. Valdivieso is one of the few Chilean women writers to deal with women's issues in her writings.

La brecha, novela. Prologue by Fernando Alegría. Santiago: Zig-Zag, 1961. Paperback, 142 pp. Well-developed novel of a rebellious woman who struggles to assert her individuality and freedom in the patriarchally oriented Chilean bourgeois milieu. Her struggle leads her to terminate an oppressive marriage and to define her own role in society. Important in the development of Chilean feminine literature, as it breaks new thematic ground.

Las noches y un día, novela. Barcelona: Seix Barral, 1971. ISBN 8939-1971, paperback, 256 pp. Particularly interesting in its structure. The different fragments relate the present and the past of the character-narrators -- an old man and two lovers -- who, against the background of the 1964 Chilean presidential campaigns and their involvement with the left, try to assert their own identities.

Los ojos de bambú, novela. Prologue by the author. Santiago: Zig-Zag, 1964. 246 pp. Interesting novel of a ficticious famous Chilean painter who is invited to spend a year working in China during the cultural revolution. Her bourgeois and western upbringing make it impossible for her to fit in, or to understand China's social and cultural changes and the sacrifices it requires from individuals.

La tierra que les di, novela. Santiago: Zig-Zag, 1965. Paperback, 190 pp. Each chapter deals with the effects an overpowering mother has had on each member of her family, belonging to the Chilean economic aristocracy. Their moral decadence and the auctioning of the family landholdings after the mother's death symbolize their vengeance. The novel clearly is a denunciation of the ethical bankruptcy of the economically privileged Chilean social strata. PRL

VALES DE RODRIGUEZ, Sofía Estévez y (see **ESTEVEZ Y VALES DE RODRIGUEZ, Sofía**)

VALLBONA, Rima (see **ROTHE DE VALLBONA, Rima Gretel**)

VALLE, Agripina Montes del (see **MONTES DEL VALLE, Agripina**)

VALLE, Jimena del (Chile, twentieth century)

Amaneció

En silencio, novela

VALLE, Lila del (Chile, twentieth century)

Distinto, poemas

VALLE, Luz del (Guatemala, twentieth century)

Flores de mi alma para Trujillo y otros poemas

El milagro de septiembre, juguete escénico en un acto

VALLE, María del (pseudonym: see **ALVAREZ CABUTO, María Angélica**)

VALLE, Silvia del (Chile, twentieth century)

Escrito en la arena

VALLE SILVA, Luisa del (Venezuela, twentieth century)

Amor; poemas 1929-1940

En silencio, poesía

Humo; poemas 1926-1929

Luz; poemas 1930-1940

Poesía, includes Ventanas de ensueño, Humo, Amor, Luz, En silencio, y Sin tiempo y sin espacio

Sin tiempo y sin espacio, poesía

Ventanas al azul

Ventanas de ensueño, poesía

VALLS, Julia A. De (see **DE VALLS, Julia**)

VANEGAS, Ana (Colombia, twentieth century)

Anochecer en la alborada, novela

VARELA, Blanca (Peru, b. 1926). Born in Lima, she has lived in Washington, D.C., and Paris where she was associated with Simone de Beauvior. While in France, Surrealism made a permanent imprint on her poetry. She has two children from her marriage to the prestigious Peruvian painter Fernando Szyszlo. She has published four volumes of poetry, is fluent in both French and English, and is currently the director of Fondo de Cultura Económica in Peru.

Canto villano, poesía. Lima: Arybalo, 1978. Paperback, 50 pp. This collection of thirty-six poems, divided into five sections of varying length. It confirms Varela's preference for a poetic form with no capitals nor any punctuation, except for occasional periods. It continues her sarcastic unsentimental tone through conscientiously irreverent imagery and self-deprecation. The poet only takes pride in disdainfully yet agonizingly transcending her own experience. The title suggests skeptical optimism.

Ese puerto existe y otros poemas. Prologue by Octavio Paz. Xalapa, México: Univ. Veracruzana, 1959. Paperback, 99 pp. Available in major research libraries. Paz' eight-page prologue situates the author among young Spanish American poets living in Paris after World War II, surrealistic in spirit and indebted to the Andalusians of the Generation of 1927. The first two parts contain ten and eleven long, free-verse poems, seemingly separated according to somnambulistic associations with Paris and Peru. Four much longer poems follow, divided into several parts, with the same type of surrealistic imagery, but more in a quasi-narrative form.

Luz de día. Lima: Rama Florida, 1963. Paperback, 59 pp. Illus. by Fernando Szyszlo. Available in major research libraries. Dedicated to Octavio Paz, a two-page quasi-prologue cryptically explains the intellectual attitude which has resulted in a pervasively iconoclastic yet hopeful tone in her poetry. Varela postulates a particular "order" of spiritual growth in order to attain a solidly self-assured posture: despair, acceptance of failure and faith. The first section contains six selections in poetic prose; the second includes fifteen free-verse poems. Surrealistic imagery pervades throughout the poet's self-search in the absence of a "you" and the constant passing of time. Index.

Valses y otras falsas confesiones, poemas. Lima: Instituto Nacional de Cultura, 1972. Paperback, 89 pp. Available in major research libraries. This collection is divided into fifteen sections, most of which consist of a single poem; four sections contain several interrelated poems, e.g., "Auvers-sur-Oise" where the overriding image is music in monologues of inspirational self-doubt, or in a dialogue with a discouragingly deaf partner or self. The initial poem alternates poetry addressed to the lover with prose descriptive of the poet's experience in New York. Only one poem expresses some social concern lamenting hunger in the world. Most of the poems evince terrible resentment toward God, the former lover or a transcended self. A singular sign of optimism appears in the image of children playing in the dirt. SHA

VARELA Y VARELA, Olimpia (Honduras, twentieth century)

Corazón abierto, poemario antológico

VARGAS FLOREZ DE ARGÜELLES, Emma (Colombia, twentieth century)

Luz en la senda, poemas

Melodías del alba

VARIN, Stella Díaz (see **DIAZ VARIN, Stella**)

VAZ FERREIRA, María Eugenia (Uruguay, 1880-1925)

Los cálices vacíos por Delmira Agustina. La isla de los cánticos por María Eugenia Vaz Ferreira. Montevideo: Centro Editor de América Latina, 1968. 72 pp. [See annotation under AGUSTINI, Delmira.]

La isla de los cánticos, poesía

La otra isla de los cánticos

Los peregrinos, teatro

La piedra filosofal, teatro

VAZQUEZ, María Esther (Argentina, b. 1934). Short-story writer, essayist, poet, newspaper woman, Vázquez graduated from the Facultad de Filosofía y Letras, Universidad de Buenos Aires. She has travelled through Europe, the United States and Canada at the invitation of Departments of Cultural Affairs of different countries to offer seminars and lectures. She is an active participant in congresses and symposia. Beginning in 1972 she has conducted an special weekly interview session called "Instantáneas" which appears in the Sunday Literary Supplement of La Nación.

Invenciones sentimentales, cuentos. Buenos Aires: Emecé, 1980. First Prize from Depuytren Foundation and First Prize from the Municipality of Buenos Aires for the biennium 1980-1982.

Los nombres de la muerte, cuentos. Buenos Aires: Emecé, 1964. Prize from the Fondo Nacional de las Artes. The basic theme of these fourteen short stories is personal identity. A few of them are fantastic short stories.

Noviembre y el ángel, poesía. Buenos Aires: Kraft, 1968. First prize from the Municipality of Buenos Aires. Collection of lyrical poems.

Para un jardín cerrado, cuentos. Buenos Aires: EUDEBA, 1970. A touch of magic endows these short stories with a poetic tone. EA

VAZQUEZ GOMEZ, Esperanza Guerrero de (see **GUERRERO DE VAZQUEZ GOMEZ, Esperanza**)

VEGA, Ana Lydia (Puerto Rico, b. 1946). Vega studied literature at the Universities of Puerto Rico and Aix-en-Provence and currently teaches at the University of Puerto Rico. She was a founding member of the journal Reintegro. Several of her short stories have won prizes in literary contests. Her second book, Encancaranublado y otros cuentos de naufragio won first prize in the Casa de las Américas contest for 1982. Almost all her stories deal with female characters and women in their social context.

Encancaranublado y otros cuentos de naufragio. 2nd ed. Río Piedras, Puerto Rico: Antillana, 1983. Paperback, 141 pp. Divided into three sections, each of the first two "Nubosidad Variable" and "Probabilidad de Lluvia," includes six short stories and the last ("Napa de vientos y Tronadas," is a single story. All deal with the life, history and culture of the Caribbean, mostly the Spanish-speaking Antilles. In the first narrative, "Encancaranublado," three men (a Haitian, a Dominican, and a Cuban) are united in a boat seeking refuge in Miami. At the end they symbolically enter an American ship where, together with Puerto Ricans, they encounter prejudice and oppression. Havana, San Juan, Jamaica and Port-au-Prince are the most frequent settings for the stories. Most of the narratives refer to contemporary situations. Her style is full of colloquial expressions, humor and irony.

Vírgenes y mártires, con Carmen Lugo Filippi. Río Piedras: Antillana, 1981. ISBN 84-499-4932-7. Paperback, 139 pp. The book includes six short stories by each author and a final story written by both. The joint effort is unique in the history of Puerto Rican narrative. The book explores different images of women, particularly those held by men: virgins and martyrs. Lugo's stories rely on the reproduction of the language of mass media and on the way women are expected to act and to think according to "feminine" magazines. Vega's strength lies in the rhythmic qualities of her language and in her use of a vocabulary and syntax that recreate popular speech patterns. ILJ

VELAS PALACIOS, Matilde (Argentina, twentieth century)

Añoranzas, novela

Cartas de amor

La dicha ajena

VELASCO, Blanca Ocampo de (see OCAMPO DE VELASCO, Blanca)

VELASCO, Isabel (Chile, b. 1940). Velasco has been an active participant in the Society of Chilean Writers where presently she is the secretary-in-chief. She also organizes frequent poetry workshops in the city of Santiago where she resides. The fundamental themes of her poetry deal with the loneliness of the woman who has not chosen for herself the prescribed, assigned role of wife and mother. Her books of poetry are extremely well-received among the young women in Chile.

Cardos, poesía

Del silencio. Santiago de Chile: Nascimento, 1980. Paperback, 81 pp. Thirty poems unified by the common theme of silence, and the lack of communication between people, especially lovers. The recurrent images of voiceless bells and silenced people give this book a coherent unity. A particular fascination with perfectly regulated verses gives a unique quality to the brief and rather cryptic poems of the collection. A subtheme of this book deals with the concept of alienation in a woman's existence, mainly since people do not hear the female voice. MA

Sol, ¿dónde estás?, poesía

Tú, ayer, poesía

VELASCO Y ARIAS, María (Argentina, twentieth century)

Claras mujeres argentinas, motivos juglarescos

Cien apólogos rioplatenses para chicos y grandes, fábulas

Orgías del sábado, relatos

VELASCO Y CISNEROS, Isabel (Cuba, 1860's-1916)

Expansiones

VENTURINI, Aurora (Argentina, twentieth century)

El ángel del espejo, poemas

Carta a Zoraida, relatos para las tías viejas

Corazón de árbol

Jovita la osa y otros cuentos

Lamentación mayor, poemas

Versos al recuerdo

VENTURINO, Alice Lardé de (see **LARDE DE VENTURINO, Alice**)

VERA, Carmen Agüero (see **AGÜERO VERA, Carmen**)

VERA, María Luisa (Mexico, twentieth century)

　　Arcilla, versos

　　Cuentos de extramuros

　　Poemas de niños tristes

　　Yunque, versos

VERBEL Y MAREA, Eva C. (Colombia, b. 1856)

　　Ensayos poéticos

　　El honor de un artesano, drama inédito

　　María, drama inédito

VERGARA, Anamaría (Chile, b. 1931)

　　Manifiesto diario, poesía

　　Tierra áspera, poesía

VERGARA, Marta (Chile, b. 1898)

　　Circunstancias, novela

　　Memorias de una mujer irreverente

VEYRO, Blanca Rosa (Mexico, twentieth century)

　　El curandero

VIAL, Magdalena (Chile, b. 1921)

　　Cantábile, poesía

　　Clausura del sueño, poemas

　　Dibujo en el agua, teatro

　　Humo, teatro

　　Lluvia adentro, novela

　　Ojivas, poemas

　　Procedimiento equivocado, teatro

　　Reloj, prosa

VIAL, Rosa de (Chile, twentieth century)

Antología poética

La voz de los siglos, poesía

VIAL, Sara (Chile, b. 1931)

La ciudad indecible, poesía

En la orilla del vuelo, poesía

Un modo de cantar, poemas

Viaje en la arena, poesía

VIAL DE UGARTE, María Mercedes (Chile, twentieth century)

Amor que no muere, novela

Cosas que fueron, novela

VIAL E., Magdalena (Chile, twentieth century)

Lluvia adentro

Reloj; Punto muerto

VIANA, Luz de (pseudonym: see **VILLANUEVA DE BULNES, Marta**)

VICENS, Josefina (Mexico, twentieth century)

El libro vacío, novela

VICENS, Nimia (Puerto Rico, b. 1914)

Anémona nemorosa

Canciones al mundo, poesía

VICIOSO, Sherezada (Dominican Republic, b. 1948; also Chiqui). Chiqui
Vicioso spent several years living in New York City before rediscovering that
her roots are in her native land of the Dominican Republic. She currently
lives there where she is a social worker. Viaje desde el agua, a collection of
poems, is her first published volume. She is particularly interested in the
role and assessment of the woman poet. Her poetry reflects her belief that
poetry should include the concerns of the poet's daily life.

Viaje desde el agua, poesía. Santo Domingo: Visuarte, 1981. 70 pp.
This is a collection of poetry written between 1977 and 1981. The
poems, usually written in a conversational, antipoetic tone, primarily
reflect the poet's concern for people, general and specific, and her
emotional response to them. This volume, a refreshing addition to the
new generation of poetry in the Dominican Republic, is available only
through a limited printing by the publisher. ASL

VICTORIA, Alejandra (pseudonym: see **BUSTAMANTE, María Teresa
de**)

VICTORIA, Laura (pseudonym: see PEÑUELA DE SEGURA, Gertrudis)

VICTORIA DE REUS, María López de (see LOPEZ DE VICTORIA Y BARBE, María)

VICTORIA Y BARBE, María López de (see LOPEZ DE VICTORIA Y BARBE, María)

VICTORIA Y FERNANDEZ, Magda López de (see LOPEZ DE VICTORIA Y FERNANDEZ, Magda)

VICUÑA, Cecilia (Chile, twentieth century)

> Saboramí, español e inglés (bilingual). Trans. Felipe Ehrenberg. Cullompton, England: Beau Geste, 1973.

VIDAL, Marzo (pseudonym: see BOHORQUEZ, Abigael)

VIDAL, Teresa (Chile, twentieth century)

> Vertiente, poemas

> La vocación

VIDELA, Graciela Albornoz de (see ALBORNOZ DE VIDELA, Graciela)

VIDRIO, Lola (Mexico, twentieth century)

> Don Nadie y otros cuentos

VIEIRA, Maruja (Colombia, b. 1922)

> Campanario de lluvia, poesía

> Ciudad remanso, prosa

> Clave mínima, poesía

> Palabas de la ausencia, poesía

> Los poemas de enero, poesía

> Poesía

VIEYRA, Adelia (Argentina, twentieth century)

> Crónicas de un indiano en la corte de Carlos V (quinto)

> El vencedor del tiempo

VILALTA, Maruxa (Spain - Mexico, b. 1932). She was born in Barcelona. Her parents fled the Spanish Civil War to settle in Mexico. She is a drama critic and scenery designer as well as an avant-garde dramatist. She has also written novels, short stories and scripts for radio, television and cinema. Her plays have won prestigious prizes. Some of them have been translated into Catalan, English, French, Italian and Czeckoslovakian.

Antología de obras en un acto, selección de Maruxa Vilalta

Cuestión de narices, teatro

Los desorientados, teatro

Un día loco, teatro

Dos colores para el paisaje. México: B. Costa Amic, 1961. 184 pp.
Vilalta's early novel is almost mathematically balanced and the thesis
is undisguised. An idealistic history professor is contrasted with a
hustling, materialistic business man. Each one attains a different kind
of success, according to his own views. Vilalta's later works,
particularly her dramas, reveal how greatly she has matured since her
first publications.

Esta noche juntos, amándonos tanto, farsa trágica

Historia de él, teatro. México: Difusión Cultural/UNAM 1978. 59 pp. It
is interesting to note that a drama as avant-garde and impressionistic
as Historia de él won the Juan Ruiz de Alarcón prize accorded by the
Mexican Association of Theatrical Critics as the best play of 1978.
Scenes are shifted on stage, a ballet is performed, the actors behave like
robots. They don and doff masks, they exchange roles and their
dialogue is played on tape recorders. The theme of domination,
nevertheless, is artfully woven through the tumultuous action.

Nada como el piso 16 (diez y seis). México: Joaquín Mortiz, 1977. 94 pp.
The dictatorship of big business is exposed in the drama which won
prizes for the best work by a Mexican dramatist in 1975 both by the
Mexican Association of Theatrical Critics and the Union of Critics and
Chroniclers of the Theatre. The setting is a New York penthouse where
three characters, a tyrannical industrialist, his submissive mistress and
a captive electrician are the objects of Vilalta's sharp, well-drawn
satire.

El 9 (nueve), teatro

El otro día la muerte, teatro. México: Joaquín Mortiz, 1974. 94 pp. In
her prologue Vilalta affirms that she wants to treat not only death but
also life. Her four short stories on the theme of death are a mixture of
Surrealism and reality. They deal with death through war, through
dictatorship and through seeking one's own death. Death personified
may be enticing. Neither time nor place are designated; the
nightmarish atmosphere is brilliantly sustained.

Un país feliz, teatro

Soliloquio del tiempo, teatro

Teatro/Maruxa Vilalta. México: Fondo de Cultura Económica, 1962.
485 pp. Six full-length dramas and a trilogy of one-act plays prove that
Vilalta is definitely an anti-traditional playwright. Her plays are
generally not confined to any specific time or place. There is little or no
psychology in Vilalta's treatment of her characters. She is more
interested in dialogue than in action, more concerned with exposing the
evils of society than in suggesting solutions. Her dramas are more
thought-provoking than entertaining. GB

La última letra, monólogo

VILARIÑO, Idea (Uruguay, b. 1920). Vilariño's poetry is filled with deep anguish and a desolate vision. She studied literature in Montevideo and started writing poetry in 1945. Her poetic language has evolved from hermetic, richly imagistic renderings to a more rigorous, economic expression. Vilariño is also active as a literary critic and has published works on Julio Herrera y Reissig and on the sociological and linguistic implications of the tango.

Cielo cielo, poemas

Grupos simétricos en poesía

Nocturnos, poemas. Buenos Aires: Schapire, 1976. Paperback, 72 pp. 1st printing, 1955. Pain and an intense awareness of solitude are expressed in these short, minimal poems. Images of night and darkness pervade the text suggesting the anguish the speaker endures when she seeks answers to the problems of identity, the loss of love and mystery of death. Valuable for college literature courses.

Paraíso perdido, poemas. Montevideo: Número, 1949. Paperback, 15 pp. Contains poems from two collections. A sense of loss and despair runs through the seven lyrics which make up this volume. "Paraíso Perdido" is undoubtedly the best-known lyric in the collection. In this poem the speaker rejects a world she envisions as impervious to suffering and longs for the paradise of light, love and security which was her childhood. The verbal expression is stark, stripped of punctuation.

Pobre mundo

Poemas de amor. Buenos Aires: Schapire, S.R.L., 1972. Paperback, 72 pp. This collection explores the themes of solitude in love and the impossibility of communication. In this work she comes to the full realization that the absence of love can be equated with nothingness; it is existential obliteration. Like most of her later poetry, she uses a stark free verse. Valuable in college literature courses.

Poesía, 1941-1967

Por el aire sucio, poemas. Montevideo: Número, 1951. Paperback, 33 pp. These fourteen poems evoke the darkest moods of the mind. Exclamatory and intensely personal in tone, they convey a sense of neglect and despair over death and over the transcience of anything human. Unlike earlier hermetic lyrics, these are clear, compressed and deliberately epigrammatic. A case in point is provided by the poem "Eso" where the concern with conciseness is presented with unusual force.

La suplicante

Tangos

30 [Treinta] poemas. Montevideo: Tauro, 1967. Paperback, 30 pp. Contains poems from other collections. IR

VILLALTA, Manuela de Blanco (see **BLANCO VILLALTA, Manuela de**)

VILLANUEVA, Margos de (see **REINBECK DE VILLANUEVA, Margos**)

VILLANUEVA, Margos Reinbeck de (see **REINBECK DE VILLANUEVA, Margos**)

VILLANUEVA DE BULNES, Marta (Chile, b. 1894; pseudonym: Viana, Luz de)

La casa miraba al mar, novela y cuento

Frenesí, novelas cortas

El licenciado Jacobo, cuentos largos

No sirve la luna blanca, cuentos

VILLANUEVA MATA, América (Venezuela, twentieth century)

Voz de mi silencio

VILLANUEVA Y SAAVEDRA, Etelvina (Bolivia, twentieth century)

Sueño y canción, poemas

VILLAR, María Angélica (Argentina, twentieth century)

Día en la noche, poemas

Pasos para un travesía, poemas

VILLAR BUCETA, María (Cuba, b. 1899)

Unanimismo, poesía

VILLARAN, Consuelo María Eufrosina (Peru, early twentieth century; pseudonym: Rimac, Flor del)

Neurosis, novela

VILLARINO, María de (Argentina, b. 1905)

Antología poética

Calle apartada, poesía

La dimensión oculta, cuentos

Elegía del recuerdo, poesía

Los espacios y los símbolos

Junco sin sueño, poesía

Luz de memorias, autobiográfico

Memoria de Buenos Aires, relación

Pueblo en la niebla, cuentos

La rosa no debe morir, novela

La sombra iluminada, poemas

Tiempo de angustia, poesía

VILLARREAL, Concha de (Mexico, twentieth century)

El desierto mágico

Musa mestiza, poemas

Tierra de Dios, novela

VILLEGAS, Maruja González (see **GONZALEZ VILLEGAS, Maruja**)

VITALE, Ida (Uruguay, b. 1924). First marriage to Uruguayan literary critic and writer Angel Rama. Second marriage with Uruguayan poet and literary critic Enrique Fierro. Translator of many works from French, Italian, English, Portuguese and German. Recognized literary critic and journalist. Selected poems translated in English, Italian, Russian. Publications in: Crisis, Eco, Poesía, Plural, El Sol, and Sin Nombre, among other magazines and journals.

Cada uno en su noche, poesía. Montevideo: Alfa, 1960. The poetic design of Vitale's poetry begins to be clearly delineated in this volume of twenty-seven new poems. It also includes three selections from her first book of poems, La luz de esta memoria, and five from her second collection, Palabra dada. This characterizes Vitale's books of poems; she incorporates with great care selected poems from previous works into a new volume, seeking thematic unity.

Fieles. Mexico: Universidad Nacional Autónoma de México (UNAM), 1982. ISBN 968-58-0406-0, 97 pp. Another edition: (Mexico: El Mendrugo), Author's edition, hardback, n. pag. This collection is an anthology selected by Vitale that contains poems from three books dating from 1953 to 1972 (Palabra dada, Cada uno en su noche, and Oidor andante), plus all the poems of Jardín de sílice, first published in Venezuela, with limited circulation. Excellent selection of Vitale's poetic work.

Jardín de sílice, poemas. Caracas: Monte Avila, 1980. Paperback, 91 pp. This collection of thirty-eight poems in three sections is Vitale's strongest evidence of the excellence of her poetry. Her carefully wrought poetic system explores and confronts different levels of perception for the representation of experience together with the representation of this experience by means of the elaboration of a tight and coherent lyric discourse of a strongly contained anguished tonality.

La luz de esta memoria, poesía. Author's edition. Montevideo: La Galatea, 1949. Paperback, 47 pp. First collection of poems by Vitale. The central theme of this brief collection of fifteen poems is the reconstruction of the memories of love and desire of a nostalgic and at times anguished voice that forsees the future with trepidation.

Oidor andante, poesía. Montevideo: Arca, 1960. Paperback, 79 pp.
Another edition: (Mexico: Premiá), ISBN 968-434-261-6, paperback, 69
pp. This collection of forty-nine poems marks a new point of maturity in
Vitale's poetic system. Here the poetic word begins to question its
validity, and the validity of language to redesign experience and reality.
The title of this book points to the position of the poetic voice, the one
who wanders about listening to the world outside, constructed from the
world inside. MGP

Palabra dada, poesía

VITERI, Eugenia (Ecuador, b. 1928). The recipient of numerous literary
prizes, Viteri has made many outstanding contributions to Ecuadorian fiction
during the last thirty years. The prevailing theme in her works has been that
of the daily frustrations and tensions experienced by people living in the
urban sectors of society.

A 90 (noventa) millas solamente, novela. Quito: Casa de la Cultura
Ecuatoriana, 1969. 191 pp. This novel is about a Cuban youth who
abandons her native island during the early Castro years. As time goes
on, the novel's protagonist rejects life in Miami and begins to dream of
her return to Cuba. Despite the novel's somewhat simplistic dichotomy
(i.e., the United States as "evil" and Cuba as "good"), Viteri's
descriptions of the Cuban exile's struggle to adapt to a new lifestyle are
effective. An interesting feature of the novel is how Viteri questions the
traditional roles played by women in society.

Las alcobas negras

El anillo y otros cuentos. Quito: Casa de la Cultura Ecuatoriana, 1955.
117 pp. In the best tradition of Horacio Quiroga, the most salient
feature of this collection of stories is its conciseness and clarity of
purpose. Jealousy, compassion for one's fellow man, the search for love
and companionship are constants in Viteri's stories.

Cuentos escogidos

Doce cuentos. Quito: Casa de la Cultura Ecuatoriana, 1962. 95 pp. The
gallery of characters in this collection of stories clearly illustrates
Viteri's ability to write socially committed literature that transcends
the local setting and speaks to the concerns of all people. Viteri is
especially at her best when writing about the daily struggles confronted
by average, everyday people.

Los zapatos y los sueños. Guayaquil: Casa de la Cultura Ecuatoriana,
1977. Paperback, 117 pp. As is typical of Viteri's other stories, this
collection also deals with the everyday struggles that beset man and
that frequently are overcome by one's ability to imagine a better world.
MH

VIVAS BRICEÑO, Clara (Venezuela, b. 1896)

A la sombra de nuestros héroes, poemas

Ala y musgo

La carta, versos

<u>Gracia plena</u>, romance

<u>La quimera imprevista</u>, poemas

<u>Simón Bolívar, libertador de América</u>, anagrama

VIZCARRONDO, Carmelina (Puerto Rico, b. 1906)

<u>Minutero en sombras</u>, cuentos

<u>Poemas para mi niño</u>, poemas

<u>Pregón en llamas</u>, poemas

W

WALKER, Rosa Cruchaga de (see **CRUCHAGA DE WALKER, Rosa**)

WALKER DE SERRANO, Elisa (see **PEREZ WALKER DE SERRANO, Elisa**)

WALLS, Isabel Figueras de (see **FIGUERAS DE WALLS, Isabel**)

WALSH, María Elena (Argentina, b. 1930). A poet and children's writer. Prior to Hecho a mano, her poetry expresses private preoccupations of love and death, but she then changes her language and themes to become a prolific writer of poems, songs, and stories for children and young adults which are more important than her work for adults. The didactic nature of children's literature is the impetus for her consciousness-raising tales. The popularity of her books is evidence by the number of re-editions.

Angelito. 3rd ed. Illus. by Jorge R. Serrano. Buenos Aires: Estrada, 1977. Hardcover, n. pag. A didactic tale with catchy rhymes and brilliant illustrations for toddlers and beginning readers. An angel is sent down to earth by his superior to tame the feisty Juancito, who becomes controllable only upon learning that he has a guardian angel. The familiar Christian symbol is more representative of socialization than of religious doctrine.

Apenas viaje, poemas. Buenos Aires: El Balcón de Madera, 1944. Paperback, n. pag. A pamphlet of five poems for adults. Walsh affirms the splendor of nature and of God, the certainty of death, and the poet's ineffability. The poems, mostly sonnets, function as a life cycle, evoking the viaje from adolescence to death. Nature imagery and allusions to the creative process dominate these sonnets and quartets. Reprinted in Otoño imperdonable.

"Baladas con Angel" in Argumento del enamorado por Angel Bonomini y Baladas con Angel por María Elena Walsh. Buenos Aires: Losada, 1952. Paperback, 137 pp. These ballads project the romantic theme that the lovers are the only people in the world, and that the permanence of their love will ultimately lead to death. The lover, whose tribute to Walsh is the first part of the book, is the source of life; love's plenitude is described in traditional nature imagery. Such a total abandonment to an individual is rarely expressed in her later poetry.

Cancionero contra el mal de ojo. Photographs by Sara Facio y Alicia D'Amico. Illus. by María Cristina Brusca. Buenos Aires: Sudamericana, 1976. Paperback, 100 pp. Many of the poems in this cancionero for adults demonstrate the poet's social commitment and clarity of language. Straight-forward though playful, and diverse in her criticism, Walsh denounces such things as woman's imprisonment in her own home, those who pray to "San Dinero," and the bombing of Hanoi. Walsh directly addresses her sympathetic reader throughout.

Casi milagro, poemas. Montevideo: Cuadernos Julio Herrera y Reissig, 1958. Paperback, n. pag. Four poems elaborate the romantic preoccupations previously established: the relationships between God and nature and between poetry and nature, love and the absence of love. Walsh experiments with the sonnet sequence and lyric form also representative of her early stage. The poems of this pamphlet were later published in more accessible collections, Otoño imperdonable and Hecho a mano.

Chaucha y Palito. Drawings by Vilar. Buenos Aires: Sudamericana, 1977. Paperback, 169 pp. Seven long fairy tales for juvenile and young adult readers, set in a modern context of urban growth and computers. The last story, "El cuento de la autora," is an excellent biobibliographic presentation of the author to her readers. Walsh talks of her youth, the wars of her childhood, her first publications, and travels to the United States. By mentioning writers and historic events, she clearly tries to stimulate in her young readers the desire to use reading as a vehicle for learning about historical and contemporary issues, and to integrate literature and daily life.

Cuentopos de Gulubú, cuentos para niños. Drawings by Juan Carlos Cavallero. Buenos Aires: Luis Fariña, 1966. Paperback, 92 pp. A collection of sixteen humorous stories for toddlers and young children set in the imaginary forest of Gulubú. Imaginative illustrations, suspense, and the intimate tone of an author very concerned with the enjoyment of her public make these short tales delightful reading. Written in a colloquial style and meant to be read aloud.

Dailán Kifki, narrativa para niños. 4th ed. Drawings by Vilar. Buenos Aires: Sudamericana, 1974. Paperback, 176 pp. Pure fun and games for young and juvenile readers. Dailán Kifki is an elephant left on the stoop of a little girl's house. Narrated in a first person that directly addresses the reader: "¡Imagínense! ¿Se imaginaron? ¿Se imaginan qué problema?" Each of the forty-eight chapters is an anecdote of their adventures together: Dailán's elephant-sized stomach-ache, Dailán stuck in a tree, a helpful fireman, the flying elephant and fireman team, a trip to the forest of Gulubú (Cuentopos de Gulubú), the girl's reunion with her mother, and her marriage to the fireman.

El diablo inglés, cuento. 3rd ed. Illus. by Raúl Fortin. Buenos Aires: Estrada, 1977. Hardcover, n. pag. A consciousness-raising tale of Tomás, a young vagabond guitarist who, lost in the forest, meets a red-skinned, English-speaking man he believes to be the devil speaking devil-language. The man disappears and Tomás sees boats on the river and an army of "red devils." Tomás sensibly heads to the city to exchange his guitar for a gun, to fight the "diablos de chaqueta colorada y ojos como diamantes . . . soldados ingleses." The youth's call to arms is a strong statement on the part of Walsh against cultural and linguistic imperialism. Incorporates narrative, dialogue, and poetry. Although meant to be read aloud to toddlers, this would be an entertaining story to include in an anthology for beginning and intermediate Spanish courses.

Hecho a mano, poemas. Buenos Aires: Luis Fariña, 1965. Paperback, 132 pp. Medium-length poems for young adults and adults. This collection marks a turning point in Walsh's poetry. The tone has become much more conversational and narrative, and the narrator appeals to the readers by drawing them into the poem. Although there is still a hint of earlier, more complex lyricism and imagery, an overall sense of seriousness and simplicity in both language and subject matter dominates. New themes pay tribute to everyday experiences, such as advertising propaganda, city life, and bureaucracy.

Juguemos en el mundo, poemas. 3rd ed. Buenos Aires: Sudamericana, 1977. Paperback, 72 pp. While many of the thirty-one poem/songs are whimsical, several express a social commitment not present in Walsh's earlier, more private poetry. Popular rhyme schemes, direct language, and everyday themes are indicative of Walsh's resolution to dedicate her song to humankind. Her new critical stance is evident, for example, in her ironic treatment of the injustices of the business world and the police. Both commitment and whim are to characterize her future writing.

Otoño imperdonable, poemas. 4th ed. Buenos Aires: Sudamericana, 1970. Paperback, 69 pp. Originally published in 1947, Walsh wrote these doleful poems between the ages of fourteen and seventeen. Relying on traditional forms and especially the sonnet, Walsh's early preoccupations reflect a fear of the inevitable: the relationship between existence and death, the lack of poetic expression and the pain caused by this silence. Recurring symbols of autumn -- wind, cold, night -- illustrate the overall sense of death and stagnation. A feature of this edition is "Otros poemas (1947-1949)," eleven poems previously published in Apenas viaje, Baladas con Angel, and Casi milagro.

El país de la geometría, cuento. 3rd ed. Illus. by Néstor Luis Battagliero. Buenos Aires: Estrada, 1977. Hardcover, n. pag. A short, attention-grabbing story of a geometric world constructed and ruled by King Compass, who sends all his military subjects in search of the elusive "source of inner happiness," the Round Flower. He only ultimately finds the mysterious figure by dancing, and thus drawing the very flower on the floor with his compass-feet. A colorfully-designed story of instructional value. Meant to be read aloud, suitable for up to age ten.

El reino del revés, poemas para niños. 8th ed. Drawings by Vilar. Buenos Aires: Sudamericana, 1976. Paperback, 97 pp. Humorous poems and songs, some almost non-sensical. Designed to be read aloud to very young children, the rhymes and verbal trickery create a musicality that is the collection's predominant feature. Vilar's superb drawings make this an outstanding book for toddlers.

La sirena y el capitán, cuento. 3rd ed. Illus. by Mirtha Castillo. Buenos Aires: Estrada, 1977. Hardcover, n. pag. Fairytale of a singing mermaid who lives in the Paraná River who travels freely in pre-Hispanic America. Confronted unwittingly by a bumbling sea captain, the leader of a group in search of gold and glory, she is captured as his bride. All the creatures of the land then unite against the barbarian and free her. Alternates poetry and dialogue with narrative, creating an oral quality. Colorful, eye-catching illustrations. Suitable for reading aloud to toddlers and for beginning readers. This didactic interpretation of the Conquest would be a good reading to anthologize for beginning and intermediate Spanish courses.

Tutú Marambá, poemas. 13th ed. Drawings by Vilar. Buenos Aires: Sudamericana, 1976. Paperback, 96 pp. Real geographic locations are mixed with fantastic people, animals, and situations in this collection of poems for children (ages two to six). Among trips to the dentist, puppet shows, and monkey families, the poem/songs are unified in their goal of musicality and fun. Excellent illustrations.

Zoo loco, poesía. 4th ed. Drawings by Vilar. Buenos Aires: Sudamericana, 1970. Paperback, n. pag. These limericks treat animals, including the usual fantastic repertoire of cat pianists and canaries that drive. The introduction explains the author's intention to write limericks in Spanish, and points out their similarity to Spanish American coplas for their foolishness or outright lies. These poems are not without their social criticism: e.g., a sad female dolphin is depicted alone and bored in her kitchen with the dishes piled up in the sink. Vilar's collage technique utilizing photographs adds a sense of realism to the drawings. CW

WARNKEN, Marta Herrera de (see **HERRERA DE WARNKEN, Marta**)

WASLEY, Agnes (Chile, b. 1922)

La quinta estación, poemas

WEBER, Delia (Dominican Republic, b. 1900)

Antorchas vivas, poemas

Apuntes, poemas

Dora y otros cuentos

Encuentro, poemas

Salvador y Altemira, drama

Los viajeros, poema dramático

WEINSTEIN, Lytia (Chile, b. 1923)

Amorosa, poemas

Como la vida, cuentos

Donde tu voz no llega, poemas

WIEZELL, Elsa (Paraguay, b. 1927)

Barro de estrellas, poemas

El canto y la luz

El duende fugitivo

Eco tridimensional, poesía

Lirondela

Mensaje para hombres nuevos

Orbita de visiones

Palabras para otro planeta

Poema ultrasónico

Poemas ciegos

Poemas de un mundo en brumas

Por las calles de Cristo

Puente sobre el Tapecué, poemas

Sembradores de sol, poemas

Temblor de acacias, poemas

Tiempo de Amor

Tronco al cielo, poemas

Virazón, poemas

WILMS MONTT, Teresa (Chile, 1893-1921)

Anuarí, cuentos

Cuentos para los hombres que son todavía niños

Lo que no ha dicho, recopilación

X

XENES Y DUARTE, Nieves (Cuba, 1859-1915). Xenes was born on a farm near Havana. Her rural surroundings inspired her early poems. She moved to the capital of the Island when she was nineteen. There she joined the famous literary <u>tertulias</u> held in Havana, organized by the intellectuals of the epoch. Her poetry appeared in the most important newspapers and magazines. Xenes gained the admiration of her colleagues for the intensity and sincerity of her verse. She became one of the best known female writers of the Cuban Romantic period. The influence of Bécquer can be found in her work, particularly in her love poems.

<u>Poesías</u>. La Habana: El Siglo XX, 1915. Prologue by the poet Aurelia Castillo de González. Her poetry was published posthumously by her colleagues in the National Academy of Arts and Letters, of which she was one of the founders. Xenes has two main themes: love and patriotism. She has been considered the most erotic female writer of the Cuban Parnassus during the Romantic period. She paved the way for the later erotic poetry of Delmira Agustini and Alfonsina Storni. In her work she also shows concern for moral values and contempt for false religion. SMA

Y

YAN, Mari (pseudonym: see YAÑEZ BIANCHI DE ECHEVERRIA, María Flora)

YAÑEZ, María Flora (see YAÑEZ BIANCHI DE ECHEVERRIA, María Flora)

YAÑEZ, Mirta (Cuba, twentieth century). As a student of literature at Havana University she won a poetry prize in 1971 for her book Las visitas. In 1976 her short stories Todos los negros tomamos café were published. Yañez belongs to the recent group of short story writers whose themes describe the new process of the Cuban Revolution. She sees the Revolution as the future of the Cuban people. Her poetry is innovative, her narrative tends toward realism. In both genres she keeps an intimate tone.

Todos los negros tomamos café, cuentos. La Habana: Arte y Literatura, Instituto Cubano del libro, 1976. Paperback, 113 pp. These short stories deal with life in Cuba's mountainous region, the experiences of the people who inhabit that area (identified as "la Sierra" or "Mayarí arriba") and the stories they tell. The title is a line from a popular song; it is placed in contrast to the production of coffee in the sierra. Each of the ten stories is preceded by a first person monologue, which also closes the book. These monologues serve as a frame to the stories and at the same time tell a story that unifies the whole: that of the persona, the narrator who encounters and describes this rural world and works in the coffee fields.

Las visitas, poemas. Colección Premio. La Habana: Comisión de Extensión Universitaria, 1970. Paperback, 53 pp. Illustrated with photographs of Old Havana. Written in free-verse form, this series of poems tries to reconstruct the old city of Havana, searching for its secret life in the stones, corners and old houses. The Moorish, Baroque, Neo-classical and Art Nouveau architectural features are seen as part of the present life of the city and its people. The poems are short; language is prosaic, with few metaphors. ILJ

YAÑEZ BIANCHI DE ECHEVERRIA, María Flora (Chile, b. 1898; pseudonym: Yan, Mari; also Yañez, María Flora)

El abrazo de la tierra, novela

Las cenizas, novela

Comarca perdida

¿Dónde está el trigo y el vino?, novela

Espejo sin imagen, novela

El estanque, cuentos

Juan Estrella, cuentos

Mundo en sombra, novela

El peldaño, novela corta

La piedra, novela

El último faro, novela

Visiones de infancia, autobiografía

YANEZ COSSIO, Alicia (Ecuador, b. 1929). One of Ecuador's major contemporary novelists who has the ability to treat local problems and situations in a universal context. The multiple interpretations that are possible upon reading her fiction illustrate a new stage in Ecuadorian letters that transcends the socially oriented works of the 1930's.

El beso y otras fricciones, cuentos. Bogotá: Paulina, 1975. 83 pp. This collection of short stories has as its common theme the dangers of dehumanization in a world of computers, automation, and nuclear reactors. Set in a futuristic context of interplanetary communication, each story questions whether or not man will be able to preserve essential human and ethical values so as to avoid being destroyed by his own scientific inventions.

Bruna, Soroche y los tíos, novela. Quito: Casa de la Cultura Ecuatoriana, 1973. 346 pp. This novel deals with a young woman who rebels against the patriarchal structures of society. In her search for a new lifestyle, numerous characters from the protagonist's past are presented as models either to reject or to emulate. This novel is considered one of the major narrative works published in Ecuador during the 1970's.

De la sangre y el tiempo, poesía

Luciola, poesía

Más allá de las islas, novela. Quito: Colegio Técnico "Don Bosco," 1980. 137 pp. This novel consists of a collection of characters who flee to the Galápagos Islands in search of immortality. As is the case in Yánez Cossío's other works, one also encounters here a condemnation of societal values which deny man his sense of human dignity. The quest for fulfillment takes place in an atmosphere characterized by dreams and surrealistic qualities that frequently make the distinction between reality and irreality indiscernible.

Poesía. Quito: Casa de la Cultura Ecuatoriana, 1974. 74 pp. Poems which stress two major themes: a mother's love and concern for her children; and Yánez Cossío's anguish over the poverty and injustices which continue to victimize so much of the world.

Yo vendo unos ojos negros, novela. Quito: Casa de la Cultura Ecuatoriana, 1979. 291 pp. This is a novel which reiterates Yánez Cossío's deep concern over women's place in modern society and the need to overcome the taboos and traditions which continue to stifle growth and development. Along with the work's feminist orientation, the author also presents the protagonist's struggle within the context of a capitalist society that tends to sacrifice human values for the gold and glitter of consumerism. MH

YCAZA, Rosa Borja de (see BORJA DE YCAZA, Rosa)

Z

Obras reunidas

La tumba de Antígona

ZAMORA, Bernice (United States, twentieth century)

Restless Serpents, bilingual

ZAMUDIO, Adela (see **ZAMUDIO-RIBERO, Adela**)

ZAMUDIO-RIBERO, Adela (Bolivia, 1854-1928; also Zamudio, Adela)

Cuentos breves

Ensayos poéticos

Intimas

Novelas cortas

Peregrinado

Ráfagas

Rendón y Rondín

ZANI, Giselda (Uruguay, b. 1909)

Por vínculos sutiles, cuentos

ZANZI, Blanca Bidart (see **BIDART ZANZI, Blanca**)

ZAPATA, Dolores Correa (see **CORREA ZAPATA, Dolores**)

ZAPATA ARIAS, Irene (Colombia, twentieth century)

Negro, no mueras por las calles, poesía

ZAVALA, Iris M. (Puerto Rico, twentieth century)

Barrio doliente, poesía

Escritura desatada, poesía

Kiliagonía, novela

Poemas prescindibles

Que nadie muera sin amar, poesía

ZENDEJAS, Josefina (Mexico, twentieth century)

El caracol que habló, cuentos para niños

Como un viento cualquiera, poemas

Los crótalos del aire, poemas

Desde un bache hasta la luz, cuentos de Nema

Es mi sangre, lecturas para jóvenes

Esplandor de la angustia, poemas

La fingida laguna, cuentos de Nema

Gusanito, poemas en prosa

Hora del optimismo, poemas

Llagado acento, poemas

El muñeco de nieve, cuentos para niños

Pirripipi, cuentos para niños

El ritmo de los días, poesía

Semillas de luz, cuentos de Nema

Semillas, pensamientos

Vidas mínimas

ZENDEJAS, Sara Margarita (Mexico, twentieth century)

Plomo

ZENNER, Wally (Argentina, twentieth century; pseudonym)

Antigua lumbre, poemas

Encuentro en el allá seguro, poesía

Magnificat

Moradas de la pena activa, poemas

La niña y el cielo

Soledades, poemas

ZENTENO DE LEON, Esmeralda (Chile, b. 1880;   pseudonym: Zouroff, Vera)

Liberación

Martha

El otro camino, novela

ZERTUCHE, Sofía (Mexico, twentieth century)

El infierno está aquí, novela

ZILVETTI VALDIVIESO, Irma Almada de (see **ALMADA DE ZILVETTI VALDIVIESO, Irma**)

ZOUROFF, Vera (pseudonym: see **ZENTENO DE LEON, Esmeralda**)

ZUÑIGA, Olivia (Mexico, twentieth century)

Amante imaginado, poemas

Los amantes y la noche, canto

Entre el infierno y la luz, poemas

La muerte es una ciudad distinta

Retrato de una niña triste

Appendixes

PARTIALLY ANNOTATED LIST OF ANTHOLOGIES

Note: Some bibliographies and other reference books are included here.

Album poético-fotográfico de las escritoras cubanas. Ed. D. García de Coronado. Habana: n.p., 1868. Another edition: (Habana: El Figaro, 1926).

Alma y corazón: antología de las poetisas hispanoamericanas. Ed. Catherine Perricone. Miami: Universal, 1977.

Antología de la poesía femenina argentina, eds. J.C. Manbe and A. Capdevielle. Buenos Aires: Ferrari Hermanos, 1930.

Antología de la poesía femenina chilena. Ed. Nina Donoso Correa. Santiago de Chile: Gabriela Mistral, 1974. 279 pp.

Antología de las escritoras argentinas: 1840-1940. Ed. Elisa Ruiz. Buenos Aires: Centro Editor de América Latina, 1980. Paperback, 180 pp. Anthology in very economical edition of Argentina's women writers, many of whom were unknown to most critics, then and now. Contains letters, poems, short stories, fragments of novels and essays, some of which would be very useful in class. A second volume is promised in the last introduction, but in 1986, it has not yet appeared. Most useful are the editor's introductions which give a short bio-bibliographical sketch of each writer. Recovering lost women writers would be much easier if each Spanish American country had an anthology such as this one. The title is somewhat confusing (on the cover it is listed as: J.M. Gorriti, C. Duayen, M. de Villarino y otras: Las escritoras 1840-1940), since this is only one volume in a large series on Argentinean literature put out by Centro Editor. NSS

Antología de poetisas americanas. Ed. J. Parra del Riego. Montevideo: García, 1923.

Antología femenina. Ed. F. Santelso. Los Mejores Versos de las Mejores Poetisas. Mexico: LUX, 1938.

Las argentinas, de ayer a hoy. Ed. Lily Sosa de Newton. Buenos Aires: L.V. Zanetti, 1967. 237 pp. Besides an introduction on the "Dilemma of

Today's Women," this book on the feminine impact throughout the history of Argentina, is divided into ten chapters. The first four deal chronologically with the participation of women in various political and cultural events up to the end of the nineteenth century. The next five chapters analyze specific areas pertaining to women in the twentieth century: "Feminism in Argentina," "Women in Education," "Female Correspondents and Writers," "Women in the Arts and Sciences" and "Working Women." The concluding chapter reflects very briefly on the international progress of the status of women in comparison to Argentina. Contains extensive bibliography and an index of all women cited. It received honorable mention from the Argentinian Society of Writers (S.A.D.E.) in 1967. SHA

Así escriben las mujeres. Ed. María Elena Togno. Buenos Aires: Orion, 1975. Paperback, 189 pp. This collection published in celebration of the International Year of Women (1975) contains short stories by the following Argentinean writers: Poldy Bird, María Angélica Bosco, Silvina Bullrich, Lilian Goligorsky, Liliana Heckler, Luisa Mercedes Levinson, Marta Lynch, María Ester de Miguel, Silvina Ocampo, María Rosa Oliver, Olga Orozco, Syria Poletti and Hebe Uhart. A one-and-a-half-page prologue by M. Elena Togno makes two important points: 1) the obstacles to active participation in "forbidden areas" impelled women to create fiction; 2) numerous novels by men about the opposite sex provide women with the experience of fiction which they would subsequently utilize in their literary production. Each short story is preceded by very brief information on its author. SHA

Bibliography of Hispanic Women Writers. Eds. Norma Alarcón and Sylvia Kossnrr. Chicano-Riqueño Studies Bibliography Series, No. 1. Bloomington, Ind.: Chicano-Riqueño Studies, 1980. 86 pp. A bibliography of the criticism listed in the MLA Bibliography for about a hundred Spanish American women writers, as well as some from Spain. DEM

14 (Catorce) mujeres escriben cuentos. Ed. Elsa de Llarena. Mexico, D.F.: Federación Editorial Mexicana, 1975. Paperback, 190 pp. According to the cover of 14 mujeres, Llarena is editor of El Rehilete (a literary magazine), co-director of Imaginaria and of Folios, the organ of the Asociación Mundial de Mujeres Periodistas y Escritoras. Llarena has published Prosas, Cuentos cortos, Durero, maestro grabador and a collection of children's stories, Ayotzin.

> The anthology offers twenty-four short stories by fourteen twentieth-century Mexican women writers, including such well-known authors as Rosario Castellanos, Elena Poniatowska and Elena Garro as well as several less well-known writers. The stories treat feminist, indigenista and other social issues as well as psychological and existential conflicts. They reflect a variety of writing styles and technical tendencies typical of twentieth-century writing, and this makes the collection highly appropriate both for courses on women writers and for those on modern Latin American narrative. Includes a short editor's preface. NGD

Chicanas Speak Out. N. Y.: Pathfinder Press, 1971.

Contemporary Women Authors of Latin America: New Translations. Eds. Doris Meyer and Marguerite Fernández Olmos. Brooklyn College Humanities Institute Series. Brooklyn, N. Y.: Brooklyn College, 1983.

Cuentos desde el taller, Taller "Leonar Alonso" dirigido por Syria Poletti. Ed. Syria Poletti. Buenos Aires: Plus Ultra, 1983. ISBN 950-21-0467-6, 158 pp. This short story collection is the result of one of Poletti's workshops which she named after a recently deceased participant, Leonor

Alonso. Poletti's first prologue explains the origin of the workshop and evaluates its accomplishments. The second prologue is a brief allegory of the art of writing. Seven stories by Leonor Alonso follow, introduced by Poletti's poetic eulogy of the author. The other five workshop participants--Mireya Soldano de Prol, Ilda Haidé, Arditte de Daiban, Lidia Risotto de Levi, Mabel Rivera, and Velia Malchiodi Piéro--contribute four stories each, preceded by an imaginative autobiographical account. All the selections represent extraordinary talent in Poletti's students. Index. SHA

The Defiant Muse: Hispanic Feminist Poems From the Middle Ages to the Present. A bilingual anthology. Eds. Angel Flores and Kate Flores. New York: Feminist, 1986. ISBN 0-935312-47-1, ISBN 0-935312-54-4. Paperback, 144 pp. Although it is difficult to find out anything about the life of Kate Flores, we know that she is a poet and translator of poetry from Spanish, French and German. She also has taught at Queens College. Her book, Relativity and Consciousness, was recently published by Gordian Press. Educated in the United States, Angel Flores received his Ph. D. from Cornell University in 1947. He continued his studies in Spanish as an Associate Professor at Queens College (1948-1952) in New York where he later became Professor Emeritus of Romance Languages and Comparative Literature. He is author or editor of twelve anthologies of poetry in translation. Not only has he studied Spanish literature, but he has written and edited some books on Marxism and Franz Kafka.

This tremendous array of bilingual Hispanic poems depicts many feminists' views of their oppressed lives. Upon reading the thorough introduction, one becomes attuned to the feminists and their task to free themselves from the overpowering influence of male poetry and the male-imposed belief in women's innate inferiority. These poems present womens' concerns principally in Spanish, Argentinian, Mexican and Puerto Rican societies. Many of the poets discuss women's exclusion from military service, their exploits in war, their love for national heroes and their limited choice between positions within the church or marriage. These poems cover many centuries and these issues change as each society changes. Aside from the choice of poems, a brief biography of each poet helps the reader to put each work into its context.
                                                                          CK

Cuentos: Stories by Latinas. Eds. Alma Gómez, Cherríe Moraga, and Mariana Romo-Carmona. Brooklyn, New York: Kitchen Table, Women of Color Press, 1983. ISBN 0-913175-01-3, 241 pp. Alma Gómez, born of Puerto Rican parents, grew up in the Caribbean section of New York City's Lower East Side. Her occupations have included: writer, teacher, consultant, social work administrator. Cherríe Moraga, poet and writer, was born in Los Angeles and now lives in Brooklyn. Mariana Romo-Carmona emigrated from Chile in 1966 and now lives in Boston. She is a writer, editor and has worked in radio.

Cuentos includes short stories by twenty-four Latinas now living in the United States. The authors come from New York, Texas, and California in the United States and from Puerto Rico, Brazil, Chile and Cuba. The stories, written in Spanish, English or a mixture of both, reflect the experience of Latinas as United States. Third World women are: "an exiled people, a migrant people, mujeres en lucha." The book is divided into three sections: 1) women who do not fit society's mold; 2) growing up -- the battle for identity; and 3) sexuality -- breaking out of the limits defined by culture. An excellent collection representing a wide variety of female experience. Contains an introduction by the editors and a glossary of Spanish expressions. NM

Detrás de la reja. Eds. Celia C. de Zapata and Lygia Johnson. Caracas: Monte Avila, 1980. 400 pp. Historical Introduction by Zapata. Thematic and stylistic commentary by Johnson. The most complete critical anthology of Latin American women prose writers available until now. Excluding the three stories from Brazil, most of the stories come from Mexico (six) and Argentina (five), with a few each from Uruguay (three), Chile (two), Costa Rica (two), Cuba (one) and Venezuela (one). Of exceptional literary quality and strikingly homogeneous in their treatment of intimate personal themes, with the exception of Rosario Castellanos' preoccupation with social conditions. The volume is organized thematically according to the age and civil status of the female protagonists. SEM

Diccionario biográfico de mujeres argentinas. Ed. Lily Sosa de Newton. Buenos Aires: Plus Ultra, 1980. Paperback, 533 pp. Available commercially. This second edition extends and brings up to date the information of the first one of 1972. A two-page introduction explains the author's original intention to limit her work to outstanding women in the past. Once her historical research was complete, the author decided to incorporate important women still alive. These contributed their own vitae. The dictionary thus provides a comprehensive outline of the evolution of Argentinian women. Numerous writers are included. A few are notably missing: Libertad Demitrópoulos, Griselda Gambaro and Olga Orozco. SHA

Diez escritoras ecuatorianas y sus cuentos, ed. Michael H. Handelsman. Guayaquil: Casa de la Cultura Ecuatoriana, Núcleo del Guayas, 1982. 171 pp. This anthology serves as a companion to Handelsman's two-volume study of the prose writings of Ecuadorian women authors, Amazonas y artistas (Guayaquil, 1978). For each of the ten contemporary escritoras represented here (Carmen Acevedo Vega, Zoila María Castro, Aída González Harvilán, Violeta Luna, Estela Parral de Terán, Mireya Ramírez, Lupe Rumazo, Fabiola Solís de King, Eugenia Viteri, and Alicia Yánez Cossío), there is a brief biographical sketch followed by two short stories. In an introduction Handelsman comments on the prejudice that still exists against women writers and the obstacles and criticism that they face in the exercise of their craft. MSA

10 (Diez) mujeres en la poesía mexicana del siglo XX. Compiled by Griselda Alvarez. Mexico: Secretaria de Obras y Servicios, 1974. 151 pp.

Escritoras de América, catálogo. Ed. Aurora Fernández y Fernández.

Five Women Writers of Costa Rica: Short Stories by Carmen Naranjo, Eunice Odio, Yolanda Oreamuno, Victoria Urbano, and Rima Vallbona. Ed. Victoria Urbano. Beaumont, Tx.: Asociación de Literatura Femenina Hispánica, 1978.

Florilegio de escritoras cubanas. Ed. A. González Curquejo. 3 vols. Habana: El Siglo XX, 1910-1919.

La guirnalda literaria, Colección de producciones de las principales poetisas y escritoras contemporáneas de España y América. Guayaquil: Calvo, 1870.

J.M. Gorriti, C. Duayen, M. de Villarino y otras: has escritoras 1840-1940. [See annotation under Antología de las escritoras argentinas: 1840-1940.]

Las mejores poetisas colombianas. 3rd ed. Bogotá: Minerva, 1936.

La mujer en la poesía chilena, 1784-1961, antología. Compiled by María Urzúa. Santiago, Chile: Nascimento, 1963.

La mujer en las letras venezolanas: homenage a Teresa de la Parra en el año internacional de la mujer: Catálogo exposición hémero-bibliográfica, 5-26 octubre 1975. Caracas: Impr. del Congreso de la República, 1976. 176 pp.

La mujer por la mujer. Ed. with Prologue by Juana Robles Suárez. Mexico: Pepsa, 1975. Paperback, 186 pp. The unifying theme of the anthology is woman's life experience: the pain of childbirth and of motherhood (M. Lynch, "Sala de guardia"), man's attitude towards women (Sor Juana, "Redondillas"), woman's incommunication and solitude (C. Lispector, "Lazos de familia"), the need for illusion and phantasy (G. Mistral, "Todas íbamos a ser reinas;" M. Jara, "La camiseta"), woman's social engagement (V. Parra, "Yo canto la diferencia") and her apprehension of different levels of reality (S. Ocampo, "Autobiografía de Irene"). It is a useful primary source for a course on Latin American women's literature. PRL

Mujeres chilenas cuentan. Ed. Chela Reyes, Prologue by Vicente Mengod. Santiago: Zig-Zag, 1978. Paperback, 96 pp. The eleven short stories anthologized are of irregular quality. Lacking thematic unity, the obvious intent of the book is the present a sample of Chilean women's short story writing. The best stories are those of E. Cerda, "Roberto Pampa, profesión marino," dealing with a young boy's yearning for the sea; O. Arratia's "El niño grande," on the relationship of a father with his handicapped and dying son; V. Cruzat's "Perder Asis," about the transforming powers of imagination; and M. Allamand's "El niño de las ovejas," which captures well the atmosphere of the Chilean countryside. The Prologue reviews each story; an epilogue provides bibliographic information on the authors. PRL

Mujeres en espejo, I: narradoras latinoamericanas, siglo XX. Ed. and Introd. by Sara Sefchovich. Colección Narrativa Latinoamericana. Mexico: Folios, 1983. ISBN 968-478-021-4, paperback, 224 pp. Selections from twenty-five Spanish American prose writers and one Brazilian translated into Spanish. Many of the most important writers from Argentina (five) or Mexico (eight), plus one or two from each of ten other countries. DEM

Open to the Sun: A Bilingual Anthology of Latin American Women Poets. Ed. Nora Jácques Wieser. Van Nuys, CA.: Perivale, 1980. ISBN 0-9122-88-16-7, 279 pp. Includes representative poems of nineteen twentieth century women poets, selected from among the best-known and from the not-so-familiar poets of the last three decades. The editor is to be praised for the high quality of her selection, which minimizes repetition of the usually printed poems in the case of the established figures, and avoids trivial or merely militant themes in the case of the younger authors. The English versions, which have been made by different translators, are generally good although some errors have slipped through. The general introduction and the introductions to each author are concise, informative, and helpful. Suitable as textbook for college courses. MF

Other Fires, Short Fiction by Latin American Women. Foreword by Isabel Allende. Selection, introd., some trans. and notes by Alberto Manguel. New York: Clarkson Potter, 1986. ISBN 0-517-55870X, paperback, 222 pp. Contains some Brazilian writers and the following Spanish Americans: Armonía Somers, Marta Lynch, Alejandra Pizarnik, Angélica Gorodischer, Vlady Kociancich, Inés Arredondo, Albalucía Angel, Amparo Dávila, Elena

Poniatowska, Silvina Ocampo, Liliana Heker, Elena Garro, Beatriz Guido, Lydia Cabrera, and Rosario Castellanos. DEM

Parnaso femenino. Ed. E. Esquiu Barroetavena. Buenos Aires: Argentinidad, 1936.

Pasos en la escalera. La extraña visita. Girándula. Aval de Agustín Yáñez. México, D.F.; Porrúa, 1973. 188 pp. A collection of twenty-one stories, in which each of the seven authors contributes a story under each of the three titles. Conceived and presented as an exercise in literary art, each author utilizes different subject matter and demonstrates her particular style. The stories are written by Guadalupe Dueñas, Angeles Mendieta Alatorre, Mercedes Manero, Margarita López Portillo, Carmen Andrade, Beatriz Castillo Ledón, and Ester Ortuño. Dueñas is the lead writer in each section and perhaps the most inclined toward a subjective, fantasy world. This work should be of interest to the general public, as well as to scholars interested in the process of literary creation and its treatment in literature, in addition to collective efforts by women. EE

Poesía de autoras colombianas. Selection and notes by Eddy Torres. Bogotá: Kelly, 1975. 333 pp. Published under the auspices of the "Oficina de Divulgación de la Caja de Credito Agrario, Industrial y Minero," to celebrate the 1975 International Year of the Woman, this anthology is divided into six parts. Three historical and literary periods of Colombian woman's poetry are covered: the colonial period (one poet), the nineteenth century (five poets), and the twentieth century (thirty-one poets). The selection of authors and works, as well as the Prologue by Eduardo Carranza, and the editor's explanatory remarks represent an excellent and much-needed introduction to the field. Among the most striking works are those by Emilia Ayarza de Herrera, Agueda Pizarro, María Mercedes Carranza, and Olga Elena Mattei. A valuable and useful addition for students of Hispanic women's literature.
ED&ME

Poesía femenina guatemalense. 2 vols. Guatemala: n. p., 1977.

Poesía feminista del Mundo Hispánico (desde la Edad Media hasta la actualidad). Ed. Angel Flores and Kate Flores. Serie la Creación Literaria. Mexico: Siglo Veintiuno, 1984. 285 pp.

Poetisas americanas, Ramillete poético del bello sexo hispanoamericano. Ed. J. D. Cortes. Paris: Bouret, 1875, 1896.

Poetisas contemporáneas mexicanas. 2 vols. Ed. Josefina Zendejas. Mexico: Ideas, n.d. [1944].

Poetisas de América. Ed. María Monvel [Tilda Brito de Donoso]. Santiago de Chile: Nascimento, 1929.

Poetisas mexicanas, siglos XVI, XVII, XVIII y XIX. Prologue by J. María Vigil. Mexico: Secretaría de Fomento, 1893.

Poetisas mexicanas: siglo XX. Ed. Héctor Valdés. Mexico, D. F.: Universidad Autónoma de México, Dirección General de Publicaciones, 1976. Paperback, 227 pp. Includes a selection of poems by seventeen modern Mexican women poets. A short biographical/critical sketch precedes each poet's work. The editor's introduction declares as his purpose the collection of works by women which have been difficult to obtain. The poetic modes of expression range from the mystical to the personal and confessional to the intellectual, the erotic and the folkloric. An excellent sampling of the richness and creative energy of the work of modern Mexico's women writers. Suitable especially for courses in modern Latin American women writers. Also contains a bibliography of books of poetry by each of the writers.   NGD

La sartén por el mango, encuentro de escritoras latinoamericanas. Eds. Patricia Elena González and Eliana Ortega. Ave. González 1002, Rio Piedras, P.R.: Huracán, 1984. ISBN 0-940238-72-1, 173 pp.

Selección poética femenina, 1940-1960. Ed. Martha Giménez Pastor.

Spanish American Women Writers. Ed. Lynn Ellen Rice Cortina. New York: Garland, 1983. ISBN 0-8240-9247-3, hardbound, 292 pp. A bibliographical research checklist, ordered sequentially by countries, includes a name index for quick verification of its 1994 entries. Useful as a preliminary resource. Includes women who are not necessarily known as authors, thereby attempting to provide a context of literary activity that supposedly makes for a richer checklist. Cortina mentions the book's dual shortcomings in its Introduction, namely its being biased and incomplete. Sometimes Cortina enters pseudonyms, date and place of publication, and the work's genre; sometimes she does not; and although she orders the writers by country of birth, in the case of some who have published in a different country, there may not even be a cross-reference to indicate this. For example, Nicaraguan-born Claribel Alegría appears solely in El Salvador, her adopted country. It would be difficult to locate Marta Traba, who shows up under "Tain de" rather than "Traba" as she is better known; Cuba's beloved Haydée Santamaría inexplicably appears as "Santa María." VM

26 (Veintiséis) autoras del México actual. Eds. Beth Miller and Alfonso González. Mexico: Costa-Amic, 1978. 463 pp.

The Web; Stories by Argentine Women. Translated and edited by H. Ernest Lewald. Washington, D. C.: Three Continents, 1983. ISBN 0-89410-085-8, hardbound, 170 pp. Biographic introductions and stories by Luisa Mercedes Levinson ("The Clearing," "Mistress Frances"), Silvina Ocampo ("The Prayer"), Silvina Bullrich ("The Lover," "Self Denial"), María Angélica Bosco ("Letter from Ana Karenina to Nora," "Letter from Nora to Ana Karenina"), Syria Poletti ("The Final Sin"), Beatriz Guido ("Ten Times Around the Block," "Takeover"), Marta Lynch ("Bedside Story," "Latin Lover"), Amalia Jamilis ("Night Shift," "Department Store"), Eugenia Calny ("Siesta"), Luisa Valenzuela ("Change of Guard"), Cecilia Absatz ("A Ballet for Girls"), and Reina Roffé ("Let's Hear What He Has to Say"). MB

Woman Who Has Sprouted Wings: Poems by Contemporary Latin American Women Poets. Ed. Mary Crow. Discovery Series. Pittsburgh: Latin American Literary Review Press, 1984. ISBN 0-935480-14-5, paperback, 168 pp. Thirteen Spanish American poets (and one Brazilian) are included: Alejandra Pizarnik from Argentina; Delia Domínguez and Violeta Parra from Chile; María Mercedes Carranza from Colombia; Rita Geada and Nancy Morejón from Cuba; Rosario Castellanos, Ulalume González de León and María Sabina from Mexico; Cecilia Bustamante and Raquel Jodorowsky from Peru; Claribel Alegría from El Salvador; and Circe Maia from Uruguay. Preface by Joanna Bankier. Introduction by Mary Crow. All poems are presented in Spanish and in English translation. Each poet is preceded by a biographical note. DEM

Women in Hispanic Literature: Icons and Fallen Idols. Ed. Beth Miller. Berkeley: University of California, 1983. ISBN 0-520-04367-7. Paperback, 373 pp. Comprises seventeen essays on Hispanic women writers and images of women in Spanish and Latin American literature. Chronologically, the essays treat periods from the Medieval to the modern. Directed to a general scholarly audience as well as to Hispanists. All quotations in Spanish are translated into English. The editor's introduction discusses a wide range of women's issues in the context of Hispanic literatures. Includes title, name and subject index. An important contribution to the study of women in Hispanic literatures. NGD

Women in Spanish America: An Annotated Bibliography from Pre-Conquest to Contemporary Times. Ed. Meri Knaster. Boston: G. K. Hall, 1977.

Women Novelists in Spain and Spanish America. Ed. Lucía Fox-Lockert. Metuchen: Scarecrow, 1979. In this English-language survey of Hispanic women novelists, the author has selected nine Peninsular and thirteen Latin American writers and one of their works. These range from the seventeenth to the twentieth century. Included is biographical data, plot summary and an incisive critical analysis of each categorized by "family," "social class," "sexuality" and "message." The comprehensive introduction briefly summarizes each writer and her importance as a representative of the feminist ideal. A bibliography, footnotes and index makes this a valuable work for those interested in an overall view of Hispanic women writers as well as specific points of interest. PS

Women's Voices from Latin America: Interviews with Six Contemporary Authors. Ed. Evelyn Picón Garfield. Detroit, Michigan: Wayne State University, 1986. Illus., ISBN 0-8143-1782-0, 190 pp. Includes a Preface, Introduction, Further Readings. Each interview is preceded by a photograph and a brief biography of the writer. Bibliographies of works by and about each author are grouped together at the end. The authors included are: Armonía Somers, Griselda Gambaro, Julieta Campos, Elvira Orphée, Marta Traba, and Luisa Valenzuela. DEM

AUTHORS BORN BEFORE 1900

Note: This list only contains authors for whom a birthdate is known and listed in the bibliography. They are listed under their complete name.

ACEVEDO DE CASTILLO, Olga
ACEVEDO DE GOMEZ, Josefa
ACOSTA DE SAMPER, Soledad
AGOSTINI DE DEL RIO, Amelia
AGURTO MONTESINO, Claudina
AGUSTINI, Delmira
ANABALON, Luisa
ANAYA DE URQUIDI, Mercedes

BARRAGAN DE TOSCANO,
    Refugio
BAZAN DE CAMARA, Rosa
BENITEZ, María Bibiana
BERNAL, Emilia
BETANCOURT DE BETANCOURT,
    Isabel Esperanza
BETANCOURT FIGUEREDO,
    María de
BOLIO DE PEON, Dolores
BORRERO, Juana
BORRERO DE LUJAN, Dulce María
BRANNON DE SAMAYOA, Carmen
BRITO DE DONOSO, Tilda
BRUNET, Marta

CABELLO DE CARBONERA,
    Mercedes
CABRERA, Lydia
CADILLA DE MARTINEZ, María
CAIÑAS PONZOA, Angeles
CAMACHO DE FIGUEREDO,
    Pomiana
CAMARILLO DE PEREYRA, María
    Enriqueta

CARRERAS DE BASTOS, Laura
CARVAJAL, María Isabel
CASTELLANOS DE ETCHEPARE,
    Delia
CASTILLO DE GONZALEZ, Aurelia
CASTILLO Y GUEVARA, Madre
    Francisca Josefa
CATALINA DE JESUS, sor
CEPEDA, Cecilia
CESPEDES DE ESCAÑAVERINO,
    Ursula
CID BAEZA, Astensia
CORREA ZAPATA, Dolores
COX STUVEN, Mariana
CRUZ, María
CUELLAR, Francisca Carlota

DAVILA DE PONCE DE LEON,
    Waldina
DENIS DE ICAZA, Amelia
DIAZ DE RODRIGUEZ,
    Albertina
DIAZ DE SCHTRONN, Zoraida
DULCHE ESCALANTE, Catalina

ECHEVARRIA DE LARRAIN, Inés
ELFLEIN, Ada María
EMILIANI IMITOLA NINFA, María
ERAUSO, Catalina
ESPINOSA DE RENDON, Silveria
ESTEVEZ Y VALES DE
    RODRIGUEZ, Sofia
ESTRADA MEDINILLA, María
EULATE SANJURJO, Carmen

FARIAS DE ISSASI, Teresa
FERNANDEZ DE TINOCO, María
FIGUERAS DE WALLS, Isabel

GAMERO DE MEDINA, Lucila
GARAY, Nicole
GARCIA COSTA, Rosa
GODOY ALCAYAGA, Lucila
GOMEZ DE ABADIA, Herminina
GOMEZ DE AVELLANEDA Y
    ARTEAGA, Gertrudis
GOMEZ MAYORGA, Ana de
GOMEZ SANCHEZ, Enriqueta
GORODISCHER, Angélica
GORRITI, Juana Manuela
GRILLO DE SALGADO, Rosario
GUERRA, Rosa

HALL DE FERNANDEZ, Elisa
HERNANDEZ DE ARAUJO, Carmen
HURTADO DE ALVAREZ, Mercedes

IBARBOUROU, Juana de
ISAZA DE JARAMILLO MEZA,
    Blanca

JARAMILLO GAITAN, Uva
JUANA INES DE LA CRUZ, Sor

LABARCA HUBERTSON,
    Amanda
LASTARRIA CABRERO, Berta
LE QUESNE, María Antonieta
LLORENS TORRES, Soledad
LOPEZ DE VICTORIA Y BARBE,
    María
LOPEZ DE VICTORIA Y
    FERNANDEZ, Magda
LOZANO, Abigaíl

MACHADO DE ARREDONDO,
    Isabel
MANSILLA DE GARCIA, Eduarda
MANSO DE NORONHA,
    Juana Paula
MARIA DE LA ANTIGUA, Madre
MARIN DEL SOLAR, Mercedes
MARMOL, Adelaida del
MARRERO Y CARO, Rosa
MATAMOROS, Mercedes
MATTO DE TURNER, Clorinda
MELENDEZ, Conchita
MENDEZ DE CUENCA, Laura
MENENDEZ, Josefa
MONTENEGRO DE MENDEZ,
    Dolores
MONTES DEL VALLE, Agripina
MORVAN, Henriette
MURILLO, Josefa

NEGRON MUÑOZ, Mercedes
NIETO DE HERRERA, Carmela

OBALDIA, María Olimpia de
OCAMPO, Victoria
ORREGO DE URIBE, Rosario

PADILLA DE SANZ, Trinidad
PALMA Y ROMAN, Angélica
PARRA CERDA, Vicenta de la
PARRA SANOJO, Ana Teresa
PEREZ DE ZAMBRANA, Luisa
PEREZ Y MONTES DE OCA,
    Julia Luisa
PRIETO DE LANDAZURI,
    Isabel A.

RODRIGUEZ, Catalina
RODRIGUEZ DE TIO, Lola
ROQUE DE DUPREY, Ana

SALMERON ACOSTA, Cruz María
SANSORES PREN, Rosario
SANTA CRUZ, María de
SANTA CRUZ Y OSSA, Elvira
SOTO Y CALVO, Edelina
SOTOMAYOR DE CONCHA,
    Graciela
STORNI, Alfonsina
SUAREZ, sor Ursula
SUCRE, Dolores

TADEA DE SAN JOAQUIN, sor
TAGLE, María
TAPIA DE CASTELLANOS, Esther
TORRENS DE GARMENDIA,
    Mercedes

UREÑA DE HENRIQUEZ, Salomé

VALDES MENDOZA, Mercedes
VAZ FERREIRA, María Eugenia
VELASCO Y CISNEROS, Isabel
VERBEL Y MAREA, Eva C.
VILLANUEVA DE BULNES, Marta
VILLAR BUCETA, María
VIVAS BRICEÑO, Clara

WEBER, Delia
WILMS MONTT, Teresa

XENES Y DUARTE, Nieves

YAÑEZ BIANCHI DE
    ECHEVARRIA, María Flora

ZAMUDIO-RIBERO, Adela
ZAMUDIO, Adela
ZENTENO DE LEON, Esmeralda

CLASSIFIED LISTING OF AUTHORS BY COUNTRY

Note: Authors with pseudonyms or alternate forms of names are only listed under their complete name here. To find a complete name, look up the other form in the body of the bibliography. Authors may be listed under more than one country if they lived outside of their country of origin.

ARGENTINA

ABELLA CAPRILE, Margarita
ABSATZ, Cecilia
ADLER, Raquel
AGÜERO VERA, Carmen
AGUIRRE, Dora de
ALBORNOZ DE VIDELA, Graciela
ALCORTA, Gloria
ALMADA DE ZILVETTI
    VALDIVIESO, Irma
ALVAREZ, Marta
ALVAREZ DE TOLEDO,
    Luisa Isabel
ALVAREZ REYNOLDS, Mercedes
ALVEAR, Elvira de
ANCHORENA DE AZEVEDO, Inés
ARZON, Anadela
ASTRADA, Etelvina
ASTRADA, María Nélida

BARBITTA COLOMBO, Adela
BARRA, Emma
BARRAGAN, Lida
BAZAN DE CAMARA, Rosa
BELTRAN NUÑEZ, Rosario
BEMBERG, María Luisa
BERTOLE, Emilia
BERTOLE DE CANE, Cora María
BIAGONI, Amelia
BLANCO AMORES, Carmen
BLANCO AMORES DE
    PAGELLA, Angela

BLANCO VILLALTA, Manuela de
BOMBAL, Susana
BORNEMANN, Elsa Isabel
BOSCO, María Angélica
BOTTINI, Clara
BRUMANA, Herminia
BULLRICH PALENQUE, Silvina

CABALLERO, Teresa
CALANDRELLI, Susana
CALNY, Eugenia
CAMPO, Margarita del
CAMPOS, Alicia
CANDEGABE, Nelly
CANTO, Estela
CAPMANY PUCCIO, Mireya
CARLO, Adelia di
CARNELLI, María Luisa
CARNELLI DESPOSITO,
    María Cristina
CARRASCO, Ofelia Judith
CARTOSIO, Emma de
CASCO DE AGNER, Margarita
    del Carmen
CASTELLANOS, Carmelina de
CHOUCHY AGUIRRE,
    Ana María
CORTINA, María Teresa
CORTINAS, Laura
CRESTA DE LEGUIZAMON,
    María Luisa
CRUZ, Josefina
CRUZ DE CAPRILE, Fifa

CUELLAR, Aída
CUTANDA, María Concepción

DALMAU DE SAN TESTEBAN,
    Emma Teresa
DEMITROPOLOUS, Libertad
DE VALLS, Julia A.
DE VATCH, Laura
DHIALMA TIBERTI, María
DIEGO, Celia de
DOMINGUEZ, María Alicia
DOS SANTOS, Estela
DOUMERC, Beatriz
DUHART, Sara María

ECHEVARRIA DE LOBATO
    MULLE, Felisa Carmen
ELDELBERG, Betina
ELFLEIN, Ada María
ELGUL DE PARIS, Marta
ELORZA DE ORTI, Ana Manuela
ESPINDOLA DE PASCUAL
    ROMERO, Sofía
ESTRELLA, María del Mar
ESTRELLA ALONSO, Josefina
EZEIZA GALLO, Carmen N. de

FERRARIA ACOSTA, Eloísa
FERRE, Patricia
FIGUERAS DE WALLS, Isabel
FINKEL, Berta
FLOREZ DE RIZZOLO,
    María Esther
FRUCTUOSO DE SCHVARTS,
    Josefa A.
FRUNIZ PAZ, Martha Noemí
FUENTES MOLINA, Perla
FUSELLI, Angélica
FUTORANSKY, Luisa

GALLARDO, Sara
GALLARDO DE ORDOÑEZ,
    Beatrix
GALLARDO DE SALAZAR
    PRINGLES, Justa Beatriz
GAMBARO, Griselda
GANDARA, Ana
GANDARA, Carmen
GARAY, María Consuelo
GARAY MUÑIZ, María
    del Carmen
GARCIA COSTA, Rosa
GARCIA DE LA MATA, Helena
GIL, Marta Nélida
GIMENEZ PASTOR, Martha
GOMEZ PAZ, Julieta
GORRITI, Juana Manuela
GRANATA, María

GUERRA, Ana María
GUERRA, Hilda
GUERRA, Rosa
GUIDO, Beatriz

HARRIAGUE, Magdalena
HECKER, Liliana
HERMOSO, Fernanda

ISRAEL DE PORTELA, Luisa
IZAGUIRRE, Ester de

JAMILIS, Amalia
JARQUE, Delia
JURADO, Alicia

KRAPKIN, Ilka

LAHITTE, Ana Emilia
LANGE, Norah
LARDE DE VENTURINO,
    Alice
LEVINSON, Luisa Mercedes
LOPEZ DE GOMARA, Susana
LOPEZ GARCIA DE
    PERALTA, María
LOUBET, Jorgelina
LUJAN, María Diana
LUZ, Alba
LYNCH, Marta

MALHARRO DE CARIMATI,
    Victorina
MALINOW, Inés
MANSILLA DE GARCIA,
    Eduarda
MANSO DE NORONHA,
    Juana Paula
MARPONS, Josefina
MAURA, María Elena
MEDINA ONRUBIA DE
    BETONA, Salvadora
MERCADER, Martha
MIGUEL, María Esther de
MOLLOY, Sylvia
MORA Y RIERA, Argentina

NAVARRO, Ada
NUÑEZ, Zulma

OCAMPO, Silvina
OCAMPO, Victoria
OCAMPO DE PERA,
    María Ofelia
OLIVER, María Rosa
OLIVIERI, Marta
OROZCO, Olga
ORPHEE, Elvira

PADILLA, Lila
PALISA MUJICA DE LACAU,
    María Hortensia
PANCHECO DE PANCHECO,
    Carmen
PASAMANIK, Luisa
PEREZ DE MONTI, Luisa María
PICHETTI, Leonor
PIZARNIK, Flora Alejandra
POLETTI, Syria
PUENTES DE OYENARD, Sylvia
PUJATO CRESPO DE CAME-
    LINO VEDOYA, Mercedes

RAFFO, Hortensia Margarita
REYES ORTIZ, Marta
RODAS, Virginia
ROFFE, Reina
ROTZAIT, Perla
RUBERTINO, María Luisa

SALOTTI, Martha
SANDOR, Malena
SCHAPIRA FRIDMAN, Flor
SCHULTZ CAZANUEVE DE
    MANTOVANI, Fryda
SEIBEL, Beatriz
SELVA MARTI, Ana
SILVA NOCEDAD, Lucrecia
SOFOVICH, Luisa
SOLA DE SOLA, Emma
SOLARI, Zita
SOSA DE NEWTON, Lily
SOTO Y CALVO, Edelina
STEIMBERG, Alicia
STORNI, Alfonsina
SUAREZ, Isabel Estrella de
SUAREZ, María del Carmen

TAMPIERI DE ESTRELLA,
    Susana
TAPIA DE LESQUERRE, Lola
THENON, Susana

VALENZUELA, Luisa
VAZQUEZ, María Esther
VELAS PALACIOS, Matilde
VELASCO Y ARIAS, María
VENTURINI, Aurora
VICUÑA, Cecilia
VIDAL, Teresa
VIEYRA, Adelia
VILLAR, María Angélica
VILLARINO, María de

WALSH, María Elena
WEINSTEIN, Lytia
WILMS MONTT, Teresa

ZENNER, Wally

BOLIVIA

ANAYA DE URQUIDI,
    Mercedes

BEDREGAL DE CONITZER,
    Yolanda
BRUZZONE DE BLOCH, Olga

CABRERA DE GOMEZ REYES,
    Adriana
CARDONA TORRICO, Alcira
CASTELLANOS DE RIOS, Ada
CUELLAR DE TORRICO, Yolanda

ESTENSSORO, María Virginia
ESTENSSORO MACHICADO,
    Angélica

GUTIERREZ DE CALDERON, Ana

ZAMUDIO-RIBERO, Adela

BRAZIL

ALVES PEREIRA, Teresinha

CHILE

ACEVEDO DE CASTILLO, Olga
ACUÑA, Beatriz
ADRIAZOLA, Ximena
AGOSIN HALPERN, Marjorie
    Stela
AGUIRRE, Isidora
AGUIRRE, Margarita
AGUIRRE VIGOUROUX, Berta
AGURTO MONTESINO, Claudina
ALBALA, Eliana
ALDUNATE, María Elena
ALLAMAND, Maité
ALLENDE, Isabel
AMUNATEGUI, Amanda
ANABALON, Luisa
ARRATIA, Olga
ASTORGA, Irma Isabel

BENNET, Daisy
BLANCO, Marta
BOMBAL, María Luisa
BORDES, Inés
BRANDAN, Matilde
BRITO DE DONOSO, Tilda

BRUNER, Carmen
BRUNET, Marta
BUSTAMANTE, María Teresa

CALLEJAS, Mariana
CARRASCO, Margarita
CARRASCO DE BUSTAMANTE,
    Catalina
CARREÑO FERNANDEZ, Yolanda
CASANOVA, Cecilia
CASTILLO, Carmen
CELIS, Gloria
CERDA, Eliana
CESPEDES LIARTE, Gioconda
CHAMBERS, Nancy
CID BAEZA, Astensia
CODINA DE GIANNONI, Iverna
CONTRERAS FALCON, Victoria
CORREA MORANDE, María
CORVALAN POSSE, Stella
COX BALMACEDA, Virginia
COX STUVEN, Mariana
CRUCHAGA DE WALKER, Rosa

DEL RIO, Ana María
DIAZ-DIOCARETZ, Myriam
DIAZ VARIN, Stella
DOMINGUEZ, Delia
DONOSO CORREA, Nina

ECHEVARRIA DE LARRAIN,
    Inés
ECHEVERRIA DRUMOND,
    Liliana
ELIM, Miriam

FLORES AEDO, Juana

GAETE NIETO, Carmen
GALAZ, Alicia
GARFIAS, Mimi
GEEL, María Carolina
GERTNER, María Elena
GEVERT, Lucía
GODOY, Tamara
GODOY ALCAYAGA, Lucila
GODOY GODOY, Eliana
GOMEZ - CORREA,
    Wally de
GONZALEZ, María Rosa
GREVE, Escilda

HAMEL, Teresa
HERRERA, Sara
HERRERA DE WARNKEN,
    Marta
HUNEEUS DE CLARO, Ester

JARA, Marta

JAUCH, Emma
JODOROWSKY, Raquel

KNEER, Luisa

LABARCA HUBERTSON,
    Amanda
LADRON DE GUEVARA,
    Matilde
LAGOS GARAY, Yolanda
LASTARRIA CABRERO, Berta
LATORRE, Marina
LEIGHTON, Marcela
LE QUESNE, María Antonieta
LEZAETA, Gabriele
LOPEZ PUELMA, Lucía
LOYOLA, Adriana
LUJAN, Monica

MADRID, María Cristina
MARIN DEL SOLAR, Mercedes
MATTE ALESSANDRI, Ester
MENARES, María Cristina
MENENDEZ, Josefa
MERANI, María
MERINO GONZALEZ, Laura
MIRANDA, Marta Elba
MOLINA, Paz
MORALES, Violeta
MOREL, Alicia
MORENA LAGOS, Aída
MORENO, Inés
MORVAN, Henriette
MUNITA, Marta de

NAVARRO, Eliana
NAVARRO DE CASTRO,
    Rebeca

ORJIKH, Victoria
ORREGO DE URIBE, Rosario
OSSA DE GODOY, Blanca
OSSANDON, Francisca
OYARZUN, Mila

PARRA, Violeta
PAULO, Valería de
PAUT, Elisa de
PELLEGRIN, Mariluz
PERALTA, María Isabel
PEREZ WALKER DE SERRANO,
    Elisa
PETIT, Magdalena
PINCHEIRA, Dolores
PINO, Tegualda
PIWONKA, María Elvira
PRATS BELLO, Ana Luisa

RENDIC, Amalia

REPETTO BAEZA, Leticia
REQUENA, María Asunción
REYES, Chela
REYES, María Esperanza
ROEPKE, Gabriela

SANHUEZA, Eugenia
SANTA CRUZ Y OSSA, Elvira
SEÑORET, Raquel
SEPULVEDA, Ximena
SILVA OSSA, María
SOLARI, Olga
SOTOMAYOR DE CONCHA,
    Graciela
SUAREZ, Mariana
SUAREZ, sor Ursula

TADEA DE SAN JOAQUIN, sor
TAGLE, María
TEJEDA, Patricia
THEIN, Gladys
TORRES, Maruja
TURINA, Pepita

URIBE CASANUEVA, Inelia
URZUA, María
URZUA DE CALVO, Deyanira

VALENZUELA ALVAREZ,
    Mercedes
VALLE, Jimena del
VALLE, Lila del
VALLE, Silvia del
VELASCO, Isabel
VERGARA, Anamaría
VERGARA, Marta
VIAL, Magdalena
VIAL, Rosa
VIAL, Sara
VIAL DE UGARTE,
    María Mercedes
VIAL E., Magdalena
VILLANUEVA DE BULNES,
    Marta

WASLEY, Agnes

YAÑEZ BIANCHI DE
    ECHEVERRIA, María Flora

ZENTENO DE LEON,
    Esmeralda

COLOMBIA

ACEVEDO DE GOMEZ, Josefa
ACOSTA ARCE, Conchita

ACOSTA DE SAMPER, Soledad
ANDRION DE MEJIA ROBLEDO,
    Rita
ARANGO, Esther

BARCO DE VALDERRAMA,
    Lucy
BLANCO, María Teresa
BUITRAGO, Fanny

CAMACHO DE FIGUEREDO,
    Pomiana
CARRANZA, Maríamercedes
CASTELLANOS, Dora
CASTILLO Y GUEVARA, sor
    Francisca Josefa
CEPEDA, Cecilia
CHAMS, Olga
COCK DE BERNAL JIMENEZ,
    Lucía
CORREA DE RINCON SOLER,
    Evangelina

DALL, Gloria
DAVILA DE PONCE DE LEON,
    Waldina
DIAZ, Anita
DIAZ DE CASTILLO DE OTERO,
    Margarita

EASLEY, Marina
EASTMAN, María
EMILIANI IMITOLA NINFA,
    María
ESPINOSA DE CUSAN, Cecilia
ESPINOSA DE PEREZ, Matilde
ESPINOSA DE RENDON,
    Silveria

FLOREZ, Magdalena
FLOREZ FERNANDEZ DE
    SERPA, Paz

GARCIA DE BODMER, Helvia
GOMEZ DE ABADIA, Herminia
GOMEZ MEJIA, Carmen de
GONTOVNIK, Mónica
GRILLO DE SALGADO,
    Rosario
GUTIERREZ ISAZA, Elvira

HERRERA DE RODRIGUEZ
    URIBE, Leonor
HURTADO DE ALVAREZ,
    Mercedes

ISAZA DE JARAMILLO MEZA,
    Blanca

JARAMILLO DE CASTRO,
    Margarita
JARAMILLO GAITAN, Uva

LASCARRO MENDONZA,
    Elvira
LLERAS RESTREPO, Isabel
LLONA, María Teresa

MATTEI DE AROSEMENA,
    Olga Elena
MATTU, Olga Elena
MONTES DEL VALLE, Agripina
MUJICA, Elisa

NILO, Mariela del

OCAMPO DE SANCHEZ,
    Natalia
OCAMPO DE VELASCO, Blanca
OSPINA DE NAVARRO, Sofía

PEÑUELA DE SEGURA,
    Gertrudis
PEREZ, Cecilia
PINZON CASTILLA DE CARREÑO-
    MALLARINO, Isabel
PIZARRO DE RAYO, Agueda

RESTREPO DE MARTINEZ, Rosa
RESTREPO DE THIEDE, María
RUBIO DE DIAZ, Susana

SANCHEZ LAFAURIE, Juana
SANCHEZ MONTENEGRO,
    Blanca de
SANTOS MILLAN, Isabel
SAÑUDO DE DELGADO,
    María Isabel
SENIOR DE BAENA, Lilia
SENIOR DE CARRIZOSA,
    Zita
SILVA DE CAMARGO, Esther
SOTO, Carmelina

TAIN DE TRABA, Marta

URIBE DE ARENAS RUIZ,
    Maruja
URIBE DE ESTRADA,
    María Helena

VALENCIA, Angela de
VANEGAS, Ana
VARGAS FLOREZ DE
    ARGÜELLES, Emma
VERBEL Y MAREA, Eva C.
VIEIRA, Maruja

ZACS, Vera
ZAPATA ARIAS, Irene

COSTA RICA

BARRANTES, Olga Marta

CARVAJAL, María Isabel
CASTRO DE JIMENEZ, Auristela

DOBLES YZAGUIRRE, Julieta

FERNANDEZ, Janina
FERNANDEZ DE GIL, Zeneida
FERNANDEZ DE TINOCO,
    María

GONZALEZ, Edelmira
GONZALEZ, Luisa
GUARDIA, Lilly

NARANJO, Carmen
NIETO DE MADRIGAL, Carmen

ODIO, Eunice
OREAMUNDO, Yolanda

PINTO, Julieta

ROTHE DE VALLBONA,
    Rima Gretel

URBANO, Victoria

CUBA

ACOSTA, Ernestina
AGÜERO, Omega
AGUIRRE, Mirta
ALONSO, Dora
ALVAREZ, Consuelo
ALVAREZ RIOS, María
ANTUÑA, Rosario

BARROS, Silvia
BERNAL Y AGÜERO, Emilia
BETANCOURT DE BETAN-
    COURT, Isabel Esperanza
BORRERO, Juana
BORRERO DE LUJAN,
    Dulce María

CABRERA, Lydia
CAIÑAS PONZOA, Angeles
CAMPOS, Julieta
CAPOTE DE AGUILILLA, Araceli
CASTILLO DE GONZALEZ, Aurelia

CASUSO, Teresa
CEPEDA, Josefina de
CESPEDES DE ESCAÑA-
    VERINO, Ursula
CHACON NARDI, Rafaela
COLLAZO COLLAZO, Eulalia Nila
CORDERO, Carmen
CORTAZAR, Mercedes
CUZA MALE, Belkis

DIAZ CASTRO, Tania
DIAZ DE RODRIGUEZ, Albertina
DOMINGUEZ ROLDEN, María
    Luisa

ESCANDELL, Noemí
ESTEVEZ Y VALES DE
    RODRIGUEZ, Sofía

FERIA, Lina de
FERRER, Surama
FIGUEROA, Esperanza

GARCIA MARRUZ, Fina
GARCIA TUDURI DE COYA,
    Mercedes
GEADA, Rita
GOMEZ DE AVELLANEDA Y
    ARTEAGA, Gertrudis
GUTIERREZ KAHN, Asela

IÑIQUEZ, Dalia

JAUME, Adela

LLANA, María Elena
LLEONART, Yolanda
LOYNAZ DE ALVAREZ DE
    CAÑAS, Dulce María

MACHADO DE ARREDONDO,
    Isabel
MARMOL, Adelaida del
MARRERO Y CARO, Rosa
MARTINEZ, Angela
MATAMOROS, Mercedes
MENDEZ CAPOTE, Renée
MORALES DE ALLOUIS,
    Hilda
MORANDEYRA, Mary
MOREJON, Nancy

NIETO DE HERRERA,
    Carmela
NIGGEMAN, Clara
NUÑEZ, Ana Rosa
NUÑEZ, Serafina

OLEMA GARCIA, Daura

OLIVER, Carilda

PADILLA, Martha
PERERA SOTO, Hilda
PEREZ, Emma
PEREZ DE ZAMBRANA, Luisa
PEREZ Y MONTES DE OCA,
    Julia Luisa
PORTAL, Herminia del
POTTS, Renée
PRADO, Pura del
PRIDA, Dolores

QUINTANA, Caridad

REXACH DE LEON, Rosario
RIERA, Pepita
ROBLES, Mireya
RODRIGUEZ, Catalina
RODRIGUEZ, Clotilde del Carmen
RODRIGUEZ ACOSTA, Ofelia
ROJAS, María Teresa de

SABAS ALOMA, Mariblanca
SALADO, Minerva
SANCHEZ DE FUENTES,
    María
SANTA CRUZ, María de
SIMO, Ana María
SOLAR, Carmen
SOLDEVILLA, Loló de
SORAVILLA, Lesbia
SOTO DE SEGURA,
    Estrella
SUAREZ, María Dolores
SUAREZ-RIVERO, Eliana

TAMAYO, Evora
TEJERA, Nivaria
TORRENS DE GARMENDIA,
    Mercedes
TORRES, Araceli

VALDES MENDOZA, Mercedes
VALDIVIA, Omara
VELASCO Y CISNEROS,
    Isabel
VILLAR BUCETA, María

XENES Y DUARTE, Nieves

ZALDIVAR, Gladys

DOMINICAN REPUBLIC

CARTAGENA PORTALATIN,
    Aída
CASTELLANOS, Colombina de

CONTRERAS, Hilma

GOMEZ DE READ, Ernestina

LAMARCHE, Martha María

MEJIA, Abigaíl
MILLER, Jeanette

NIVAR DE PITTALUNGA,
    Amada

UREÑA DE HENRIQUEZ,
    Salomé

WEBER, Delia

ECUADOR

ALVAREZ DAVILA, Nadya

BORJA ALVAREZ, Aída
BORJA DE YCAZA, Rosa
BORJA MARTINEZ, Luz Elisa

CASTILLO, Laura del
CASTRO, Zoila María
CATALINA DE JESUS, sor
CELI DE BENITEZ, Eloísa
CORDERO DE ROMERO, Aurelia
CORDERO Y LEON,
    Ramona María

ECHEVERRIA LOPEZ, Maruja
ESPINEL, Ileana
ESTRADA DE RAMIREZ PEREZ,
    Aurora

GONZALEZ DE MOSCOSO,
    Mercedes

HIDALGO DE CHIRIBOGA,
    Alicia

IDOBRO, María Angélica
IZA, Ana María

KATZ, Elsa

LUNA, Violeta

MARTINEZ DE TINAJERO,
    Blanca
MUÑOZ DE MERCHAN,
    Isabel

PINO DESANDOVAL, Hylda

RUMAZO, Lupe

SOLIS DE KING, Fabiola
SUCRE, Dolores

UGARTE DE LANDIVAR, Zoila

VACA DE FLOR, María, Natalia
VITERI, Eugenia

YANEZ COSSIO, Alicia

EL SALVADOR

ALEGRIA, Claribel

BRANNON DE SAMAYOA,
    Carmen

DURAND, Mercedes

GUERRA, Dora

RUKAVISHNIKOVA-DARLEE,
    Irina

GUATEMALA

ACUÑA, Angelina
AGUIRRE, Lily
ALARCON DE FOLGAR,
    Romelia
AREVALO, Teresa

BERNAL DE SAMAYOA, Ligia
BURGOS, Elizabeth

CAMACHO FAHSEN DE
    AGUILERA, Isabel
CASTEJON DE MENENDEZ,
    Luz
CRUZ, María

DENIS DE ICAZA, Amelia

ECHEVERS, Malin d'
ESCOBAR THORBURN,
    Elizabeth

FERGUSON, Gloria

HALL DE FERNANDEZ,
    Elisa
HERRERA, Marta Josefina

JUAREGUI MONTES, Rosa

MOLINA DE RODRIGUEZ,
    Blanca Luz
MONTENEGRO DE MENDEZ,
    Dolores
MORALES TINOCO DE
    MARROQUIN, Clemencia

PARRA CERDA, Vicenta de la
PAZ Y PAZ, Leonor

QUIÑONEZ, Delia

RINCON DE MCDONALD,
    Sonia
RODRIGUEZ CHAVEZ, Elisa

TEJADA MILLA, Mercedes

VALENTI, Walda
VALLE, Luz del

HONDURAS

CARDONA, Adylia
CASTAÑEDA DE MACHADO,
    Elvia

DIAZ LOZANO, Argentina

GAMERO DE MEDINA,
    Lucila
GUILLEN DE RODRIGUEZ,
    Maribel

MARTINEZ, Celina

PAUL MEJIA, Gloria

SUAREZ, Clementina

VARELA Y VARELA,
    Olimpia

MEXICO

ACOSTA ANGELES, Helia Diana
ACOSTA DE BERNAL, Catalina
AGUIRRE, Ingrid Dolores
ALARDIN, Carmen
ALEMAN DE QUIJANO,
    Laura Elena
ALEMANY, Ofelia
ALMAZAN DE PEREZ BARRERA,
    María Helena
ALVAREZ, Gloria de

ALVAREZ, Griselda
ALVAREZ, Luisa María
ALVAREZ DEL CASTILLO DE
    CHACON, Graciana
AMOR, Guadalupe
ANDA, María Elena de
ANGELES, Isabel de los
ARIAS, Olga
ARREDONDO, Inés

BANDA FARFAN, Raquel
BARRAGAN DE TOSCANO,
    Refugio
BASURTO GARCIA, Carmen
BATIZA, Sarah
BERMUDEZ, María Elvira
BERTHELY JIMENEZ, Lylia C.
BOBES ORTEGA, Evelina
BOHORQUEZ, Abigael
BOLIO DE PEON, Dolores
BRAVO ADAMS, Caridad
BRITO SUMARRAGA, Sahara
BROOK, Paulita

CAMACHO DE SALAZAR
    PEREZ, Isabel
CAMARRILLO DE PEREYRA,
    María Enriqueta
CAMPOBELLO, Nellie Francisca
    Ernestina
CAMPOS, Julieta
CARDENAS, Nancy
CARMEN, María del
CARREÑO, Rosa de
CARVAJAL, María Isabel
CASTELLANOS, Rosario
CASTILLO LEDON, Amalia de
CASTRO DE PEÑALOSA, Dolores
CASTRO LEAL, Paloma
CHOPITEA, María José de
CHUMACERO, Rosalía d'
CORBO FAURÉ, Estela
CORNEJO, María Isabel Eloísa
CORREA ZAPATA, Dolores
COX, Patricia
CROSS, Elsa
CRUZ DE MORENO, María de la
CUELLAR, Francisca Carlota

DALTON, Margarita
DAVILA, Amparo
DELALKE, Gemma
DELAVAL, Alicia
DOLUJANOFF, Emma
DUEÑAS, Guadalupe
DULCHE ESCALANTE, Catalina
DURAND, Luz María

ELIZONDO, Hortensia
ENGEL, Lya
ESCANDON PREVOWSOIR,
    Gemma Violeta
ESPEJO, Beatriz
ESTRADA MEDINILLA, María

FARFAN CANO, Isabel
FARIAS DE ISSASI, Teresa
FERNANDEZ, Zoila Amable
FERNANDEZ DE CORDOVA,
    Olivia
FERNANDEZ DE LOMELI
    JAUREGUI, Emma
FOPPA, Alaíde
FORMOSO DE OBREGON
    SANTACILLA, Adela
FRAIRE, Isabel
FRANCIS SORIANO DE
    SOTRES, Susana
FUENTE, Carmen de la

GARCIA, Soledad
GARCIA IGLESIAS, Sara
GARCIA ROEL, Adriana
GARCIA SANTOS DE CUEVAS,
    Raquel
GARRO, Elena
GARZA RAMOS, Corina
GIL, Minerva Alicia
GLANTZ, Margo
GODOY, Emma
GOMEZ MAYORGA, Ana de
GOMEZ REINA, Irena
GOMEZ RUL, Ana María
GONZALEZ DE LEON,
    Ulalume
GONZALEZ MALDONADO,
    Rosario
GREENBERG S., Paulina
GUERRERO DE VAZQUEZ
    GOMEZ, Esperanza
GUTIERREZ SUAREZ,
    Emma E. de
GUZMAN E., Julia

HERNANDEZ, Luisa Josefina
HERNANDEZ, María de Lourdes
HERNANDEZ DIAZ, Celia de
HIDALGO, María Luisa

ITURBIDE DE LARIS RUBIO,
    Sara
IZQUIERDO ALBIÑANA,
    Asunción

JUANA INES DE LA CRUZ,
    sor

LAFARJA DE CRUZ, María
    de la Luz
LA TORRE, Josefina Muriel de
LLACH, Leonor
LLARENA, Elsa de
LOMBARDO DE CASO, María
LOPEZ PORTILLO, Margarita
LUZ PEREA, María

MAIRENA, Ana
MAR, María del
MARIA DE LA ANTIGUA,
    madre
MARIN, Guadalupe
MAURIES, Blanca B.
MELENDEZ DE ESPINOSA,
    Juana
MELO DE REMES, María Luisa
MENDEZ, Concha
MENDEZ DE CUENCA, Laura
MENDIETA ALATORRE,
    María de los Angeles
MENDOZA, María Luisa
MENDOZA LOPEZ, Margarita
MERINO, Adriana
MEZA, Otilia
MICHELENA, Margarita
MOLINA, Silvia
MONDRAGON AGUIRRE,
    Magdalena
MORA, Antonieta
MORA, Carmen de
MUÑIZ, Angelina
MURILLO, Josefa

NAJERA, Indiana E.
NAVA, Thelma
NIETO DE DIEZ, Catalina
NIETO DE SANCHEZ, Rosa

OCAMPO, María Luisa
OCHOA, Enriqueta
OCHOA, Rosa Margot
ODIO, Eunice
O'NEILL, Carlota
OREAMUNO, Yolanda
ORTEGA, María del Carmen

PACHECO, Cristina
PACHECO DE HAEDO,
    Carmelinda
PALACIOS, Adela
PALAVICINI, Laura
PARODI, Enriqueta de
PAZ PAREDES, Margarita
PEREZCANO DE JIMENEZ
    ARRILLAGA, Josefina
PONIATOWSKA, Elena

PRIETO DE LANDAZURI,
  Isabel A.
PUYHOL, Lenica

QUINTANA, Elvira

RABELL,Malkah
REINBECK DE VILLANUEVA,
  Margos
REYES, Alicia
REYES, Mara
RICO, Carmen de
RICO, Dina
RIESTRA, Gloria
RODRIGUEZ PUYHOL, Esther
ROSA, Lilia
ROSENZWEIG V., Carmen
ROSS, María Luisa

SALAS DE CALDERON, Gloria
SANSORES PREN, Rosario
SELIGSON, Esther
SIERRA, Tina
SILVA, Teresa de
SOLAR, Adriana
SUAREZ, Josefina
SUAREZ, María

TAPIA DE CASTELLANOS,
  Esther
TERRES, María Elodia
TORRES, Eugenia
TOSCANO, Carmen
TREJO, Blanca Lydia
TREVIÑO CARRANZA,
  Celia

URIARTE, Chayo
URIARTE, Yolanda
URIBE, Rebeca
URQUIZA, Concha
URUETA DE VILLASEÑOR,
  Margarita

VALENCIA, Tita
VERA, María Luisa
VEYRO, Blanca Rosa
VICENS, Josefina
VIDRIO, Lola
VILALTA, Maruxa
VILLARREAL, Concha de

ZAMBRANO, Esperanza
ZENDEJAS, Josefina
ZERTUCHE, Sofía
ZUÑIGA, Olivia

NICARAGUA

ALEGRIA, Claribel

BELLI, Gioconda

DENIS DE ICAZA, Amelia

NAJLIS, Michèle

SELVA DE IBARRA, María de la

PANAMA

AGUILERA DE SANTOS,
  Luisa Victoria
ALVARADO DE RECORD, Elsie

CAMARANO DE SUCRE,
  Yolanda

DENIS DE ICAZA, Amelia
DIAZ DE SCHTRONN, Zoraida

GARAY, Nocole
GUARDIA DE ALFARO, Gloria
GUARDIA ZELEDON, Gloria

OBALDIA, María Olimpia
OCHOA LOPEZ, Moravia
OSSES, Ester María

PORTOCARRERO DE
  CHAMORRO, Bertilda

ROJAS SUCRE, Graciela

SIERRA, Stella

PARAGUAY

CHAVEZ DE FERREIRO, Ana Iris

ESPINOLA, Lourdes
ESTIGARRIBIA DE
  FERNANDEZ, Graciela

GOMEZ SANCHEZ, Enriqueta

IZAGUIRRE, Ester de

PLA, Josefina

WIEZELL, Elza

PERU

ABADIA -EGUI, María de Jesús
ACOSTA, Sofía A.
ALDUNATE DE ALBA, María
    Luisa
ALVARADO RIVERA, María J.
AMAT Y LEON DE BOGGIO,
    Consuelo
ARAMBURU LECAROS, Elena
ARCINIEGA, Rosa

BALUARTE, Amparo
BAZAN MONTENEGRO, Dora
BELEVAN, Enriqueta
BUSTAMANTE, Cecilia

CABELLO DE CARBONERA,
    Mercedes
CALLER IBERICO, Clorinda
CAMPO Y PLATA, Graciela del
CARRILLO, Sonia Luz
CARVALLO DE NUÑEZ, Carlota
CASTELLANOS ARGÜELLES
    DE MOLLOY, Lucila
CERNA GUARDIA, Rosa
COLMENARES DE FIOCCO,
    Delia

ELGUERA DE MACPARLIN,
    Alida
ESPINOSA DE MENENDEZ,
    Leonor

FONSECA RECAVARREN,
    Nelly
FOX-LOCKERT, Lucía

GALLARDO, Delia María
GARRON DE DORYAN,
    Victoria
GONZALEZ CASTRO,
    Esmeralda

HELFGOTT, Sarina
HERRERA DE ANGELES,
    I. Orfelinda

JOFFRE DE RAMON, Sara

MACEDO C., María Rosa
MATTO DE TURNER, Clorinda

PALMA Y ROMAN, Angélica
PORTAL, Magda
PORTOCARRERO, Elena
PRADO, Blanca del
PUGA DE LOSADA, Amalia

REYES, Doris
RIESCO MALPARTIDA
    LUSZCZYNSKA, Laura
RODRIGUEZ PARRA DE GARCIA
    ROSELL, Elisa

SAKS, Katia
SALAZAR, Ina

VARELA, Blanca
VILLARAN, Consuelo María
    Eufrosina

PUERTO RICO

AGOSTINI DE DEL RIO, Amelia
ARRILLAGA, María
ARZOLA, Marina

BABIN, María Teresa
BENITEZ, María Bibiana
BERIO, Blanca Teresa
BONNIN ARMSTRONG, Ana Inés
BURGOS, Julia de

CABALLERO, Pepita
CADILLA DE MARTINEZ, María
CADILLA DE RUIBAL,
    Carmen Alicia
CASANOVA-SANCHEZ, Olga
CASAS, Myrna
CEIDE DE LOEWENTHAL, Amelia
CHIESA DE PEREZ, Carmen
CLAUDIO DE LA TORRE,
    Josefina A.
COLLAZO, Paula
CORON PELLOT, Carmen
CRUZ DE BECERRIL, Dominga
CUCHI COLL, Isabel

DAVILA, Amparo
DAVILA, Angela María
DEMAR, Carmen
DROZ, Vanessa
DURAN, Ana Luisa

EULATE SANJURJO, Carmen

FELICIANO MENDOZA, Esther
FERNANDEZ DE LEWIS,
    Carmen Pilar
FERRE, Rosario
FIGUEROA, Loida
FILIPPI LUGO, Carmen

GALLEGO, Laura
GARCIA RAMIS, Magali

GARDON FRANCESCHI,
   Margarita
GARRASTEGUI, Anagilda
GAYA DE GARCIA, María
   Cristina
GONZALEZ MALDONADO,
   Edelmira

HERNANDEZ DE ARAUJO,
   Carmen

LICELOTT DELGADO, Edna
LLORENS TORRES, Soledad
LOPEZ DE VICTORIA Y
   BARBE, María
LOPEZ DE VICTORIA Y
   FERNANDEZ, Magda
LOPEZ SURIA, Violeta

MATTEI DE AROSEMENA,
   Olga Elena
MELENDEZ, Concha
MOLINA, Marina

NEGRON MUÑOZ, Mercedes
NOLLA, Olga

OCHART, Luz Ivonne

PADILLA DE SANZ, Trinidad
PALMA, Marigloria
PEREZ MARCHAND, Lilianne
PUIGDOLLERS, Carmen

QUIÑONES PEREZ, Marta
   Magaly

RAMIREZ DE ARELLANO,
   Diana
RAMIREZ DE ARELLANO
   DE NOLLA, Olga
RAMOS COLLADO, Liliana
RIVERA, Etnairis
RODRIGUEZ DE TIO, Lola
ROQUE DE DUPREY, Ana

S. DE LERNIER, Clara Luz
SALGADO, Teresina
SANFIORENZO, Carmen
SILVA, Margarita
SILVA DE MUÑOZ, Rosita
SOTOMAYOR, Aurea

TIO, Elsa

VICENS, Nimia
VIZCARRONDO, Carmelina

ZAMBRANO, María
ZAVALA, Iris M.

SPAIN

ARZOLA, Marina

MUÑIZ, Angelina

PERI ROSSI, Cristina
PLA, Josefina

SOFOVICH, Luisa

VILALTA, Maruxa

UNITED STATES

AGOSIN HALPERN,
   Marjorie Stela
AGOSTINI DE DEL RIO, Amelia
ALVAREZ, Rosa Elvira
ALVES PEREIRA, Teresinha
AZEVEDO, Idilia

BLANCO, María Teresa

CASTILLO, Amelia del
COLLAZO G., Josefina
COTA-CARDENAS, Margarita
CUZA MALE, Belkis

DAVIU, Matilde
DIEZ DE RAMOS, Nena

ESCANDELL, Noemí
ESPINOLA, Lourdes

FOX, Lucía

GONZALEZ DE RAGGI,
   Ana Hilda

NEGRON, Delis
NIGGEMAN, Clara
NUÑEZ, Ana Rosa

PERERA SOTO, Hilda
PIZARRO DE RAYO, Agueda
PRIDA, Dolores

REXACH DE LEON, Rosario
RIESCO MALPARTIDA
   LUSZCZYNSKA, Laura
RODAS, Ana María

ROTHE DE VALLBONA,
  Rima Gretel

SAKS, Katia
SANCHEZ, Rosaura
SUAREZ-RIVERO, Eliana

URBANO, Victoria
UTRERA, Esther

VALDIVIA, Omara

URUGUAY

ACOSTA DE SANCHEZ, Azulina
AGUIAR, Marta
AGUIAR DE MARIANI, Maruja
AGUILERA DOMINGUEZ, Mirta
AGUSTINI, Delmira
ALVAREZ CABUTO, María
  Angélica
ALVAREZ DE TOLEDO, Adelaida
ARZARELLO DE FONTANA, Sofía

BACELO, Nancy
BERENGUER BELLAN,
  Amanda
BIDART ZANZI, Blanca
BOLLO, Sarah
BRINDIS DE SALAS, Virginia
BRUM, Blanca Luz

CACERES, Esther de
CALCAGNO DE CIONE, Catita
CARRERAS DE BASTOS, Laura
CASAL, Selva
CASAL DE SANCHEZ, Marynés
CASTELLANOS DE ETCHEPARE,
  Delia
CASTELLANOS DE GALLINAL,
  Elina
CASTELLO, Lucía

ETCHEPARE HENESTROSA,
  Armonía

FERRARI DE PLAZA, Angélica
FERRAZ DE GADEA, María Julieta
FIGUEREDO, Amalia de
FUENTE, María Angélica de la

GENTA, Estrella
GILIO, María Esther
GONZALEZ DE LEON, Ulalume

GONZALEZ VILLEGAS, Maruja
GRAVINA TELECHEA, María F.

HERRERA, Silvia

IBAÑEZ, Sara de
IBARBOUROU, Juana de
IZCUA BARBAT DE MUÑOZ
  XIMENEZ, María del Carmen

LAGO DE FIRPO, Sylvia
LAMAS DE SAENZ, María Luisa
LAZO, Loreley
LEON, Margarita de
LLANA BARRIOS, María Esther
LOPEZ CRESPO, Iris de
LUISI, Luisa
LUJAN REYES DE GUADALUPE,
  María de

MACHADO BONET DE
  BENVENUTA, Ofelia
MAIA, Circe
MEDEIROS, María Paulina
MENENGHETTI, Cristina
MIERS, Reyna
MIRANDA, Paula
MOLLA, Rosana

ORGAZ DE CORREA LUNA,
  Delia

PATERO DE IBARRA,
  Graciela
PEREZ DE PASTORINI,
  Eloísa
PERI ROSSI, Cristina
PIAGGIO, Edda
PORRO FREIRE, Alicia

ROMERO, Chita
RUSSELL, Dora Isella

SAENZ, Raquel
SILVA, Clara
SILVA BELINZON, Concepción
SILVA DE MAGGI, Marinés

TESTA, Celia

VAZ FERREIRA, María Eugenia
VILARIÑO, Idea
VITALE, Ida

ZANI, Giselda

VENEZUELA

ALLENDE, Isabel
ALVAREZ, Mariela
ARIAS DE CABALLERO,
     Blanca Graciela
ARVELO LARRIVA, Enriqueta

BENCOMO, Carmen Delia
BETANCOURT FIGUEREDO,
     María de
BRANDT DE RICARDO, Blanca
BRIGE, Carmen
BRUZUAL, Narcisa

C. DE ARVELLO, Clotilde
CARVAJAL DE AROCHA,
     Mercedes
CASTILLO, Regina Pía

DAVIU, Matilde

GRAMCKO, Ida

LERNER, Elisa
LIMA DE CASTILLO,
     Polita de
LOZANO, Abigaíl

MACHADO DE ARNAO, Luz
MADRID, Antonieta
MENDOZA SAGARZAZU, Beatriz

MONTSERRAT, María de

ONTIVEROS Y HERRERA,
     María G.

PALACIOS, Antonia
PARRA SONOJO, Ana Teresa
PEREZ GUEVARA DE
     BOCCALANDRO, Ada

SALMERON ACOSTA,
     Cruz María
SCHÖN, Elizabeth
SILVA DE REYES, Clara
STALK, Gloria

TARAN, Ana Enriqueta
TAYLHARDAT, Concepción de
TERAN, Ana Enriqueta
TERAN, Cora de

VALLE SILVA, Luisa del
VILLANUEVA MATA, América
VIVAS BRICEÑO, Clara

INFORMATION NOT AVAILABLE

OTERO JOY, Sarah

QUIÑONEZ, Isabel

DRAMATISTS

Compiled by Jean Graham

Note: This list contains the authors whose included works were described as "teatro," "teatral," "comedia," "pieza," "tragedia," "drama," or "dramático."

ACOSTA DE SANCHEZ, Azulina
AGOSTINI DE DEL RIO, Amelia
AGUIRRE, Isidora
ALBORNOZ DE VIDELA, Graciela
ALONSO, Dora
ALVARADO RIVERA, María J.
ALVAREZ RIOS, María
ALVES PEREIRA, Teresinha
ARAMBURU LECAROS, Helena

BABIN, María Teresa
BARBITTA COLOMBO, Adela
BARRAGAN DE TOSCANO, Refugio
BARRANTES, Olga Marta
BARROS, Silvia
BASURTO GARCIA, Carmen
BATIZA, Sarah
BELTRAN NUÑEZ, Rosario
BENCOMO, Carmen Delia
BERNAL DE SAMAYOA, Ligia
BERTOLE DE CANE, Cora María
BETANCOURT DE BETANCOURT,
    Isabel Esperanza
BETANCOURT FIGUEREDO,
    María de
BIDART ZANZI, Blanca
BOHORQUEZ, Abigael
BOLLO, Sarah
BRAVO ADAMS, Caridad
BRITO SUMARRAGA, Sahara
BROOK, Paulita
BRUZUAL, Narcisa

BUITRAGO, Fanny

CABRERA DE GOMEZ REYES,
    Adriana
CALCAGNO DE CIONE, Catita
CALNY, Eugenia
CARDENAS, Nancy
CARREÑO, Virginia
CARREON GUTIERREZ,
    María Luisa
CARRERAS DE BASTOS, Laura
CARVAJAL DE AROCHA,
    Mercedes
CARVALLO DE NUÑEZ,
    Carlota
CASAS, Myrna
CASTAÑEDA DE MACHADO,
    Elvia
CASTELLANOS, Rosario
CASTILLO LEDON,
    Amalia de
CHOPITEA, María José de
COLMENARES DE FIOCCO,
    Delia
CORTINAS, Laura
CUCHI COLL, Isabel

DAVILA DE PONCE DE LEON,
    Waldina
DIEGO, Celia de
DONOSO CORREA, Nina
DULCHE ESCALANTE, Catalina

ENGEL, Lya

FARIAS DE ISSASI, Teresa
FERNANDEZ DE CORDOVA, Olivia
FERNANDEZ DE LEWIS,
    Carmen Pilar
FERRARI DE PLAZA, Angélica
FERRAZ DE GADEA,
    María Julieta
FINKEL, Berta
FONSECA RECAVARREN, Nelly
FORMOSO DE OBREGON
    SANTACILLA, Adela
FOX-LOCKERT, Lucía
FRUCTUOSO DE SHVARTS,
    Josefa A.
FUSELLI, Angélica

GALLARDO, Delia María
GAMBARO, Griselda
GARCIA SANTOS DE CUEVAS,
    Raquel
GARRO, Elena
GENTA, Estrella
GODOY, Emma
GOMEZ DE AVELLANEDA Y
    ARTEAGA, Gertrudis
GONZALEZ DE MOSCOSO,
    Mercedes
GRAMCKO, Ida
GUERRA, Rosa
GUERRERO DE VAZQUEZ
    GOMEZ, Esperanza
GUILLEN DE RODRIGUEZ, Maribel
GUZMAN E., Julia

HELFGOTT, Sarina
HERNANDEZ, Luisa Josefina
HERNANDEZ DE ARAUJO,
    Carmen
HERRERA DE WARNKEN, Marta

IBARBOUROU, Juana de

JOFFRE DE RAMON, Sara
JUANA INES DE LA CRUZ, Sor

KATZ, Elsa

LAHITTE, Ana Emilia
LERNIER, Elisa
LEVINSON, Luisa Mercedes
LIMA DE CASTILLO,
    Polita de
LOPEZ CRESPO, Iris de
LOPEZ DE VICTORIA Y BARBE,
    María
LOUBET, Jorgelina

MAIRENA, Ana
MANSILLA DE GARCIA,
    Eduarda
MARPONS, Josefina
MARRERO, Carmen
MATTEI DE AROSEMENA,
    Olga Elena
MATTO DE TURNER, Clorinda
MEDINA ONRUBIA DE BETONA,
    Salvadora
MENDEZ, Concha
MERCADER, Martha
MONDRAGON AGUIRRE,
    Magdalena
MORENO, Inés

OCAMPO, Silvina
OCAMPO, Victoria
OCAMPO HEREDIA, María Luisa
O'NEILL, Carlota
ORJIKH, Victoria

PALMA, Marigloria
PARRA CERDA, Vicenta de la
PATERO DE IBARRA, Graciela
PETIT, Magdalena
PLA, Josefina
PORTOCARRERO, Elena
PRATS BELLO, Ana Luisa
PRIETO DE LANDAZURI,
    Isabel A.
PUJATO CRESPO DE CAMELINO
    VEDOYA, Mercedes

REINBECK DE VILLANUEVA,
    Margos
REQUENA, María Asunción
REYES, Chela
REYES, Mara
ROEPKE, Gabriela
RUBERTINO, María Luisa

SANDOR, Malena
SANTA CRUZ Y OSSA, Elvira
SCHÖN, Elizabeth
SCHULTZ CAZANUEVE DE
    MANTOVANI, Fryda
SEIBEL, Beatriz
SOTOMAYOR DE CONCHA,
    Graciela
STORNI, Alfonsina

TEJADA MILLA, Mercedes
TORRES, Eugenia

URBANO, Victoria
URUETA DE VILLASEÑOR,
    Margarita

URZUA DE CALVO, Deyanira

VALLE, Luz del
VAZ FERREIRA, María Eugenia
VERBEL Y MAREA, Eva C.

VIAL, Magdalena
VILALTA, Maruxa

WEBER, Delia

TRANSLATIONS AND BILINGUAL EDITIONS

Note: Starred items are annotated in the Partially Annotated List of Anthologies or in the body of the bibliography. Bracketed items mix Spanish and English in the same work.

ANTHOLOGIES:

Contemporary Women Authors of Latin America: New Translations. Eds. Doris Meyer and Marguerite Fernández Olmos.

[Cuentos: Stories by Latinas. Eds. Alma Gómez, Cherríe Moraga, and Mariana Romo-Carmona.*]

The Defiant Muse; Hispanic Feminist Poems From the Middle Ages to the Present, a bilingual anthology. Eds. Angel Flores and Kate Flores.

Five Women Writers of Costa Rica: Short Stories by Carmen Naranjo, Eunice Odio, Yolanda Oreamuno, Victoria Urbano, and Rima Vallbona. Ed. Victoria Urbano.

Open to the Sun: A Bilingual Anthology of Latin American Women Poets. Ed. Nora Jácquez Wieser.*

Other Fires, Short Fiction by Latin American Women. Ed. and trans. by Alberto Manguel.*

Woman Who Has Spouted Wings: Poems by Contemporary Latin American Women Poets. Ed. Mary Crow.*

The Web; Stories by Argentine Women. Trans. and Ed. by H. Ernest Lewald.*

Women's Voices from Latin America: Interviews with Six Contemporary Authors. Ed. Evelyn Picón Garfield.*

INDIVIDUAL AUTHORS:

ALEGRIA, Claribel

Flowers from the Volcano / Flores del volcán.*

ALLENDE, Isabel

The House of the Spirits.

ALVAREZ DE TOLEDO, Luisa Isabel

The Strike.

ALVES PEREIRA, Teresinha

Help, I'm Drowning.

¡Hey, Mex!

While Springtime Sleeps.

ASTRADA, Etelvina

Autobiography at the trigger.*

BARRIOS DE CHUNGARA, Domitila

Let Me Speak / Testimony of Domitila, a Woman of the Bolivian Mines.

BOMBAL, María Luisa

House of Mist.

New Islands.

The Shrouded Woman.

CASTELLANOS, Rosario

The Nine Guardians.

CORPI, Lucha

[**Palabras de mediodía, Noon Words**.]

COTA-CARDENAS, Margarita

[**Puppet**.]

CUCHI COLL, Isabel

The Student's Sweetheart.

DIAZ LOZANO, Argentina

>**And We Have to Live**.

>**Enriqueta and I**.

DUARTE DE PERON, Eva María

>**Evita: Eva Duarte de Perón Tells Her Own Story**.

ESPINDOLA, Lourdes

>**Womanhood and Other Misfortunes**.

FERRE, Rosario

>**La muñeca menor / The Youngest Doll**.*

FRAIRE, Isabel

>**Isabel Fraire, Poems**.

GARRO, Elena

>**Recollections of Things to Come**.

GILIO, María Esther

>**The Tupamaro Guerrillas**.

>**The Tupamaros**.

GODOY ALCAYAGA, Lucila

>**Crickets and Frogs: A Fable**.

>**The Elephant and His Secret: Based on a Fable by Gabriela Mistral**.

>**The Mystery: Five Songs of Motherhood**.

>**Selected Poems of Gabriela Mistral**. Trans. Doris Dana.

>**Selected Poems of Gabriela Mistral**. Trans. Langston Hughes.

GOMEZ DE AVELLANEDA Y ARTEAGA, Gertrudis

>**Belshazzar**.*

>**The Love Letters of Gertrudis Gómez de Avellaneda**.

GUIDO, Beatriz

>**End of a Day**.

>**House of the Angel**.

IBARBOUROU, Juana de

Angor Dei.

JESUS, Teresa de

De repente / All of a Sudden.

JODOROWSKY, Raquel

Ajy Tojen.

JUANA INES DE LA CRUZ, sor

The Pathless Grove, A Collection of Seventeenth Century Mexican Sonnets of Sor Juana Inés de la Cruz.

Sor Juana Inés de la Cruz, Poems.

A Woman of Genius: The Intellectual Autobiography of Sor Juana Inés de la Cruz.

LLONA, María Teresa

Intersection / Encrucijada.

MADRID, Antonieta

Naming Day-by-day / Nomenclatura Cotidiana.

MAIRENA, Ana

Majakuagymoukeia.

MATTO DE TURNER, Clorinda

Birds without a nest.*

MONDRAGON AGUIRRE, Magdalena

Someday the Dream.

OCAMPO, Victoria

Victoria Ocampo: Against the Wind and the Tide.

O'NEILL, Carlota

Trapped in Spain.

PARRA SANOJO, Ana Teresa

Mamá Blanca's Souvenirs.

"**Las Memorias de Mamá Blanca**, A Translation with Introduction and Notes."

PASAMANIK, Luisa

The Exiled Angel.

PETIT, Magdalena

La Quintrala.

PIWONKA, María Elvira

Selected Poems.

PIZARNIK, Alejandra

Alejandra Pizarnik, A Profile.

PONIATOWSKA, Elena

Massacre in Mexico.

RIERA, Pepita

Prodigy.

ROBLES, Mireya

Tiempo Artesano / Time, the Artesan.

ROEPKE, Gabriela

The Dangers of Great Literature, A Lecture in One Act.

Three Non-Shakespearean Plays in One Act.

A White Butterfly.

STORNI, Alfonsina

Alfonsina Storni: Argentina's Feminist Poet, The Poetry in Spanish with English Translations.

UMPIERRE-HERRERA, Luz María

[**En el país de las maravillas**.]

[**Una puertorriqueña en Penna**.]

VALENZUELA, Luisa

Clara: A Novella and Thirteen Short Stories.

The Lizard's Tale.*

<u>Other Weapons</u>.*

<u>Strange Things Happen Here; Twenty-six Short Stories and a Novella</u>.

VICUÑA, Cecilia

<u>Saboramí</u>.

ZAMORA, Bernice

[Restless Serpents.]

KEY TO CONTRIBUTOR INITIALS

AA	Ana María Alvarado
AMA	Angela McEwan-Alvarado
AP	Amanda Plumlee
AS	Arlene O. Schrade
ASL	Anita K. Stoll
AT	Alexanda Tcachuk
BM	Barbara Morris
BTO	Betty Tyree Osiek
CK	Caragh Kennedy
CS	Cynthia Steele
CW	Catharine Wall
DEM	Diane E. Marting
DK	Dennis Klein
DM	Doris Meyer
EA	Esther A. Azzario
ED	Elisa Dávila
EE	Elizabeth Espadas
EFS	Erica Frouman-Smith
EPG	Evelyn Picón Garfield
FO	Felicidad Obregon
GB	Grace M. Bearse
GFW	Gloria Feiman Waldman
GH	Gina C. Hardalo
GM	Gabriela Mora
HP	Hilda Peinado
ILJ	Ivette López Jiménez
IR	Irene Rostagno
IV	Ileana Viqueira

JG	Jean Graham
JM	Joan F. Marx
JP	Juan José Prat
JZ	Joseph W. Zdenek
LD	Lee Dowling
LFL	Lucía Fox-Lockert
LGC	Lucía Guerra-Cunningham
LGL	Linda Gould Levine
LK	Ludmila Kapschutschenko
LP	Luisa M. Perdigó
MA	Marjorie Agosín
MB	Mary Berg
ME	Miriam Ellis
MF	Malva Filer
MGP	Magdalena García-Pinto
MH	Michael Handelsman
ML	Monique J. Lemaitre
MSA	Melvin S. Arrington, Jr.
MQG	Sister María Cristina Quiñónez-Gauggel
NE	Noemí Escandell
NG	Norma Grasso
NGD	Nancy Gray Diaz
NL	Naomi Lindstrom
NM	Nancy Mandlove
NSS	Nancy Saporta Sternbach
PF	Patti Firth
PK	Patricia N. Klingenberg
PRL	Patricia Rubio de Lértora
PRP	Phyllis Rodríguez-Peralta
PS	Patricia J. Santoro

RA	Raysa E. Amador	SSR	Susan Schaffer
RI	Raúl Inostroza	ST	Susan Tritten
RRV	Rima R. de Vallbona		
		TA	Teresa R. Arrington
SC	Susana Castillo	TF	Tanya Fayen
SEM	Seymour Menton	TR	Timothy J. Rogers
SHA	Susana Hernández-Araico		
SMA	Sarah Marqués	VB	Virginia M. Bouvier
SMI	Sharon Magnarelli	VM	Virginia Moore
SS	Stacey Schlau		
SSO	Sylvia Sherno	YGR	Yolanda García-Reynero

INFORMATION ABOUT
CONTRIBUTORS

Note: Annotators are alphabetized by their final last name unless their names are hyphenated.

MARJORIE AGOSIN, Wellesley College. Author of: <u>Las desterradas en el paraíso: María Luisa Bombal</u>. (MA)

ANA MARIA ALVARADO, Rutgers University. Author of critical essays on Latin American literature, short stories, journal publications. (AA)

RAYSA E. AMADOR, Adelphi University. Research on: the XVI Chronicle of the Conquest and colonization of the New World; Latin American women and the television soap opera. (RA)

MELVIN S. ARRINGTON, Jr., University of Mississippi. Author of various publications (articles, reviews, translations) on colonial, nineteenth- and twentieth-century Spanish American literature. (MSA)

TERESA R. ARRINGTON, University of Mississippi. Author of articles on Hispanic linguistics and foreign language teaching methodology. (TA)

ESTHER A. AZZARIO, Wayne State University. Retired from Wayne State, Azzario researches Argentine literature. (EA)

GRACE M. BEARSE, Radcliffe College. Areas of research: Latin American women writers, Chicano literature. [Deceased. -- Editor] (GB)

MARY BERG, University of California, Los Angeles. Author of articles on García Márquez, Cortázar, Borges, Bombal, and Lugones. Areas of research: nineteenth and twentieth century Latin American fiction. (MB)

VIRGINIA M. BOUVIER, Washington Office on Latin America. Author of: "Alliance or Compliance: Implications of Chilean experience for the Catholic Church in Latin America." (VB)

SUSANA CASTILLO, San Diego State University. Area of research: Latin American theater. (SC)

ELISA DAVILA, State University of New York, New Paltz. Author of: "El poema en prosa en Hispanoamérica posterior al Modernismo" (Tinta). Area of research: "Poesía viva hispánica en los Estados Unidos." Also compiling an anthology of contemporary women poets of Latin America. (ED)

NANCY GRAY DIAZ, Rutgers University, Newark. Author of dissertation: "The Radical Self: Metamorphosis to Animal Form in Modern Latin American Narrative" and articles on modern Latin American literature.
(NGD)

LEE DOWLING, University of Houston. Author of articles published in Hispania, Language and Style, and Hispanic Journal. Area of research: Latin American colonial literature. (LD)

MIRIAM ELLIS, University of California, Santa Cruz. Author of translations of Gioconda Belli in Revista Mujeres, 1984-85; work in progress: Latin American Women poets since 1950: A Bilingual Critical Anthology."
(ME)

NOEMI ESCANDELL, Westfield State College. Author of two collections of poetry: Ciclos and Cuadros: Area of research: Contemporary women novelists of Latin America, Spain, and the United States. [See annotation in body of bibliography.] (NE)

ELIZABETH ESPADAS, Wesley College. Author of articles on contemporary Spanish and Spanish American literature. (EE)

TANYA FAYEN, State University of New York, Binghamton. Translator of Harlem de todos los días by Emilio Díaz Valcarcel. Areas of research: the influence of Faulkner and Sur on Latin American writers. (TF)

MALVA FILER, Brooklyn College of The City University of New York. Critical edition of Pueblo en la niebla by María de Villarino. Author of articles and books on Latin American literature. (MF)

PATTI FIRTH, Rutgers University, New Brunswick. Translator of Spanish American poetry. (PF)

LUCIA FOX-LOCKERT, Michigan State University. Author of Women Novelists in Spain and Spanish America, El rostro de la patria en la literatura peruana, Ensayos hispanoamericanos and creative works. See annotation in body of bibliography. [See annotation in the body of the bibliography.] (LFL)

ERICA FROUMAN-SMITH, C. W. Post Center of Long Island University. Area of research: contemporary women novelists of Latin America. (EFS)

MAGDALENA GARCIA-PINTO, University of Missouri, Columbia. Editor for poetry from Uruguay and Paraguay for the Handbook for Latin American Studies. (MGP)

YOLANDA GARCIA-REYNERO, University of California, Los Angeles. Areas of research: contemporary Latin American and Chicano literature.
(YGR)

EVELYN PICON GARFIELD, University of Illinois, Urbana - Champaign. Author of Women's Voices from Latin America: Interviews with Six Contemporary Authors; ¿Es Julio Cortázar un surrealista?; Julio Cortázar;

Cortázar por Cortázar; Las entrañas del vacío: ensayos sobre la modernidad hispanoamericana, with I.A. Schulman. (EPG)

JEAN GRAHAM, University of California, Los Angeles. Actress and teacher. Areas of research: modern Latin American theater and novel. (JG)

NORMA GRASSO, Stockton State College, Pomona, N. J. Area of research: Argentine literature. (NG)

LUCIA GUERRA-CUNNINGHAM, University of California, Irvine. Author of Mujer y Sociedad en América Latina; La narrativa de María Luisa Bombal; Más allá de las máscaras (novel). (LGC)

MICHAEL HANDELSMAN, University of Tennessee. Author of works on Ecuadorian literature and Latin American women writers. (MH)

GINA C. HARDALO, Institutional Services, Houston Public Library. Area of research: currently involved in analysis of the Spanish titles owned by the Library Resource Center. (GH)

SUSANA HERNANDEZ-ARAICO, California State Polytechnic University. Areas of research: Spanish Golden Age literature, Latin American literature with special interest in contemporary women writers. Susana Hernández-Araico's annotations were carried out with the support of a generous grant from the Southern California Conference on International Studies (SOCCIS). (SHA)

RAUL INOSTROZA, California State University, Long Beach. Author of El ensayo en Chile desde la colonia hasta 1900; articles and book reviews on Latin American literature, linguistics, and foreign language teaching. (RI)

IVETTE LOPEZ JIMENEZ, University of Puerto Rico, Bayamón. Author of "Julia de Burgos: los textos comunicantes;" "Papeles de Pandora: devastación v. ruptura." Area of research: Caribbean women writers. (ILJ)

LUDMILA KAPSCHUTSCHENKO, Rider College. Author of El laberinto en la narrativa hispanoamerican contemporánea. (LK)

CARAGH KENNEDY, University of California, Los Angeles. Area of research: Latin American films. (CK)

DENNIS KLEIN, University of South Dakota. Area of research: Latin American literature. (DK)

PATRICIA N. KLINGENBERG, University of Tulsa. Author of "The Grotesque in the Short Stories of Silvina Ocampo" and "The Fantastic in the Short Stories of Silvina Ocampo," articles in Letras Femeninas. (PK)

MONIQUE J. LEMAITRE, Northern Illinois University. Author of Octavio Paz: Poesía y poética; "Estructura e Ideología en algunos textos de Roque Dalton," Institute for the Study of Ideologies and Literature, 1985. (ML)

PATRICIA RUBIO DE LERTORA, Skidmore College. Author of La Nación 1970-1973: bibliografía de la literatura chilena; co-author of: Carpentier ante la crítica: bibliografía comentada and Diccionario de términos e "ismos" literarios. (PRL)

LINDA GOULD LEVINE, Montclair State College. Author of <u>Juan Goytisolo: la destrucción creadora</u>; <u>Feminismo ante el franquismo: entrevistas con feministas de España</u> (with Gloria Waldman); critical edition of <u>Reivindicación del Conde don Julián</u>. (LGL)

NAOMI LINDSTROM, University of Texas at Austin. Author of <u>Macedonio Fernández</u>; Co-editor of <u>Woman as Myth and Metaphor in Latin American Literature</u>. (NL)

ANGELA McEWAN-ALVARADO, Los Angeles County Superior Court (Interpreter). Translator of stories by Carlota Carvallo de Núñez (Peru) and of the biography of Emilia Pardo-Bazán by Carmen Bravo-Villasante. (AMA)

SHARON MAGNARELLI, Albertus Magnus College. Author of <u>The Lost Rib: Female Characters in the Spanish American Novel</u> and numerous articles on contemporary Spanish American novel and theatre. (SMI)

NANCY MANDLOVE, Westminster College. Area of research: contemporary women poets of Spain and Latin America. (NM)

SARAH MARQUES, Marymount College. Author of <u>Arte y sociedad en las novels de Carlos Loveira</u>. (SMA)

DIANE E. MARTING, University of California, Los Angeles. Author of articles on Sor Juana, María Luisa Bombal, Luisa Valenzuela and "Female Sexuality and Feminism in Selected Twentieth Century Novels of Latin America," Diss. Rutgers University. (DEM)

JOAN F. MARX, Muhlenberg College. Dissertation on Elena Garro. Area of research: Spanish American literature. (JM)

SEYMOUR MENTON, University of California, Irvine. Areas of research: Spanish American short story, Cuban prose fiction, the Colombian novel, the Guatemalan novel and the Costa Rican short story. (SEM)

DORIS MEYER, Brooklyn College. Author of: <u>Victoria Ocampo: Against the Wind and the Tide</u>; co-editor of <u>Contemporary Women authors of Latin America: Introductory Essays & New Translations</u> (2 vols.) (DM)

VIRGINIA MOORE, Rutgers University, New Brunswick. Area of research: Spanish American literature. (VM)

GABRIELA MORA, Rutgers University, New Brunswick. Author of: <u>En torno al cuento: de la teoría general y de su práctica en Hispanoamérica</u>. (GM)

BARBARA MORRIS, University of California, Los Angeles. Author of "Reading a Legend: Camila O'Gorman by Bemberg and Molina" (article). Area of research: Hispanic film and literature. (BM)

FELICIDAD OBREGON, Montclair State College (New Jersey). Area of research: Spanish literature. (FO)

BETTY TYREE OSIEK, Southern Illinois University. Annotator for the <u>Handbook of Latin American Studies</u>; book in progress on Rosario Castellanos. (BTO)

HILDA C. PEINADO, University of California, Los Angeles. Special interest in Chicana writers. (HP)

LUISA M. PERDIGO, St. Thomas Aquinas College. Author of articles on: Octavio Paz, Vicente Huidobro, Braulio Arenas, Enrique Goméz-Correa, Jorge Guillén, and Eugenio Florit; original poetry. (LP)

AMANDA PLUMLEE, Davis & Elkins College. Author of a book review of Episodios folklóricos y otras crónicas by the Ecuadorian author Franklin Barriga López. (AP)

JUAN JOSE PRAT, University of California, Los Angeles. Areas of research: Spanish popular literature and medieval traditions. (JP)

SISTER MARIA CRISTINA QUIÑONEZ-GAUGGEL, Fundação Tecnológica e Educacional Clarice Lispector (Belo Horizonte, Brazil). Area of research: women in contemporary Latin American society, especially Brazilian, Argentinean and Honduran. (MQG)

PHYLLIS RODRIGUEZ-PERALTA, Temple University. Author of: José Santos Chocano; Tres poetas cumbres en la poesía peruana. (PRP)

TIMOTHY J. ROGERS, Miami University. Author of critical studies in contemporary Hispanic poetry and translations of Hispanic poetry. (TR)

IRENE ROSTAGNO, Santiago de Chile. Area of research: Spanish American literature. (IR)

PATRICIA J. SANTORO, Rutgers University, New Brunswick. Area of research: the transformation of novels into (Spanish peninsular) films, specifically: Los santos inocentes; La familia de Pascual Duarte and La colmena. (PS)

SUSAN C. SCHAFFER, University of California, Los Angeles. Area of research: contemporary Mexican narrative. (SSR)

STACEY SCHLAU, Westchester University. Areas of research: Spanish American female narratists; narrative theory; women and religious genres; Caribbean literature; women in the Third World. (SS)

ARLENE O. SCHRADE, University of Mississippi. Author of "Sex Shock: The Humanistic Woman in the Super-Industrial Society" in Monster or Messiah: Computer Impact on Society; text materials (Spanish, Spanish/English bilingual) published for grade levels four to University; consultant/contributor to: Women in World Areas: Latin America, forth-coming. (AS)

SYLVIA SHERNO, University of California, Los Angeles. Recent areas of research: contemporary Peninsular poetry, including the poets Blas de Otero, José Angel Valente, and Gloria Fuertes. (SSO)

CYNTHIA STEELE, Columbia University. Areas of research: Mexican literature; Latin American women writers; indigenista fiction. (CS)

NANCY SAPORTA STERNBACH, Smith College. Author of a study of women writers and protagonists in Spanish American modernismo; articles on Latin American feminism and feminism in Argentina. (NSS)

ANITA K. STOLL, Cleveland State University. Areas of research: twentieth century Latin American literature and Golden Age drama. (ASL)

ALEXANDRA TCACHUK, Rosary College. Areas of research and publication: immigration movements into Argentina and how they are reflected in literature; Argentine women writers. (AT)

SUSAN TRITTEN, Miami University (Ohio). Area of research: Spanish American women writers. (ST)

RIMA R. [ROTHE] DE VALLBONA, University of St. Thomas. Author of Yolanda Oreamuno and La obra en prosa de Eunice Odio; Mujeres y agonías (short-stories) and Las sombras que perseguimos (novel). [See annotation in body of bibliography.] (RRV)

ILEANA VIQUEIRA, Universidad de Puerto Rico, Río Piedras. (IV)

GLORIA FEIMAN WALDMAN, York College. Author of: Feminismo ante el franquismo; Teatro contemporáneo; and various articles. (GFW)

CATHARINE WALL, Modern Language Association. Area of research: the relationship between the literary and visual arts. (CW)

JOSEPH W. ZDENEK, Winthrop College. Areas of research: García Lorca, modern drama, pedagogy. (JZ)

ABOUT THE EDITOR

DIANE E. MARTING has been a Fulbright Grantee, former Acting Director of Women's Studies at Livingston College, Rutgers, and former Instructor of Spanish, Portuguese, and Women's Studies at Rutgers University and the University of California at Los Angeles. She has translated Octavio Paz for *Signs* and Rosario Castellanos for *A Rosario Castellanos Reader*. Her articles have appeared in *Boletin de Literatura Comparada*, *The Review of Contemporary Fiction*, and *Alba de America*, and she is the compiler and editor of "Spanish America," a chapter in *Women Writers in Translation: An Annotated Bibliography, 1945-1982*.